25 YEARS
OF ROCK 'N' ROLL

COMPILED BY THE EDITORS OF *GOLDMINE* MAGAZINE

Published by

 krause publications

700 E. State St.
Iola, WI 54990-0001

Front Cover Photo Copyright: Chuck Stewart
Book Cover Photo Copyright: Ron Pownall/Star File

Please call or write for our free catalog. Our toll-free number to place an order or obtain a free catalog is 800-258-0929 or please use our regular business telephone 715-445-2214 for editorial comment and further information.

Library of Congress Catalog Number: 98-86936
ISBN: 0-87341-688-0
Printed in the United States of America

INTRODUCTION

I was an inattentive high school freshman when a question briefly pierced through my fog of boredom. "What makes art classic?" the teacher asked. While I remember her name today only for the ingnominy of having sat through a year of her lectures, this particular lesson made an impression. "It's timeless and universal," she said, offering the stock answer to her own question. We were reading Homer, who could hardly have seemed less relevant at the time, but her statement explained the appeal of *Led Zeppelin IV* to me quite well.

Although rock 'n' roll in the Reagan era was still not accepted as established culture (the President himself had been involved in the anti-rock movement of the 1950s), it still seemed that the music had a grain of the timeless and universal in it. Some of it, I thought, was classic in the Platonic sense of the word — dare I admit I learned anything that fateful freshman year of high school.

That year set me on the path to where I am now, an editor for a publication whose purpose is to keep the history of rock 'n' roll alive and to provide music collectors a way to connect with each other.

Over the past 25 years, *Goldmine* has published interviews with many of the people who have helped make rock 'n' roll great. Some of the best of those are reproduced here for the first time since their original publication, along with a CD featuring some of the artists whose work stands the test of time.

I'm not sure if anyone will still be listening to rock music in another 25 years, let alone 250 or 2,500 years — when rock 'n' roll will be as old as Homer is now — but recently I was given a clue. A *Goldmine* writer and I were discussing "Dyslexic Heart," a song by Paul Westerberg, former lead singer of the much-loved Replacements. "I love you, I hate you, I've got a dyslexic heart," he sang, and suddenly I found myself drawn back to that freshman year of English. Looking in a musty bookshelf in my spare room, I found a very yellowed book of Greek and Roman literature.

"I loathe and love, but why I cannot tell/I simply feel that way and suffer hell."

Catallus, somewhere around 60 B.C., must have been going through a Westerbergian gloom. Maybe it's better stated the other way around.

Either way, we haven't come as far in the last couple of millennia as we think. There are more buttons to push, but people are still people. As rock music becomes an accepted — even respected — part of our culture, it seems that what most rock 'n' rollers sensed early on, and what I began to sense those years ago, has been borne out: Rock 'n' roll is very much a real art form and is definitely here to stay.

In 2,000 years, rock music may yet have the power to grip an adolescent imagination and not let go for a lifetime or so. Even if it doesn't, I'm still happy to help preserve it on a stone tablet like this one.

—Irwin Soonachan, Associate Editor, *Goldmine*

TABLE OF CONTENTS

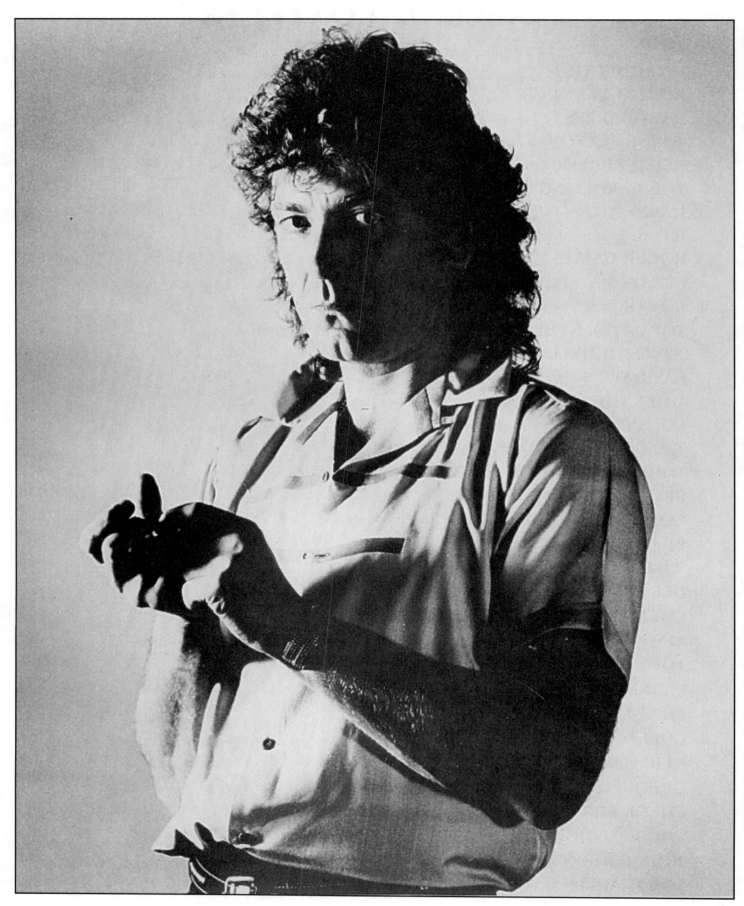

Robert Plant

By Ken Sharp
August 6, 1993

Hey, hey, mama, said the way you move, gonna make you sweat, gonna make you groove." Those immortal lyrics from Led Zeppelin's "Black Dog" may seem banal on paper, yet when delivered with unparalleled passion and fury by Robert Plant, everyone goes home satisfied. In the annals of hard rock history, no singer has been more imitated and revered than Robert Plant. Plant, with his long, unfurling golden tresses, bountiful charisma, sexual magnetism, and unmistakable bluesy vocal acrobatics, was the perfect prototype for a hard rock singer.

The saga of Robert Anthony Plant began in the industrial town of Birmingham, England. Born August 20, 1948 in West Bromwich, Staffordshire, England, Plant was the son of a civil engineer. Plant credits Terry Foster, a local white blues guitarist from Kidderminster, with turning him on to blues. Honing his burgeoning vocal chops at the Seven Stars Blues Club in Stourbridge, Plant ripped it up on such blues classics as "Got My Mojo Working." Hooked on the awe-inspiring sounds of blues masters Robert Johnson, Howlin' Wolf, Sonny Boy Williamson, Willie Dixon, and Muddy Waters, Plant worked with a number of little-known groups such as the Delta Blues Band, the New Memphis Bluebreakers, the Black Snake Moan, Banned, Hobbstweedle, the Tennessee Teens, and the Crawling King Snakes.

Plant, known in his local environs as "The Wild Man Of Blues From The Black Country," later went on to form his own group, the Band Of Joy. Specializing in covers of many of Plant's favorite West Coast groups, including Moby Grape, Love, Buffalo Springfield, and the Jefferson Airplane, the troupe also included Plant's long-time friend, drummer John Bonham.

During this period, Plant recorded several one-off CBS singles, including one with Birmingham-based group Listen (formerly the Tennessee Teens), a remake of the Young Rascals "You Better Run." In 1967, Plant cut two solo singles for CBS Records, "Our Song" b/w "Laughing, Crying, Laughing" (which reportedly sold a measly 800 copies) and "Long Time Coming" b/w "I've Got A Secret." Additionally, Plant recorded a track called "Operator," which appeared on a double anthology album by British blues pioneer Alexis Korner. Slogging it out on the club circuit, it seemed Plant was headed nowhere fast.

Meanwhile, Jimmy Page, fresh from the breakup of the Yardbirds, was looking to put together the ultimate supergroups. The first addition to Page's dream band was top session player John Paul Jones (Herman's Hermits/the Rolling Stones/the Yardbirds/Donovan) on bass. Page then went hunting for his vocalist. Legend has it that he first approached then-hot British blues-rocker Terry Reid to assume lead vocal duties for the soon-to-be-dubbed Led Zeppelin. Unable to take the job, Reid recommended a promising unknown singer named Robert Plant, who was then playing with Korner.

Just when it seemed this young, virile singer was destined to wallow in obscurity belting out the blues in the Midlands, Page rescued him, checking out this unknown sensation at a teacher's training college near Birmingham. Page was suitably knocked out, but not completely sold; he was a little perplexed that such an abundantly talented singer hadn't been discovered yet. But Page soon discovered, after inviting Plant back to his home, that he had found a kindred musical spirit. Ever the loyal friend, Plant recruited childhood pal John Bonham into the fledgling group, and Led Zeppelin was born, the name provided by punster Keith Moon of the Who.

From the opening raw notes of "Good Times, Bad Times" on from the band's self-titled debut album, issued in 1969, the music world was never the same. Led Zeppelin made their American debut in Denver, Colorado on December 26, 1968. In no time at all, Zeppelin went from being second on the bill to Vanilla Fudge to their undeniable status as America's premiere concert attraction and one of the most influential bands in rock.

Plant's creative role with Led Zeppelin—particularly on the songwriting front—was minimal at first; he didn't find his voice as a songwriter until penning the lyrics for the elegant "Thank You," a song written for then wife Maureen. Plant's flowery poetic lyrics, best exemplified by "Kashmir" and "Stairway To Heaven," juxtaposed with the sonic assault of Page's lethal guitar riffs, proved the soundtrack for the '70s. At their peak, Zeppelin manager Peter Grant predicted in the May 1973 issue of *Financial Times* that the band would earn $30 million in the following year. The immense popularity of Led Zeppelin was so far-reaching that the daughters of then-U.S. President Gerald Ford told talk show host Dick Cavett that Zep was their favorite rock group.

A dizzying rapid-fire succession of sold-out tours, multi-platinum albums, and a career that balanced equal doses of decadence and transcendent splendor, marked the career of Led Zeppelin. It was Satyricon come to life.

Yet just when it seemed everything the group touched turned to gold, a black web of tragedy enveloped the band. In August 1975, Plant and his wife were involved in a serious car accident while on vacation in Rhodes, Greece. A period of agonizing recuperation followed, with Plant recording all his lead vocals for the group's 1976 album *Presence* while on crutches. Then, to make matters worse, two years later, while on tour in New Orleans, Plant received the horrifying news that his beloved five-year old son Karac had died. The group's U.S. tour

was abruptly canceled and Plant went into seclusion with his family.

It would be another year before the band regrouped to record the magnificent *In Through The Out Door* album. Issued in September 1979, the album would sadly prove to be the band's swan song. Having just completed a SRO European tour, Led Zeppelin was gearing up for their first live shows in America in over three years.

Sadly, the group never made the trek to the U.S. On September 25, 1980, drummer John Bonham was found dead at Jimmy Page's new home, the Old Mill House, in Mill Lane, Windsor, choking on his own vomit after a long-night of hard drinking. Devastated, the band issued a press release which stated, "We wish it to be known that the loss of our dear friend and the deep respect we have for his family, together with the sense of individual harmony felt by ourselves and our managers, have led us to decide that we could not continue as we were."

With Led Zeppelin a non-entity, Plant threw his heart and soul into his first solo album, *Pictures At Eleven*, which was released in July 1982. Produced by Plant, the record burst with daring innovation and sheer electricity. A fierce declaration of purpose, it reaffirmed Plant's undying belief in rock 'n' roll. It even included an affectionate nod to his former comrades with the Zeppelinesque "Burning Down One Side." Yet Plant was inexorably driven to create new music, not coast on the coattails of Zeppelin's signature sound.

It wouldn't be until the release of his second solo effort, 1983's *The Principle Of Moments* (his first album issued on his own record label, El Paranza, distributed by Atlantic), that Plant returned to live performances. Supported by a band that comprised Robbie Blunt on lead guitar, keyboardist Jezz Woodroffe, bassist Paul Martinez, and guest drummer Phil Collins, Plant's first solo tour began on August 29, 1983. A side project, the retro Honeydrippers, found "Percy" in eternal '50s mode, belting out much loved gems from his youth. The album found Plant teaming up once again with Jimmy Page, along with such other notables as Jeff Beck and Nile Rodgers.

Surprisingly, the mini-album *The Honeydrippers, Vol. 1* was a smash. Hitting #4 in Billboard in 1984, the LP sported a cache of engaging tracks, among them the #25 "Rocking At Midnight" and a splendid rendition of the Phil Phillips chestnut "Sea Of Love," which reached #3 in Billboard, higher than any Zeppelin single had ever placed (although, admittedly, Led Zeppelin was the consummate album group).

Other extra-curricular vinyl exploits include the one-off *Crawling King Snakes*, an incarnation which included Plant and drummer Phil Collins, who recorded a cut for the *Porky's Revenge* soundtrack. Plant's most esoteric and underrated solo work, *Shaken N' Stirred*, followed in June 1985. Featuring the semi-hit "Little By Little," the album, while not a major success, was an unequivocal artistic triumph.

The ghost of Led Zeppelin still haunted Plant's career, though. Five years after their last performance together, Led Zeppelin, with the addition of drummers Tony Thompson and the ubiquitous Phil Collins, reunited on July 13, 1985 for the worldwide benefit ever Live-Aid. With only one hour of rehearsal time, Led Zeppelin hit the stage at Philadelphia's J.F.K. Stadium to the rollicking, brutal sounds of "Rock And Roll." All good intentions aside, the performance was not up to par, marred by Page's out of tune guitar and Plant's hoarse voice, ravaged by weeks of live solo dates.

Yet Led Zeppelin's appearance at Live-Aid brought the former band mates closer. Unity between Plant, Jimmy Page, and John Paul Jones was so strong that the band even convened in January 1986 in Bath, England to work on new material for a new Led Zeppelin album. Sadly, the project quickly fell apart.

Plant, blessed with a spanking new band including keyboardist Phil Johnstone, returned with a bang with the *Now And Zen* album, his most successful solo opus to date. The album whole-

heartedly embraced the Zeppelin myth on such tracks as "Tall Cool One" (featuring Zep samples from "Whole Lotta Love" and later used in a Coca-Cola commercial, much to the consternation of Plant's devout following), "White, Clean and Neat," and "Heaven Knows." To cap off the Zeppelin aura, Jimmy Page added scorching guitar solos to "Tall Cool One" and "Heaven Knows."

Paul returned the favor by singing and co-writing "The Only One" on Page's debut solo album, *Outrider*. Much to the thrill of Plant-o-philes everywhere, he hit the stage in 1988 with a generous helping of Led Zeppelin songs that occupied the set. Prior to this tour, Plant had steered clear of playing any tunes from the hallowed Zep canon of material.

In the midst of Plant's 1988 solo tour, Led

Photo/Chuck Boyd/Flower Children

9

Zeppelin reunited once again, this time with John Bonham's son Jason behind the drum kit. The occasion was Atlantic Records' 40th Anniversary Concert, held at New York's Madison Square Garden on May 14, 1988. Despite several problems with the sound, the band ran through a ragged yet charming thirty-minute set which included such timeless gems as "Heartbreaker," "Misty Mountain Hop," Plant favorite "Kashmir," "Whole Lotta Love," and "Stairway To Heaven." With a cover story in *Rolling Stone*, platinum album, and SRO tour, Robert Plant was once again atop the hard rock fiefdom, right where he belonged.

1990's *Manic Nirvana* album followed up the overwhelming success of *Now And Zen*, offering a sumptuous wealth of adventurous and raucous cuts including the pulverizing "Hurting Kind (I've Got My Eyes On You)" and a frenetic cover of Kenny Dino's "Your Ma Said You Cried In Your Sleep Last Night." Another whirlwind tour followed, this time taking in many small towns across America. Plant went as far as dubbing the jaunt "The Rand McNally Tour."

June 1993 saw the release of Plant's sixth solo album, *Fate of Nations*. From the mesmerizing Middle-Eastern intrigue of "Calling To You," to the pastoral acoustic textures of his cover of Tim Hardin's "If I Were A Carpenter,"

Fate of Nations is Plant's most assured and effortless recording to date. Unlike many of his contemporaries, Plant hasn't lost his passion for rock 'n' roll. Endlessly exploring new boundaries and possibilities within his new music and continually reinventing himself, Plant continues to be a vital force in the music world today.

The unforgettable legacy of Robert Plant's work as a member of Led Zeppelin and as a solo artist speaks for itself—loudly. While Plant imitators such

as Whitesnake, Great White, and Kingdom Come are among the innumerable acts that have haunted the airwaves with their unflagging desire to replicate every nuance of his vocal style, there's only one Robert Plant. He is a true rock original, unwilling to live in the shadow of his former band, and unrelenting in his quest for artistic and transcendence.

Goldmine: When did you first realize you had made it in America with Led Zeppelin?

Robert Plant: When Linda Winters said she'd come back to the hotel, I knew that something was going to happen. The earth was going to move and stuff and hey, presto, a second later it did.

But seriously...

On a serious level I don't think that I can remember. Every town that we played in viewed us with a kind of strange distance initially when we started playing. We were supporting Iron Butterfly or whoever it was, and what we were doing wasn't particularly that different to Cream or other people, but the structure and actual presentation of the thing was quite a bit different, although the weight of the thing was similar.

So I guess there was a kind of strange period of observation and then suddenly we found' We started in Denver, Colorado on December 26, 1968 and by the time mid-January had arrived, (due to) the power of the underground radio—the equivalent of college radio or whatever now—the word had spread and we got this remarkable kind of anticipation, which was phenomenal. It was something I obviously could never have anticipated.

Do you get a bigger rush hearing your new songs on the radio or the older stuff?

Well, the biggest thrill is to hear the current material. However, I'm always proud. It's such a gas to be in this country. There's such a kind of bump when you start talking about music here. The reaction to music, whether it's Led Zeppelin or not, is incredible and it makes me so happy.

How did you approach your latest album, Fate of Nations*?*

I brought the whole record and the whole attitude really from the relief zone, that kind of place where you pull in when you're really tired and you

get some new power. I think at the end of the Manic Nirvana tour I went straight back to England. I played with some major weighty guys like Faith No More, the Black Crowes, and Alannah Myles, and I really wanted to go someplace and pick up the thread. I thought that my music was powerful. I thought that *Manic Nirvana* was very edgy, very aggressive, and very demanding on songs like "She Said," "Watching You," and "Anniversary."

I was really quite agitated as a guy. But when I got home I was satiated. I had my fill. I'd done it all. I'd sung and sung and sung, I'd gone to Muskogee and come home. I was on the tour that time forgot, with Faith No More opening up for me in a school gym. But I got home and started leaning back and wanted to know what do I wind down to and, you know, it can only be honest music, non-compromised and non-contrived.

So I found those old records of mine, like Moby Grape, and my memory started moving back to a kind of pastoral time when I wasn't trying too hard. I wasn't trying to keep up with anybody. I was just singing and writing lyrics like "Over the Hills and Far Away" and "Misty Mountain Hop," which, now they're cute. But then that was the best I could do. So I went back to the misty mountains. I drove into the hills and stayed in little tiny places and got up in the morning before the sun came up and hung out and just absorbed it all again.

And I found that it was all still there, all that inspiration. In fact, it's like a well, it doesn't dry up. It's just sort of an area that really inspires me so my whole music on this album comes from that sort of finding that easy path, that natural energy area that made me start writing the lyrics the way I've written them and developing a thing with new guys, to a degree.

Is the band pretty much the same as it's been for the last few records?

What you don't see from the credits on the record is that there's four guys drumming. There's Richard Thompson, Kevin MacMichael from Cutting Crew, Francis Dunnery from It Bites, and Doug Boyle, who was with us before but he's not now. There's me playing guitar. I played sitar on one track that's not on the album.

Is it going to be B-side?

I don't know. It's called "Hey Jane." It's really

cute. It's like a hippie anthem.

Did you play a real sitar or a coral sitar?

Oh, a real sitar! I bought one in India and took it all the way back to England. I even bought a seat for it on the plane. I'd been recording with these Indian guys recently on "Network News" and "Calling To You." I got into the whole kind of Indian musician thing in England.

Back with Led Zeppelin, you and Jimmy Page were quite into Indian music. What led you into that initially?

It's another blues form. It's got all those blue notes (imitates Indian music sounds). It's got all those quarter tonic wails. It's great.

When you start writing for a record, are you writing solely for yourself or do you have the audience in mind as well?

Yeah, I have written for the audience. That's why with the *Now And Zen* album, when I used "Tall Cool One" and all the Zep samples and stuff, there was a sense of humor in that. The sense of humor had to be a continuum. You don't take yourself too seriously but I did want desperately to be up there among the big boys 'cause I am a big boy.

But, you know, this time and probably last time too, with *Manic Nirvana*, with a different music form, this is for me. I don't give a hoot about anybody else, really. I'm talking this up now because I want it to be a success and I believe there's great songs here that mustn't be buried. It's for me. It's for me and it's for the guys who wrote it and it's for the people who want to hear "If I Were A Carpenter." It's beautiful.

What led you to cover Tim Hardin's "If I Were A Carpenter" on the new record?

Yeah, "Carpenter." Strong stuff, beautiful and so sweet. Some of my friends say, "Wow, you haven't sung like that since Zep or since very early Zep." It's not innocence, it's just inspired. I was the most impressionable English would-be hippie. I was like a weekend hippie. I thought that the insinuation of the music then was very honest and there wasn't a rock god in sight. There was nobody strutting around in a very expensive suit pretending that it's

all new. It was all great stuff and people were inventing themselves and then moving along and doing some new shit that nobody ever heard of. In the middle of it all was Hendrix, the real king.

Did you ever see Hendrix live?

Yeah. I saw him in a club in New York. We used to jam there at night. I got a twinkle in my eye because I was there and I watched Bonzo (John Bonham, the late Zeppelin drummer) play unbelievably with Hendrix and Buddy Miles. But that was what you do. On the last tour I used to go out with the Black Crowes to clubs when we were touring in Canada. They were the only people who would let me play guitar on stage so we went out at night and I sort of became Neil Young, playing those kind of weird solos.

There's an innate sense of spirituality which pervades Fate of Nations, *especially on "I Believe," which sports some gorgeous falsetto singing.*

The whole thing is supposed to be lifting people up a bit without doing it by torment or without doing it by insinuating some kind of macho deal. I just suddenly became Glen Campbell on "I Believe" (laughs). It was such a cute move, the chords were, and I wanted to not have too many words, just something minimal. My best bit of singing on the record, I think, is at the end of "Come Into My Life," where the girl stops singing and the drums give way and you've just got a hurdy gurdy churning away. Maybe it's a snare drum, I can't remember.

Some of the vocal phrasing on the end of "Great Spirit" is great. It's unusual. I never thought I would sing like that but I guess I was visited for a minute.

Do you still surprise yourself as a songwriter?

I think the vocal phrasing on "Calling To You" is really strange. It's unusual because it's crossing an unusual time signature and it's a very, very tough, an uncompromising song with that violin solo at the end by Nigel Kennedy. That and the vocal and chorus on "Memory Song." Just the invention of the melody line. Not how great it is but just it was a neat thing to come up with.

Since becoming a solo artist, you've certainly become tremendously involved top to bottom with a song's creation and final version on a record. When you come up with a song now can you visualize how it's going to sound fully produced?

Not really, no. Halfway through this record I got the plot. And I went, "this is it." I want to use a lot of acoustic stuff, mandolin. I wanted to give it a trademark. I remember when Zep III (the *Led Zeppelin III* album) came out and everybody went, "Aww." And then we carried it along with "Battle Of Evermore" and "Stairway," that acoustic/electric marriage and the abstract lyrical content. I think that it's a kind of landscape of sound and color that I really have been trying to develop here and still keep it in the main pop idiom, but not lying on my back and opening my legs too much.

That brings up the point that there's almost a mythical view of Robert Plant, the blond god with his shirt off, strutting around on stage. You're probably embarrassed to look at the pictures!

No, no! It was a weird thing to do but it was hot at those gigs. It was tongue-in-cheek. We were always giggling. Basically what happened was, I left some shirts in the hotel room and then so did Iggy (Pop). But about all these other guys who left their shirts at the hotel, I don't know. It was part of the kind of obvious macho strut that went with singing.

There was always a little wink on your part, where others bought into the macho thing completely.

Yeah, but we also wrote songs that were buying into it, like "Hot Dog" and "D'yer Maker," "Down By The Seaside." There was loads of stuff that came through, like "Black Country Woman," "Boogie With Stu," loads of bits and pieces that were around, saying that this is also quite funny. "Your Ma Said You Cried In Your Sleep Last Night."

"Wearin' And Tearin'?"

No, "Wearin' And Tearin'" wasn't funny. It was a definite slam. There was nothing funny about it, at least lyrically and emotionally for me—I was furious. It's all about drug abuse. The whole song is just my abhorrence that the use of the drugs distorted the joy of the music.

Nowadays in the rock world, new hard rock singers are often compared to you. Back when you started out in the '60s, what singers were you compared with in the press?

In America then, the whole pop scene had only just transcended from the English post-Beatle boom. So the West Coast music, you had (Jim) Morrison and the Doors and we were definitely not alike at all. And as far as other front men go, can I say that the Airplane had Grace Slick, Big Brother had Janis, Country Joe was a bit of a struggle to do that one. So I don't know, I suppose it was (Roger) Daltrey. There was nobody, really, who was actually doing that strut stuff. Daltrey used to spin his microphone around and around and around, which I thought was really cool. I tried it a couple of times with disastrous results. I got arrested in some state for knocking a cop out.

Listening back to some of your older songs, do they take on a different meaning for you?

No—very nice question—but no because the songs were very much of a pop sort of thing. The thing about English pop around the time you're discussing is that it wasn't cerebral. The lyrical content didn't have the abstractions. That's why I was so turned off by (Love's vocalist) Arthur Lee, Buffalo Springfield, with "For What It's Worth." I was using my head. Head music, man. Underground. When I was seventeen making records, we weren't thinking like that. I hadn't written any poetry or anything then. I didn't know how to combine abstraction and ambiguity and epithets, stuff that you can't really say what it's all about. I mean, what in heaven's name is "Stairway" all about? I don't know.

Sometimes it's best to leave the interpretation open...

I actually do know what it's about. But if I wake up and ask myself the question, I don't know because it's always shifting—the idea of what it's all about. So I couldn't write like that then. I was a kid and I just wanted to go (sings), "Hey, hey mama'" because that one I do know; that's easy.

By the way, have you heard Tori Amos's version of "Whole Lotta Love"?

Yeah. She's great, isn't she?

She told me how much she loved you, growing up.

And I love her and I told her I loved her.

Tori said when she was age thirteen you were the man she wanted to lose her virginity to.

But how disgusting that she waits all these years to tell me that. She told me that and I said, "What a fine time to tell me," because she's older than that now. I said to her, "Don't let a few years come through your wishes and my ability" (laughs). But she ran away to Germany and left me standing all alone with my award in my hand 'cause I met her at the *Q* (U.K. rock magazine) award ceremony. I saw her and said I want to be her friend so I lost twenty pounds and told her I'd never leave her.

On the whole, are you satisfied with your vocal work on your solo albums?

Every time I make a record I make it on the back of doing nothing but writing. So I go into the studio and maybe I've only sung for an hour a week before. So I've got to try and get my voice in some kind of slick order. I never do it the right way around. So I've never got the best vocal performance on a record. It's crazy. There's so many singers I know in the same position. You should actually go and work out somewhere but I can't stand in a field and sing, "There's a lady who's sure." But do you know what I mean? It's hard work.

When you began playing music and singing, at one point did you get the bug and say, "This is it, music is going to be my lifeblood"?

What happened was, I stood in for a guy who had a bad throat when I was in school and my friends were in a band and they were doing all this kind of Jackie DeShannon stuff like "Needles And Pins" and all that, 'cause the Searchers had all these hits. It was all pretty static music, sort of maroon suits with black velvet collars, a bit like the Beatles in Hamburg.
Anyway, this music was a bit too stiff, a bit too anally retentive. There was something up their bottoms. They were just standing there like the Searchers did. And I went, "What about 'Got My Mojo Working' by Muddy Waters." They said, "Well, what's that?" And I said, "Play a 12-bar in Eat This tempo." And I counted it out and started singing it and soon as I started being able to wail with my voice rather than stick with a straighter melody. Then the heavens opened and that was it. I thought

this was great, I could go (sings) "I Can't Quit You Baby." I can bluff this or I can mean it or I can make it sail or fly or dive or stand still.

Can you recall the first time you made money from singing?

We used to get about eight pounds a night supporting all kinds of major American acts. That was quite later on. I must have been sixteen then and we'd play in dance halls where Solomon Burke would come through or Wilson Pickett. When we used to play the festivals in the late '60s and early '70s with Zep, those guys were still banging around on these big shows. So you'd have the Doors, Janis, Zep, the Youngbloods, Wilson Pickett, B.B. King, John Lee Hooker, Creedence Clearwater. This would be one show. Tommy James. All on the same bill.

There's not a day goes by that I don't wish I had the chance to have seen some of those shows first-hand.

Well, everybody who's into music wants to have been there at that time. My deal is that I'm too young, too. (Jimmy) Page is a bit older than me and had been over here with the Yardbirds so he'd seen all that West Coast stuff.

From that West Coast sound, what groups do you most wish you had seen?

I never say Moby Grape. I'd have love to have seen them. I'd like to have seen Buffalo Springfield because I think their material was so kind of heady. They were doing stuff like "Flying On The Ground Is Wrong," "Broken Arrow," "Bluebird," "Expecting To Fly." "Broken Arrow" is brilliant. I thought, "Wow, this band is amazing." Neil Young has carried on all the way through from that point in time. All the way through, never flinches, straight ahead. Always moving: *Zuma, Rust Never Sleeps*. Tireless and brilliant and animated and Scorpio and fantastic.

Keith Richards spoke of his desire for rock 'n' roll to evolve and not be solely a music for youth. You can be older and still vital playing like Muddy Waters until you drop. Do you feel that way?

I saw Keith play just before Christmas in England and he was absolutely brilliant. He had Steve Jordan on drums. It was fantastic and he was so happy. And when the Stones go out again, he won't

Photo/Chuck Boyd/Flower Children

be that happy. And Jagger's made a record that could stand up and he could have stood up with his record but he's not going to do anything and it's mad. To spend so much time doing that and to find in the end that you just say, "Hey, that's it, now I'm going back there."

Keith is so accomplished and so there—and the way he played his chords and he kind of brought the plectrum up in his right hand. It was tremendous. I was so pleased. I've never really had much to do with the guy. We didn't really have any affinities back then. I really wanted somebody to wail the blues in that band like Otis Rush might have done. We were kind of rubbing along like this in the same space but miles away, in the same margin but different parts of the page. I'm so pleased Keith has made those two (solo) records. They're so refreshing in the middle of the kind of trumped-up pop, which is now starting to fade.

Just the fact that a band like R.E.M. can be popular is healthy.

For me, with the time that I've spent writing songs and performing, it would be ridiculous if the only thing that I could do is just stand there in some aging rock pose and say "Hey, this is what I do." You know what I mean? The thing is, you don't have to do all these macho things to appeal to people. There is a certain amount of style and anti-style to all aspects of commercial pop music'that you become "happening" by accident but the accident becomes contrived as soon as it's realized. There's very little spontaneity about it.

15

The music that you love and that I love came by sheer accident and was performed in an environment where nobody expected... Nobody expected the Electric Prunes to have their first hit—or the Thirteenth Floor Elevators—so really, a lot of those times were much more honest. I think no matter how unusual or how the scene is changing—it has, thank goodness—and there's a lot of rock puppets now who must be sitting in their dressing rooms wondering what the walkup's going to be like at the gig, if anybody's going to show. That can only be good because they've been there too long. They went to the wardrobe and pulled out Page's clothes and put them on.

You've got to say something and keep it positive and also a little bit of an imagination comes in handy, a bit of originality. But it still becomes a bit of a contrivance as well because anti-hip becomes hip. And you see the way videos are structured and you know we're all still going for the same thing; it's just making sure the way you keep your dignity and you make it fresh.

You once said the Now And Zen *album closed a chapter for you and the* Manic Nirvana *album opened a new one. What did you mean by that?*

It's the end and the beginning; *Now And Zen* just really showed the possibilities with tracks like "White, Clean And Neat" against "Why," two radically different tracks on an album that is different in every area. I'd broken the pain barrier in the writing capacity with new people. I was able to look at them and make mistakes. Everybody could make the biggest mistakes ever. It didn't matter about me being anybody special. The whole game was up and a new game had begun and it was great. I can't think of doing anything else because this is so formative.

One of your most memorable solo videos was for "I've Got My Eyes On you," with the professional wrestlers. It was very surreal and strange.

That was the idea of the guy who did the video. He was the guy who did the original Zep covers way back. He was from Hipgnosis. He did *Zep II, Zep III, Houses Of The Holy, Physical Graffiti,* and all that. *Principle Of Moments.* He did the "Heaven Knows" video in Morocco and stuff, and "Big Log" and the "In The Mood" video as well. We just make silly films.

What was your first stab at writing lyrics? Was it "Thank You" from Led Zeppelin II*?*

No. It was for "Good Times, Bad Times." Songwriting can be a cleansing—or at least it allows me to say what I want to say without me sort of saying, "My baby, she done left me, oh shit." Or, "I wish my baby would done leave me."

A lot of the '50s stuff does have great simplistic lyrics.

Oh yeah. "Mystery Train," great. Little Junior's Blue Flames, 1951.

Speaking of '50s music, I know you're a huge Elvis Presley fan. How did you get involved in (the tribute charity album) The Last Temptation Of Elvis?

It's nothing to do with liking Elvis, and in fact in a way the title is not that good for Elvis but it's great for the charity. (British journalist) Roy Carr I know very well. He's (British music paper) *NME*'s musicologist and freak and a good friend. He approached me and asked me if I wanted to do an Elvis tune from the movies and I didn't know whether to do something like "Viva Las Vegas" or "Do The Clam" or "Slicing Sam" or "Did You Ever Get One Of Those Days." I picked "Party" because I wanted to make it into a psychobilly kind of thing, and I used a guy from Johnny Kidd and the Pirates on guitar named Mick Green. Have you heard it?

Oh, yeah.

It's great. I think Holly Johnson's version is awful. That's awful. It's so cheesy, it's terrible. But there's plenty of room for cheese.

Didn't Led Zeppelin meet Elvis?

It happened because we were selling tickets faster than he was and he wanted to know why and who are these people; that was basically what he wanted to know. But he'd got a friend from Germany from the army days, a kid I think he'd adopted who was a Zep freak. So he was there and we all went to the hotel and met him and had a great time.

I can't really talk in great detail about it; it would take hours. But the great thing about the whole meeting was that Elvis's sense of humor was sharp as a razor and his actual street sensitivity was really fine-tuned. But he was surrounded, as everybody knows, by a kind of a sugar-coated existence. If we could have taken him out of the hotel with us and said, "C'mon, we'll take you down to some den of iniquity that we know just down the strip," he would have been fine. He could have been rescued.

The funniest thing about the whole night, apart from the fact that he stayed with us for two hours and he normally only saw people for ten minutes because we were all having a great time, is that our manager, Peter Grant, who weighed about 360 pounds at the time, walked in and sat down, but not looking properly, and he ended up sitting straight on Elvis's dad's lap, which was hilarious because he nearly broke Vernon's legs.

So it was a good way to start the evening. We just talked about Elvis impersonators and Zeppelin impersonators. We didn't know it was going to happen then but we said it might. We sang together; it was great because Zeppelin said, "We don't do soundchecks very often and when we do they're very disgusting because we only do your songs," and he said, "Oh yeah, which ones do you like?" And I said, "I like (sings), 'Treat me like a fool, treat me mean and cruel but love me.'"

So we go in and say goodbye and it's an hour later and we've had a drink and a laugh and I'm in the corridor getting to the elevator and Elvis calls me back and he sang it to me down the corridor. He sang the first bit and there's me singing the answers to him. It was great! It's like he should have came away with us or someone else and gone away from all those wallies.

Tell us about some of your post-Zeppelin appearances with Jimmy Page. First off, what are your recollections of (the 1985 charity concert) Live-Aid?

We weren't together. I was hoarse. Page's roadie had just took the guitar out of the case and just didn't tune it up so it was terrible, really. Now, of course, we should have done it, but in a way we had to be the tools of everybody's desires. That's the thing about a reunion, is that you end up being more for people's property. Your decisions are always based around other people's emotions. You can't live life and operate just on your own selfishness but at the same time you don't have to be a slave to it all.

And I suddenly saw myself up there re-igniting all the legends and dreams. Golum the medieval one was there, and Strider and Gandalf and the Butter

Queen and the Chicago Plaster Casters and everybody was there all put back together again and I grinned because I could see it all like a never-ending journey.

How about (the) Knebworth (Festival in England) when Jimmy Page joined you for several numbers?

It worked well because I was playing with my band and Jimmy joined me in the situation where everything was covered. We knew what we were doing, we knew it would sound good. We'd taken all the physical and logical efforts to make it sound good in a modern arena rock 'n' roll situation. And we tuned up. It had to be right. It was a case of putting the story straight for Jimmy as well because he didn't sound good the last two times (Live Aid and Atlantic Records' 40th Anniversary concert in New York) 'cause he had a fucking dumb road manager who he just couldn't get rid of. You can't have a career destroyed by a fit of nerves and a bad roadie. So it was really good.

What's the writing process like with (band member) Phil Johnstone?

The way it works is it's very quick. You just say "Public Enemy, think about it," and then there it comes. The thing about it being premeditated is that it is premeditated but it's a little extravaganza. It's four minutes of like a ludicrous department over here swinging around to some acoustic stuff which could never be premeditated. I mean, a song like "Liar's Dance," it's impossible to get too technical or career-oriented about something like that.

What was the first song you wrote with Phil Johnstone?

"Tall Cool One." In one afternoon we wrote that and "White, Clean & Neat." Not bad for an afternoon's work. I'm not a great songwriter per se. I hadn't ever been eloquent enough to write lyrically about political problems or my feelings or anything like that, but I feel I'm probably touching on the Alan Freed syndrome, something really close to my heart, rock 'n' roll roots and the kind of misinterpretation by the authorities and stuff.

Speaking of rock 'n' roll roots, are the Honeydrippers (Plant's short-lived post-Zeppelin rockabilly/R&B experiment) finished?

I don't want to bring back the Honeydrippers for years yet, and when I do, I'd like to be doing it in a very rock 'n' roll way. The thing is, if I use those elements and bring them into what I do anyway, then that satisfies my yen.

One of your favorite recordings is "Love Me" by the Phantom. Who's the man behind the mask?

They say that it was Pat Boone's kid brother but I don't think it was. I did an interview in New York and a guy sent me a Phantom album. I haven't played it yet but I will soon. What I liked about it was that it was so ramshackle and everything was so over-affected that you had to search to find out what the fuck what going on inside the song. In the middle of it all there's a radical singer huffing and puffing and swaggering and swirling and twirling his hips and grinding himself into infinity, who now drives a truck somewhere in Illinois, probably. The Meteors did a version of it, a psycho-billy version, but it ain't so good.

What's the best rumor you've ever heard about yourself?

Hah! That I stabbed somebody in the Atlanta airport and I was arrested. I read it in the local newspapers in England; that was a funny one. But the usual one is like I'm having a love affair with somebody from the Bangles or something like that.

Fairly recently a collection came out in England with a newly discovered Band of Joy (Plant's pre-Zeppelin band) track that was found. What can you tell me about it?

There are several Band of Joy tracks that I've got. I think the one on that record is called "Adriatic Sea View." Actually, it's a version of "Sweet Mary Blues" by Leadbelly. That's the song Leadbelly wrote for Governor Pat O'Neef after he (Leadbelly) was jailed for murder, and he sang it to the judge and the guy let him out from jail and paroled him. It's great; it's ridiculous.

One of your most underrated albums was Shaken N' Stirred. *How do you assess it today?*

It was some kind of real milestone and masterpiece, probably more in terms of musicianship more than anything. It wasn't a commercial record

and we were lucky to get the kind of radio reaction we got. People did actually enjoy it to a degree. I toured with it and that was the last tour I did with the other band. I've stopped denying things from the past. I've kind of cleansed myself of all those problems.

"Heaven Knows" is one of your most popular solo songs yet you didn't write it. How did you find the song?

That was one of the 110 demos I heard for the *Now And Zen* album. What attracted me to the song was the kind of mood and the drama and the whole lure of the song. It's a sexy song.

When they took the structure of "Heaven Knows" and they played it to me, it's "Kashmir." The chord progression, if you slide down and play it at a different tempo, it's "Kashmir."

And I said, "You bastards! What thieves!" And they said, "Yeah, and you didn't thieve?" So we thieve together now. All the kind of love of Led Zeppelin and that thing is confined to one or two areas of the musical sensibility department. What I'm trying to do is trying to live life without Zep. *Now And Zen* was a very important record because it does have all the Plant/Zeppelin elements without Zeppelin, but with contemporary computers chattering, drum samples, and it is a ballsy record.

Jimmy Page plays a great solo on that.

The studio afternoon with Jimmy could have been a lot more relaxed. Everyone from everywhere in the building came and were kind of climbing off the walls as he played over the top of the song. The session took about three hours for him to do two solos. Most of the time we were hampered by the fact that everybody was so keen. There were people showing up, tour managers who were just going off to work with Yes, who suddenly turned up to say goodbye. It was very funny, clamorous, and it could have been a bit more comfortable.

You returned the favor when you appeared on "The Only One" from Jimmy Page's Outrider solo album.

"The Only One" is humorous from my angle because I called it "The Only One." I had to call it that. In exchange for his endeavors on my record I said I'd sing a song, but he omitted to tell me that it hadn't been completely written yet. So he gave me the back track and I went, "Oh, I don't hear anything." And he said, "No man, that's for you." And I thought, well, that's a bit of an emotional blackmail there because I was in the middle of making my own record, but I took it home. (recites some of lyrics:) "It's all it fits, it's all that ever really, really was and who could resist because you're the only one." It's funny but of course it's very serious.

Twenty years after Led Zeppelin played London's famed club the Marquee, you returned to play there as a solo act. What was that like for you?

I was petrified. I mean, going back and playing somewhere which is a bit bigger than my dining room is a bit of an odd choice to do. But I wanted to do it because I have to distance myself to a degree from the big event. Ten weeks at Wembley, the Dire Straits approach, is wonderful. If I can ever aspire to it and develop and regain an audience properly instead of meandering around on the perimeter of rock 'n' roll saying, "I'm the king of anti-pop," if I could do that then that's great. But if I could do it so it's not so much like going to work. I think a lot of musicians tend to make it going to work almost, and I don't do that.

Being a member of the "legendary Led Zeppelin," have there been exceedingly high expectations placed on you as a solo artist?

Sure. See, media and my approach to my career, a lot of reporters don't think or do their homework. They think, "Oh, he was in Led Zeppelin and we'll ask questions about him going

back." And really, the media keeps playing on the fact that it could reform. Somebody could rebuild Stonehenge but it's not gonna happen. Like Spinal Tap. I mean, wouldn't it be just like that, everybody's granddads going out on tour again getting lost looking for the stage.

Obviously you saw the movie This Is Spinal Tap. *I ask a lot of musicians to share their most "Tappish" touring experiences. Do any come to mind?*

Well, you know the one about getting lost on the way to the stage? That's where they got it from, I'm sure. A lot of that stuff is from when we toured with the Fudge (Vanilla Fudge). We did get lost. We used

to play Baltimore Municipal Auditorium or whatever it was and there was a way under the street from the hotel to the gig where you could actually go on this path under the road. We wound up in some bloody kitchen where some guy went (imitates drunken guy with American accent), "Hey, man, have you come for the rubbish?" I said, "No, do I look like I'm dressed for rubbish calling? I've come to give it out."

So anyway, all those things, loads of things. Richard Cole, who was the tour manager in Zep. In those days we traveled in a station wagon on the first or second tour of America. That's the best way to travel and also you could communicate. It got a little harder later. We were in San Francisco looking for the Fillmore. We were down somewhere by Fisherman's Wharf in the fog in this Oldsmobile cruiser, me and Bonham fooling around in the back and Jimmy saying, "Close the window. My hair, my hair!" (laughs). Cole was backing up and suddenly the car wasn't going anywhere but he was accelerating really hard and he backed up on the capstan, those things that they tie up the boats with. Had he missed that by nine inches either side we would have reversed quite merrily into the San Francisco Bay.

Ricardo (Cole) could never find anything. He never knew where anything was. So this kind of information he gave to these various people who've written books is phenomenal because if he couldn't find his way around a town he'd been to 400 times, how could he remember all this stuff with such clarity and dialogue as well?

I guess if you treat it as a fictional story with some basis in fact, it's okay.

Yeah, well, the fact is that the people were there and they don't say anything now. It's easy to talk like that 'cause there's nobody going to refute it.

While we're spinning weird tales, what were some of the weirdest concert bills you've been part of?

Woody Herman played with Zeppelin, an odd combination. We played with Roland Kirk at Winterland in San Francisco. He played three instruments at the same time. It was that time though. John Paul Jones was experimenting in one corner and Roland Kirk was playing three instruments in the other. Some strange stuff.

Paul McCartney has fans of his work with Wings who aren't too aware of the Beatles. You must have some big Robert Plant solo fans who judge you on your work today, not the past with Zeppelin. How does that make you feel?

It's all right. I don't have to complete with one part of my career with the other or worry too much about the attention factor because I'm doing this anyway. And I'm doing it whether people like it or not. I'm very proud of the whole Zep thing because I've now grown up and I can look back at it without intimidating my career.

One of my favorite headphone songs as a kid was "What Is And Should Never Be." It was a mindblower for a ten-year old kid. What goes through your mind hearing a song like that today?

"What Is And What Should Never Be" is such an important song for me at that time in my life. It was about a girl who I loved so dearly and have loved since regularly and surreptitiously. It was so cheesy. (Sings) "Into a castle I will take you'" But it's like the whole fairy tale imagery was saying, "Baby I've just got to have you." I remember the session, I remember cutting it, I remember thinking about her, and I remember the first time that I played it to her.

On the last two solo tours, you've played Led Zeppelin songs live again. What prompted your reconciliation with the past?

I had to distance myself from the whole Zeppelin thing. I had to be seen not walking away but respectfully tipping my hat to it. But meantime I was in the Band of Joy before that and I sang (Jefferson Airplane's) "White Rabbit" and "She Has Funny Cars." So I've got to get back into being Robert Plant because otherwise what am I going to do? I can't just sing "Stairway To Heaven" for the rest of my life to keep everybody happy. So I did distance myself and I did pretend that I didn't really have much time for it but I had to do that to shut people up for awhile. It didn't work; they just shut up when they were around me.

Are you flattered by the Zep imitators such as Whitesnake, Kingdom Come, and Great White, or do you laugh?

I laugh. You've got to have a laugh. However, a seventeen-year-old kid who sees Robert Plant on the cover of *Rolling Stone*, or whatever, says, "Hmmm, he doesn't look like the king of cock rock but that German immigrant who sings with Kingdom Come does. I'll butt him and I'll go with that because I want to be seen to be associating myself with young virile rockers." Unfortunately, young virile rockers, from what I remember, came up with something quite original. That was great. I'm concerned with doing something fresh and they're concerned with aping me and Jim.

Ray Charles

By Johnny Etheredge
September 13, 1985

Ray Charles is one of the handful of musicians who has been so successful, for so many years, in so many different fields of music, that his name is a household word. He is admired by people of all ages and of all classes. He is revered by fans of rhythm 'n' blues, rock 'n' roll, soul, jazz, pop, and country. To call Brother Ray a living legend is almost an understatement. He is a performer of nearly mythical stature.

Ray Charles Robinson was born in 1930 in Albany, Georgia. (Ray dropped the "Robinson" early in his career, so he would not be confused with the boxer, "Sugar" Ray Robinson.) When only a few months old, Ray moved with his mother to Greenville, Fla., about 30 or 40 miles from the Georgia border. It was in this rural community that Ray first heard music, in the Shiloh Baptist Church. Ray recalls that the music was simple, with no instrumental accompaniment: "Preacher sang or recited, and the congregation sang right back at him."

Ray was introduced to another kind of music at the Red Wing Cafe. Run by a man named Mr. Pit, the Red Wing Cafe was the center of the black community in Greenville. Says Ray: "When you walked into the cafe you saw two things—right off—which shaped me for the rest of my life. Talkin' 'bout a piano and a jukebox." Ray was only three years old when Mr. Pit introduced him to the piano, letting young Ray try to imitate the boogie-woogie riffs that Mr. Pit laid down. Ray heard more boogie-woogie on the jukebox, along with the down-home country blues by the likes of Washboard Sam, Tampa Red, and Blind Boy Phillips.

Ray was blinded at age seven. Doctors have since told him that his blindness was probably caused by a form of glaucoma. He was educated at the St. Augustine School for the Blind in Florida. It was there that he received his formal training in piano, sax, trumpet, composition, and Braille music notation. Orphaned as a teenager, Ray decided not to return to school. It was time to make it on his own as a professional musician. He gigged around Florida with a variety of different types of bands, including—at one point—an otherwise all-white western swing band. In 1946, in Orlando, sixteen-year old Ray auditioned for Lucky Millinder's band. Lucky told him: "You ain't good enough, kid. You don't got what it takes."

By 1948, Ray decided that he had done as much as he could do to further his career in Florida. He not only wanted out of Florida, he wanted out of the South. He wanted to get as far away as he could from where he was. So he asked a friend to look at a map of the United States, and pick out the large city that was further away from Florida than any other city in the country. So it was in Seattle, Washington that Ray's career really got underway. Of course, he had already been a professional musician for several years by the time he hit Seattle. But it was in Seattle that Ray first formed his own trio. And it was while in Seattle that Ray signed his first recording contract, with Swingtime records of Los Angeles.

Small, piano-led combos featuring easy-going, smooth vocals, such as the groups led by Nat "King"Cole and Johnny Moore (featuring Charles Brown vocals) were very popular on the West Coast in the late '40s. Ray was trying to make a living, so he immediately adapted himself to this style. If you'll check out Ray's early recordings for Swingtime, you'll find that these recordings, both vocally and instrumentally, sound remarkably similar to records then being made by the King Cole Trio. At the time, Ray took great pride in his ability to perfectly imitate the sound of Nat Cole.

In 1952, Atlantic Records bought out Ray's Swingtime contract for $2,500. Ray's earliest recordings for Atlantic were still in the Nat Cole/Charles Brown mold. After some unsuccessful sides for Atlantic, a turning point came late in 1953. In New Orleans, Ray arranged and played piano on a session that produced Guitar Slim's "The Things That I Used To Do" for Specialty Records. That record—much more bluesy, raunchy, and "soulful" than anything else Ray had previously recorded—

became a giant hit for Slim. Ray must've seen the handwriting on the wall.

For the first time in his career, Ray demonstrated his remarkable musical versatility, and the ability to adapt himself to a variety of styles that would manifest itself time and time again in the years to come. It is probably this versatility—more than anything else—that has earned for Ray the title "the Genius." Beginning in 1954, Ray's records were infused with what has since become known as "soul." Ray went back to his musical roots, and merged the first two musical styles that he had ever heard. He joined gospel music to the blues, emphasized the beat, and in so doing became a pioneer of what would come to be known as rock 'n' roll. Ray left the Nat Cole imitations behind him. He began singing in his own natural voice, in a style that was probably heavily influenced by gospel singers like Alex Bradford. And his songs—mostly originals back in the mid '50s—were little more than gospel chord progressions behind secular lyrics.

In the period between 1954 and 1957, Ray introduced such instant classics as "It Should've Been Me," "I Got A Woman," "This Little Girl Of Mine," "Greenbacks," "Drown In My Own Tears," and "Hallelujah, I Love Her So." And while Ray's songs were topping the rhythm 'n' blues charts of the day, they were also being covered by a slew of rock 'n' roll artists, like Elvis, the Everly Brothers, Eddie Cochran, and Jerry Lee Lewis, to name but a few.

In the late '50s, Ray's band was playing a dance somewhere in the Midwest. The dance was scheduled to last until 1 a.m. With twelve minutes left to go in the dance, Ray and the band ran out of material. They had gone through their whole repertoire. So Ray told the band—which by now included his female backing group the Raelettes—to simply pay attention and follow him. He started riffing at the keyboard and ad-libbing some lyrics. The band members found their places and fell in. The Raelettes began repeating Ray's lyrics back to him, just as the congregation must have answered the preacher at the Shiloh Baptist Church. The crowd's reaction was so wildly enthusiastic that Ray repeated the number on the nights that followed, refining the lyrics and the riffs until the song was polished into a finished product. He recorded it in 1959. "What'd I Say" became his biggest hit to date, and placed Ray at the top of the pop charts for the first time. ("Swanee River Rock" had snuck into the bottom of the Top 40 in 1957, then dropped out again after one week.)

After the success of "What'd I Say," ABC Records made Ray an offer he couldn't refuse, an offer that Atlantic couldn't match. Ray left Atlantic Records with a remarkably varied catalog to his credit. There were all those rhythm 'n' blues classics. There were a couple of straight jazz albums, featuring Ray's piano work and occasionally his alto sax. One of Ray's last Atlantic LPs, *The Genius Of Ray Charles*, was about equally divided between big band swing and lush, string-backed ballads. At Ray's last Atlantic session, he recorded his first country song, Hank Snow's "I'm Movin' On"— shades of things to come.

There are some people who may feel that ABC Records may have "changed" Ray Charles, by burdening him with producers who forced him to record "pop" product. Ray has always been pretty much his own producer, choosing his own material and arrangements. This had been the case during his tenure with Atlantic, and it continued to be the case at ABC. During his first several years with ABC, Ray's output was an extension of the varied styles with which he had experimented at Atlantic. In 1960 and '61, Ray had giant hits in several different styles. The string-laden "Georgia On My Mind"gave Ray his first bona-fide No. 1 record. But the rhythm 'n' bluesy "Hit The Road, Jack" also hit No. 1, and Ray cracked the Top 10 with a big band swing arrangement of "One Mint Julep."

By 1962, Ray had established himself as a multi-talented performer. And though he may have been hard to classify, I don't think anyone at this point would've thought of Ray as a country singer. But you have to remember that Ray was a country boy. In the rural South where Ray grew up in the '30s and '40s, country music—or hillbilly music, as it was then known—saturated the airwaves. And Ray had always had a fondness for this music, just as he enjoyed many other styles of music. The idea of doing a country album was something that Ray had on his mind from the very beginning of his association with ABC. But since he was new to the label, he thought he would hold off on pursuing that idea until he had established some sort of track record with ABC.

Having compiled a successful track record indeed, he decided it was time to tell ABC that he was now going to do a country album. The resulting album, *Modern Sounds In Country And Western Music*, (and the 1963 follow-up, *Modern Sounds In Country And Western Music, Volume Two*) didn't really feature Ray performing in a new "style." He swung on some of the cuts, and on others he crooned soulfully, against a backdrop of strings. These albums were unique because of the source of the material. Here was a cat who was best known as a rhythm 'n' blues singer, singing songs written by hillbillies. Ray tackled material composed by the likes of Hank Williams, Ted Daffan, Floyd Tillman, and Jimmie Davis. And once again, in terms of record charts and record sales, Ray topped anything he had done previously. Ray's version of Don Gibson's "I Can't Stop Lovin' You" earned him his first certified gold million-selling single.

Ray continued to enjoy a great amount of success on record well into the late '60s. And although he has not been a major factor on the charts since then, he has consistently made great music. He has interpreted material ranging from Buck Owens to Lennon-McCartney to George Gershwin. And the results are always satisfying.

In 1971, Ray began distributing his own product on his Tangerine label (named after his favorite fruit). In 1977 he resigned with Atlantic. If I had to be stranded on a desert island with only one Ray Charles cut, it would have to be his late-'70s version

of "Blues In The Night"on Atlantic, from Ray's 1979 *Ain't It So* LP. Times may have changed, and the pop charts may no longer hold a place for Ray Charles, but this record proved that Ray had not lost one iota of "soul"and feeling and emotion and guts over the years.

And most recently, in 1983, Ray signed with Columbia records. His first LP release for Columbia, *Wish You Were Here Tonight*, was a straight country album, much more authentically "country"-sounding than any of his early '60s ABC material. Of course, I'm talking modern "Nashville Sound" country, but it is indeed country. The album—and two singles from the LP—made respectable showings on the country music charts in 1983. And in 1984, a duet with George Jones called "We Didn't See A Thing" had put Ray in the Top 10 of the country singles chart for the first time in his career. But it really doesn't matter on which chart Ray Charles may happen to be in vogue at any given time. Be it rhythm 'n' blues, pop, jazz, or country, there is a unifying thread that runs through all of Ray's music. Ray always sounds like Ray.

Ever since he left the Nat Cole imitations behind him in the early '50s, Ray has managed to conquer these varied fields of music on his own terms. If I may borrow the title of one of Ray's recordings, his music always sounds "From The Heart." Honest, soulful.

Goldmine*: I just read your autobiography that you published in the late '70s,* Brother Ray. *What made you decide to become an author?*

Ray Charles: Well, I don't think of myself as that. The only thing I truly think of myself as is, hopefully, a good entertainer. But an author, no. All I did was to try to straighten out some facts. I've seen a lot of people that I knew very, very well, very close to me, and things were happenin' to them. And so I thought, well, right or wrong, I'm going to write a book. And the things I've read and heard that were wrong, I'll correct. And the things that people didn't know, I'll try to straighten them out, too.

You spend most of your life on the road. After thirty-five years, why are you still up to that?

Well, because I can't stay in one city and really do what I wanna do. And not only that. Even if I could do that, I wouldn't want to do it. I truly enjoy goin' different places and seein' different people. True, sometimes it can bring about a little hardship. Because sometimes it can go a little further, or can get a little more difficult to do than you want. But let's face it, when you're blessed doin' what you really truly love doin', I mean, my God, don't you know it's gonna cost you something? You know what I mean? Really. I hear too many people who have to work. They gotta live. And every day of their lives they do jobs, and they really don't care about it. And yet I feel, honestly, the people are with me and they've been with me, they support me, and I'm doin' what I love doin.' So it's worth it for me to go, and I meet people, and I guess I'm just vain enough to want to get as many people as I can. (Laughs).

For twenty-five years, you've had the title "the Genius." How do you feel about that?

First of all, I didn't give that title to myself. And truly, I think it's a great compliment. I mean, it's a wonderful thing to have people feel that way about you. That's really putting you on a high pedestal. But I never thought of myself as a genius. In fact, I know without a doubt I'm not a genius. I mean, I don't kid myself. But I feel good that the people love what I do so much that this is the kind of compliment that they bestow upon me. It's really beautiful. But I'm truly just a plain cat, man. I think I do what I do well, and that's probably it. Of course, the main key to me is that everything I do, it's truly what I feel. And if people, as it turns out, just happen to feel what I feel, then it sort of works out nicely.

You had a great deal of success in the early '60s doing pop versions of country songs. And now your most recent Columbia LP and singles have put you in the country charts for the first time. Do you consider yourself to be a "country" singer?

Well, as I said, I try to entertain. I always have to come back to that one word. Because I do love different kinds of music. I've always loved country music. I was reared in the South. And in the years when I was comin' up, they didn't have what they call soul stations those days. Not even "race" stations, which was race music or somethin,' you see. So I heard an awful lot of country western music on the radio. Although, on the jukebox in my neighborhood I would listen to blues and things like that. Even today, I'm this way: I love good music. I

don't care where it comes from. Whether it's classical... and people misunderstand. They think just because it's classical, or just because it's an opera, that it's gotta be good. There's been some awful operas written, don't fool yourself. Some terrible classical music written. The thing of it is, music is such a big tree, with so many branches. And of course, as you know, you can find some good and bad in every art, whether it's painting, or sculpture, or whatever. And I think that for me, I enjoy good classical music, I enjoy the blues—love to sing the blues. I love to play good jazz. I love to take a country song—I'm not a Charlie Pride, I mean, I don't think of myself as a country singer—but I love to take country music and sing it my way. You know, put my own self into it and make it become me. That's what I enjoy doing.

When you look back at a career of milestones, like "I Got A Woman" in the mid-'50s, or "What'd I Say" in the late '50s, or the ABC sides in the early '60s, what are the high points to you? What are your proudest accomplishments?

You know; you mentioned some of them just then. Let me say that as a youngster comin' up, there were things that I wanted to do. For instance, I wanted to make a record someday. Now can you imagine a kid, nine years old, sayin' "Oh, if I could just make a record." 'Cause in my mind, that was really the ultimate of success. I mean, that would really be saying that you was really into what you was doing, you really was into music. And I thought if I could make a record, that would prove I was great. So the day when I made my first record was a big thing, number one. Or I'd tell myself "Oh, if I could just play in Carnegie Hall one day," or "If I could just have my own band one day, or my own trio." Which is what I first started with, a trio. Then I had a small band. And then I said "Oh, I hear so much that could be done with a big band, I'd love to have a big band." You know, these are things that I wished for.

And then when I started making records, I said "Wouldn't it be nice one day if I could honestly win a Grammy." And then one year Sinatra and I had a little thing where we were both nominated for the best male vocalist, or something, and I won by four votes. Isn't that great to do that? You know, to be in competition with the best in the world. That's it to do that.

Things have happened to me in my life, I have to

tell you. In spite of tragedies and I've had many tragedies in my life, truly—but on the other hand, I've had many things happen to me in my life that the public made me feel... I would've never dreamed. There was no way I would've even thought about, truly. I had a thing that they did in Georgia for me, where they honored the song "Georgia" as the state song. They already had a state song, but they took it away and used my version. I mean, if anybody had told me this would happen in the state of Georgia! What can I tell you?

I'm just grateful to the public for making it all possible. And that's not just sayin' somethin', it's the truth. I just love people. You know, at the beginning of the conversation, you mentioned that I've been out here all these years. I've spoken to many people who say "Well, you know, ever since I can remember, there's been a Ray Charles in our house." And you know, that's a great feeling to have people say that to you.

You're not a prolific composer, but the lyrics that you do write seem to be quite easy to relate to, or "true-to-life." Do you feel that you have a knack for that?

Well, I try to think about "everyday." Because every day I see the lives of people, I'm among people. It's the same as someone who writes for soap operas. You see life, and you put it in your songs. It doesn't mean that everything you sing about has to necessarily have happened to you. But life is life. And the most common thing among people is love affairs. You know, falling in and out.

Speaking from the point of view of a black musician whose career spans the years from the late '40s to the '80s, you must have noticed a great change in the way black music is accepted by the masses.

I think what has happened is that more people have become aware, not so much of my music, but of black music period. Because of many white artists who have taken black music and "presented" it—if you want to put it that way—to the masses. And these artists, of course, they said "This is who I listen to. I listen to B.B. King, I listen to Muddy Waters, I listen to Ray Charles," and da-da da-da da-da. So naturally, the other populace began to say "Maybe we'll start to listen, too." And so I think there was an evolution that did take place. You see, musicians get among themselves. I mean, blacks

among whites and whites among blacks. And so what happened is, what I was doing, you had people come along like Elvis Presley, and the guy that did "Blue Suede Shoes," and the Beatles and folks like that, and they made the masses more aware of the music.

How about your plans for the future. Will you keep making music?

I make music because I breathe... Music to me is the same as my breathing. It is not separate. It's not something I do on the side. When people ask me when am I gonna retire, there ain't no retirin.' I can't retire. How can you stop breathing? When I retire from music, I'll be gone. I mean, that'd be the end of me, truly. I just hope that I can continue to inspire young people to play good music. And I hope that I continue myself to make people feel good with my own music. And if I'm able to do that, then truly, that's the key to me.

Shane Fenton

By Dave Thompson
March 27, 1998

On February 23, 1963, the Beatles were in the English midlands town of Mansfield, cowering in their dressing room while the Granada Theatre fell under a state of siege. There were girls screaming everywhere, and as one local musician sat backstage with the bands, having made his own way in over the roof behind the chip shop(!), Paul McCartney happened to mention they were starving.

"So I went back home," the visitor remembers, "over the roof again, and through the chip shop, and told my mother all about it. She made them up a picnic basket full of food—containers of hot soup and piles of salmon sandwiches, which I took to them backstage, again going over the roof. And they were absolutely knocked out."

They certainly were. Indeed, a full decade later, Paul McCartney would still remember the struggling young singer and his impromptu act of famine-relief; he remembered this good Samaritan's name; and he might even have remembered his story. Because it really wasn't the sort of tale which one forgot in a hurry.

Johnny Theakstone was the forgotten man of early British rock 'n' roll. Many others vie for the title, but none of them even come close. Dead before his seventeenth birthday; unknown and therefore, publicly unmourned; Theakstone nevertheless would live on when his group, Shane Fenton and the Fentones, persuaded roadie Bernard Jewry to slip into the title role to help them through a crisis... and then he died again, when Fenton's own star slipped into obscurity, and the singer reinvented himself as glam rocker Alvin Stardust.

Lining up as Theakstone (vocals), Gerry Wilcox (guitar), Mick Hay (rhythm guitar), future Hollies drummer Bobby Elliott, and a bassist remembered only as Bonny, it was late in 1960 when Johnny Theakstone and the Tremoloes recorded an audition tape for the BBC late in 1960. The Corporation was constantly on the look-out for new acts to guest on the weekly *Saturday Club* show, and though the chances of being accepted were staggeringly slight, Theakstone was convinced his Tremoloes were equipped with virtually everything it took to succeed—except for a name.

Adopting "Shane" from the writing credits of a recent Gene Vincent single, and "Fenton" from a garage he passed on the way home from a gig, the newly named Shane Fenton and the Fentones dropped their precious tape in the post, and waited. They were still awaiting a reply when Theakstone died.

As a child, Theakstone had suffered a prolonged bout of rheumatic fever, an illness which so weakened his heart, roadie Jewry mourned, "that he should never have been doing the sort of things he was doing with the group. He was going out to work during the day, and then in the evening he'd go off to do a gig and sometimes not return home again until four in the morning. But no one ever stopped him because that was the life he loved."

The first sign that anything was wrong came when Jewry dropped by Theakstone's house one evening to pick him up for a show. "I found him sitting on the settee in the lounge, with blankets wrapped all around him, very ill and too weak to stand." Jewry stood in for him on stage that evening, and when Theakstone was admitted to the hospital, he continued to deputize.

"And then one day there was a knock at the door and it was Cliff Hardy, who was the local Musicians Union branch secretary. 'Johnny died last night.'"

The effect on the group was shattering. "We thought the best thing to do would be to fold it up out of respect for Johnny's mum. And then... about a month after Johnny's death... a letter arrived from the BBC saying they liked the tape we sent them, and were now offering us a studio test.

"Johnny's mum came round to see us and said she'd been turning it over in her mind, and didn't want us to give up now, just as the BBC had shown interest. 'I'd like you to carry on. It was Johnny's life. He would have wanted you to do that.' So we got the group together again, and then she came to see us again and said, 'would you be offended if I asked you to use Johnny's name?'"

Jewry said he wouldn't. He became Shane Fenton that same afternoon.

The newly reconstituted Shane Fenton and the Fentones sailed through the audition, early in 1961, and duly appeared on *Saturday Club*. Before the end of the day, the show's M.D., Tommy Sanderson, had become the Fentones' manager; by the end of the week, he had landed them a deal with EMI.

September, 1961, saw Shane Fenton and the Fentones release their debut single, the stirring "I'm A Moody Guy," backed by the old music hall favorite "Five Foot Two, Eyes Of Blue." Days later, on October 3, the band received its media launch, at the Center of Sound in central London. They made their television debut on *Thank Your Lucky Stars*, and the record, as Jewry put it later, "...was away." It eventually peaked at #19 on the British chart, and nobody doubted that a new star had been born—nobody, that is, apart from the record buying public. They were never convinced by this latest beat sensation, and the more they saw of them, it seemed, the less certain they were.

Through early 1962, Shane Fenton and the Fentones slugged around the UK, aboard one of the legendary Larry Parnes' package tours, sharing the bill with Billy Fury and the Tornadoes, Karl Denver and Peter Jay. But though their live show went over well, three successive singles passed by unnoticed: "Walk Away" and an early cover of "It's All Over Now" for the full group, and the instrumental "Lover's Guitar" by the Fentones alone.

June brought a respite within this gathering gloom, when the still memorable "Cindy's Birthday" returned the band to the upper echelons of the chart. But then it was back to square one as "Too Young For Sad Memories" and "I Ain't Got Nobody" sunk successively into oblivion, to be joined by another of the Fentones' instrumental efforts, "The Breeze And I."

"One moment our career was taking shape, and we were going steadily upwards," Jewry would recall, "and then within a matter of weeks, it was all over. We just couldn't get work. Promoters only wanted to book you if you came from Liverpool, and they could plaster this all over their posters." It didn't even matter that the Fentones, during their few weeks of glory (actually it was months of glory, but it seemed a lot less), had played all the future hotbeds of Merseybeat, "and knew what the music was all about." They had, quite simply, happened too soon. "Our timing was wrong."

That fact was brought home to them when the Beatles played Mansfield, and Jewry rushed home to get them some food. That night, he experienced what it was like to be at the top of the game. The following month, however, Shane and his Fentones were reminded of what it was like at the bottom,

when they set off on another Parnes package, way down the bill behind Joe Meek's Tornadoes, Rolf Harris and Joe Brown.

It was the last thing they would ever do. In April, 1963, Shane Fenton and the Fentones broke up, and Jewry headed off to a solo career which was no more rewarding than his band act. "A Fool's Paradise," a wryly ironic title for a man who still dreamed of stardom, flopped that same month; "Don't Do That" went belly-up in July. The only bright spot on the horizon was when he met Iris Caldwell, the Liverpudlian ballet dancer who would become his wife, and who had her own tale of Merseybeat-derived woe to tell —her brother was Rory Storm, the man who could, and maybe should, have beaten the Beatles to the top.

For a time, Jewry moved into management, linking with Tommy Sanderson to oversee Bobby Elliott's new band, the Hollies. But the following year he was performing again, as the husband and wife duo "Shane Fenton and Iris" took their song-and-dance routine through the cabaret clubs of northern England. And when 1972 brought Jewry a brand new record deal, he'd been Shane Fenton for so many years he didn't even dream of finding another name to play with.

His manager, Hal Carter, however, did, and a year or so later, as the singer's new single, "My Coo Ca Choo," awaited its release, he unveiled the new alias. Shane Fenton, Carter argued, was yesterday's papers, and as the newly christened Alvin Stardust took his first steps back on stage, Jewry literally reveled in the mysterious new identity he and Carter had created.

A star with no past, a man with no reputation, a leather clad, black gloved demon who stalked British pop television and refused to smile or even answer questions. It was true, Stardust chuckled, as he prepared for another sinisterly appareled television performance, the BBC's immortal *Top Of The Pops*, nobody had an inkling who he was—or ever had been.

And then another of the show's guests walked by. Former Beatle Paul McCartney glanced over at Alvin, then paused for a moment, knowing he'd seen that face somewhere, but not quite able to pinpoint where.

Then he burst into a sudden grin, and raised his voice over the buzz of the crowd. "Hey, Bernie! Is your mum bringing down the hot soup and salmon sandwiches tonight?"

Photo/Chuck Boyd/Flower Children

Keith Richards

By Andrew Edelstein

May 1983

If Mick Jagger is the heart of the Rolling Stones, then lead guitarist Keith Richards is certainly the soul. He's considered the musician's musician in the Stones—as well as one of rock's best guitarists, period. But he's also the one whose controversial behavior, including a decade-long bout with heroin addiction, has fixed him in the public's eye as the bad boy of the Rolling Stones.

But in the past couple of years, Keith has cleaned up his act. He claims to have kicked the smack habit and in public he appears considerably healthier and more robust than he has in the past. This was especially noticeable during the band's 1981 American and 1982 European tours. The former can be seen in cinematic close-up in the Stones' latest film, *Let's Spend The Night Together*, which chronicles that tour.

Richards was in New York in mid-January to promote the film. During a one-hour interview at the Plaza Hotel, the thirty-nine-year-old Richards talked freely and easily about the state of contemporary music, the Rolling Stones' place in musical history and his own plans.

Goldmine: It seems ironic that your current movie takes its name from the same tune that caused such an uproar sixteen years ago when Ed Sullivan made Mick Jagger change the lyrics of "Let Spend The Night Together" to "Let's Spend Some Time Together."

Keith Richards: The rest of the band wasn't singing, so we didn't give a damn whether you changed a lyric—we didn't consider it to be an incredibly moral stand, that we'd be selling out if we did it. But by telling us to do this, those people actually, in fact, enhanced the thing they were trying to avoid. By trying to avoid somebody, they end up tripping up everybody.

I always remember when we'd do the Sullivan shows, there'd be these hushed, reverent tones the minute he walked into the studio. And he'd say "the Bible Belt, the Bible Belt." It's the one phrase that sticks in my mind—"sorry, boys, we can't do it. We have to consider the Bible Belt."

Obviously, a lot has changed since then, especially music itself. Regarding the state of popular music right now, the hottest sound seems to be techno-pop. What do you think of it?

Some of the sounds are interesting, but what it shows the most is that the music business hasn't changed a bit. As soon as there's one innovation, immediately everyone has to make a formula out of it on the theory that if you can sell it once, you can sell it again. It shows that the music business, although it progresses in one way, still operates behind the scenes in a very traditional Tin Pan Alley-type of way.

Synth-pop is essentially a merger of rock and disco. In that respect, I see "Miss You" as being a kind of pioneer recording in bringing these two genres together.

In retrospect, yes. At the time, no. I think the Stones tend to react as well as act and disco was what was happening then. At the time we were making it, we didn't see it in that light. In hindsight, yes. But at the time we were doing it, we were never aware that it was a wedding between rock and disco. It's one of those by-products that is noticed later on. It was kind of a landmark.

As one of rock's most influential guitarists, do you think synthesizers are gong to replace guitars?

No, even though synthesizers seem to be very popular right now. The guitar, apart from its musical worth and versatility, also has a mystique about it—the way it looks and plays—that is very central to rock 'n' roll. It's pretty much always going to be the central core of most rock 'n' roll.

We first used synthesizers in the early '70s to augment our sound, but I could never see us adding synthesizers to our lineup permanently.

So you think the popularity of groups like Duran Duran and the Human League is not going to be long-lasting.

31

I don't see it as any major shift in music. I think that audiences aren't particularly interested in how a sound is made or what instrument it's made on. If it sounds good to them, then that's really as much as they care to know. Most people don't break down records into instruments. The making of a record is still basically putting a few instruments together and making what comes of that speaker one sound.

If you think back to any given period, ninety percent of the music has been crap and has had a huge following. Like when we started the Dave Clark Five, Herman's Hermits—an awful lot of rubbish came out of that period. It's the other ten percent that's interesting and the thing that makes you want to carry on.

What's happening with the Stones now? Are you doing any solo work?

No. It's full speed ahead on the new Stones album.

What's the new album going to be like?

It's difficult to tell right now because the material is now in a very raw state and also we're continuing to write and change as we go along. It's never a conscious decision about the way material is when the Stones go into a recording studio. The Stones go in and then halfway through a song, somebody realizes that it sounds better turning the beat around or slowing it down. It's the same way that "Sympathy For The Devil" started as sort of a Bob Dylan ballad and then turned into a Samba. We like to have a song grow in the studio.

If we can go back to when you were growing up, you were a fanatic for rhythm and blues. But it seems that kids today don't have that passion for—or the exposure to—black music. Why do you think that is?

That's due to the radio as well as a change in black people. The atmosphere in which blacks live in America hasn't really changed that much, but it's not the same high-pressure cooker atmosphere of the post-war period which tended to produce the incredible burst of energy in music. Our interest in it was

purely due to the fact that when rock 'n' roll burst on the scene, when you happened to find out exactly who was doing the best records, it happened they were black artists. That's the way us English groups got into it. Apart from one or two white people, rock 'n' roll was played best by black people—Chuck Berry, Little Richard, Bo Diddley.

There still seems to be a real color bar in America, you would think that by the late '60s and early '70s

that would be a thing of the past. But black people are not making an identifiable sound of their own now. Prince is hardly as mind-shattering or interesting as when Little Richard or Otis Redding or Chuck Berry first appeared. It's quite a white influenced sound. Black music is no longer as identifiably black as it used to be.

It seems to me that during the past five years or so, many groups—especially the early punks—made a point of saying they weren't influenced by black music.

That's their own problem. Either that or the fact that they don't think they're being influenced by black music, when in actual fact, the music, being based very loosely on stuff we did and the influences of other '60s white groups, is, although they don't realize it, a once-removed copy of black music. It's white kids copying white kids, copying black kids.

But your heart is still with the R&B of the 1950s?

Of course. But I always also listen to everyone else, from Ludwig Van Beethoven on. The longer you get into something, the more you tend to listen to everything around you.

As a record collector, could you name the five favorites in your R&B collection?

That's a tough one. Bob and Earl's "Harlem Shuffle," Wilson Pickett's "Midnight Hour,"any one of the first four or five Otis Redding singles, anything by the early Coasters or Drifters with Clyde McPhatter. It's hard to pick five actual titles because those people were producing so much great stuff. Chuck Berry's marriage of lyrics to tuneful blues patterns was devastating when he played guitar in the way he chose to do it.

Speaking of record collecting, did you know that the original cover of Satanic Majesties now goes for as high as $50?

I didn't realize it was that high.

There seems to be a resurgence of interest in that period of music. Does it surprise you that there's all this interest in the psychedelic '60s?

You kind of forget that the kids growing up since then have no doubt a totally different perspective than we do. To us, what might seem to be a crazy phase, is when they were born. And you can never really try and understand exactly how they see that period compared to how we see that period.

What do you think of all the bands—both in the mid-'60s and more recently—who have modeled themselves after the 1965 Stones?

Now we're used to it, but there was a time when we used to say "let's spot the Mick Jagger and the Keith Richards character in that group." In a way, it's a mixture of cynicism and flattery. In a way you're kind of pleased about it; it's always great to know you've influenced so many people. It's also that you realize that what you were doing didn't come out exactly as you wanted it.

It's strange when you see these influences because it doesn't seem that we've been around that long. Sometimes it seems like a few days. When we actually started to cut our first record, we had the feeling that this is really the beginning of the end, because in the early '60s, even if you were a success, ninety-nine percent of all recording acts lasted eighteen months to two years. We felt that it would be over before we really got going, so it was very strange that we just kept going.

Does it bother you when people say "How can you be almost forty and still playing rock 'n' roll?"

No. It hasn't bothered Muddy Waters or Chuck Berry very much. I'd like to be playing as well as them at sixty—and no doubt people will be asking me the same thing then. But as long as I can play well and improve in my own life, then damn it, I'll be playing.

Ron Wood recently, quite unsuccessfully, tried teaching a one-night course in New York. Do you see yourself teaching a course like him?

I don't think so. My idea of teaching is keeping a lot of snotnosed kids in line and I never see it as more than that. I don't think I have capabilities or patience to explain how I've done things because a lot of times I don't know why I've done some things myself.

You've always had a reputation for candor. It doesn't seem to bother you playing your life out in public.

The main reason I'm open about my life is to avoid people snooping around, looking for bodies in closets that aren't here. I'd rather have everybody know what's happening to me. There it is—warts and all.

Do you see your son Marlon (who's thirteen) quite often?

Yes, quite a lot; he's a good friend of mine.

What kind of music does he like?

Like all kids, he likes what's current on the radio, but naturally, he listens to the Stones because he's been on the road with the Stones since he was a year old—he likes reggae, the Coasters, the things we went through.

What music is interesting to you today? You mentioned Prince before.

Prince vaguely, not particularly. But when he played with us, he couldn't hold the crowd—maybe he was too young or it was too big a crowd, even though it is a difficult thing to open for the Stones. I was impressed by the Stray Cats—they're gonna be great in a few years. I'm glad our judgment was correct when we chose them to be our opening act.

Who have you been listening to?

Really I haven't heard that much except for the Stones—I've been too busy writing, recording, touring. I have listened to a few tunes that have come in to us from unknown people, but I can't mention any names right now.

What are the most satisfying Stones albums to you?

In retrospect I suppose *Exile On Main St.*, *Beggar's Banquet*, *Some Girls*, *Let It Bleed*. In the '60s, *Aftermath* was particularly satisfying to me at the time. I don't like *Goats Head Soup* and *It's Only Rock & Roll* because they were done during such a stormy period for us. We were uprooted from England. Mick Taylor joined the group; it took us awhile to settle down to a new Nomadic way of living. A lot of energies were used up in different things during that period.

What do you think of Satanic Majesties *in retrospect?*

It's grown on me. It was the one Stones album that I never listened to for years and years and then a few years ago I put it back on the turntable and it was a lot more interesting than I thought it was. It is kind of the maverick of the lot.

Keith, thanks for your time.

this issue's Five Star Record

heymarty@mail.wwnet.net

© MARTY WINTERS VW T998

A DILEMMA: HOW TO CHOOSE JUST ONE FRANK ZAPPA ALBUM FROM HIS ASTOUNDING AND VARIED OUTPUT TO SUBMIT HERE?!... TO LOVINGLY RENDER AND SLOBBER OVER WITH GENEROUS (AND WELL-DESERVED) PRAISE?!! HOW?!! WELL, FIRST OF ALL, I ONLY OWN A HANDFUL OF ZAPPA LP'S — AND SINCE THE MATERIAL HERE IS LIMITED TO MY PERSONAL COLLECTION THE CHOICES WERE IMMEDIATELY PARED DOWN TO MOTHERS OF INVENTION DEBUT LP "FREAK OUT" (1966), "STUDIO TAN" (1978),

DESPITE VERY LITTLE FORMAL MUSICAL EDUCATION, ZAPPA BECAME ONE OF THE MOST PROLIFIC COMPOSER/PERFORMERS IN MODERN ROCK HISTORY! HE RECORDED DOZENS OF ALBUMS OF ORIGINAL MUSIC, RAN HIS OWN RECORD LABELS (ZAPPA, BIZARRE & DISCREET) AS WELL AS SERVING AS PRODUCER AND DIRECTOR OF TWO ROCK FILMS BASED ON HIS LIVE CONCERTS AND ROAD TOURS: "200 MOTELS" (1971) AND "BABY SNAKES: THE COMPLETE VERSION" (1979)!!

FRANK ZAPPA
HOT RATS

HIS MOST COMMERCIALLY SUCCESSFUL LP "APOSTROPHE" (1974), ANOTHER MOTHER'S LP "OVERNIGHT SENSATION" (1973) AND THIS LP FROM 1969: "HOT RATS" ON THE BIZARRE/REPRISE LABEL!! SO, I HAD AN ALL-ZAPPA LISTENING EVENING AND I WAS STRUCK BY THE TIMELESS BRILLIANCE OF "HOT RATS"! NEARLY 30 YEARS LATER, IT STILL STANDS UP AS ONE OF THE MOST ENTERTAINING AND ORIGINAL JAZZ/ROCK FUSION LP'S EVER RECORDED! AND, ALONG WITH FRANK'S BLISTERING, INVENTIVE, UNMISTAKABLE GUITAR SOUNDS, IT FEATURES AN ALL-STAR LINEUP OF MUSICIANS WITH VIOLIN PLAYING BY SUGARCANE HARRIS AND JEAN LUC PONTY, SHUGGY OTIS ON BASS AND CAPTAIN BEEFHEART VOCALIZING ON THE ONLY NON-INSTRUMENTAL TRACK — "WILLIE THE PIMP".

I SAW "200 MOTELS" AT A MIDNIGHT SHOWING AROUND 1976 OR '77 AND I HAVE TO ADMIT IT PUT ME TO SLEEP! (OF COURSE IT COULD ALSO HAVE HAD SOMETHING TO DO WITH THAT SIX-PACK AND BOONE'S FARM I HAD CONSUMED PRIOR TO THE SHOW!) ANOTHER FOND ZAPPA MEMORY INVOLVES DRIVING TO DAYTONA BEACH FOR SPRING BREAK AROUND THAT SAME TIME WITH "APOSTROPHE" LOOPING ENDLESSLY THROUGH THE 8-TRACK TAPE PLAYER — THE TAPE (I'M ASHAMED TO CONFESS) PILFERED ON A DARE FROM A LOCAL DEPARTMENT STORE!!

ZAPPA DIED IN 1993 AT AGE 52 OF PROSTATE CANCER.

☆ ☆ ☆ ☆ ☆

THE COVER ON MY COPY IS KINDA TRASHED, BUT THE ALL-IMPORTANT DISC IS CLEAN AND PLAYS GREAT!!

The Top 15 Most Valuable American Rolling Stones Records

Compiled by Tim Neely from the *Goldmine British Invasion Record Price Guide*

Key: For many listings, you'll see a letter or two before the title. These designate something special about the listing as follows:

B: for LPs, a record listed as stereo has both mono and stereo tracks on it, and as far as we know none of it is rechanneled stereo.

DJ: some sort of promotional copy, usually for radio stations, and not meant for public sale.

M: for any record pressed in both mono and stereo, a mono record.

P: for LPs, a record listed as stereo has some tracks in true stereo and some tracks in rechanneled stereo. The stereo or the rechanneled tracks are often listed below.

PD: picture disc (artwork is actually part of the record).

PS: for 45s and some EPs, a picture sleeve (this is the value for the sleeve alone, combine the record and sleeve value to get an estimated worth for the two together). UK EPs are assumed to have a picture sleeve unless noted.

R: for LPs, a record listed as stereo is entirely rechanneled stereo.

S: for any record pressed in both mono and stereo, a stereo record. Either the entire record is known to be true stereo or we don't know whether it's all stereo. In general, rechanneled stereo was not used in the UK.

	Label, Catalog #		Title	Value
1.	London LL 3402	M	12 x 5	$10,000
	Maroon label with "London" unboxed at top; possibly unique blue vinyl pressing.			
2.	London 909	PS	Street Fighting Man/No Expectations	8,000
	Ultra-rare picture sleeve; only about a dozen copies are known to exist.			
3.	London NP 1	M	Big Hits (High Tide and Green Grass)	6,000
	With two lines of type on the front cover, all in small letters.			
4.	London NPS 3	PD	Through the Past, Darkly (Big Hits Vol. 2)	6,000
	Prototype picture discs that used the cover art from "Big Hits (High Tide and Green Grass)" either on one or both sides.			
5.	London 9641	I	Wanna Be Your Man/Stoned	4,000
	Stock copy of their first US record, which was quickly pulled from the market.			

6.   London LL 3375   DJ   England's Newest Hit Makers—
                                          The Rolling Stones   3,000
       *White label promo; "London/ffrr" pressing, manufactured in UK for export to
       the US.*

7.   London RSD-1   DJ   The Rolling Stones—The Promotional Album   3,000
       Counterfeits exist of this rare promo (US version).

8.   Rolling Stones 19309   PS   Beast of Burden/Before They Make Me Run   1,200
       One of the rarest picture sleeves of the 1970s.

9.   London 2PS 606/7   S (2)   Hot Rocks 1964-1971   1,000
       *With alternate mixes of "Brown Sugar" and "Wild Horses" unavailable else-
       where. The date "11-5-71" is in the Side 4 trail-off area.*

10.   London PS 539   Beggars Banquet   1,000
       *Manufactured in UK with US labels for export to Japan; with interview flexi-
       disc in picture sleeve.*

11.   Abkco MPD-1   DJ   Songs of the Rolling Stones   500
       A 1975 promo-only issue.

12.   London 9725   PS   Heart of Stone/What a Shame   500

13.   Rolling Stones COC 59100 M   Sticky Fingers   500
       White label mono promo; no stock copies were released in mono.

14.   London 905   PS   We Love You/Dandelion   400

15.   London PS 375   R   England's Newest Hit Makers—The Rolling Stones 300
       *Dark blue label; lower left-hand corner of cover advertises a bonus photo.
       Much scarcer than the mono version because it didn't come out in rechan-
       neled stereo until late 1964, several months after the original.*

37

Photo/Henry Diltz

Harry Nilsson

By Dawn Eden
April 29, 1994

Harry Nilsson, as any fan knows, loved the movies. In life, he could do a credible Stan Laurel. In death, he cannot help but be Orson Welles's *Citizen Kane*. It seems as though everyone who had contact with Nilsson, however fleeting, has a story to tell, and each story only adds to his mystery. Considered one of rock's most literate songwriters, Nilsson had only a ninth-grade education and denied that he was any great reader. A man whose supposed party exploits fed rumor mills for years, he struck close observers as just what both he and his friend John Lennon claimed to be: a pussycat. He alienated some adults with his occasionally foul-mouthed lyrics, yet he won the hearts of kids and kids-at-heart with his sweetly innocent concept album *The Point*. Finally, despite the fact that he offered no apologies for his past behavior (including his yearlong "Lost Weekend" with Lennon), he was, in his later years, the model of a devoted family man. His life would not be more difficult to analyze if his last word was "Rosebud."

When Goldmine last caught up with Nilsson, on January 7, 1994, the singer was trying as hard as he could to camouflage his flagging health. Although Nilsson's words make it clear that he was, as he put it, "not long for this world," physically and spiritually he projected an image of resolute strength. It was a shock to many, not least of all this writer, when he died only eight days later.

Nilsson's first words into *Goldmine*'s tape recorder were a lengthy quote from his favorite article about himself: Derek Taylor's liner notes to Nilsson's 1968 album *Aerial Ballet*. Although the notes included the famous statements, "Nilsson is the best contemporary soloist in the world. He is It. He is the something else the Beatles are. He is The One" (words which would be mere hyperbole were they not this side of "true"), Nilsson quoted instead from the opening of the essay:

"Slanted-patterned parking lot and the children in the cars of many colors were whining 'Why' and 'When' and stout the bouncing bobbing frozen-food-faced ladies in wobble-pink capris were roller-curling their basket-way to the fat and hungry Riviera trunks and we, store-sullen men, waited in the scorching smog-stained sun on various vinyl-shining seats when I button-pushed into a seventeen-bar song-snatch and Timothy, eight and bright, said, 'Oh, you're smiling now, why? Oh why? Why...' the song had said: 'He met a girl the kind of girl he'd wanted all his life. She was soft and kind and good to him and he took her for his wife. They got a house not far from town and in a little while the girl had seen the doctor and she came home with a smile. And in 1961 the happy father had a son...' Such a fragment of song it was and from whom? It was new and hardly anything is new! And how could something come so strong and sudden so swiftly to snap the sad and slumberous Safeway stupor? Hayes, who rides the discs like Joel McCrea, said, '"1941," by Nilsson.' Oh, yes, he said, '"1941," by Nilsson.' Nilsson. 'Nilsson' he said, again, and told us it was good, and that was why we smiled, Timothy—we smiled because it was good..."

If one looks past the very '60s references to pink capris and Riviera cars, it is obvious why Nilsson felt so complimented by Taylor's words. It is the best description ever of that timeless feeling, the thrill that comes from hearing a pop song so exciting that it leaps out of the radio and into your long-term memory. Nilsson's "1941" came out in 1967, a year when the airwaves were cluttered with groundbreaking music of every sort. Yet, amid a radio landscape of "new" Dylans and "new" Beatles, Nilsson made an immediate impression upon Taylor and others in the know, because, through his creative magic, he was truly new.

He was born Harry Edward Nilsson III (not Nelson, as has been reported) on June 15, 1941—Father's Day—in the Bushwick section of Brooklyn, New York. Nilsson's best-known quote about Bushwick, a notoriously tough neighborhood, termed it "a crummy place to grow up if you're blonde and white." His father left his mother in 1944, so Harry spent most of his childhood with his mother and his younger half-sister. The family lived in an upstairs apartment at 762 Jefferson Avenue, along with Harry's maternal grandparents, two

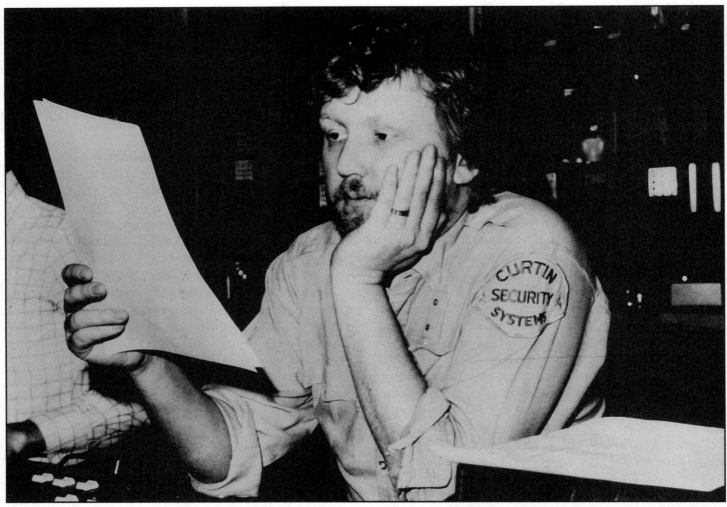

uncles, an aunt, and a cousin.

One of his earliest musical influences was his own mother, Betty, who wrote two songs which Nilsson later recorded. "She wrote 'Marching Down Broadway,'" Nilsson said, "which Irving Berlin offered her a thousand bucks for, I found out. She thought he wanted the whole song, so she said no. He may really have wanted the whole song, so she said no. He may really have wanted it; I've heard stories about him. Then she wrote 'Little Cowboy.' That was about the extent of her songwriting. I think she wrote poetry at night, you know, and things like that. She once wrote something which she sent to a publisher, called 'I Think I'm Going Mad,' and they sent it back and said, 'So do we!'"

In early 1952, Nilsson, his mother and sister took the long bus ride to San Bernardino, California, home of Betty's brother, John, and his wife, Anna. They stayed there for a month and then moved to the nearby town of Colton, where they lived in a trailer on the parking lot of the railside diner where Nilsson's mother waited tables.

As one might gather by now, Nilsson, despite growing up in the '50s, did not have a Norman Rockwell childhood. He had a total of six step-fathers, and his mother constantly had problems with alcohol and money. In late 1956, Betty moved herself and the children back East, to Long Island, to avoid prosecution for forged and bounced checks. They moved in with Betty's sister and her husband, Aunt Cissy and Uncle Fred, and slept in the family's basement and attic during that cold winter. Nilsson started school there after the new year and became very popular, making the baseball and basketball teams. His teenage life seemed to be achieving some semblance of normalcy.

Nilsson's mother and sister moved out of Fred and Cissy's home in early 1957, but Nilsson stayed there in order to complete the school year. When summer arrived, he was allowed to stay on at the home, provided he use the salary from his job as a caddy to help with household expenses. However, that June, around the time of his sixteenth birthday, he was fired after getting into a fight while on the job. When his uncle said that he couldn't afford to keep Nilsson on at the house, the dejected teenager decided to hitchhike to Los Angeles and rejoin his mother and sister, who had returned there a month before.

Nilsson returned to L.A. to find that he was on his own. His mother was in jail, presumably having been caught up to her old tricks with bad checks. Nilsson took a job at the Paramount Theater, which he later recalled was the fourth largest theater in the world. "They used to have live stage shows with all the rock 'n' roll bands, and they had a piano in the basement. So these guys passing through, the Sparrows or something, would show me some chords."

During this same period, Nilsson became taken by the explosion of great rock 'n' roll and R&B music on the airwaves. "I had this beat-up little radio that I used to listen to late at night. I had to listen to it late at night. I listened to a guy name Dick Hugg, 'Huggy Boy.' It was an all-black station. He played the Olympics, the Coasters, Ray Charles—he played Ray Charles's 'I've Got A Woman!' When I used to go to sleep, if that song came on the radio, no matter how low the volume, I would hear it, wake up, and listen to it and go, 'Yeah!'"

In the summer of 1958, Nilsson took time off from the Paramount and moved back in with his uncle John and Anna, the relatives who housed the Nilssons when they first came West in 1952. He worked pumping gas at the station owned by John, who was a mechanic. John also was a major musical influence on Nilsson, teaching him how to sing harmony. During this period, Nilsson started listening to the Everly Brothers and formed a singing duo with his best friend, Jerry Smith. "We were the poor man's—we were somewhere between the Everly Brothers and Jan and Dean, actually," Nilsson said.

After spending the summer with his uncle John, Nilsson resumed working at the Paramount. "The theater promoted me to assistant manager and sent me to San Francisco to work at a theater that they owned up there. I worked there for a year and then I came back down to act as temporary manager, to close down the L.A. Paramount Theater, 'cause they were tearing it down to 'pave paradise and put up a parking lot,' as Joni Mitchell sang.

"When we closed the Paramount (circa 1960), the cashiers who worked for me were all getting jobs at a bank, and I said, 'Hell, if I'm their boss, I know how to count money, I can reconcile the balance. I'll apply.' So I lied on my application and told them I

graduated high school.

"Got a job at the bank; I took some tests, and I came out very high in the computer area. They were just starting computers. They said, 'Do you have any interest in computers?' I said, 'This is a dream come true. You bet!'

"So I got the job, kept the job. They found out I didn't graduate from high school and they called me in to fire me. I said, 'Look, I've done a good job. You know I have. I haven't been late,' and all that stuff. I cried tears and I said, 'Look, I had to do it, otherwise I wouldn't be able to get a job.'

"They really liked me, so they went out on a limb. They said, 'Okay, you're on probation for six months.' So I said, 'All right,' and I worked really hard for the six months, and they just kept me on and eventually I was in charge of the place when I left."

During the early 1960s, Nilsson began to build a career in music. Since he worked the night shift at the bank, his days were free for hanging around music biz offices. With his natural charm, he made many connections just from spending time in waiting rooms and befriending office personnel. The fall of 1960 saw him singing demos for songwriter/producer Scott Turner. According to Nilsson, Turner paid him five dollars for each of the eleven songs (all Turner compositions) that Nilsson recorded. Years later, Turner decided to capitalize on Nilsson's success by releasing the demos (filled out by studio musicians). He telephoned Nilsson to work out payment. Nilsson later claimed to have told Turner, "You already paid me. Five dollars a song. That was our deal." The "album" came out in two different pressings. If this story, as told by Nilsson, is true, then Turner must have made back his fifty-five dollars many, many times over.

One of the legends surrounding Nilsson is that he never performed any live concerts.

He was very proud of the fact that, with all his fame, he remained an amateur (no, amateurish) at live performance. While that claim is mostly true (save cameos at Beatlefests and such, plus the specials he did for the BBC), Nilsson, when pressed, admitted having done a show with Jerry Smith. "We did one," he chuckled and corrected himself, "well, we did half of one. There was an oldies but goodies type show, a road show with all rock 'n' rollers: the Safaris, the Elegants, Don and Dewey. This promoter, Hal Ziger, needed an act to fill in for the Safaris. We said, 'Okay. What do we sing?' He said, 'Whatever the heck you want! It pays fifteen dollars.

Do you want it?'

"So, came the night, we had to be at (a bar at) 35th and Weston, which is a tough area, South Central L.A. We got there at eleven in the morning for some reason. They were still cleaning out the bar. It stunk of whiskey. It was a black bar, in a black neighborhood. Pretty soon the musicians all started showing up, carrying their guitars and cases and everything, and we were scared to death. We didn't know what the hell we had gotten into. Then they said, 'Okay, bus time!' So we get on the bus and the first thing the driver does, he looks back at everybody, then he looks toward us and says, 'Back of the bus!' We were the only white guys there! And everybody cracked up, saying, 'Hey, that's all right, man, you're all right. You can sit here if you want. He's just being friendly, you know.' It was hysterical. We drove to a place right outside of San Diego called National City, to this big auditorium there. It seated about a couple thousand people, and the audience was all black.

"When it was our turn to go on, we went, 'Holy Jesus, what have we gotten ourselves into now?' We had bought some blue corduroys and blue sweaters like the Kingston Trio." Nilsson laughed and added, "Alpaca sweaters! And the gig was paying, don't forget, fifteen dollars. So we went out and there were howls of laughter. I mean, that place went nuts! We were scared; we'd never done anything like this before anyway, and this was really scary. And I looked at Jerry and he looked at me and we both looked at each other in fear. We didn't look at the audience, just at each other! We sang, 'If I Had A Hammer.'"

Nilsson laughed at the weirdness of it all. "Now, if they had had hammers, they would have killed us! They started laughing, and at the end of it they roared approval. They were screaming and clapping, all in fun. And I said, 'That's it,' and he said, 'That's it. We're outta here.'

"So we got the first bus back to L.A., where we found our Volkswagen trashed," Nilsson said, "so the whole thing cost me a car, the Alpaca sweater, and then, on top of that, I gave a check to Hal Ziger. I said, Here's ten dollars back. We only did one song. Since I gave him his money back, my amateur status was still intact," Nilsson concluded, chuckling proudly.

In 1963, Nilsson's songwriting and recording career gained steam, thanks largely to his creative partnership with songwriter John ("Good Golly Miss Molly") Marascalco. "John Marascalco

deserves a lot of credit," Nilsson observed. "He was the first guy to loan me three hundred bucks, and he also took me into the fold to write songs with him."

Together they wrote "Groovy Little Suzie," which, Nilsson admitted, "sounded exactly like 'Good Golly Miss Molly." The similarity must have appealed to Little Richard, for he wound up recording the song. Nilsson recalled that when he sang the song for Richard, the flamboyant star told him, "My, you sing good for a white boy!"

Marascalco, besides being the first major businessperson to recognize Nilsson's songwriting talent, also financed Nilsson's first professional recording efforts, a pair of singles released on independent labels. Neither disc made waves, but Nilsson was glad to get the experience. The first one, "Baa Baa Black Sheep," came out on Crusader Records. Since Nilsson did not care to use his real name, he used a joke name based on the "sheep" concept, "Bo-Pete."

The record itself came about from a chance meeting between Nilsson and a girl group. "I was in a little studio one day," he said, "hanging around, doing demos, and I heard these teenage girls walk by singing four-part harmony. They called themselves the Beach Girls. They had this quality to them that was so raw and natural, and I thought, 'Ooh, that's cool!' So I was working on 'Baa Baa Black Sheep,' and I said to the girls, 'Here, come here a sec,' and I started to play the song. I said, 'You do the backgrounds, like the Raeletts or something.'" The song garnered a smattering of local airplay, enough to merit a Bo-Pete follow-up: Nilsson's own version of "Groovy Little Suzie" coupled with "Do You Wanna (Have Some Fun)," on the Crusader offshoot Try.

One day, Nilsson was hanging around Ziger's office, shooting the breeze with the promoter's secretary, a woman named Sonny, when a breathless music publisher rushed in. As Nilsson later told the story, "He said 'Sonny! Quick! Do you know where I can get a singer? Just somebody who could sing this song. I'm doing a demo and I gotta get it over to (Mercury executive) Jack Tracy today.' She said, 'Him.'

"He said, 'Can you sing?' I said, 'Well, what have you got?' He played this awful song called 'Wig Job,' because wigs were getting popular again, flips and all that, you know? 'So there goes my baby with a brand new lo-ok/Got all the fellows in the neighborhood ho-oked/Wig Job.'

"I said, 'What are you gonna use on the other side?' He said, 'Anything you want.' I said, 'Well, I have this little song I was writing...' This was before I started writing good songs. It was 'Donna, I Understand.'" Recalling it, Nilsson laughed at the silliness of the title. "And the guy at Mercury said, 'I like the singer and I like the song "Donna," but the other side I don't like!'

"So, as a result of that, I got signed to Mercury, and I said (to the song plugger), 'Bye!' They kept me on the label for a year and they didn't put anything out, and finally they put that one single out." Since the label thought that "Harry Nilsson" sounded too much like a middle-aged Swedish business-man, the single came out under the name "Johnny Niles."

Throughout Nilsson's early recording career, he kept his night job at the bank. "I worked there every night, from five o'clock 'til about one o'clock. I'd get off around quarter-to-one if I was lucky. I'd race to a bar and fortify myself, and then race back to this office which I was allowed to use because I cleaned the windows for them when they weren't working one night. I washed all the windows and they couldn't believe it. I made the

Photo/Henry Diltz

place spic and span. They said, 'Boy! No one's ever done anything like that for us. Here, here's a key.' That was Perry Botkin's office." Perry Botkin, Jr. was a successful songwriter, arrange and music publisher.

In late 1964, Nilsson hooked up with Phil Spector. It was an interesting meeting of minds; Nilsson, who was just beginning to blossom, and Spector, who was at his artistic and commercial peak. Nilsson

was recording a demo at Gold Star, which was also Spector's studio of choice. "Phil was walking down the hallway and he heard my demo and he said, 'Who's that?' Turns out that Perry Botkin used to publish Phil when Phil was a teenager, and he said, 'That's Harry Nilsson.' Phil said, 'That's a good song. Did he write it?' Perry said, 'Yeah—well, he and I wrote it,'" Nilsson said.

The next thing Nilsson knew, the First Tycoon of Teen phoned him to suggest that they meet, and the two started to write together. The pairing resulted in three songs: "This Could Be The Night," recorded by the Modern Folk Quartet, and the Ronettes numbers "Paradise" and "Here I Sit." As Nilsson recalled, the latter tune's lyrics presaged Nilsson's later toilet humor songs such as Son Of Schmilsson's "I'd Rather Be Dead"; "It was taken from a men's room wall; 'Here I sit, broken hearted/Fell in love, but now we parted—instead of 'farted.' 'Couldn't see the writing on the wall—' If that isn't enough of a hint! I did a record with Chere with Phil, 'A Love Like Yours,' I called us Nilssonny and Cher!"

Spector, for reasons best known to him, chose not to release the MFQ's "This Could Be The Night" at the time. (It can now be heard on the Spector boxed set, Back To Mono) The classic pop song became legendary in L.A. pop circles and a particular favorite of the Beach Boys' Brian Wilson, who has reportedly made attempts at recording it over the years. ("This Could Be The Night" has the rare distinction of being in Wilson's permanent memory. In March of this year, during his appearance at New York's Algonquin Hotel, he was unable to recall some of his own songs, but acceded enthusiastically to a request for that Nilsson tune.)

Near the end of 1964, Nilsson's Mercury contract ran out, and he was picked up by Tower, a new arm of Capitol. "I had T-1; the first contract ever signed on Tower," Nilsson claimed. Unfortunately, Tower, like Mercury, quickly forgot about its new signee. "They kept me under wraps for a year and didn't do anything, so I said, 'Please let me get out of this contract. You're not recording me. Get me out.' So, finally, we had one session. The reason we get that was George Tipton put up his life's savings, 2,500 bucks, and we recorded four tracks and we sold them to Tower." Tipton, who went on to become a highly-rated arranger, was then a music copyist in Perry Botkin's office. Reflecting upon Tipton's investment in his career, Nilsson said, "That's what I call belief. He took that money and he paid for the session, which he arranged, his first arrangement.

"Tower also bought some other demos by the New Salvation Singers, which was the group that another guy in Botkin's office had, and I sang along with the group for free." Nilsson noted that Tower later reissued those recordings to capitalize upon the fame that he had acquired as a hit song writer. "Suddenly, because I had a hit song as Harry Nilsson, the group became credited as 'Harry Nilsson and the New Salvation Singers!'"

During this period, Nilsson supplanted his bank income by recording commercial jingles. His voice was heard on commercials for Ban deodorant ("Ban won't wear off as the day wears on") and Red Roof Inns (an Elvis-style "Look for the Red Roof"), among others. He also recorded a song that was used in an episode of the popular TV show "I Spy."

Like most other songwriters of the mid '60s, Nilsson changed his writing style in the wake of the Beatles' success. However, with Nilsson it was not just a case of emulating the Fab Four purposefully. In fact, when he first heard them, he was filled with jealousy. Fortunately, by the time the Beatles released *Rubber Soul*, Nilsson had learned to stop worrying and love the Fabs. Something about the group struck a very special chord within him, as though they were his kindred spirits. Their sheer creativity inspired him to stretch his own artistic boundaries.

Nilsson continued to spend his after-work hours in Perry Botkin's office, writing songs. "I remember

one magical day," he recalled with a hint of wonder, "I wrote three songs in one night: 'Without Her,' '1941,' and 'Don't Leave Me.' In one night. And I realized then that I would never write another bad song.

"The next day, they came into the office and I said, 'Listen to what I did last night.' I had put the songs on tape. They said, 'You wrote those last night?' The guy from across the hall had a publishing company, and he said, 'Id like to buy that one, "Without Her," for $10,000.' They sold it to him, thinking they had all these other songs on mine, so it was great. Then Glen Campbell recorded 'Without Her' and they heard about it first, so they said to the guy across the hall, 'We'll give you your ten grand back.' They gave it back, plus five. They put the song back in their catalog and then sold the catalog for $150,000!

"The guy across the hall had insisted than I do a demo on 'Without Her' an octave down and never go for the high notes because, he said, no one could sing those. I sad, 'You're crazy. I just sang it.' He said, 'You can, but you can't show that to an artist who can't hit those notes.' As a result, Glen Campbell heard the version with the lowered notes and he sang it down there."

Nilsson soon became a "happening" songwriter, and his tunes were picked up by everyone from Jack Jones to Billy J. Kramer, Sandie Shaw to Fred Astaire, and Herb Alpert to George Burns. Artists began to chart with his songs, including the Yardbirds with "Ten Little Indians" and Canadian folkpunk singer Tom Northcott—with the excellent Leon Russell—produced "1941."

Around the beginning of 1967, Nilsson ran into an old friend, Chip Douglas of the Modern Folk Quartet, at the L.A. industry hangout Martoni's. "I said, 'Hi, Chip! What are you doing?' 'I'm producing these guys.' I said, 'I'm sorry, who are these guys?' He said, 'These are the Monkees.' I had heard all the publicity about them, but I didn't know what they looked like. I said, 'Oh, fantastic!' They were doing their first or second album. Chip said to the Monkees, 'Harry is a fantastic writer. I would like to take him into the studio and let you hear a couple of tunes of his.' I said, 'Sure, I'd love to.' He said, 'Would you come over now?" I said, 'Yeah I'd love it.' Especially because I'd heard rumors that they were going at four million record sales out of the box.

"So I sang seven, eight, or nine songs, and Mike Nesmith said, 'Man, where the fuck did you come from? You just sat down there and blew our minds like that. We've been looking for songs, and you just sat down and played an album for us. Shit! Goddammit!' He threw something on the floor. And he went and got Micky (Dolez) and he said to him, 'Would you listen to this man? Listen to that!' Micky gave a surprised laugh, and Davy (Jones) started laughing over one song, and it was like the three of them were just out of their tree. Only Peter Tork couldn't give a shit."

Although popular wisdom has it that Nilsson was signed to RCA in the wake of the Monkees' recording "Cuddly Toy," Nilsson's first recording session for the label was in February of '67, two months before the Monkees recorded his song. Nilsson commonly warned journalists not to assume anything about him, but it seems safe to assume that RCA caught the buzz created by Perry Botkin's office, which happened to be on the same floor as the label.

The story goes that RCA signed Nilsson to a $75,000 contract, but Nilsson's side of the story was that they signed him for "zero". Although the truth may be in between, Nilsson's figure sounds probable, since in February 1967 he was still, commercially if not artistically, an untested property.

The title of Nilsson's first album, the October 1967 release *Pandemonium Shadow Show*, was taken from the book *Something Wicked This Way Comes*, by one of his favorite authors, Ray Bradbury. Legend has it that Nilsson originally wanted to title the album after the book itself, but legal considerations prevented his doing so. (It is also hard to imagine RCA getting worked up over the idea.)

In spite of Nilsson's previous recordings for Mercury, Tower, and small labels, he considered *Pandemonium Shadow Show* his true debut. It is not hard to see why. For one thing, it was the first record of his to make the most of his three octaves-plus voice. Many listeners, particularly those in the industry (who were practically the only ones who heard the album at its time of release) were stunned by the way that the multi-tracked Nilsson could make himself sound like anything from a gospel choir to the bigger-than-God Beatles. In addition, unlike Nilsson's previous efforts which were tailored for the disposable pop market, *Pandemonium Shadow Show* had an odd feel: contemporary, yet timeless. Such praise may sound like hype, but one listen to the album shows that, with such songs as "Without Her," "1941," and

"Cuddly Toy," it sounds startlingly fresh.

Although *Pandemonium Shadow Show* missed the charts, it was received enthusiastically by critics and others in the know. One person who fit into both categories was past and future Beatles' press agent and music columnist Derek Taylor. As Taylor would later relate in his liner notes to Nilsson's second album, *Aerial Ballet*, he was so thrilled with *Pandemonium Shadow Show* that he ordered up an entire box of LPs so that he could turn others on to his new discovery.

As 1968 rolled around, the biggest development in Nilsson's business life was that he had finally gotten the courage to quit his job at the bank. He was in his tiny office at RCA when he learned of the Apple press conference that made him, at least temporarily, a household word. "It was the second largest press conference since World War II," Nilsson recalled. "They asked the Beatles, 'Who is your favorite American artist?' John said, 'Nilsson.' And a few seconds later some guy asked Paul, 'Who is your favorite American group?' and Paul said, 'Nilsson.' Then there was a hubbub throughout the room: 'Nilsson' 'Oh, yeah, the group from Sweden.' Nobody knew what it was."

It was at this time that Nilsson made his famous decision not to perform. "The phone started jumping off the hook. They called RCA to say, 'I'd like to talk to someone about Harry Nilsson.' And RCA would ring them to my phone. I had asked for an office in my contract, because I was used to being in an office, you know? And I said, 'Hello?' 'Yeah, this is Tony Green, I'm from the NME,' or something. He said, 'I'd like some information about Nilsson.' And I said, 'Yeah?' 'Can you tell me where he's appearing?' I said, 'I'm not.' 'Oh, is this Nilsson? Oh! Uh, sorry! Listen, I just called because we're doing an article on you and we're trying to find out more about you. You've only had one album out?' I said, 'Yeah.' He said, 'Where are you playing?' I said, 'I'm not.' This is just after I left the bank! He said, 'Oh, uh, well, where did you play last?' I said, 'I haven't.' Then he said, 'Well, where are you planning to play next? What's your next gig?' I said, 'I don't have any plans.' He said, 'Oh. Where did you play last?' I said, 'I haven't!'

"He said, 'You've never performed?' And I said, 'No. My amateur status is still intact, thank you.' And the guy went—you could hear him!—each one of these callers about the same press conference, they all went, 'Whoop!' And I thought, 'Ah! Mystique! This is good. I'm the guy who doesn't perform. Good! leave it in!' Like the one-name joke. That was Rick Jarrard's idea, because Harry sounded like, you know, Harry. At the time, there were eighteen television commercials like, 'Haaarry, take out the gaaaarbage!' Rick said, 'Harry's a funny name. It's so New York. "Haarry," it's a drone name.' So, anyone who asked about my performing, I would answer the same way: 'I'm not, I haven't, I don't.'

"They'd say, 'Why is that?' I said, 'Um, I don't know.' And sometimes I'd say, 'I'm doing something the Beatles can't have done.' 'What's that?' 'Not perform,'" Nilsson said.

There is another story, which Nilsson also told writers, which places the Beatles' admiration for Nilsson at an earlier date than the Apple press conference. Since this story conflicts directly with the Apple story, and since there are only a handful of people alive who know exactly what took place, one hopes that an accurate chronology will some-day surface. Story #2 has it that Derek Taylor first heard Nilsson in the spring or summer of 1967, before *Pandemonium Shadow Show* was even released. He brought demos of the album to Nat Weiss at the Beatles' management company, NEMS. Nilsson was introduced to George Harrison (then staying on L.A.'s Blue Jay Way), as NEMS attempted to seduce the singer away from RCA. According to this story, Nilsson was slow to decide. As soon as he made his mind up to say "yes," Beatles manager Brian Epstein died, and, the offer ended as NEMS fell into disarray.

Not long before or after the Apple press confer-ence, Nilsson got an unexpected phone call on Monday morning at seven. As he later told *Rolling Stone*, the call began like this:

"Is this Harry? This is John."

"John who?"

"John Lennon."

"Huh?"

"This record (*Pandemonium Shadow Show*) is fuckin' fantastic, man. I just wanted to say you're great."

After exchanging a few more pleasantries, the two said goodbye. The next Monday morning at seven, Paul McCartney called, also to rave about the album. Nilsson later claimed that he got all dressed up the following Monday morning and waited by the phone, expecting, in vain, that Ringo would call.

A few months later, Derek Taylor invited Nilsson to fly over to London to attend some of the Beatles'

recording sessions. Nilsson sat in on what became known as the *White Album* sessions and spent some quality time with John Lennon. He played Lennon his just-released second album, *Aerial Ballet*, from which Lennon especially liked "Mr. Richland's Favorite Song" (named after record promoter Tony Richland). Recalling those times with Lennon, Nilsson told Rolling Stone, "I really fell in love with him. I knew he was all those things you wanted somebody to be."

At the time that Nilsson visited the Beatles, he was working on the soundtrack to the Otto Preminger movie *Skidoo*. Released at the end of 1968, the film was a bizarre attempt at psychedelic extravagance, with an all-star cast that was mostly well over thirty: Jackie Gleason, Carol Channing, Groucho Marx (in his last screen appearance), Burgess Meredith, and Peter Lawford, among others. Nilsson wrote the entire score, including background music and pop numbers. Most unusu-ally, in a cinematic first, he sang the entire closing credits. Although the film was recently revived to an enthusiastic audience at New York's prestigious Film Forum, it has never attained more than a small cult following. As critics David Ehrenstein and Bill Reed wrote in their book *Rock On Film*, "They weren't ready for it in 1968, and they still aren't."

Nilsson himself made a cameo appearance in *Skidoo* as a prison "Tower Guard" on LSD. Since he had never taken acid, he played the role as though he were drunk. An astute viewer will catch him doing a quick Stan Laurel shrug.

Nilsson began recording *Aerial Ballet* (named after his grandparents' turn-of-the-century trapeze act) before *Pandemonium Shadow Show* even came out. One of the songs he chose for the album was the Fred Neil tune "Everybody's Talkin'," which he recorded in November 1967. Nearly one year later, when *Aerial Ballet* came out, RCA released "Everybody's Talkin'" as a single. While it made plenty of noise on regional charts, even reaching #51 in *Record World*, the single's time had not yet come. It slipped by *Billboard*'s Hot 100, despite five weeks of "Bubbling Under."

Aerial Ballet began with "Good Old Desk," a song which, like "Cuddly Toy," was much misinterpreted. Once again, the source for the misinterpretation was Nilsson himself. "After I wrote the song," he told *Goldmine*, "somebody asked me what it was about and I said, 'I don't know.' Then I realized what the initials were." Viewers of the television show "Playboy After Dark" witnessed Nilsson tell Hugh

Hefner, with a straight face, that the song's meaning was in its initials—"God." Nilsson admitted to *Goldmine*, "I bullshitted him. I thought it was funny. Nobody else thought it was funny!" Meanwhile, the catchy melody of "Good Old Desk" was not lost on English popsters the Move, whose songwriter Roy Wood lifted its bridge for his song "Blackberry Way," which became the group's only U.K. #1 hit.

Nilsson was very embarrassed at the mention of his 1960s television appearances, which included spots on German television and on the U.S. sitcom "The Ghost And Mrs. Muir." Referring to the latter show, Nilsson later explained to the British press, "I was advised to have a manager, so that year (1968) I had one. He suggested I accept the part. So I just went on and did what they told me. It was awful!"

Nilsson's best contribution to '60s television was "Best Friend," the theme he wrote and sang for The Courtship Of Eddie's Father. Considering that it was one of his best-known songs, it is surprising that Nilsson never put it on record. The reasons for its non-release are probably due, at least in part, to legal and technical considerations. The recording of "Best Friend" used on the TV show was owned by the show's producers and not by Nilsson or RCA. Since the song was written as a theme and not as a commercial tune, it is short; its only verses are the ones heard on the show. In Nilsson's later years, he was impressed by the song's lasting popularity, and he attempted to re-record it for his final, unreleased album. (At the time of his last interview, he had not yet re-recorded it to his satisfaction.)

According to legend, it was Nilsson's inexhaustible booster Derek Taylor who helped him get his next break by playing Aerial Ballet for director John Schlesinger, who was auditioning music for the film Midnight Cowboy. When the word was out that Schlesinger needed songs, responses came from everyone from Joni Mitchell to Bob Dylan ("Lay Lady Lay"), to Randy Newman (reportedly, "Cowboy"). Nilsson himself hoped for his own composition "I Guess The Lord Must Be In New York City," but Schlesinger's final choice was Nilsson's version of "Everybody's Talkin'."

When it came out as a single off of the soundtrack in August 1969, one year after it had "Bubbled Under" and nearly two years after it was recorded, the world finally heard LA.'s best-kept secret. An international smash, "Everybody's Talkin'" reached #6 on *Billboard*'s Hot 100. The *Midnight Cowboy* soundtrack, spurred by the single's success, sold over one million copies and stayed on the Top 200 for fifty-seven weeks. The following March, "Everybody's Talkin'" won Nilsson his first Grammy, for "Best Contemporary Vocal Performance, Male."

Even before "Everybody's Talkin'" hit, 1969 was a banner year for Nilsson. That March, Three Dog Night hit #55 with the *Aerial Ballet* song "One." A million-seller, "One" was a breakthrough for both the group and the songwriter.

Nilsson's third album, Harry, followed close on the heels of *Midnight Cowboy*. It spawned a Top 40 single, "I Guess The Lord Must Be In New York City," proving that the song originally written as a movie theme could succeed on its own. Although Harry did not include "Everybody's Talkin'" (fans would have to buy the *Midnight Cowboy* soundtrack or *Aerial Ballet* for that), it became Nilsson's first hit album, reaching #120 during its fifteen weeks on the charts. It came at an important time for Nilsson, for it showed "Everybody's Talkin'" listeners, who had been attracted by his singing voice, that he had a unique songwriting voice as well.

Nilsson later noted that his album catalog tended toward trilogies. There is a point to that (no pun intended), for *Harry* seems in many ways like the final chapter in the trilogy that began with *Pandemonium Shadow Show*. Its songs are linked by a theme of retrospection, from the haunting "Mourning Glory Story" (which Nilsson later admitted was unwittingly influenced by the Beatles' "For No One"), to the wistfully childlike "The Puppy Song" (originally written for Mary Hopkin). In addition to ending a cycle, the album also began one, with Nilsson's first of many great Randy Newman covers, "Simon Smith And His Amazing Dancing Bear."

Nilsson followed *Harry* with a project close to his heart, *Nilsson Sings Newman*. Released in February 1970, the album stands apart from the rest of Nilsson's catalog, or anyone's catalog, for that matter. Its uniqueness comes from the fact that it is a true meeting of minds, each one of them a great songwriter and artist.

By 1970 Randy Newman was well-known in industry circles, with one solo album to his credit as well as many songs recorded by others, but commercially he was an unproven quantity. It would not be until the end of that year, after *Nilsson Sings Newman* came and went, that Newman would have his first major hit song in the United States, Three Dog Night's version of "Mama Told Me Not To Come." It was a daring move of Nilsson's to record an entire album of Newman's songs, and one which ultimately widened the audience for Newman's music. Although *Nilsson Sings Newman* did not chart, it was lauded by the press, earning more than one citation for "Album of the Year."

Nilsson Sings Newman is centered upon Newman's songs, Nilsson's voice, and Newman's own piano work. In some ways it is more a Newman album than a Nilsson album, because the delicate arrangements make the songs the star. Nilsson's own style was particularly compatible with Newman's. Listening to this album, and especially comparing it with Newman's own versions of the songs, the respect Nilsson felt for Newman is strongly evident. Nilsson's own personality comes through in the vocal arrangements. As with the previous albums, all the background voices, from the "female soul singer" to the "barbershop quartet," belong to Nilsson. On songs such as "Love Story," he created the perfect blend of romance and irony, qualities which are very present in Nilsson's own songs.

Nilsson later recalled how much effort went into that collaboration, as well as how tedious things got for his partner: "Randy was tired of the album when we were finishing making it, because for him it was just doing piano and voice, piano and voice, over and over and over. But I needed that practice because I needed to learn the songs inside and out the way that he knew them, but do it my way so that it (stylistically) matched both of us. Once I got the take down, I knew what I was going to do with it later. He didn't."

Nilsson spent much of 1970 working to bring another pet program into fruition, an animated musical TV special, aimed at children of all ages, called "The Point!" He was inspired by the idea that everything was pointed. Well, it seemed profound to him at the time, as he later explained: "I was on acid and I looked at the trees and I realized that they all came to points, and the little branches came to points, and the houses came to point. I thought, 'Oh! Everything has a point, and if it doesn't, then there's a point to it.'" Kids, don't try this at home.

Broadcast in early 1971, with story and songs by Nilsson and narration by Dustin Hoffman, "The Point!" was a cross-generational hit, just as Nilsson had hoped. The soundtrack album, which was narrated by Nilsson, reached #25 during a thirty-two-week chart life and launched the Top 40 hit "Me And My Arrow."

Nilsson knew that, with his current success, fans would search for his first two albums, and he wasn't pleased. After completing "The Point!," and before beginning his next new album, he returned to the studio to tinker with his old tapes. The result was June 1971's *Aerial Pandemonium Ballet*, a collection of remixed and retooled versions of tracks from *Pandemonium Shadow Show* and *Aerial Ballet*. Although the new versions mostly retailed the feel of the originals, Nilsson added some creative twists, such as a canny allusion to "One" in the tale of a star's fall from grace, "Mr. Richland's Favorite Song." Included on the album was a retooled version of "Daddy's Song," a tune which was originally included on *Aerial Ballet* but was yanked from it when RCA feared competition from the Monkees' version. Although *Aerial Pandemonium Ballet* was no smash, it sold better than either of the albums it compiled, reaching #149 on the Top 200.

In June 1971, Nilsson went back into the recording studio after a year-long absence to make the album that would become his all-time best seller, *Nilsson Schmilsson*. The album, Nilsson's first album of mostly original, non-soundtrack material in the two years since *Harry*, was done at London's Trident Studios, with a producer who was new for Nilsson, Richard Perry. From its hilariously homey cover photo to its tongue-in-cheek title, *Nilsson Schmilsson* was a surprising change from Nilsson's previous records.

The greatest surprise was that Nilsson had made such a great artistic leap. Nilsson later observed, "I really needed it, too. That was exactly what I was hoping would happen. That album was a great meeting (of minds) ... I was so glad to meet Richard Perry, because he was thinking the same thing I was thinking at the same time: now let's go to work and do some rock 'n' roll and get down!"

It was while in England that Nilsson heard and recorded the Badfinger song "Without You." While the Badfinger version (on their 1970 album *No Dice*) stands on its own, there is no question that Nilsson's version was the definitive one. The emotional centerpiece of *Nilsson Schmilsson*, "Without You," deserved all its success. It topped the U.S. charts for four weeks and the U.K. charts for five, selling well over one million copies and earning Nilsson his second Grammy.

Nilsson Schmilsson spent nearly one year on the charts, reaching #3, going gold, and spawning two more hit singles, both penned by Nilsson: "Jump Into The Fire" and "Coconut." The hard-rocking "Jump Into The Fire," which today would be called "alternative," was a completely left-field choice for a follow-up to "Without You." Fortunately, fans took it on its own merit and sent it up to #27. To this day, it is the only hit to feature a bass detuning. Nilsson, when later presented with the contrast between "Jump Into The Fire" and his earlier work, answered, "My earlier stuff had the same soul in it, only it was more subtle."

Nilsson Schmilsson was still on the charts in July 1972 when the artist released his next album, *Son Of Schmilsson*. RCA chose the single "Joy" to coincide with the release, not a wise move, as "Coconut" was still in the Top 40 and, moreover, "Joy" was not the most commercial song on the album. (It wasn't the least commercial one either; that honor forever goes to "You're Breakin' My Heart.") The single missed the charts entirely. Fortunately, the label realized its mistake and quickly spun off the poppier tune "Spaceman."

The only *Son Of Schmilsson* song to hit the Top 40, "Spaceman" reached #23. The follow-up, "Remember (Christmas)," was a minor hit that

winter, edging up to #53. *Son Of Schmilsson* was a profitable album for Nilsson—it hit #12, spent thirty-one weeks on the chart, and went gold—but there was something about it that put off buyers who had been drawn to Nilsson by "Without You."

That something had to do with Nilsson's heavy use of both bathroom and bedroom humor, often within the same song. Although finding reasons why records do or don't sell is a largely futile pursuit, it is safe to say that one song in particular, "You're Breakin' My Heart," dispelled the romantic image that Nilsson had created of himself. Today, the song sounds almost quaint, but in those pre-punk days of 1972, when pop lyrics rarely got racier than Melanie's "Brand New Key," many buyers were forever put off by Nilsson's enthusiastic use of the f-word.

In late 1972, Ringo Starr, who was by then a close pal of Nilsson, invited him to play the title role in a campy horror movie that Starr would produce, *Son of Dracula*. When the film came out, most assumed that Starr got the idea from Nilsson's vampirish album cover for *Son Of Schmilsson*, but the truth is even spookier: Starr got the idea for the film before he even saw Nilsson's album. Since Nilsson was doing most of his recording in London, and since so many of his friends were there, he bought a flat on Irzon Place, in fashionable Mayfair. Throughout the '70s, the flat served him well, but more than once, when he lent it out friends, it became the site of tragedy. Mamma Cass died in his bed there, in July of '74. Four years later, legendary Who drummer and close Nilsson pal Keith Moon died there as well, in the same bed. Fortunately for Nilsson, Pete Townshend was kind enough to buy the place from him after Moon's death, so that Nilsson would never have to see the flat, or the bed, again.

Although Nilsson claimed not to believe jinxes, he told *Goldmine* that his London flat had bad vibes from the start. "It was just a typical London flat, but it was in a great neighborhood. It was across from the Playboy Club, diagonally. From one balcony you could read the time from Big Ben, and from the other balcony you could watch the bunnies go up and down.

"Robin Cruickshank was Ringo's partner at the time, and he did interior decorations, furniture and stuff. I said to Robin, 'Just do whatever kind of decorating you want to do with it. I'll sign a blank check, you fill it in. Have you ever had a dream design you wanted to do? Use this place, 'cause I'm only going to be using it six months out of the year.'

So I came back to London six months later and it was all done. There was a ribbon on the door there to welcome me; they had fresh fruit in the fridge. I looked around and I said, 'This is incredible.' This flat had felt wallpaper—bright, royal blue with yellow, red and green felt stripes. It was like, 'Wow! Where am I?' It was all steel, chrome and glass. Everything was purchased for the space.

"I went to check out the bathroom, and there was a beautiful glass tub with a design of scenery of trees and bushes cut in. But then there were two sinks and two mirrors. I looked into one and there was a picture of an apple tree, and the other one was a hangman's noose. I called Ringo and said, 'I don't think this is too funny. Do you mind?' He said, 'What?' I said, 'The hangman's noose in the bathroom.' He said, 'What? Hold on a second—Joan, have someone go over to Harry's place and put up something else—Don't worry, Harry, I didn't even know about it. Robin must have done it.' So I said, 'Thanks,' and he sent over a nice apple tree mirror to take its place. But ever since that day something struck me. It's like whistling in the graveyard, but ... then, when Cass died, it was, like, wow. Then when Keith died—Those phone calls (notifying me) were devastating, you know?"

In March 1973, while planning got underway for *Son Of Dracula*, Nilsson recorded an album as different from *Son Of Schmilsson* as champagne is from Ripple: *A Little Touch Of Schmilsson In The Night*. As with the transition from *Harry* to *Nilsson Sings Newman*, he once again followed a hit album with one that was a labor of love. It started when Nilsson approached his friend Derek Taylor about doing an album of standards. Taylor suggested bringing in arranger Gordon Jenkins, a living legend best known for his work with Frank Sinatra. With Taylor producing and a twenty-six piece orchestra backing, Nilsson recorded the songs which he had always loved, from Gus Kahn and Walter Donaldson's "Makin' Whoopee" to Bob Cole and Rosamond Johnson's "Lazy Moon." The latter song was Nilsson's favorite of the album, as it has been sung previously by his idol Oliver Hardy. (In fact, the album's cover featured Nilsson reprising the thumb-as-lighter gag from the Laurel and Hardy classic *Way Out West*).

Even for those who knew Nilsson's earliest albums, *A Little Touch Of Schmilsson In The Night* was a stunner. It succeeded on a multitude of fronts: as a document of the best music of a bygone era, as a work of art (of Jenkins's witty-yet-delicate arrangements), and, perhaps most importantly to listeners, as the ultimate makeout album. The first album of Nilsson's to contain no vocal harmonies, it let his voice stand alone as an instrument worthy of interpreting the work of Tin Pan Alley's greatest writers. Derek Taylor, in his liner notes, reiterated his claim that Nilsson was "the best contemporary singer in the world." The album's greatness dared listeners to disagree.

Released in the summer of 1973, *A Little Touch Of Schmilsson In The Night* only managed to make it to #46 during its seventeen-week U.S. chart run. It fared better in the U.K., where it made #20. RCA released one single, "As Time Goes By," which crawled up to #86 on the Hot 100. Today, in light of such successful albums of the '80s and '90s as Linda Ronstadt's *What's New*, Annie Lennox's *Diva* and the *Sleepless In Seattle* soundtrack (which popularized Jimmy Durante's version of "As Time Goes By"), it is obvious that Nilsson was ahead of his time.

Son of Dracula disappeared as soon as it saw daylight in the summer of 1974. The soundtrack, featuring Nilsson songs and dialogue from the film, fared slightly better, reaching #160 and spinning off a Top 40 single, "Daybreak." The song would be the last hit of Nilsson's lifetime.

Around the beginning of 1974, Nilsson renewed his friendship with John Lennon, who was in Los Angeles recording with Phil Spector for what would become the album *Rock And Roll*. Lennon had recently separated from Yoko Ono and taken up with May Pang, and the period of drinking and debauchery that ensued became known as his "Lost Weekend."

The most famous incident from this period was that notorious night at the Troubadour, an L.A. club which was packed with celebrities and fans there to see the Smothers Brothers' comeback. Among those celebrities were Lennon and Nilsson, and they were too drunk to care about who the audience was there to see. They were dying to be noticed; Lennon even sported a tampon on his head. What they did and said has been described elsewhere and is largely unprintable here (for example, Lennon told a Smothers Brother to have intercourse with a bovine creature). The upshot, which made headlines worldwide, was that the man with a tampon for a hat and the man with a voice that was, like Modess, "soft as a fleecy cloud," were ejected from the premises.

Nilsson later complained to *Rolling Stone*, "That

incident ruined my reputation for ten years. Get one Beatle drunk and look what happens!" Even in his last interview, he was defensive: "It still haunts me. People think I'm an asshole and a mean guy. They still think I'm a rowdy bum from the '70s who happened to get drunk with John Lennon, that's all. I drank because they did. I just introduced John and Ringo to Brandy Alexanders, that was my problem.

"(My association with) John Lennon hurt me a lot, with the bad press. But on the other hand, I owe John everything. I had signed an agreement with RCA for a new, $5 million contract and they had reneged on it; the new president didn't sign it. I had been saying, 'The contract's binding. We'll take you to fucking court, man.' And the president had said, 'It's not binding here.' And there was this question of jurisdiction and all that stuff, and I was prepared for a fight.

"I said to John, 'I just got $5 million, and they took it away from me, like that.' He said, 'Ah, they're all fuckers, Harry. They're all fuckers.' He said, 'Just go down and tell the guy he's a fucker.'

"So I went down to RCA. We'd been up all night long and it was now ten in the morning; both still drunk, with shades, hats, dark jackets. The secretary said, 'Mr. Glancy, uh, Harry Nilsson and John Lennon are here to see you, sir.'

"'What?' Boom! Door, opens immediately. We walk in. There we are, you know? In every office, heads are turning to look at us. He said to John, 'Hi! How are you doing, sir? Would you like a cigar?' John said, 'No, thanks. I'd take a brandy.' So we had a brandy, and John said, 'Look, it's about Harry. You know, you've only ever had two artists on your label: Elvis and Harry. He told me what you're paying him. Look, for that money, I'll sign it. You've got an artist! Pay the two dollars!' 'Pay the two dollars' was like saying, pay the parking ticket, rather than fight City Hall. He said, 'I'll sign with you, for that kind of money.'

"When the guy heard that, his mind went 'Bing!' Dollar signs! So he said, 'Well, we'll have to get the contracts together.' I said, 'No, no. They're on the tenth floor. They're in Legal. Ask Dick Etlinger, in Business Affairs. He's the guy.' So he calls up and says, 'Do you have the Nilsson contract? Could you bring it up here?' Because he didn't want to look like an asshole in front of John.

"They brought up the contract. I said, 'All you have to do is affix your signature where it says "President." Just write your name on it.' He said, 'Okay,' and he did it, right in front of John. John

made me $5 million that minute. I looked at John for a minute and I almost cried. Then I said, 'I'd like four copies.' I gave one to John, one to me, one in the hotel safe, and I sent one out to California. And that's how I got to be a multi-millionaire. Thank you very much, John!"

Lennon decided to produce Nilsson's next album, and Nilsson, not surprisingly, was all for it. The result was the underrated *Pussy Cats*, released in August 1974. (RCA rejected Lennon and Nilsson's original title, *Strange Pussies*.) Listening to tracks such as the Jimmy Cliff cover "Many Rivers To Cross," it is easy to understand why so many fans were cross, for Nilsson literally lost his voice during the recording sessions.

Although one of his vocal cords was ruptured and bleeding, Nilsson refused to let on just how much pain he was in, fearing that John would stop the sessions. As a result, the album's booze-drenched, gut-wrenched feel is closer to that of the post-punk efforts of the Replacements or Alex Chilton than it is to anything else by Nilsson. It reached #60 on the Top 200, aided no doubt by the prominent placing of Lennon's name on the cover.

By the time of Nilsson's next album, 1975's *Duit On Mon Dei*, Nilsson's voice had returned, although it occasionally took him some effort to bypass its rough edges. Nilsson's original title for the album, which RCA rejected at the last minute, was the tongue-in-cheek *God's Greatest Hits*, *Duit On Mon Dei*, and the album that followed, *Sandman* (1976), seemed as though they were part of the trilogy that started with *Pussy Cats*. Unfortunately, as far as the public was concerned, any similarity between the three was purely coincidental. Neither album broke the upper half of the Top 200. Nilsson was justifiably angry, as he told *Goldmine*. "I'm getting pissed off because three of my best albums—*Duit On Mon Dei*, *Sandman*, and *Pussy Cats*—got totally overlooked. And yet there are songs on there that I wish I wrote. Well, I did!"

Nilsson's next album, *That's The Way It Is* (1976), was his most blatantly commercial effort to date, composed mainly of covers of oldies and newies. It seemed a little strained, but still had some classic Nilsson moments, particularly his version of Randy Newman's "Sail Away." The album fared poorly, reaching #158 during six weeks on the Top 200, but Nilsson had a major success that year in the British stage production of "The Point!" Starring the Monkees' Micky Dolenz and Davy Jones, "The Point!" ran at London's Mermaid Theatre and was well received, spawning an original cast album.

The 1977 album *Knnillssonn* (pronounced "Nilsson") was Nilsson's last for RCA and, in his opinion, his best. All-original, it was his most consistent rock album since *Nilsson Schmilsson*. By this point, Nilsson's happy marriage to his third wife, Una, had caused him to cut down on the partying. As a result, *Knnillssonn* is extremely well-thought out, from its Agatha Christie-influenced "Who Done It" (no relation to "Ten Little Indians") to Nilsson's most beautiful love song in years, "All I Think About Is You."

When *Knnillssonn* came out, RCA assured Nilsson that it would receive the kind of heavy promotion befitting such a hit worthy album. That was in July. The next month, Elvis died. Another label might have been able to promote a current artist's album and milk a dead superstar's catalog at the same time. Unfortunately, RCA was not another label. *Knnillssonn* did do better than all Nilsson's other records since *Pussy Cats*, reaching #108 on a ten-week chart stay, but that was not good enough for Nilsson, who began looking for a way out of his contract.

January 1978 saw RCA release the soundtrack to the Gene Wilder film *The World's Greatest Lover*, featuring the Nilsson vocal "Ain't It Kinda Wonderful." A few months later, someone at the label, unbeknownst to Nilsson, decided to fill in the gap between the artist's albums. The resulting compilation, *Greatest Hits*, was a factor in Nilsson's decision to leave the label.

When *Goldmine* brought up *Greatest Hits*, handing Nilsson the album's cover, he could not contain his fury. "Look at this. This is RCA for you," he said. The front cover photograph is the back of a man, presumably Nilsson, looking at his reflection in a mirror. The back cover is the same man's face, holding the mirror so that it covers nearly all his features. "That's not me," Nilsson fumed. "Now, do you think RCA has got any fucking soul whatsoever, when they do shit like this? I begged them in the very beginning, 'Don't ever put out a best-of album until I'm dead or I'm off the label.' And, no, they sneak this out and don't tell me about it, and hire a guy to look like me, and then they took an old picture of me and reversed it and put it in the mirror. How about that for trash?" Ironically, *Greatest Hits* was Nilsson's last Top 200 album, hitting #140 in a five-week chart stay.

Although Nilsson did not release any records in 1979 (perhaps because he was working out his

release from RCA), he was busy working with old friend Perry Botkin, Jr. on a new musical, *Zapata!* The show opened the following year at the Goodspeed Opera House in Connecticut, but failed to move on to Broadway; 1979 also saw director Robert Altman commission Nilsson to write the songs for the movie *Popeye*. The soundtrack, released in December 1980, featured the film's stars, rather than Nilsson himself, singing Nilsson's tunes. Nilsson did record his own demos of the songs, tapes of which reportedly exist.

In 1980, Nilsson signed to Mercury Records and released one album, *Flash Harry*, which was available in Europe and Japan but not in the United States. His only album released under the full name "Harry Nilsson," it is his rarest work and also his least appreciated. Although *Flash Harry* had its merits, it left reasonable doubt as to whether Nilsson could still successfully stretch his talent to album's length.

The fact was that Nilsson, after *Flash Harry*, was no longer interested in making albums anyway. Rock 'n' roll would always be a part of his life, but his family needed him and he wanted to, in the words of his friend Ringo's album title, "stop and smell the roses." Thus began one of the most active rock "retirements" since David Bowie called it quits.

The death of Nilsson's beloved friend John Lennon inspired him to, for the first time in his career, use his celebrity to draw attention to a cause. He not only joined the National Coalition to Ban Handguns, but became its most active and prominent spokesman. He used every available platform to broadcast the message of gun control, from Beatle fan conventions to the halls of Congress. In his last interview, he spoke passionately about the cause. "The world is full of fear," he noted. "I wasn't aware of how much fear there was, until this last couple of years—that the world is on the brink of chaos. Every human being at any given moment can go mad. And that's one of the reasons we've got to get rid of the handguns. I think that the President should write an executive order declaring a national state of emergency—24,000 handgun deaths every year—and actually, physically ban handguns. Give everybody six months to turn them in. When they do they get a tax credit. The remaining handguns are to be collected—all registered guns, period.

"Now, that will leave only the bad guys with the guns but now we will know who to identify. You have the right to self-defense, but you don't have the right to carry arms if you're not in the militia. The Second Amendment says, "A well-regulated militia being necessary to the security of a free state"—well, we have that. It's called the National Guard, established in 1912. So if you want a gun, join the National Guard and you'll get to shoot their guns. Another alternative is, if you have a gun, then you must keep it at the gun store and only use it for target range shooting."

In the early '80s, Nilsson, after loving movies all his life, ventured into the production field. He formed Hawkeye Entertainment with legendary writer Terry Southern (Candy), and they had moderate success with several projects, most notably the Whoopi Goldberg vehicle *The Telephone*. On the musical front, although he was officially "retired," he could no more avoid musical involvement than Elizabeth Taylor could avoid marital involvement. Among his many projects, he helped write and produce songs on Ringo Starr's album *Stop And Smell The Roses* and himself recorded songs for compilation albums and soundtracks.

As the '90s rolled around, Nilsson began to seriously consider making a new album. The idea came from necessity, as all of Nilsson's RCA money had been stolen by an unscrupulous financial adviser (who was convicted and sent to prison). By that time, along with wife Una, he had six children at home, plus he had an independent son from his previous marriage. In addition, he was diagnosed with diabetes and related ailments, and became increasingly aware of his own mortality.

An unwelcome turning point occurred on Valentine's Day, 1993, when Nilsson suffered a massive heart attack. After he survived miraculously, he started writing and recording in earnest, hoping for a hit that would secure his family's financial future. He also lobbied RCA to release a three-disc compilation of his work. Nilsson took the time to sequence the projected discs, and came up with a fitting title: *Personal Best*.

At the time of the *Goldmine* interview, RCA was insistent upon a two-disc set, and was not receptive to Nilsson's track sequence or his title. The label's seeming indifference to Nilsson's wishes hurt him deeply. "They don't understand," he said, sounding pained. "I only have three albums left in me, period. This is the twilight of my career. I have one shot left.

That's to do this album I'm doing—and two more, hopefully—and this (three-disc) compilation to explain who I am to the listening public, because they've never put it all together. This is my opportunity to put it all together, the way I sequenced it. My list. Schindler's list. And I'm telling you, it breaks my heart, and it's already twenty percent dead, okay? It's breaking my heart, to have to go through this nonsense. I went through this when I was a boy, I went through this when I was a man, with RCA doing things like that. Just once, I would like them just to bend. One time. One time!"

A few days after the interview, this writer spoke with Nilsson by telephone, for the last time. Nilsson said that he had decided not to fight RCA's wishes for a two-disc set, and he was working on trimming down his proposed three-disc track sequence to make up for the change. He hoped that the label would accept his new sequence, and the Personal Best moniker. He sounded less bitter and more upbeat, speaking enthusiastically of the autobiography which he started. Two days later, on January 15, 1994, after completing the vocal tracks for a new album, he died of a heart attack.

Nilsson told *Goldmine* that he would like to be remembered for his best lyrics, such as these which he quoted from *Sandman*'s "Flying Saucer Song":

"Late last night, in search of light, I watched a ball of fire streak across the midnight sky. I watched it glow, then grow, then shrink, then sink into the silhouette of morning. As I watched it die, I said, 'Hey, I've got a lot in common with that light. That's right. I'm alive with the fire of my life, which streaks across my span of time and is seen by those who lift their eyes in search of light to help them through the long, dark night.'"

The flying saucer image combines themes which were central to Nilsson's life and music: light, love, and hope, bordered by darkness, loneliness, and the scythe of time. From Nilsson's heady superstar days, to his years of devoted fatherhood, he did everything with the fervent intensity of a man who lived every day as though it were his last. It was this man who, in January 1972, during the height of his fame, told *Newsweek*, "I do believe that most men live lives of quiet desperation. For despair, optimism is the only practical solution. Hope is practical. Because eliminate that and it's pretty scary. Hope at least gives you the option of living."

R.E.M.

By Marianne Meyer
July 1983

Kudzu. For those rockers who are not up on their Southern vegetation, kudzu is the strange, hay-like growth that seems to be overrunning the cover of *Murmur*, the second I.R.S. Records release from the Athens, Georgia-based group R.E.M.

Guitarist/chief spokesman Pete Buck explains: "We wanted something definitely Southern for the album cover, and kudzu is. Eleanor Roosevelt brought it to America from China in her wisdom, to shore up erosion. She didn't realize that one acre of kudzu has one root, so it does nothing for erosion, and it just kills every plant it can touch. And nothing kills kudzu—you can burn it to the ground, and a week later it's back."

Sounds like a flawed metaphor for the local music scene growing up in the Southeast states, eh?

A batch of diversely talented musicians-bands like Pylon, Love Tractor, the Method Actors, and, of course, R.E.M., spreading determinedly out of their original homeland to head off the erosion of corporate radio glut, while remaining true to a shared vision (the root, if you will) of good, glorious pop music.

But no, R.E.M. is not a band big on metaphors. Even the name, most commonly associated with the sleep state in which dreams occur, was not chosen to give a handle to the group's often drifting imagery and pop psychedelia sounds.

"We write in our sleep. That's how we all walk around," laughs Mike Mills, the group's boyishly attractive bassist, but even he stresses the need for individual interpretations.

"When you put the record on, it's a chance to let your mind go. You don't have to think of anything in particular."

Still, it's hard not to see connections, like rampant kudzu, winding throughout the group's history. Take this interview, for example.

Sprawled about a Holiday Inn room in Nashville, Tennessee, the four members of R.E.M. (vocalist/lyricist Michael Stipe and drummer Bill Berry round out the crew) are preparing to open for the English Beat, I.R.S. labelmates, on the third anniversary to the day that R.E.M. first played together at a friend's birthday party.

While the Vanderbilt University auditorium is a lot bigger than the now-condemned church that housed the initial performance, the birthday girl has driven up for the occasion with a female companion (the manager's girlfriend) who did the back cover photography for their *Chronic Town* EP.

In the course of the show, they will invite members of Nashville's own Jason and the Scorchers to join them onstage. And here, sitting in on the discussion, is Scorchers' manager Jack Emerson, who met R.E.M. on their first-ever road trip, when they played—you guessed it—here in Nashville.

It's a kudzu-like logic that pulls everything together, despite Stipe's casual insistence that "the word haphazard is tantamount to the R.E.M. saga."

Okay, then. A recap, sans metaphor, of R.E.M. history: Stipe and Buck lived together in "a monstrous old church (Buck's words) with a huge back room, no ventilation, and lots of strange foreign animals."

With "honorary residents of the church," Mills and Berry, who moved in "after leaving school; and that's a euphemism, I don't think it was voluntary," the quartet practiced for three weeks, wrote about eighteen songs, mixed in some '60s cover tunes, and played for 500 or so friends at the aforementioned birthday party. They liked what they heard, so the band kept plugging in for local concert dates.

Then came the first road trips. "We could only go out on weekends," then-student Mills explains, "because of school, so we found all these towns that we could drive to that never had out-of-town bands except for the big arena type bands."

In an effort to relay the band's sound to club owners, they made an independent single, "Radio Free Europe"/"Sitting Still," and included rock critics throughout the country in a promotional mailing blitz. To them, it was still a bit of a lark.

"Once we started making records," recalls Buck,

"we said, 'This is really fun, let's make another,' and we recorded *Chronic Town*."

Mitch Easter's North Carolina home studio provided the setting. "It's the funkiest little place, in his parents' house, with dogs all over the place and his mother who makes you coffee and donuts," is how Buck describes it. Meanwhile, rock critics started jumping on the band-wagon, and R.E.M. found their 45 popping up on 1981 10 Best Lists. The major labels jockeyed for position and, after a brief flirtation with RCA, the band chose to sign with the funky/plucky I.R.S. team.

"I.R.S. was about the boundaries of the biggest label we wanted," reveals Buck, no fan of the corporate music machine. "Every band they have is really good. Maybe not all of them are to my taste, but they show real intelligence in signing them."

I.R.S. took the already completed EP, cover graphics and all, and released it untouched by corporate hands. It generated more than enough critical acclaim to surround the *Murmur* follow-up with rumors of being 'The next big thing.' A murmur of pressure, so to say, that the band will have none of.

"We never think about delivering anything," Buck stresses. "We try to please ourselves before we please anybody else. The only thing I do worry about a little bit is that people are gonna have their ideas of what we are so inflated by the time they hear this basically simple record, that it's gonna spoil whatever interest they might have in it."

Basically simple? Hard to accept, given such R.E.M. attributes as:

(A) Stipe's understated but obviously well-read lyrical abilities, shining through in such intriguing titles as "Moral Kiosk" or "Wolves, Lower;"

(B) a production style that includes the tripping effects of psychedelia without knob-twiddling indulgence;

(C) the punk-powerful but controlled rhythmic fury of Berry and Mills; and,

(D) Buck's ringing Rickenbacker guitar, recalling the Byrds in their melodic prime.

A complex eclecticism, even for its simple sound, but Buck shrugs off the praise: "One critic called us the 'great hopes of pop' so we tried calling ourselves the 'great popes of hop' for a few weeks."

It's a self-deprecating wit that holds even when Buck receives direct praise for his guitar sound's great traditional merits.

"Everybody mentions all the historical antecedents," he admits, "but the reason I play like that is that it's a simple way to play. I'm no great guitar player by any stretch of the imagination. I have really good taste and no talent."

The band as a whole echoes the description for themselves, citing influences as diverse as Pere Ubu, the Ink Spots, New York Dolls, and Velvet Underground, while their professional experience goes back only so far as the first party gigs.

"We learned to play by playing together," Buck continues, "and the more we play together, the more we know we can do."

The LP proves the truth of his statement. There's a greater variety to the compositions (check out the sunny pop of "We Walk", the darker "Talk About The Passion"), a more confident mix that plays up both the group's new confidence in the studio, and Stipe's growth as a vocal force.

An enigmatic sort whose soft-spoken intensity off-stage belies his frenetic presence on-stage, Stipe is still coming to grips with the glare of the spotlight.

"I was terrified of having a four-piece band with a frontman," he remembers, "and I was pretty horrified at having the vocals mixed way up on the EP, so when we did it, I would sneak over and push them down. It was a group decision to bring the vocals up a little bit on the LP."

Likewise, the group prefers to play down its own importance in a musical scene that they are actually in the forefront of.

Emerson will jump in to call them "The hardest working band in the Southeast for the past two years," and credits R.E.M. with "helping to establish a circuit where bands can actually make a living, proving you don't have to go the bullshit route to make things happen."

But Buck demurs. "We didn't set this up. We were just one of the first bands in the South to tour outside of New York and our hometown."

To Stipe, too, it's more a question of sharing R.E.M.'s experiences with other bands. "If you screw with us, the next band from the Southeast is probably friends of ours, and they're gonna know about you."

And what we know about R.E.M., if the group has its way, will focus firmly on the music it creates. Four fellows of considerable Southern charm and hospitality (even the silent Berry, who opens up when the tape recorder is turned off), they prefer to keep a low profile, image-wise.

"It's anti-image, if anything," Buck explains. "We're not trying to market ourselves as pop personalities. We'd just as soon people listen to the records and appreciate them for the songs. By not really having an identifiable personal image, it keeps the emphasis on the music."

But just like the metaphors that cling to the group's "haphazard" history, that evening's performance replayed significance above and beyond the sheer musical power of R.E.M.

As the crowd joyously bopped in the aisles in celebration of hometown talent, one was reminded of Buck's words on the Do-It-Yourself movement, which his band so clearly illustrates: "There's a small but real appreciative audience where we're working," he'd said earlier. "The people who come to the clubs and hole-in-the-wall ex-biker bars are real interested in the music and real knowledgeable fans. And there's thousands of great American groups now who are not in the major leagues. They don't have to go to some big slick guy with a $1,000 lunch budget to make a great record, and they don't have to hit the top of the charts to be a success."

Or as Stipe puts it, slipping himself into metaphor, "That huge sea cow that was the record industry has been harpooned and is losing blood quickly."

But the music, the dancing, and the pure delight of being there as both take place never dies. Kudzu anyone?

Photo/Chuck Boyd/Flower Children

Roger Daltrey

By Ken Sharp
July 8, 1994

With his powerful and versatile voice, long golden tresses, and a particular knack for microphone-twirling, Roger Daltrey, through the words and music of Pete Townshend, was one of the most prominent rock mouthpieces of the '60s and '70s. While the immortal lyric "Hope I die before I get old" was written by Townshend, it was Roger Daltrey who delivered that line with snarling angst and compelling conviction. Later on it was Daltrey, too, who first gave voice to Tommy, Townshend's landmark rock opera—the image of Daltrey, resplendent in miles of fringe, working the stage at Woodstock, remains one of the more indelible in rock 'n' roll.

Rising from the ashes of a working class background in London's rough and tumble Shepherd's Bush district, Daltrey was an outlaw who made good. By his own admission, rock 'n' roll saved his life. And what a rich and fruitful life he's packed into the last half-century.

Daltrey, Townshend, Keith Moon, and John Entwistle—the Who—revolutionized the world of rock with a supersonic juggernaut of sound and fury. When Townshend executed one of his trademark windmills, often bloodying his fingers in the process, he did it as if his life depended on it.

And it did. The Who's visceral sound was a dizzying assault on the senses marked by Townshend's perceptive and ground-breaking songwriting, Moon's manic runaway-train style of drumming, Entwistle's virtuoso bass prowess, topped off by Daltrey's ever-present swagger and defiant braggadocio.

Meanwhile, tales of the Who's off-stage exploits are legendary; hotel owners to this day shudder at the mention of the group's name. Massive stage destruction was a Who specialty, with smashed Rickenbacker guitars and demolished Premier drum kits commonplace. Yet despite the band's plunge into Dionysian bouts of debauchery, the Who were the genuine article, a pure, well-oiled rock 'n' roll machine. At the apex of their popularity, there was no match for the Who as a live entity.

Fraught with triumph and tragedy, the story of the Who is well-documented and needs no retelling. [For the complete history, Who aficionados should seek out Richard Barnes' excellent tome, *Maximum R&B* (Eel Pie Publishing, 1982)].

Over the course of their wild and woolly career, the Who issued over a dozen-studio albums. Their biggest hit album was 1973's *Quadrophenia*, which reached #2 on the *Billboard* charts. Daltrey's solo career, meanwhile, has been a mixed bag. Releasing eight solo albums, Daltrey, more often than not, mined decidedly un-Who-like terrain and was met with lukewarm commercial response in America. Daltrey's luck as a solo act has been better in England, where he scored a Top-Five hit with "Giving It All Away."

He's also found success as a thespian with impressive roles in such films as *Tommy*, *McVicar*, and *The Three Penny Opera*. A versatile actor, for Daltrey it's all been a sideline to the work that matters most to him, the Who.

The Who epitomize the term rock-legend. Inducted into the Rock and Roll Hall of Fame on January 17, 1990, the Who's colorful and vital legacy lives on through such disparate bands as U2, KISS, and Pearl Jam, among many others. Their place in rock history is unassailable. Along with the Beatles and the Rolling Stones, their seminal body of work remains a benchmark by which all rock 'n' roll bands are measured.

1994 has been a busy year for Roger Daltrey. In February he staged two standing-room-only "Daltrey Sings Townshend" tribute shows at New York's prestigious Carnegie Hall. A star-studded bill showcasing such guests as Lou Reed, Alice Cooper, Pearl Jam's Eddie Vedder, and the Spin Doctors, and featuring the Juilliard Orchestra, a live album and home video culled from those performances has just been issued on Continuum Records, Daltrey's current label affiliation.

Most recently, Daltrey embarked on an extensive

U.S. tour, taking the "Daltrey Sings Townshend" show on the road with a special guest, former Who bassist John Entwistle. Unlike the celebrity-packed Carnegie Hall affairs, Daltrey will sing all of the material on this trek.

And on the Who front, due out in July is a four-CD box titled *30 Years Of Maximum R&B* (MCA Records), which brings together a wealth of digitally remastered Who classics along with various "odds and sods."

Goldmine sat down with Roger Daltrey recently for an exclusive conversation.

Goldmine*: How do you feel you've evolved as a vocalist over the past thirty years?*

Roger Daltrey: It's very difficult for me, being the guy who sang all those songs. First of all, you have to understand that I'm like anybody else. When I hear my voice on a record I absolutely loathe my voice. I cannot stand my voice. So listening back to songs I sang twenty years ago, it does sound like someone else and I can appreciate it for the first time. I don't know many singers who actually do like the sound of their own voice.

Do you remember the first time you heard the Who on the radio in America?

It was when we came over to do the Murray The K show and "Happy Jack" was a hit and they were playing that on the radio along with "I Can't Explain," "My Generation," and "Substitute."

Was there a moment you felt the Who had broken through here?

Listen, I never, ever thought about getting a second job. Once we came to America it always felt like we'd made it, even though we were playing pissholes most of the time (laughs). It always felt like that was the breakthrough. It was a period where every time we came back more people came to see us and it just snowballed and snowballed.

It's hard to believe now, but when the Who first started out, you were competing with groups like Herman's Hermits.

Yeah, it went the other way for them (laughs). Every time they came back they were less and less (popular).

You once said rock 'n' roll saved your life. How did it do so?

I think I would have been jailbait. I've always said that. We weren't wealthy but we definitely weren't poor. We were incredibly rich because there was a wonderful community in Shepherd's Bush, where I grew up. All my friends were into villainy and crime (laughs).

But it wasn't like it was today, with all the drug problems. It was petty thieving and just general larking about. A lot of my friends ended up robbing banks. I used to like a lot of excitement. Rock 'n' roll gave me all of that and I could do it legitimately. Well, kind of legitimately.

London's Marquee club was a great training ground for the Who in the early '60s.

We played there every Tuesday night. When we first did the job, Tuesday was a slow night; that's why they let us in there. God, they didn't know what hit them (laughs). We were just a pub band. We were big in our own little area. But the great thing about the Marquee was that the West End of London, it was like the whole of England goes out from the West End of London. So it expanded our audience potential by literally a million. And that in itself was very useful. I have to tell you, and I don't mean this as sour grapes or anything, but it is hard to play for fans who see you all the time; makes it much harder.

Their expectations are higher.

Yeah, you can never satisfy them. I call it fan fatigue. I went to see Bob Dylan last year, who I think is absolutely incredible, but he suffers from his audience. I mean that nicely. I know without our fans and the devotion of our fans we wouldn't be here. I don't mean to put them down, but I'm just stating a fact that it is hard to play to people that see you all the time and it takes a lot of fun out of it in some ways.

What do you recall about recording the group's first album, The Who Sings My Generation?

Well, for the *My Generation* album, there was nothing to be nervous about in them days. We used to take every day as it came. Every day was just a gig and I think we did the recording between gigs, literally. We did the whole album in two afternoons. We did the album in two afternoons and by the end of the week we were playing the stuff onstage. That's how wonderful it was in those days.

A big change from today, where it takes two days to get a drum sound.

Oh God, that's what killed it for me.

"I Can't Explain" was a cop of a Kinks-styled song, which Pete has since confessed. Was there a rivalry between the Who and the Kinks?

We were London bands but there was camaraderie. There wasn't any rivalry. If there was, it was all friendly but whatever band you were in, you were the best!

Why did Jimmy Page play rhythm guitar on "I Can't Explain" and the Ivy League do background vocals?

Well, Shel Talmy didn't think that Pete's lead guitar playing was up to it and he didn't think our backing vocals were up to it. He was right about the backing vocals (laughs). And obviously in those days you weren't in overdub facilities. You made the record and that was it. So if you wanted to put a solo on you had to do it when you were doing the record.

Are those early days a blur for you? It's well-known that Keith Moon didn't even remember playing on the "Substitute" session. He didn't think it was him.

(laughs) I think if Keith Moon was here today and you asked him to recall most of his early life or most of his life, he wouldn't be able to recall it. I always used to develop a cold going into the studio. We always used to record in the afternoons. We used to be playing all night. We never used to stop playing.

So it was always a nightmare for me anyway, because my voice never used to warm up until about nine o'clock at night, which is when we usually went on stage. So I used to sound like a foghorn. I used to sound like I was singing at the end of a tunnel but I guess it's all part of growing up.

Was "Substitute" a quick track to cut?

Yeah, "Substitute" was quick. All those tracks were quick. The first slow track that we did was "I Can See For Miles." I mean, slow; it took a whole day (laughs), and most of that day was taken up on doing the harmonies. I mean, the actual track and

the lead vocal was done literally in a couple of hours and then we spent eight hours overlaying harmony after harmony after harmony. It was the ace future single that didn't do that well.

But in America…

It was a big single in America but the rest of the world they didn't seem to take to it at all. I still think it's probably our best single. I really love it. The energy of that record is incredible.

One of my favorites is "The Kids Are Alright," which balances the power of the Who with a gorgeous melody. Do you recall recording that track?

That just is all part of my memories of the *My Generation* album. Like I say, it was done in two afternoons. I don't particularly remember any songs.

How did the band come to cover Martha and the Vandellas' "Heatwave"?

In the early days, before Pete started to write prolifically, we used to listen out for all obscure American records. Every group in England, after the emergence of the Beatles, groups like us, got into Tamla-Motown. Almost every group played "Heatwave." But we just stuck with it longer than most (laughs).

I can't remember half the names of the people we used to copy. James Brown was one. It was the extension of the Chicago blues. When we first heard James Brown, it was the next step in the ladder and it all made sense. He was doing songs like "Please Please Please." Marvin Gaye, "Baby Don't You Do It." We used to do a lot of James Brown, Martha and the Vandellas stuff, Doris Troy, we used to do quite a bit of hers. Wilson Pickett. We did some Major Lance songs, but I can't remember what they were.

How would Pete present new songs to the Who?

In those days I don't think there were even demos. I can't remember. "I Can't Explain" was a demo, I think. I'm very vague on that. "Anyway, Anyhow, Anywhere" wasn't a demo because we wrote that on stage at the Marquee. We literally wrote it on stage. He had a thing going on guitar and we started putting lyrics to it. Pete had the basic verse structure and I think I wrote the bridge and bits of the chorus. He would do this bit and I would say, "What about that bit?" and we put this bit and that bit and the song came together like that. And we recorded it the next day; that's why there's no demo of it.

Do you wish you had written more songs with Pete?

Of course I do. Of course I do.

Why didn't it happen?

Well, he's an insular guy and it probably wouldn't have been as good as it turned out if I had. I wish I could write with him now.

You started out on lead guitar in the Detours and Pete played rhythm. Why did it take so long for you to play guitar on stage with the Who? I think you started to play guitar live on the 1982 tour.

It was confidence. I had to work. The Who in those days were incredibly poor. They were still at college and school. I was making guitars and I was a metal worker and if you ever see sheet metal workers' hands, you've never seen so many cuts in your life. You're better off being a brick layer if you're gonna play guitar than a sheet metal worker. So it became just impossible to play in the end and my confidence totally went. I can still do it. Again, it's confidence. Part of the early Who career was all about knocking people's confidences out.

Did you have any Spinal Tap moments in the Who?

We lived the life with Keith Moon. It was all Spinal Tap magnified a thousand times.

People have surmised that Pete became an over-achiever due to his inferiority complex about his looks and his rather large nose. That's why he resorted to windmills and smashing guitars, to take attention away from his looks and place it more on his total physical being. Do you agree?

Well, it seems to me that whole theory bears no sense at all. To take away from his appearance, it seems to me that he was trying to attract attention (laughs). That's a complete paradox, isn't it (laughs)? I think Pete did have a hard time as a kid with his appearance. But don't all kids have a hard time? God, I had a hard time too. I was little with

bow legs and rickets. I used to get picked on like everybody else used to get picked on. That's how I learned to look after myself.

But contrary to what some people seem to think, I was never a bully. I was just a hard man. I seem to have read somewhere recently where Pete suggested that the first time he met me I punched him in the nose at school. Well, that is quite honestly not true. I met Pete first when he came to one of our rehearsals with a guitar. I saw him at school, he was a character. You could hardly miss him. But he loves to make those kind of stories up and we have had a lot of fights in the past and I did used to rule the band with an iron fist.

But the band needed it! The band wouldn't have

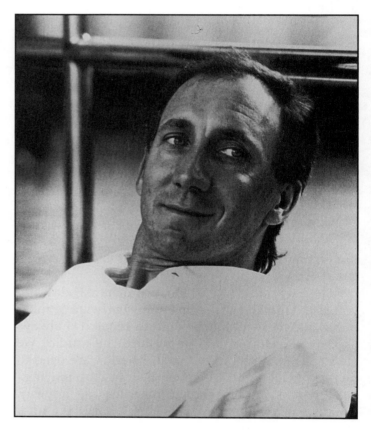

gotten anywhere. And he now readily admits that he would have laid in bed all day if I hadn't dragged him out of bed and forced him to come to a gig. So I don't make any apologies for that behavior. That was what was necessary at the time.

Pete once said that he really admired your change in the band from a somewhat hard character to "Peaceful Percy."

"Peaceful Percy," yeah. Well, they threatened to

kick me out, that's what it was! I didn't want to do anything else in my life except be in this band. Even though I used to fight with them, it was the (kind of) fights that you had with a girlfriend you loved.

Pete said he admired you making that change because it proved how much you loved the Who.

My love for the band is still there. It hasn't changed; maybe that's why it's so painful these days.

Was that a difficult thing to supersede your leadership in the band?

It was never down to leadership. I didn't ever want to be the leader. I wanted to be in a band that shared ideas and were in it together. More of the battles were down to the fact that Pete did actually want to be the fucking leader. That's really what it was about. Up 'til then we didn't really have a leader and it was going pretty good. I feel it went downhill during the later part of the '70s, when Pete actually attained that position of being the leader and being the insular writer, writing everything, producing demos and, "This is what we play." That's when the band started to die as far as I was concerned, that's when we ceased to be a band.

Around what album would this be occurring?

It was around *Who By Numbers*.

The Who covered two Rolling Stones songs, "Me Last Time" and "Under My Thumb." Why did you do those?

They'd been jailed. Keith and Mick had been jailed for smoking grass, or had been caught with cannabis anyway, and we did it as a gesture. All the proceeds were gonna go to legal things to mount a campaign to get them out. We thought it was a disgraceful sentence.

They're neat covers.

Yeah, they're almost as good as the Stones (laughs). It was fun to sing somebody else's song. And they got jailed in the afternoon the previous day and we went in the studio eight o'clock the next morning to record that. John was on vacation so Pete played the bass.

One of my favorite music promos is for "Happy Jack," a precursor by many years to the MTV-styled music video. Where was this zany clip shot?

That was filmed in Robert Stigwood's office in London, which was completely trashed (laughs). He was not a happy man. That cake went everywhere. We didn't eat much of it. It seemed to go everywhere but our mouths. It was directed by Michael Lindsay-Hogg. He directed my pay-per-view this time. He did all the great Ready Steady Go stuff. He was the best rock or pop director for that time.

In the film for The Kids Are Alright *there's another zany clip where Keith is walking around like a mechanical robot with the music of "Cobwebs And Strange" playing. But that wasn't the original music for it, was it?*

It was for "Call Me Lightning." We filmed that in Los Angeles in a warehouse. We were just bored one afternoon and we had to get something out because we were on tour with Herman's Hermits.

What do you recall about playing the Monterey Pop Festival?

God, that was a good day. Monterey I remember, but I seem to remember the Fillmore West, that we played the week before Monterey. That was much more memorable for me. The first time in San Francisco. They were good gigs. Monterey was kind of a drugs blur (laughs). But my most affectionate picture of it is just before we went on stage. The dressing rooms were under the stage and there was a jam session going on with Hendrix. Brian Jones was there and Mama Cass. There was Townshend and Moon and everybody was bashing and crashing something. Janis Joplin was there. Hendrix was doing some Beatles song, "Sgt. Pepper," and this jam just went on and on. It was better than any of the things on the show. It was amazing.

Is it true there was an argument between Pete and Jimi Hendrix about who would go on first?

Well, that was between them. I don't think there was an argument.

For the Happy Jack *album everybody in the band was contracted to come up with two songs each. You only came up with one, "See My Way."*

My song is the demo. The Who never recorded my song. It's basically the demo I did over at Pete's. It's Pete and me. They were war days with me and the guys. The whole album was tongue-in-cheek, that album. The only thing that I remember about that album is the mini-opera.

"A Quick One" is amazing. Whose idea was it to do a mini-rock opera?

Kit Lambert's. Kit's father was a very famous English composer and he started the Covent Garden Opera House. His name is Constance Lambert, so Kit was educated in classical music. He was an incredibly intellectual man. He loved pop music! He loved pop singles, he loved rock 'n' roll. He always saw it could do much more than it was actually doing. It was always his dream.

He hated what classical music had become, the fact that it had become pompous for this overfed middle class with their noses in the air. Most of the composers like Mozart wrote those songs for the people and it was the pop music of its time. Kit hated what classical music had become so he always wanted to give rock a bigger foundation. Although he loved the three-minute single and I still do, I think it's one of the things that's sadly missing in popular music. The three-minute single is something completely magical. Kit always thought what the music was saying could actually do so much more than it was doing at the time.

Indicative of the perfect three-minute single is "Pictures Of Lily." It's probably less than that.

It probably is. "I'm A Boy," they're all two thirty, two minutes forty-five seconds.

I was psyched to see the Who do "Pictures Of Lily" on the 1989 tour.

I have problems singing it now. My voice just cannot sing that song; the sound of my voice isn't the same anymore. I think "Pictures Of Lily" is a great song. It's another rip-off from the Kinks. I tried to get Ray Davies to sing that song at Carnegie Hall but he couldn't do it. He was doing two shows at Wembley and he just couldn't take the time out of his schedule. He sent me a great note.

Think about Ray Davies singing that and it would be more of a Kinks songs than it ever really was a Who song.

One of the lost gems from Happy Jack *is "So Sad About Us."*

It's a great song. It's very melodic but there's an angst behind it. I can't really remember whether Pete wrote it as a single for the Merseybeats and they did it first, or whether we did it first and then they covered it. I know they covered it and had a hit single from it. I think that's one of the few hit singles Pete's had with any other artists.

What do you remember about the Who's appearance on the never-aired Rock And Roll Circus TV show?

Not a lot. The grass was good (laughs). I felt that we did a fairly reasonable performance of the mini-opera. Brian Jones wasn't in good shape in those days, sadly. But it was one of those memorable times. Again, the director for that was Michael Lindsay-Hogg.

And John Lennon was on the show as well.

Yeah, Lennon was on that show.

The Who opened for the Beatles in Blackpool and also at the NME Poll Winners Concert. I missed out on all those great bills.

You didn't really miss much. You couldn't hear fuck-all, anything apart from the screaming. All you could do was to see them. We were backstage when the Beatles were on and you could just about hear a noise. It was just literally screaming. I got on great with Lennon. I got on really good with him. Keith got on great with Ringo, and George is a lovely guy. I've known Paul for thirty years. Paul loved the Who. He did a lot for our career over here in America. Him and Paul Simon.

Paul Simon?

Paul Simon was the first guy to bring us here. He made Murray The K aware of us and he (Murray) brought us over for his Easter show.

When you appeared at the RKO Theatre in New York for the Murray The K shows, is it true that you used to torment him by wearing monster masks?

We did everything to Murray The K. I broke every

microphone on the show and the last one left was his own personal gold-plated microphone. We would do four or five shows a day. But they were two songs (each show). We used to do something like "Substitute." We always used to do "Generation." We'd do one song and then smash all the gear up. And we had Bobby Pridden backstage permanently gluing guitars back together.

Speaking of smashing guitars, the Who's appearance on the Smothers Brothers' TV show is legendary. Someone had to lose their hearing with the explosion that Keith caused. Did that catch you off-guard?

Oh, yeah.

Did you know what Keith was up to?

No. He just got the pyrotechnic guy drunk and paid him a few hundred dollars and the guy put on four or five times the amount of charge that should have been there. It went off like a grenade. It was a huge explosion, huge! I mean, the Smothers Brothers nearly got sacked for that. They got into a lot of trouble for that. We did "I Can See For Miles" and "My Generation" and that was live vocals too. That's a live vocal to a track on both those songs. I used to sing live quite a lot on those TV shows.

Tell me about the 1968 tour of Australia that you did with the Small Faces. I heard it was a totally wild tour.

It was crazy because Australia was really a backward country then. We couldn't afford to take our own equipment so we had to hire what was there. We used these systems from, like, World War II; it was the P.A. It was unbelievable! And the Aussies at that time had no sense of humor and they threw us out after three weeks. They didn't like us at all. The Small Faces were fun to be with. We did that whole tour with them.

Did you play at all with them in London?

No, not in London. They were looked at in those days as much more of a pop group than we were. We were too rough at the edges to be a pop group. We were too fucking ugly (laughs).

Well…

(Laughing) This is a statement of fact!

How'd you wind up being the one smothered by the Heinz baked beans on the cover of the Sell Out album?

I was the last one to be done. They all grabbed the easy ones and I was basically last and they thought, "Oh, we'll let Daltrey get in the tub of baked beans." It was awful. I got very sick because they had just got the bloody things out of the freezer. So they were freezing cold. Then I think it was Moon who had the bright idea about putting an electric fire around the back of the tub. I was cooking, one half of me was cooking. My feet was freezing and it made me very ill (laughs).

Who came up with the idea for all the phony adverts on The Who Sell Out?

Chris Stamp. It was Chris' idea, because at that time we relied heavily on the pirate radio stations. You have to understand that at that time in England (in stuffy voice) the BBC Broadcasting Service, they played probably two rock 'n' roll records a day! That was it. So all these kind of renegade people set up in ships off the shore and beamed in rock 'n' roll. And it was incredible because for the first time ever we had DJs who were just so happy to be playing the music they loved.

It was so different from today, where you get DJs who are told what to play because of the marketing and all this shit. There's a few left, like (WNEW-FM, New York's) Scott Muni, who play what they love. But in those days it was really special. That album was recorded when the government had brought in legislation to sink them. They said, "You can't broadcast." They did some international thing where they had to go so far off shore that it became almost impossible for them to survive. *Sell Out* came out literally within the first week of them being turned off. To placate us the government gave the BBC their own pop station and it was awful.

The jingles on Sell Out were fake, of course, but the Who did a real Coca-Cola jingle.

Yeah, we did a Coke jingle. Coca-Cola are crazy for not digging that one out because it's a great jingle. "Things Go Better With Coke."

Didn't Pete also do an Air Force commercial?

Yeah, he did that. (In loud voice) Yeah, get killed

in Vietnam, join the Air Force! (laughs) It's easy to put it down in retrospect but we weren't aware of all the politics. We were English and that's no excuse but we were.

How do you assess the Sell Out *album?*

I love *Sell Out*, I think it's great. I love the jingles. The whole thing as an album is a wonderful piece of work. The cover. Everything about it. It's got humor, great songs, irony.

Around this time the Who were viewed as raking in the dough but in reality you were in great debt. It seemed the more popular the band became, the poorer you were. Was it because of destroying all the equipment and the hotel rooms?

Yeah, you have to remember that Keith was inventing the rock 'n' roll lifestyle at that time, which was a very expensive occupation.

Were there any hotels that welcomed the band?

Oh, in the end they did. When we used to pay the bills in cash they used to welcome us back. There were some hotels where I think Keith paid to have the whole hotel decorated. They put him in the worst room in the hotel knowing full well that he would smash the hell out of it and we'd pay in cash and they'd redecorate the room. And the next time we came back they'd put him in the next really bad room (laughs).

Did you ever participate in any of the craziness?

No, I was two years older than the other guys. I was a war baby. My family were a lot poorer than they were. I'd had to fight too hard for anything I had in my life and to smash things up for me... I had to work too fucking hard to get 'em. I just couldn't do that. I was something in me. I didn't want to be that destructive.

The mini-pop opera "A Quick One" wasn't new to the band but Tommy *as a full statement was revolutionary. When Pete first played you the songs...*

He didn't play us the songs. He had one song called "Amazing Journey." It was Kit Lambert's idea to do the full rock opera and basically the story line of *Tommy*, the holiday camp, was Keith's idea. The actual story line is more Kit Lambert than Pete Townshend. You don't very often hear Kit Lambert's name mentioned when it comes to *Tommy* these days, but I haven't forgotten.

In that time period there were a few concept albums, things like the Small Faces' Ogden's Nut Gone Flake*, the Kinks'* The Village Green Preservation Society *and, of course,* Sgt. Pepper*. Do you think that also had an effect in opening up the waters for an album like* Tommy*?*

Sgt. Pepper is a collection of songs, top-and-tailed by a great song. But there isn't really an overall concept to *Sgt. Pepper*. It's just a series of great songs. When you really think about what it's saying, there's a great song saying, "This is Sgt. Pepper's Lonely Hearts Club Band" and it starts and it ends with the same song.

Well, maybe Ogden's *and* Village Green Preservation Society *are more along those lines.*

Well, they are but they came out after *Tommy*. [Ed. note: *Actually, they both came out several months before* Tommy.] I mean, *Tommy* was the first one to come out with an actual story line where the narrative was followable or almost followable, where one part of the narrative in one song would be picked up again in the next song. *Tommy* was the first album to do that.

What did you think of the new song "I Believe My Own Eyes" that Pete wrote for the Broadway play of Tommy*? Was it a song the Who could have done?*

Of course it was a song the Who could have done. Whether we would have done it, I don't know. I have to be very careful what I say about *Tommy* on Broadway because I hate hurting people's feelings in the press, because I know what it's like to read things about yourself in the press that hurt. It's not nice. I don't like *Tommy* on Broadway at all. I like the music, I'm pleased with Pete's success, but I don't like what they've done to it. Why they couldn't have adapted more of Broadway for *Tommy* than *Tommy* for Broadway. But who am I to knock it? It's a huge success.

Did you like Pete's new song?

I don't think I should comment.

I saw the Disney Channel's Tommy *special and, to be totally honest, I felt there were too many interviews with the Broadway cast and crew and not enough of the Who.*

They know fuck-all about *Tommy.*

It was interesting in the special how you said Tommy *wasn't based on you at all, and then Pete said it was based on you and him, and John thought* Tommy *was you as well. Is this how things always operated in the Who, with everyone having different perceptions?*

You have to understand that Pete writes his best material when he's writing through a third person, and that person was always me. And let's be honest, what would *Tommy* have been if it wasn't recorded in the first place by a bunch of lunatics like the Who? Here was a band that, at the time they recorded *Tommy,* was probably two million dollars in debt. No other band would be prepared to take those kind of chances. When you think back to what could have happened if *Tommy* had been recorded by another band that wasn't prepared to take those chances, it might have been nothing at all, that record.

If Tommy *had been a failure, would the Who have broken up?*

No. I don't think there's any way it could have failed. We don't know failure in this band. We didn't know failure. We got to know it a little after awhile but at that time there was no such word.

But Pete used to literally write his best stuff when he was writing about a character that he could see very, very clearly from outside of himself. When he gets introspective it turns into melodramatic dross. And some of it's really good and I admire his courage for doing that. So, I'm not putting him down for that but he writes his best stuff when he's writing for a figure beyond himself. And I was that figure. And of course I personified Tommy, I was the guy who used to play the part. I played the damn part for five years. I slogged my balls off around the world sweating it out. People thought I was Tommy. I used to get called Tommy in the street.

What do you recall about performing Tommy *at New York's Metropolitan Opera House?*

Well, I mean it was just another gig to me. That was how I used to feel about everything. I never used to be impressed with any of that shit. It's a hole with a stage! So it had chandeliers, so what!

Did the band have anything to do with the Tommy *album cover?*

No, it was Mike McInnerney who did that and I think it's an incredibly good cover. He mostly worked with Pete and Chris.

Was playing at Woodstock as miserable as it has been reported for the Who? The best part about it had to be when the sun came up while you were playing.

The only reason it was a miserable experience as far as I was concerned was, to be honest, being an artist you always want to give your best. By the time we got on the stage we were in no condition whatsoever to play a show.

Because you were spiked?

Well, nobody spiked us, everybody was spiked! I mean, everything was spiked (laughs) and we were there for like ten hours before we were onstage and you had to drink something in ten hours. So that's the only area where you can say it was a miserable experience because I couldn't perform my best.

But let's be honest. Woodstock did our career an immense amount of good. And the fact, like you said, the sun came up on the "See Me, Feel Me" bit was extraordinary. It really was like a gift from God.

Live At Leeds is viewed as the definitive live album by the Who but there were a lot of songs from the show left off the album.

I've always wondered why and I must dig out the rest of that show. I mean, Live At Leeds is the end of a two-and-three-quarter-hour show. It's just the jamming bit at the end (laughs). The whole rest of the show is hardly there.

Like the opener, "Heaven And Hell"?

That's right. I must dig them out one day. I think some of that stuff is going to be on the boxed set.

The Who live at the Fillmore East is one of the best live Who gigs. It's circulating among collectors.

Well, some of our bootlegs are better than our records (laughs).

Did you ever perform "The Seeker" live?

Yeah, we used to play it live. I've always found it a bit ploddy. It's a real late '60s rhythm. I don't like it that much.

Tell me about Pete's unfinished Lifehouse project. Some of the Who's best songs, like "Pure And Easy," were earmarked for that record.

The whole problem with Lifehouse was that the concept was too ethereal. Music-wise it was some of the best songs Pete's ever written. But the narrative, again, wasn't very strong. We would have needed another three years working on it before recording it to make it complete.

Would you have liked some of the tracks destined for Lifehouse to have been included on Who's Next*?*

You know, what would it have changed? *Who's Next* is a great album in itself. What would it have changed to have a song like "Pure And Easy" on it? Not a lot. It would have just made it a longer great album. So what! It didn't matter.

Were you intrigued by the new sounds Pete was getting for Who's Next *with his Arp 260 synthesizer?*

I used to hate that fucking thing. Oh, God, it used to drive us nuts! All it could do is go "weeeeing..." (imitates high-pitched sound). I mean, I could do the same with a paper and comb (laughs).

Did you enjoy the loops on "Baba O'Reilly"?

The loops were great. "Won't Get Fooled Again" has an organ, it's not a synthesizer at all. The fucking synthesizer used to drive me fucking nuts! I used to love "Bargain" but I hate the solo (imitates the solo with goofy voice). It's like someone with a belly ache! Can you imagine what that would be like with a great guitar solo? That's what I hated, any excuse

except to play a great guitar solo! I mean, let's be honest, what would you have preferred to hear? (laughs)

A wailing lead?

Can we have these answers in the interview? (laughs) So, I really did loathe this machine.

Didn't you record some tracks at Mick Jagger's house?

We did it at Stargroves. Jagger had this big old house out in the country and they used to have a mobile studio. We recorded "Won't Get Fooled Again" there and quite a lot of other stuff too. It was good because we were kind of hanging out. What's great about *Who's Next* is that it was the only album where we played all the stuff extensively on the road before we went in to record it. We played all those songs over and over again. They were our songs. They weren't just Pete's songs. That's the difference with *Who's Next*. We had that freedom to do that. We were never allowed that freedom after that.

Where was the front cover shot?

The front cover is a composite with the background put on. The big concrete block photo was taken just outside of Sheffield. I don't think it's there anymore. They used to pick these big blocks to hold slag heaps from mine shafts. They used to put these big concrete blocks in there to stop them from slipping. It was just there on this big black mountain of slag. There was this big white concrete block sticking out.

And you all had bladder problems that day.

That's right! It looked like a great place to piss!

I know you're unhappy with the Quadrophenia *album, due to the mix.*

I love the album but I still think *Quadrophenia* should be remixed. I've never heard a good mix of it. It's incredibly weak, it's thin. I've heard what's on the tapes. It lacks the real power that I know is there from hearing it in the studio. I always remember when I first heard the record I thought, "Oh, dear, maybe I should have another listen to it." I think a lot of the vocals are very low.

Did you like John Entwistle's remix for the Quadrophenia *soundtrack album?*

No, not at all. I hated it. Everything was totally out of balance. I think that's even worse. I mean, it's just all bass. It doesn't work having a lead bass guitar. You just lose a lot of the guitar power. I think it needs a great mixer, someone like Mutt Lange, to do it. I think you would be surprised if you knew what was on there.

How come "Love Reign O'er Me" onstage is 25,000 times more powerful than "Love Reign O'er Me" on the record? We're playing exactly the same stuff and singing it the same way, it's just not coming across on the record with that power. The whole *Quadrophenia* thing was great in one way because I had my own studio at the time and I was running the songs down in the studio at home before I got to the studio with the Who. That helped a lot on that record. I think vocally on that album I do some vocal acrobatics.

Didn't you have a lot of technical problems on the 1974 Quadrophenia tour?

Yeah. That was before samplers and all these things. We had to put all those sounds on tapes and again I used to hate it. Once you were playing with a tape, that's when it started to die for me. You were no longer free to do what you felt like doing. You'd be stuck into this thing. I worked for the sound. I made the sound bigger and we were still a four-piece but it didn't work creatively for me at all.

Wasn't that the tour where Lynyrd Skynyrd was the opening act?

Yeah. They were good guys. We used to find bands on the road and if we liked them we'd take them. All of them made it. They all became huge bands. James Gang from Cleveland. Lynyrd Skynyrd. They were no one when we first saw them. They were great guys, lovely guys. And they were a good band too. I'm glad they're still playing.

You had a major fight with Pete while recording "5:15." Did the band ever get along?

We got along very well. Everybody talks about this big fight. It wasn't a big fight. We were rehearsing *Quadrophenia* and we had a film crew to film the rehearsal. We'd played almost the whole of *Quadrophenia* and this film crew were all sitting on their trunks watching the show without a camera turning! So I just said, "For fuck's sake, when are you lot gonna start filming? You're waiting for me to wear my voice out so you can film me when I'm flogged out! *Quadrophenia* is a hard piece of work to sing, I don't want to sing it twice."

And Pete came over to me and started poking me: "You do as you're fucking told." He was on his brandy and he started poking me in the chest. And the roadies, 'cause they know what I'm like—if I ever get rolling, I'm a little tiger—they all jumped on me! They're holding me down (laughs). Pete hits me with his Gibson across the shoulder while I'm being held and then he starts spitting at me, calling me "a little cunt." And then he says, "Let the little cunt go, I'll fucking kill him."

So they let me go and he threw two punches. One went to one side of my head and he throws the other one and it goes to the other side and he was throwing a right at me and he was totally off balance and I hit him with an upper cut and he went six inches off the ground and passed out. And I had to escort him to the hospital because I thought I killed him! No one was sorrier than I was. But it wasn't a big fight. He was pissed and he thought he could fight me and he can't fight me (laughs). I mean, you have to know how to fight.

Did the press make out the Townshend vs. Daltrey feud to be more than what really existed?

Of course they did. We used it too. We were guilty of it. But it's not important. It wasn't a big fight. It was like the wife hitting you with a frying pan. The next minute you're in bed fucking each other to death (laughs).

Tell me about the time when Keith Moon passed out at a gig in San Francisco and a nineteen-year old drummer from the audience named Scott Halpin played with the Who.

We've got a video of that on the new video that's coming out.

Tell me about that show in San Francisco.

What do you do when your drummer is passed out on literally the third song in the show? You're just about to premiere your new work, *Quadrophenia*, which is a difficult piece anyway. There you are and you have 14,000 raving fans. We weren't quitters. So I stood at the front and said, "Is there a drummer in the audience?" Simple as that. And they all lined up and we picked one out and we basically had a jam session. The audience was happy. Keith was happy, he was out of his brain (laughs). John was unhappy because Keith smashed his French horn (laughs).

What's in the plans for the live video?

Well, there's a boxed set coming out with some different tracks that have never been out there before and some tracks that have been remastered so they do sound better. There's a video going with it of all unreleased Who live stuff. There's the Who at the Isle Of Wight, there's the Who in Chicago in '75 and the thing at the Cow Palace when Keith passed out. There's stuff back in '66 in Finland. All live.

Any out-of-the-ordinary song selections?

The trouble is our catalog is known to death. There's not really any out-of-the-ordinary stuff.

"Tattoo"?

Well, that's all on there, yeah. The video is three hours. It's done. I was gonna get involved with it but I decided that the Who today are too painful. I really did.

In what sense?

It's incredibly sad. It should never have been a sad ending but for John and I it is. It just is.

On a happier topic, what did you think of Keith's lone solo LP, Two Sides Of The Moon*?*

Well, only Moon would have the balls as a drummer to make an album where he sings! And I love it for that. And I love "Don't Worry Baby." He loved the Beach Boys. I'm producing a film about Keith at the moment and I was thinking about calling it "The Last Beach Boy." That's all he ever wanted to do was be in the Beach Boys. He never wanted to be in the fucking Who, we played rubbish! (laughs) So we used to do "Barbara Ann" to keep him happy. "Moon's in a mood, quick, play 'Barbara Ann'!" (laughs) And "Bucket T," that was another one that would keep him happy for six months.

Do you like the Odds And Sods *album?*

I like *Odds And Sods*. I love "Relay." [*Editor's note: "The Relay" was not included on* Odds And Sods *but was rather a single.*] I loved "Put The Money Down." I think they're great tracks. I think "Relay" is a fabulous track. I'm gonna do "Relay" onstage on my tour. I might do it acoustically.

You spoke of Who By Numbers *as the record where Pete took over the leadership role and that's when the rot set in, but it's a brilliant album.*

I like it.

Do you like the cover?

No. It was a good idea but I think John can do better than that. I think there's some really great tracks on that album. "Dreaming From The Waist" is a great track. "How Many Friends." I love "Blue, Red and Grey;" that's one of my favorite tracks.

"Success Story" is another gem.

We really used to let John choose the songs he wanted to do. The trouble is, when John wanted to do his songs, John had to sing them and unfortunately, John has this habit of singing incredibly out of tune (laughs).

Is that true?

Is it true? Are you fucking deaf? (laughs) Sometimes he sings all right, but if you notice I'm singing behind him, shadowing him every way. He's just gone deaf. He's a good singer, John, I love his voice. I love all his songs. I think one of the sad things about John's writing is his best work was done on an album called Smash Your Head Against The Wall, which I think he should re-record. And if he does I'd like to sing some of it.

I think me and him as a collaboration could do something really good. I'm working with him at the moment. He's gonna guest with me on some shows on my tour. Not all of them, some of them. And I'm gonna talk to him about it because I really do feel for John, because when the Who ended that was the end of John's life. He's very much a muso, unlike myself, where I have an acting career and there are other things I do. He's a fabulous bass player. He's got such a unique sense of humor, incredibly dark. I mean, Siouxsie and the Banshees made a whole career out of *Smash Your Head Against The Wall.* Listen to the melodic form of that music. Exactly the same as Siouxsie and the Banshees ten years later.

For the Who Are You *album, I know you had some problems with producer Glyn Johns.*

I had a punch-up with Glyn Johns, mainly because he put strings on John's track "Had Enough." I went into the studio in the afternoon the day before they put on the strings. I thought, "Fucking hell, strings on a Who track!" When I heard it, it was just slushy strings and I don't like slushy strings.

I don't mind orchestras. I like them triumphant. There's things you can do with strings that can be really good and exciting but what he'd done on this I didn't like. He said, "What do you think?" And I said, "Don't like it much." And he went up the fucking wall. So I think he smacked me and I smacked him and that's how we were in those days. No big deal. I've read his recollections of those events about him always trying to get me to sing different. That's bollocks! There's not one rock 'n' roll singer who's ever sung in more different styles than I have.

Don't give me that bullshit! From "Tattoo" to "Behind Blue Eyes," with that softness and vulnerability, to "Who Are You." Don't give me that shit that he was trying to do that, he wasn't.

It's just that I disagreed with him about the direction of the album. I still don't think that Glyn was the right producer for that album. He was the right one for *Who's Next*, because we had already done all that kind of pre-production work and all he had to do was mike it up and get it down on record and mix it. I do like the record but basically the mixes are down to Jon Astley, they weren't down to Glyn Johns at all. I love "Music Must Change" and I love "Who Are You."

Why didn't Keith play drums on "Music Must Change"?

He just couldn't get it together. That was just when he was really bad on the alcohol. He'd just started to go for a cure.

Around this time, Keith was given a promo job with Shepperton Studios. Was he being phased out of the group?

We wanted to get him back to England because he was killing himself back in Los Angeles, and we brought him back there and let him deal with that job. He loved to be in the press and the press loved Keith. He was a journalist's dream. There was always something to write about and if it ever got dull, he'd invent something to write about.

So it was done for that reason. I've read in Dave Marsh's book where it talks about John and I wanting to get Keith out of the band. It's really not true. You have to remember that most of that book is really an interview with Pete, when Pete was very bad on drugs. By Pete's own admission, he's a compulsive liar.

The truth of what was happening there is we had to make a record and we had to get it finished. John and I were quite prepared to get in another drummer to finish the record, which is not the same as getting Keith out of the band. It was a totally different thing. It was totally, totally untrue.

This had been going on for a long time where we had to deal with these problems. When Keith took the overdose of the monkey tranquilizer in San Francisco and we seriously had to consider what we could do. We had this whole tour booked, can we do it? Keith couldn't even walk for three days then. We did seriously consider getting another drummer in to get us through. You do those things to keep together as a band but you never, ever talk about getting rid of the bloke. I mean, the Who without Keith Moon? Who do they think we are, fucking mad? There's no truth in that at all. But I will admit to saying that we might have to get another drummer in to finish this record.

Moon's playing on Who Are You *is great.*

Oh, yeah, but it was hell to get it. He could be good for an hour.

Did he know his playing had deteriorated?

Oh, yeah, and he was so sad about it. He was so upset. He used to cry. Nobody knew more than Keith. It used to break his heart.

When Keith died, was that a phone call you knew was going to come one day?

Well, the truth is, with Keith it was a phone call that we knew was going to happen one day. He lived nine lives and I'd seen him nearly die several times. When people talk about living on the edge, they don't know what living on the edge is like until they had seen how Keith Moon used to live. I've never met anyone who lived like Keith Moon. He really lived on the fucking edge, oh, yeah.

If you could see him today what would you say to him?

That I love him and I miss him. I really miss him, God, I miss him. The world misses him. He was a wonderful human being. Although he had this narcissistic streak in him, his main aim was to entertain people. Mostly at his own expense, and in the end at the expense of his own life.

Do you regret going with Kenney Jones as a drummer for the Who?

Oh, I do, he said, thinking very hard (laughs). He had to ponder this question (laughs). I just felt that Keith was such an extraordinary drummer, to try and replace him was just ridiculous. We had the

chance then to be completely free to do literally anything. We could have added what we liked. We could have done so many experiments. We could have added a string fucking quartet if we wanted to.

People were expecting nothing because the Who that people had known at that point had stopped. We just filled the gap and pushed it back into the same slot with a drummer who was quite obviously the complete wrong drummer. No one supported me at the time, including most of the fans. I used to

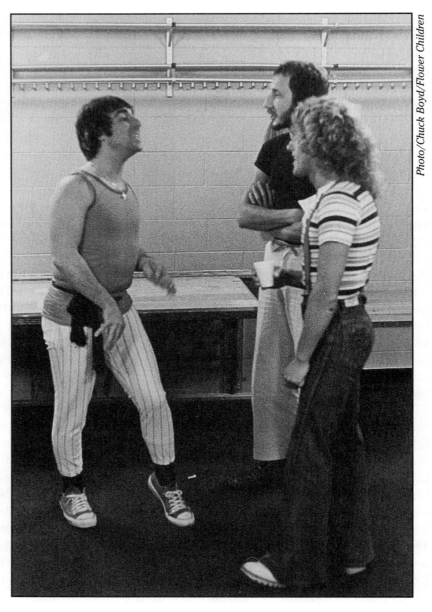

Photo/Chuck Boyd/Flower Children

get real vehement letters from fans saying how could I be so nasty to Kenney. I was never nasty to him. I was just stating my feelings about this because I don't feel he's the right drummer.

I'm not saying he's a bad drummer. I'm not saying

he's a bad guy. I didn't dislike the guy, but I just felt he wasn't the right drummer for the Who. It's like having a wheel off a Cadillac stuck onto a Rolls Royce. It's a great wheel but it's the wrong one. I took a lot of shit over that from fans and from everyone.

What would you have done for a drummer?

We could have just hired and fired. For fuck's sake, the world is full of drummers! I think my argument was justified when finally in '89 you heard us playing with a drummer, Simon Phillips, that had the fluidity and technical ability of Moonie. He could throw it all over the place and keep it together. They realized what had gone wrong back in '82. The role that Keith used to play on the drums wasn't just to keep a rhythm, it was to link what Pete and John used to play.

We not only had an extraordinary drummer who played all the things you would expect in all the wrong places, we also had this bass player playing lead bass all of the time. And we had a guitarist who sometimes played lead and sometimes played incredible rhythm.

Moon's function wasn't to go "boom-chick, boom-chick, boom-chick." He used to play that way because it used to tie the whole thing up. As soon as you put Kenney Jones... all he used to do was (imitates drum fill) and boom-chick, boom-chick, boom-chick; it was fucking horrible! It used to drive me crazy! I used to want to die on the stage. I was gonna buy him a pair of brushes (laughs).

Fifteen years ago the film The Kids Are Alright *was released. How do you view the film today?*

I can't be objective about it. To me it was wonderful to see. It was Moon's film. I love it for that. I don't think it was well-directed or even well-put together as a piece of footage on Keith Moon and the band. It's all right. What I like about it is it's completely unpretentious. I don't think anyone can deny that.

Any thought on releasing the Who's full show at the Isle Of Wight festival?

Who would buy it? When people say to me, "Why don't you do more obscure stuff?" you have to realize that the people who would like the obscure stuff are not everybody. You can't please everyone all the time so you try and please yourself and do a cross-section of stuff. Do a bit for you, a bit for you, and a bit for you.

Back in 1979, Pete had said that the Cincinnati tragedy (when eleven Who fans were trampled to death in the rush to get into the arena) was a somewhat positive event because it made the band reassess its view toward its audience. It was a very controversial statement at the time.

I should think it fucking was. He didn't lose his family, did he? I think it might have made him reassess because he was quite heavily into drugs at the time. We didn't find out until after the show (about the tragedy).

Was there any thought to canceling the tour?

What would have been the point in stopping? It's like somebody getting killed in a car crash on the way to a Frank Sinatra concert. I mean, what can you do? In the end we're all responsible for somebody farting in Tokyo, if you believe the theory of chaos. What would have been the point? If it happened when we were in the hall and we could have controlled a situation, then I would have felt totally different. Totally different and totally responsible and held my head and said, "This is the end."

But the fact is, it happened before; I wasn't even at the hall. You have to remember it would have been an even worse catastrophe if we hadn't played that night. That's why they didn't tell us. There would have been a total riot. There had already been those people killed on the way in. There could have been more people killed on the way out.

I think that there were some people who should answer to it. I don't know whether they did. It's all in the past now. I can live with my conscience on it. But as far as it being a good thing, what a load of bollocks! That's a really bad choice of words.

Face Dances was a more polished Who album. Do you like the album?

I love *Face Dances*. I love all the songs on *Face Dances*. Imagine if they had been played with a great drummer, as they are when we play live now with a drummer like Simon Phillips or whoever I take on the road with me on my tour; you can hear what the potential of that album could have been. Listen to the drums on that album and you tell me if they're any fucking good. As a fan yourself and someone who is writing this article, do you think they're any fucking good?

It's not Keith Moon.

But are they anything? (laughs) It's music, for God sakes. Is it good drumming or bad drumming? It's fucking awful drumming. Because you love the group so much it still doesn't excuse it. The fact that I liked the guy didn't excuse me from having to say, I'm sorry, but his fucking drumming stinks!

Do you think that with Face Dances *and* It's Hard…

It's Hard should never have been released. I had huge rows with Pete. Pete had just come off detox and he was really looking for help. We did *It's Hard* in the studio and the band was rehearsing before Pete got out of the clinic just to try and keep a vibe up, to try and support Pete. But when the album was finished and I heard it I said, "Pete, this is just a complete piece of shit and it should never come out!"

Why did it come out?

It came out because, as usual, we were being manipulated at that time by other things. The record company wanted a record out and they wanted us to do a tour. What I said to Pete was, "Pete, if we'd tried to get any of these songs onto *Face Dances*, or any of the albums that we've done since our first fucking album, we would not allow these songs on an album! Why are we releasing them? Why?" Let's just say that was an experience to pull the band back together, 'now let's go and make an album.'

What did he say?

"Too late. It's good enough, that's how we are now." I hated it. I still hate it. Hate it, hate it, hate it!

Didn't Pete have a lot of problems writing songs for the album?

He had a lot of problems writing for a long time for the Who.

Creative friction has always led the Who to do their best work.

Well, obviously, the best work comes out of friction. Creative friction is the most stimulating environment for artists to work (in). It's when you get a morass of mediocrity it becomes like a soft sponge and sucks all the energy out of anything. That's one

thing the Who, fortunately, never had to deal with. It was always creative friction and that's had a lot to do with the success of the band. If we hadn't had the creative friction, we would have been Herman's Hermits (laughs).

It seemed, though, that the band was getting along well during the Face Dances/It's Hard *period. Do you think this lack of friction affected the quality of those albums?*

We were getting along well. We were trying to support a man we thought we were going to lose. He was very badly into drugs. This wasn't just an alcoholic binge. This was someone who was kind of nodding out on the big one. [*Ed Note: Daltrey is referring to Townshend's admitted heroin use.*] You try and pull together. You avoid all of those situations which can make people go back on that. So maybe we were too soft. Maybe the lack of the in-fighting did help to destroy the band. I don't think it did. I think Pete had already made up his mind.

There was supposed to be a followup studio album to It's Hard.

That's right. We finished the farewell tour. And we had one more album to deliver and Pete went away and said he was gonna start writing it. If you've ever tried to come in and co-write with Pete and inquire how things were going, you'd have the door slammed in your face. He worked himself into an insular situation, as far as we were concerned.

It used to be incredibly difficult to sit down feeling useless because you can't do anything until Pete's done it. That is not easy work, believe me. It's much harder to do nothing than it is to be in there, beavering and trying to do something. That's the kind of position he put us in. Then, halfway through '83, he came to us and said, "No one's phoned me up and asked me how it's going." And that came out of the blue because up until then, if we would have phoned him up, he would have told us to piss off! (laughs) He said, "I'm gonna finish the band." And that was the end of it.

So I said to him, "If you can't write, let's all sit in a room. If we look at four walls, let's give it two or three weeks and take our instruments. I'm sure we'll come up with something good, Pete."

But it didn't work. He was not prepared to share, which is very sad. That's why I feel, for me the end of the Who was very sad, because it ended up in almost a very selfish exercise. But I suppose we were all being selfish. I'm being selfish for wanting to keep it going. As much as I think that Pete has written some incredible songs, some incredible songs, the magic that the band gave those songs far outweighs the importance of those songs.

That chemistry was a gift from the heavens. It really was. For us four people to meet up and be able to create that, something that came from Pete on one level and take it to the next level, I've always seen that as the important thing.

Is there one Pete Townshend song that he did on his solo album that you wished you sang in the Who?

Psychoderelict would have been a great Who album. *Psychoderelict* for me was fatally flawed because it was obviously autobiographical, even down to the woman, for fuck's sake, which is what's been going on. It's all out in the open now. It's been in the papers in England. It's fatally flawed because he didn't have the balls to act the character on the record, so then it becomes just pretentious.

If the Who had gotten hold of that, it would have cut that pretense out, and he would have written for me in the third person. It would have given it a different strength. It would have been a great Who album.

How about something like "Rough Boys"?

Well, "Rough Boys" is a gay song. When he initially wrote that he sent that to me for my next solo album and said, "I've written this song for you." I've still got the note and the demo. I can't kind of get to grips with *The Iron Man* album. I think "The Sea Refuses No River," the Who would have really ripped that one up. A lot of *Empty Glass* would have been a great Who album. It could have been a great, great album. It was a great album by Pete, but if you add the magic of the Who, it would have been better.

Was it fun to reunite for Live Aid?

No, it was not fun at all. I didn't want to do it with Kenney Jones. We got on there and all the power went off and it was a nightmare. A good cause but…

The Who were inducted into the Rock and Roll Hall of Fame in 1990. What does that mean to you?

What the fuck is it? I mean, Pete was once quoted as saying "It's a Hard Rock (Café) without all of the hamburgers." It ain't even the Hard Rock at the moment (laughs). (Note: Daltrey is referring to the fact that the Hall of Fame building does not yet exist.) I was honored to be with those artists, yeah, but I'm not so sure about some of the other names that were mentioned when we were there (laughs).

Every artist, I'm honored to be on the same planet with them, but some of the industry people that get mentioned at those functions… I find it very difficult when I hear people talking about their good old mates from the old days and mentioning names and I know these people have ripped off artists that I've known very well, and unfortunately some aren't with us now. And you think, do I really want to be in the room with some of these fucking people?

The 1989 tour must have been a happy time for you.

Fabulous. I loved every minute of it. Physically, I was in bad shape for that tour. Very bad shape. I had something wrong with me that had been with me from birth on the inside that all of a sudden had come to life. It was called a mermangioma, which is a bunch of varicose veins in my guts. I'm okay now; I had it all cut out.

On that tour when I started singing and all the blood would go down 'cause you start pumping your diaphragm, this thing would blow up like a balloon. It stopped me eating. I lost so much weight. God, I was ill on that tour. But the singing was wonderful. And the crowds got me through it. Again, I loved doing *Tommy* when we did it. I didn't like all the guest stars. I'm not that kind of singer. I need to warm up and stay there. Oh, man, is it hard work!

The Who reunited for Pete's Iron Man *album and performed "Dig" and the old Arthur Brown hit "Fire."*

I liked the tracks. I was a little bit concerned with the motivation behind doing them. All of a sudden we're not good enough to be around for fucking twelve years and then we're good enough to be on a record. I kind of felt a bit used. Pete tends to do that.

Well, the record didn't sell that well.

The record didn't sell that well, but isn't it a lesson in humanity? I do feel with interviews with Pete in the last ten years he's been almost trying to deny the Who, anything that the Who had to do with his career, and I find that very sad.

I was taken aback by reading the recent Rolling Stone article on the upcoming Who box, with Pete saying he didn't think the Who were very good.

I think what he's trying to say is he was wonderful and the Who were a piece of shit. Don't you get that feeling?

I got the feeling now with his major success on Broadway that he's trying to distance himself from the Who. Anyhow, what went through your mind on opening night of the "Daltrey Sings Townshend" show?

Well, sheer terror the first night, mainly because we didn't have time to get a run-through of it. It was the first time that we had put the whole show together. And believe me, it's a lot different playing with seventy musicians (than) it is with seven.

What acts were you trying to get for the show that didn't work out?

Ray Davies tried to do it and couldn't. I tried for Bruce Springsteen. His wife just had a baby and that put him out. Bonnie Raitt I would have liked. I did try for Garth Brooks. I wanted him to do "Generation" since he fucking nicked all our guitar smashing (laughs). He's made a good living out of it.

You were happier with the second night?

Oh, yeah. I've never known any new venture show that we've set out on where the first night has been any good. Imagine seeing that show five nights in, woo, would it be good. It was a really difficult one to get together. It's hard.

Why wasn't Eddie Vedder in the pay-per-view?

He's a star.

Now you're going out on a "Daltrey Sings Townshend" tour.

After doing the Carnegie shows, and like I said the first night we had to wing it because mainly we didn't get a run-through. But the second night really did kick in. A lot of people said to me, "You've got to do this again. You've got to let other people hear this." Who music isn't like any other music. I can't sing those songs the same because I don't feel the same, but it doesn't make the way I sing them now any less valid. When you're middle-aged, you're no longer angry. It doesn't mean you're less passionate. It's just the anger becomes something else.

I think if you're still angry at fifty, it's very unbecoming (laughs). Something's really fucking wrong. So John will be a special guest on the tour and maybe I'll pick up a few people on the way. I'd like to try and work in conjunction with local radio stations and pick up some new talent in the areas to play some of the early songs. There'll definitely be an orchestra. I will be singing all of the songs. I'll be easier than me walking on and off (laughs). We've got some other songs to do. The Eddie Vedder spot I'll do on my own. So that's a nice little section. It'll be interesting. I'll probably do forty shows. The tour starts in May. We'll be playing sheds and theaters. It'll be really good.

It's good you're bringing John along.

He needs to play and I need to sing. Listen, this is the last chance in my life that I'm gonna get to do it so I'm just gonna go for it.

When's the album from the Carnegie Hall show coming out?

It'll be out in May. (Ed. Note: It's been pushed back to July.) Although I miss Pete physically not being there, within the sound you don't miss him. I mean, on the last tour he played acoustic guitar. You could hardly hear him most of the time. This won't sound like the Who. It can't be the Who. The Who's dead. But if you wanna hear those songs sung and done well, but differently and dramatically... It's wonderful, wonderful music. It's going to be a fucking good night out.

Any chance for a Who reunion show this year? Pete talked about the possibility of it in Rolling Stone.

Oh, yeah, he just wants to use us. I don't want to be in a band like that; he uses us like that. I want to be in a band that's a band. I want to be in a band that gives me something in my life, not that he can use as a toy on a piece of string like a fucking yo-yo. I want to be in a band that exists. Not that existed then, and he can pick up and use it like a piece of toilet paper.

If Pete asked you to do some shows for a Who reunion, would you do it?

No. No, I wouldn't do it. I would not do it. It's got no meaning doing it as the Who. Me doing this has got more meaning because it's different. You've never heard those songs done that way. They're all very, very different and the sound is very different.

The orchestration is very different. But for the Who to do that again... I mean, for what?

What did Pete say to you after the Carnegie Hall show?
He didn't say anything.

Who's in the band for your U.S. tour?

We've got five musicians this time out. Ringo's son, Zak Starkey, is on drums. Guy Fletcher from Dire Straits is on synthesizer, Simon Townshend (Pete's brother) on guitar and backing vocals. Geoff Whitehorn's on lead guitar and we haven't selected a bass player yet. Of course, Jody Linscott will play percussion. John "Rabbit" Bundrick will play keyboards and Billy Nichols will be on backing vocals.

Quite a large band.

You should see the orchestra!

Who's producing the live album?

Bob Ezrin, great guy. He just finished Pink Floyd's *The Division Bell.*

If you had to excise a few Who songs from the band's catalog that you think are real stinkers, what would you select?

I wouldn't say anything. I haven't recorded anything that I'm ashamed of. I mean, *It's Hard*, I'm not ashamed of that for any other reason than it's a sub-standard record and it shouldn't have come out.

Lastly, what Who songs do you wish you'd written?

Maybe "Behind Blue Eyes" or "Won't Get Fooled Again" because they mean so much to me. They mean a real lot to me. I would have liked to have written those two.

Curtis Mayfield

By Craig Werner
July 4, 1997

Curtis Mayfield's voice sinks to a whisper as he recalls the lyrics from one of his greatest songs: "I've got my strength and it don't make no sense not to keep on pushing." If you're looking for a one-sentence summation of what soul music is all about, it would be hard to do better. It's a vision that inspired the marchers of the sixties and continues to speak to many wandering the wilderness of the nineties. Mayfield savors the line: "Keep on pushing."

Lying on his side on a hospital bed in the sunlit study of his comfortable suburban Atlanta home, Mayfield traces the music he helped shape to its sources in the black church: "Gospel was your foundation, and there's been many a song coming from the black church."

As for the specific connection with "Keep on Pushing:" "It was probably subconscious. All you had to do was just change some few lyrics. 'Keep on Pushing' was intended, written as a gospel song. But all I needed to do to lock it in with the Impressions was say 'I've got my strength' instead of 'God gave me strength and it don't make sense.' I've got my strength. Nothing else needed to be changed."

Meditative, often poetic in his response to questions about his music, the black freedom movement, and the sources that gave strength to both, Mayfield quotes his own lyrics frequently. The man given credit with providing much of "the soundtrack of the civil rights movement" has been paralyzed, physically, since a light-rigging fell on him during an outdoor performance in 1990. But his eyes shine with an undiminished intellectual and spiritual clarity. When Mayfield speaks, his words resonate with the spiritual power that has allowed black folks to survive four centuries of storm without surrendering the vision of a better, calmer world. His dignity and eloquence evoke images of an urban elder, an American griot passing the heritage of the ancestors down to a community in need of sustaining wisdom.

Mayfield smiles at the image of himself as sage: "I wouldn't make the choice myself. I just believe in living because I'm just a man. I'm certainly no saint, never have been. I've always wanted to do more or less the right thing with living. Do unto those as you'd have them do unto you, that was more or less my church motto and that always made proper sense."

Mayfield pauses to gather his breath; his health keeps him from speaking or singing for extended periods. His Grammy-nominated 1996 album *New World Order* would be a remarkable achievement for any artist. But for a man who can only record a few lines at a time, it's something close to a miracle.

"I don't like to appoint myself to nothing, knowing I'm no better than anybody else. But it always makes me feel good to know I try to do the best I can and those who might observe say 'Hey, I can take a little something from that person.'"

In the time since Mayfield first appeared on the Chicago music scene in 1958, he's given many things to many different people. The great records he made with the Impressions—"People Get Ready," "I'm So Proud," "We're a Winner"—inspired the movement at its peak during the mid-sixties. "This Is My Country" and "Choice of Colors" kept the faith even as the Movement began to dissolve in paranoia and violence after the assassination of Martin Luther King. The funk he laid down for his independent Curtom label during the seventies showed what black power might mean economically and creatively. *The Super Fly* soundtrack broke down the blaxploitation film genre in terms that apply equally to gangsta rap. Sampled echoes of his riffs help keep hip-hop from losing its history and its soul. His songwriting contributed to the success of a parade of singers including Jerry Butler, Jan Bradley, Gene Chandler, Major Lance, Aretha Franklin, Mavis Staples, Rod Stewart, Donny Hathaway, the Five Stairsteps, Deniece Williams, En Vogue and dancehall reggae stars Chaka Demus and Pliers. His guitar work influenced Jimi Hendrix; his religious vision inspired Bob Marley. Poet, elder, political conscience for a generation, Mayfield remains a wellspring of one of America's most important cultural traditions.

Marley, who grew up in Jamaica listening to the Impressions on Miami radio stations, paid tribute to Mayfield in "One Love/People Get Ready." Marley's Rastafarian anthem and Mayfield's soul classic share a vision of community that remains crucial in a time of racial polarization and spiritual despair. Fully aware of the brutal histories of blacks throughout the diaspora, both Marley and Mayfield offer a healing vision that reaches out across racial lines. Recalling that he wrote "People Get Ready" in a "spiritual mind," Mayfield emphasizes its openness: "It doesn't matter what color or faith you have. I'm pleased the lyrics can be of value to anybody."

Mayfield's "spiritual mind" found its rhythm on the streets of black Chicago where he grew up and began his career. Born June 3, 1942, Mayfield can't remember a time when he wasn't listening to gospel music: "Most of my young life it was almost automatic. Most black folks connected one way or another with the quartets and the little chorus groups and what have you." Most immediately, Mayfield experienced the music that resounded out of the gospel church presided over by his grandmother, A.B. Mayfield: "My grandmother was working to become a minister back in the early fifties. And so I saw a lot of church. We had a little storefront place. It was known as the Travelling Souls Spiritualist Church. And so it was just automatic for us young kids. We had Sunday school every Sunday, so after we'd come up in age of course we'd heard a lot of gospel music."

If his grandmother provided the religious center of the family, Mayfield picked up his earliest musical inspiration from the male relatives who introduced him to the gospel quartet tradition that exerted a profound influence on the Impressions.

"My grandfather and my uncle, they were affiliated with my grandmother but they were into the music. They listened to a lot of old timers like the Original Five Blind Boys and the Dixie Hummingbirds. All of them, the Soul Stirrers when Sam Cooke was there as a young kid. There was a lot of music. We actually started out óthat was my foundation more or lessóconnecting music with the church."

Not surprisingly, Mayfield's own career began in a family-based gospel group, the Northern Jubilee Gospel Singers. Composed of Jerry Butler, Mayfield, cousins Sam, Tommy, and Charles Hawkins, the group performed in the highly competitive Chicago quartet scene of the late '40s and early '50s. Unlike most Chicago quartets, the group was based on the north side; after a number of early moves Mayfield's family settled down in the Cabrini-Green housing project, which had not yet turned into the emblem of urban despair it was to become during the seventies. Although Mayfield's father left the family when the singer was an infant, his mother helped develop his deep love for language. He fondly recalls that his mother "was very much into poetry. She also liked symphonic music. She wrote poems herself and had a lot of books of poetry which I used to read all the time. She read me Paul Laurence Dunbar, Dr. Seuss, limericks. These became the foundations for my hook lines and rhythmic patterns."

Testifying to the role the women in his family played in nurturing his talent, Mayfield dedicates his collection of poems and lyrics, *Poetic License* (Dove Books, 1996) to the "Memory of Grandmother Sady Washington and Reverend Annabell Mayfield" and "My Mother, Marion Pauline Washington."

Mayfield emphasizes the role the black community as a whole played in his upbringing: "I was fortunate enough to be amongst a lot of folks who helped to strengthen my mental abilities as a youngster. I learned through the streets and through the wise old people. I used to love to listen to old folks. Though you have to sort things out and make certain amends because a lot of what they say's BS." He chuckles softly and continues: "But there's a lot of truth to it too. You know, everything in its place. That's more or less how I got my learning, talking to elderly people who'd had to do the same because of the times. Even prior to my time that was the only way to get a learning. And still they managed to do well for themselves."

Pondering the contrast between the support he received during his childhood and the frequent isolation of poor black communities today, Mayfield reverts to the voice of the elder.

"The young ones have lost the presence of the older people; that and the family. I even watch it with my own family; the suffering back then in my early years."

Without romanticizing an era when the population density of Chicago's black belt reached an incredible 300% of legal capacity, Mayfield remembers the '40s and '50s as a time of communal sharing: "Mostly everybody that had a little something or that had a little home or even an apartment, they had grandfathers, they had uncles and aunties, and many times those people lived right within the same household. And of course the women had their men and everybody had the support and took

what little you might have to make it work for everybody."

Mayfield links the values of post-war black Chicago to those of the rural south where most of the older generation had grown up: "Down south everybody had their pigs and chickens and everything to make it. It worked, you know."

He considers what happened to that sense of shared struggle, a sense of connection at the center of gospel music, the freedom movement, and most of his own songs: "As you got older you began to see a different way of life, and the men and the women, they became divided. The man go his way and you could see families just sort of deteriorating simply because they didn't have that background. A lot of kids can't look back one generation. If you were to put a family tree together you don't know from nothing, so many ins and outs."

Shining out beneath the stocking cap he always wears during public appearances, Mayfield's eyes take an intense sadness. He concludes his meditation on the trouble he sees by considering the ambiguous role of individualism in black communities: "Everybody wanted to become individuals, independent individuals. Which has its place. But to have a foundation you need a very strong beginning and you have to know where you come from."

For the young Mayfield, gospel music balanced the need for individuality—finding his own voice—with a strong sense of how the individual fit into a vital group. Embracing individuality was crucial for a community struggling against stereotypes, prejudice, and invisibility. But to embrace raw individualism—a sense of self divorced from community grounding—amounted to spiritual suicide.

The Chicago of Mayfield's childhood presented a setting that encouraged both individuality and

community. Recently, scholars of African-American culture have begun to recognize the cultural activity that took place in the city from the mid-thirties to the mid-sixties as a "Chicago Renaissance" equivalent in importance to the better known Harlem Renaissance of the '20s. Like Harlem, Chicago hosted thriving literary and intellectual scenes; Richard Wright, Gwendolyn Brooks, Margaret Walker, Nella Larsen, and Leon Forrest are only the most prominent of the Chicago-based writers. But what set the Chicago Renaissance apart was the music that surrounded the young Mayfield and the countless Chicago-born musicians of his generation.

In addition to the gospel and pop scenes, Chicago played an important role in the history of ᷾ and the blues. Pianists Herbie Hancock and Ramsey Lewis, who helped attract a pop audience to jazz during the '60s and '70s, grew up alongside experimental musicians such as Anthony Braxton, Muhal Richard Abrams, and the members of the Art Ensemble of Chicago. Mayfield emphasizes Chicago's role as a "blues town, with McKinley Morganfield (Muddy Waters) and Little Walter and all those guys" and credits the rich musical scene with providing him a constant source of fresh musical ideas: "I had so much to go back on for ideas and sounds and rhythms and feels."

The deepest of those ideas and rhythms came from gospel music. At the outset, gospel provided a way for enlivening a spiritual experience that sometimes eluded the younger members of the church. With a smile, Mayfield says: "Whereas the preaching would kind of tire you out and put you to sleep, the music was kind of an outburst just full of love, so that would build your heart up." Soon, however, music took on a more central role in Mayfield's life. As the youngest member of the Northern Jubilees, he developed the distinctive, near-falsetto style that made his mature singing so distinctive. "My cousins had formed the group and I couldn't wait for a chance to sing with them. I was maybe seven when they got started and I guess within a few months I found that I could carry a tune. I had just an automatic high pitched voice being that young. I fit right in as a tenor singer."

In his brilliant book *You Send Me: The Life and Times of Sam Cooke*, Daniel Wolff describes how the competitive nature of the gospel quartet scene challenged singers like Ira Tucker, Clarence Fountain and Claude Jeter to develop their style to the highest possible level. Although Mayfield never really did battle with the giants of the quartet tradition, he credits his exposure to the scene with helping advance his musical awareness.

"As churches grew, our church anyway, the church had plenty of little affairs with other churches and we'd go visit other churches and they'd visit us and every church would have a group, a young kid singer vocalist or someone who was singing music. So we got a lot of that. A lot of acappella and group singing and that was good for the youngsters. That would build your heart up."

As a member of a relatively small congregation, Mayfield had little direct contact with the major stars of the gospel highway, but he listened to their records constantly, especially those put out on "Specialty Records, the old black and white label." Fondly recalling "the old victrola" that occupied a prominent place in the Mayfield apartment, he credits the records with establishing the love for harmony that echoes through from "Gypsy Woman" and "I'm So Proud" down through "No One Knows About a Good Thing" and "Back to Living Again," two of the strongest cuts from *New World Order*.

"We heard plenty of church music, plenty of harmonizing, so I think that was more or less how I built up my foundation. I was never really a lead singer but to hear these people sing the way I always wished I could sing, to go so deep and then so high, just so strong. Those guys could belt out a tune. That was just good singing and good music. I was a quartet man, the four and five man groups." Mayfield pauses and you can almost hear the chords fill the air. "When it comes to quartets, it could even be barbershop. I just loved harmony. So

that's where the foundation was laid down for me."

If Mayfield's foundation lay in gospel, doowop provided an equivalent influence on the secular side of his sensibility. Throughout the '50s, Chicago was home to a thriving doowop scene that developed groups such as the Flamingos, the Spaniels, and the Dells, whose sweet harmonies and gospel intensities paralleled those in Mayfield's gospel soul. Like most big city doowop scenes, Chicago's South Side featured highly competitive street corner singing. Paralleling the competition between gospel quartets and anticipating later forms such as hip-hop freestyling, doowop groups would battle for control of street corners where they could attract an audience and establish a reputation. In Robert Pruter's definitive study *Doowop: The Chicago Scene*, Reggie Smith, a member of the Five Chances, remembered Mayfield's incursion on the group's turf at Forty-fourth and Prairie: "Curtis Mayfield was living around there before his mother and him moved to Cabrini-Green. His mother had bought him a banjo, something of that sort. He used to come around beating on the banjo and we'd tell him to get away from us with all that noise, cause we're trying to sing (but) he went on to beat us to death. There was a lot of talent come through our area."

Both the gospel and doowop scenes centered on the South Side black belt, but the near North Side where Mayfield moved was by no means a musical wasteland. The Cabrini-Green doowop scene revolved around the recreation center in Seward Park, which provided rooms for groups to practice in. Billy Butler, one of several North Siders who later recorded Mayfield compositions, described Seward Park to Pruter: "We were all into trying to sing. That was the only thing to do really...the area didn't have street gangs at the time. Everyone would form a group and go into Seward Park."

The most popular North Side doowop groups included the Van Gayles, Serenades, the Capris, the Players and the Medallionaires. Herbert Butler, a member of the Players, told Pruter of the competitive energy in the Seward Park Center: "At that time everybody sang. You know that Major Lance lived right down the street and Curtis Mayfield right on the next street... Everybody who was anybody would rehearse there... They had like seven rooms and you could come in and tell which room which group was gonna be in, because people would be hanging around the doors or rooms would be full and they would not be letting anybody in."

Even before he joined the Northern Jubilee Gospel Singers, Mayfield toyed with secular music. While attending the West Side Grammar School, he formed a short-lived group called the Alphatones with schoolmates Al Boyce and Dallas Dickerson. But the real move toward popular music came when Jerry Butler, who had sung with the Northern Jubilees, invited his friend to join the Roosters, who would soon change their name to the Impressions. The original members of the Roosters—Sam Gooden, Emmanuel Thomas, Fred Cash and brothers Richard and Arthur Brooks—had moved from Chattanooga to Chicago, where they brought Butler into the group. Aware of Mayfield's ability to harmonize and play guitar, Butler convinced the other Roosters to give his friend a chance. "I had known Curtis from church," Butler told Pruter, "and we sang in various choirs together and so I persuaded him to join us...So he joined the group and we really started to get an identity...a sound of our own."

Mayfield dropped out of Wells High—"I'm not recommending that to anyone," he cautions—and devoted himself to music. He laughs when he remembers his early days in the group, especially the reception the down-home Roosters received from the more urbane Chicago audiences.

"Down south they been the Roosters and a Chick because they had a lady singer with them. So they come to the big north with that Roosters name. We couldn't get through a song after we told the audience the name. They'd be crowing and making all kinds of barnyard sounds." Mayfield credits Eddie Thomas, who later became his partner at Curtom, with coming up with the name that stuck. "We were doing a little show somewhere when Eddie decided he wanted to manage us and his first statement was 'we gotta do something with that name. You got to make some kind of impression.' And we just said, yeah, that's it. So that's how the title for the group came about."

Although the Impressions were aware of both the gospel and doowop scenes, their music never belonged in either camp. From their first recordings, they combined elements of gospel and pop music in a manner pioneered by Ray Charles and Sam Cooke, who left the Soul Stirrers in 1957 to pursue a solo career.

"At first it was strange listening to Ray Charles. He's been singing gospel all his life even though his music's considered rhythm and blues. He just changed the lyrics but never changed his way of singing, which you could hear was out of the church."

Mayfield and Butler paid close attention to Cooke's crossover success: "Oh yeah, I was a Sam Cooke fan. With the Northern Jubilees we admired the Soul Stirrers so much and tried to duplicate some of their sounds. Incidentally, the way Sam voiced his music was taken from an elderly man with the Soul Stirrers, but of course Sam Cooke was Sam Cooke. Sam found himself singing those gospel shows where he was able to ad-lib and do all the things he did so well. But when 'You Send Me' came out, man, we thought it was just a fantastic piece of music. I loved it."

It was almost accidental that the Impressions' first record, which featured Butler as lead vocalist, captured the gospel soul sound that would be the group's signature. It was virtually a fluke that the group signed with Vee-Jay in the first place. Mayfield recalls that a major snowstorm hit Chicago the day they were scheduled to audition for Chess Records.

"The snow was about five feet to walk through when we went to Chess Records and knocked on the door," Curtis told Alan Warner. "I guess there was a secretary in there, but no one would let us in. So we turned around and what's across the street: Vee-Jay Records. We just went right across through the snow, dragging our amplifier and guitar. Ewart Abner was upstairs and the A&R man, Calvin Carter—they let us in. It must have been a weekend, no one was really working, and we sang ('For Your Precious Love') for Calvin right on the steps. He loved it. About a week later, I was in the studio for the first time. And that's really how we got off."

Carter provided a slightly different version of story in an interview with *Chicago Tribune* writer Clarence Page: "They sang about five or six numbers and sounded pretty good, but I was not hearing that thing that sounds like money in the bank. On a hunch, I told them, 'Sing something you're ashamed to sing! Sing something you don't usually feel like singing in public.' So one of them told the rest, 'Hey, how about that spiritual thing we worked out?' The rest of them argued about it, but they finally sang it. It was a beautiful ballad. It was called 'For Your Precious Love.' It sold over nine hundred thousand copies on its first issue."

Written by Butler and the Brooks brothers, "For Your Precious Love" introduces several elements of the gospel soul style Mayfield later brought to perfection. A powerful bass line and softly strum-

ming guitar provide a deceptively peaceful setting for Butler's solemn testifying. The call and response between the lead vocalist, whose baritone contrasts with Mayfield's sweet tenor, and the background chorus emphasizes the cut's gospel roots and points toward the production techniques Phil Spector used for pop gospel masterpieces by Ben E. King ("Stand By Me") and the Righteous Brothers ("Ebb Tide").

Ironically, the success of "For Your Precious Love" contributed to the break-up of the group. Mayfield attributes the problems to Vee-Jay's desire to market Butler as the star of the act. "They chose to put out the record as 'Jerry Butler and the

Impressions'," he observes. "So when the record came out that way, all the attention went to Jerry, the fan mail, the way the disc jockeys announced it. It kind of created a tension with the fellows." Although Butler's decision to pursue a solo career sidetracked the Impressions for several years, Mayfield views the change as "a blessing in disguise." As he told Pruter, "When Jerry left it allowed us to regroup and start getting into our own selves, and it allowed me to generate and pull out my own talents as a writer and a vocalist."

Mayfield emphasizes that there were no hard feelings with Butler: "It wasn't Jerry. We were always close." In fact, even after Butler left the group, the Impressions sometimes benefited from his name.

"Nobody was really aware of the Impressions. Sometimes we did gigs in little towns as Jerry Butler and the Impressions and Sam would do 'For Your Precious Love'." When Vee-Jay dropped the post-Butler Impressions after a couple of unsuccessful singles ("Seniorita I Love You" and "That You Love Me"), Mayfield went on the road as Butler's guitarist.

Cutting him off from most of his familiar social networks, Mayfield's apprenticeship with Butler sparked his development into a mature songwriter.

"During those times of my life I was sleeping with my guitar and writing every feeling. Anger, love, everything in my life would come out on paper. I found it worked great for me because it was always there." Mayfield considers the role songwriting played in his personal development: "It was even an escape if I was hurt too bad or if something wasn't going right. I could always retire to writing my sentiments and my personal feelings. A lot of times those songs were mostly for me. I was the one trying to learn the first lesson because I didn't have the answers." Mayfield pauses. "My fights and arguments, even with God, went down on

paper. Why, when. Why, what. Well, this is how I feel about it."

Between 1960 and 1963, Mayfield's meditations helped keep numerous Chicago singers on the charts. The Sony/Okeh CD *Curtis Mayfield's Chicago Soul* documents the brilliant string of songs Mayfield wrote during the first half of the sixties. His beautiful soul ballad "He Will Break Your Heart" gave Butler his first number one R&B hit and made the pop top 20. Whenever Butler seemed to be losing steam, he turned to his old friend, who responded with "Find Another Girl," "I'm a Telling You Now," and "Need to Belong." The songs recorded by his former high school classmate Major Lance ("Think Nothing About It," "Um um um um um um," and the dance hit "The Monkey Time"), Billy Butler & the Enchanters ("I Can't Work No Longer," "Nevertheless I Love You," and "I Found

True Love"), and proto-feminist Jan Bradley ("Mama Didn't Lie") show Mayfield maturing into a songwriter capable of competing with the work coming out of New York's Brill Building and Berry Gordy's Motown.

Mayfield dismisses any suggestion of a rivalry between the Chicago soul industry and Gordy's cluster of Detroit-based labels.

"It wasn't really a rivalry," he says. "Those guys were just so much admired and they were so big, there was no need. The best I could do was learn something from them. What with Berry Gordy, Smokey Robinson, they had fantastic writers over there and all you could do was admire those folks for the contribution they made to America. That was a heck of an era, the Motown era."

The best of Mayfield's early '60s work, most notably the records he made with Gene Chandler, stands up with the pop sound coming out of Detroit. Best known for "Duke of Earl," Chandler's ability as a soul performer shines through more clearly on Mayfield compositions "What Now," "Think Nothing About It," "Man's Temptation," "Just Be True," and "Rainbow." As Mayfield told Pruter, "Gene seemed to sing my songs in his own way, and he had such an enthusiasm for them. He was a seller of them. Whatever it was, even if the song wasn't the best, Gene just had a way of putting himself totally into a tune…He always was capable of putting his own influences, his own feeling, into a tune, but also being true to the original intention of the writer."

As a songwriter, Mayfield provides a refreshing exception to a history littered with the tragic stories of gifted craftsmen who fell victim to predatory record labels and failed to profit from their genius. His ability to keep control of the rights to his songs, which enables him to live in financial comfort even though he can no longer tour, didn't happen by accident. Mayfield thinks back on his experience as a young songwriter in the highly competitive New York scene of the '60s: "I got hold of those rumors listening to the old folks. There was a place there, an old landmark right in the Square at 1615 Broadway. At one time that was all music and publishing and all your big publishers, all they had to do was hang around that area."

Mayfield remembers the scene as a multi-racial one which both united and divided songwriters in their struggle for economic rewards.

"When you come down in the streets around that building, you'd run into young people, black,

Italian, Hispanic, it didn't matter. They were all peddling their songs. If they had a decent song, they could run up to the publisher and sell it for twenty dollars. Of course the publisher would take it lock, stock and barrel."

Even success didn't guarantee security. Mayfield continues: "Maybe they'd go up to fifty or 100 dollars if you got a little hot streak going for yourself, but nobody ever owned nothing except those big guys who had the money. You saw so many people all over the country; people used to come down out of New York and Chicago and they'd run down to Nashville and buy songs. Well many of those songs became great, great hits. Those were the times of real publishers because they really did promote the sheet music. Publishing companies are now more or less holding companies."

Aware of the exploitation suffered by his elders, Mayfield explored ways of establishing control over his own economic fate.

"It was important to me to own as much of myself as I could. So I found out where the Library of Congress was and how to record my own publishing company. Turned out it cost nothing to do either one."

Over the years, Mayfield established several publishing companies, including Chi-Sound (established 1965), Curtom's publishing arm Camad (1968), and Mayfield Music (1975), where he continues to publish today.

Mayfield credits his publishing ventures with enabling him to withstand the financial stress caused by the accident that ended his performing career. When Rod Stewart's version of "People Get Ready" and En Vogue's remake of "Giving Him Something He Can Feel," a song Mayfield wrote for Aretha Franklin, became smash hits, Mayfield collected substantial royalties. Similarly, he benefits whenever hip-hop producers enrich their records with samples from "Freddie's Dead," "Superfly," or any of Mayfield's other classic records. Mayfield expresses satisfaction with the way the record industry has come to terms with sampling: "James Brown's voice sort of taught everybody to work it out and get your credits. His 'owwwws' were the whole record, they were on everything. But now it's been standardized and one must be given the proper credits. It becomes a residual for you even if it's not just but one beat. So it works out where you can make a decent living."

Mayfield maintains a deep empathy for the writers and singers who lost control of their material.

Despite his relatively secure economic position, he joined in a 1995 class action suit filed to gain remuneration and a pension fund for soul acts exploited by unscrupulous labels. There's an uncharacteristically hard edge in Mayfield's voice when he observes that "Publishing was the foundation of large estates I found out as I got older. And learning the value of that I found it's better to keep your song and bargain with them and try and be strong and resist taking the 100 or 500 or whatever it might be. The value is in you the person, so own what you do as best you can."

He expresses particular concern for artists who no longer own the rights to records sampled by hip-hop acts: "Not all of that is properly standardized and anyone who uses a rhythm piece out of a song or something, whoever owns the masters has the right to collect residuals. Even if it's a voice, the money goes back to the label. Whoever owns the master owns the right to collect residuals."

Reiterating the need to "own as much of yourself as possible and believe in yourself as you do your dream," Mayfield refers to the law suit: "That's why I did it. I'd always hear the old guys saying you gotta pay your dues. Yeah, I paid my dues; a lot of people paid their dues. It's true, you do have to pay your dues, but sometimes you pay so much out that you find you have to buy yourself back if you could afford to do so."

By 1961, Mayfield had saved enough money to stake the Impressions to a second shot. "I saved a thousand dollars working with Jerry Butler as his guitarist. When I was with Jerry all I did was sleep with my guitar and write songs. So I went and got the Impressions and took them to New York and we recorded our first record on ABC Paramount, 'Gypsy Woman.'" A haunting erotic ballad backed with an infectious castanet rhythm, the song rose to #2 on the R&B charts and #20 on the pop charts. It was followed by a string of hits including "It's All Right" (#1 R&B, #4 pop), "I'm So Proud" (#2 R&B, #14 pop), "Keep on Pushing" (#1 R&B, #10 pop), and "Amen" (#17 R&B, #4 pop).

Mayfield credits arranger Johnny Pate with helping develop the Impressions' distinctive sound. "He was a musician's musician. He wrote great blues from way back, was an upright bass player, and an arranger. That was my first introduction to arranging. Everything prior to that was just head sessions where we just used rhythms. Just nail the rhythm and get it through. But Johnny gave me my first encounter with real arranging and along with Riley

Hampton, who I used on the first Curtis album, he was the love of my life as far as real arrangers go."

Pate's approach to arranging shines through clearly on "Amen," one of the few Impressions hits not written by Mayfield. Mayfield remembers seeing the movie *Lilies of the Field* and telling Pate he wanted to record the song: "Watching Sidney Poitier, I thought it was a great movie and we just had to sing that song. So Johnny helped put our own interpretation on it." Following a majestic horn introduction, Pate organizes the song around a series of call and response patterns, between individual voices and harmonizing group, between horn section and vocal lines.

Built on Mayfield's gospel foundation, the call and response style defines the approach to gospel soul the group first developed in "It's All Right." Mayfield, who enjoys remembering the origins of his songs, credits Fred Cash with inspiring the lyrics for "It's All Right."

Mayfield told interviewer Alan Warner: "We were in Nashville, Tennessee, at a gig; we'd already done the first set, and we had about an hour before the second. It was a nice, warm night, and we went out front of the club and were sitting in our station wagon—myself, Fred, and Samuel Gooden. I got to talking and running off at the mouth and just dreaming about ideas and things that might happen to us in the future. Fred kept answering back to me, 'Well, all right, well, that's all right,' you know. Before I knew it, it rang in my head. We had a real hook line, 'It's All Right,' so I said, 'Say it's all right.' Before we knew it, we had actually written two thirds of that tune right there in the car! We could have gone on stage for the next show and sang it!"

Emphasizing the collaborative process he'd picked up in gospel and the Chicago studios where he worked as a session man, Mayfield points out that the recorded version of "It's All Right" owes something to Pate and, less directly, blues singer Bobby "Blue" Bland: "I'd also say Bobby 'Blue' Bland made a great contribution to this song, too, because he had a song out ('That's the Way Love Is') which had such delightful horn movements in it. I asked Johnny to listen to that song and maybe lock in with some of the horn structure. Anyway it just worked out perfect."

Complementing the call and response arrangement, "It's All Right" introduces the distinctive vocal style that sets the Impressions' gospel soul apart from the styles coming out of Motown or the R&B-based Stax studio in Memphis. Describing the switch-off lead style that made the new three-man Impressions' sound so distinctive, Mayfield reflects on the curious difference between sacred and secular traditions.

"It was probably original in R&B and contemporary music, but there was nothing original about it if you ever sang gospel. In gospel, you knew how to sing lead and also how to incorporate yourself into the group, how to blend in. Sometimes everyone would come out and sing harmony with a portion of the lead."

As he told Robert Pruter, "It made us a three-man group stronger than we were as a five-man group. It locks everybody in; you really know where the voices are...When you have four or five men, if one moves up, the other doesn't know where to go. Of course, other groups imitated us."

The style works perfectly on "Keep on Pushing" and "People Get Ready" where Gooden's resonant bass voice and Adams' stronger tenor add power to Mayfield's delicate leads. Gooden and Adams remained in the group after the Brooks brothers and Thomas left the group in 1962, an event Mayfield attributes to the fact that "my own music and personal creations were so dominant and our styles had just become somewhat different. It just wasn't their music."

Determined to realize the new sound's potential, Mayfield and Eddie Thomas laid the foundation for the Impressions' success while both were still working for Jerry Butler.

"Eddie was still driving for Jerry, his valet more or less, and I was his guitarist. Eddie was such a hustler man. Everywhere we went, anything even looked like an antenna, maybe five or ten miles away, we'd come on and Jerry would hustle 'Gypsy Woman' to whoever was there." Thomas's success in getting airplay reflects a radio world not yet locked into tight playlists and formats. "Country and western, gospel, any kind of station, didn't matter what the format was. Eddie would pull over and take us to the station. People just appreciated you coming in and making the stop, so they'd give you a play. So that's how we began to build up 'Gypsy Woman' and finally it broke out and began to do very well in Philadelphia."

The hard work paid off, enabling Mayfield to take the reformed Impressions on the road.

"So then I was able to move away from Jerry and we started performing as a group and it allowed Eddie to move away from being a valet and driver and to become a promotion man for ABC-Paramount. Later he became their first black national promo man."

There's a hint of nostalgia in Mayfield's voice when he concludes: "The country was our neighborhood. We were putting on 150,000 miles a year."

If the Impressions' sound was beginning to assume its classic form on the early singles, the group's first albums on ABC-Paramount, the group's label up until the birth of Curtom in 1970, reflect an uncertainty about creative direction and marketing strategy. Released in 1963 to capitalize on the success of "It's All Right," their self-named debut album shows their continuing affinity with doowop in the rich harmonies and teen-oriented lyrics of "Sad, Sad Girl and Boy" and the lovely "Grow Closer Together." Strikingly less successful, the follow-up LP, *The Never Ending Impressions*, suggests that the Impressions, like the Sam Cooke who could release the uninspired *Live at the Copa* at the same time he was writing soul classics like "Bring It On Home to Me," aspired to the Las Vegas lounge circuit. "I'm So Proud" strikes a discordant note in a set that includes Duke Ellington's "Satin Doll," Kurt Weil's "September Song," and a cover of the Trini Lopez hit "Lemon Tree."

With *Keep on Pushing* (1964) and *People Get Ready* (1965), the group, supported by Pate as full-time arranger, finally settled on the gospel soul sound that spoke so clearly to the freedom movement. Even as the Impressions experimented with Motown dance music ("I Love You (Yeah)") and James Brown R&B ("Somebody Help Me"), *Keep On Pushing* makes brilliant use of the African-American tradition of masking, which dates back to slavery. Faced with certain punishment if they expressed anger or planned resistance, blacks developed codes that enabled them to communicate among themselves without attracting white attention. Frequently they hid "political" messages beneath surfaces that the masters heard as statements of religious faith or longing. The classic example is the spiritual "Swing Low Sweet Chariot," which whites heard as a yearning for reward in a better world. For black listeners aware of the masked meanings, however, the song served as a call to escape on the underground railroad, the abolitionist chariot swinging down to carry them to the relative freedom of the North.

Gospel singers, most of whom grew up in segregated situations nearly as oppressive as slavery, adopted similar strategies. When Mahalia Jackson envisioned the day she'd "walk in Jerusalem" or Sam Cooke invited you to "come go with me to that land," black listeners understood the political message clearly. During the freedom movement, the masks began to come off; leaders such as Martin

Luther King, Jr. and Fannie Lou Hamer relied on music to transform terrified individuals into a cohesive community with the strength needed to march out and face police dogs, fire hoses, and the Ku Klux Klan.

Mayfield was natural heir to the tradition of using religious images to express far-ranging social agendas. But he was entering into the pop culture of the early '60s which maintained its placid surface by refusing to mention religion or politics, especially if the stance was anywhere to the left of "The Ballad of the Green Berets." Combining gospel and R&B strategies, Mayfield devised a brilliant solution. Like Ray Charles, he freely altered religious references to fit a secular vocabulary. Adapting Mahalia

Jackson's strategy to R&B style lyrics, he wrote songs that could be heard as simple love songs even as they bore witness to the deeper love that inspired the movement.

"Keep on Pushing" exemplifies the approach. No one fighting the good fight in Mississippi or Alabama or Chicago had any doubt what Mayfield was talking about. When Mayfield urged his people to get ready for the "train to Jordan," he tapped into the same energy that powered the underground railroad's "chariot." Even when the connection with political masking was less direct, the Impressions celebrated the emotions that gave the movement strength: love, a profound sense of connectedness, the belief that somehow things would work out. Overflowing with the joy of feeling accepted, "I'm So Proud" anticipates the central impetus of a black power movement that was still in its infancy when the song was released in 1964.

As the movement gathered strength, the Impressions succeeded in speaking more directly without attracting significant resistance, at least until 1968 when several radio stations, including Chicago's number one rated WLS, banned the distinctly uplifting "We're A Winner." Mayfield attributes the banning to the song's "social conscience; it was about a mass of people during the time of struggle, and when it broke it was so much out of the ordinary. It had a little gospel feeling and it sort of locked in with the movement of equality. It wouldn't be what you could call a crossover record during those times, but the demand of the people kept it struggling and happening, and it's still one of my favorite tunes."

As close to pure gospel as anything that ever made the pop charts, "People Get Ready" overcame programmers' resistance and brought the call-and-response voice of the movement to the Top 20 in 1965. Mayfield describes how the song's "nice, spiritual gospel feel dictated the words, which came from the inspiration of the church and different sermons. It just all came together properly."

From the opening bars of the song—a gospel hum carried along by bells, Pate's beautiful horn chart, and Mayfield's delicately syncopated guitar chording—the cut defuses possible resistance. Bringing a healing vision to a community poised on the edge of rioting, the song welcomes anyone willing to do the right thing onto the "train to Jordan" while warning "there's no hiding place against the kingdom's throne." When the song ends with "you don't need no ticket, you just thank the Lord," you can almost believe that the promise of the movement would be fulfilled.

Mayfield called and the movement responded profoundly. Several movement veterans have referred to him as the man who wrote "the soundtrack for the movement." Mayfield demurs: "Somehow here lately I've been getting a lot of credit for being the one who more or less laid the soundtrack for civil rights. I don't know who even gave me that title. It's not totally true, but I'm honored to think that some of my music was appropriate and could lock in with what was happening."

Certainly Mayfield was deeply committed to the movement. "As a young man I was writing songs like 'Keep on Pushing' and 'This Is My Country' and feeling all the love and all the things I observed politically." Mayfield's voice trails off as he considers the connection between his music and the political energy of the Sixties. When he speaks again, he seems to be picking up a thought in midstream. "Of course with everything I saw on the streets as a young black kid, it wasn't hard during the latter Fifties and early Sixties for me to write through my own heartfelt way of how I visualized things, how I thought things oughta be."

Profoundly political, but never narrowly ideological, Mayfield's sense of how things ought to be took shape both within his own community and in response to the calls of the leaders.

"When you're talking about songs such as 'We're a Winner,' that's locked in with Martin Luther King. It took something from his inspiring message. I was listening to all my preachers and the different leaders of the time. You had your Rap Browns and your Stokeley Carmichaels and Martin Luther Kings, all of those people were there right within that same era. They get their credit and rightfully so."

But Mayfield insists that the real strength of the movement lay in the commitment of the larger community, the local people he refers to as "the invisible heroes."

Even as cries of "Black Power!" began to drown out the earlier movement's calls for "Freedom Now!," Mayfield maintained a gospel-tinged vision of interracial harmony. Closer to King than Malcolm X in sensibility, he emphasizes that the movement's successes required cooperation and shared struggle.

"People of all colors were trying to push this along ever since there's been a slavery. Not just the minority or blacks. Everybody in this country at one time or another has been a minority, wherever they come from. We just made a good loud noise as far as congregating. From out of that came a lot of my songs. So I'm just happy that maybe I made a bit of a tribute during my time in that particular era."

It's probably impossible to understand Mayfield's gospel soul apart from the political energy of the movement. Both emerged at a unique moment in American history. For a brief moment, a substantial majority of blacks managed to balance a deep sense of connection to traditional communities with a real desire to move closer to an American mainstream where blacks and whites would interact more freely and equitably. Martin Luther King's dream was, as he told the world, "very deeply rooted in the American dream." Survival in America didn't necessarily imply selling out, bleaching your soul. For that same brief moment, a significant number of whites seemed willing to respond to the vision of democracy and equality. White listeners attracted by the subversive sounds of Motown, which masked the voice of black Detroit with pop lyrics and production, frequently moved on to the gritty sounds coming out of Stax in Memphis or to Mayfield's gospel soul. Adding some white folks to your audience didn't require surrendering your voice. And it held out a healing vision of possibility that nostalgia cannot bring back.

The moment didn't last; riots and assassinations swept the cities, Richard Nixon rode a "southern strategy" rooted in racial antagonism to the White House, the movement veered sharply toward a nationalist ideology that rejected gospel and the blues. In the words of Maulana Karenga, one of the leading theoreticians of the Black Arts Movement, they were "invalid; for they teach resignation, in a word acceptance of reality—and we have come to change reality." Although the black community declined to abandon the traditions that had allowed it to survive slavery and segregation, Karenga's words represented a real challenge to the vision of "It's All Right" and "People Get Ready."

Mayfield responded in a measured fashion, accepting certain aspects of black power while reasserting the gospel vision. The covers of the first two Impressions albums released on Curtom reflect a new, more aggressive social stance. Their ABC-Paramount covers show the group dressed in suit jackets and ties; on *This Is My Country*, they wear turtlenecks and stand in the rubble outside a ghetto tenement. On *The Young Mod's Forgotten Story*, they pose in stylish leather jackets and the sailor's caps

associated with the emerging black scene. Mayfield embraced the fashion elements of black power without qualification: "It was a great opening: the style, the clothes, the wide pants, and the long German coats. Everything sort of fell in and it hit a real nice fashion. To be fly was to be, you know."

More importantly, Mayfield responded to the black power movement's call for uncompromising confrontation with the history of racism and oppression. In the 1968 single "This Is My Country" (#8 R&B, #25 pop), Mayfield testifies to "three hundred years of slave driving, sweat and welts on my back" but goes on to reassert the gospel vision, now stated in unmasked political terms: "This is my country." It's an uncompromising rejection of anyone—Elijah Muhammad as well as George Wallace—who would deny blacks full participation in American society.

"Some people think we don't have the right to say it's my country."

Similarly, the first cut on the *This Is My Country* album calls on the "invisible heroes" of the movement to fill the vacuum created by the assassinations. Backed by an arrangement that combines blues guitar and bass with gospel tambourine and organ, "They Don't Know" reassures those who feel despair over having "lost another leader" that they aren't alone. Reminding his listeners that "every brother is a leader," Mayfield promises "our love is gonna help the world be free."

Mayfield's late '60s work drew criticism, most of it respectful, from some black power advocates, who typically showed better taste in music than their theory allowed. Never confrontational in style, Mayfield responded to the criticism with music that reiterated his major points. "Choice of Colors" (#1 R&B, #21 pop) rejects unthinking racial hatred—"How long have you hated your white teacher"—while endorsing the black power call for unity and respect: "Can you respect your brother's woman friend, and share with black folks not of kin?" The clinching lines keep the faith in the open vision of the earlier movement, seeing the path to a better society in "a little more education, and love for our nation."

If Mayfield continued to resist separatism, his involvement with the Curtom label—named for Mayfield and his business partner Eddie Thomas—shows a deep understanding of the black power movement's call for economic self-determination. As early as 1966, Mayfield had begun exploring the possibility of establishing an independent label. His first two attempts—the "Windy C" and "Mayfield" labels—went under as a result of distribution problems, as had Thomas's self-named label. Nonetheless, they provided Mayfield and Thomas with invaluable experience with the business and production aspects of the music industry. By 1968, when the Impressions' contract with ABC-Paramount was about to expire, the partners were ready to devote themselves wholly to Curtom. As Mayfield told Pruter, he gave the industry another

shot because "I wasn't a quitter. Sometimes these things are like marriages. You don't give up wanting to be in love and having the best you can expect, just because your marriage fails."

For more than a decade, Curtom provided an emblem of the real potential of black power, financially and artistically. The label's financial success resulted from a series of astute decisions made in collaboration with business manager Marv Stuart, a young white man with a background promoting rock acts. Mayfield credits Stuart with a major role in Curtom's success. As Mayfield told Pruter, "as green as he was, he was very ambitious. I taught him the record business, and how to relate to people...through his own know-how and his own go-gettingness, he learned. He was able to find weak spots in Curtom and he turned them around."

One of the best decisions focused on Mayfield's own career. Although the Impressions' first three Curtom albums made the charts, none rose into the top hundred. As Stuart told Cary Baker, "I told Curtis, 'Everyone makin' it was a singer-songwriter, Curtis. You're an artist, you should go out on your own.'" The decision paid off immediately. Mayfield's solo debut, *Curtis*, made the Top 20; each of his first five solo efforts made the Top 40, capped by the *Super Fly* soundtrack which reached number one. Mayfield recalls his initial surprise at the success of his solo projects, which he pursued in part because: "I was just spreading myself too thin, trying to do everything at Curtom and still going out on gigs with the Impressions...I never really intended to leave permanently. But when the *Curtis* album came out, we all of a sudden discovered we had two hit acts."

Alongside its two showcase acts, the Curtom roster boasted a number of solid artists, many of whom had been discovered and developed by Mayfield. The Curtom Story, a two-disc import set released on Britain's Charly label, provides a fascinating overview of Mayfield's activity as musician, writer, and producer. The songs Mayfield wrote during the late '60s and early '70s uphold the high standards he established writing for Butler, Chandler, and the Impressions. Mayfield devoted a great deal of attention to the Five Stairsteps, a pre-Jackson 5 style family group whose hits included Curtis' compositions "Don't Waste Your Time," "Don't Change Your Love," and "Stay Close to Me." In addition to the biggest hits of the Five Stairsteps, the Impressions, and Curtis as a solo act, the Curtom set showcases performances of vintage Mayfield compositions by

Holly Maxwell ("Suffer"), Baby Huey & the Baby Sitters ("Might Mighty Children"), Curtis' old friend Major Lance ("Must Be Love Coming Down"), Love's Children ("Soul Is Love"), the Staple Singers ("Let's Do It Again"), Mavis Staples ("A Piece of the Action"), and two acts including the young Donny Hathaway: the Mayfield Singers ("I've Been Trying") and Donny Hathaway and June Conquest ("I Thank You").

Mayfield first met Hathaway, who he honors as "a young genius," when the Impressions were performing at Washington's Howard University, where Donny was a student.

"Donny was originally out of St. Louis and he was at Howard studying music. He'd come out of the church too but his family got him into the university. So he went back to the long-haired classical music and learned to play that piano any way you could imagine. So I was playing at Howard and he came to the theater with a couple of his singers. They were all majoring in music."

Hathaway impressed Mayfield with both the breadth and depth of his musical knowledge.

"He had a lot of learning in him but he was instilled with a lot of depth of the religious feeling of black music. This fella, you could just talk to him over the phone and play him a piece of music and he could call out every chord and every movement and where the fifth was and the augmented and tell you what key it was in." Mayfield pauses in admiration: "He really baffled me. I always admired people that could do that because I never had that kind of learning and it was just amazing."

Flattered by Hathaway's request for permission to name the group the Mayfield Singers, Curtis attended a campus performance and immediately signed them to a contract: "They were singing like the Fifth Dimension before there ever was one. So of course I signed them up and we got a chance to make a couple of recordings. That's how I came to know Donny. Of course he was an arranger and he just wiped the studio musicians out. He was so intellectual with the music. We got some of our people for the records out of the Chicago Symphony and oh, he had them kicking. All those little new ideas he'd learned in his writing. It was just a delight for the old timers to come in and hear this new kind of music and to see this youngster just making his way. He was destined to be somebody big."

While Curtom boasted a solid roster of artists, the label's success rested primarily on Mayfield's own recordings, many of them arranged by Hathaway. One of the great albums of the '70s, *Curtis* features Mayfield classics "(Don't Worry) If There's a Hell Below We're All Gonna Go" (#3 R&B, #29 pop) and "We People Who Are Darker than Blue." The album includes several cuts in the gospel soul vein, most notably the inspirational "Move On Up," one of Mayfield's most frequently sampled songs. But there's no question that the compelling funk grooves laid down by Mayfield's band, especially in performances such as the one documented on the *Curtis/Live!* album, were primarily responsible for the new level of success. Part of the success resulted from Mayfield's increasing appeal to an audience attuned to the psychedelic rock coming out of San Francisco. On both *Curtis* and *Curtis/Live!*, Mayfield's guitar playing takes on a more aggressive edge, reflecting a stylistic call and response with Jimi Hendrix. Hendrix credited Mayfield as a significant influence on his guitar playing, a connection that comes through clearly on "Little Wing" and "Electric Ladyland." Mayfield, who experimented with feedback and distortion on his early '70s solos, saw Hendrix's explorations as part of a shared attempt to free music's connecting energies: "Jimi's approach to music transcends racial barriers. His imagination spoke to people on a deeper level than that. With the psychedelics and what have you, he was almost like a scientist, studying the effects."

Mayfield views the move toward funk as a natural extension of his Chicago heritage.

"For me it was just the way. I had my guitar and of course I was out of Chicago and, along with the gospel, I heard plenty of rhythm and blues and blues per se by Muddy Waters and Little Walter."

Mayfield's experience playing the blues as a session man with several Chicago labels introduced him to the improvisational musical approach he would develop in the early '70s.

"I felt really good to be appointed to play a couple of sessions with Jimmy Reed." Mayfield pauses to sing a few lines of one of Reed's classic blues and resumes: "Everybody had to circle him like he was the fire and we was circling around him to get warm. We all watched his mouth and watched his guitar because he was one of those guys that bars meant nothing to. He may change right in the middle, he may go back to the one and then back to the bass. But you had to watch him and keep tempo and change when he changed." Mayfield smiles, remembering Reed's notorious inability to remember the words to his songs. "Of course he could never remember his lyrics so his wife was always feeding him the words. If you listen to the old Jimmy Reed stuff, you can hear his wife singing right behind him. But they sold records. He was Jimmy Reed."

Mayfield feels that exploring the possibilities of funk improvisation gave his music a more distinctive sound.

"I just had another way of coming off with my music and it did appear to be just a little bit different. I'd never taken any music lesson so I didn't really know the forms, eight bars, sixteen bars, this, that. So I played and wrote as I felt it." Less conventionally structured than the songs Mayfield wrote for the Impressions, the new sound challenged his musicians. "I didn't get slack from the musicians but even they would make comments that 'gosh this is a terribly strange key to play in, what did he do?' They just had to follow as I wrote it and I wouldn't dare let them change it. Always at the end it would turn out and everybody would say, 'Wow, that's happening.'"

Mayfield hastens to credit the musicians who played on his Curtom albums with their contributions. Upon the mention of guitarist Phil Upchurch, bass player Lucky Scott, and percussionist "Master" Henry Gibson, his voice took on a special richness.

"They were always my main sources. Philip. I've known Philip since I don't know when, since I was about fifteen or sixteen. He was playing guitar with all the artists on Vee-Jay and Mercury and Okeh, all the main people at Chess. He was one of the best."

Similarly, Mayfield remembers Gibson, whose congas provide one of the signatures of the funk albums, as someone who's "been with me all the way up till a few months prior to my having the accident. I always had Lucky and Henry. I owe them a great bunch of gratitude because they helped to make my sound whatever it was."

The mention of Lucky Scott took Mayfield's mind back to the early days of the Impressions. "Lucky was the nephew of Sam Gooden, he was just a baby then. When we came out in 1958, Lucky and his brother were in diapers. Gotta mention his brother Benny Scott. The family called him Porky, but now he's known as Lebron Scott. Lucky grew up seeing us doing our thing and somehow he picked up a bass and he worked himself to a point where when the time came we had to bring him in. He died last year, I'm sorry to say."

Mayfield remembers that Lucky joined the band as the result of an automobile accident "where all of our band members were destroyed in a car accident somewhere in Georgia. That was a heavy blow because we all were close." Mayfield breathes deeply and resumes: "That's when Lucky came in to play with us. It was right around the time of 'We're a Winner.' For some reason he had a style come out of the church where everything he played felt good. Lucky was one of the members of my band not only on the road but in the studio from that time even through *Super Fly* when I was out on my own. All those movie soundtracks, he made great contributions. Lucky was always there."

Just as Mayfield's music took on a harder edge in the funk period, his lyrics began to focus on the disturbing aspects of what was happening in the black community and the country as a whole. The ominous rolling bass at the start of "Hell Below" underscores a sound montage based on the Book of Revelations before exploding into Mayfield's reverb-laden warning to the "sisters, niggers, whities, jews, crackers." Although the tone of his '70s work is sharper and less optimistic, Mayfield sees very little change in his approach to songwriting.

"Really I'd found myself very early. I was writing songs when I was maybe twelve. Some of them were gospel, and even though the later ones were different, it really stayed the same. My songs always came from questions that I need answers for, even for myself."

If the '70s songs sound different, the difference reflects the new questions Mayfield was asking himself.

"I was observing things, what happened politically, what was in the paper, what was on television. Asking what things were wrong that oughta be right. It was just straight from the heart and I didn't have answers all the time."

Mayfield wanted his songs to help other people think through problems from their own angles: "The songs were food for thought, I hoped my music was inspirational in manner. It could speak in a dialogue that makes you think for yourself. What would I do if I seriously gave this some thought?"

Increasingly, Mayfield's songs challenged his audience to think about racial polarization and the increasing problems of inner city black neighborhoods. His solo albums confront the blues realities of drug addiction ("Stone Junkie"), racial paranoia ["Mighty Mighty (Spade & Whitey)]" and the continuing theft of land from American Indians ("I Plan to Stay a Believer"). The vastly underrated song "The Other Side of Town" addresses the spiritual despair of poor black communities, many of them even more isolated than they had been nearly two decades earlier when the Brown vs. Board of Education decision promised an end to segregation. The haunting version of "Mighty Mighty (Spade & Whitey)" that opens *Curtis/Live!* condemns the racist "stupidness we've all been taught" and asserts: "really ain't no difference, if you're cut you're gonna bleed." Asking the audience if he can "get a bit deeper," Mayfield echoes James Brown: "I got to say it loud, I'm black and I'm proud."

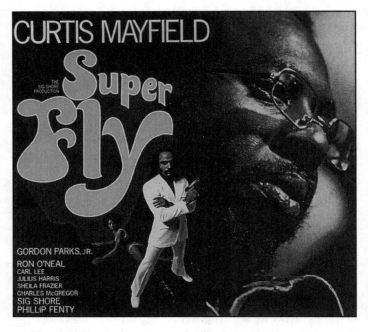

Mayfield's balancing of black self-assertion and racial openness reaches deep into the gospel tradition, which recognizes that the ability to accept others, to live out the democratic vision, requires self-acceptance. The same combination of perceptions recurs in the two singles from the *Roots* album, "We Gotta Have Peace" (#32 R&B, #115 pop) and "Beautiful Brother of Mine" (#45 R&B). A masterful combination of Mayfield's gospel and funk styles, "Beautiful Brother" holds out a vision of a community coming to terms with the real meaning of the slogan "black is beautiful": "Together we're truly black power, learning to love by the hour."

Even though Mayfield continued to advance his vision of love and acceptance, the emphasis on black power and social problems may have contributed to the difficulty he had crossing over to white audiences as a live performer. His solo albums sold well to white listeners. But for some reason, attempts to book Mayfield into rock venues elicited little response from audiences who eagerly embraced other artists experimenting with combinations of rock, funk, and soul. In 1969, Mayfield played the Fillmore West on a bill with Santana and Ike and Tina Turner. In 1972, he was booked into Chicago's version of the Fillmore, the Aragon Ballroom. Neither crossover attempt worked. Chicago promoter Jerry Mickelson offered an explanation that rings hollow in light of the success of Sly Stone and Jimi Hendrix with similar crowds: "You learn the market. Take Curtis Mayfield. He was hotter than a pistol, and he died in the Aragon. So we learned that you can't do a black act up there."

Mayfield's failure to cross over as a performer seems particularly baffling in light of the massive success of his movie soundtracks, beginning with *Super Fly*, which stayed at the top of the album charts for four weeks during 1972. Mayfield takes great pleasure in remembering the moment when he realized the degree of his success as a soundtrack writer.

"I was standing in Chicago right on State Street, the main street in the Chicago theater district, right there in the loop. And I looked out and right there I could see the marquee for three of my movies at the same time, *Super Fly*, *Let's Do It Again*, and I think it was *Claudine*. Right there in my home town. So you know I felt like a big man."

Between 1972 and 1977, Mayfield wrote the music for a half dozen soundtracks, performing the music himself on *Super Fly* and the underrated *Short Eyes*, one of the better films in the prison movie genre. Complementing Miguel Pinero's brilliant script, the *Short Eyes* soundtrack features "Do Do Wap Is Strong in Here" (#29 R&B), one of Mayfield's strongest late '70s compositions. Varying widely in quality, Mayfield's collaborative soundtracks included *Claudine* (1974) and *Pipedreams* (1976), both performed by Gladys Knight and the Pips; *Sparkle* (1976) with Aretha Franklin; *A Piece of the Action* (1977) with Mavis Staples; and *Let's Do It Again* (1975) with the Staple Singers. Both Aretha and Mavis Staples would later reunite with Mayfield on *New World Order*, where Aretha makes a brief cameo while Mavis Staples' background vocals add spiritual depth to "Ms. Martha," a bluesy response to the gospel standard "Mary Don't You Weep."

Remembering his work with the Staples took Mayfield back to memories of Chicago's gospel scene and reminded him that the title cut from *Let's Do It Again*, one of the group's most successful records, almost never got recorded. The problem related to the Staples' gospel background. Mayfield remembers the Staples from his younger days in Chicago.

"They started out with the church music, gospel music, and they'd already built a great following and name for themselves. So they of course made their crossover. But they always wanted their music to be inspirational. So their style didn't really change too much. They simply found a music that spread them out, allowed them to make a better living."

The problem with "Let's Do It Again" lay in the song's obviously sexual lyrics. Mavis Staples remembers her father's reluctance to record a song that "was definitely more explicit than anything we'd ever done before. Pops didn't want to sing it at first." Fortunately, Pops Staples had an affection for Mayfield that stemmed from the early '60s when the Staples and Impressions lived in the same South Side Chicago neighborhood.

"We would always talk and then we'd run into each other on the road," Mavis recalled. "Pops was crazy about Curtis. They'd talk and when we started doing those message songs, I remember Curtis telling Pops 'You know, Pops, you got a thing there and I'm gonna do me some of those songs.' And Daddy said, 'Yeah, that's what I tell the songwriters. You write for us, you read the newspaper. That'll tell you what to write.'"

So Mayfield was in a unique position when the problem over the soundtrack arose. Mavis recalls the crucial conversation.

"Pops would say, 'Curtis, I ain't gonna say that 'funky' stuff. You know me, Curtis, I don't sing songs like that.'" Mavis' voice takes on Mayfield's rhythms when she recounts how Curtis finally won her father's approval. "Curtis said, 'Oh Pops, please, Pops, it's just a movie score. It ain't like your regular stuff. You're just doing it for a movie.'" Mavis chuckles, "When Daddy said all right, I said 'Lord, Curtis, you have done something ain't nobody but you could do. Ain't no way Pops was gonna say 'funky.'"

When the single sold over two million copies, everyone concerned was happy that Mavis and Mayfield had carried the day.

Mayfield's soundtrack work, especially on *Super Fly*, brings the tension between commerce and values into sharp focus. Mayfield jumped at the chance when producer Sig Shore asked him to write the soundtrack for what would become one of the definitive films of the blaxploitation genre.

"I can recall having received the *Super Fly* script from Sig Shore and (screenwriter) Philip Fenty at the Lincoln Center in New York. I was performing there and they brought this script in between shows and wow, was I so excited. I'd written a song just flying back home from New York. It took me hardly no time to prepare the songs and that's how it began. It was different, it was wearing a new hat. I was fulfilling the dreams of many agents and writers and people who are of the business."

The songs Mayfield wrote in that burst of creative activity, especially the title cut (#5 R&B, #8 pop) and "Freddie's Dead" (#2 R&B, #4 pop) earn the *Super Fly* soundtrack a place alongside Isaac Hayes' *Shaft* and James Brown's *Black Caesar* as the pinnacles of blaxploitation funk.

From almost the moment the movie was released, however, audiences recognized a dissonance between the movie's celebration of drugs and sex, and the message of Mayfield's soundtrack, which clearly identifies the "Pusherman" as community enemy number one. Mayfield remembers his surprise at the way director Gordon Parks Jr.'s treatment transformed the meaning of Fenty's script: "For me when I first was reading it, it read very well. I mean all this was reality. We're not trying to sell it, but we're telling it to you like it is. But reading the script didn't tell you 'and then he took another hit of cocaine' and then about a minute later 'he took another hit.' So when I saw it visually, I thought 'this is a cocaine infommercial.' That's all it was." Mayfield considers his words carefully. "I don't know whether that was intended or not. It was a great beginning and introduction of cocaine to a lot of people. No one really knew about cocaine at the time. Of course it was going to grow anyway whether there was *Super Fly* or not. But it was a great opening."

Rather than backing out of the project, Mayfield set about creating what amounts to a masked dialog with the surface message. "I made the commitment and of course I wasn't going to let go of my chance to do a movie. Yet I didn't want to be part of that infommercial. So it was important to me that I left the glitter and all the social stuff and tried to go straight in the lyrics. I tried to tell the stories of the people in depth and not insult the intelligence of those who were spending their money. That was an actual effort on my part."

Mayfield's efforts were aided by the fact that the music hit the charts prior to the film's release.

"We made the whole soundtrack for about $35,000, which is unheard of," Mayfield recalls. "And then I released it three months prior to the movie coming out so when the kids got in there they knew the music."

The strategy meant that even though the film includes only an instrumental version of "Freddie's Dead," audience members familiar with the single could juxtapose the film's images with Mayfield's sober reminder that it all leads to meaningless violence, community destruction.

Mayfield reiterates that the script itself tells a story similar to the one in his lyrics: "I didn't put (the movie's main character) down. He was just trying to get out. However his deeds weren't noble ones. But he was making money and he had intelligence. And he did survive."

Mayfield emphasized the point by concluding the title song with a moment that could be described as gospel funk. While Pate's orchestration fades out over one of the decade's catchiest rhythmic grooves, Mayfield repeats the line "trying to get over" again and again, bringing "Super Fly" into dialogue with the gospel classic "How I Got Over." Mayfield clearly understands the struggles of the brothers and sisters on the streets as part of a shared history extending back to slavery:

"He did survive," he repeats. "In that time and era, most times the black guys don't make it through the movie. For most black folks in that time and era, just making it was tough. So this guy did what he did and he was true to himself and he got out and kept his life. So that was noble to a lot of people that was going to see the movie anyway."

The struggle to survive, to find a way of moving beyond mere survival, continued to command Mayfield's attention on *Back to the World*, which reached number sixteen in 1973. One of Mayfield's most consistent albums, *Back to the World* reworks the basic concept of Marvin Gaye's *What's Going On* (1971). Like Gaye, Mayfield tells the story of a black veteran returning home from Vietnam to encounter a community on the verge of collapse. He recalls that the inspiration came from his experience performing at military bases.

"I wrote *Back to the World* because we'd played some bases in France, England, Germany and that was a very popular common saying. 'I'll be glad when I get back to the world,' which meant to them coming back home to America. And so I wrote that

song as my own interpretation of what the war was all about."

Mayfield quotes a few lines from the title song: "Crawling through the trees, sucking mud up to my knees, fighting them, fighting this damn war. Wondering if the Lord even knows what it's for. Do you really think God could ever forgive this life we live." His face takes on an expression mixing anger and sadness as the lyrics blend back into his thoughts on what the vets found when they returned home. "Then you get back to the world and you wonder what it's all for. You can't get a job. You're being robbed. Your woman that was there two or three years, your woman's long been gone. And of course, all these different things were part of the times. So all you could do was deal with the questions and answers of how you might try to reasonably work it out so you could live with it."

The concern with finding a way to live with it—to reconnect with your woman, your community, the spirit—differentiates *Back in the World* from *What's Going On*. Injecting gospel intensities into the dense orchestral textures and funk rhythms, Mayfield focuses on the vet's changing psychological responses. In contrast, part of what makes *What's Going On* an unquestioned masterpiece is Gaye's concentration on the complicated social crosscurrents sweeping through the inner city and the country as a whole. Mayfield acknowledges the social forces in "Back to the World" and "Future Shock" (#11 R&B, #39 pop), but concentrates on the vet's struggles with despair ("Right On for the Darkness") and the renewal of hope he finds when he turns to his "heavenly Father" in "Future Song (Love a Good Woman, Love a Good Man)." Where Gaye concludes *What's Going On* with the near-desperation of "Inner City Blues"—"makes me wanna holler"—Mayfield resolves *Back to the World* with the up-beat "Keep on Trippin'." As always in Mayfield's music, what black intellectual Cornel West calls the "audacious hope" of the gospel vision shines through the darkness.

Super Fly and *Back to the World* mark the peak of Mayfield's popular success. Through the remainder of the '70s, he continued to produce solid music. Almost every album contains memorable cuts, some in the funk style, some soft ballads recalling his work with the Impressions. *Sweet Exorcist* (1974) includes the driving "Ain't Got Time" and "Kung Fu" (#3 R&B, #40 pop); two of Mayfield's most beautiful love songs, "Only You Babe" (#8 R&B) and "So In Love" (#9 R&B, #67) highlight *Give*

Get Take and Have (1976) and *There's No Place Like America Today* (1975). The yearning "Show Me Love" combines with Curtis' version of "Sparkle" and the title cut to make *Never Say You Can't Survive* (1977) his most satisfying non-soundtrack album of the late '70s.

The decline in consistency in Mayfield's albums, like the decline in his popularity, had several sources. His soundtrack work demanded an increasing amount of attention and many of his best songs—"Let's Do It Again," "Giving Him Something He Can Feel"—were recorded by other artists. In itself, that was nothing new. But Mayfield believes that the multiple pressures of running Curtom ultimately infringed on the quality of his music.

"What was happening during those times was that I was wearing too many hats. I was going on the road, doing movies, trying to keep my career going strong, making decisions in the studio for many a person. I was trying to handle all my personal affairs and watch out for the money."

Gradually, the financial pressure of running the company came to dominate Mayfield's attention. He admitted to Pruter that "I began to allow other people with bad decisions to influence me. That was probably no good for me, the company, and for the customer that had so much expectations for me. The whole name of the game was to make money, too. The investors want to hear one thing— 'I want to make money.' Probably what people should have done, and I probably should have done myself, was just laid back and kind of watch things for a while."

Rather than laying back, Mayfield made a somewhat desperate attempt to tap into the disco market. In retrospect, Mayfield finds the late '70s slightly amusing.

"Those were some strange times for me. I had done so well for myself for such a long time. You know I was spoiled."

He laughs, thinking about *Heartbeat*, which was produced by Norman Harris, Bunny Sigler, and Ronald Tyson, who had played a major role in the success of the Philly International label.

"It was definitely a good experience. You're always walking that tightrope of what is commercial to the fans and then whether you're expressing yourself independently as a creative person. Sometimes you have to..." Mayfield pauses and then reiterates the central role financial concerns played in Curtom's decisions during the late '70s. "Of course you have to look at it as a business. It is

a business. And those who actually spend the money and invest, the stockholders and the people like that, they may not even listen to the music. The bottom line is what do I get out of it. So you're somewhere in there trying to express yourself in order to prove yourself. To show your own value, you must make hit records. It just can't be me me me. That always fails. Every once in a while even the best of the best have to say, okay maybe I better let somebody who's proven themselves with a new track record do something to keep me going."

Although the Philly-produced *Heartbeat* (1979) and *Do It All Night* (1978), which Mayfield produced himself, are generally viewed as his weakest albums, Curtis refuses to condemn the attempts.

"It wasn't so bad. I liked the music. It was strange how *Heartbeat* worked out. The hit record from that album, "Between You Baby and Me" (#14 R&B) that I did with Linda Clifford, was the one track that was my own creation." Mayfield chuckles. "So I felt good about that. And yet I have experienced other people's styles and how other people interpreted me as a vocalist and as an artist. But they never could express me the way I expressed myself."

Summing up his disco period, Mayfield draws the conclusion that "I learned from that that all my life the music I made only sold when I was being me, when I was just being Curtis. When I tried to be other than what I was, you could forget it. I had to be me to be a singer at all. I wasn't knocking down anything, but it was just that little style and just from the heart, that high vocal." Mayfield laughs again. "Thank God I had microphones 'cause I wasn't a strong singer. But everybody seemed to like that falsetto."

The final albums of the Curtom years— *Something to Believe In* (1980) and *The Right Combination* (1980), a collection of duets with Linda Clifford—reflect Mayfield's search for a new source of vitality. Both musically and lyrically, the duets wander. The effective moments are almost all intensely personal, holding out the promise of romantic love as shelter from the gathering storm. But the gospel soul belief in the power of love, the sense that the connection between two human beings prefigures a broader social transformation, retreats in the face of personal weariness and political defeat.

Although it received little attention, *Something to Believe In* provides a fascinating, and frequently moving, sense of Mayfield's response to the changing times. The first cut on the album, "Love Me,

Love Me Now" opens with the sound of a police whistle over a string-washed dance beat that recalls the disco of *Heartbeat* and *Do It All Night*. Even as Mayfield repeats the line "come dance with me," however, his repeated cries of "love me baby" communicate a depth of isolation unlike anything in his earlier music. The remake of "It's Alright" underscores the changes in Mayfield's energy since the high point of the movement. The Impressions' version of the song radiates an energy of connection, especially when the three voices come together at the ends of lines. The 1980 recording accentuates the distance between the lead singer and the female backup singers, who sound like they're located in a different room. You can feel the call and response fundamental to gospel politics and the freedom movement falling apart. But if "It's Alright" suggests that Mayfield has lost control, the best songs on the album—"People Never Give Up," "Never Stop Loving Me," and the achingly beautiful "Something to Believe In"—demonstrate his profound understanding of the gospel vision. Even as he stands alone on the dance floor, contemplating the inevitable collapse of the disco community, Mayfield testifies to the power of love. But, whatever the lyrics may claim, the message of the album comes through clearly: with Reaganism on the horizon, nothing's really going to be all right.

The weariness at the heart of *Something to Believe In* had accumulated over two decades of hard work, decades during which Mayfield helped define the cultural feel of two distinct eras in black politics. Carried along by the energy of the freedom movement during his years with the Impressions, Mayfield engaged the potential and problems of black power as clearly as any musician of his generation. By the early '80s, however, Ronald Reagan occupied the White House, black music—even disco—was falling off the charts, and Mayfield decided it was time for a change.

First, Mayfield disbanded Curtom, which had peaked financially and creatively in the mid-'70s. By the end of the decade, Mayfield, Clifford, and the funk-disco group TTF were the label's only successful acts. When Mayfield sold Curtom's distribution rights to RSO in 1979, it marked the effective end of the label, which formally ceased operation in 1980. At the same time, Mayfield decided to move permanently to Atlanta, where he had maintained a second residence since 1967. He explains the move in terms understandable to anyone who's ever experienced a Chicago winter.

"That Chicago weather. Man, man. That hawk'll get you," he says, using the local nickname for the arctic wind that blows off Lake Michigan. "Atlanta had trees, space, some of those things you want to have. It was a good place for the children."

The final change concerned Mayfield's musical direction. Freed from the burdens of running Curtom, Mayfield signed with the Boardwalk label where his music recovered some of its vitality. Although *Love Is the Place* (1981) and *Honesty* (1982) are markedly uneven—"they didn't want to do an album that was a hundred percent Mayfield"—the Boardwalk albums re-established Mayfield on the R&B charts with the gorgeous falsetto ballad "She Don't Let Nobody But Me" (#15). They also include Mayfield's strongest social commentary since *Back to the World* in the Impressions-style "Come Free Your People" and "Dirty Laundry," an incisive criticism of Reagan-era political corruption. A musical setting based on harmonica and steel guitar gives a deceptively soft, near-country feel to Mayfield's uncompromising condemnation of greed and hypocrisy: "Dirty laundry in the country/ can't trust our Uncle Sam/ broken link, future sinking, and no one gives a damn."

Painfully aware of the self-destructive forces turning some inner city neighborhoods into war zones, Mayfield expresses a deep sympathy for the despair of young people deprived of a sense of a brighter future. He sees the million man march as a logical response to the Reagan years.

"You might sense a mass of people wanting to find some answers. That's really what a lot of young blacks and young people in poverty want. They need answers. You're not the smartest person in the world. It don't look like through schooling itself, with what's happening in the schools, you're going to be. You need answers."

Mayfield, who approved Spike Lee's request to use four of his songs—"Keep on Pushing," "People Get Ready," "We're a Winner," and "New World Order,"—in his film on the million man march, *Get On the Bus*, continues: "How do you get from here to there when you want to be a righteous person? I don't want to do crime, hey that's risky, and it takes smarts to even do that. So the young kids need something to believe and to prove and to be proven to that it works." Mayfield traces the source of the problem to the hostile political forces he addressed in "Dirty Laundry": "The bigotry, the discrimination and the selfishness and the greed. All these things really come from the top down. Those at the bottom of the totem pole don't have things. They have to carry the load by sweat and labor, cheap labor. Whether they're black or white, they're being manipulated by the higher powers that be."

At that point in our interview, a fly found its way in from outside and began circling Mayfield's head. When Curtis blew at it to shoo it away, I was shocked to realize that I'd been so caught up in his presence, the melody and power of his words, that I'd forgotten about his physical condition. Yet Mayfield talks freely and honestly about his physical condition and the accident that caused it.

Mayfield was just taking the stage at an outdoor concert at Wingate High School in Brooklyn on August 13, 1990 when a strong wind blew a light tower over on him, crushing several vertebrae.

"I knew what had happened right away and the first thing I told myself was just to stay alive."

Once his condition stabilized enough for him to be transferred, Mayfield underwent extensive therapy first at Atlanta's world-class Shepherd Spinal Center. Finally, he was able to return to his home where he gradually adjusted to life as a quadriplegic.

"At first I thought since I was paralyzed, there wouldn't be so much pain," he says. "But I found that aches come and go. I have a lot of complications, the effect of low blood pressure, chronic pain, things no one really could see or would even know unless you were around people with spinal cord injuries. I'm trying to maintain the status quo but the hardships are many as are the complications. Sometimes you don't have answers."

Yet, Mayfield says, he generally avoids depression.

"I think my spirits are maybe even higher. It's like I died and woke up to see this wave of love from so many people I knew and people I didn't know. Of course it doesn't mean you don't every once in a while find a tear in your eye. Your body does not allow you to do many things that your mind says. Your mind always says 'I'm ready, let's go.' You have to deal with it; you have to learn patience. It's tough being a person who totally has to rely on someone else when you've been independent all your life."

Prior to the accident, Mayfield's career had settled into a relatively quiet groove. After the death of Boardwalk president Neil Bogart, Mayfield attempted to revive Curtom. The climate for independent labels had changed drastically by the '80s, however, and Mayfield wound up signing a distribu-

tion agreement with Ichiban Records. The best cuts from the two resulting albums, *We Come in Peace with a Message of Love* (1985) and *Take It to the Streets* (1990) demonstrate Mayfield's continuing ability to write love ballads ("Baby It's You, #69 R&B); funk ("Do Be Down"), and social commentary ("Homeless"). But throughout the decade, he found his greatest popularity with European and Japanese fans.

"You have to remember that when I was having all my hits in the States, my records really weren't being exposed properly in Europe," Mayfield told British rock critic David Nathan at the time. "So maybe this is like a catch-up situation. People seem more loyal in Europe. I see some of the same faces at my concerts each time I come over and that's a comfortable feeling."

As the '80s drew to a close, Mayfield immersed himself in several projects, including a return to film. He contributed music to the soundtracks of *I Mo Git U Sucka* and *The Return of Superfly*, which includes a collaboration with rapper Ice-T on a remake of Mayfield's classic funk cut. On "I Mo Git U Sucka," Mayfield plugs in with the angry political energy of the emerging hip-hop scene, singing: "It's gonna take a revolution to change the institutions." In 1987, he collaborated with English ska group the Blow Monkeys on "Celebrate (The Day After You)," a strong political statement criticizing the conservative policies of Margaret Thatcher. The fateful Brooklyn performance was one of a series intended to prepare Mayfield's band for another European tour.

The one thing Mayfield regrets about life since the accident is that he can no longer play guitar:

"I always had a different guitar style. I tuned it to the key of F sharp, which is a Spanish tuning. I found later it was all the black keys on the piano. Being self-taught I never changed it. It makes me sad I'll never be able to teach that to anybody. For expression and harmony, my guitar was like another brother to me. I mourn my guitar to this day."

Mayfield takes pride in his ability to provide for his family despite the injury.

"You just try to do the right thing for all that are immediate to you. My particular thing is how, within my limits, to still find ways to earn a decent living, just prove to myself that I'm doing the best that I can do." He says with satisfaction: "How many fifty-four-year-old quadriplegics are putting albums out? You just have to deal with what you got and try to sustain yourself as best you can and look to the things that you can do. So that's how I'm looking at things. I'm devoting what time I have to my children."

The post-Christmas clutter in Mayfield's home (this interview was conducted in February) bears witness to the importance of children in Mayfield's life. Five of his ten children still live at home, amidst framed photographs, mildly Afrocentric art prints, and an extensive library. "I'm trying to get the rest of them out of here to college," he laughs before paying tribute to his second wife, Altheida, whose strength helped see him through his darkest moments.

"I got a very strong woman. You never know who's going to take that stand and say, 'hey, I'll do it.' Nobody wants to do it, but she's been around six years."

While the joy he takes in his family remains crucial to Mayfield's spirit, he also appreciates the recognition he has begun to receive for his contributions to American music. He was inducted into the Rock and Roll Hall of Fame in 1991, the NAACP Hall of Fame in 1994 and the Soul Train Hall of Fame in 1996. He received the Grammy Legend Award (1994). Two tribute albums, *People Get Ready* (Shanachie) and *All Men Are Brothers: A Tribute to Curtis Mayfield* (Warner Brothers), feature performances of Mayfield songs by a who's who of the rock and soul worlds including Aretha Franklin, Bruce Springsteen, Stevie Wonder, Jerry Butler, Stax guitarist Steve Cropper, B.B. King, Jerry Butler, David Sanborn, and Whitney Houston. *I'm So Proud: A Jamaican Tribute to Curtis Mayfield* includes recordings of Mayfield's compositions by Bob Marley and the Wailers, The Heptones, and Marcia Griffiths. Rhino Records has released a three volume box set *People Get Ready!: The Curtis Mayfield Story* along with two single-disc compilations, one focusing on the Impressions and the other on his solo work. Britain's Charly label has reissued most of Mayfield's catalog, including all the Curtom material, and compiled three greatest hits albums representing the different periods of his solo career. VH1 produced an hour long documentary on Mayfield as part of its "Legends" series.

Without question, however, *New World Order* marks the real triumph of Mayfield's recovery. Nominated for a Grammy on the basis of quality rather than sentimental appeal, the album calls forth a real sense of wonder. It's a dangerous word, hard to take without irony. But it's the right word.

As consistent as any of Mayfield's previous albums—and it's only fair to remember that consistency was never the hallmark of an artist who created so much for himself and others—*New World Order* advances Mayfield's gospel vision into the '90s.

"Fusing elements of hip-hop on this CD was not so much a concession to the times, as much as it was a connection to the times," he says. "We all have to grow. You have to stay true to yourself while recognizing and acknowledging what's going on now."

The album's contemporary feel results in part from the contributions of co-producers including Organized Noize, best known for their work with TLC, Roger Troutman, the guiding spirit of Zapp, Narada Michael Walden, and hip-hop pioneer Darryl Simmons, who Mayfield credits with convincing him to return to the studio.

"Fortunately we had a lot of the young people who always admired my work, so they could put music together that was of the '90s and all I needed to do was just lay my signature down. They're all great producers and have great ideas but they were all very kind and always left the parts for Curtis."

The creation of *New World Order* serves as testament to the advances in studio technology. Mayfield's health makes it hard for him to sing more than a couple of lines at a time. Throughout most of the recording sessions, he lay on his back to conserve energy. Nonetheless, he feels the album represents his true voice.

"Mostly what I had to change was I don't have the ability to sing the high falsetto nor do I have strength to really sing a song on stage as a performer. I could never do it."

But sophisticated techniques for "punching in"—combining lines recorded at different times—leave no audible evidence of the way the songs were recorded. Mayfield appreciates the advances in recording technology since he was last in the studio.

"Two of the songs Roger Troutman did with me, he came right into my house with a little box of a console and a hard drive and I sang the two songs in bed. He ran it right in here into my speakers. I didn't have to move, he put a mike in front of me and I sang 'We People Who Are Darker than Blue' right here."

The spiritual vision of *New World Order* circles back to the gentle clear-sighted gospel soul of the mid '60s Impressions. Obviously written with his physical condition in mind, "Back to Living Again" speaks equally to the political needs of black America as it seeks to renew its sense of purpose in the aftermath of Reaganism. "The Got Dang Song," "Ms. Martha" and the soulful remake of "We People Who Are Darker than Blue" grapple with the continuing realities of poverty and despair. But images of rebirth resonate throughout the album, most notably in the title song. Happy with *New World Order* as a direct expression of his real voice, Mayfield views it as a reaffirmation of the faith that carried him through good times and bad: "Lyrically, my philosophy hasn't changed. The concept of peace, love, get it together and maybe there'll be a new world order."

When I ask about future plans, Mayfield says that *New World Order* may well be "the last album."

"At this point in my life I'm just glad that I was able to do *New World Order*. That's not to say I might not do a little something with someone else. But I'm fifty-four years old and I've been doing this since I was seven, professionally since I was fifteen. I turned sixteen in the Apollo Theatre. I'm a fighter but it's best at this point to go on and retire and be appreciated for whatever you have done."

Mayfield's been talking for over two hours. When his assistant Sylvia greeted me on my arrival, she'd warned me his health usually prevented him from talking for more than thirty or forty minutes. "You got me in a good long wind, man," Curtis said as I rose to leave. "As I sum it up, I just want folks to say he didn't do bad with his life in inspiring others. My music was hard and soft but never harsh. I think that's what allowed me to stay in the business."

Roy Orbison

By Jeff Tamarkin
October 1979

Roy Orbison is an interviewer's dream. Not only is the man gracious, he is more than willing to volunteer information about himself and his long, illustrious career as a pop singer. Orbison loves to talk, and he does so in an articulate, clear, and interesting manner. He is modest about his influences on rock music, and often apologized for what he called "ramblin' on" during our conversation. Each time, I was quick to assure him that I was fascinated by what he had to say, and had no intentions of stopping him. The following is the text of my ninety-minute talk with one of the greatest voices and finest personalities rock music has ever known.

Orbison has seen his share of hard times: He lost his first wife in 1966 and two children in 1968; he recently underwent open heart surgery; and his career, though it has been good to him, has given him less than he deserves in terms of commercial success and public recognition. While his former labelmates from Sun Records—Elvis Presley, Johnny Cash, Jerry Lee Lewis, Charlie Rich, and others—went on to amazing successes, Orbison was relegated to accepting a position as a cult figure, respected greatly by those who knew of him, but evading the mass adulation his one-time cohorts long ago earned. Sure, Orbison had his hits—"Only The Lonely," "Crying," "Pretty Woman"—but his last major smash was in 1964. Since then, Orbison has worked steadily but released new music only sporadically, maintaining a career built on his considerable reputation. Still, a mark of the man's character is that he refuses to submit to becoming just another "oldie" on the circuit, and that he shows no bitterness when he speaks, preferring to forge ahead, thankful that he has come this far.

In what may be the greatest jolt to Roy Orbison's career in several years, Elektra/Asylum Records recently signed the legendary performer and released his first significant album of new material in almost a decade. *Laminar Flow* is the name of the record, and at first listening, it is apparent that "The Voice" is as strong as ever, and that Orbison is far from being a washed-up has-been.

This interview took place in June at the Elektra/Asylum offices in New York.

Goldmine: *When did you actually start singing and writing songs?*

Roy Orbison: The beginning of everything, it sounds trite, is that my father gave me a guitar when I was six years old... I told him I wanted a harmonica. He asked me if a guitar would be okay instead, and I said sure. Then we moved to Fort Worth, Texas, and my mother and father started working in a defense plant. This only has a bearing because every night a cousin or uncle or friends would come by, and play and sing. So I learned very quickly that if I learned to play this guitar and sing fairly well, I got to stay up later than the rest of the kids, and actually be a part of the festivities. It had such a profound effect on my life, because these people didn't know what was going to happen to them. So they partied heavy and played heavy.

How old were you at this time?

I was six to seven. The topic of conversation was either music or it was about the war. So, I'm still a historian and still a music maker. I then visited a radio station in Kermit, Texas, KVWC. I'd go down every Saturday to do their jamboree thing, and became a regular, me and a fellow called "Stan the Man." Then, when I was ten years old, I won a medicine show contest, tied with a fellow who was fifteen years old. I won $7.50 and he got $7.50. Then we moved to the oil fields of West Texas, and I played and sang for the school and things, and then formed a group.

What kind of material were you performing then? Was it straight country music?

Generally, it was country, but by the time I had the group, I guess when I was about fourteen, we were doing things like "Lady of Spain" and "In The Mood," and pop stuff as well. Whatever was current in country, we had to do it. As soon as it faded away, we'd drop it. We toured for the principal of the school. He was running for Lion's Club governor. So, we played here and there, and some people asked us to play a dance one evening. I was going to say, "We've played all that we know," and they said "We'll pay you $400 if you come play." So I said, "We'll be there!" I amplified the guitar, and we had a drummer already.

I'll make a jump from there. I went to college, and I did nothing at college except play the guitar, really, and learn that that wasn't what I wanted to do. That was Northern Texas University. Pat Boone was there at the time, and he'd made a record. So I wanted to make a record. Elvis Presley had started recording at that time. We were very close to Dallas, Texas and he (Elvis) would play a place called the Big D Jamboree. So, my second year of college, I went to Odessa Junior College, which was very near my home town of Wink (Texas), and I started a couple of television shows. We would play honky tonks, and promote them on the television show. The fellow took the bar and we would take the door, and charge a dollar a person and make a little money. I had heard these boys at school who had written a song called "Ooby Dooby." So I took it to Clovis, New Mexico, and made a record of it at Norman Petty's studio, (Ed. Note: Prior to its appearance on Sun, Roy Orbison and The Teen Kings' earlier recorded version of "Ooby Dooby" appeared on the small Southern independent Jewel

label.) and then sent it to Sam Phillips. Sam said come on down, so we made that record and went on our first tour; me and Johnny Cash, Carl Perkins, and everybody. We wound that first tour up in Memphis, and Elvis Presley came to the show and was introduced at intermission, and we started kind of running around together.

I've heard that you weren't especially fond of the song "Ooby Dooby," even though it was your first hit.

Elvis and I both thought that everything we did for Sun was not good, for the longest. We both did the same thing, though, in about 1970. The era of instant history started. Everybody was very interested in the Sun period. And since it seemed to be so important, and everybody was very concerned, they wanted to know the "ins" and "outs" of everything. I started playing "Ooby Dooby" on the shows. Elvis started doing "That's All Right" and a few of his things. So we didn't acknowledge (the Sun era) until 1970-ish, until it became popular to do so. That "instant history" thing is still very important. All of a sudden, that period of 1960-64 was important, and I seem to be very important in that era. That was supposedly my time. Then the Beatles had their time, and so forth and so on. Being part of history was very important, because so many people in music, whether they enjoy what I do or not, know that I've paid my dues.

Yet, you've said often that you won't play the oldies circuit, the package shows.

Right. You see, the thing was, when they asked me to do these oldies things, most of the people that were on the shows, one artist in particular, quit recording before I had my first hit. So I asked the performers, "Where do I fit in this picture, of a '50s show, for instance?" Because I didn't have a hit, a big enough hit, 'til the spring of 1960. And they couldn't answer that satisfactorily. Also, I still had current records internationally. I still had a hit somewhere in the world, not all the time, but from time to time. In 1971-72, even 1973-74, in Australia, I had one of the biggest records ever there. So, I just didn't fit in there. If they had said that "We have people from '56-'60," then you're gonna have the Beatles, or people from that era, represented so and so...(but) it didn't make any sense. Also, I guess a little ego had something to do with it; I didn't want to be an "oldie".

Most of the people who got their start at Sun—yourself, Carl Perkins, Jerry Lee—are still going strong.

And Johnny (Cash). We were all playing long before we started recording, and that is very important. It's not something that we all of a sudden decided to do and then did it and it worked. I had twelve years' work behind me before I made my first record.

Did you ever have any formal vocal training?

No, I was in the school group, but is was a small school and I didn't listen much to whatever music

theory was going on. I didn't have the opportunity. I was in West Texas, and there wasn't much to do there except play football, and drive sixty miles to get a hamburger. I've never had any vocal training, and I've never studied my vocal range to see what it spans. And when I write songs, I could score them, but I don't. I just do it from memory, because if I can't remember it, I don't expect anybody else to. I do the words and music at the same time, and remember them. I don't use a recorder, because it's a little bit inhibiting. I don't think I've lost anything by not doing that.

Just by being associated with Sun, you've sometimes been labeled a rockabilly singer. That seemed to be a mistake in your case, except for your very early stuff.

Well, it was a strange term to me. The first time I saw it written was on an import EP. There were four songs, and it had a picture of a hillbilly with a corncob pipe and a hillbilly hat. And it said "rockabilly" and "hillbilly rock." And of course, the country singers objected to being called hillbillies. They're country singers now as opposed to country and western, even. We didn't object to it, we just didn't know what it was. We didn't know, for instance, that we were creating anything. We were doing our own thing, and didn't know that it was a small circle of some importance until 1970.

How do you feel about the way that whole style developed? It mushroomed, and it's still going strong now, perhaps stronger than ever.

I feel very very good about it, very fortunate to have been there. We were all there under adverse circumstances for the time. By that I mean we were being paid less than most artists, than any artists. That's why we all left. It wasn't because we weren't getting what was standard. It wasn't that we felt that we were better than anybody, but we weren't getting what they were getting in Nashville, for instance. So, each and every one of us did migrate to Nashville.

So, when did the people at Sun actually realize that they were bigger than they thought they were?

I don't think they realized it 'til about 1970, maybe '69. When Johnny Cash re-did a song called "I Walk The Line," it was a big hit all over. And from that, and through his television show, he got his first number one pop record, which was "A Boy Named Sue." And that's marvelous. Because that was hard times for all of us (during the Sun era). I don't think Elvis made any money at Sun to speak of. I think Johnny made more than any of us at Sun. Jerry Lee probably did. I didn't make much, and Carl didn't make much.

That's so hard to believe now, when you look back at the impact the music had, that nobody made anything from it.

Yeah, because later, when everybody did start doing well, to have been under one roof (in the Sun days) was really something. I'm proud of it.

If everybody had stayed at Sun, it might have turned into a multi-million dollar company.

Oh sure, they could have bought all the record companies there were.

How did you feel, back in 1969-70, when Creedence Clearwater Revival had a hit with "Ooby Dooby," and especially recently, when Linda Ronstadt had a smash with "Blue Bayou?"

That makes me feel good. That's one of the things that you get. It may sound corny, but that's one of the better things you get from being in the business. When you write a song, you have your feeling about it...and when you record it, but it's practically in solitude—there's very few people there to say "That's terrific" or whatever. You only know if it's a million-seller. That's a sign that it had to be good. When you step on stage it's the ultimate, because you get instant response when you do something.

You get instant applause, and when you do something wrong, you get the feedback from that, too. But along the line, the money goes to the account, and it goes other places. You don't walk around with money stuffed in your pockets. If you work as hard as a lot of us do, you don't have time to enjoy hot sports cars and all that stuff, you know? What does count are some of the awards you get, and people recording your stuff, or stuff that you were involved with. That helps monetarily, of course, but it's also the supreme compliment. It's magnificent that a song that I wrote back in '61 was the song of the year.

Of all the songs of yours that others have recorded, what is your favorite?

"Blue Bayou," for sure.

You've been nominated for country awards, but you've never really been a strict country singer. How do you see your position in the country music field?

I don't know, it's strange, because I've never had a hit country record. Take "Only the Lonely" for instance. At a later date, Sonny James recorded "Only the Lonely" and it was a hit country record, number one. And a girl named Arlene Hardin recorded "Lovin' Man" which was "Pretty Woman," but about a man. It was a top ten country. Of course, Linda's was country and pop, a top ten record. But I have never had a country hit record. We're talking about a good deal of time here, from 1956 to now. A lot of people have gone from what's called pop or Top 40 to middle of the road stations or country stations, and they do play my records. People who used to play them still play them. So, I think I have a super good following—I think, I'm not positive—in the country field, and I'm proud of that. But the only measure I would have had of my status in country music would've been how many hit records I've had in country music, and I've never had one.

I just see myself basically, well, it's hard to see myself objectively...other people have said that I'm "The Big O," "The Voice," "The Beat Ballad King," stuff like that. And they've said bad things, too. I think there is country influence in what I've done, but there's also a lot of Spanish influence and Mexican influence. I lived fairly close, well nothing's close in Texas, but fairly close to the border, and heard a lot of Mexican music, and that influence is there. Plus, very much like an artist would do today, he would singing everything that was currently popular, to satisfy the audience. So, I was getting everything and singing everything. But I don't have one big influence, but a lot of great influences.

One last question about the '60s period. I've heard that "Only The Lonely" was a song you originally did not intend to record yourself, but to sell to someone else, like Presley.

What we did was this. Joe Nelson and I wrote "Only The Lonely," and we were on our way to Nashville. We had two or three other songs. We had just gotten out of the Army. It was early in the morning and I'd driven from West Texas. We got there about six in the morning, so I sent a note by the gateman, and he sent a note back saying that he had the whole troop in there, at Graceland, and they were all still asleep, that he would see me in Nashville. So, I wanted to play him the song, and had it been later, and had he heard the song and wanted it, he could have had it. But he didn't get to hear it. Then, I played it for Phil Everly, and I'm not sure whether he thought I was pitching it to him or not. I just played it for him because I was proud of it. Had he wanted it, he could have had it. But he didn't say, one way or another. So, I went in and recorded it and two other songs, and it happened to be that big. So, in actual fact, I guess you could say that, as it happened, I had to record "Only The Lonely" myself to get it done, not properly, but to get it done. Everything was lovely after that, it was terrific.

Those early songs were always written out of your personal experiences, rather than as an observer, a third party?

Yes, they were written after the event. You may have heard of people who, in the midst of a broken love affair, they'll write a great song; well, in my midst of broken love affairs, I can't sleep, I can't think, I can't eat. So how you gonna write a song? But later, when I'm content, I can write a happy song, sad song. I can reflect on what happened. So, like, "Working For The Man," that song was inspired by when I was working in West Texas, and "Cryin" was a true experience. And so was "Running Scared." But it was years later.

When did you start becoming so huge in Britain?

That would have to return with "Only The Lonely" because that was in the charts so long. It was roughly like this: number one for sixteen weeks, and number two for sixteen weeks. So it was a strong international song, and that set the tone for the whole career. Had the song only been a hit in America, I probably would not have been an international artist.

So, by the time you went over there to tour with the Beatles (1963), you were already very well established as a hit-maker?

Oh, yeah. It was a hit and miss proposition. "Only The Lonely" was super big, "Blue Angel" wasn't quite so big, "I'm Hurtin'" wasn't as big. Then, "Cryin" got back to the top ten, "Running Scared" got to number twelve, and "Dream Baby" was number one. And by the time I got to England with the Beatles, I had "In Dreams," which was number three. I had a big log of hits, and they were very excited to see me. And they still are to this day. It's practically the same way in the States. I usually play places I've played before. I don't know why it happened, but if I played a place, I always checked up to see if I was pricing myself out of the business or not. And I always wanted the promoter to make money. So I was always invited back to these things. So, I still play the same places in Canada, And generally for the same promoter that I did in '63. And the same places in America. The American situation is very much like the English situation. I still play places that I've always played. But, I haven't played Chicago still, and I had never played in Los Angeles.

The only time I've seen you live was in 1977 in San Francisco.

At the Old Waldorf. That was the start of what we're doing now. People in the audience came back. The Eagles, and I don't know who all. And they said, "When are you coming to L.A.?" So I did go, and I filled Santa Monica Civic, and we even broke a seventeen-year record there, for mail-in things. So, that showed me that there was some sort of popularity there, and as basis for continuing, and that it wasn't like an oldies thing. It didn't seem to be. It was like "An Evening With Roy Orbison." I was on a tour of the West Coast, and had just bypassed L.A., for some reason or the other. I had been touring America since about 1974 or 1975. It's hard to cover, it's so vast. You can do five dates in Australia and you've covered the whole country. And it's the same size as the States, but it's a different situation. I figure if you played every town where it was possible to draw 3,000 people, in America, it would take you a lifetime and you would still not manage it. So, it always amuses me when someone says, "We're gonna tour America next year."

Do you hit the small towns or do you stick to the cities?

No, I always do the small towns as well, the reason being that, back in West Texas, no one ever came to play. And I always resented that just because it was a small place...now, I didn't mind driving the sixty or seventy miles, because, like I said, we did that just to get a hamburger. But in the back of my mind, I think I made a commitment then, which may sound hokey, that if I ever was successful, I would play small towns as well as big towns. So I always play the big cities and small cities.

This is going back to the British tour again. When you went over there in 1963, were you prepared at all for what was happening over there?

No. My fan club president said, "You'll be touring with the Beatles. They're the hottest act in England. So, everybody will see how good you are." She was

biased, naturally. I left my clear glasses on the plane, and I was very frightened to go on stage for many reasons. First of all, I was in a foreign country. Second of all, I'm always nervous before I go on.

Then, I had these dark glasses. And I managed a dozen or so encores; in fact, they were still shouting for me as the Beatles were playing. For a while. Then it was one constant scream.

Roy Orbison

You opened for them? I always thought you headlined that tour.

Well, no. They came to me and said, "Look, since you're making all the money, let us close the show." And I said, "Let's wait 'til after rehearsal." It was in fact, my show. I said after we had equal billing—I've forgotten whether it was Roy Orbison/Beatles or Beatles/Roy Orbison—I said, "I'll let you know after rehearsal." I did my rehearsal, and then they did theirs. They were doing "Twist And Shout," and things like that; "Money." Every song they played was up. So it didn't make sense to me to go on after all this rocking music, and do ballads. I only had "Dream Baby" and "Candyman" to play up. I told them they could close the show. It helped them. They did overcome the "We want Roy, we want Roy" after I had left. They were frightened each night, but it helped both of us, because it was the right set-up for them and for us.

You must have been amazed when about a year later, the Beatles broke the way they did. And that you had your biggest hit with "Pretty Woman" right in the heart of the Beatlemania thing.

Yeah, that year, in '64, "It's Over" was my first release that year. It was the first number one single by an American in England since '62, I think... Then, "Pretty Woman" came out, and it was number one here and there at the same time. That was the first time that had happened since 1961. So, for the first years, '64 and '65, they were the number one vocal group in the world, and I was the number one male vocalist in the world. So, their coming to America didn't do anything but help me, that year. Their biggest year was my biggest year in the States. My touring internationally and then touring in the States is very much like an international artist would come here from some other country, You probably wouldn't get to see them in their home country; they'd come here to tour. I got caught up in a thing where if I went to a foreign country and did well, they say, "Will you come back next year?" And I say, "OK, I'll come back next year." With all of this to do, it was very hard to play New York. I was invited to play at least twelve times, really important things in New York. And each time, I was committed, and couldn't make it. Same way with L.A. and Chicago. Really, there was no method to the madness.

Were your records still strong overseas after "Pretty Woman?" They didn't register very highly here after that.

Yeah, they were still strong internationally as late as a couple of years ago. They did a collection of the hit things, and it broke in at number one in England. I didn't sanction that, but they did it. So they withdrew it and we renegotiated. They put it back and it went back to number one.

That was all early material?

It was early material, but let's see, the last chart record here was in 1968. After "Pretty Woman" was "Crawling Back," "Cry Softly," things like that. Overseas there were a lot of number one hits—"Too Soon To Know," things like that. So, at about the time of, when I lost my wife in an accident, in 1966, and then my two children in a fire in 1968, for about, effectively from 1966 to 1969, I was touring and all. But I wasn't concerned about what records were released. Then I was with a recording company that was being bought and sold at the time: MGM. I tried to get out of that thing from 1970 to '73 or '74. I made one LP in 1974 for Mercury, I think, and one in '75 or '76 for Monument. And that was it from 1970 until now.

But all the time, I would go to Australia and I'd have a hit record. They gave me gold records three times running for the same song. And the last time I was in Australia, they gave me fifteen gold albums and one platinum album. And I still have, in a London safe, from the last trip over, two or three gold albums there, which are scattered hits. I quit in 1972, internationally, releasing anything. So this is the first really important thing (*Laminar Flow*) in seven years or so.

So what have you been doing, mostly?

Touring and recording, but not releasing. And writing still. And today, if I had to do a show, let's say next week, I could call my group and it should be good. That's what I've been up to for a couple of years, going back. I was looking for the right company and the right booking agent, the right set-up, the right everything. I've had two or three tours, in different sections of the U.S., since 1964.

Do you have a tour planned for the future?

111

We're considering it.

Will you play clubs or concerts?

We may do clubs after concerts. I think if you're going to do what I call an "in club," the only thing that would make that special is if you did that after a concert. If you did it before, I think it would just be an industry thing or an ego thing. But it seems to me natural to do a concert. I've been doing concerts anyway.

Let's move on to your new album. How did you get involved with Elektra/Asylum records?

I was looking for companies that were big and little at the same time, if that makes any sense. A company that was small enough, but with a lot of push. There were three or four around, and I figured this was the best one. Not too much personnel, not too many acts, where you wouldn't get lost, but where it's still considered a major label.

When did you begin work on Laminar Flow?

We started October, November. I started writing a little bit, and listening to songs. We actually started the recording in January. We refreshed February 15.

Were the songs on the album written specifically for the record, or had you been performing some of them already?

One of them I had written earlier, a few months earlier. One I wrote specifically for the album, and one was fairly current. The other stuff...my concept for an album is to do everything from a beat ballad all the way up to a real rocker. I also didn't want to write the whole album, because I would have taken longer. I wanted to do some things that current successful writers were doing, songs that have been hits recently. So I picked songs from those writers.

Did you choose all the material yourself, or did your producers (Clayton Ivey and Terry Woodford) pick some?

The producers provided some of the material for me to listen to, but I had the final say on all of it.

How did you hook up with them?

They happened to be in Los Angeles the same time that I was. We were introduced, Terry Woodford and I, and he told me how great he was. I said, "Well, I'll come see you." So I went down to Muscle Shoals, Alabama, and I liked the way he talked. And I met his partner, Clayton Ivey, and found out very quickly that he was a genius on the keyboards. I meet very few geniuses. Terry was terrific, he knew what he was doing, then they came to my house. We talked and we said, "Let's go try." Before we knew it, we had it done. I say "before we knew it" because we were going to do a couple of things to see if we worked well, and we worked so well that we got the whole thing by the 15th of February.

Did they influence the arrangements and all, or was that all your doing?

Clayton did a lot of what he called "setting a groove." We'd get a groove going, and I would sing. When we all felt comfortable, we did it that way. It wasn't arranged beforehand. We would just try, and sometimes if it wasn't right, we didn't do it. The ones that were right we put on the album.

Has there been a single chosen from the album?

They sent out "Easy Way Out," which is a disco-type thing. And I think we're going to try to send out another song. Hopefully, we can release two or three things, because there's been an absence, on my part, of material. And in the marketplace, there are people who would play this or that or vice versa. And we've got a lot of stuff on the album for them to play.

How did you feel about doing a disco-type thing?

We actually didn't set out to do a disco thing. I don't know yet that that's pure disco, because I don't know what that is, really. But it sounded good. When I hear the piano and the drums playing what they're playing, it's really strong to me. And the song has a little bit to say. But, not knowing what it is, I think we could say we realized after it was done that you could disco to the song. But we didn't sit down and say, "Let's do a country song, or a disco song," or so on. We just put all these grooves, what they call a groove and what I call a feel, all out with a good range of tempos and attitudes.

What about the song an the album, "Hound Dog Man?" That's a tribute to Elvis, isn't it? How did that come about?

"Hound Dog Man" was...we were sitting around singing songs and playing tapes and things like this in a log cabin. A guy sang this song, and they said "How would you feel about doing that song?" I said, well, first of all I wouldn't want to get in on any exploitation. Elvis and I were too close. And in the second place, I said "When was the song written?" And they said, "A couple of years back." So it was written before Elvis died, and there had to be a rewrite of the song. So, when it was rewritten, I said, "Yes, I'd like to do it."

Your wife (Barbara) was given co-credit for writing the song.

Yes. It was so close to me that it was hard to record. It was even hard to sing, but it was a thing where it was like from me to Elvis. And I think I've told a few people that I don't mind if no one else hears it. It was just a thing that I did from me to him. Although you could say, "Well, you put it out on an album, to sell. How can you say that?" But that's my telling about that.

What was your relationship with Elvis in his last years?

Very close, all the way through. We had two photographs taken together, one in 1956 and one in December before he died. So I guess that would have been twenty years apart that the photographs were taken. We were very close because we were the two from Sun who went more pop than country. And I did a film for MGM; he did his films for MGM. And we recorded at the same studio, we had the same manager initially. We did the same first tour. We would send messages.

And you're about the same age.

Right. There's a lot of sameness. We were very kindred souls, Elvis and I.

What were you doing when you heard that he died?

It was the night of my Santa Monica performance.

The fellow asked me, did I want to cancel? And I told him no. I would like to have canceled the show, but I'll worry about it later, meaning that I didn't want to worry about it at the time. I went ahead and did the concert, ostensibly to take my mind off what had happened. Then it came down later.

Did it affect your performance?

No, the performance was glorious. People were so responsive that they just lifted me up. It was like a standing ovation before I sang. I didn't mention about it at the show. I did the Liberty Bowl, which was a tribute to Elvis. I asked the family about it first. It was done in Memphis, his home town. His father was in the press box.

You know that his father died yesterday.

Yes I heard it on the airplane. Vernon was there, and Charlie Hodge. It was a real thing for Elvis. Then on his birthday, I did a thing which I at first thought was a tribute to Elvis on his birthday. (Ed. Note: This was the NBC-TV presentation, "Nashville Remembers Elvis," aired January 8, 1978.) It turned out to be "Nashville Salutes Elvis" on his birthday, that kind of thing. It didn't come out as it was presented to me. That's why I was a little hesitant on the "Hound Dog Man" song. I wanted it to be in the right context. I don't see everybody that I know often, but from time to time, I'll see one of the Beatles—Ringo here and Paul there. And I see the Beach Boys from time to time. I guess everybody that I've been associated with that's still around, I see from time to time. It's that kind of thing. I don't think any entertainer can keep close relationships, if you're traveling. Even Johnny (Cash) and I don't see each other maybe but four or five times a year. And we're next door neighbors! I may see him in the car coming or going and we wave, but I only see him that much. He's out of town and when he comes home he wants to rest. Then I'm out of town.

How much time out of the year are you touring now?

Up until we started this album project and I signed with the company, I would say it's averaged six months out of the year, from 1961. As little as two months on the road and as much as ten months. Ten months was too heavy, and seven months in a row once, with nine days off. I would like for it to be no more than three or four months now. So I'll try to plan it that way.

Did you know when you signed to E/A that Jerry Lee was also on the label?

I didn't know, but it is a strange coincidence. When I signed...we went to Los Angeles to play the record for them, they were in the process of releasing the Jerry Lee album. I didn't know that he had signed.

You had open heart surgery not long ago. How did that affect your career?

Yes, when I was doing the thing at the Liberty Bowl, I ran up to the P. box, and it's a long way. When I got to the top, I was feeling quite woozy. I mentioned it to my wife, and we went to Honolulu, checked into a hospital intensive care and nothing. No signs of anything. Went back to Nashville checked in, and no signs of anything. They said "Go home, watch the Super Bowl." Then, that Wednesday, I had open heart surgery. Ninety days later, I was playing a show in Winnipeg, Canada, and I did a week thing in Vancouver. It affected me greatly. I could think better, I could see better, and I had greater perception. It increased the blood flow. I wasn't getting all the oxygen to the thinker that I should have been getting. But it was all very clear to me what to do.

This is another subject completely, but are you aware that John Belushi did an impersonation of you on "Saturday Night Live"?

Yeah, yeah, this Newman gal, Laraine Newman, held up this placard that held a gold record in it, with a pair of glasses mounted on it. I was going to tell my wife, "Get in touch with those people, I need some more of those glasses." She (Newman) started this thing by saying "Now I know ten thousand musicians intimately, but I'm not a groupie. But there's this one person, Roy Orbison..." and Belushi went on to do the thing and it was fabulous. I called them up to thank them, and they wanted to know whether to put me through to the legal department, was I offended? And I told them, "No, I wasn't offended," that I loved it! So it was terrific. I was rolling.

Did they invite you to play on the show?

I was going to do the show before the open heart surgery. We probably will do something on the show in the fall.

Would you do material from the new album or the old songs?

I don't know yet. We may do a little shtick. I probably will talk to them and see what they want to do.

When you do go out on the road, will you still do most of the old stuff, or new material?

Oh yeah, I'll always do the old stuff. That's been a lifetime dream. I remember very well going out on stage with one hit record, and then seeing the star come on with five or six or ten. And I said, "One day I'll be able to do that." So I still do all that I can. The show started out being fifteen minutes long, then twenty, then thirty. At last count, it was an hour and forty-five minutes. I still had a few more to go. So, when I say all of them, I still do the bigger ones. But that is my show. If I get a couple of hit records off this album, I'll include them. I went through, on the Beatles tour, "In Dreams." That's as far as it would take me. The next year was the Beach Boys tour, and I went through "It's Over," because it was the first part of the year. The next year I played with the Rolling Stones and I could do "Pretty Woman." When I get the hit, I tuck her in there!

Why, in your own opinion, didn't you have any more huge successes after "Pretty Woman," which was your biggest hit?

It's very strange. The very next record didn't sell anything; in fact, nobody knows the title of the next record on Monument. Then we released another on Monument. It had to be somebody's fault somewhere. The reason I say that is because you would have pre-orders of a hundred thousand coming off of that. But, the next record didn't sell that. It didn't. Then when I re-signed with MGM, I did have three or four more hit records. Not of the magnitude of "Pretty Woman," but then that was the biggest seller. I set a big precedent with "Only The Lonely" when it went two million. The next one after that was a million, and the one after that 600,000. And I said, "I'm on my way out again." Then "Running Scared" came out and hit it. So, I don't know the reason would be for that. It's strange. If I knew the secret...

This is a tough question. If you could look back at the last twenty years and try to sum up objectively your own influence on music, where do you see yourself?

That's a very tough question. The only thing that I could say about that would be what people say and do, what my contemporaries say and do. When I say my contemporaries, they might not be as old as I am, or some of them might be older, but they're still doing well. For instance, when Linda did "Blue Bayou," that would have been an influence. Peter Asher is her producer, (and) we toured together when he was with Peter And Gordon... At a birthday party for me that the Beatles came to in 1964 (Paul couldn't make it because he was dating Jane Asher), so the influence is personally and professionally...I hope they've been for the good, that's all I can say about it.

One influence I see is that you brought complexity to rock music. You were one of the first to do complex arrangements vocally.

Yes, the expansion. Maybe I expanded things a little bit.

The average, quote, "rockabilly singer" could have never done what you did.

Maybe I did add another dimension. I don't know exactly how to put it.

Can you see doing this for the rest of your life?

I think so. My voice is as strong as it ever was, even stronger now. I do realize that you have to warm up a little bit now. I never do. I just go out and sing. I think I'll always be a studio artist. And I think I'll do the touring for another four or five years, at least. Then I think, I think from what I know now, as opposed to what I knew ten years ago or twenty, that I would try to pass along some of the things I've learned to younger talent; maybe be a producer. I think I could be great at that. That's what I'll probably do. I'll never be an old man. My father called me the other day, on my birthday, and he said, "How old are you?" And I said, "Dad, you know how old I am." He said, "No tell me how old." So I told him, and he said, "You're almost as old as I am." And I said, "That's right." He learned to fly when he was forty-three, and got his pilot's license. And he bought a mini Harley Davidson when he was fifty-one. So he's still rockin' and I'll still be rockin'."

Top 25 (plus) Most Collectible Country Western Records

by Fred Heggeness

The list below considers only records that are country western; not those that might be crossover rock or rockabilly. Therefore, Elvis, Roy Orbison, the Johnny Burnette Trio, and so on are not on the list. If crossover records were part of the list, Presley would rank twenty titles worth $2,000-4,000 each; Roy Orbison and the Teen Kings would rank $6,000 and $2,000; Paul McCartney $3,000; and Carl Mann, Ray Smith, and Bill Haley $2,000 each. The "Jamboree" LP is valued at $5,000 and the Billy Barrix rockabilly Chess 45 at $7,500! Also not included in the list below are the Fendermen, Charlie Feathers, Lou Giordano, and Buddy Holly.

	Label, Catalog #	Title	Value
1.	Abbott 5001	Jim Reeves Sings (Mono only)	$1,500

Very rare and very much in demand. Most of the tracks were released as singles, but the album is impossible to find at any price!

2.	Radio Show 1477	Here's To Veterans (Merle Haggard)	1,500

So what's the big difference between this $1,500 disc and show 1454, which is the same show but a different record? Glad you asked! Show 1477 features the Beatles on the other side. Enough said!

3.	Starday 101	Grand Ole Opry's New Star (George Jones)	1,200

George's first album, also his rarest. Some of these tracks were released as singles.

4.	Victor 6000	Blue Yodel No. 12 (Jimmie Rodgers)	1,000

Released as a picture disc in 1935, this gem is very collectible among fans of all music formats. This title was also released as a (non-picture disc) regular 78rpm, Victor 24458, worth at least $100. Look for all Jimmie Rodgers records to rise fast in value, as he is the "Father of Country Music!"

5.   Columbia 2601   Rock'n Roll'n Robbins (Marty Robbins)   800

Marty's first album is his only solo 10-inch LP. Features many of his collectible rockabilly tracks. Valued here at $800, you'll probably have to pay more if you are buying!

6.   Sun 1265   Jerry Lee Lewis' Greatest (White promo label version)   800

His second Sun LP was released as a promo, unlike the first (Sun 1230). Very rare. The stock copy of Sun 1265 is worth $250!

7.   Sterling 201   Calling You (Hank Williams)   750

Available as an original 78rpm record in 1947. This is Hank's first recording.

8.   Sterling 204   Wealth Won't Save Your Soul (Hank Williams)   500

Hank's second 78rpm. Two versions, both worth $500 each. One version reads on the flip side, "When God Comes and Gathers His Jewels." The other version reads on the flip, "When God Comes and Fathers His Jewels."

9.   Sterling 208   I Don't Care If Tomorrow Never Comes (Hank Williams)   500

Still 1947, Hank's third release, also only on 78rpm.

10.   Coral 57235   Moon Over Mullican (Moon Mullican)   500

Price is for the stock copy, rarer than the promo. Great music too!

11.   Bat 1001   Waylon Jennings At JDs   500

His first LP is very rare. Reissued first on Sounds 1001, worth $200 and later on Vocalion in 1969, still collectible at $30-40.

12.   Capitol promo 1384   Rockin' With Wanda (Wanda Jackson)   500

This price is for the yellow promo label version. Classic album! Stock copy is listed later. Its reissue as a Starline label version is still collectible at $50.

13.   RCA Victor Thesaurus Series   Hank Snow   500

Promo collection of ten albums from RCA Victor Music Service to radio stations. You'd be lucky to find one, let alone all ten! When word gets around about this set, its value will skyrocket!

14.   RCA Victor Thesaurus Series   Sons Of The Pioneers   500

Promo collection of eleven albums from RCA Victor Music Service to radio stations. Again, you'll be lucky to see just one disc of the set!

15.   Columbia 21496   The Sun Keeps Shining (Everly Brothers) (45 rpm)   500

Yes, the Everly Brothers are rock crossover. But this is a country record! It's also their first and only release on Columbia. Very rare on the red label. The white promo label version is much easier to find, but still worth $250.

16.   Sterling 210   Honky Tonkin' (Hank Williams)   400

This is the final Sterling 78rpm release and the easiest to find. The Sterling 78s are a great investment if you should get the opportunity!

117

17. Capitol 1384   Rockin' With Wanda (Wanda Jackson)   400
     The stock copy. Promo version is listed above.

18. Coral 57235   Moon Over Mullican (Moon Mullican)   400
     *Price is for the blue promo label version, more common than the stock copy,
     which is ranked above.*

19. Atlantic 1503   Arkansas Twist (Bobby Lee Trammell)   400
     *Again, is this country or rockabilly? You buy it for $400 and listen to it, then
     let me know. Still, it's a great album!*

20. BBC Transcription Disc (Johnny Cash) (Radio show)   400
     *Not just a radio show, it's a country artist live in a rock concert format, it's a
     British release of an American artist for the American radio market, and it's
     the rarest and most collectible of all radio series. Also, it's very rare within
     the series, and there may be fewer than ten copies of this LP left. Yes, $400 is
     a very conservative price!*

21. Antone's 6000   Old Time Favorites (Bob Wills)   400
     *Were you a member of the Bob Wills Fan Club in the early '50s? This 10-inch
     LP was sent to you as a gift.*

22. Antone's 6010   Old Time Favorites (Bob Wills)   400
     *A second gift from the club. Bob Wills died in 1996, which may give these 10-
     inch LPs a boost in value.*

23. Philips 1970   Lonely Weekends (Charlie Rich)   400
     *This LP was country/rock crossover like most of the Sun label artists and
     releases. Philips Records was owned by Sam Philips, who also owned Sun.
     Charlie Rich can be considered a genuine country artist.*

24. American Eagle Features Marty Robbins (Radio show)   300
     *Three-LP set features live music from Marty Robbins and other country artists,
     recorded in the early '80s. Live radio shows featuring top country artists will
     always be a good investment!*

25. MGM 107   Hank Williams Sings   300
     From 1952, this is Hank's first LP and is a 10-inch version.

26. MGM 168   Moanin' The Blues (Hank Williams)   300
     *This 10-inch LP was also released in 12-inch format with both a 1956 yellow
     label version and a 1960 black label version. The 12-inchers are worth $150
     and $25.*

27. MGM 202   The Hank Williams Memorial Album   300
     *Another 10-inch LP re-released as a 12-incher worth $150 (yellow label) and
     $25 (black label).*

| 28. | MGM 203 | Hank Williams As Luke The Drifter | 300 |

Released in 1953 as a 10-inch LP. Again, later versions are 12-inchers worth $150 (yellow label) and $25 (black).

| 29. | MGM 242 | Honky Tonkin'(Hank Williams) | 300 |

Hank coined the phase "Honky Tonkin'" and this is the first record released with that title. It's another 10-inch LP with 12-inch re-releases.

| 30. | MGM 243 | I Saw The Light (Hank Williams) | 300 |

Only one version of this 10-inch LP was pressed. Later versions are 12-inchers. One has a green cover and yellow label and is worth $200, another version has a church on the cover and a yellow label, worth $150. The black label version goes for $25.

| 31. | MGM 291 | Ramblin' Man (Hank Williams) | 300 |

The last of the 10-inch LPs. Later 12-inch versions worth $150 and $25.

| 32. | MGM EP 1623 | It's Only Make Believe (Conway Twitty) | 300 |

The first MGM EP for Conway Twitty, yellow label 1958 release. Later EPs on the MGM label are worth up to $250 each.

| 33. | Imperial 3004 | America's Favorite Folk Artist (Slim Whitman) | 300 |

This 10-inch LP was released in 1954 and is very hard to find. Love him or hate him, this is a classic LP. Another 10-inch LP on RCA Victor (3217) was released in 1954 and is worth $200.

| 34. | Brunswick 55130 | Jole Blon (Waylon Jennings) | 300 |

Waylon's first record, recording during his association and membership with Buddy Holly & the Crickets. Holly plays guitar on this release. The $300 price tag is for the maroon-colored label stock copy. The promo version lists at $250!

Charlie Feathers is considered rockabilly but I think many will agree that he belongs on the list above. "Tongue Tied Jill," a maroon-colored label 45 rpm on Meteor (5032) is worth over $1,000! Other versions on Meteor range in value from $300-750, including 78s. Sun label 78s and 45s by Feathers range from $400-750 each. The Flip label, pressed by Sun, ranges from $500-750 for "I've Been Deceived" (Flip 503).

You'll discover that the twenty-nine-plus highest priced records in this book are either rockabilly or rock crossover country songs (like Elvis). The country western-only artists don't rank until Jim Reeves's Abbott LP is listed at $1,500. Rockabilly and rock crossover records represented the bridge of country western music changing to rock and roll. Most rockabilly records were released in 1958, give or take a year.

Also listed at $1,500 is the Merle Haggard radio show. The reason for that high price tag is the Beatles show on the flip side.

Photo/Henry Diltz

Joni Mitchell

By William Ruhlmann
February 17, 1995

On the cover of her seventeenth album, *Turbulent Indigo*, released by Reprise Records on October 25, 1994, Joni Mitchell placed a carefully rendered reproduction of one of Vincent Van Gogh's more shocking paintings. In late December 1888, in what his sister-in-law called "a state of terrible excitement and high fever," the tortured painter cut off a piece of his right ear and offered it as a gift to a woman in a brothel. Back from the hospital in January, he noted simply in a letter to his brother Theo, "I have a new portrait of myself for you."

In the painting, Van Gogh appears in an overcoat, wearing a fur-covered hat, the right side of his head wrapped in a bandage. But unlike other self-portraits, this one shows us a tranquil Van Gogh, one who looks calmly, stoically off to the side of the picture, an expression that makes the white cloth we know is covering his mutilated ear all the more disturbing. It's as if, having indulged in this desperate, outrageous act, he is, for the moment, perversely satisfied. For her album cover, Joni Mitchell recreates the painting with one dramatic change: she substitutes her own face for Van Gogh's.

That this successful fifty-one-year-old singer-songwriter of the late twentieth century should identify so closely with the suicidal thirty-five-year-old painter of the late nineteenth century will not be a surprise to anyone who has followed Mitchell's career. Reacting to shouted song requests from her audience at the Universal Amphitheatre in Los Angeles in August 1974, at the height of her popularity, a slightly annoyed Mitchell said, "That's one thing that's always, like, been a major difference between, like, the performing arts to me and being a painter, you know? Like, a painter does a painting, and he does a painting. That's it, you know? He's had the joy of creating it, somebody buys it, somebody buys it again or maybe nobody buys it and it sits up in a loft somewhere till he dies. But he's never—nobody ever says to him—nobody ever said to Van Gogh, 'Paint a "Starry Night" again, man!(Laughs) You know? He painted it; that was it."

Then she sang one of her best-known and earliest songs, "The Circle Game."

Though Mitchell begins the comment stating that there is a difference between the performing arts and what we might call the "compositional" arts, as an artist who has spent an equal amount of time in each, she has struggled to combine them. While her natural inclinations led her to painting early on, she found greater popular success as a songwriter and singer, but pursued that course without losing the Van Gogh-like perspective of an artist whose only true allegiance is to the art itself.

In that sense, her musical career has been misunderstood, at least from her way of looking at it. A conventional viewpoint, taken by most observers, is that Mitchell emerged as a songwriter in the late 1960s, notably with Judy Collins' hit version of her song "Both Sides, Now," then achieved increasing success as a performer during the wave of singer-songwriters in the early 1970s, along with James Taylor, Jackson Browne and others, culminating in the million-selling 1974 album Court and Spark.

But following that triumph, Mitchell turned away from her lyrical concern with adult romance and her musical interest in folk-pop melodicism, and toward more obscure poetic lyrics and jazz, so that she also turned away from much of her audience. In the last twenty years, she has continued to release albums to a steady, if relatively small, audience and has been kept on major record labels due to long personal associations and the prestige of her name. Her long-time friend David Geffen, for whose Geffen Records label she recorded from 1982 to 1991, told New York Daily News staff writer Jim Farber in 1994, "Even though we lost money on every one of her records, we always treated Joni as one of the most important artists in the world."

And certainly it is as an artist that Mitchell sees herself. Her early career was not a steady, unbroken climb to popularity, but rather one in which Mitchell frequently felt unsuited and which she came close to abandoning several times. Her work, the momentum of that career and the unpredictable tides of musical fashion may have placed her at a commercial and critical pinnacle in 1974, but that can be seen now more as a happy aberration than the execution of a deliberate plan—happy because it consolidated her standing in such a way that she has been able to continue to work as she chooses at a certain level of recognition, while many of her peers have faced compromises and reduced exposure in the ensuing decades.

If, twenty years on, we are still inclined to think of her early work—songs such as "Both Sides, Now" and "Big Yellow Taxi" and albums like *Blue*—as her most impressive, nevertheless such efforts as *The Hissing of Summer Lawns*, much criticized upon release, have proven influential, and even *Turbulent Indigo*, which has turned out to be one of Mitchell's poorest sellers, was able to stir up controversy for its songs about current social problems and scandal.

Twenty-six years after most listeners got their first introduction to Joni Mitchell through Judy Collins' hit recording of "Both Sides, Now," a significant audience still looks forward to hearing what she has to say, and for a songwriter, that's a triumph. As she prepares to make her eighteenth album, with some songs already written (though it may be 1997 until we hear them), she seems to have less in common with Van Gogh, who committed suicide at thirty-seven, a little over a year after painting the self-portrait she evokes on the cover of Turbulent Indigo, than with another acknowledged influence, Pablo Picasso, who lived happily into his nineties and continued painting until the end.

But now let's go back to the beginning. Joni Mitchell was born Roberta Joan Anderson on November 7, 1943, to a mother who was a teacher and a father who had left the Royal Canadian Air Force to become the manager of a grocery store, in Fort McLeod, a town in the southern part of the province of Alberta, Canada, that had been established as an outpost by the Northwest Mounted Police in 1874.

Alberta, the westernmost of the so-called "prairie" provinces of Canada, sits north of the states of Washington, Idaho, and Montana and even today has a population density of less than ten people per square mile. To call it remote is an understatement.

Joanie Anderson (she would become Joni Mitchell upon her marriage in 1965, and we will refer to her by her more familiar name from here on) was raised in the somewhat less remote city of Saskatoon in the next province to the east, Saskatchewan. Saskatoon (which in 1991 had a population of 186,000) was settled in 1883. It is the largest city in the province and the site of the University of Saskatchewan, which makes it more of a cosmopolitan place to grow up in Fort McLeod. But "remote" is still the operative word.

"The town I lived in was a small third-world town," Mitchell told psychologist Jenny Boyd, Ph.D., for her book *Musicians In Tune: Seventy-Five Contemporary Musicians Discuss The Creative Process* (written with Holly George-Warren, Fireside, 1992), "the mail still came at Christmas on open wagons drawn by horses with sleigh runners."

Boyd writes that Mitchell displayed creativity early on and that that creativity was encouraged by her parents "until they no longer approved of her means of expression and withdrew their support." But that early support helped her overcome the disapproval of her peers, who shunned her for being different.

"In my early childhood, because I was creative— I was a painter always—I had difficulty playing with the other children in the neighborhood," Mitchell told Boyd, "just because my games they couldn't get in on."

Mitchell also showed an early interest in music: At seven she asked her parents for piano lessons. But she showed more interest in composing her own music than in practicing classical pieces, as the result of which "my teacher rapped my knuckles with a ruler and said, 'Why would you want to compose when you could have the greats under your fingers?'" she recalls in an interview with the author conducted for this article in New York in October 1994.

As a result, she abandoned the lessons. "So, my first love of music was cut off at an early age by bad education," she said.

"...But I still used to sit down and compose my own little melodies," she told Boyd. "That's what I wanted to do, to compose...I thought I was going to be a painter when I grew up, but I knew I could make up music; I heard it in my head. I always could do it, but it was discouraged."

That very discouragement seems to have acted as a stimulus, however. In discussing the development of creativity, Mitchell told Boyd that what keeps many people from being creative is a fear of failure, a disinclination to take risks. "You have to be able to go out on a limb," she said. "...To innovate, you have to have a certain kind of fearlessness. I think it helps if at an early age you got used to being shunned and you survived that. If you had to fight some things in your childhood, you now can stand alone."

Another thing Joni Mitchell had to fight in her childhood was the polio epidemic that swept Canada when was nine. She contracted a slight case of the paralyzing disease, and it was feared that she would not walk again. Though she recovered, some of her muscles were permanently atrophied in ways that would affect her performing style later on.

As she moved toward adolescence, Mitchell maintained her interest in art, and it was expressed especially in an interest in clothes and fashion. "As a child, I harbored the idea of becoming a fashion designer," she said. "I drew cut-outs. I'd dress dollies. Through every class, my mother saved some of them, and they're kind of interesting to look at now. I made my own clothes. So, fashion was a thing interested me in my early teens ...I had my own column in the high school paper, 'Fads And Fashion.' It was pretty fluffy."

Her other main interest, she noted, was "rock 'n' roll dancing...I had an added advantage that I was a night owl and that radio stations shut down about midnight locally and there was a strong broadcast from a station in Texas that would wave in and out, and you could hear songs that were coming that wouldn't be there for four months, so you almost had a crystal ball and you could predict the hits in the future in a miraculous way."

Mitchell's interest in music and dancing brought her in contact with some of the rowdier elements of society. "I gravitated to the best dance halls from the age of twelve to the age of sixteen," she says. "Not that I liked beer, but we would go from time to time to the bootleggers, and the bootleggers were also brothels. Like any young black trumpet player in the south, like John Handy or any New Orleans musician who knew he was a musician at an early age, somehow I was drawn to where the music was best, and it's always in the roughest areas. And yet, the street had heart then, and a child, a baby, a clean-looking baby was not molested. If anything, they were very protective. First of all, they'd say, 'Get her out of here,' or, if I insisted on remaining, they'd make sure that someone saw me safely to the bus.

"So, even the toughest areas—which I went to for the music and the booze or whatever, or to see people drinking, not necessarily because I cared to drink myself, to see life—were very protective and generous to me. My street experience was not anything like what the streets are now, with cocaine and white slavery and so on. But I (saw) a lot of life, and I (had) a lot of difficult, I (became) an unwed mother, and all of the travail and the white-trash prejudice that accompanied that."

Though this seems to be the first time Mitchell has spoken in an interview about her teenage pregnancy and the child she gave up, she has referred to the incident in song. "Little Green," on the 1971 *Blue* album, concerns the subject ("Child with a child pretending/ Weary of lies you are sending home/ So you sign all the papers in the family name/ You're sad and you're sorry, but you're not ashamed/ Little green, have a happy ending"), and it comes up again in "Chinese Cafe" on the 1982 album *Wild Things Run Fast* ("We were wild in the old days/ Birth of rock 'n' roll days/ Now your kids are coming up straight/ And my child's a stranger/ I bore her/ But, I could not raise her").

Mitchell not only saw the seamy side of the entertainment world on the streets of Saskatoon, but was also aware, even then, of the trappings of celebrity that accompanied the singers of the songs she heard on the radio as well as other entertainers, and she strongly disapproved of the loss of privacy. "I wrote a poem in, I guess it was grade ten, about the age of sixteen, about Hollywood, called, 'The Fish Bowl,'" she said, and then recites: "The fish bowl is a world reversed where fishermen with hooks that dangle from the bottom up reel down their catch without a fight on gilded bait. Pike, pickerel, bass, the common fish, ogle through distorting glass, see only glitter, glamour, gaiety, fog up the bowl with lusty breath, lunge towards the bait and miss and weep for fortune lost. Envy the goldfish? Why? His bubbles break 'round the rim while silly fishes faint for him and say, 'Oh, look there, he winked his eye at me!'"

She laughed, and continued, "So, with this young insight, it was really ironic that I would enter into this world."

The first real step she took toward entering into that world was learning to play a stringed instrument. "There came to my hometown at college—I was still in high school—a different kind of party," Mitchell recalled, "where people sat around and sang." This was, of course, the folk music boom, finally making its way to Saskatoon. "It was a different way of partying than I was used to, which was dancing and drinking beer," Mitchell said, "and I kind of took to it. But a lot of time there was no accompanist; no one seemed to play an instrument.

So, I got it in my mind that I wanted to learn to play guitar. Well, I borrowed a guitar from somebody, but the action was incredibly high. It was an old orchestral F-hole rhythm guitar, basically, and I couldn't press the strings down. My fingers were bleeding. It was intolerable."

Mitchell turned to her parents, but they hadn't forgotten her previous flirtation with music. "My parents, my mother in particular, said, 'Oh, if we buy you a guitar, you'll just abandon it. You never follow anything up. It'll be just like the piano,'" Mitchell recalled. "So, I started saving up, but I couldn't save up fast enough. Guitars were fairly expensive. But I managed to scrape up $36 to buy myself a baritone ukulele. That's what I started on.

"About six months later, I was playing accompanying some kind of bawdy drinking songs at a wiener roast, which was our teenage form of entertainment—go out in the bush with some beer and sit around a campfire and sing songs—when I was overheard by some—they seemed like old people, but they were young people, really. They were, like, in their early twenties, and they worked for a television station in Prince Albert, Saskatchewan, and they thought I was really good. So, they took off this moose-hunting program (moose hunting is big up there), *Field & Stream*-type of show, which came on late in the evening, and they stuck me on. I'd be eighteen at the time and playing this baritone ukulele for about six months, and I think it was about an hour long.

"In the meantime, my friends, who knew me as a rock 'n' roll dancer and kind of an enjoyer, found this change kind of hard to relate to, 'cause the songs at that time (were) folk songs and English ballads, and, you know, women's English ballads are always, 'the cruel mother,' and there's a lot of sorrow in them. But they had beautiful melodies, that was the thing, and I always loved melody. Melody is generally melancholy and sad, and the text that accompanies it must be the same.

"So, this kind of joyous, fun-loving creature became this earnest creature. This transformation had taken place, and I think a lot of people had a hard time with that transition. I know some of my best dance buddies would say, 'Put that thing down. We're gonna drag you onto the dance floor.' 'No, no, no,' I was clinging to it (the ukulele) in the corner, saying 'Leave me alone.' I introverted into this intimate relationship with this stringed instrument."

Mitchell did not, however, expect to make a career out of music. In 1963, at the age of nineteen, she enrolled at the Alberta College of Art in Calgary, returning to the western province of her birth.

"All my live I was waiting to study painting," she said. "When I got there, the teaching was as disappointing as the piano was. If you had any hand-eye control, and if you already knew how to render tonality and you'd made these simple observations, there was almost a prejudice levied against you, and it was considered that you should go into commercial art because, basically, the age of the camera had come, and Greenberg was kind (i.e., art critic Clement Greenberg, who championed what he called "post-painterly abstraction," notably in his 1961 book Art And Culture) and de Kooning (i.e., painter Willem de Kooning, a leader of the school of abstract expressionism), and all the profs were pouring paint down inclined planes, and they were basically resentful or prejudiced against someone who had drawing ability. I would say, out of 150 new students, there were only about four of us that had that. A lot of them had entered into art school, I think, for the lifestyle or the idea of becoming an artist, and the profs seemed to figure that they were better suited knowing nothing to be implanted with their love of abstract painting.

"Well, I developed a prejudice towards it and a kind of a rebellion, and I took to playing in the coffee houses north of there in a city called Edmonton and one in Calgary called the Depression, and the two interests began to kind of conflict."

For Mitchell, who turned twenty in October 1963, pursuing a career as an artist turned out to have two drawbacks: "the lack of classical training at the school, and also the fact that, in Canada, art was looked on more as a vocation than the important and great thing that it is," she explained. "Truth and beauty? No, no, they viewed it more as a trade. It was stuck in between auto mechanics and cafeteria cooks in training."

In 1964, Mitchell got on a train and went east to Toronto to attend the Mariposa Folk Festival and see folk singer Buffy Sainte-Marie. On the way, she wrote her first song "Day After Day." She did not return to college. As she put it, "I allowed my disappointment in the education offered me to lead me to the East Coast, where there were seventeen thriving coffee houses in Toronto."

In his book, *Neil Young: Don't Be Denied* (Quarry Press, 1992), John Einarson provides a description of the thriving music scene in Toronto in 1964. "The 'scene' of Toronto music at that time was the Yorkville district," Einarson wrote. "Within the downtown Yorkville village district, a two block stretch between Avenue Road and Yonge Street one way, and Davenport and Bloor Streets on the other side, some ten to fifteen different coffeehouses could be found amid the closely-knit artistic community that thrived there. On any given night one could easily hear the strains of Eric Andersen, Tom Rush, or Odetta wafting from these tin enclaves. These coffeehouses were literally houses, old, brick two and three story homes with folk singers or small groups performing in the front room or basement."

And there wasn't only folk music, as Levon Helm recalled in his book *This Wheel's On Fire: Levon Helm And The Story Of The Band* (written with Stephen Davis, William Morrow and Company, 1993). "It was a great time to launch a band in Toronto," noted Helm, who was a member of Ronnie Hawkins' rockabilly—playing Hawks then, "because the place was jumping. On a weekend night on that Yonge Street strip you could catch Oscar Peterson, Carl Perkins, Ray Charles and his band, Cannonball Adderley, Charles Mingus. You could see a local band like us or one of our competitors, the Paupers. There was a folk music scene...And it wasn't just music. Toronto was also the publishing, fashion, and style capital of Canada. The city was swinging at least a year before so-called Swinging London."

Sounds great, but for twenty-year-old Joni Mitchell there was just one problem. "When I got there," she recalled, "it cost $160 to get into the (musicians) union, which was a fortune for me; just an impossible goal. And there wasn't much scab work around, and coffee house doors slammed in my face, and it was pretty insulting. There were some dues in that town."

She stuck it out, however. As Einarson put it, "Living in one of the dozens of communal pads on Huron Street in the village, Joni perfected her...craft in the coffeehouses at night, working during the day at a Simpsons-Sears department store to pay the rent."

Apparently, there was more department store than coffee house work, but, "then I finally found a scab club in Toronto that allowed me to play," Mitchell told Joe Smith in his book *Off The Record: An Oral History Of Popular Music* (Warner Books, 1988). "I played for a couple of months.

"In 1965, I was playing in the cellar where they kept the Canadian talent and where the imported American talent played upstairs," she said, elaborating, "and I met a folk singer named Chuck Mitchell. I was at an indecisive time in my life, and he was a strong force. He decided he was gonna marry me. So, he dragged me across the border, and he got me some work, and we were kind of quickly married. It was not a marriage made in heaven. He was relatively well-educated. He was in contempt of my lack of education and also my illiteracy. I did all my book reviews (in school) from *Classic Comic Books*, and I had a kind of a contempt for what I called pseudo-intellectuals, and in a way I was right. I mean, I was developing as an original, unschooled thinker, and I had the gift of the blarney. I had a gift of metaphor. But he kind of ridiculed me in the same way that (Canadian prime minister) Pierre Trudeau ridiculed his wife Margaret when she wrote her book. He said, 'My wife is the only writer I know who's written more books than she's read.' So, there was this aristocratic—the educated pride versus the uneducated, and that marriage didn't last very long."

It did last for almost two years, however, and they were important years in Joni Mitchell's development. For one thing, she began to write songs in earnest. "I began as a folk singer," she said, meaning a singer of traditional folk songs. "I would say I was a folk singer from 1963 until '65. '65, when I crossed the border, I began to write. Once I began to write, my vocal style changed. My (Joan) Baez/Judy Collins influence disappeared. Almost immediately when I had my own words to sing, my own voice appeared."

Writing also led Mitchell to her own guitar sound, based on unusual tunings and conditioned by a physical infirmity. "The moment I began to write, I took the black blues tunings which were floating around," she said. "Tom (Rush) played in open C. Eric Andersen showed me an open G, which I think is Keith Richards' tuning, he mainly writes in that. Then there was D modal. Buffy had a couple of original tunings. But I began to experiment because my left hand is somewhat clumsy because of polio. I had to simplify the shapes of the left hand, but I craved chordal movement that I couldn't get out of standard tuning without an extremely articulate left hand. So, to compensate for it, I found the tunings were a godsend. Not only that, but they made the guitar an unstable thing, but also an instrument of exploration, so that you could put the thing in a new tuning, you had to rediscover the neck, you'd need to search out the chordal movement, and you'd find five or six chords, and then there was the art of chaining them together in a creative manner. It was very exciting to discover my music. It still is, to this day."

"Her unusual tunings and lilting voice drew the attention of those in the know who tipped her to be a future major talent," wrote Einarson. "Unfortunately, not enough people took notice of her genius to keep her in Canada." Chuck and Joni Mitchell moved to Detroit, where Chuck was from, in late 1965.

Unlike nearly all aspiring songwriters, the Mitchells put their business together properly at the start. "The one thing I had was my own publishing company," Joni said. "Chuck and I set up two publishing companies. That was at his instigation. That was very insightful." Joni's company was called Siquomb Publishing, and the name came from one of her many writing projects. As she would explain on Philadelphia radio station WMMR in March 1967, she was writing a mythology, the names of its various members derived from acronyms based on descriptive phrases. There were, for instance, a race of miniature women, the Posall ("Perhaps Our Souls Are Little Ladies"), and men, the Mosalm ("Maybe Our Souls Are Little Men"). Siquomb was the queen of the mythology, her name meaning, "She is Queen Undisputedly of Mind Beauty."

Indisputably, Siquomb saved Joni Mitchell from the kinds of schemes that typically rob songwriters of their work. One of her first songs was "Urge For Going," which eventually concerned romantic parting, though in its original form it was about the difficulty acoustic folk performers were starting to have finding places to play in the wake of the fold-rock movement ushered in by Bob Dylan's decision to use an amplified backup band. "The clubs were going electric," she recalled, and the first draft (of "Urge for Going") was about that: 'I've got the urge for going, but there's no place left to go.'"

Another early composition was "The Circle Game," Mitchell's song about a young boy's rites of passage. It was inspired by another song, Neil Young's "Sugar Mountain." Mitchell had met Young in 1964 at the Fourth Dimension folk club at the University of Manitoba, and encountered him again in the Yorkville district of Toronto in 1965. Young, a member of the Squires rock 'n' roll group, had written "Sugar Mountain" on his nineteenth birthday, November 12, 1964, as a lament for the approaching

end of his teenage years ("You can't be twenty on Sugar Mountain.") Mitchell took the story to its logical conclusion, but offered hope. "So the years spin by and now the boy is twenty/ Though his dreams have lost some grandeur coming true/ There'll be new dreams, maybe better dreams and plenty/ Before the last revolving year is through."

And then there was "Both Sides, Now." The obvious influence for its theme was the music of Bob Dylan, especially his 1964 album *Another Side Of Bob Dylan*, with its songs in which the singer disavows previous beliefs, especially "My Back pages." In Mitchell's hands, the theme takes on less political, more aesthetic form, as she gives us poetic descriptions of clouds, love, and life, then strips the poetry away in favor of stark disillusion, only to reject that, too, and conclude that she still doesn't know them at all.

Here were found the basic themes of her early songwriting. Over and over, she wrote about aging and disillusionment, though frequently hanging back from outright pessimism. "I think at twenty-one I was quite old," she said. "'Both Sides, Now' is like an old person reflecting back on their life. My life had been very hard. I had gone through a lot of life. When Chuck Mitchell and I wrote 'Both Sides, Now,' he said to me, 'Oh, what do you know about life, you're only twenty-one.' But I knew a lot about life. I'd gone through a lot of disease and personal pain. Even as a child. I'd had three bouts with death. I was not unaware of my mortality. But somehow, still, I was very young for my age, in spite of my experience."

Based in Detroit, Chuck and Joni Mitchell traveled to folk clubs in the northern Midwest and along the East Coast, and when they were at home, they played host to fellow folk musicians in town to play the Chessman, the local folk club.

"In Detroit, everybody was kind of scuffling, and we had a big apartment, Chuck and I, so we billeted a lot of artists," Mitchell said. "Eric Andersen stayed there, and Tom Rush stayed there. It was a fifth floor walkup in the black district; basically, it was two white blocks, Wayne campus housing. The rent was really cheap, and we had three or four bedrooms in this old place. So, artists stayed with us frequently. I was just beginning to write, and Tom, I think, first carried off 'Urge for Going.' So, he played that around, and the next time he came to play the Chessman, he said, 'You got anything else?' and I played him some songs. It was usually the one that I thought was too feminine, a little too light for a man to sing, that I withheld—'Any more?' 'Well, yes, this one, but it's not right for you'—'The Circle Game' or something—'That's the one I want.' So, he'd cart that off, and in that way the songs became known in places that I hadn't gone. There were no records."

Soon enough, however, there were records. The first, curiously enough, was by country singer George Hamilton IV, who cut "Urge for Going." In a March 1967 live appearance, introducing the song, Mitchell told her audience, "It's currently on the country hit parade. However, I don't think it really is a country song, if you can classify songs. As a matter of fact, it's~1#13 with a bullet. That means it's moving up rapidly. It's by a fellow named George Hamilton IV. The song is by me, but he does it, with Chet Atkins and whole Nashville chorus and a Carter Family type and all sorts of people and a recitation and electric rock 'n' roll mandolin. But originally the song went like this..."

Hamilton's cover of "Urge For Going," released as a single by RCA, entered Billboard's Hot Country Singles chart for the week ending January 21, 1967, and peaked at #7 during a twenty-one-week chart run. (Unless otherwise stated, all chart figures cited here will be from *Billboard*, as reported in Joel Whitburn's various chart books, published by Record Research, Inc. On occasions when a record performs better on charts published by the rival trade paper *Cash Box*, this will be noted.)

Mitchell isn't sure how Hamilton got hold of the song, but she credits Tom Rush, who may also have pitched it—unsuccessfully—to Judy Collins. "At one point, George came to Detroit, and I remember meeting him," Mitchell said, "but I think he must have heard the song first from Tom."

By the time "Urge For Going" had ended its chart run, other Joni Mitchell compositions were coming onto the market. In February, Vanguard Records released Canadian duo Ian and Sylvia's *So Much For Dreaming* album, containing their rendition of "The Circle Game." In June, Vanguard released Buffy Sainte-Marie's *Fire And Fleet And Candlelight* LP, which included "The Circle Game" and "Song To A Seagull."

"I picked up music more for fun," Mitchell said. "I had no ambition to make a career of it at all." But when her songs started to become popular, this changed. "Of course, once I began to write my own songs, I was slightly ambitious for them," she admitted. "I was a stage door mother to them. I wanted to display them. I thought that this was a

superior work to selling women's ware, which was all I was really trained for. I had a grade twelve education. So waitressing, hairdressing, that was about all. This was slightly more lucrative and lot more fun at the club level."

And at the club level, her increasing renown as a songwriter was boosting her as a performer, helping her break the one city she'd been having trouble playing, New York. "I had difficulty initially in finding work in the clubs (in New York)," Mitchell said, "but I had a kind of a circuit on the Eastern seaboard from Miami to Boston, and a little bit in the Midwest around the Detroit area. New York was difficult without a record. The major clubs were hard to crack until some people started singing my songs. When Buffy and Tom Rush initially began to play (them), then the circuit that they played on opened up to me because they were kind of a herald of the writer of these songs. So, 'Circle Game' and 'Urge for Going,' (Dave) Van Ronk was 'Both Sides, Now' (which he retitled, "Clouds") and 'Chelsea Morning,' all helped to make club work possible for me."

This, in turn, seems to have given Mitchell the impetus she needed to split up with her husband and go out on her own. The dramatic circumstances of that move suggest it was anything but an amicable parting.

"I was in the middle of a poker game some place in Michigan late in the evening," Mitchell recalled, "and I turned to a stranger, basically, next to me, and I said, 'I'm leaving my husband tonight. Will you help me?' We rented a U-Haul truck. We drove back to Detroit.

"I had polio, and a lot of the muscles in my back are deteriorated. So, you can imagine the will. I separated what I considered was a fair split, fifty percent of the furniture, and the stranger and I hauled it on our own backs down a fifth floor walkup in the middle of the night, and I moved out. The song 'I Had A King' kind of tells a bit of the aftermath of that. I moved to New York. I moved to West 16th Street, and I set out looking for work in that area."

Despite the success she had found with her songs and the increased club work, Mitchell was not naive about her chances for making it big in the music business. She considered those chances small, and, in fact, in 1967, the year of the *Summer of Love*, the year of *Sgt. Pepper*, the chances for a songwriter with only an acoustic guitar could not have been considered very great. The people who were recording her songs were folkies, none of them big sellers, all of them essentially sideswiped two years earlier by the rise of folk-rock, which was itself already giving way to other pop trends.

Mitchell could see all this by the time she got to New York. "I came in late," she said. "Basically, clubs were folding, and bands were the new things, and I wasn't ready for a band. It would take me five albums to find a band that could play with me without squashing the intricacy of the music."

At this point, though, she wasn't thinking about five albums, or even one. "Record companies offered me terrible slave labor deals in the beginning, and I turned them down," she said. "I turned down Vanguard. They wanted three albums a year or something. In the folk tradition, they come and stick a mike on the table in front of you, and they collect it in an hour, and that's the album. And that output—I already saw Buffy struggling under the weight of it. So, I thought, no way. This'll take the fun out of it. There's no remuneration. It was a terrible contract, the highlight of which was, they would provide little folding table-top cards that said I was a vanguard artist, and it would have driven my price up slights, I guess. To be a recording artist, I could have made a little more in the clubs, but not that much, and it would have required that I have a manager."

A manager was another thing she didn't want. "Of course, the managers wanted a big hunk of (my song publishing), and I turned down a lot of managers," Mitchell said. "I said, no way, this is my little business. You're not writing these songs. It's kind of like the story of the little red hen. You know, 'Who will help me sow the wheat?' I didn't understand the way that management was structured at that time."

Nor did Mitchell understand how she was going to make it when she was perceived as a folk singer, even if she had ceased thinking of herself that way. "I looked like a folk singer, even though the moment I began to write, my music was not folk music," she said. "It was something else, maybe closer to German lieder, or it had elements of romantic classicism to it." Nevertheless, it sounded to a lot of people like folk music, and folk music was on its way out.

"I wasn't keen waiting for my big break or anything," Mitchell said. "As a matter of fact, I entered into the game thinking that this was the tail end of an ear. The minimum wage at that time was $36 a week, you could barely eat and pay your rent on it, and I was able to make about $300 a week in the clubs. Traveling, of course, ate up some of it. But I had no manager, I had no agent, I had no liens on me. So, I viewed it initially as a way to get a little nest egg ahead, and then I would fall back on salesmanship. I would go back into women's ware. My idea of a little bit ahead was the rent paid and enough for the next month, like, $400 in the bank."

In fact, she achieved her goal in 1967. "That's probably the richest I ever felt," she recalled, "because after I had my recording deal, I had a lot of people on my payroll, and unless you're an arena artist, it's a lot of work, and everything you do is self-promotion."

Despite that $400 nest egg, Mitchell kept accepting engagements, including, in the early fall of 1967, an offer by British-based American record executive and producer Joe Boyd to undertake a brief tour of Great Britain. "Joe set up a tour with the Incredible String Band, and some isolated little gigs without them in small coffee house," she recalled.

Boyd was especially interested in Mitchell as a songwriter, and he arranged a U.K. publishing deal for her with Essex Music. She left a ten-song demo tape with Boyd, who played it for his clients, the folk-rock group Fairport Convention. Fairport recorded a demo of "Both Sides, Now" at sessions for their debut single, "If I Had A Ribbon Bow," released in November. "I Don't Know Where I Stand" and "Chelsea Morning" would turn up on their debut album, *Fairport Convention*, released in June 1968, and they added "Marcie" and "Night In The City" to their concert repertoire.

(In January 1969, they would include "Eastern Rain," a song Mitchell herself has never released officially, on their second album, titled *What We Did On Our Holidays* in the U.K. and *Fairport Convention* in the U.S.)

"The first time I heard 'Both Sides Now,'" Judy Collins wrote in her autobiography, *Trust Your Heart* (Houghton Mifflin Company, 1987), "was on the phone in 1967 during the middle of the night. I got a call from Tom Rush, who was very excited. Tom, a great fan of Joni's, had earlier introduced me to her and to her fine song 'The Circle Game.'

"'Joni has a new song, and I want you to hear it. I think you'll love it.' He put Joni on the phone, and she sang 'Both Sides Now.'

"I immediately fell in love with the song and knew it was a classic. I had to sing it."

Judy Collins recorded "Both Sides Now" (while Van Ronk had changed the title completely, Collins merely removed the comma after "Sides") on September 28, 1967, at Columbia Studios in New York with a string arrangement by Joshua Rifkin, who played harpsichord on the track. Collins also recorded Mitchell's "Michael From Mountains," and the two songs were used as the opening tracks on either side of Collins' album *Wildflowers*, released in November.

Like Joan Baez, Judy Collins had begun as a singer of traditional folk songs and, in the wake of the folk songwriter boom led by Bob Dylan, begun to champion the work of new writers. Unlike many of her folk peers, she had neither ignored the rise of folk-rock in 1965 nor entirely given in to it, instead branching out into tasteful arrangements and adding theater music to her repertoire. She had been rewarded in 1967 by the audience that greeted the LP *In My Life*, making it her most successful album so far. *Wildflowers*, on which she introduced both Mitchell's songs and her own, was intended to consolidate that success and extend it. It would.

Photo/Henry Diltz

Mitchell, meanwhile, was still having some trouble with the New York club circuit, and beginning to think that maybe having a manager wouldn't be such a bad idea. "I had a hard time playing in New York," she said. "I cried and pleased, said, 'I'm good, I'm good.' I had no manager to, like, front for me. Finally, this place (the Cafe Au Go Go) hired me as an opening act to an opening act. Ian and Sylvia were the headliners, and there was a comic in the middle and I was in really foot-soldier position. I had all of the songs at that point that would constitute my first two albums.

"Elliot (Roberts) came in. He was a manager of comics. He came in to hear the comedian, Howard Hesseman. And people were talking, you know, the opening act to the opening act, nobody was really listening to me. Elliot thought that, God, this girl is really good. Why is nobody listening to her?"

Elliot Roberts (both Elliot Rabinowitz in the Bronx), then working at the William Morris Agency, represented a new type of manager, appropriate to the new type of entertainers who were emerging in the second half of the 1960s. For one thing, he didn't want a piece of Mitchell's publishing. As he told Steve Chapple and Reebee Garofalo for their book *Rock 'N' Roll Is Here To Pay: The History And Politics Of The Music Industry* (Nelson-Hall, 1977), "People see now that they can become millionaires by doing it right. People used to think you had to beat someone for all their publishing to hit the jackpot. We showed them that it was the other way around. If you left the publishing there and did the right thing by the artist, and the artist was good, then you'd make it."

Beyond that crucial matter, Roberts was ready to adapt himself to the special needs of his clients. "Let's say you wanted me to manage you," he said. "Well, we'd have to get together. I'd have to find out what you wanted, and what you're like, whether you're abrasive and hard, or soft and sensitive. I'd have to find out what you're capable of. Whether you can go on all these interviews or whether you would get shell-shocked. All this varies from person to person. It's all in the person. What do you want to be? Do you want to retire in three or four years? You know, that's all part of it. It depends on what the person wants."

What Roberts found out initially was what Joni Mitchell didn't want. "He pitched being my manager, and I said, 'I don't need a manager. I'm doing quite nicely. Why should I cut you in?'" Mitchell recalled. "But he was a funny man. I enjoyed his humor. So, I said, 'Okay, let's do a trial run. I've got a gig coming up in the Midwest near Detroit. Why don't you accompany me, and we'll see how we get along?'" The resulting trip, which, according to Roberts, began the next day, sounds like a folkie version of This Is Spinal Tap, but it solidified their relationship.

"We went to this town, Ann Arbor, Michigan," Mitchell recalled. "Pot was legal there, and Elliot was a pot smoker, but people were very secretive about that. He was also dressed in a suit with silk shirts with his initials on the pocket. She was (his friend and later partner David) Geffen at that time. They were very Madison Avenue.

"So, we get to this hotel, and it's before the gig, and we don't let each other know that we smoke pot. But I get to his room, and I can smell that he's been smoking pot, and he's got a towel under the door and everything, and I realize that he's as bad as me. He has no mechanical aptitude. He can't find the light switch, he can't turn his TV set on. Anyway, we end up on our way to this gig. We get lost in the hotel. The hotel was like kind of a square donut shape, and we literally could not find our way out (laughs), and we wandered through soup kitchens and all kinds of places, and he was so funny.

"When we finally got to this club, it was packed not only to capacity, but there were people standing in the back. It was the biggest crowd I ever drew at that point. I got up on the stage and I sang my first song, and there was, to me, a thunderous reception. I broke out into a wide grin, and my upper lip stuck to my gums and I couldn't get it down! I had to peel it with my tongue. Elliot was doing loud shtick from the audience. He was making a lot of jokes and everybody was giggling 'cause everybody knew why. And so, I said to him, 'Okay, you're my manager.' I enjoyed his company on the road so much. He was good, and I was a great straight man for him. So, in this way we began."

Roberts quit his job at William Morris and began working full-time for Joni Mitchell. His first goal, of course, was to obtain a record contract for her. But if independent folk labels like Vanguard were interested, the majors were not. Roberts tried Columbia Records, the home of Bob Dylan, with its self-professed talent scout of a company president Clive Davis. They weren't interested, maybe because Roberts' friend David Geffen was pitching them another female singer-songwriter, Laura Nyro, who they signed instead.

Roberts next tried RCA. "We brought them Joni songs and demos," he told Chapple and Garofalo, "and they said, 'That's nice, a girl and some songs, but it's not making it. We're looking for the Rascals or Wilson Pickett.'"

Many people are credited with "discovering" Joni Mitchell, from Tom Rush to Joe Boyd to Elliot Roberts, and Mitchell graciously admits them all. "These all, in their own way, were kind of discoveries," she said when the list was read off to her. But it would take one more discoverer to get her career going.

On October 16, 1967, in Los Angeles, David Crosby made his last recording session with the Byrds. Crosby, the son of a Hollywood cinematographer, had made his way through the folk music boom of the early 1960s with a love for harmony, jazz chords, and unusual guitar tunings. In 1964, in the wake of the British Invasion, he formed a group with fellow folkies Jim (later Roger) McGuinn and Gene Clark. By 1965, with the addition of the rhythm section of bassist Chris Hillman and drummer Michael Clarke, they were the Byrds, America's primary answer to the Beatles and among the sounds of folk-rock with their ringing version of Bob Dylan's "Mr. Tambourine Man."

But by the fall of 1967, Gene Clark was gone, their singles were struggling to make the Top 40 and a rivalry had grown up between McGuinn, lead singer on the Byrds' hits, and Crosby, who wanted more room for his own often daring compositions, including "Triad," a song in praise of a menage a trois. This all come to a head at the end of October, when the other Byrds bought Crosby out and fired him.

Photo/Henry Diltz

At loose ends, Crosby went to Coconut Grove, one of his old haunts in southern Florida. "When I was down there as a folkie, I used to do all kinds of sailing," he wrote in his autobiography, *Long Time Gone* (written with Carl Gottlieb, Doubleday, 1988).

"At least one of us was always working at a boat rental yard, so we'd get permission to take them out at night and sail around Biscayne Bay all night long, smoking joints and laughing like fools and having a great time. After the Byrds, I came down and hung around, looking for a boat. Wasn't quite sure how I would get it, but I knew something would turn up that would be right."

Actually, two things turned up. One was a sailboat called the Mayan, and the other was Joni Mitchell. "I was playing the Gaslight South," she recalled. "He came into the club one night and was very interested in my tunings."

There was a little more to it than that. "Right away I thought I'd been hit by a hand grenade," Crosby told biographer Dave Zimmer (Crosby, Stills & Nash: The Authorized Biography, with photography by Henry Diltz, St. Martin's Press, 1984). "Her voice, those words...she nailed me to the back of the wall with two-inch spikes. I went up to her afterwards and said, 'You're incredible.' She said, 'You really think so?'"

Roberts had not accompanied Mitchell to Florida, instead flying to California for a meeting with West Coast-based Warner Bros. Records. Warner Bros. was the one major label interested in signing singer-songwriters. Over the next few years, the company would record folkies like Tom Paxton, Gordon Lightfoot, and Eric Andersen, after their initial deals had ended, ex-group leaders like John Sebastian of the Lovin' Spoonful, Neil Young of Buffalo Springfield and Van Morrison of Them, James Taylor, whose career had been fumbled by the Beatles' Apple label, and such homegrown talent as Randy Newman and Van Dyke Parks.

Such as the direction provided by label head Mo Ostin, who had come into the company in 1963 from Frank Sinatra's Reprise label when Warners bought it. Warner-Reprise hadn't been able to come up with much to challenge the British Invasion (though it had joined it by licensing the Kinks for American distribution), but with laudatory selectivity, the company enlisted the services of one of the major San Francisco acid-rock groups, the Grateful Dead, plucked Frank Zappa and the Mothers from the faltering hands of MGM, and picked up the Jimi Hendrix Experience for the U.S. The result was an eclectic roster far removed from the less discriminatory habits of labels like Columbia and its "throw 'em against the wall and see what sticks" philosophy.

(Record executive Joe Smith, who brought the Dead to Warners, told Chapple and Garofalo that the company's signings did not reflect a deliberate decision to contract singer-songwriters, but rather "the personal tastes" of Ostin and himself.)

None of which is to suggest that, when Mo Ostin agreed to sign Joni Mitchell for a $15,000 advance, he knew exactly what he was getting. Probably, her first album would have been tricked out with folk-rock arrangements if it hadn't been for David Crosby, who came in to produce it. "To many corporate executives, I looked like a second-generation Judy Collins or Joan Baez because I was a girl with a guitar," Mitchell explained. "The same thing they do to young women now, they liken them to me. (Did someone say "Tori Amos"?) So, basically, they wanted a folk-rocker. David believed in my music as it was. He knew that it was taking that some place, but it didn't look like it was taking it that some place, and the people in power couldn't really hear that it was taking it some place. As a matter of fact, I was an oddity on the scene."

Mitchell, with Crosby in tow, arrived back in New York and met with Roberts in his office on West 57th Street. "He was," Roberts said in Long Time Gone, "the first hippie that I met in that era." The three took off for California to record Mitchell's first album.

Under Crosby's laissez-faire production style, the album was cut quickly at Sunset Sound in Los Angeles. Far from a folk-rock record, it featured Mitchell alone on guitar and piano. The only added instrumentation was some bass guitar played by Stephen Stills of Buffalo Springfield, who were recording at the studio next door. Also in the Springfield, of course, was Neil Young, Mitchell's old friend from Canada, and they were able to renew their acquaintance. Roberts, meeting these various artists for the first time, would wind up managing all of them.

The album was finished by February, when Mitchell took off for her club circuit back on the East Coast, starting in Ottawa. While there, she was introduced to Graham Nash, who was on tour with the Hollies and had heard of her from his friend Crosby.

When Mitchell got back to Los Angeles, Crosby set out to showcase her to various people in the business, playing an advance copy of her album or having her sing in person. In Long Time Gone, Roberts describes one such impromptu concert. "Sure, they played (disc jockey) B. Mitchell Reed's

house too. David invited some people over one day. I remember Cass (Elliot) was there, John Sebastian, Michelle Phillips, about seven or eight people, all heavy players. David says, 'Joan,' and called Joni out. She was upstairs and came down with her guitar and she played eight or nine of the best songs ever written. The next day B. Mitchell Reid talked about it on the radio, how there was this girl in town named Joni Mitchell that's recording an album and there's nothing he can play now, but whenever this album comes out, it's going to be one of the great albums of all time. David set it up so that when the album finally came out, everyone in L.A. was aware of Joni Mitchell. The first club date we played, at the Troubadour, was standing room only for four nights, two shows a night."

The Hollies, meanwhile, arrived in L.A. on tour, and Nash came to see Crosby, setting off a turn of events that would inspire several songs. "I was living with David," Mitchell said in Long Time Gone. "Graham and I had had kind of a ill-fated beginning of a romance because we had met in Ontario...

"He ended up at David's place and I was staying with David until my house was ready. Graham came down sick in David's house and I took him home to my new house to play Florence Nightingale. At first it wasn't really for romance's sake... I took him home and was looking after him and I got attached—here was a mess. What was I going to say? I'm kind of going with David and we sort of staked claims, but I'd written all these independent songs, trying to explain my position to him; that I'm still in an independent mode. But I got really attached to Graham and I guess that's the first time I harbored the illusion of forever. I really felt for the first time in my life that I could pair bond."

"I went with her," said Nash, "and I didn't leave for a couple of years."

The author if "Triad," meanwhile, said, "The thing with Joni and Graham was that I felt great about it." Crosby went back to his old girlfriend, Christine Hinton. And the world was treated to such songs as Mitchell's "Willy," Nash's "Our House" and Crosby's "Guinnevere" (which is partially about Hinton, partially about Mitchell).

Joni Mitchell was released in March 1968, and the first thing to say about it is to confirm that the title was *Joni Mitchell*. The album's cover, a painting by Mitchell surrounding a tiny photograph of her, features a grouping of birds that spell out the words "Song To A Seagull," the title of one of the songs. Not only has this led many people to call the album Song To A Seagull, but several reputable rock 'n' roll history books (one example being *The Rolling Stone Rock & Roll Encyclopedia*, edited by Jon Pareles and Patricia Romanowski (Rolling Stone Press/Summit Books, 1983)) list two different albums, one called *Joni Mitchell*, the other *Song To A Seagull*.

Mitchell, when informed of this, expressed surprise. "People can't see them," she said of the birds, "and the 'L' (of Seagull) is cut off, 'cause even the graphic department, they didn't see it either. It's called *Joni Mitchell*."

To anyone who had been attending Joni Mitchell's club performances, the album must have been a surprise, at least in terms of the song selection. First, her best-known material—"Urge For Going," "The Circle Game," "Both Side, Now"—was nowhere to be found. Nor were some of her lighter, funnier songs. Instead, more recent material, the "independent songs" she had been writing while living with Crosby, were here, arranged in a loose story line that followed her recent history. "Part One," the first side, was titled, "I Came To The City," and began with "I Had A King," her account of her split with Chuck Mitchell, followed by songs reflecting on city life. "Part Two," subtitled, "Out Of The City And Down To The Seaside," included songs like "The Dawntreader," and life on Crosby's boat, "The Pirate Of Penance" and "Cactus Tree," about "a man who's been out sailing" and "a lady in the city."

Whatever else such an arrangement of material may have meant, it presented a different Joni Mitchell from the one audiences were used to in clubs, where her sense of humor and wit balanced the ornamentation and preciousness of some of her lyrics. "See, there you're looking at a slightly different form," she explained. "An album was basically twenty-two minutes per side. In a club, you're writing for sets, which are a little longer. I forget now—it's so long since I played a club set—but I think it was about ten songs, maybe fourteen songs. You're doing three and four sets a night, and some people are staying for two sets, so there has to be some variation between sets.

"Also, as an entertainer, you're looking to keep your audience awake, and so there's kind of little comedic things like 'Dr. Junk The Dentist Man' and funny little songs from back where I felt, I need a laugh here, this is too much drama, and none of those things found their way onto albums. I must have twenty or thirty songs prior to the first album that never were recorded."

Later, when Mitchell began to introduce some of her humor on records, it sometimes contributed to the critical backlash she suffered in the late 1970s. Though she is referring to Crosby's preservation of her acoustic presentation, one of the comments she makes in *Long Time Gone* about the album is telling:

"...The way you enter the game in this business is usually the way you stay. It takes a lot to break typecasting and the way you come into the game is crucial, which was something I didn't realize at the time. In retrospect, I realize the importance of it."

Actually, at the time, *Joni Mitchell* didn't get that much attention. It entered the charts on May 18 at #197 and peaked three weeks later at #189, lasting a total of nine weeks near the bottom of the Top 200.

But other events were conspiring to put Joni Mitchell before the public. For one thing, the musical climate, which, only the previous fall, had seemed to favor psychedelia and the elaborate eclecticism of Sgt. Pepper, had changed in favor of her approach. Bob Dylan's comeback album, *John Wesley Harding*, released the last week of 1967 on the same day as Leonard Cohen's debut LP *Songs Of Leonard Cohen*, countered the new complexity with a new simplicity. Soon after, Simon and Garfunkel topped the charts with *Bookends* and the soundtrack to The Graduate, and soft, quiet folkie music seemed to be back.

At the same time, Mitchell's folkie champions continued to record her material. April saw the release of Tom Rush's *The Circle Game*, containing the title track, "Tin Angel" and—finally—his version of "Urge For Going." Rush's album hit #68. The same month, Dave Van Ronk and the Hudson Dusters released their self-titled album, featuring "Chelsea Morning" and the song he insisted on calling "Clouds."

But the biggest factor in broadening Joni Mitchell's exposure was Judy Collins. After its release in November 1967, her *Wildflowers* LP, containing Mitchell's "Both Sides Now" and "Michael From Mountains," had enjoyed a curious chart history. Most albums of the time had a simple sales profile: a couple of weeks after release, they would enter the charts and rise to a peak, then gradually fall back down and off the list.

Not *Wildflowers*, the sales profile of which would have looked like a mountain range rather than a single spire. It entered the charts of January 6, 1968, at #145 and rose up the chart for the next several weeks, peaking at #47 on March 9. It then began to drop, but reversed itself after hitting a low at #67 on April 13 and slowly began to rise again. On June 22, it hit a new high of #43, and it rose to #36 by July 13 before starting to sink again, but it remained in the Top 50 for the rest of the summer.

On September 21, it suddenly dropped from #45 to #76, seeming to indicate that, thirty-eight weeks into its chart run, it was finally running out of gas. But it continued to bounce around in the lower half of the Top 100 for the next several weeks, and it was

at #60 on November 2, the day that a single of "Both Sides Now," released nearly a year after the album on which it appeared, entered the *Cash Box* singles chart at #19 and made *Billboard*'s Bubbling Under The Hot 100 chart at #120.

Curiously, *Wildflowers* started to slip as "Both Sides Now" went up the singles chart, but on November 23, as "Both Sides Now" made the Top 20, it jumped twenty places to #48, and by December 14, it had hit a new peak at #31, while *In My Life*, Collins' previous album, had re-entered the charts. On December 21, "Both Sides Now" peaked at #8 on the Hot 100, and the following week, *Wildflowers* celebrated a full year in the charts by reaching its final peak at #5 on the LP chart.

"Both Sides Now" became an instant standard, appearing on albums by at least fifteen different artists in 1969 alone, and it is no doubt the most widely recorded song Joni Mitchell ever wrote. It has been recorded by Frank Sinatra, Bing Crosby, Neil Diamond, Andy Williams, and Willie Nelson, among many others.

The situation did not go unnoticed at Warner Bros., of course, but the way the company chose to exploit its association with the hit offended its artist. In explaining the context of this incident, we must begin by noting that the late 1960s was a strange time in American life and 1968 was the strangest year of the time period. Unrest over the Vietnam War, coming on the heels of the Civil Rights movement, and paralleled by the counter-cultural trends in lifestyles, combined to make things tough on everybody—hippies, straights, blacks, whites.

Even record company executives who, as always, just wanted to sell records. The good news was that, in the aftermath of the British Invasion, record sales were booming. The bad news was that record companies found themselves signing artists they didn't understand who played music they didn't like and selling it to an audience they didn't know. The counter-culture, which bought the lion's share of the records, also seemed to be a bunch of anti-capitalist revolutionaries. The record companies tried to appease them.

Lenin pointed out that capitalists will sell you the rope you can then use to hang them with, and the record companies were trying. (Any similarity the reader may perceive to the current gangsta rap music scene is strictly coincidental, but not at all surprising.)

One place where the company meets the consumer—or tries to—is in advertising, and you can see the strain in the record company ads of the day. The most notorious example is Columbia Records' "The Man Can't Bust Our Music" campaign that sought to align the label's acts and the label itself with the revolution and somehow escape the onus of being part of the establishment.

Warner Bros. took a slightly different approach. Its ads, designed by Stan Cornyn, were intended to appeal to the sly, irreverent side of the counterculture. For example, when Randy Newman's debut album failed to sell despite glowing reviews in 1968, Warners took out an ad in the trades under a headline reading, "Want a free album? Okay." The ad noted that the company was unable to sell the album, had hundreds on hand, and would give a thousand of them away free, to those who sent in an enclosed coupon. The tone of the ad copy was satiric: at one point, it speculated about what would happen after the offer was over: "Which brings us to the age-old dilemma: can the girt who gave it away ever hope to sell it?"

Today, such a remark might get somebody sued for sexual harassment, and that brings us to Joni Mitchell, who also had a poor-selling album in 1968, while her song "Both Sides Now" (not contained on her record) became a big hit for Judy Collins. This inspired Cornyn to write an ad with a headline reading, "Joni Mitchell is 90% virgin."

The point, if you read the copy, was that Collins had sold ten times as many records as Mitchell had, but the headline statement flagged a part of Joni Mitchell's image that has both helped and hurt her, and that she has never entirely escaped.

In fact, Mitchell brought it up in her *Goldmine* interview, noting that, in an earlier interview as part of the press junket she's been on promoting Turbulent Indigo, she was "confronted" with a copy of the ad in Toronto, as well as Cornyn's followup ads, "Joni Mitchell takes forever," bemoaning the time it took her to finish records, and, announcing tile release of her second album, "Joni Mitchell finally comes across."

"I must have seemed very peculiar to them," Mitchell said of Warners. "I had an innocence. By that time, I'd be about twenty-five, but I felt and looked about sixteen. So, I think that innocence is—they want—the temptation with innocence is to corrupt it, and since I was not corrupting myself—I wasn't showing my tits, I had very low necklines, but they were demure. In a way, they didn't really know what to do with me. I was neither an anarchist nor—I wasn't rough-mouthed. I was a Canadian girl.

Not that it wasn't within me, under the right circumstances. But under the wrong circumstances, if I was rough-mouthed, I would embarrass people because of their view."

Mitchell acknowledged that this innocent image had its advantages, just as it had back in Saskatoon when she was a teenager. "People tended to be protective of me," she said, "and even in the scene when cocaine was around, people would shelter me from it. Everyone would be doing it, but they wouldn't do it in front of me. So, somehow or other, I brought out protectiveness in people well into my thirties, which was all right. It helps you survive some pretty tough situations."

But Mitchell did not feel protected by the Warners ads, and they would be one reason she left the company in 1971.

Meanwhile, Roberts put her on the road to take advantage of her increasing success on records. In September 1968, she was in London at the Royal Festival Hall, appearing with Al Stewart and Fairport Convention in "An Evening of Contemporary Song." In December, she played the Miami Pop Festival, appearing before 100,000 people. On February 1, 1969, she made her debut at Carnegie Hall in New York.

In the midst of touring, she found time to cut her second album, which, despite her objection to Dave Van Ronk's title change, was called *Clouds* and finally contained her version of "Both Sides, Now." Indeed, the album was a combination of older songs like "Chelsea Morning" and "I Don't Know Where I Stand" and newer ones that frequently took direct, personal glimpses at romance. "I Don't Know Where I Stand" is perhaps the most telling statement of romantic doubt ever committed to disc, and girls everywhere copied out the lyrics and sent them to insufficiently attentive lovers. (Unfortunately, the author can cite personal experience on this point.) "The Gallery," meanwhile, was a dissection of the techniques of a subtle Romeo—no matter how the other lines change, the phrase "Turn down your bed" remains in every variation of his line.

On May 1, Mitchell taped an appearance on "The Johnny Cash Show," her network TV debut. It was broadcast on ABC on June 7. The show also featured a rare appearance by Bob Dylan, who Mitchell met for the first time.

Clouds entered the charts on June 14 at #93, ninety-six slots higher than her previous peak, and reached #31 on July 19, lasting a total of thirty-six

weeks. This time, when Judy Collins released a one-off single of "Chelsea Morning" in July, Mitchell's own version also was available. (It hit #78 in August and turned up on Collins' *Living* album in the fall of 1971, where, of course, it was heard by Bill and Hillary Clinton, who later named their daughter after it.)

Mitchell's friends and lovers Crosby, Stills, Nash, and Young had formed a group by the summer of 1969, and Mitchell, currently living with Nash and handled by the same management (Roberts had by now formed a company with David Geffen called Geffen-Roberts), frequently traveled with them. During the first weekend of August, she performed at the Atlantic City Pop Festival in New Jersey, where she quickly discovered that playing to an audience of a quarter-million was quite a different experience than playing to a rapt club crowd. Attempting unsuccessfully to grab the attention of the noisy festival-goers with her soft, acoustic songs, a frustrated Mitchell stormed off the stage after offering only a few songs, commenting something to the effect that if they weren't interested, neither was she.

Two weeks later, she was with CSN&Y in New York, but as reports of the first chaotic day of the Woodstock festival came out, it was decided that she would not accompany them to the site. She was scheduled to appear on Dick Cavett's talk show on the Monday night after the weekend festival, and it was feared they might not be back in time. Also, as she told Dave Zimmer, "I was the girl of the family

and, with great disappointment, I was the one that had to stay behind." (As it turned out, Crosby, Stills and Young appeared on the Cavett show with her.)

Stuck in a hotel room while history was being made in the mud at Yasgur's Farm, Mitchell found inspiration. "The deprivation of not being able to go provided me with an intense angle on Woodstock," she told Zimmer. "I was one of the fans. I was put in the position of being a kid who couldn't make it. So I was glued to the media. And at the time I was going through a kind of born-again Christian trip—not that I went to any church; I'd given up Christianity at an early age in Sunday school. But suddenly, as performers, we were in the position of having so many people look to us for leadership, and for some unknown reason, I took it seriously and decided I needed a guide and leaned on God.

"So I was a little 'God mad' at the time, for lack of a better term, and I had been saying to myself, 'Where are the modern miracles? Where are the modern miracles?' Woodstock, for some reason, impressed me as being a modern miracle, like a modern-day fishes-and-loaves story. For a herd of people that large to cooperate so well, it was pretty remarkable and there was tremendous optimism. So I wrote the song 'Woodstock' out of these feelings, and the first three times I performed it in public, I burst into tears, because it brought back the intensity of the experience and was so moving."

"Woodstock" is actually something of a throwback to Mitchell songs like "Both Sides, Now" and "The Circle Game," both in its sense of disillusionment and longing for an idealized world, and in its circular imagery.

Mitchell continued to tour with CSN&Y, opening for them at the Greek Theatre on the campus of UCLA on August 20, and at the Big Sur Folk Festival in September. Like Woodstock, that festival was taped, and it would result, more than a year later, in Mitchell's feature film debut, Celebration At Big Sur (1971), one of many festival documentaries released in the wake of the success of Monterey Pop and Woodstock. Mitchell's "Song To Aging Children," meanwhile, turned up on the soundtrack of a movie version of Arlo Guthrie's story song "Alice's Restaurant," in theaters in the fall and in the charts, up to #63. The version was sung by one Tigger Outlaw.

In two years, Joni Mitchell had gone from being the opening act to an opening act in a Greenwich Village club to being a worldwide headliner. But by the beginning of 1970, she had been on the road for a year, and it had become too much. On February 17, after appearing at the Royal Albert Hall in London, she announced that she was quitting live appearances.

Asked to compare the club work, which she seemed to enjoy, with the concert work, which she clearly did not, Mitchell said, "It's not the number of the people, because it all abstracts, but you can't see faces from the big stage, and you're subject to severe adjudication, and it's not as much fun. I never liked the big stage. The looseness and the heart went out of it for me.

"I got to the point where I kept asking my manager at that time, 'Let me quit, let me quit,' and he couldn't understand it till he came out one night for 'Circle Game' and it was towards the end of the show, and he saw my knuckles were white on the strings. It was very, very unpleasant for me to be up on that stage. There was no rapport. It didn't feel friendly."

In fact, there was even more to it than that, as she explained to *Musician* magazine's Bill Flanagan in an interview conducted in the fall of 1985 and later published in his book *Written In My Soul: Rock's Great Songwriters Talk About Creating Their Music* (Contemporary Books, 1986). "I really enjoyed playing clubs for about forty people," she said. "I liked being center of attention. It was like being the life of the party. That I could handle. When it got to the big stage, I found that I didn't enjoy it. It frightened me initially. I had a lot of bad experiences, including running off many a stage. I just thought it was too big for me, it was out of proportion. This kind of attention was absurd."

Part of the reason Mitchell didn't trust the adulation was that it came for the same performances that had attracted only scant attention before. "I don't like receiving things that don't mean anything," she said. "I couldn't get work in these little piddling clubs, and then I couldn't believe that suddenly overnight all these people loved me for the same songs. These same people sat in clubs when I was the opening act and talked through my show. Now suddenly they were rapt? I wanted to see where they were at. I wanted to show them where I was at."

In showing them, Mitchell moved toward the nakedly personal songs on her next several albums, songs that, rather than alienating her audience, cemented their commitment to her, so much so that it is this material that most of her long-time fans love the most.

Meanwhile, on March 11, Mitchell won a Grammy Award for Best Folk Performance for *Clouds*. The same month, Crosby, Stills, Nash and Young released their version of "Woodstock" as the lead-off single from their album *Deja-vu*. It hit #11 on May 9. And also in March, Reprise released Joni Mitchell's third album, *Ladies Of The Canyon*.

It is said that the average recording artist has about an album and a half's worth of material when signed to a record company. The first album uses up the strongest songs, the second is a combination of the weaker ones and quickly composed filler, and by the time of the third album, the artist is faced with writing a whole album for the first time—the result being that most artists make good first albums and mediocre second albums, and the third album is where they separate the men from the boys.

Joni Mitchell had been so prolific in her early years as a writer, however, that her third album, like her second, was a combination of old and new. "Morning Morgantown" and "Conversation" were a couple of years old, "Ladies Of The Canyon" and "The Priest" more than a year old, and the rest seemed to have come since the last album. This allowed the listener the unusual opportunity of hearing her growth as a writer over a significant period of time on a single disc, as if it were a retrospective rather than a new album.

And the growth was obvious. The new songs included "For Free," in which she compared her career unfavorably to that of a street musician—as stark an expression of her new commitment to strip herself bare before her audience as could be imagined, at least in professional terms. There were also "Willy" and "Rainy Night House," strikingly confessional songs, "Woodstock," and the simultaneously playful and cautionary "Big Yellow Taxi."

There had also been a real musical leap. After crediting Crosby as producer on her debut, Mitchell had left off a producer credit on *Clouds*, and she did so again here, but in addition to her own voice and instruments, she brought in some harmony singers, a cello played by Teressa Adams, Paul Horn on clarinet and flute (notably on "For Free"), Jim Horn on baritone sax, and Milt Holland on percussion. All this was part of finding accompaniment that wouldn't lose the subtleties of the music. Here, she did it by using instrumental colors selectively. Later, she would grow bolder.

Ladies Of The Canyon entered the charts on April 11, and rose to #27, a new peak for Mitchell doubtless aided by the release of "Big Yellow Taxi" as a single. Unfortunately, Mitchell's version had to compete with a cover by the Neighborhood, and her version went to only #67, while theirs got to #29 (#24 in *Cash Box*). At least she controlled the publishing. (On December 23, *Ladies Of The Canyon* went gold, signifying sales of half a million copies. Eventually, it would be certified platinum for sales of a million copies, making it one of Mitchell's two best-selling albums.)

Despite her concert retirement in February, Mitchell was back on stage in August at the Isle of Wight festival, but she must have wished she hadn't returned. A year after Woodstock (and the Atlantic City debacle), it had become clear that not every festival was a celebration of peace and love, and at this one, a man jumped on stage during Mitchell's set and shouted, "This is just a hippie concentration camp!" Mitchell burst into tears.

After that, she seems to have gotten off the road and taken an extended rest in Europe, while writing songs for her next album. Meanwhile, Matthews Southern Comfort, a group led by former Fairport Convention singer Ian Matthews, scored a #1 hit in the fall in England with "Woodstock," as the movie of the festival hit theaters. In the U.S., Matthews' version had to compete against one by the Assembled Multitude, which came out first and got to #79 (#78 in *Cash Box*). Nevertheless, Matthews' version, coming after the first of the year, got to #23 (#17 in *Cash Box*), making it the third chart version within a year.

The next time fans got to hear Joni Mitchell's voice, it was singing backup to James Taylor on Taylor's hit version of Carole King's "You've Got A Friend," which appeared on his *Mudslide Slim And The Blue Horizon* album in April 1971, was released as a single in May, and hit #1 on July 31. Taylor and Mitchell appeared on stage together in London in a concert broadcast on the radio and widely bootlegged under such titles as It Takes Two To Tango ("I sound like I'm on helium," Mitchell said of the show, "I've got this high, squeaky, girlie voice."), and Taylor was also heard on Mitchell's fourth album *Blue*, released in June.

If what she was trying to do was show herself to her audience, Mitchell succeeded completely with *Blue*, her first album to consist almost entirely (with the exception of the four-year-old "Little Green") of newly written material. In the intoxicating infatuation of "All I Want" and "A Case Of You," the playful rejection of "Carey," the unhappiness

and self-pity of "Blue," "California," and "River," and the bitterness (still, incredibly, mixed with hope) on "The Last Time I Saw Richard," Mitchell drew unusually revealing self-portraits and performed them with emotional urgency.

Mitchell explained to Bill Flanagan the circumstances under which the album was made. "I'll just tell you what you have to go through to get an album like that," she said. "That album is probably the purest emotional record that I will ever make in my life. In order to get that clean...you wouldn't want to walk around like that. To survive in the world you've got to have defenses. And defenses are necessary but they are in themselves a kind of pretension. And at that time in my life, mine just went. They went and you could call it all sorts of technical things. Actually it was a great spiritual opportunity but nobody around me knew what was happening.

"All I knew was that everything became kind of transparent. I could see through myself so clearly. And I saw others so clearly that I couldn't be around people. I heard every bit of artifice in a voice. Maybe it was brought on by nervous exhaustion. Whatever brought it, it was a different, undrug-related consciousness...I was so thin-skinned. Just all nerve endings. As a result, there was no capability to fake. The things that people love now—attitude and artifice and posturing—there was no ability to do those things. I'll never be that way again and I'll never make an album like that again."

At the same time, Mitchell recognized that *Blue* was a breakthrough in terms of her communication with her audience, that it helped define what her relationship with listeners should be. This she explained to Jenny Boyd, saying, "On a spiritual or a human level, I have felt that it was perhaps my role on occasion to pass on anything I learned that was helpful to me on the route to fulfillment or happy life. (That includes) anything that I discovered about myself, like 'I'm selfish and I'm sad' (a line from "River"), which are unpopular things to say. By giving the listener an opportunity then to either identify, in which case if he sees that in himself he'll be richer for it, or if he doesn't have the courage to do that or the ability, then he can always say, 'That's what she is.' So I feel that the best of me and the most illuminating things I discover should go into the work. I feel a social responsibility to that; I think I know my role. I'm a witness. I'm to document my experiences in one way or another."

These are Mitchell's reflections in the '80s and '90s on *Blue* and its aftermath. At the time, of course, the album was much closer to her experience, and its confessions must have been painful. But the pain conveyed itself to her listeners. *Blue* earned rave reviews from unusual quarters. *Rolling Stone*, which had not taken her seriously until now, devoted a long review by Timothy Crouse to singing its praises, and Robert Christgau, no friend to singer-songwriters, also was impressed.

The album was also an impressive seller, breaking into the charts in July and going to #15, although only "Carey" became a minor singles chart entry (#93 in *Billboard*, #92 in *Cash Box*). It went gold in November and later joined *Ladies of the Canyon* as a million-seller.

In July, Mitchell toured the U.S. with Jackson Browne, who would not release his debut album until January. She was romantically linked to him, as she had been to James Taylor, and of course to Graham Nash and David Crosby, and in its year-end issue, *Rolling Stone* referred to her as a groupie and named her "old lady of the year." She didn't speak to the magazine for the next eight years.

Despite her popular success, Mitchell seems to have given serious thought to retiring from music in 1971-72, taking time off to go back to Canada (where she bought property and built a house in British Columbia) for an extended period. One thing she did do was leave Warner-Reprise after four albums. Geffen and Roberts founded Asylum Records in 1972 to record acts they believed in and couldn't sell to existing labels, among them Jackson Browne and the Eagles. Roberts told Chapple and Garofalo that other reasons for the founding of their own label included an intention to "minimize the contractual pressures on singer-songwriters who wanted to work at their own speed" (their words), and to avoid the kind of demeaning ads labels that Warners took out on their artists. (So much for "Joni Mitchell takes forever.")

Therefore, Mitchell's fifth album, *For The Roses*, released in October 1972, sixteen months after *Blue* (which, in the early '70s, was a longer hiatus than usual), appeared on Asylum Records. When it did, it became apparent that, if Mitchell hadn't retired before, she

Photo/Henry Diltz

might very well now. On the title track, she condemned "people who have slices of you from the company," who "toss around your latest golden egg," and even when she wasn't being that specific, the album was full of self-questioning.

Told that the record sounds like an announcement that she was retiring, Mitchell agrees. "I did that," she said, "and I might not have come back. That was a swan song all right, of sorts, and I didn't think I'd ever come back. I built myself a stone house in a place where the landscape had infinite variety and moods and was enough to be a companion to a solitary. I armed myself with *Thus Spake Zarathustra*, which was my bible for that time period. It was the perfect companion to a convalescent and a solitary, and it was the only thing I had to keep me from feeling completely isolated.

"I bought out all the psychology and the philosophy department of two major bookstores—before they went computerized and their shelves narrowed down—in Los Angeles, and I sat out there in the bush throwing those books at the wall, saying, 'Bullshit, bullshit.' I couldn't see myself (in the books). It was all so archaic. It was all so dated, the knowledge. I kept saying, 'Western philosophy is in its infancy.' It just didn't apply, so much of it. Especially the tail end of Freud. Jung, here and there—synchronicity, that was interesting. But the dream symbolism; you couldn't apply either of those dream interpretation ideas to my dreams."

Having rejected most of Western thought, seeing through the music industry came easily to Mitchell. "That was, like, spiritual/material conflict," she said, "and I was mad at the business. 'For The Roses' puts that out fairly clearly. As a matter of fact, (Atlantic Records head) Ahmet Ertegun came up to me afterwards, and he'd heard the song, and said, 'Joni, you're the only artist that knows what's going on.' I was living with Geffen at the time, and I said, 'That's not true, Ahmet. You underestimate your artists.'"

Whatever it had to say lyrically, musically For The Roses was Joni Mitchell's most accomplished record yet. She had stripped her sound down for *Blue*, but on For The Roses, she used a rhythm section consisting of jazz bassist Wilton Felder of the Crusaders and drummer Russ Kunkel of the L.A. studio band the Section, which frequently backed up people like James Taylor. Legendary guitarist James Burton (heard on records by Rick Nelson and Elvis Presley) played on one track, and Stephen Stills was credited as "Rock 'n' Roll Band" on another.

But the most notable instrumentalist was "Tommy Scott," who played reeds and woodwinds throughout. Scott, a twenty-six-year-old Los Angeles native, would help Mitchell finally to put together a successful hand sound over the next few years.

For The Roses earned positive reviews and was a commercial success. It was prefaced by a single, "You Turn Me On, I'm A Radio," whose B-side contained a non-LP recording of one of Mitchell's earliest songs, "Urge For Going." The single reached #25 (#20 in *Cash Box*), Mitchell's first Top 40 hit, and the album got to #11 and went gold in two months.

In 1973, Joni Mitchell found herself back in the Warner Communications empire when the company bought Asylum Records, merged it with Elektra Records, and put David Geffen in charge of an entity called Elektra-Asylum Records. Meanwhile, British fans waiting for a new album could enjoy the unlikely cover of "This Flight Tonight" from *Blue* performed by hard rock band Nazareth, which became a #11 U.K. hit in the fall.

In December, Asylum anticipated the release of Mitchell's sixth album with the up-tempo single "Raised On Robbery," a rollicking number that featured guitar playing by the Band's Robbie Robertson. The single hit #65 (#50 in *Cash Box*).

It was followed, in January 1974, by Court And Spark, which would turn out to be Joni Mitchell's critical and commercial apex. For the record, Mitchell was accompanied by a collection of fusion jazz musicians, including Felder and Joe Sample of the Crusaders, guitarist Larry Carlton, and members of Scott's band, the L.A. Express.

"I had no choice but to go with jazz musicians," Mitchell told Bill Flanagan in 1985. "I tried to play with all of the rock bands that were the usual sections for James Taylor when we made our transition from folk to folk-rock. They couldn't play my music because it's so eccentric. They would try, but the straight-ahead 2/4 rock 'n' roll running through it would steamroller right over a bar of 3/4. My music had all these little eccentricities in it, and it would just not feel right to me. Finally one bass player said, 'Joni, you know really you should be playing with jazz musicians.' People used to call my harmony weird. In context of today's music, it's really not weird, but it was much broader polyphonic harmony than was prevalent ten, fifteen years ago. Now, much of it has been assimilated.

But they couldn't figure out how to play those chords. In the standard tuning they're really virtuosic chords. The way I'm playing them in open tuning, you can do it all with one finger. So with a simple left hand I was getting these chords that I liked the sound of, but which look like minor ninth inversions. Write these chords out and they have long names. So that's when I started playing with the L.A. Express."

Later on, Mitchell's turn to jazz musicians would cause her music to change in ways less acceptable to the critics and the public, but on *Court And Spark* the fusion musicians helped create a jazz-pop style that captivated her listeners.

Lyrically, the acceptance the album received was not hurt by her having lightened up somewhat, treating both her romantic ("Help Me") and social/business ("Free Man In Paris") concerns with a little less seriousness. "Help Me," which became a #7 hit, treated infatuation engagingly rather than threateningly and had a strong hook, while "Free Man In Paris," which hit #22, was written in the voice of David Geffen, wistfully wishing for a way out of "stoking the star maker machinery." Elsewhere, Mitchell came off as more philosophical than bitter.

The result was her best reviews ever. "She's the best singer-songwriter there is right now," wrote The *Village Voice*'s Robert Christgau, and the New York newspaper's critics' poll named *Court And Spark* the best album of 1974. Behind its two Top 40 singles, the album hit #2 in the charts, going gold the month of its release.

Mitchell toured arenas backed by the L.A. Express and also appeared with Crosby, Stills, Nash and Young during their reunion tour of stadiums in the summer. During a series of dates, August 14-17, at the Universal Amphitheatre in L.A., she recorded most of the songs for a live album, *Miles Of Aisles*, released as a two-LP set in November. The album showed her growth as a performer and allowed her new, larger audience a chance to hear her older work. It was a measure of her popularity that it hit #2 and went gold soon after release, with "Big Yellow Taxi," released as a single for the second time, reaching #24.

On March 1, 1975, Mitchell and Tom Scott won the Grammy Award for Best Arrangement Accompanying Vocalists for the song "Down To You" on *Court And Spark*. She also had been nominated for Album of the Year, Record of the Year, and Best Pop Vocal Performance, Female.

In 1975, she worked on the followup to *Court And Spark*, finally turning up in public at Bob Dylan's Rolling Thunder Revue shows in the fall, first as a spectator and later onstage.

The Hissing Of Summer Lawns, her eighth album, was released in November. Musically, Mitchell again employed a mixture of friends like Graham Nash, David Crosby and James Taylor, along with various fusion jazz musicians, except for the track "The Jungle Line," which featured her singing over "the warrior drums of Burundi."

Lyrically, however, *Hissing* was a departure, and that was what caused critics palpitations, with Christgau, for example, calling her "a West Coast Erica Jong" (Jong was the author of the '70s best-selling novel *Fear Of Flying*).

In 1985, Mitchell explained to Flanagan that *Hissing* represented a return to an older approach. On her first three albums, she noted, she had often employed fictional characters, but, starting with Blue and running through *For The Roses* and *Court And Spark*, "I went through a period where I wrote very personal songs. I did a series of self-portraits, scrapings of the soul, and I went through that for a long time. By the time I got to *The Hissing Of Summer Lawns*, I was back to doing portraits again. By that point, people were used to me being a confessional artist and the result of that subtle change was a lot of people didn't like *Hissing* because if I was saying 'I'm like this,' that 'I' could either be them—if they wanted it to be—or if it got too vulnerable, they could go, 'It's her.' But the moment I started doing portraits again, saying 'you,' a lot of people saw themselves more than they wanted to. Then they would get mad at me."

The reputation of *The Hissing Of Summer Lawns* has risen over the years. For example, *The Rolling Stone Record Guide*, edited by Dave Marsh with John Swenson (Random House/Rolling Stone Press, 1979) awarded the album only two out of a possible five stars. (In her interview with Flanagan, Mitchell referred to *Rolling Stone* as "the... rag that kind of started the war against me.") But thirteen years later, in *The Rolling Stone Album Guide*—edited by Anthony DeCurtis and James Henke with Holly George-Warren (Random House, 1992)—it is upgraded to three-and-a-half stars. Christgau even upgraded it from a B- to a B in his book *Christgau's Record Guide: Rock Albums Of The '70s* (Ticknor & Fields, 1981). And artists such as Prince have cited it as a favorite.

Mitchell agrees that such belated vindication is

encouraging, but remains wounded by the initial reception. "It hurt," she said. "Well, it was trying to get me or something, I don't know."

Despite the bad press, *Hissing* was a commercial success, hitting #4 and going gold a month after its release, while "In France They Kiss On Main Street" went to #66 (#55 in *Cash Box*) as a single.

Mitchell wrote her next album, *Hejira*, during a cross-country road trip. She resurfaced in November 1976, playing at a "California Celebrates The Whale Day" benefit on the twentieth and participating in the Band's Last Waltz show on the twenty-fifth. *Hejira* was released the same month.

Again, Mitchell teamed with players like Larry Carlton, Victor Feldman, and members of the L.A. Express, but *Hejira* was a sparer effort than its immediate predecessors, and listeners were struck by the innovative bass playing of Jaco Pastorius, who was heard on four songs.

"The first time he came in, I had never heard him play," Mitchell wrote in a tribute to Pastorius after his death that was published in the December 1987 issue of *Musician* magazine and reprinted in the book *The Jazz Musician*, edited by Mark Rowland and Tony Scherman (St. Martin's Press, 1994).

"Everybody'd heard my lament about the trouble I was having. I was trying to find a certain sound on the bottom end, going against the vogue at the time. It's very difficult to buck a vogue. Bass players were playing with dead strings; you couldn't get them to change, to get a round, full-bodied tone. I liked that old analog, jukebox, fifties sound-upright bass, boomier. In the Sixties and early Seventies you had this dead, distant bass sound. I didn't care for it. And the other thing was, I had started to think, 'Why couldn't the bass leave the bottom sometimes and go up and play in the midrange and then return?' Why did it have to always play the root? On 'The Jungle Line' I had played some kind of keyboard bass line, and when it came around for (L.A. Express bassist) Max Bennett having to play it, he just hated it. Because sometimes it didn't root the chord, it went up into the middle. To him that was flat-out wrong. To some people it was eccentric. So when Jaco came in, (L.A. Express drummer) John Guerin said to me, 'God, you must love this guy; he almost never plays the root!'"

Lyrically, Mitchell returned to the "I" for much of *Hejira*, once gain inviting her listeners in to her own personal reflections, and despite the lack of a hit single, the album hit #13 and went gold in a month. Mitchell was nominated for a Grammy Award for Best Pop Vocal Performance, Female, for the album, losing to Linda Ronstadt and *Hasten Down The Wind*.

Critics also responded positively, seeing the album as something of a return to form, although Christgau, for one, worried about the significance of her self-examination. "The reflections of a rich, faithless, compulsively romantic female are only marginally more valuable than those of her marginally more privileged male counterparts, especially the third or fourth time around," he noted.

Chapple and Garofalo, whose book, *Rock 'n' Roll Is Here To Pay*, was being written about this time (it was published in 1977) also comment on Mitchell's wealth and isolation, questioning her relevance and her ability to identify with the real experiences of her audience. "Will she cope with the grittiness of life in the United States," they asked, "or stay, sighing, in Laurel Canyon? For Joni Mitchell is an extremely isolated rock star. She rarely tours. She does virtually no interviews. Perhaps she is an inherently shy person, but her isolation is certainly encouraged by her manager, Elliot Roberts, who long ago stopped her interviews... Joni Mitchell, as Roberts is quick to point out, is a wealthy woman. It is too easy for her to assume the role of the rich hippie."

It is, of course, a typical reporters' conceit that a public figure should be described as isolated simply because she declines to talk to reporters. Doing interviews may be a way of talking to the public, but except in a very limited sense (even if you assume, as reporters do, that their questions reflect what the public is interested in) they do not constitute listening to it.

Nevertheless, the criticism reflected Mitchell's tendency, despite the more personal tone of *Hejira*, to approach lyrics more from a poetic than a communicative angle. Once, she had been an artist with whom you identified, but now she was becoming one you merely admired from afar.

And with the release of the hour-long two-LP studio album *Don Juan's Reckless Daughter* in December 1977, even that admiration came into question. The album contained several extended compositions, notably the sixteen-minute "Paprika Plains," allowing Mitchell's jazz sidemen, especially Pastorius, to stretch out. Despite the album's length, Mitchell seemed to have less material than usual—of the ten songs, one was an instrumental and another was a studio version of "Jericho," which had appeared on *Miles Of Aisles* three years before. Nevertheless, the length allowed reviewers to speak of the album's pretentiousness and indulgence. Fans made it another gold album (Mitchell's last), but it only reached #25.

In April 1978, the movie and soundtrack of *The Last Waltz* appeared, featuring Mitchell's second feature film appearance as she sang the *Hejira* song "Coyote."

The same month, she met with jazz composer/bassist Charles Mingus, terminally ill with Lou Gehrig's disease. Mingus wanted to create what Mitchell later described as "a piece of music based on T.S. Eliot's *Four Quartets* and he wanted to do it with—and this is how he described it—a full orchestra playing one kind of music, and overlaid on that would be bass and guitar playing another kind of music; over that there was to be a reader reading excerpts from *Quartets* in a very formal literary voice; and interspersed with that he wanted me to distill T.S. Eliot down into street language, and sing it mixed in with the reader." (This is from Mitchell's interview with Leonard Feather printed in the September 6, 1979, issue of *Down Beat* magazine, as quoted in *Mingus: A Critical Biography*, by Brian Priestley (Da Capo, 1982).)

Mitchell read Eliot's long poem, she told interviewer Cameron Crowe in *Rolling Stone* in 1979, and told Mingus, "I'd rather condense the Bible." Mingus then asked Mitchell if she would write lyrics for six melodies of his. Working first in New York (he was living at Manhattan Plaza, she at the Regency Hotel), then at Mingus's home in Mexico, they completed much of the work before Mingus' death on January 5, 1979, In June, Mitchell released an album called *Mingus* featuring the new songs, plus such familiar Mingus tunes as "Goodbye Pork Pie Hat."

"...Although the Joni Mitchell recordings can hardly be considered part of the Mingus canon," wrote Brian Priestley, "it is worth noting that her lyrics for 'Goodbye Pork Pie Hat' are far superior to those recorded by Rahsaan Roland Kirk, and her singing is almost good enough to make one think of Sheila Jordan or Annie Ross. And the restrained but distinctly space-age bass playing of Jaco Pastorius, which, fittingly, dominates the album, could never have existed but for the influence of Mingus on those who have influenced Pastorius."

Perhaps recognizing the dicey commercial prospects of such a project, Mitchell took the extraordinary step of agreeing to an interview that would be published in *Rolling Stone*, her first extensive question-and-answer session in more than a decade. The album actually charted higher than *Don Juan's Reckless Daughter*, getting to #17, though it became her first album since *Clouds* not to go gold.

Mitchell also launched a tour, backed by a band including Pastorius, guitarist Pat Metheny, keyboard player Lyle Mays, and saxophonist Michael Brecker. In September, they were filmed and recorded at a performance at the Santa Barbara County Bowl.

The result, released one year later, was the two-LP live album *Shadows And Light* and, in December 1980, a TV special on the Showtime cable television network. The album hit #32, while its single, a version of Frankie Lymon and the Teenagers' "Why Do Fools Fall In Love" featuring the Persuasions, bubbled under the Hot 100 at #102.

Shadows And Light completed a phase in Mitchell's work that had begun with *The Hissing Of Summer Lawns*, and she made several notable changes in presenting her next album, *Wild Things Run Fast*, which appeared in October 1982. For one thing, she split with her manager, Elliot Roberts, after seventeen years and, after a brief period without management, took on Peter Asher, who handles such artists as James Taylor and Linda Ronstadt. On November 21, she married bass player Larry Klein at Roberts's home in Malibu.

Klein appeared on the album in place of the increasingly undependable Pastorius. *Wild Things*, which was released by Geffen Records (still under the Warner Communications umbrella), was a more rock-oriented, up-tempo collection than Mitchell's more jazz-oriented works of the second half of the '70s. It also, unusually for Mitchell, contained two cover songs, the '50s ballad "Unchained Melody" (in a medley with her own "Chinese Cafe"), and "(You're So Square) Baby, I Don't Care." The latter, best known as one of Elvis Presley's recordings for Sun, became a #47 chart single, and the album itself hit #25.

Mitchell undertook an extensive tour to promote the album that lasted for much of 1983. She was backed by a four-piece band consisting of guitarist Mike Landau, keyboard player Russell Ferrante, Klein on bass, and drummer Vinnie Colaiuta; 1984 saw the release of a one-hour home video, "Refuge Of The Roads," filmed on the tour and directed by Mitchell. This seems to have been the last extensive touring Mitchell has undertaken, though she has played isolated shows in the last decade.

Wild Things had been the first album to contain a producer's credit since Mitchell's debut—she was credited as producer. For her next album, *Dog Eat Dog*, released in October 1985, Mitchell shared production duties with Klein, Thomas Dolby, and Mike Shipley. And she brought in several guest stars, including Michael McDonald, Don Henley, and James Taylor, for a set of songs that took on a variety of social concerns, from smoking to evangelism. By now, her audience had dwindled to a dedicated core who were still able to give the album nineteen weeks on the charts and a peak at #63. "Good Friends," the duet with McDonald, released as a single, made #85 in *Cash Box*.

Mitchell was involved in the charity activities prevalent among pop performers in the mid-'80s, with mixed results. She appeared on the Canadian Ethiopian relief record "Tears Are Not Enough." On June 15,1986, she was a last-minute addition to an Amnesty International concert at Giants Stadium, in New Jersey, thrown on as a set-change interlude between headliners the Police and U2. The result was a three-song set (including the premiere of "Number One," which would appear on her next album) greeted by an impatient, teenage audience with something less than complete graciousness. But Mitchell, who doubtless would have run off crying at such an experience fifteen years before, persevered and even found positive things to say in a post-set interview with Pat Benatar on the live MTV broadcast.

Mitchell was not much heard from in 1987, except for an appearance on the Herbie Hancock-hosted Showtime music series "Showtime Coast To Coast," on which she appeared playing with David Sanborn and Bobby McFerrin. Her fifteenth album, *Chalk Mark In A Rain Storm*, was released on March 22, 1988. Here, she seemed to be trying to catch up with the production and sound of such '80s peers as Peter Gabriel, who turned up dueting with her on the opening track, "My Secret Place." Don Henley, Billy Idol, Tom Petty, and Willie Nelson also appeared on the album, on which Mitchell took on Native American concerns ("Lakota") and covered such songs as "Cool Water" and "Corrina, Corrina" with revised lyrics. Reviews were mixed, and the album peaked at #45. Mitchell was nominated for a Grammy Award for Best Pop Vocal Performance, Female, for the album, losing to Tracy Chapman's "Fast Car."

On July 21, 1990, Mitchell appeared in Berlin, singing the song "Goodbye Blue Sky" at the massive live staging of The Wall organized by former Pink Floyd leader Roger Waters. Released on video and disc in September, *The Wall—Live In Berlin* hit #56.

Mitchell's sixteenth album, *Night Ride Home*, was released February 19, 1991. It was described by Mark Coleman in *The Rolling Stone Album Guide* (which awarded it four stars) as not "so much a comeback as a chance to catch up with a long-lost confidante," containing "Mitchell's most tuneful material since *Court And Spark*... Like her old pal Neil Young," Coleman concluded, "Joni Mitchell has managed to forge a mature style from the raw material of her youthful follies."

The album reached #41. (Geffen issued a special limited edition version in a black cardboard package containing a set of photographs featuring Mitchell's face superimposed on landscape scenes. Geffen also released a 45-minute home video titled *Come In From The Cold* containing five music videos relating to *Night Ride Home* and three relating to *Chalk Mark In A Rain Storm*.)

More changes marked the run-up to the release of Mitchell's latest album, *Turbulent Indigo*. She spent a year in litigation to end her contract with Geffen Records (which had been sold to MCA), and then re-signed to Warner Bros., appearing in photographs with label heads Mo Ostin and Lenny Waronker just prior to their messy departures from the company. On the day before recording for the album commenced, she split from her husband, Larry Klein, though Klein co-produced and played on the record.

The resulting album is reminiscent of *Dog Eat Dog* in its taking on of various social concerns. "Very outward, this album," Mitchell noted, "and angry." Of the songs, she said, "They're not cynical. They're candid photographs, basically, don't you think? That's what they are. The songs that I'm writing for the next album (some of which were previewed at the Edmonton Folk Festival last summer) are quite different. I have two already, and they're of a different quality already. So, you kind of get ahead of yourself.

"I think that this was a clearinghouse," she continued, returning to *Turbulent Indigo*," and also that I saw so much injustice levied at women this time. I always hung with men all my life, and I've always felt that the better way than the feminist stance, which is pointing outward and saying 'them' and 'us,' was a dialogue between a man and woman, like, 'What's wrong here?' Working closer, working with rather than pointing at would be more effective. Let's come to a greater understanding. Are we really that different or is it sociologically imposed?

"After all, we all began as women. We developed in our different ways after that, but we all began—Don Juan, in the (Carlos) Castaneda books, says that the universe is basically feminine, that the whole thing is like a birthing creature, and this hostility towards the earth and towards the feminine—if the Orientals and the Indians view the sky as masculine and the earth as the bearing female, you're raping the bearing female. We've lost our holisticness."

The album drew some criticism for its forthrightness, notably on the spousal abuse song "Not To Blame" (which has been linked to Jackson Browne's alleged abuse of ex-girlfriend Daryl Hannah despite Mitchell's denial) and the anti-advertising (and other things) song "Sex Kills."

"One of the reviewers I spoke to—and I don't watch television that much—said, 'Oh, but all these issues have been on "Oprah," and you don't want to hammer them in,' Mitchell noted. "I thought, well, gee, I'm unaware of that. I'm sure that everything you could write about is a cliché, and somebody's heard it way too much. But maybe there's another way to put it. You can't give up on it or dismiss it as a theme or say, 'We've heard that too much.'

"I'm very surprised at the positive reception that this album has received among my friends, almost immediately, relative to other projects of mine for a long time. Instead of, 'Oh, there's Joni, she's suffering again,' it shows me that the world must have touched and hit against people now long enough."

Even looking outward, then, Mitchell again is hitting listeners directly. If she sees life as difficult for others, her own last few years, which have included medical problems and tax disputes, haven't been easy, either, and much of this comes out on *Turbulent Indigo*.

"Somebody told me—some Harvard grad was given this axiom—basically what he said was that, in your teens and twenties, that is your lyric period, and then from your thirties through your forties, that's your epic period as you begin to experience things again and again," Mitchell said, "like Leonard (Cohen)'s line, 'Are my lessons done? No, do them all again.' That was a thirties writer's statement. Then, as you approach your fifties and for the rest of your life, now you're developed into a tragedian. Your irony should be in full bloom at this point. I don't think I could have tackled 'Job' (the album-ending song "The Sire Of Sorrow (Job's Sad Song)") as a song until now, that I've lived enough life to have been to the pit, figuratively speaking, enough times to be able to empathize fully with that position of bereavement and temptation to lose faith."

And in such a way, Mitchell keeps faith with listeners who have looked to her for a quarter century as a gauge for their own development. "You can still choose your side, acting with humanity, but what's the use?" Van Gogh wrote to his brother just before committing suicide. For Joni Mitchell and her audience, there still is a use in choosing, and on the last page of the CD booklet to *Turbulent Indigo*, Mitchell is seen holding her painting of herself as the mutilated Van Gogh, but wearing a smile.

Ray Davies

By Ken Sharp
March 1, 1996

The role call is staggering: Lennon/McCartney, Jagger/Richards, Pete Townshend, Marriott/Lane, each an amazing and influential songwriter in his own right. Standing among them as a peer, however, is Raymond Douglas Davies, perhaps the quintessential British rock songwriter. He is truly one of a kind. Davies' seminal work in the Kinks chronicled the working class, a celebration of the joys and melancholy of day-to-day living.

From "Well Respected Man" to "Dead End Street," "Autumn Almanac" to "Shangri-La," Davies was a magnificent observer of British life. Never comfortable in the spotlight or hanging out with his fellow rock peers at such "in" London clubs as the Ad Lib and the Speakeasy, Davies, in the '60s, spent most of his time burrowed away in his cozy semi-detached home in London, busy working on the next Kinks classic.

The fall of 1995 saw the U.S. publication of *X-Ray* (The Overlook Press), an autobiography of sorts from Davies. Juxtaposing the narrative of a teenage reporter (the young Ray Davies) interviewing a rock star in his golden years (the old Ray Davies) with an intriguing sci-fi flair, *X-Ray* is an hilarious, and often brutally honest, account of Davies' childhood and his glory years with the Kinks, who are still going strong more than thirty years on.

To promote the book, in an unprecedented move delighting all Kinks fans, Davies hit the road for an intimate solo tour in America and Europe where he mixed select readings from *X-Ray* with a generous overview of the Kinks's vast catalog, including the airing of many seldom-performed gems like "Two Sisters, " "Dead End Street," "Village Green," "Set Me Free," "See My Friends," "I Go To Sleep," "Tired Of Waiting For You," "The Money-Go-Round," and "Harry Rag," sprinkled with several splendid new songs like "Animal," "Julie Finkel," and "To The Bone."

Goldmine spoke to Ray Davies in October 1995 during his American solo tour. He offered candid and thoughtful observations on topics ranging from the aborted first recording of "You Really Got Me" to a prospective CD-ROM release of *The Village Green Preservation Society*, one of the Kinks's best-loved albums of the '60s.

Goldmine: *How long did it take for you to write* X-Ray?

Ray Davies: 1988 they (Viking, his English publisher) asked me to do it. I was living in Ireland when they asked me to write the book but I refused at first because I didn't want to write just an autobiography about myself; it's just facts and figures. I came up with the idea of me as a young person meeting me as an old person, which allowed me to step back and look at myself objectively and the band, as well, more objectively. I found that in interviews I'd done before, I always phoned up the next day and I asked the press person to cut bits out. So I adopted a journalistic style in pulling bits that I might cut out.

Was it difficult writing the book?

It was difficult at first but I wrote a two-page treatment. I didn't want to write the book they wanted. I pitched an idea to them. I always kept that handy when I lost the thread. I'd pick it up and put it down when I was on tour or in the studio. Then I'd come back to it and read those two pages and get back into the swing of it. It was good for me to have that discipline.

When you had the finished copy of the book in your hands, did you have the same feeling as completing a great song?

I was looking for the typos (laughs). It was like holding that first record and seeing your name on it. I still get that with records. This was different because this book suddenly came to life. I didn't decide to finish it until the beginning of last year (1994). They said they wanted it out at a certain time and I suddenly got into it then and did it.

147

Not too long ago you were questioning whether you'd come back to America again. Why?

What, a couple of years ago?

Yeah.

Well, I felt I'd lost touch with America and the people. That first experience we had in America hit me quite hard. We never really knew what it was about. (The Kinks were banned from America for a few years in the late '60s due to a union problem they encountered while performing here.) The first time we toured America was a catastrophe. I think that stayed with me for a long time. Being banned hit us at a crucial time in our career, all our special years when we had those hits and we couldn't get back here.

I thought our last album we did (*Phobia*) was good, but it was misconceived by the record company. The Kinks are a rock band and it's very difficult to put the songs into that context. They wanted songs in it that were more my sort of songs. I think they wanted a solo record, quite frankly. But you can't compromise a rock band. You've got to go in there and make a rock record. So I think it fell between two different styles and as I was the producer and I had to come over here and play the tapes for the president of the company and all that, I felt like I was working too hard. It should be fun.

I knew that they picked the wrong singles and everything. It was just a disaster. I thought maybe this was it and I should never come back here again. I didn't follow my instincts and my instincts were when I first signed with that company (Sony) it was wrong, and I got out quick. I wish we could have gone in there in a different way. We went in there with blazing guns and everyone ran in there sort of shouting out and stomping around as if it was going to be the next big thing and I just wanted to make a record. There's a tendency now in the music biz to decide how you're going to market a record before you hear it.

Is that good?

No. You can only hype something when you know what the strength is. The problem with the Kinks is that we have been hyped the wrong way at the wrong time. The way we did it was we had to re-establish our fan base and all that. Bands build their own audiences their own way and that's the only way you can do it. It

Photo/Chuck Boyd/Flower Children

can't be manufactured by a marketing person. I think that had a kickback to me after that tour here and I broke my foot and I had a couple of broken toes and all that shit. I did a bit of damage inside of me, I think, and I felt like quitting it for a while.

I went back and did some teaching. I taught songwriting, but you can't teach songwriting. I taught it in England. That went good. I've done that for three years now. I did one before I came over here. It's Eastern Arts, in East Anglia, and there's one in Devon where they do writers' courses there and they do another one in Yorkshire. I did these in East Anglia and it was very good. You get interesting people there, some famous people who come there just to mix with other writers.

Tell us about some of the new songs you performed in your solo show. "Animal" and "Julie Finkel" come to mind. Are these songs for a solo album or the Kinks?

After the last record company experience I had, I'm not positioning them anywhere. I just play the songs until they become songs. A couple of them tonight were stronger than they were last night. I thought of other things to put in them now when we get a chance to rehearse next. That's the way we did "You Really Got Me." We had different arrangements of that and the recorded version of that which went out and became a hit was after like six months to a year of playing it live.

What was wrong with the first version of "You Really Got Me"?

Ah, it was Phil Spector. Echo and everything. My voice was gravely and it was all wrong.

What new songs that you played tonight will be on To The Bone, *the next Kinks album?*

Only "To The Bone" is written for the album and there's another song we've written that's gonna be on it. It's gonna be a double album over here. (Note: *To The Bone* was released as a single album in England last year.)

Your American solo tour has been a very emotional moment for fans. What's it been like for you to delve into some of your lesser known but equally important songs like "Autumn Almanac" and "Village Green"?

I mean, "Autumn Almanac" is very odd. It's not a rock 'n' roll record. It's about gardening (laughs). You can't have a more ordinary occupation than that.

Eating roast beef on Sunday...

And sorting out the leaves that fall in the autumn and sweeping them into the sack. It's about that. Also the hump-backed man I spoke about really existed and when I became really successful he came and did my garden for me.

I heard you produced "You Really Got Me" when Shel Talmy was out of the room?

Well, Shel was around. To be fair to Shel and to do him credit, he produced the worst version and the best version so he's gotta do something right. "Dead End Street" was produced by him but he wasn't there. But that was the contract. Sometimes a producer is good as a catalyst to get people to do things. I think he was effective for the time. I wouldn't listen to him now although I'd respect his opinion. It was a different thing producing then; now you've got to be part of the band.

You wrote a lot of your classic Kinks songs in your semi-detached home. Was there some tangible magic in that home?

Oh, yeah. Absolutely. The thing about finishing the book, you asked me earlier about *X-Ray* and I realized it was about my family. That's why I dedicated it to my family. I don't think I could have written all those songs without them. It was a crucial part of me. It's not a coincidence that I start my book off... see, the character in my book, the kid, the nineteen-year-old journalist, is me. And all the things I wrote about in the book which people think is a novel and I've made up are true. Every dark thing about the kid listening to people singing outside and the thing with the electricity plug, all that stuff in the early pages, the dreams and the biting your teeth and falling asleep and slightly having insomnia when you're a kid, all that stuff's true. And it was easier for me to approach that by writing in that style.

It's interesting that this kid, if you read the book, he talks about his family that was dissolved and taken apart. And that's because I feel that my family is finished. It's gone. Coming from a big family and then having a band and that's it. I don't have anybody anymore 'cause my sisters were much older than I. My parents are dead, my sisters had gone away. They just had different lives. It's all part of me and I wanted it to be kind of a tribute to my family that really grew up in post-war Britain and experienced things that millions of other families did.

What did your family think when you would mention them in songs, or even title songs after them, like "Arthur"?

I did a song called "Rosie Won't You Please Come Home," which is about when my sister went to Australia. And "Come Dancing," Gwen is the sister in "Come Dancing." She's very close to me now. She's the only one who is still close to me. The big thrill for me is that she read the book. She was one of the first people to buy it. She phoned me up and told me she liked it. So whatever any critic said to me I knew she'd be my worst critic. We went to a little church school up the road and she was there before me. She's seven years older than me. But they remembered her because she was really clever. Gwen was the closest, she was seven years older than me.

I lived with Rosie. I called Rosie "Mum" until I was five years old. She came back to England and she said that and I couldn't believe that. Maybe that had a lot to do with the way my relationship with Dave was formed because I've never really remembered having a brother relationship with him. I always thought that my nephew Terry, who is Rose's son—he's only a year younger than I—I felt like he was my brother.

Did Dave read the book?

I think he's read it. He's read bits. (Ex-Kinks drummer Mick) Avory's read the book. I made Avory read it.

In X-Ray *you reveal that Mick had some pretty peculiar sexual peccadilloes.*

He's a star, he's a star (laughs). He's one of the great unsung stars of the rock world. He comes into Konk (studios) once a week and signs my pay check.

What did Mick think of the book?

I don't know what he thinks of the book. I made him look at certain sections that involve him and asked if it was accurate. He said, "Well, I'd like you to change little bits," because it was such trivial stuff, but most of it was okay with him.

Was it therapeutic writing X-Ray?

It wasn't therapeutic. It's only the fact that after I finished it, I realized what I was writing and it made me realize certain things.

In your solo show there's a lot of pent-up sexual innuendo around Mick Avory. Was that a long-standing joke between you two?

Well, Mick, he's straight. I remember when he was getting married. I went out for a drink with him and got him drunk and we went to a terrible Greek restaurant in London and I said, "Mick, this is your last opportunity, go off and turn gay." But he tried, he tried. But he just couldn't succumb to it. Now I think maybe he's having second thoughts but he's got a lovely daughter now.

Mick, as I called him in the book, I recognized him being a lonely person like me. It's not sexual innuendo. It's like people drifting, it's nothing to do with sexuality, it's people lost. Friendship is more important than anything. Mick Avory, really, in all my years when I was going up and down and being crazy and (having) these fights with Dave, he remained my friend in the band. He's still my friend. He's the only person in the world that I would allow to sign checks on my behalf. He looks after my gas bills and everything while I'm away. I let him have carte blanche because I know I can trust him. And it takes a special person and that goes beyond sexuality. It's a strange indefinable thing that friendship has that cannot be touched. References to sex taint that sort of relationship. It's asexual and I'm not condoning that but it's something that's beyond that.

I was reading an interesting quote by Pete Townshend where he complimented you by saying he'd never be the writer that you became and he also talked about how the Who and the Kinks never got much credit in light of the Beatles and the Stones. Did you ever feel the light should have shone more on the Kinks?

No, I think justifiably the Beatles got the credit

they deserved, and the Stones, for the most part. I just felt that they were led by their publicity machine a bit too much and I think deep down John Lennon and people like that would have preferred to have mixed with us a bit more. I think it was the elitist attitude that their advisors took more than the bands. I think the Rolling Stones are friendlier now to me than they were then. It's easy to say that we were all buddies.

You told a story tonight about an incident with John Lennon at a show where the Kinks were part of the bill. (In his show, Davies described Lennon checking out the Kinks from the wings, putting on an air of

superiority until he saw how well the band was going over. Afterwards, Lennon offered to write a song for the Kinks.)

Maybe he felt intimidated by us. We were the new young band in town and he was sizing us up. I always think of him as being like the older boy at school. They always give you a hard time when you go there.

Didn't Lennon love your song "Wonderboy"?

Yeah, in my book I talk about the time he was in a club and was playing and playing it. That's nice. It wasn't a big hit. I think he liked my work. I stayed at an apartment close to him in New York. It's an odd thing, this sort of rivalry that goes on in your lives. I used to see him in New York walking down the street with Yoko. I used to just wave. Then one day I was going off on a tour and I ran past 72nd Street by the Dakota and I was off jogging and I saw Yoko standing there alone and she had a kind of weird smile on her face. I'd never seen her without him before. Then I went on the tour and four days later he was dead. It's kind of weird.

I was in Paris doing an interview and they were playing records and asking me to make comments on the records and they played (Lennon's) "Starting Over" and I said, "I think it's a good record. I'm glad he's having success. It's not as good as the stuff he's done on his own."

And he said, "Don't you think it's as good?"

And I said, "Not particularly."

And the guy said—it's a French journalist—"Oh, that's interesting because he got shot this morning. He's dead."

I felt really pissed off that he did it in that way. So I went with the people who I was with to Notre Dame and I lit a candle for him. It was the only thing I could do in the circumstances. It was a big sense of loss. You know sometimes the rivals are closer to you in life than the friends.

It seems a lot of the major traumas in your life have had to do with your finances, contractual obligations, and complications. You've always been hesitant to market yourself.

I think the thing that scared me originally is that I thought it was wonderful. I just wanted to get "You Really Got Me" as a number one so I could get lots of friends and get recognition for the song, the band, and make my girlfriend happy. It ended up that I was dealing with a market that revered volume. Volume became all-important. Again, I keep going back to the book but I react against the volume. I reacted against that. I think I decided to be non-commercial. I actually believed in my stupid naive way that my friends would still be there. But when the volume falls apart, it's not a good business ethic to do that. You find that people want to buy something and be involved with something that's on a roll. I didn't really understand that business ethic and people love to be hyped.

As I said before, I only want to hype something that I think is finished and ready. Otherwise I'd be saying this is the first theater novel tour by a rock musician. I'm not doing that until I think it's right. Sometimes I fall behind the race with that. But it's just that reaction I had. I understand the realities of business, but I try my darndest to let it not influence me. But the things that fire me up to write about, I started a musical based on a big finance corporation. Finance fires me up, the power plays fire me up. Wall Street makes me interested because money is power is sex.

X-Ray finishes off in 1973. Are you planning a sequel?

I finished then for a good reason. I felt writing about the development was very important, the genesis of the band and all that, and then I realized that first curve, that bunch of songs I wrote, was about that first time finding yourself. Rites of passage and all that and developing into what can loosely be called an adult and then finishing it. And it all ended at that time. I thought it was an ideal time to end at the White City concert where I nearly died afterwards. It all seemed kind of symmetrical to me. And also going back to a journalistic thing, it would be the sort of thing in England particularly because I know we came back here in the '80s. It was the most interesting time for us, the '80s here.

Why?

It was just incredible. It was a different thing. In England I thought if a journalist came in, a tabloid-type journalist, that's what they'd write about. I combined that with my own sense that the songs related to a certain period. Then I wrote different songs after '73. I became a different person, really.

Many artists feel that success is the panacea to all their problems and insecurities. But success in itself doesn't change anything. Did you feel that way as well?

See, I was really lucky. I had a kind of troubled

childhood. I ended up going to, it's not a home, really. How can I explain it? I went to classes a couple times a week for a year or two. I had a one-on-one tutorial with somebody. This wonderful person explained to me that you probably will never get over your insecurities. And I was really young when I was told that. I got a slight advantage from that because I always remembered what she said. She was very convincing. She justified what she said. She was an extraordinarily incisive person. I think when I became an adult I still kept thinking "I'm not gonna grow up."

That's why the book is firmly rooted with a nineteen-year-old. I think that's about as developed as I've got. Maturity comes. You learn how to order food differently, you order the right wines, you know how to talk to people. But the basic matter that makes you as a person, certainly in my case, doesn't change that much from that time. It's all downhill after that (laughs).

I've heard you are planning on releasing a CD-ROM for the Village Green Preservation Society *record.*

Well, I think it's the only format I've yet discovered that could possibly not be prohibitively expensive for me to do. As a movie it would be too expensive. I thought about doing it as an outdoor rock event and taking it 'round but it's so much money and logistically it would be impossible to do without hit singles and things. It'd be a hit show. Maybe I'll write a few more things and adapt them to become hit singles.

Can you understand why many Kinks fans cite that as their favorite record by the group?

Yeah. Well, you see, think about the time I wrote it. I didn't think I'd come back to America again. In many respects my career was over. We were having hit singles but in Europe and the rest of the world and a few here, but the sales were gradually going down. I thought, well, why not write something about things you truly care about? I wrote this song about friendship, "Do You Remember Walter?" It's about a real friend that exists. To me that was all-important. I wanted a record that would not necessarily get airplay but would be played for friends and at parties—just play the record like playing a demo. (laughing) And I achieved that and it didn't get any airplay at all. It became a cult record as a result.

What's interesting is, I think the whole indie scene in Britain started out of a similar wish or desire to undersell. It became a sales ploy to sell things. I was in a very highly vamped, high profile band when I made *Village Green Preservation Society*, which is a reaction against things. Now it's becoming fashionable to make those sort of records, to actually sell lots of records. You can do that more in England. There's a whole movement over here of low-fi music that you can buy on seven-inch records, new bands starting out. It's the same sort of attitude. Now there are more people doing it.

There's a Kinks site on the Internet, and one heated discussion surrounds whether the band ever did an acid-inspired album in the '60s. In the midst of the height of psychedelia the band did an earthy, idio-syncratic album, Village Green Preservation Society. *It seems the Kinks were always operating against the times.*

I think there were elements of acid-type, not music, I suppose, it's more the intellectualizing of it than the actual application of it. It's a stubbornness, I suppose, and the sort of people I'm with, we get bored easy. If a fashion comes along we get bored with it after a day. The original band was so good. It's very rare that you can find friends that you've made in adulthood as close as the friends you had at school. You get this intuitive thing going with bands that went to school. I think we actually laughed at all the fashion things. Even when, not so much with the Beatles but the Rolling Stones did certain things, I would go, "For fuck's sake, get real!" (laughs)

We were just interested in doing our little songs. Avory wanted to be a jazz drummer. But he was happy to play my music because he felt we were on our own cause, our own campaign. It's a bad busi-ness ethic, as I said, but in a strange way it helped us. Because we were on such shitty deals, we put ourselves on forty pounds a week, which was then, for a rock star, a hundred dollars a week. We got that up right until the '80s, I think. If there was any profit at the end we'd distribute it. I didn't drive so I didn't need cars and Mick had a Morris Minor or something. Dave had a Jag, all right. He had to have that. First time I saw him driving we were scrump-ing. Scrumping is when you steal apples from a farm. We were scrumping apples on a farm and we got away and he was driving a tractor. He was about twelve.

When the Kinks were inducted into the Rock And Roll Hall of Fame, you spoke of how rock 'n' roll had become respectable and said, "What a bummer."

I was skeptical of it. I remember that night. I got to the Hall of Fame dinner and saw what a big schmoozing event it was and went back to my room. I ordered sandwiches in my room. A guy who was with me, Kenny Laguna—he's a really nice guy—he came up to my room and talked me into going back down. It all kind of resolved itself. Mick dragged me up onstage. He had a terrible suit on, this terrible tuxedo.

Was it good to see (original Kinks bassist) Pete Quaife again?

Yeah, yeah. Kinda good. Anyway I walked onstage and the people there, the first to shake your hand was Clive Davis (president of Arista Records, for which the Kinks recorded for several years) and Allen Klein (the notorious one-time business manager for the Beatles and Rolling Stones, among others). Can you cope with it? (laughs)

Do you have a different feeling about it now after playing at the opening of the museum in Cleveland?

I went there and it was under some pressure because we'd just played this show at the Edinburgh Festival, which is a theatre festival. Suddenly I got away from rock 'n' roll. I just had to do a good show. And there were theatre people coming to judge the show, not necessarily Kinks fans. And I really got a good reaction from them. Then suddenly two days later I found myself on a plane to Cleveland. It was completely different from what I'd been doing, a different mindset entirely. But I went on there and I actually felt really pleased to be there because everybody from Steve Cropper to Aretha (was there). All those people were great.

Did you have a chance to check out the museum?

Yeah, the next day I did. They're still pulling it together. It's a wonderful building. But they haven't got the exhibition together yet. You can only see so much of Pete Townshend's suit or Keith Moon's outfit and Elvis Presley's Las Vegas gear. What we're going to build there is a front room with my piano in it, my parents' piano. I'm trying to track down the green amp (which Davies discusses in the book) but I don't think I'll ever find that.

Maybe it vaporized.

No, someone stole it.

Do you think your songwriting process is different now than the way you used to write in the early days?

I think a big mistake is you become an academic about all these things, analyze things. That's why I trust my subconscious. I don't say that in the show for effect. I really think it is smarter than I am. My subconscious tells me lots of things, dreams and instinctive things.

Are you a good judge of your material?

I am before I go into the studio with it. You get into the studio and you hype yourself up just to get through the session and you think things are better than what they are or worse than what they are. Usually I think they're worse. The only true judge is to judge a song just on piano or guitar or whatever. That's why it's interesting developing these songs this way, these new songs.

The new songs are changing in each show?

They're not changing, I'm not doing radical changes. But I'm finding out which bits are consistently good (laughing) and which bits are consistently bad and when I get the next chance to sit down, I'll change them.

In your book, you speak about being obsessed with the movie Charley Varrick. *Do you still struggle with remaining independent?*

I think that commerce dictates art. It always has done. You go right back to Rembrandt, he painted those pictures because he got commissioned. I think an artist needs a commission. In many respects an artist needs something to say "fuck them" to. Only Bach can write for God totally. Bach wrote for the glory of God. Maybe you'll get the isolated guys like Van Gogh. In the modern world you have to write for a corporation and ultimately there's always one out there for you. The great thing about being a maverick is that I think of myself now as a recording artist, like an independent filmmaker. I'm not tied to a studio but if I have a project I like, I'll get finance from different sources and make the movie and put it out on the independent circuit.

I think that's going to apply more and more in rock music because the artist who has got a home for all his records is very lucky. Bruce Springsteen is very lucky to be at Columbia. He'll be there longer than the people running the company. Warners are like that, they're good to some artists. The Kinks just got off to a bad start and we inevitably end up in this torn situation where we're between the strength of the artist and the people providing the finance.

Which record label is releasing the next Kinks album, To The Bone, *in the U.S.?*

I'd love to have my own label, but quite honestly, there's so much administration involved in it. I had Konk in the 1970s. I had one of the first independent labels of this modern era, I suppose. We did really well but I found the administration impossible. And to be an artist as well, you just can't cope with it. But now I think I've got it knocked. I think I can cope with it. I've got advisors around that can deal with things.

In X-Ray, *you speak of being secretive about "Waterloo Sunset." Why?*

It started as a real personal song. Writing that was like your question earlier about writing the book and what did I feel when I finished it. I knew I'd done my best work. It was a good piece of work when I finished the song, not when I made the record. I wanted to keep it inside me, keep it for me. It's a very selfish thing and also very stupid, lack of business sense. That's why I took my time making it and I gradually let it out in small bursts because everybody had to like it in the band. Avory had to like it, Quaife, Dave had to like it. In the end everybody though it was great.

Were you happy with it as a record?

Well, you can always change things. I'd pump the bass up a bit (laughs).

this issue's Five Star Record!

© MARTY WINTERS
1996

ARETHA FRANKLIN'S 1969 LP ON ATLANTIC RECORDS "SOUL '69"! THIS LP FEATURES RICH BIG BAND ARRANGEMENTS BY ARIF MARDIN, AND MANY VETERAN JAZZ MUSICIANS, INCLUDING DAVID "FATHEAD" NEWMAN, KING CURTIS, ERNIE ROYAL, URBIE GREEN, FRANK WESS, AND PEPPER ADAMS (FROM HIGHLAND PARK, MICHIGAN) ON BARITONE SAX! ARETHA ADDS HER TOUCH TO HITS OF THE DAY, SUCH AS "TRACKS OF MY TEARS" AND "GENTLE ON MY MIND"!

SHE ALSO SINGS A TOUCHING, BEAUTIFUL VERSION OF "CRAZY HE CALLS ME," SAM COOKE'S "BRING IT ON HOME TO ME", "ELUSIVE BUTTERFLY" AND "TODAY I SING THE BLUES"! ARETHA IS ABSOLUTELY AT THE HEIGHT OF HER SINGING SKILLS HERE — IN COMPLETE COMMAND OF THE ENTIRE EMOTIONAL SPECTRUM! THE BACKING VOCALS ARE COMPLETELY TASTY AS WELL!

HER LPS ON ATLANTIC FROM THE LATE '60's TO THE EARLY '70's ARE MY FAVORITES! I LIKE HER GOSPEL LPS, TOO! BEFORE SHE RECORDED FOR ATLANTIC, ARETHA MADE SEVERAL ALBUMS FOR JOHN HAMMOND AT COLUMBIA RECORDS!

THIS DISK ITSELF IS IN GREAT CONDITION.!! THAT'S RIGHT — NOT EXACTLY MINT— BUT IT PLAYS JUST FINE! THERE'S A SLIGHT RING WEAR ON THE COVER, AND SOMEBODY WROTE THEIR INITIALS ON THE BACK AND ON THE LABEL IN BALLPOINT! THE CORNERS ARE KIND OF SCUFFED AND ROUNDED, TOO... AND THERE'S A TINY SAW MARK RIGHT HERE!!

IN THE 1980's ARETHA CHANGED LABELS AGAIN, THIS TIME TO ARISTA! IN LATER YEARS SHE HAS RECORDED DUETS WITH ANNIE LENNOX, GEORGE MICHAELS, WHITNEY HOUSTON, ELTON JOHN, LARRY GRAHAM AND PETER WOLF!! SHE'S ALSO RECORDED WITH THE LIKES OF DIZZY GILLESPIE, CARLOS SANTANA AND KEITH RICHARDS!

☆☆☆☆☆

Mott The Hoople

by Dave Thompson
July 1998

Even today, looking back from a distance of almost thirty years, it was a marriage made in the most mystifying Heaven. On the one hand, there was Shadow Morton, one of the undisputed legends of pop production history, the master who drew mignon magic from the Shangri Las; on the other, there was Mott The Hoople, mordacious rock 'n' blues miscreants, untamed and untamable, vibrant and violent. What could they possibly have had in common; what could they possibly have found to talk about?

For the Mott boys, of course, it was enough just to be there, to draw from the same wellspring of inspiration that Morton had always untapped for his clients, to ask about favorite old records and effects. But for Morton, still struggling to prove himself in the new age of rock more than five years after he helped to create it, what was Mott but another crazed English beat group, and not even one of the famous ones.

They were inexperienced, too. Vocalist Ian Hunter himself confessed, "We didn't understand the techniques of a studio. If something (went) wrong, we just had to cope."

Even with all the experience in the world, Morton couldn't have known what he was getting himself into.

Yet together, this so unlikely pairing was to create one of the classic sounds of the earliest 1970s, a record which combined everything either party had ever thought was sacred about rock 'n' roll, and which sounded like nothing they had ever done before.

"Midnight Lady" rarely makes it onto die hard fans' "Best Of Mott The Hoople" collections. It is seldom held up as a shining example of Shadow Morton's greatest creations. Most people don't even know it exists. But from the churning guitar lines which ride across the verses, to the mock-gospel "na na nas" which sharpen up the hook; from the piano/organ duet which pins the instrumental break, to the scorching Mick Ralphs solo which duels along beside them; and on to the fade-out which comes so frustratingly early—because it's obvious that the session only got wilder after that—"Midnight Lady" remains so unfathomably contagious that you just know its makers were built for success.

Little more than nine months later, Mott The Hoople broke up. Of course it was only a temporary situation. Within days, they were rehearsing a new song, "All The Young Dudes;" within days, too, they'd lined up the song's author, David Bowie, to produce them. His management had landed them a brand new record deal; his example was teaching them a whole new approach. And by mid-summer, 1972, Mott had one of the fastest-selling singles in Britain, and were Top 40 bound in America. The events of the previous twelve months seemed far, far away.

Mott The Hoople had been around since mid-1969; the union between vocalist Ian Hunter, an itinerant pianist/guitarist with a thick curls, impenetrable shades and an absolute Bob Dylan fixation; and the Silence, a Hertfordshire-based rock 'n' blues band whose sheer persistence, rather than their musical vision, was responsible for them signing to Island records.

Their mentor there was producer Guy Stevens; it was he who introduced Hunter to the band, in a last ditch attempt to give the Silence their own recognizable identity. It was he, too, who rechristened them Mott The Hoople, lifting their name from a William Manus novel. And for three years since then, Mott had been pounding the boards with a grim tenacity which refused to bow down to even the most adverse circumstances. And things were adverse.

Engulfed, as drummer Dale "Buffin" Griffin explained, "in an endless whirlwind of sweaty, jam-packed gigs the length and breadth of the British Isles, with increasingly large crowds of dancing dervishes, leaping, raging, wilding-out, and passing-out, through late 1969, 1970-71, we all but wore our own grooves in the British motorway system."

But while the band's concert ticket sales went through the roof, their record sales barely registered. Three albums had passed to almost zero commercial response: in 1970, their eponymous debut, eyecatching with its Escher lizard jacket and a fiery take on "You Really Got Me," made #66 for one week in Britain and #185 in America. "That means five people bought it, and ten more heard it on the radio," bassist Pete "Overend" Watts shrugged when he was reminded of this years later.

Mad Shadows, Mott's contribution to the early '70s heavy metal catalog, did better: it got to #48 on the British chart, doubled its predecessor's chart life, and gave the band an anthem they'd still be playing at the end of their career, the redoubtable "Walkin' With A Mountain."

And *Wildlife*, the group's third album, did better still. It soared to #44, and remained on the listings for two weeks as well. But such observations are relative. "Mott The Hoople was a cult band," Hunter once reflected. "We didn't go out of our way to do anything special."

So why, he mused of their live support, "did we get this fanatical following?" And what—with their albums having had so little lasting impact—were they going to do to consolidate it? Well, they could try to score a hit single. The group had never had a serious stab at the singles chart—indeed, two years had elapsed since their first and only British 45, the first album era "Rock 'n' Roll Queen." And having already rejected every track on *Wildlife* as being either utterly unsuitable, or obviously impractical, the band turned their attention to even newer material.

According to Hunter, Mott had already booked the necessary studio time long before the song which would become their new single was written. Touring the U.S. in May, 1971, the opportunity arose to go into the studio with Shadow Morton, at a time when the only band he'd produced in years was Barefoot Jerry. "(So) we got on a plane and went straight to Long Island to record this thing I wrote on a bog (the lavatory) in New York. We rammed through it, all out of tune, but we needed a single. It had a catchy 'na na na' bit, so we thought it was commercial."

Steve Marriott, in town with Humble Pie, was roped in to sing some backing vocals, and in October, Island unleashed "Midnight Lady" as Mott The Hoople's new single. And at first, it looked as though the gesture was going to pay off. Buffin continues, "sales were so promising that the BBC gave us a slot on Top of the Pops. The day after the show aired, the single stopped selling." And that was such a remarkable feat, he continued, that "this

should be in the *Guinness Book of Records*."

It avoided the chart with grim resolution then, but "Midnight Lady" did find its way onto a British K-Tel hits collection—albeit amongst the make-weight misses which the licensing majors used to slip in alongside the big names. And by the time Mott came to record their own next album, *Brain Capers*, "Midnight Lady" was not even considered for inclusion.

But they never forgot the song. Over the next year or so, it remained a regular in their live set, and when a radio broadcast crew turned up at the Tower, Philadelphia, on November 29, 1972 to record the night's proceedings, "Midnight Lady" was ready to meet America.

It was the last song of the set—"We're gonna go after this," Ian Hunter warned a surprisingly luke-warm audience, "so if you don't start enjoying your-selves now..." The crowd obeyed, just as Hunter knew they would.

"Midnight Lady" may not have sold a bean in Britain, but the idiot "na na na" chorus got the crowds going every time, which is why the song was chosen for a single in the first place. Three minutes long on vinyl, in Philadelphia it stretched to five, and there were other nights when it lasted even longer, as band and audience locked into one another, to clap and chant the night away, daring the other to tire and start slowing. "I can't hear ya!" Hunter complained as the Philadelphia audience began to warm up. "Louder!"

Today, of course, "Midnight Lady" is deeply enshrined within Mott The Hoople's legend. In the post-Dudes dawn of 1972, Island (Atlantic in the U.S.) included it on the *Rock 'n' Roll Queen* compi-lation of the band's pre-Bowie best... and it wasn't just a token rarity, thrown on to ensnare collectors. It deserved the honor wholeheartedly. The likes of the title track, "Death May Be Your Santa Claus," "Thunderbuck Ram," the uncompromisingly brief "Wheel Of The Quivering Meat Conception," and the correspondingly elongated live romp through "Keep On Knocking," all shone with the latent promise which was Mott's all along, but which needed Ziggy's magic touch to translate to the fore.

"Midnight Lady," on the other hand, transcended that rough potential altogether, and pinpointed the future there and then. Just over one year later, Mott The Hoople was back on Top Of The Pops. And this time, their sales went through the ceiling.

this issue's

Five Star Records
© MARTY WINTERS MW 1997

TODAY'S TOPIC: "ALBUM COVER ART AS SATIRE — OR: IS IMITATION *REALLY* THE *SINCEREST* FORM OF FLATTERY?"

IN THE '80'S ALPERT RECORDED WITH JANET JACKSON AND U2!

A&M SP 4110
HERB ALPERT'S TIJUANA BRASS
A TASTE OF HONEY ★ TANGERINE
LOVE POTION #9 ★ LEMON TREE
LOLLIPOPS AND ROSES ★ PEANUTS
WHIPPED CREAM & OTHER DELIGHTS
A&M RECORDS

THIS IS THE ONE THAT *STARTED IT ALL* — HERB ALPERT'S *MILLION-SELLING LP* FROM *1965* ON *A&M RECORDS* (CO-FOUNDED BY *ALPERT*) — WHICH FEATURES THE *GRAMMY AWARD-WINNING* HIT *"A TASTE OF HONEY"!* ALBUM DESIGN CREDITS GO TO *PETER WHORF GRAPHICS* — AND EVEN THOUGH IT'S *STILL PRETTY LISTENABLE,* YOU *GOTTA* REMEMBER *THIS* ONE FOR THE *NAUGHTY PHOTO* ON THE *COVER!* IT GIVES ME A *SWEET TOOTH* LIKE I *NEVER HAD BEFORE!*

AND, IT HAD TO BE AT *LEAST PARTIALLY RESPONSIBLE* FOR A *PORTION* OF THE *MILLIONS* OF *COPIES* THAT WERE *SOLD!!* I'M *ALMOST CERTAIN* IT'S *STILL AVAILABLE* ON *CD!*

SWEET CREAM & Other Delights
CONTAINS THE SMASH DISCO SINGLE "I DON'T KNOW WHAT I'D DO"

I BOUGHT THIS RECORD *STRICTLY* FOR THE *COVER!* *SWEET CREAM* WAS A *DETROIT-BASED GIRL SINGING GROUP* AND THIS *1978* RECORDING FEATURES A *SLEW OF LOCAL MUSICIANS!* IT'S *PRETTY FORGETTABLE* FOR THE MOST PART, BUT *OBVIOUSLY* THEY EXPECTED A *BEAUTIFUL NAKED WOMAN* COVERED WITH *WHIPPED CREAM* TO SELL A *FEW COPIES!!* MM-MMM!

PAT COOPER
SPAGHETTI SAUCE & OTHER DELIGHTS
FRANK GAUNA
UNITED ARTISTS

THIS *COVER* (*PHOTO* AND *DESIGN* BY *FRANK GAUNA*) TO *PAT COOPER'S SECOND LP* IS CLOSER TO *PURE SATIRE* AND FEATURES *PAT* COVERED IN *SPAGHETTI* AND *SAUCE* HOLDING *BREAD STICKS* INSTEAD OF A *ROSE!* *SIDE ONE* IS *STAND UP COMEDY* RECORDED *LIVE* AND *SIDE TWO* IS A SERIES OF *EXTREMELY SHORT NOVELTY SONGS* — *"PEPPERONI KID"* & *"POPPA'S HOME-MADE WINE"* AMONG THEM! TO BE *HONEST,* I DON'T FIND THIS STUFF VERY *FUNNY,* BUT THEN, I'M *NOT ITALIAN* AND I'M *NOT* FROM *BROOKLYN!*

PAT COOPER'S LATEST *CLAIM TO FAME* IS A SERIES OF *UGLY APPEARANCES* ON THE *HOWARD STERN SHOW!*

☆ ☆ ☆ ☆ ☆

CONCLUSION: *"HOMAGE* OR *FAUX PAS?* *YOU* DECIDE!"

Ian Anderson

By Irwin Soonachan
May 22, 1998

Only one man could possibly be playing the flute in the band that's rehearsing inside the empty Duluth, Minn., Civic Center. The oh-so-familiar strains of "Living In The Past" are an obvious clue that Ian Anderson has entered the building, but no one who works there seems to think so.

"Hi. I'm here to speak with Ian Anderson."

"I'm sorry, there's no one by that name here."

"But that's him playing in the auditorium."

"I'm sorry, that's someone else playing."

Time for a different tack.

"Well, may I please speak with Jethro?"

"Sure, he's right inside."

In 1998, as Ian Anderson celebrates the thirtieth anniversary of his band's first record, *This Was*, he finds himself synonymous with the prog-rock beast he largely created. The image of Anderson, in a pair of tights, perched on one leg while playing the flute, is one of the most identifiable in rock 'n' roll. Now Anderson, who named the band after an eighteenth century agronomist, is forever married to the image.

But more than twenty years after an era which saw Jethro Tull become popular enough to sell out the Los Angeles Forum each night of a five-night stand, Anderson finds the band playing smaller venues like the one in Duluth, and unable to sell out.

Anderson's ability to work a crowd, though, remains largely intact (as does his ribald on-stage sense of humor), and the old war horses of the Tull live canon carry the day. Joined by longtime guitarist Martin Barre, a Tull member since their second record, and a cast of younger musicians, Jethro Tull can still produce a very energetic show. The Midwestern audience was nonplused by the rarities, sitting stone-faced through a Rashaan Roland Kirk cover dating from *This Was*, but were stoked by the classics. By the end of the concert, they had left their seats and collectively rushed to the front of the auditorium for a predictable yet still innervating finale of "Aqualung."

He no longer traipses around in tights and spends a bit less time balanced on one leg, but Ian Anderson is still a formidable performer and one of rock music's few iconoclasts. He spoke with *Goldmine* shortly before his Minnesota appearance.

Goldmine*: Even when you started back in 1968, you were pretty public about staying away from drugs, groupies, and that sort of thing. What led you to say that?*

Ian Anderson: Immaturity and naiveté led me to say it because I thought it might make some difference. But, of course, I guess fifty percent of people that might have read something that I said regarding my stance on unbridled sexual activity and particularly on all the dangerous chemical drugs, I suppose fifty percent wouldn't have believed me, would have thought I was just lying and the other fifty percent probably would've thought I was not a real man, or not a real rock musician because rock musicians are supposed to do that.

One of the band was asked by a customs agent with the U.S.A. this morning on our return to the U.S.A. from Canada, "When were you last in jail?" or "When were you last arrested?" I think was actually the comment. That seemed very strange because in his twenty-nine years of traveling to North America, Martin Barre has not only not been arrested, but to my knowledge, has never been involved in any kind of a fracas with anybody over anything. It's just making the assumption that if you're a rock musician... when as he said, "What do you do?" and he said, "I'm a musician," he said, "When were you last arrested?" You can get pretty angry about being pigeonholed in that way. Guilty at something, before you started. It's unfortunate.

In 1968, it must have taken a lot of guts to come out and say that.

No, it didn't take a lot of guts at all. I thought it was a perfectly sensible thing to do, to let folks know that not all musicians were necessarily given to extreme behavior or dangerous or suicidal behavior. But remember that back then, and we're not really talking about 1968, more 1969 and '70, I saw a number of people disappear.

I played on the same concert at the Isle Of Wright Festival in 1971, I believe, that was Jimi Hendrix's last major appearance. It certainly was one of the last appearances of Jim Morrison of the Doors. I'm not sure who else on that (bill) has snuffed it through drugs, drink, or excesses, but there are probably quite a few other casualties. I remember Keith Moon, he was on that show; he's not here any more for exactly the same reasons.

I guess there were probably a few people that were on the bill that night who drank or drugged themselves to death one way or another, and I think that's very sad.

I miss Jimi Hendrix; I didn't know him well as a person, but I miss his music enormously. I feel angered by the leeches and the parasites that surrounded Jimi Hendrix during the time that I did know him and worked on a lot of concerts with him. I saw that coming because of those kind of people, that entourage, that dangerous group of people that make themselves indispensable, and who are basically there to feed to the ego of the artist and feed his appetite for destruction, which is so often the case.

However, I stopped winching about drugs and stuff when I realized that people by and large didn't believe me anyway, so I've just kept quiet about it.

I still haven't smoked marijuana or taken cocaine or anything else at all. I'm not saying I wouldn't do it; I'm not against it on moral grounds, I'm against it on common sense grounds, 'cause I'm probably the kind of guy who, if I did that stuff, I would kill myself. I would end up overdoing it. So I stay away from it.

I mean it took me about thirty years to quit smoking. I have to assume that my likelihood of psychological, if not physical, dependence, on other chemical substances might well be the same. But to me it's just a question of common sense... If I knew for sure that I was the kind of guy who could smoke a couple of joints and sniff a bit of cocaine and shoot up heroin once a week, and it was just all under control, and it was as brilliant as people tell me that it is, maybe I would do it. But how can I possibly know that I'm that kind of guy? Because there aren't many of those kind of guys.

What are some of your musical influences?

Some of the most important ones are the ones I started with, which were Muddy Waters and Sonny Boy Williamson and Howlin' Wolf and even the pop guys like Bo Diddley and Chuck Berry, just for a little while. But then it kind of moved more into the slightly more ethnic things. I didn't get to hear—because we didn't know about them then—people like Robert Johnson or Son House, or the real guys way back in the very early days of gramophone recording. We didn't know about those guys in the north of England in the mid-60s. But we did get to

hear about people like Sonny Terry and Brownie McGhee.

We got to hear about some of those folks when we were school boys, and it was very exciting, in a dangerous and mysterious way. That kind of music had such passion and such soul, such earthiness in relation to the jolly, quaint folk culture of the U.K.

I came from Scotland so I grew up with an awareness of some Scottish traditional folk songs and the kind of tacky and popular music up there. So when I heard what sounded to me like folk music that had a lot more real guts to it, it was very exciting. I'm not particularly wild about pop music in the sense of chart pop music, but the folk music forms and even the urban folk of Muddy Waters, that rang very live bells to me as being something that... I knew I didn't want to try make a living being a black guy, because I didn't think I was going to be very successful. I did, however, feel I would make a living being a musician, using the influences of that music, and some of the improvisational inspiration that came from a lot of those early players, who clearly were not masters of their instruments. Because what they did was something that transcended mere technical proficiency; it was beyond that.

What about the jazz guys? You covered a Rashaan Roland Kirk song ("Serenade To A Cuckoo") on your first record. Were you influenced by him at all?

Well no, I listened to Roland Kirk. I refuse to call him Rashaan Roland Kirk because at the time I listened to him, and at the time I met him, he was just called plain old Roland Kirk. His motivation for changing his name, presumably, is that he suddenly discovered Islam at some point in life and went a bit overboard, and he got fairly testy, or so I hear. When I met him he was a very charming man, I only saw him once...

Was that at Newport?

Yes. Well, it was one of the Newport festivals... It was on the road, I think. Actually, it was in Miami, rather than Newport. But it was the first time around in the U.S.A. I wouldn't say he was an influence, other than he was the first flute player I ever heard at the time I'd just got a flute. I didn't start playing flute until I was twenty. He was an influence, in the sense that he dictated a way, an aggressive way of playing the instrument, which was easy for me to work on.

My main influence as a flute player is actually Eric Clapton, because before I heard Roland Kirk I was listening to Eric Clapton with John Mayall's Blues Breakers and thinking, "Wow, I wish I could play guitar like that." Well, I tried, and I couldn't. So I quit playing guitar and switched to the flute. But of course, the things I learned to play on the flute were very much the eclectic blues mix that was the Eric Clapton of that period. That was the stuff I played. So you could say my main influence as a flute player was Eric Clapton. Which is true. It's not just a smart thing to say, but that is the case.

I haven't really been influenced by any flute players other than just that moment of Roland Kirk giving me a song, just because it was the first thing I ever heard and it stuck in my head and I thought, "Well that's a fun little thing to do that I can just about learn to play."

You're on your umpteenth North American tour, but are you used to Americans yet?

I think it's taken me a long time to get used to, not to North America or its cultural diversity, but it has taken me a long time to get used to American personalities and to be more comfortable with and more appreciative of the genuine and open, if rather outgoing, sort of general banter and fun that people present to you.

I'm not a particularly outgoing sort of person; I'm relatively private in my private life. I find sometimes, American personalities will be, for a lot of British people, will be just a little bit too big and loud and forceful. But for the most part, I think it's meant in a very gentle and generous way. It just comes across with rather more decibel force than perhaps it was intended. It's taken me a while just to get used to the fact that you're not bad guys; we just have to wear earplugs sometimes and get used to the jargon, which I think is probably one of the things that bothers me a little bit.

I think there's kind of a semantic smokescreen going up around the U.S.A., has been for a while. In back of these seats all you hear now is "have a nice day." It's all this stuff that flies out of people's mouths; they don't really think what it means.

One of the latest real irritations is when people say, they talk about something and they allude to something else, and they say "as far as something something." What they mean is "as far as something something something is concerned," that's the actual English phrase. But they leave out the connection, they can't be bothered with that. It's like having a sentence and forgetting to put a period at the end and going on to the next one. Every time I hear this, it makes me really mad for some reason. You're using something from the English idiomatic... but you're not using it properly. You're actually using only half of it and then you must wander up into something (else), and grammatically, of course, it doesn't make sense. It is incorrect grammar.

English people sometimes say that Americans don't have as good a sense of humor or that they don't understand English humor. Yet your humor has always gone over very well with American audiences.

I think when we first came over here we saw it first-hand, the very tenuous relationship of British humor with the mass American audience.

I'm one of the people who put some money into the Monty Python film called *Monty Python and the Holy Grail*. I saw the preview with the Led Zeppelins and the Pink Floyds and all the people who put up the money for the film; we all went to see it. But it was just a rough cut, without titling or anything.

I knew it was going to do well, but I was looking forward to seeing the finished cut movie, the credits, and the final performance all wrapped up with a pink ribbon. So I went to see it a few months later when it opened in New York.

I was sitting in the movie all the way in the back—it's funny sitting in a movie theater that's half-empty, or half-full, depending on your point of view—watching Monty Python's new movie. It was unbelievable because every time we laughed at an obviously funny bit, the entire theater was completely silent and looked at us as if we were from Mars. Then, in other places that completely baffled us, when we were just paying attention to what was going on, suddenly the American audience would laugh at something, and we'd think, "What the fuck are they laughing at?" And it was

really quite amazing that they would find different things funny, but quite clearly they found them (Monty Python) funny... Yes, America gets the point.

Canada, for example, loves Mr. Bean, and Mr. Bean, to me, is bad. For the first five minutes of the first time that I ever saw Mr. Bean, I thought it was moderately amusing. But now, I wouldn't (just) like to kill Mr. Bean, I would like to hang him up by his horrible little shoes and just mercilessly beat him to death. Of course, I don't really mean Mr. Bean, I mean Rowan Atkinson (who plays Mr. Bean), that's who I would like to kill, 'cause I hate Mr. Bean and I wish it would go away. A lot of people find it tremendously funny. I haven't.

In 1993, you said that you only saw yourself performing in Jethro Tull until 2001. Are you going to stand by that?

I wouldn't say I would only see myself performing in Jethro Tull, but I think the likelihood is that Jethro Tull as an entity will go on for a few more years. Quite clearly, there is life for all of us outside that particular grouping and that particular commitment that I guess we have to each other. As it's happened during the last two years, it's just about all we've done, we've done an enormous amount of touring.

We will be working in the studios, doing some new music, some of it solo projects stuff, some if it band stuff. Whatever it is, there is this sort of need, I think, as you get older, to find other ways to express music that is perhaps, of a sort that... There's nothing you can't do within the structure of the group Jethro Tull, but if it doesn't deviate too much from the kind of expectations of the audience.

I think maybe, after all this time, it's not really fair to expect people to go out and buy a record under a certain banner and then find out that the taste of that particular cornflake has dramatically changed. You owe them a little bit of consistency of style, consistency of type of musical product, because they will buy it on faith.

Where do you see yourself going musically and artistically from here?

What I think I would like to do, is... I actually like two kinds of songs.

One is observational songs about other people, which I rather like doing, because it's a bit like being a landscape painter or a portrait painter, because you're taking things and you're trying to bring those into some sort of focus and through words and music you express something that is really quite a pictorial idea of somebody. You're giving people a picture postcard of a scene or a personality or a circumstance, quite observational.

The other sort of stuff is the more personal reaction to something, the personal emotional stuff. That is generally, for me, harder to write about because it's harder to find the vocabulary to express those ideas without falling into the cliché traps of pop and rock music. There are only so many ways to say I love you, frankly; I think they've all been done in every language to the point where there are few new ways to express the simple and most universal emotions. So they're very hard songs to write, to me, at any rate. Sometimes people might manage to do it, but for me that's a hard thing to do. However, that's perhaps my little musical goal, if you like, to do lyric writing to be...

As you might have already guessed, when I do start talking, I tend to talk too much, not too little and I do the same thing when I'm writing lyrics. I tend to write too many lyrics rather than too few. Just absolute enthusiasm and trying to get all the ideas in. I think my goal would be to be more concise, more sparse in my writing and present things that were more of a personal nature, were more subjective and more emotional, but without piling it on.

Where you can go for the rich texture, the richer ideas, are in the observational writings, that's when you can be more dense in your use of the language; the musical language, too, not just the lyric writing. Somehow there you can pile the paint on to the canvas in heftier, meatier layers, but in the emotional stuff, less is more. I think that's what I've learned; now I have to learn to put it into practice.

So will there be a Tull album in 1998?

Well, there will certainly be an album in the end of August, or the beginning of September, but whether it's a Jethro Tull project or an Ian Anderson one, it all depends on what gets finished first. They're about neck and neck in terms of material and demos and things at the moment, so we'll just see which makes it out into the world first.

Mick Fleetwood

By Frank Harding
October 2, 1992

Goldmine: *You arrived in London with a set of drums at age fifteen, and were discovered by Peter Bardens. Soon after, you joined his band the Cheynes, who backed the Ronettes in support of the Rolling Stones' second British tour of cinemas in 1964. What impression did the Rolling Stones leave on you at the beginning of your career?*

Mick Fleetwood: Well, it was all very exciting in terms of it was our first excursion on what would be considered a major tour. So that was all very new. The Stones were a band that, you have to remember, we knew about before they made it, so it wasn't as daunting in aspect as it would have been if we would have come in cold and the Rolling Stones were on the charts, and it's the first we'd known of them. Had that been the case, it would have been that much more daunting. However, they were literally sort of on top of the world or about to become massive. It was my first exposure to fanatical fans ripping vans apart, which included ours. If you had long hair you were to be ripped apart, so it was, all that and above.

In terms of the question being what impression they gave, one of the main things was that I befriended Brian Jones on that tour. He was a charming chap at that point and—I don't think this is any revelation, but I'd like to go on record saying it—it was very apparent that Brian was the real nuts and bolts of that band at that point. He enjoyed the most adulation on stage, which drove Mick Jagger crazy. You could tell even then.

They were pretty wild but they hadn't made the transition into what, shortly after that, was to become a real scene. They were young, we were young, and it was a great tour. Mick Jagger was fairly aloof, as he still is today, I feel, and having seen them years later, the essence of what they represented still holds true. I remember going to see them when Mick Taylor was with them—I forget what tour it was—in Boston, and I went backstage and it was actually, I suppose thinking about it, very similar only much bigger. Mick Jagger was still very aloof, and you were aware of him being more aloof.

Keith Richards was as crazy as he always was, but you were aware that this guy is more crazy. And there was little Mick Taylor, basically lost, being eaten up.

And that's what happened in a way to Brian. I think he was very sensitive and God knows there's been enough things written about it, but it really was like that. It didn't surprise me at all what happened to him. But right then and there he was the Rolling Stones.

In 1967 you found yourself in the Bluesbreakers and met up with two people that were to have a profound effect on the rest of your life, Peter Green and John McVie. Was the musical connection instant?

Certainly with Peter. John I'd known through the years 'cause we used to play on the same bill quite often and John was always "in John Mayall" and it was always like there would be three or four bands and John would always be heading the bill.

Peter was already a friend of mine. I already knew about him musically and he was growing at an incredible rate, to the point where it was very evident he was becoming a power unto his own self musically. John McVie—our friendship was consummated in terms of just being together, and we were very close, and basically still are in terms of our friendship's never changed. It's always been there and one doesn't necessarily draw on it very often. Like now I don't spend much time with John, but whenever we do, it's absolutely a given, and never ever to this day been shaky. John, much like myself, is a follower, a musical follower, and I think I could speak for him.

Peter was someone that was just very natural. He encouraged me musically one hell of a lot. He understood, where other people didn't understand, what I had to offer. So I'll always be grateful for that. He would always stick up for me, as would John, because not being technically very proficient at all, that can sometimes go unnoticed. However, through the years, thank goodness, how I play has been at least acknowledged.

So would it be true to say Peter helped you with the feel of music?

Absolutely. Emotionally, yeah, exactly that.

You ended up forming Fleetwood Mac with Peter, then recruited Jeremy Spencer, and temporary bassist Bob Brunning, and that lineup played the Windsor Festival. Jeremy Spencer was a character, to say the least. How did you get on with him?

Well, I roomed with Jeremy and, if you like, I became his foil. The very nature of what Jeremy—certainly in those days and basically for the duration of the time he was with Fleetwood Mac—was known for, was he did Elmore James, and that was basically about it. That's what he did, and that was what Fleetwood Mac was. The bulk of the first album was Jeremy Spencer.

So in that regard, when you look at it, probably his most powerful moment in Fleetwood Mac is when it started, because Peter absolutely didn't want to be known as the leader of the band, and so forth, and Peter wanted Jeremy to front the band. He didn't want to be construed as the new Jeff Beck, or the new Eric Clapton, and all that was very real to Peter. Hence I think Peter made pretty darn sure that he pushed Jeremy out front as much as he could, and no matter how much Jeremy was pushed out, Peter would always have the power he did. He was most definitely the leader of the band. Jeremy did his rendition of Elmore James and that's how he was as a person. He was a mimic, really. He was like a wonderful actor and became believable.

Did Jeremy play a major part in Fleetwood Mac's early days?

Very much so. He was the center of the stage presence of the band. If one could construe that we ever had a stage act, it would have been in the time that Jeremy was with us. It went on from just stage pranks, and then became the thing people came to watch Fleetwood Mac for. So there again, Jeremy actually was really instrumental in giving us the attention, over and above the musicianship of the band.

And he caused you to get banned from gigs?

Yes, from the Marquee. He did the old thing with Harold the dildo, and it got more and more outrageous, until he got us banned. He could get really obscene. Jeremy and I often used to travel to gigs in my car. I managed somehow to always have a decent set of wheels. This one time we all stopped off at my parents' place in Salisbury, and he was an outrage, to the point where he got us in trouble with the police for crude and lewd behavior, twelve-year-old girls being confronted with a dick hanging out the side of the car! Actually very funny, but I suppose not very funny, in terms of what was really going on. So he was a wild, wild guy.

Then on the other side was this little homebody that would forget about the fact that we were doing gigs, making cups of tea, and listening to Rick Nelson in his little bed sit that he was living in with his wife Fiona, totally in a dream world. He had no worries, would never worry about equipment or anything, "Jeremy, you've got five strings on tonight." "Oh, yeah, but I can play 'round that."

But when he hit the stage he really became another person, and his character was normally one that was very quiet, meek, and mild. However, he was horribly sarcastic to the point of being vicious, and of course he couldn't handle that himself. He could dish it out, but he couldn't take it, which I suppose comes from insecurity. A funny little guy!

Bob Brunning was Fleetwood Mac's bassist for three odd-weeks. When the Mac part of the band, John McVie, joined, you spent almost a year together touring, making a debut single and album. You have been described as the tightest rhythm section in the world. What do you think it is about John and your playing that defines the backbone sound of Fleetwood Mac?

I think that both me and John, if you like, suffer, and sometimes I think John suffers more than I do. But I know that feeling, and I, to this day, am not actually that confident about what I do. I think that because of that, it's created a style of playing where I don't crave to be ambitious musically at all, because I feel I'll screw it up. So therefore, I don't go for things which are usually not necessary. Musical ego just doesn't enter into the equation with me and John at all, and I think that has become the magic and the strength of both of us together. Alone I don't think we actually do feel strong.

I think we are two musically insecure people that have become secure together. The marriage is a very real thing. John doesn't realize what a good bass player he is, and, to that extent, I have to say that just from people liking my playing, neither do I, but people tell you you are, and you go yeah, is that right?

There's absolutely no overconfidence in your playing.

I don't think so at all, because I'm still terrified of doing something wrong, so I'll go the simplest route to ensure my security.

Was the partnership between you and John an instant success?

Yeah, so much so that we became drinking buddies and just very close immediately. I sat with him on planes and buses, very close straight away.

Photo/Chuck Boyd/Flower Children

It's always been there.

John and yourself both took credit for writing "Fighting For Madge" and "Searching For Madge," on the Then Play On *album. Who's Madge?*

Madge is the original fan of Fleetwood Mac. She knew about Peter Green before Fleetwood Mac was formed and then it spilled over into when he formed Fleetwood Mac. She was about five foot nothing, very broad in the beam, one has to say, I suppose, desperately unattractive, but terribly sweet. And I don't know to this day how she functioned, how she did it, but she was basically at, more or less, every little gig we did, sometimes five in a row, and we sometimes drove her and her friend to the next show. She would never expect anything and in the freezing cold, we'd say, "Well, how are you getting home, love?" "Well, I'll start hitchhiking," and you've got to remember she couldn't have been more than about fifteen or sixteen years old at the most.

So you dedicated songs to her?

Yes, and Madge became a true legend with the band. I actually saw her on one of the last major Fleetwood Mac tours. The friend that she often traveled with, I forget her name, had terrible heart trouble. Tiny, tiny, thin thing, sadly passed away, but that was her traveling companion so it really was the odd couple.

Danny Kirwan gave the band the unique position of having three lead guitarists and songwriters. Immediately after he joined you released the single "Albatross" in England. It went to number one and became the band's first million-seller. What did he bring to Fleetwood Mac?

He first of all brought some needed relief for Peter Green musically. That's why Danny Kirwan was elected into Fleetwood Mac. It became pretty evident to me and Peter that Jeremy was not going to take the time, or be bothered about taking his music, the way Peter was thinking, into another arena creatively. He simply just wasn't going to, and so that was the main thing, creative relief for Peter Green. And then he brought his own real talent into the band, a real sense of high melody even more so than Peter.

Danny could never write words, but he was the first person in a major way that laid the grounds for, most certainly, myself and John being able to feel quite comfortable with harmony, which was not the sort of thing to be doing, the pussy side of stuff. What are you trying to do? The New Seekers or something? That, looking back on it, was Danny really contributing yet another level of musical openness that was to become a major part of Fleetwood Mac.

In 1969, with "Albatross," "Man Of The World," and "Oh Well," you were outselling the Beatles and the Rolling Stones on the U.K. singles charts. It was the most successful year for Fleetwood Mac in England. All of those singles were written by Peter Green. You became, in that point in time, pop stars. What effect did this have on Peter?

To start with, seemingly a good effect. He was very image-conscious. He was very, in the healthy sense of the word, ambitious. He knew exactly what he was doing and what he wanted to do, which also incorporated a wonderful sense of musical integrity. He never did anything he didn't want to do, but he knew what buttons to push to go that little bit further, where the element of commerciality was actually thought about. He knew how different he was, I think, and hence that the band was, and he simultaneously had a sense of social responsibility that I wasn't even aware of. I didn't even think about it.

He obviously had that, and he was using the band and his talent as a vehicle, which is actually highly commendable, although I think it ended up basically destroying him.

The end result, in terms of what success did to Peter, was that he tried too hard to manipulate the powers that be, that control the press. He was naive. I did warn him. I said, "Peter, you have to be careful venting your really innermost thoughts because you're exposing your soul to the world, and I don't think you're ready to do that," and he didn't listen. He really suffered because of that, and became disillusioned. His soul was nigh on destroyed.

A last single, "Green Manalishi," then Peter quit. Why did he leave, and what effect did that have on the rest of the band?

Mmm...Peter left—I think the window psychologically had been opened, and I have to say that acid was probably responsible. He was becoming increasingly frustrated the more success Fleetwood Mac got. We couldn't really do anything wrong, and it's like the ambition that he once had took him to the top of the mountain and then he said, well so what, and the only sort of alternative he had, basically, was to throw himself off the mount, which is what he did. He left the band. He had dreams of doing things in a different way, to the point of distraction in regard to money. Huge guilt. A psychological profile that ended, I won't say with his demise, but it certainly was the end of that person that I once knew. And he's never come back from that.

Photo/Chuck Boyd/Flower Children

As luck would have it, John's wife Christine joined the band and filled in Peter's place. Christine McVie carved her own niche in Fleetwood Mac's history. She certainly is Fleetwood Mac's leading hitmaker and songwriter by far. Did she find it easy joining an all-male group, one her husband was in, and into the shadow of Peter Green?

I think she did find it easy, actually, because she'd been working with the Chicken Shack being the only lady in the band, a band certainly of the same genre as Fleetwood Mac, a blues band. So musically, yeah, I think she felt that she wasn't threatened, that she wasn't in an arena where she had desperately to catch up with what we were doing. The ease of coming into the band was magnified even more, 'cause she was living with us all at Kiln House, and as such was very familiar with the music that was going on even to the point where she actually played on *Kiln House* with us. And yet there was that element of the commitment that she made to the band, but also was aware of, because of the marriage (to John), is this the right thing to do?

Many years later it transpired that she had second thoughts as to whether it was. I don't think she would have changed it, and it certainly was not a problem to start with. It became a problem when the road dog element in John came out. Hey, you're sharing a bedroom, you're sharing a van, you're sharing! It's a tall order to put on to anyone, and I think many years later it was just an intangible situation, where they became very unhappy.

Soon after Christine joined you lost another member. Jeremy Spencer, in the space of a few hours, changed his life, when he joined the Children of God, while you were on tour in California. You were the last person to talk to him before he left. Did you have any idea he was going to leave?

No. I knew that he was about to snap, mind you, which was basically saying the same thing. But I had no idea. When he walked out of the hotel room he was gone. I knew that he didn't want to be in Los Angeles. He didn't want to get on the plane when we left San Francisco, he thought L.A. was an evil place, and we were all on mescaline, which wasn't very helpful! They plucked him right off the streets, and as you know he had that (religious) side which was always there. His first duffel coat, I remember, had a small pocket with a Bible in it.

Jeremy's replacement gave Fleetwood Mac its first American in the band. Bob Welch wrote some great songs and brought his own individual style to the band. He never got the recognition he deserved while in Fleetwood Mac. Would you agree with that?

Yeah, I think Bob probably, to this day, lives with a slight haunting feeling of whether he should have hung in there a bit longer, 'cause when he left, the band took an upward swing that was to change the course of musical history, certainly for this band.

What was it about his playing that he brought to the band?

171

He's so individual. Bob's forte, if you like, is almost like R&B space music or something. In terms of the space music, it's reflected in his vocals and the subject matter. He didn't come from the background that we did at all. Musically he was very proficient, and he had a broad sense of understanding, which was a new influence on the band. If you like, he had to scale down his approach technically to enable him to function properly in Fleetwood Mac, and to that extent that's what he learned while he was with the band. I think it benefited his musical talent, because of that. It took a while for him to understand sometimes, that the simpler way was the best way, and I still think that's correct. That's my opinion.

During Bob's time with the band, more than a few band members came and went within Fleetwood Mac. Danny Kirwan was fired, Dave Walker and Bob Weston replaced him and didn't last long. Walker's barrelhouse boogie didn't fit, and Weston had an affair with your wife. Your manager put a bogus band out on the road. During those three years did Fleetwood Mac ever think of quitting?

No, we didn't. We did, however, agree to hang it up for a few months, and then all the management problems surfaced. No, we never did, or I certainly was not aware of that decision being made. If someone was thinking that to themselves, which I was not, to this day I've never heard it from anyone, not from John or Chris, or Bob.

You made the Bare Trees *album in England, then traveled to America to promote it. In your book you describe how the master tapes had been magnetized at the airport upon your arrival, and had to be remixed. New light was shed on this event when listening to tapes from the forthcoming boxed set.*

For years that has been an absolute heartfelt story 'cause we were in shock when we put the tapes on at Warner Brothers. We'd been mixing literally up to the time we'd got on the plane in England. We'd brought them over on the plane, and I thought putting them through one of these baggage things, something had happened. We'd lost all the top end, the high end had gone. However, during the course of putting this box together, we were re-educated to the fact we just had mixed the album with our ears closed, with cotton wood in them, or the speakers were so out of sorts at the Delane Lee studio that upon putting it on another system what was on the tape was actually on the tape. I think, hope, that's probably what happened, that the monitoring system had to have been so out, because I hate to think we were that wrong.

Bob Welch was instrumental in keeping the band together in 1974, while making the Heroes Are Hard To Find *album. Then he left the band. Why did he decide to leave at the end of the year?*

He was disillusioned. It was that time in his life when his marriage was going wrong, he was distraught and highly wound up, which is never a great time to analyze and make the decisions that he made.

He didn't see any light at the end of the tunnel, and I think the stress of the whole thing, being our front man, caught up with him. He quite simply ran out of juice or the desire to be involved anymore, and I knew he was leaving. He never said anything, but that's one person I knew that it was just a matter of counting off the calendar until he quit.

Were you conscious of looking for other musicians to join the band?

I suppose I was, in a strange way, and hence I certainly made a mental note of Stevie and Lindsey when I heard them.

The most talked about and publicized time of Fleetwood Mac, of course, is when Lindsey Buckingham and Stevie Nicks joined the band. Did they initially fit into the band? Did it gel right away?

Yeah, it did, it did. Chris (McVie) has gone on record often, saying "I want to make sure I can get on with Stevie as a woman," 'cause quite rightly there is nothing worse than two women bickering. I mean, none of us could have stood that. And they actually got on famously for many years. They were very close. They're not anymore, which is a shame, but they just grew apart.

And then Fleetwood Mac, *the slowest album to reach number one in chart history. Basically, Fleetwood Mac had been written off by many, then bounced back with one of the finest albums of the '70s. How did your record label (Warner Bros.) help or initially react to the record?*

While we were making the album and getting toward the latter stages of it, I was terrified that the record company was just going to put it out and not really understand that we all felt it was really happening. Something was afoot, something very special, and I wanted desperately for them to really support us. So much so, I went to (Warners chief) Mo Ostin and said if you don't feel the same way about this album as we do, I want you to let us off the label, which of course was very naive, but if nothing else it made it very clear just how serious we were about what we were doing. After that, they took the point and the next time, they had a disagreement about us going out playing live, before the album came out. There was a certain amount of re-education involved. There was a certain amount of them not realizing what was going on. To that end we tried to instill that, and I think they got the hook after a little while.

Then Rumours. *I know that it's been analyzed and much talked about, but why do you think it became the biggest-selling album by a rock band in music history?*

(After a long pause) Musically, it was pressing what turned out to be all the right buttons, but I think what pushed it over the top into an arena which was way above anything anybody could possibly have concocted, was the personalities in the band. The fact that Fleetwood Mac was a very real life drama certainly sustained that honesty and realness for a long time. It did, however, become a living fantasy. That's what the magical element of the band became, and I'm not complaining, but that was the aura that followed this band around for a great many years. It was basically unreal.

Obviously the live performances helped. The audience could see what was going on.

Most definitely. Absolutely. It was very, very apparent. Stevie was mainly responsible for that.

With Tusk, *the next album, a great deal was said about the cost of making this album and Lindsey's involvement. I believe you wanted to release the package as two separate albums.*

That's true. Had we done so, it would have done it, could have sort of pioneered a thing that has been done quite successfully in recent years. I think it would also have been a success right then and there, but we were advised not to do it. We were advised not even to do a double album and for good reason; the record business was in a terrible slump. The costs of doing a double album were scary.

But we went ahead and did it 'cause we had to. We literally had to, otherwise I think the band for once would have been in jeopardy. So we did *Tusk*, and it was by no means as big a success as *Rumours*. But people forget that we sold about four to five million copies, which basically is the better part of ten million albums, really. In terms of what people were prepared to pay for the package, that album is a major milestone in Fleetwood Mac's history. It was very important; it was an excursion away from the predictable, and Lindsey was certainly instrumental in perpetuating that desire. I would love to pick the best of *Tusk* and put it on an album, because I think it would make an absolutely incredible album. I like all of it, but I just know that it's something I would like to do in the future.

At the end of the Tusk tour Fleetwood Mac took a break and this marked a drastic change in the way Fleetwood Mac worked. What happened?

Well, we quite simply had enough. We were toured out, we were played out, were studio'd out. It was, and I didn't want to admit it then—enough was enough. For the first time, I ceased to manage the band, everyone had their own management situation. The whole thing was just changed after that tour. The desire for Stevie and Lindsey especially to embark upon solo careers was magnified. So we decided to hang it up for a while. We set a time period of nine months that we weren't even going to talk about what we were going to do. That was definitely the beginning of a very different set of scales.

At that point in time, you chose to do something

that was very dear to your heart and went to Africa. What was the attraction of going to Africa?

Well, strangely enough was almost more personal than musical in a way. The musical affinity was built in, but once before, when I just felt like wandering around for personal reasons (me and my wife Jenny had split up), I just disappeared. My father actually said, "Why don't you go down to visit my friend's son in Zambia?" I did and it did so much good. The end of *Tusk* had such an influence on me and I felt it was the time where I needed to take stock of what was happening. Then that desire got wound up in having something to do, and I thought I'm going to incorporate going and making this album (*The Visitor*), which I did. It took the better part of a whole year, really with me going there to negotiate with the musicians, being down there for some six weeks and then going to England for several months finishing off the project. It was my magical mystery tour.

At that point in time you renewed contact with Peter Green, and he played on your album.

I re-recorded "Rattlesnake Shake," and I knew that unless Peter at least sang on it, that it wasn't going to make it on the album. I wanted that, and he did, and it's a great version. I felt very comfortable having him on the album, it meant a lot to me.

You went straight from making a highly personal album to going immediately back into the studio with Fleetwood Mac in France, to record the Mirage *album. How did that work out?*

It was immediate. Me and Richard (Dashut) went literally from mastering the album, got into the car, drove to a ferry, arrived in the morning at the Chateau about six, ready to start that day. I felt on top of the world. Richard and I both did. We brought the album mixes and those sessions were started off with *The Visitor* being played. Lindsey particularly was very moved by what we'd done and I would probably have to say surprised, in a nice way. He was sort of blown away, which was great; it made both me and Richard, who's very much always been under Lindsey's wing creatively. It was a real statement that he had been able to make, in putting this album together with me.

Two great tracks from the Mirage *album, "Hold*

Me" and "Gypsy," put Fleetwood Mac back into the singles charts. Yet Lindsey had some reservations about the album. What do you think about the Mirage album?

Photo/Chuck Boyd/Flower Children

I think there's some real good stuff on it. I don't think there's the continuity that was needed, and to a certain extent we were backtracking a bit. And I can definitely see Lindsey being a lot more uncomfortable with that. When I say backtracking, it sounds worse than it really is. What we had decided to do was to really try to make this a band effort, that incorporated the band. That was not Lindsey. Lindsey was wanting to do everything other than that. He couldn't see a way of doing what he wanted to do with the real involvement of the band. And yet to his credit, he really tried to do that. I think the trying to do something ended up being a slight detriment to the whole thing. But I don't dislike that album at all.

You then formed a sidekick band called the Cholos, who soon afterward changed their name to Mick Fleetwood's Zoo. Why did you change the name?

I thought Cholo meant camaraderie and a lot of other wonderful things. However, I was naive enough not to realize it had very strong gang connotations. A Cholor is a Cholo, and you don't mess with them. My friend Ron Thompson, a great blues player, said, "I think you're very ill-advised to be using the name; you don't have the right," and he convinced me to change the name. We had a hundred thousand albums sitting on the shelf, with the Cholos plastered all over them. Richard Dashut came up with the title the Zoo, and to this day the band is alive and well.

Mick Fleetwood's Zoo sustained you during Fleetwood Mac's hiatus of the early '80s. How did Fleetwood Mac get back together again?

It was a long-winded process. There were probably three or four major times I felt we were about to embark on doing an album. There was a lot of sitting on a fence, particularly from Lindsey and Stevie; to be honest, the seeds were already down as to whether Lindsey even wanted to continue, although he hadn't literally said that. Some commitments were made, then broken. In the end, basically John, Christine, and myself said we're going to start.

I believe the track "Can't Help Falling In Love" had some bearing on the proceedings.

Yes, and that became the catalyst that pulled us all back together, and ironically enough Billy (Burnette) was singing on that. We had a great time, and I think Lindsey had a great time doing it. I think his pre-conceived notions of the animal he wanted to get away from wasn't as bad as maybe he'd led himself to believe, at that particular point! So we embarked upon making another album.

The result was Tango In The Night, laden with hits, and a very successful album. Did you have any idea, during the making of it, that Lindsey wanted to leave?

Yes, he made it pretty clear that Tango was his swan song. We talked about the road, and it always turned into a non-conversation. It basically didn't take a rocket scientist to read between the lines, that this guy had no desire to be involved with this band after the making of the album. That, of course, turned out to be the case.

You brought in two new members. Billy Burnette had played with you in the Zoo, and on "Can't Help Falling In Love," so he was an obvious choice. How did the band choose lead guitarist Rick Vito? Were auditions held, and was anyone else considered?

Todd Sharp was thought about. I had done a session with Rick quite a while before and I remembered his playing. I remember having a long conversation about Peter Green and I thought Rick's playing reminded me of Peter. He had a real understanding of his playing. There was a sense of connecting umbilically with Peter that he enjoyed. That's where my knowledge of his playing came from and having played with him, only briefly, I knew he had the goods as a guitar player to be worthy. And when I say worthy, it is that, because Fleetwood Mac has always had wonderful guitar players, I felt that he could more than handle it, which he did.

You did a very successful tour to support Tango In the Night, *which proved to everyone that Fleetwood Mac had gotten over Lindsay's departure. Billy and Rick fit in well. It must have felt good to be back on top.*

I think we had proved what a lot of people had assumed to be, with Lindsey gone, an impossible task. And it couldn't have been better. I think a wonderful sense of confidence was instilled in the band. Rick and Billy more than accomplished their not so easy task, having not performed on Tango, and came into the band at very short notice. I put the situation together and John and Chris okayed it. It was nice to have their support, and I was just very happy that it worked out, because it might not have. I think the fans totally understood; they were happy that the band hadn't broken up, and I think that the band hadn't broken up, and I think that enabled them to accept Billy and Rick. They were helping us out of a situation that could well have spelled the end for Fleetwood Mac.

Did Stevie have any reservations about touring?

She had some. She's always worried about her voice and that's really the main thing. Also, she was running a solo career, so she definitely had other angles involved, but when push came to shove she was always there.

Following that successful tour, you recorded and released Behind the Mask, *the first album without Lindsey. How did it work?*

I felt it worked really well. It was definitely back to a band, which I happen to enjoy. It was a lot more fun in the studio, in terms of stress. I think everyone felt very free to offer their input, maybe more so than with Lindsey, 'cause he became very opinionated, sometimes to the betterment of the band, no doubt. It was great to see Chris really coming to the fore, making that album and realizing that this woman is not just a pretty face that writes great songs, she also has a real insight into working in the studio and an insight with a lot of things musically. So, I enjoyed making the album a lot.

Do you feel your record label didn't get behind that album?

Yeah, I do. I think there was a sense of standing on shaky ground or something. I think that it's a very accessible album, not that one can sit down and just say that it should have been a success. And the bottom line, it wasn't. I do feel, however, that it was an unfortunate time in terms of the way radio was changing. There was a big move toward rap. I think the record label got cold feet. They could have been more supportive. That really is the only time I can say that they should have worked that much harder to establish Bill and Rick in the band. For whatever reasons, they thought we were on creative shaky ground. And I think they were wrong.

During the Behind The Mask Tour, *Christine and Stevie announced their departures from Fleetwood Mac. Do you think their decisions had anything to do with your book release* (Fleetwood: My Life and Adventures In Fleetwood Mac, *William Morrow and Co., 1990)?*

No, none at all.

Why did they decide to leave, or specifically not to tour with Fleetwood Mac?

I think Stevie just couldn't see how she was going to sustain her solo career, and physically she felt that she was at her wits' end, that she just couldn't do it anymore, which is understandable. Neither Chris or Stevie are spring chickens anymore. I mean, time goes by, and to that extent I understood it was a decision she made in her mind, that's what she had to do. At that particular point she went on record numerous times and certainly told me, and for whatever reasons didn't do it, but she was very, very involved in wanting to adopt a child, and take time out to be around while it was young, for a couple of years, and that meant not being able to work. She didn't do that, but that was definitely in her mind.

Stevie and Lindsey certainly have had their contribution to Fleetwood Mac well publicized. Christine has been there almost from the beginning, and indeed played on the band's second album; she's written most of Fleetwood Mac's hits. What do you think Christine contributed both personally and musically to Fleetwood Mac?

Christine's personality really tells the story. She's very warm, doesn't think of herself as anything extraordinary, is very much a team player, and at the same time, for me has the most attractive, unique female voice in the record business still. I think she is totally unique. There is absolutely no one she can be compared with that I can think of.

There are a lot of people that have wonderful voices that have elements of other singers. Christine McVie is Christine McVie, and that's her power. She's also a wonderful songwriter. She's also not a loud singer. She's not a theatrical person. I tend to be theatrical. If I wrote songs I would be

automatically a lot more noticeable than Chris. The same with Stevie, and Chris has no problem with that, and wouldn't want it to be any different. But there are times when you almost feel like educating people as to the power of this woman, and what she's meant to Fleetwood Mac.

There is a retrospective Fleetwood Mac boxed set coming out shortly. What can the fans expect from it?

I think that it is in order to do a retrospective boxed set. I'm glad of the fact that there are two areas where I think the package is going to be a really powerful one. In America, for the most part, the bulk of Fleetwood Mac fans have no idea how this band started, and I think that has got to be a story well told in this package. I also think that there's a period of our history that in Europe basically went totally unheard; that was the period when Bob Welch was with his band. I think those actually are, outside of a few things which haven't been released before, two areas that are strong points on this package.

You have the Zoo, John has John, McVie's Gotta Band with Lola Thomas, and ex-members Lindsey Buckingham and Rick Vito have their solo albums out. What is in store for your band the Zoo?

Stardom (laughs). I'm personally really excited. I think there's a real future. Like anything, if it's handled properly. I think the personalities in the band are very real, they're by no means the same and that makes for good medicine, creativity. For me it's a given, the band has a real sound to it and a person. Becka Bramlet is destined one way or another for success, and I'm just glad that seemingly it's gonna at least start, and I hope continue, with my involvement with her in the Zoo. I think she's a talent that's about to break loose. Billy Thorpe, by no means a spring chicken, is a very creative person, at last in a band, where I think a slight element of self-destructiveness is avoided, the way his career may have been gone. I know he's enjoying being in a band. And God knows it's the only way that I can function. I think we've got a great future.

So you now technically are in two permanent bands.

Technically, I'm in two permanent bands.

The Top 10 Most Collectible Fleetwood Mac Albums

by Tim Neely

Many of the American singles and albums released by Fleetwood Mac are hard to find, especially from before 1975, the year that Lindsey Buckingham and Stevie Nicks first made an impact with the band. Nonetheless, few of them are especially valuable.

That said, here are 10 that could fetch more than average to a Mac collector. This list includes only group efforts; it does not include solo works that would make this list, such as the original release of Buckingham Nicks with a gatefold; any of the singles that were released from that album; or scarce solo picture sleeves, such as Stevie Nicks' elusive "Nightbird."

They are arranged according to the near-mint (basically store-bought condition) value in the *Standard Catalog to American Records, 1950-1975*.

Key (taken from *Goldmine British Invasion Record Price Guide*): For many listings, you'll see a letter or two before the title. These designate something special about the listing as follows:

B: for LPs, a record listed as stereo has both mono and stereo tracks on it, and as far as we know none of it is rechanneled stereo.

DJ: some sort of promotional copy, usually for radio stations, and not meant for public sale.

M: for any record pressed in both mono and stereo, a mono record.

P: for LPs, a record listed as stereo has some tracks in true stereo and some tracks in rechanneled stereo. The stereo or the rechanneled tracks are often listed below.

PD: picture disc (artwork is actually part of the record).

PS: for 45s and some EPs, a picture sleeve (this is the value for the sleeve alone, combine the record and sleeve value to get an estimated worth for the two together). UK EPs are assumed to have a picture sleeve unless noted.

R: for LPs, a record listed as stereo is entirely rechanneled stereo.

S: for any record pressed in both mono and stereo, a stereo record. Either the entire record is known to be true stereo or we don't know whether it's all stereo. In general, rechanneled stereo was not used in the UK.

Label, Catalog #		Title	$ Value
1.	Epic BN 26402 M	Fleetwood Mac	100
1.	Epic BN 26446 M	English Rose	100

The above two albums are the most sought-after in the American Mac catalog. These are white label promotional copies, specially pressed in mono for radio stations. They will be indicated as such, even though they likely carry the same number as the stereo counterpart. Most of these will have "Special Mono Radio Station Copy" stickers on the front.

3.	Warner Bros. PRO-A-652	Rumours	50

A promotional 12-inch single with an embossed cover, this contains "Go Your Own Way" and "Silver Springs." As most Mac fans know, "Silver Springs" was a non-LP track until the release of the box set.

3.	Mobile Fidelity 012	Fleetwood Mac	50

One of the earliest Mobile Fidelity albums, this also is an "Original Master Recording." Versions on Reprise (it was released with two different numbers) are more common.

5.	Mobile Fidelity 119	Mirage	40

Another audiophile version, the cover will have an "Original Master Recording" stripe across the top front. Again, Warner Bros. pressings are very common.

6.	Epic BN 26402 S	Fleetwood Mac	30

The first American album by "Peter Green's Fleetwood Mac."

6.	Epic BN 26406 S	English Rose	30

The group's second American album.

6.	Blue Horizon BH-3801 (2)	Fleetwood Mac in Chicago	30

The original American pressing of this came out on the short-lived Blue Horizon label, distributed in the United States by Chess. (The original British title of this set was Blues Jam At Chess.) This is not to be confused with later issues of this same material, most notably on the Sire label.

6.	Nautilus NR-8	Rumours	30

Obviously not to be confused with the very common Warner Bros. version, this audiophile pressing will have the "Nautilus SuperDisc" logo on the front cover.

10.	Reprise RS 6465	Future Games	25

This is for the originals with a pale yellow cover. Copies with a pale green cover are common.

Brian Wilson

By Steve Roeser
November 18, 1988

There's a certain handful of people in the world of pop and rock music whose accomplishments are so awesome, talent so prodigious and artistic depth so vast, that their names have long since taken on mythic proportions. Dylan, of course, and Van Morrison come to mind. Pete Townsend and McCartney, Neil Young, Eric Clapton, Keith Richards... only a few others. In recent times, we've lost Zappa and Garcia, both of whom certainly ranked alongside these just mentioned. Smokey Robinson and Berry Gordy also require top consideration. You can probably think of a few others.

But in terms of legendary American record producers of the 1960s, there are two figures whose work stands a cut above the rest. Their recordings are still enjoyed immensely every day on the radio throughout the world. One is Phil Spector. The other is Brian Wilson. Spector started out in the late '50s as a singer and guitarist, but soon concentrated his efforts strictly on writing and producing, very successfully, for various groups, a number of which he created himself. In the process, he became a legend by the time he was 25.

Wilson also became a pop music legend by the time he turned 25, but did so by writing, producing, playing and singing for essentially one group, the

Beach Boys. There was the occasional side project for Jan and Dean, or someone else around their scene. But the Beach Boys were Brian Wilson's life. It could also be conversely stated that, especially at the outset of their career, Brian Wilson was the Beach Boys. He wrote, arranged and produced just about all of the group's early music, as has been well-documented over the past 30 years. (If you can, check out the Beach Boys' five-CD box set, *Good Vibrations*, which was released on Capitol in 1993. It's still in print, but not always easy to find.) Regardless of the combined talents of his younger brothers Dennis and Carl, their cousin Mike Love, and early "original" member Al Jardine, it is generally acknowledged that without Brian, there never would have been a group called the Beach Boys. Or, if there had been it might have been a successful local band at best, not an international phenomenon on a level comparable with the Beatles in the early-to-mid 1960s.

But, somewhat like Spector in a way, Wilson, now 53, has had to live with the widely-held notion (accurate or not, fair or unfair) that he's never done anything since 1966 that measures up to the classic recordings he made way back when. As he admits in the following interview, Brian did screw himself up on drugs in the wake of his huge success with the Beach Boys, and put himself out of commission literally for years. There was the momentary glimmer of renewed activity in the decade after he composed and created one of the most masterful pop singles of all time, "Good Vibrations." But most people preferred to write Brian off callously as just another once-brilliant drug casualty whose glory days were well behind him.

Apparently, however, someone must've forgotten to tell Brian Wilson about this theory, or at least to convince him of its validity. He has steadfastly refused to subscribe to that view of himself. He is still at it. Through good times and bad (and there have been lots of bad times, emotionally and psychologically), Wilson hasn't thrown in the towel. He has continued to write, sing and record in the studio, sometimes for the Beach Boys, but just

as often for himself. Because it is fairly obvious, to anyone who is truly interested, that music is the reason Brian Wilson is here. And that has really always been the case.

Brian Douglas Wilson was born in Inglewood (Los Angeles), California on June 20, 1942, just two days after Paul McCartney was born in Liverpool, England. That their shared time on this planet is virtually exact is a fact that is not lost on Brian himself, who felt a sense of rivalry with McCartney and the Beatles in the '60s and (gathered from some of his comments here) probably still regards McCartney competitively, even today. It is also perhaps not coincidental that Wilson, whose songs are more associated with the pleasures of summer than any other writer, should have been born on the first day of summer.

Brian often turned to others to work with him on lyrics to his songs, at the urging of his father, Murry, the manager of the Beach Boys in the beginning, after Nik Venet signed the group to Capitol Records in 1961. (Brian was producing his own group before the Beatles were even signed to EMI.) Mike Love, Gary Usher and Roger Christian were among those who wrote with Brian in the early days. The late Christian, whose collaborations with Wilson included the car songs "Shut Down," "Little Deuce Coupe" and "Don't Worry Baby," was a DJ at KFWB in Hollywood, which Brian names here as one of the stations he was attuned to growing up. Love's recent lawsuits against Wilson, seeking co-writing credit to a number of well-known Beach Boys songs, have been discussed in the music press and elsewhere, and are an ongoing topic of controversy.

After working with Tony Asher as his co-writer on the highly-acclaimed *Pet Sounds* album (which McCartney took as his cue, it's been told, to try to outdo with his *Sergeant Pepper's* concept), Brian met and began collaborating with a musician/songwriter/actor named Van Dyke Parks, introduced to him by fellow L.A. record producer Terry Melcher. This was the genesis of the infamous Smile project (original working title, Dumb Angel), a never-completed song cycle that was meant to go far beyond Brian's magnificent *Pet Sounds*. Although bits and pieces of the Parks/Wilson compositions for this great lost opus surfaced here and there in subsequent years, hardcore Brian fans, in particular, consider Smile to be nothing less than the Holy Grail of pop music treasures, and won't rest until they hear all of what still exists from those sessions.

There has been talk of either a boxed set or a CD-ROM of all the Smile tapes intended for release. But when, and in what format?

"I know a lot of people were expecting Capitol to release a Smile sessions collection in the fall of 1995," a longtime Beach Boys fan close to the scene observed. "Given the fact that there was a new record by Brian and Van Dyke—which I love and have now listened to over a hundred times—as a Brian Wilson fan, I don't feel that we have anything to complain about.

"That said," added the source, who requested anonymity, "everybody is aware of the intense interest in the Smile sessions. And right now, Capitol and the Beach Boys are formulating plans that will unfold in the near future." The longtime fan further stated that there is likely to be a definite announcement regarding Smile made by Capitol in February.

In 1988, after years of speculation about his mental and physical condition, the death of his brother Dennis, estrangement from family and the other members of the Beach Boys, as well as rampant rumors (or mostly true accounts, depending on your position or point of view) that his fife was controlled by his psychotherapist, Dr. Eugene Landy, Brian finally released his first solo album, *Brian Wilson*. Some were a bit disappointed by the results, while many others, especially the true believers in Brian's magic, found the work to be captivating and tremendous. Unquestionably there were some beautiful songs on the record, and overall it was the best work Wilson had done in ages. It was a monumental improvement over where he had dislocated himself in the mid '70s, when Brian's creativity was at such a low ebb, that he could muster nothing more imaginative than a remake of the Righteous Brothers recording of "Just Once In My Life" from 1965, a song co-written and originally produced by his model, Spector. Indeed, Brian had thought Spector's record to be so flawless, that he'd had the Beach Boys make almost an exact replica of it. Everyone knew that Brian Wilson was meant for more than that, and could do worlds better.

After a less-than-overwhelming commercial response to his solo album, and an aborted follow-up, it was another five or six years of relative obscurity for Wilson. However, Brian did have the good fortune during that time to meet up with a talented musician and record producer, who also happened to be a great admirer of his past work. That man,

Don Was, also was just then coming into his own as one of the most formidable behind-the-scenes individuals in the music business. Was and Wilson talked with one another, played some low-profile gigs together, and gradually came to know each other on a musical and personal level.

This friendship grew to the stage where Was became thrilled with the idea of using his influence to put the spotlight back on Wilson and his music. The first phase of these efforts (which included a project called *Bells Of Madness*, featuring Brian, his daughter Carnie, and Rob Wasserman, on the GRP label) culminated in the summer of 1995, when the Don Was-directed documentary film *Brian Wilson: I Just Wasn't Made For These Times* was shown to a worldwide audience via the Disney Channel.

Brian afforded Was full cooperation in the making of this film, which included newly-recorded versions of some of Wilson's finest songs, including "This Old World," "Do It Again," "The Warmth Of The Sun" and "Til I Die." In the liner notes to the accompanying album, which was released an Was's Karambolage label through MCA Records, Brian offered a special dedication to several people, including his mother Audree, his second wife Melinda, whom he recently married, and the Beach Boys. But the first person listed to whom he dedicated the album is Phil Spector.

Toward the end of the documentary, Brian is seen with Parks, and they are playing the song "Orange Crate Art," a tune which some old Brian/Beach Boys fans believe has some link to the legend of the Smile album. Maybe it does. But Parks and Wilson have both been reluctant to draw any specific analogies between their latest collaboration and the work they did together in the '60s.

Orange Crate Art may be the most unusual album project that Brian Wilson has ever been associated with. That can be stated purely from the fact that Brian's only job on the album was to sing. He did not write any of the songs. Parks wrote eight of them, used Michael Hazlewood as his co-writer on two others, one is a Hazlewood composition, and the final track is a George Gershwin piece.

Brian did not produce the album (Parks did), or arrange any of the music (Parks again). Neither did he play any instruments on the record. He used only his voice, which, before Wilson claims he caused injury to, many of us knew to be one of the most wondrous instruments in all of recorded music. That instrument, in spite of all the wear and tear, still sounds marvelous on *Orange Crate Art*.

With this album, one can sit back and enjoy Brian Wilson as the interpretive artist, filtering the work of others through his unique musical sensibility. This is a very enjoyable album that reveals brightly a different aspect of Brian's talent.

The "Brian is back" fanfare has been sounded before. Then people look around after a while, and the man is nowhere to be found. But the events of 1995 seem to tell a different story. It seems really true that this time a new chapter is being written in the life of Brian Wilson. And he is the author. He isn't letting things happen, but rather making things happen. And that's the Brian Wilson who made musical history.

The people who love Brian's music, and are inspired by his work over and over again are made to feel good, and feel happy, just to know that he is there, working. Busy doing what he is meant to do. What he was born to do. For those who know his work, it is not that Brian Wilson makes music, Brian Wilson is music. They are one and the same.

The following conversation took place in the living room of Brian's home, in the Hollywood Hills section of Los Angeles, between four and five in the afternoon on Friday, December 1, 1995. The proceedings began just moments after the interviewer had been introduced to Brian for the first time, never having spoken to him before. There were some minor audio problems experienced in the taping of the conversation but, with only slight editing of the transcription, this is more or less precisely what transpired.

Goldmine: *I've listened to the album that you did with Van Dyke. It think it's great.*

Brian Wilson: *Orange Crate Art*? It is. It's a wonderful album.

With these two 1995 releases-the soundtrack to the documentary that Don [Was] did with you, and Orange Crate Art—*it's a very encouraging sign to old fans of yours as well as anyone who loves your music, that you're working a lot again. In the case of these projects, you had Don co-producing...*

Yeah.

...and in the case of Orange Crate Art, *you didn't have to produce at all. Can people expect to see, in the coming year, you arranging and producing yourself on songs that no one's heard yet?*

Not that I know of. But maybe the Beach Boys might get an album done by the spring [of 1996].

Is there any truth to this [story] that you've been working with the Beach Boys lately?

Yeah, ah, there is. About three weeks ago we did two songs in the studio. One was for Carl, and the other is for the whole group. But Carl sang lead on the one song, called "Soul Searchin'," written by Andy Paley and me. It's got that stroll thing [Brian briefly demonstrates the beat]—you know, it's a stroll type of rhythm. And it's comin' out real good.

Did Don have anything to do with this Beach Boys project?

Ah, yeah, he's the executive producer.

He mentioned [to Goldmine in 1994] that you had worked on a recording of "Proud Mary".

Yeah.

What was your interest in doing that?

"Proud Mary"? I wanted to do it [because] I've always loved that song. I thought, "Great lyric: 'Rollin' on a river.' Great, great idea." So, we did it. We did the track, but we're not done.

So, out of that grew these new songs.

Yeah.

Is it possible that you would ever get to the point where you'd say, "I don't think I'd work with the Beach Boys again"? Could it ever get to that?

Sure it could. Absolutely, yeah. Sometimes the guys act really wise. And wise-off.

Could you foresee writing and producing for a group other than the Beach Boys?

Not really, no. I'm pretty true to the Beach Boys that way.

I want to ask you some specific questions about Orange Crate Art, *because that's mostly why I'm here. Do you feel that you're a better singer now than you were in the early days of the Beach Boys?*

No. Not at all. I don't think I'm quite as good as I used to be, because of cigarettes. They ruined my throat. I blew my throat, my voice, from cigarette smoking. I smoked for seven years, [quit] and then I started smokin' again for another three. I totally ruined my throat. I ruined my range and my timbre. The quality of my voice didn't have that sweetness in it anymore, you know? That's a very, very hard lesson to learn.

Your voice does sound very good on this record, though.

I know, but I don't think it's as good as it used to be. I don't know, maybe it is. [Brian humorously dismisses the question.]

When did you finally quit smoking?

About half a year ago. No, about four months ago.

When you are out touring and doing shows with Van Dyke, performing the songs from Orange Crate Art, *can people expect to hear you perform some of the old songs that you and Van Dyke wrote together, such as "Heroes And Villains," On Sailor"...*

Yes, maybe we will. We might do that, yeah.

Would you do any other old songs?

I'm tryin' to think I don't think so. No, I'd have to keep it more or less original material.

You don't think you'd do any of the stuff from the documentary, I Just Wasn't Made For These Times?

[In a very quiet voice] I don't know. I really don't.

The album closes with George Gershwin's "Lullaby." What effect did the music of George Gershwin have on you when you were developing as a musician?

Totally, totally I was overcome by him, by his music. I was overwhelmed.

[after a brief pause] You had a hit album in the '70s with the Beach Boys, 15 Big Ones, *which you produced, where you covered songs by Chuck Berry ["Rock A.nd Roll Music"], Fats Domino ["Blueberru Hill"], the Five Satins ["In The Still Of The Night"]. As*

a teenager, you must have been very turned on by the original R&B artists, the R&B artists that were really heavy then.

Chuck Berry? Chuck Berry is the man. Chuck Berry is the man that got me really goin' on my songwriting. There is an innovator who I thought was great. He's really great.

What did you feel about Fats Domino?

Photo/Henry Diltz

Brian Wilson: Um, I never really thought Fats Domino was that... He's not really that bad of a singer. But he's somewhat of a genius like Chuck Berry, in his own way. In his own right.

Little Richard?

Yeah, Little Richard, eh? I got a [Brian lets out a Little Richard-like whoop, circa 1956] idea from him. You'd hear that and go, "Whoa!" I remember hearing those records. His screaming thin and his yelping was funny. I learned about how to be exciting from Little Richard. His music didn't really get me that excited.

What about the black vocal groups in general? Were you very into them?

You mean like the Del Vikings, or...

The Flamingos, the Drifters...

Oh, yeah! Yeah, all those old records, totally into those records.

Living around here, what L.A. radio stations would you listen to back then?

KFWB, KRLA! Remember those?

Well, I wasn't living here then, but I heard about 'em, yeah. Um, Hunter Hancock?

Oh! You really hit it on the nerve-bone there! You've got my whole junior high trip together. [laughs] Yeah, actually, yeah. Huntin' With Hunter it was called. Yeah, I remember that.

Would he be on every night, just about?

No, I think he was on once a week. I don't know.

How about Johnny Otis? Would you listen to him?

Yeah, Johnny Otis, absolutely!

Would you watch his TV show?

Yeah, yeah.

How about Peter Potter? He was another [DJ] who had a show.

Oh, Peter Potter—something about "a hit or a miss"?

Yeah right.

Hit Jamboree or Hit Parade. Yeah, I thought it was very, very creative. I liked that a lot.

So, a lot of that music inspired you to try to get into writing?

Yeah, it does. it behooves me to try to prove myself, you know? [I've fallen short] in some ways in life , but in other ways I feel like I'm a strong man. I'm a strong kinda guy.

Do you believe that part of you, throughout your entire career, has been trying to create recordings that go beyond the best work of Phil Spector? Records such as 'Be My Baby," "Then He Kissed Me" or "You've Lost That Lovin' Feelin'"?

Yeah, sure.

When you think of records like that, and the sound that came off those records, do you feel in some ways you've been trying to match that? Match Spector's work from those early times?

[Very quietly, almost in a contrite tone of voice] Yeah...

Do you feel you succeeded, with any of your records, to…

No. But we tried.

Can you make a comment about Spector in general, and his work? How you feel about him.

Well, sure. I mean, I've always thought that he was the most important producer in the history of the whole business. His sounds were so new and inventive. He was the greatest.

There's a song on Orange Crate Art *called "San Francisco," which you've said you like a lot. You've always lived in southern California.*

Right.

Do you have a strong sense of yourself, and a personal identity, as a very Californian musician and artist?

Brian Wilson: Uh, no, not really. I think I'm well… I never really had that kind of identity crisis.

Goldmine: Do you feel you could have created a lot of the same type of music if you had lived in another part of the United States?

No, not at all. I wouldn't have been exposed to the records that I was. We got into California, got out into Los Angeles, got into some studios, and found our scene there. And we lived off that place for the whole time.

You were doing some publicity when you put out your solo album in 1988. 1 believe I saw you on Late Night With David Letterman.

I think you might have, but I don't know. [thinks a moment] This was back in 1988?

'88.

Yeah, I did. I was on there.

I watched the show, and I clearly recall you saying… You made a comment that stuck with me. You said, "There's no such thing as giving up in life." Do you remember saying that?

Yeah, right.

Is this a philosophy you've held your whole life?

I felt that… ah, no. But, uh, I heard Randy Newman. You know, at different times in my life I've had that kind of attitude, yeah.

What was it about Randy Newman's work that might have given you that?

Well, he had a song where he wrote, "When the goin' gets tough, the tough get going." And I liked that. I liked what he was talkin' about. And I got into a more tough frame of mind, you know? 'Cause he's a toughie! [Brian laughs]

Yeah, he is. He's a very creative person, too. None of the songs on this record were co-written by you, but have you been writing lately with Van Dyke, other material?

No. He wrote all the material for *Orange Crate Art.*

Will you write with him again?

[in a whisper] I don't know.

How can you compare writing with Van Dyke to some of the other many writers you've written [songs] with over the years?

He's more inventive than the other guys. He's just somebody who I think is just a little better than the rest of 'em. He has a thing goin' with music, like a little romance—a romance of making music, you know?

A couple of years ago, I saw you coming out of a movie in Santa Monica. I think you had gone to see Hero *featuring Dustin Hoffman.*

Yeah.

What is your definition of a hero?

A hero?

Yeah.

I dunno. Lemme think... a hero eh? A hero is somebody who, ah, is able to... sacrifice a little bit of his happiness in order to do some rescue some people, get things better. [That's] a hero.

Did you have any heroes when you were growing up?

Oh, God yes! Oh, are you kiddin'? My dad. My doctor, and some of the producers that I liked. Certain authority figures in my life. I've had a lot of that in my life.

Nik Venet?

Yeah! Yeah, Nik Venet was one of those kinds guys that you just had to like. There was something about him that you just liked, you know? I saw him ... at a party at his house, and I hadn't seen him since 1963, 30 years. [laughs] It was really quite a shock to see him. But I'm okay. [laughs] It was a shock, that's all.

There's also a good song on the record called "Movies Is Magic."

Yeah.

That song kind of talks about the pre-rock 'n' roll era.

Yeah

Can you recall the earliest music that appealed to you as a child? Like late '40s, around 1950 maybe, when you were only maybe eight, nine years old?

[letting out a quick sigh] Yeah, Les Paul.

Les Paul?

Yep.

Anything else? Like big band stuff...

Maybe Rosemary Clooney.

Yeah?

And also [Brian raises his eyes and emits a sharp whistle.] Glenn Miller. [laughs]

Are there particular records from that time that you recall...

No ...

... really affecting you?

No.

Did your father listen to big band radio broadcasts?

No, he didn't like that.

What kind of music would you hear him listening to?

Lawrence Welk.

Uh-huh. Would you watch that show?

Yeah, we all did. We loved it.

Uh-huh. Brian, the music, that is constantly in your head...

Yeah...

Where does that come from?

[brief pause] Um... I dunno. I guess, from the sky? I dunno... I have no idea.

Do you believe, as some composers and songwriters do, that the music is always "out there" somewhere...

Yeah.

...and that, as the artist, you merely serve as a conduit....

Yeah

through which the music is communicated...

Yeah.

...to the rest of us?

Yeah [interviewer laughs] What was the question? I'm sorry...

No, that's what I wanted to know. What do you think of that idea, that somehow the music just comes through you?

Well, it comes through me ,cause it's put through me. [Brian chuckles to himself momentarily.] And it puts me through it. It comes through me because someone puts it through me.

Who?

[sounding incredulous, at a loss] I don't know. I never knew.

Do you regard your musical ability as a gift?

Yeah, very much so. You know, everybody has music...

I saw a little piece of [TV broadcast] videotape recently, where you were talking about hearing Rubber Soul, *when you first heard it, and then you played it every night for a month, you were saying. And you particularly liked the songs "Michelle" and "Girl."*

Right.

What was it about that album that was blowing your mind so much?

Well, I liked ... probably John Lennon, you know? I don't know. I think maybe John Lennon's music kind of blew me away.

Did you watch The Beatles Anthology *that was just on?*

Um, yeah, I did, actually. Goldmine: What did you think about it?

Well, I was frightened by it, you know?

Why?

Because they had such an overly-famous kind of image, in a way. The Beatles are so famous, it's almost embarrassing, you know? When I saw the *Anthology* shows, I felt a little scared, and also a little jealous. But, mostly, proud. You know? I thought they did wonderful things. A wonderful anthology, I thought, beautifully produced... And

"Let It Be," of course, made it all worth it, for me. When they did that song… Did you see it?

Yes.

I was sittin' in a room, listenin' to [watching] the Anthology. And when Paul did "Let It Be," I mean, the whole room just felt like it was goin' up and up. Something really different, you know? Very, very spiritual. And I was very proud. It was one of the most spiritual moments of my whole life.

You could say … Are you saying you felt proud because you share in it somehow?

Yeah. Yeah, because, like, he [McCartney] was doin' that [song], and you know, like, it wasn't It puts you in awe when you hear that music, you know? And we were all in this living room—my wife, and me, and [Wilson biographer and friend] David Leaf, and his wife, Eva. And, I'm tellin' ya, I don't know about the rest of them—I didn't actually even ask anybody—but I know I didn't feel like I was on the earth. I felt like that had taken me someplace that 1, I didn't know where. You know? I couldn't believe it. "Let It Be" by the Beatles. [laughs] Kind of like, really, somethin' else.

Uh-huh…

I mean, a message song, for sure. You know, obviously…

When you say, too, you feel a little envious, or jealous…

Yeah. Of Paul.

Of Paul?

Yeah…

Ah, I think maybe some people can agree with you on that, because you inspired them, and …

Ah, ha!

…and you've never gotten the recognition on that kind of level.

No, but, you see, I don't let myself know that. It's like, I don't need to, you know? Because it would

just be aw, who cares? You know? I mean, so? Blech! You know what I mean?

Uh-huh

There's a certain naiveness about me, about my personality. I'm a little bit naive in some ways. In other ways I'm pretty smart, too. But, who knows? Go ahead.

Well, you know, the critics have certainly appreciated your music, but have you ever felt that your music with the Beach Boys has been kind of taken for granted by the public? The public at large?

No. No, we have people that still come up to us all the time and tell us that they like our music. There's still people that do that.

There's a quote in the [CD] booklet, an Old Testament quote…

Yeah…

…that begins, uh, it has something to do with "fathers."

Yeah.

When you think of your dad, Murry, do you feel thankful that he led you to pursue music, and…

Yeah. He taught me how to play the piano. He taught me how to, ah, as he calls it, "kick ass." You know? He taught me to do that. Just some basic things like, "Get in there and kick butt," or "Go out there and kick ass in football today," or "Go on down to the studio and kick Spector's butt!" He was so competitive, you know?

Uh-huh.

He was more competitive than I was. But he got the flame of the devil under my ass: "Get out there and compete!" He really knew. My dad made a great coach. He was a nice character. He was a little mean, you know, too. But he was a great, great guy. My dad was a good man.

Did you feel grateful that he wanted you to pursue [music] really heavily?

Oh, sure, he kept I mean, it was my mother, too. My dad, you see... I'll tell you what it really was. To be honest with you, it wasn't my dad that Well, yeah, it was! Because, I remember I was in the... Was it fourth grade? Or fifth grade? I was sitting in my little chair in class, right? And I started humming the melodies to songs he wrote. And I felt that, when I went to school, I was so afraid of everybody, that my dad's music got me through. When you're a little kid, and your father's music helps you through, you know darn well that's a spiritual thing, right? It's gotta be. You know that has to be spiritual.

So, you're talking about when you were 10 or 11 years old. How was [your dad's] music helping you?

0h, well–eight years old.

Okay.

It was helping me because it gave me love. You know? It was a real source of love. It really did. It was a wonderful source of love. I sang [the music, mentally] in class, and it got me far away from what the teachers were teaching. I [fell behind] a little bit in my grades, because of my preoccupation with my dad's music. But I was so preoccupied that when I'd get out of class, I'd go in the bathroom and look in the mirror [and say to myself], "Well, I've made it through so far today." I'd talk to myself, and prep for the next class, you know? I was so afraid of people, that I had to go way out of my way to completely be able to handle it.

Do you recall the record that your dad put out after the Beach Boys had hit it big?

No.

I think he had put his own personal record [album] out.

Oh, yeah! *The Many Moods Of Murry Wilson* [1967].

Yeah.

I don't know. I listened to it but I haven't... I might get it and listen to it. He might have somethin' goin' on there.

He must have been very proud of his own music

He sure was. His music was very superior. He made very superior music. [pause] He was a wonderful, wonderful man, with a great heart... and a good belt to spank with. He really spanked me hard.

[At this point, David Leaf, who is on the other side of the large living room, asks a question, and there is a brief exchange between him and Brian.]

Brian, you've written a lot of songs about girls.

Oh, yeah, of course!

And you say one of your favorites on this record is "My Jeanine."

Yeah, I love "My Jeanine." That's a wonderful song. I like that a lot.

Has anything ever inspired you to write, more than a girl? Like, any particular girl?

[sighs] Well, I never, ever, really wrote a song about a girl. I never did. I've used girls' names, like "Caroline, No," or Rhonda, you know? Or "Wendy." But they were never written for any specific girl. If I do, it's gonna have to be one of the best songs ever written. If I do write a song about a girl, it's gonna be really good. It'd be a real good song, you know?

So, whenever you wrote one of those songs, and you named it after a girl, it wasn't about a particular girl?

No, not at all.

It was about girls in general?

Yeah.

Just the beauty of...

Like "California Girls." It was kind of saying, like, "Wow!" It's a song about girls, and it is about girls, but no specific girl. [laughs] I'm sure there were girls out there named Rhonda who went, "Oh, that was written about me!" You know? [laughs]

What is there in the universe that is more beautiful

than a girl?

That is... probably the truth. Um, except [for] music. [pause] Us guys get the credit for most of the music that has been written: Gershwin, Cole Porter, you know...

Yeah. You just mentioned the song "Wendy." And you wrote that song, I guess, before you were married, right?

Mmmm... [trying to remember] No-yeah! Yeah.

Were you perhaps dreaming of having a daughter named Wendy, when you wrote that?

Nooo... I don't think so! I don't think so.

She's a beautiful girl. I saw her at the screening [of the Don Was documentary].

Yeah, she's a wonderful kid. I'm gonna cut her, I'm gonna produce her.

Really?

On their new album.

Great. It's gonna be her solo record?

No, no. She's gonna sing one cut on a new Beach Boys album. One whole cut.

And you're gonna produce that yourself?

Yeah. And it might be "In My Room," too. I don't know.

Wow, that'd be fantastic. How has your friendship with Don Was helped you to bring the scope of your music, and your past accomplishments, into perspective?

Basically, he's guided me along. He did my documentary film, and all the stuff where I needed somebody to be guiding me. I need guidance, you know? I'm all messed up, because I took a lot of drugs in my life, you know, and fried my brain. So, I have to live with the bed I made. [quietly] I took a lot of very, very potent, dangerous drugs, and you know, it fucked me up. [very quietly] But that's okay.

Do you feel that you've bounced back from that, to a large degree?

I'm trying to. I'm trying to do that, yeah. I'm in the process of tryin' to bounce back with something that... I think could be meaningful. Instead of just goin' in there, just to get through, you know? Instead of going through that so much, I like to go into life [Brian makes an additional brief comment, which is inaudible on the tape.]

You mention the song "Help Me, Rhonda." You know, I was listening to a John Lee Hooker song the other day..

Yeah?

And there's a little riff in there. Did you perhaps get part of that from a John Lee Hooker song?

I might have, yeah. [laughs merrily]

Were you into him?

John Lee Hooker? I... I don't know. Uh, this is gonna sound really stupid, but is he a blues singer?

Yeah.

Yeah, I don't think so. Maybe, maybe not. I don't know. I don't really know.

How much were you ever into the blues?

The blues... didn't do much, for me. Ray Charles did.

What was some Ray Charles stuff that you really dug?

Well, he did a version of "The Long And Winding Road." Beautiful, beautiful. "What'd I Say," "Georgia On My Mind," and all those songs.

How about, aside from Wendy, can you foresee doing a record for a solo artist, writing and producing for them?

Ah, I had thought about that I think every time I wanted to do that, I either shied away from the project, or just wasn't really able to handle what was goin' on there. So, instead, I kind of just funnel my energies into the Beach Boys. I'm sure it was cool, though.

How has it felt this year [1995], with these projects coming out, and meeting the public more again? Actually getting out, like the fact that you were at the screenings for your film, and involved with that, and doing press, and going to New York, and everything like that? Does it feel good just to get out, and be in touch with the media and the public?

Yes. It's good to be there.

Does that help your creativity?

It pushes me through, yeah. It gets me through what I have to get through.

Are you aware of just how many people out there think you're great? And that it is believed you have a special gift that is appreciated?

Some people tell me that. Um, like, my solo album was met by a lot of praise. People liked my solo album a lot. They really did.

Was it very disappointing to you that the album that followed your solo album went unreleased?

Yeah, it was stolen.

It was stolen?

Someone stole the tapes.

The master tapes were stolen?

Right, the master tapes, all, the whole library, of all... of everything to do with my second solo album, was stolen.

Where were they?

They were in our tape room, at my studio. And we sold the studio. But before we sold it, we went to take the tapes out, and we were supposed to find the ones with the, uh... it was called... Oh, what was it going to be called? I don't know.

Sweet Insanity?

Yeah, *Sweet Insanity*. Someone made off with the

tapes. Stole 'em.

Any theories about what, how that happened, or who would want to do that? Or, did they take something without knowing what it was or... ?

I don't know. I really don't know. I think someone stole them because they were jealous that... I don't know. Who knows why? All I know is, they weren't there. We couldn't find 'em. We searched the place high and low, and we did not find all those tapes. There was like a whole shelf, half a shelf worth, of master tapes, and what-do-you-call-it... So, I say to myself, "Oh, man! All that work, for nothin'?" You know? But then I said, "Well, yeah, but I had fun makin' the album, you know? So, what the heck? What's the big deal?' You know? [Brian laughs good-naturedly, as if it really is no catastrophe.]

How long did you work on it?

Oh, we must have done it for at least seven, eight months. Over half a year.

People do have, like, other generation copies of it, so it's been heard by people, right?

Oh, yeah, there are tapes, cassette tapes of it. Um, somewhere... [calling across the room to Leaf] David?

David Leaf: *Yes?*

Do you have a cassette tape of the whole *Sweet Insanity* album?

David Leaf: *Uh-huh.*

You got it all?

David Leaf: *Yeah.*

Can you bring it over sometime?

David Leaf: *Sure.*

I'd like to listen to it.

David Leaf: *Absolutely. Next time I come over.*

All right.

David Leaf: *There's some good songs on that record.*

Yeah, I know.

David Leaf: *"Don't Let Her Know She's An Angel"...*

Yup. [Leaf names a couple more titles, and Brian agrees that he thought the songs were good.] Yeah, there were some cute songs on there. It was a cute album, it really was.

Goldmine: *Who else played on it?*

Ah, there was Andy Paley, uh, a black bass player, and me, and a guitar player—I don't know, just musicians that we knew. A harmonica player. A lot of good synthesizer stuff. We had a great programmer, who knew all about it, and he made it real easy for me to do that. They say that sometimes it can get real tedious, and almost discouraging, you know? But he made it so that I wasn't really discouraged. He really helped me get it. I was real thankful that I met the guy. This guy was so... [whistles], so quick. I don't know... [Brian seems to become somewhat distracted.] But, who knows? I think maybe it scared me to think about this, because I'm goin' back a little, to a time period in my life when it was kind of hard for me. But, anyway, uh... I'd like to quit.

Goldmine: *Okay, man.*

Brian Wilson: Okay? And I thank you very much.

Goldmine Grading Guide

by Tim Neely

When it comes to records, and how much you'll get for them, remember this above all: **Condition is (almost) everything!**

Yes, it's possible to get a high price for a beat-up record, if it's exceptionally rare. But for common material, if it's not in at least Very Good condition—and preferably closer to Near Mint—you won't get many buyers. Or at least you won't the second time around. So accurately grading your discs is important, whether you're selling your records to a dealer or selling them to another collector.

Visual or Play Grading?

In an ideal world, every record would be played before it is graded. But the time involved makes it impractical for most dealers, and anyway, it's rare that you get a chance to hear a record before you buy through the mail. Some advertisers play-grade everything and say so. But unless otherwise noted, records are visually graded.

How to Grade

Look at everything about a record—its playing surface, its label, its edges—under a strong light. Then, based on your overall impression, give it a grade based on the following criteria:

Mint (M): Absolutely perfect in every way—certainly never played, possibly even still sealed. (More on still sealed under "Other considerations.") Should be used sparingly as a grade, if at all.

Near Mint (NM or M): A nearly perfect record. Many dealers won't give a grade higher than this, implying (perhaps correctly) that no record is ever truly perfect.

The record should show no obvious signs of wear. A 45 RPM or EP sleeve should have no more than the most minor defects, such as almost invisible ring wear or other signs of slight handling.

An LP jacket should have no creases, folds, seam splits or any other noticeable similar defect. No cut-out holes, either. And of course, the same should be true of any other inserts, such as posters, lyric sleeves and the like.

Basically, an LP in Near Mint condition looks as if you just got it home from a new record store and removed the shrink wrap.

Near Mint is the highest price listed in all Goldmine price guides. Anything that exceeds this grade, in the opinion of both buyer and seller, is worth significantly more than the highest Goldmine book value.

Very Good Plus (VG+): Generally worth 50 percent of the Near Mint value.

A Very Good Plus record will show some signs that it was played and otherwise handled by a previous owner who took good care of it.

Record surfaces may show some slight signs of wear and may have slight scuffs or very light scratches that don't affect one's listening experience. Slight warps that do not affect the sound are OK.

The label may have some ring wear or discoloration, but it should be barely noticeable. The center hole will not have been misshapen by repeated play.

Picture sleeves and LP inner sleeves will have some slight ring wear, lightly turned-up corners, or a slight seam split. An LP jacket may have slight signs of wear also and may be marred by a cut-out hole, indentation or corner indicating it was taken out of print and sold at a discount.

In general, if not for a couple minor things wrong with it, this would be Near Mint. All but the most mint-crazy collectors will find a Very Good Plus record highly acceptable.

A synonym used by some collectors and dealers for "Very Good Plus" is "Excellent."

Very Good (VG): Generally worth 25 percent of the Near Mint value.

Many of the defects found in a VG+ record will be more pronounced in a VG disc.

Surface noise will be evident upon playing, especially in soft passages and during a song's intro and fade, but will not overpower the music otherwise. Groove wear will start to be noticeable, as will light scratches (deep enough to feel with a fingernail) that will affect the sound.

Labels may be marred by writing, or have tape or stickers (or their residue) attached. The same will be true of picture sleeves or LP covers. However, it will not have all of these problems at the same time, only two or three of them.

Goldmine price guides with more than one price will list Very Good as the lowest price. This, not the Near Mint price, should be your guide when determining how much a record is worth, as that is the price a dealer will normally pay you for a Near Mint record.

Good (G), Good Plus (G+): Generally worth 10-15 percent of the Near Mint value.

Good does not mean bad! A record in Good or Good Plus condition can be put onto a turntable and will play through without skipping. But it will have significant surface noise and scratches and visible groove wear (on a styrene record, the groove will be starting to turn white).

A jacket or sleeve will have seam splits, especially at the bottom or on the spine. Tape, writing, ring wear, or other defects will start to overwhelm the object.

If it's a common item, you'll probably find another copy in better shape eventually. Pass it up. But if it's something you have been seeking for years, and the price is right, get it… but keep looking to upgrade.

Poor (P), Fair (F): Generally worth 0-5 percent of the Near Mint price.

The record is cracked, badly warped, and won't play through without skipping or repeating. The picture sleeve is water damaged, split on all three seams and heavily marred by wear and writing. The LP jacket barely keeps the LP inside it. Inner sleeves are fully seam split, crinkled, and written upon.

Except for impossibly rare records otherwise unattainable, records in this condition should be bought or sold for no more than a few cents each.

Other considerations

Most dealers give a separate grade to the record and its sleeve or cover. In an ad, a record's grade is listed first, followed by that of the sleeve or jacket.

With **Still Sealed (SS)** records, let the buyer beware, unless it's a U.S. pressing from the last 10-15 years or so. It's too easy to re-seal one. Yes, some legitimate never-opened LPs from the 1960s still exist. But if you're looking for a specific pressing, the only way you can know for sure is to open the record. Also, European imports are not factory-sealed, so if you see them advertised as sealed, someone other than the manufacturer sealed them.

A few notes on compact discs

In theory, a compact disc should always play-grade in at least Near Mint condition. Otherwise, it's not worth the aluminum it was pressed on.

Unless the CD came in a special package (fold-open, fold-over, colored plastic, etc.), the two areas to check for grading are its label and its insert (booklet). Except for a few labels that use custom jewel boxes, a broken, scratched, or dirty jewel box can be replaced easily with a new one.

Most collector interest currently is with promotional CDs. Again, a disc should play perfectly; assuming that most of the value lies in the condition of its packaging and artwork and the collectibility of the artist.

Used full-length commercial CDs generally sell for 50-75 percent of the new price. Dealers in used CDs will usually pay no more than 50 percent of that price, and often much less.

Photo/Chuck Boyd/Flower Children

Bill Wyman

By Dave Thompson
February 27, 1998

It has been four years since Bill Wyman left The Rolling Stones—four years during which the Stones themselves have returned to a level of productivity unseen since the '70s—yet it still seems strange to contemplate them without him.

For over three decades, The Rolling Stones represented stability in a world, not to mention an industry, where change is ordinarily the only thing you can rely on. Ronnie Wood has been onboard for twenty years, but he's still the new boy; talk about the Stones, and you're talking Mick and Keith, Bill and Charlie, two distinctly polar halves to one irrepressible whole.

Wyman's absence strikes the hardest on stage. The Stones have now completed two tours without him, visual extravaganzas which could shame the biggest budget Broadway production, but the high tech stage sets only detract from, and rarely disguise, the shattered symmetry of the musicians. Jagger is still the calisthenic ringmaster, boundlessly active, exhorting, exhausting; Richards and Wood the Dickensian duelists, still waif-haired and wiry after so many years. But Charlie's on his own now, an Easter Island statue staring grimly out to sea, waiting for another to hove back into view.

Except he knows it's never going to.

Looking back upon the most momentous decision of his entire musical career, Bill Wyman has no regrets.

"Nobody believes me," he laughs, "but it's true."

The 1980s were a strained time for the Stones. Having opened the decade with their most successful tour ever, riding the critical rejuvenation of 1981's *Tattoo You* album, the band first slipped, then slid. Relations between Jagger and Richards soured, and what little music the band contrived to record suffered accordingly. Its dynamic title track notwithstanding, 1984's *Undercover* was the most disappointing Rolling Stones album ever; three years later, the desperate *Dirty Work* was even uglier.

Jagger launched a solo career, and didn't even bother to disguise his motives: if *She's The Boss* had been a hit, the Stones would have been over. Richards retaliated in kind; an era came so close to ending right then that when Wyman got the call to reconvene, in 1988, he didn't know then whether or not he should bother.

"I was involved in opening my restaurant (the first branch of Sticky Fingers, on London's ritzy Kensington High Street); I was writing my book (the *Stone Alone* autobiography); I was working on various other projects, and then suddenly the band decided they wanted to cut another album and do a tour in 1989. So I had to decide whether I wanted to drop everything that I was halfway through, and it was a bit difficult. But Mick and Keith had got over their six year hate campaign, and it was all right for a while."

A new album, the return-to-form of *Steel Wheels*, and tours of America and Europe followed, "but we did those two tours, and after that I didn't see any reason for carrying on. We had our usual half yearly meeting to discuss what we were going to do over the next year, make some basic plans as we always do, an album in the spring, a tour in the autumn, all that kinda stuff, and I just said during the meeting, 'Look, I really want to leave.'"

Of course, Wyman was no stranger to sudden "I quit" outbursts. Ten years earlier, he had said the same thing, swearing that he was going to leave the band in 1982. He changed his mind then; the others fully expected him to change it again this time. But Wyman had made up his mind.

"They all said, 'Ah don't be daft, you're not thinking right, your head's not in the right place, you'll be all right in six months.' But I was 'No, no, I want to leave.' I had a lot of personal problems. My marriage (to teenage model Mandy Smith) had gone down the tubes. More than that, though, I didn't really see any point in carrying on, because I didn't see there was anything more to achieve with the band.

"We'd always had ambitions in the past, always had something to aim for, to try and reach for that we hadn't achieved before—a #1 record, a gold album, a biggest selling tour, most tickets sold, most T-shirts sold, a Grammy, an award, whatever. There was always something out there to aim for, but we'd kinda done it all and I didn't see any reason to continue. I'd been in the band for thirty-one years, and the only reason to carry on would be to repeat what we'd done before, and do it for the money, and I didn't really want to do that. I had more interesting and personal things that I wanted to sort out."

"Mick and Keith took it badly," Wyman reflects. "They took it as a personal slight...their pride got hurt, I think. Charlie understood because he feels the same way, kind of, but he'll jog along, and he's closer to Keith than I am, anyway. And then they got a bit bitchy, a couple of them, said a few nasty things, silly things, like 'Oh, bass playing can't be that difficult, I'll do it,' that sort of stuff. Then after about six months, I think they realized and understood—I had a baby come along, then I had a second baby come along, I was doing quite nicely with my solo and personal projects, with the restaurant and things like that, and then they started to get back to normal and nice again, and I've been quite good friends with them ever since."

According to most Rolling Stones histories, of course, that is all Wyman and the Jagger-Richard team have ever been: quite good friends. Seven years their senior (born in 1936, Wyman turned sixty-one last October), a former military man and already happily married, the erstwhile William Perks was only invited along to play in the first place because he had a spare amp. He knew nothing about the blues; he worked a steady job; and when the rest of the group wanted to go wild in the streets, he was just as likely to return home to his family. On paper, chalk and cheese made a better combination than Wyman and the Stones, but somehow he fit, musically, emotionally, and visually.

Andrew Oldham, the whipper-snapper publicist who "discovered" the group five months after Wyman's arrival, recalls the first time he ever saw the band, at the Station Hotel in Twickenham.

And so he walked—and they still weren't convinced that he intended to go ahead with it. "They just didn't believe me. They were quite nice; they left the door open right up until four months before the 94/95 world tour, and then they asked me again, and I said no, I really meant it.

"Wyman stood against the wall and, to his right, there was the kind of bass amp I'd only seen in ads before now. Both stood as still as the statue. Bill's fame would soon be built upon concentrated nonchalance and his bass in an upright shoulder-arms drill position. Before the Stones, Bill Perks had served his Queen and country through two years of national service, but he was gaunt, pale, and almost medieval. His hair seemed glued on, and his expression was frozen." His playing already locked in solid, intuitive tandem with Watts's drums, Wyman was already the stone around which the others would roll. And he played his heart out without lifting a finger.

"I always wanted to be in a band," Wyman reflects, although he admits that when he first started dreaming, bands as we know them today did not even exist. "When I was in my teens, my early teens, there weren't bands; rock 'n' roll hadn't been invented, skiffle wasn't even around. It was dance bands. I was nine when the war ended, I was thirteen in 1949, I was fifteen in 1951, and rock 'n' roll just wasn't around, so the people I heard were Les Paul and Mary Ford, all that kind of stuff."

The first record he ever bought was Paul and Ford's *The World Is Waiting For The Sunrise*, and he still remembers rushing home to play it on the family's wind-up record player.

"Johnny Ray was the first singer I saw who had a bit of balls. I saw him at the London Palladium on my grandmother's television; the kids tore his trousers off, and that was the first time I ever saw fans attack someone on stage. But all the rest of it was dance bands, from my first memories of music, what I heard on my aunt's radio, or my gran's radio, dance music by Benny Goodman, Glen Miller, and all that lot.

"There wasn't pop music; pop music was sung by very ordinary, horrible people in evening clothes, that copied American hits. Even later, that happened. You had Guy Mitchell doing 'Singing The Blues,' then when rock 'n' roll came along, Tommy Steele did it in a version which went to #1 in England, and it was bloody awful. But previous to that, you had David Whitfield and Lita Roza and Dickie Valentine, doing all these songs like 'Green Door,' 'How Much Is That Doggy In The Window,' all the Doris Day songs, all the Connie Francis songs, they were all covered by these quite ordinary, middle aged people. There was no scene."

Still he wanted to play, but it was not until he was called up for two years military service that he heard anything he'd actually want to do. "I went to Germany in July of '55, and on the American Forces Network radio which we picked up, because it was much more interesting than the British Forces Network, I heard my first ever Elvis Presley record, and my first Little Richard, Duane Eddy, Jerry Lee

Lewis. So I went off to the PX and bought these little singles, and then I had nothing to play them on because all the record players we had were the wind up ones!

"But at least we heard them on the radio, so when I went back to England, I was ahead of the rest of the pack, so I formed a skiffle group with a guy called Casey Jones, who—Clapton played in his band later on, and Georgie Fame knew him, I found out a couple of months ago. We kind of did this for a few months before I left the military, then I just tried to get together with friends and play." Wyman, incidentally, was the band's vocalist.

By 1959, Wyman was a member of the Cliftons, "a little band I got together in south London. We played a lot of black R&B music, Fats Domino, Larry Williams, all that lot, and we did okay. It kind of jogged along, but nothing was going to happen because we weren't a stunning band, we didn't have a great looking singer or anything, so we went along locally."

It was that band's drummer, Tony Chapman, who would introduce Wyman to the bass guitar; it was Chapman, too, who introduced him to what were then the Rollin' Stones.

"He came round one evening and told me there was this band looking for a bass player, and I should go and meet them. I asked what sort of music they played, and he said the blues.

"Now, I knew Fats Domino, I knew Chuck Berry, and various other people, so I did have a little sort of edge in there. I knew nothing about the blues, though, and I remember that first night when I met the Stones, at the end of the evening when Mick said 'Well whaddya think of the music?' I said 'You can't play fucking twelve bars all night.' The funny thing about that is, twelve years later, Jeff Beck said the same thing, when we had people auditioning and hanging out after Mick Taylor left. He came and played with us, then left saying, 'You can't play twelve bars all night.'

"But the moment I started to hear the blues, I just went out and borrowed tapes and whatever, and I wrote away to America for records like everyone else did, I just made a massive collection of blues, and I've loved it ever since."

The Stones, on the other hand, took a bit more getting used to. "There was me, Charlie, and Stew (Ian Stewart) working, so we had to stay pretty tidy and dress well, and we had money in our pockets; I was married with a kid just a few months old; Charlie was courting steady and he had a good job;

and Stew had a good job.

"But the other three weren't. I thought they were a load of beatniks. They were subbing off us all the time, copping cigarettes, copping money for the electricity, copping fish and chips and food, and we kind of kept them going for some months, probably a year.

"I just thought they were a bit strange, Brian, Mick, and Keith, because they weren't normal."

Sharing a decidedly downmarket apartment in Chelsea's Edith Grove, "they were in that situation where you can't be normal, because you're on starvation level, living in this terrible situation in one of the worst winters in thirty years, with no heating, sleeping all day under your overcoats just to keep warm, and you had no reason to go out because you had no money to buy anything. So you're bound to get a bit weird. But they seemed even more eccentric, because we were normal. We had to mix with normal people because we were working. They weren't; they did some very strange things—and I don't think Brian ever fully got back to normal; he was still mad at the end, bless his heart."

Formed in December, 1962; signed to Decca (London in the U.S.) in May, 1963; Top 12 by Christmas; the Rolling Stones rose up as a covers band, but they consolidated their fame as songwriters. Reiterating a story which history never tires of repeating, Keith Richards explained, "Andrew Oldham literally forced Mick and I to start writing songs..." locking them in the kitchen for a day and saying, "I'm not letting you out until you've got a song."

Richards continued, "He put it to us, 'You're gonna be dependent upon other songwriters, other people, for all the material you need...If you get used to that, you'll never get any original material, so come on, let's get it altogether. Anybody can write a pop song, I'll lock you in the kitchen.' It was a shock to us. We'd never even thought about it."

Oldham explains, "It was a process of swift elimination. Charlie and Bill were never contenders for the things my mind was sorting. Like meat 'n' potatoes, I wanted to keep things simple with Watts 'n' Wyman. And I'd already decided it couldn't be Brian."

Jagger-Richards it was then, and Oldham's intuition paid immediate dividends. In August 1964, Marianne Faithful went Top 10 with her version of their "As Tears Go By"; the following May, "The Last Time" gave the band its first self-composed #1.

But despite Oldham's instincts, Mick and Keith were not the band's only viable songwriters. Wyman explains, "Brian wanted to write, Mick Taylor did, Woody gets in much more, but there again he hangs out with Keith all night for weeks, and weeks, or he used to, so he gets a bit of one of his songs in there. I wouldn't do that. I used to go home with my family. Mick (Taylor) in fact did quite a lot of writing within the Stones—not writing, but arranging, bringing ideas in, putting middle-eights in, working out an intro, getting a riff going, and all that, but those credits are not given to you on the records."

Both "Jumping Jack Flash" and, more recently, "Too Much Blood" (from Undercover) are famously rooted around Wyman creations; both, however, are credited to Jagger-Richards, and Wyman himself simply shrugs when they are mentioned.

"I just kinda let it come and go. The 'Jumping Jack Flash' saga—that's the one that's always been credited to me, until I mentioned it in my book, and then Keith totally denied it. I've got a long memory, other people have convenient memories.

"But it doesn't matter—life goes on, you do other things. If we'd have worried about the problems we had with Allan Klein in 1972, we'd have broken up as a band. Instead we just said 'Okay, lesson learned, let's start all over again,' and that's kinda the way I always feel about things with the band; my frustrations within the band over being creative. I'd just say 'Oh well, that's the way it is, let's do something else.' I didn't get bitter about it the way maybe Mick Taylor did, and left."

He doesn't deny his own share of frustration, however.

"If you're a musician of any stature, you have musical ideas and you need an outlet. What happens in most bands, they have the facility for an outlet; John Entwistle with the Who, George and Ringo with the Beatles, all the Zeppelin people, everybody has the little bit they can do. Everybody participates, everybody chucks in.

"But with the Stones it's like a closed shop, and there's no way in. I dunno why; it was done like that in the beginning, it was kept to a Mick/Keith/Andrew thing, and the rest of us were pushed aside as non-talented I suppose, just good at our instruments, and we never ever had a chance. We'd go into the studio and sometimes they'd run out of songs, and it'd be 'anyone got a song?' So I'd go 'Yeah, I've got one we could try, it's a bit Stonesy,' so they'd say 'Okay, let's have a go at it then.' And I'd have to sing the bugger for starters, and I'd have to try and play it on the bass—if I was a piano player, it wouldn't be so bad, but we'd run through it and they'd say 'Yeah, that's okay, that's okay, we'll try that again another day,' and of course we never did. It was like one run through.

"Whereas Keith will come in with a riff and nothing else, and we'll work on that for eight hours a day for eight days, until it becomes a song, and a bloody good song, like 'Can't You Hear Me Knocking,' because everybody devotes a week's work to it. But anyone else has a song and it's all right, one shot and you never really get a chance."

"So that's why there's that thing on the Allan Klein bloody album called *Metamorphosis*, which was a one-off that we never had another go at, called 'Downtown Suzie.' And there was another one I did in Chicago, called 'Goodbye Girl,' but it was take one again. 'In Another Land' was only done for Satanic Majesties because Mick and Keith weren't there; the session was booked, and everyone was either going to go home or do something, so we did something. So there was me, Charlie, and Nicky Hopkins, and I got the Small Faces to come in, Steve Marriott and Ronnie Lane came in to help me with the vocals. Then (engineer) Glyn Johns

convinced Mick and Keith to put it on the album."

"In Another Land" would subsequently become the Stones' latest hit single—a signal honor which little else on that album even looked like achieving—but despite this one victory, Wyman was to remain frustrated in his attempts to break through the Jagger-Richard cabal for the remainder of his time with the band.

As early as 1964, in fact, Wyman was turning his attention elsewhere. He produced a single by the Cheynes, a mid-1960s R&B band featuring Mick Fleetwood, co-writing and playing on the b-side, "Stop Running Around." He also worked with the Herd, a band formed by his old friend Tony Chapman, encouraging them to record Jagger-Richards' "So Much In Love"; and a subsequent Chapman band, the Preachers, featuring a very young Peter Frampton. Wyman produced one single for that band, "Hole In My Soul."

"I've known Peter since he was thirteen; I used to use him when he was a really little boy of thirteen, fourteen, doing demos and things. He used to play wonderful innovative jazz solos, he wasn't into rock or pop then, lovely jazz things, and he used to come knocking on my door, 'Bill, can I come in and play guitar? Got any old Beatles boots you don't want?' I used to give him old shirts and jackets..." Wyman was also responsible for giving the fourteen-year-old Frampton his television debut, when the Preachers were one of several bands invited to join the Stones on their own presentation of Ready Steady Go—Ready Steady Stones. Wyman smiles, "He started to happen a bit then, and of course he went on to great heights. We've been great mates for a long time."

Following the Preachers' demise, Wyman would record an entire album with Frampton, the guitarist now being a member of keyboard player Peter Gosling's Moon's Train revue. Wyman's best-remembered excursion, however, was alongside The End, another Gosling project whose collision of contemporary pop vision was so convincing that bootlegs still appear today featuring two particular End tracks, the "Shades Of Orange" single and its b-side, "Loving, Sacred Loving," usually miscredited to an oft-rumored, but utterly mythical Stones-Beatle studio get-together.

"Or... Peter played on that *A Degree Of Murder* soundtrack which Brian did, so there's a little similarity in the keyboards, so they say they're solo Brian tracks." Wyman laughs. "In fact, it was my Mellotron which Peter was using on them both.

"The End had a lot of success in Spain and Europe," Wyman continues, proudly adding that the band's back catalog is now finally seeing reissue, albeit in limited (1,000 copies) edition vinyl only. "They put out the first one in the summer and it sold out in a week."

Wyman's relationship with the End was based around his role as an advisor as much as a producer, although he doubts whether it actually did much good. Certainly his name did not ease their passage into the big time, and he remarks wryly, "No matter who you are, it doesn't mean that it'll get played just because you're a name. It's usually the reverse, in fact; people don't want you to step out of your allotted slot, so if you're the bassist with a famous band, that's it. You're the bassist with a famous band, and people are very reluctant to really listen to what you're trying to say, because they think if it's that good, why weren't you doing it with the Stones?"

He also insists that nothing has changed in the interim. "Before I left the band, it was 'Why aren't the Stones doing that song if it's so good?' Now it's 'Why bother—aren't you a pensioner? Shouldn't you be having your feet up in an old peoples' home?'"

After one single on Philips, the End became the Stones' Decca labelmates in 1967, but the change did not affect their fortunes. "If it wasn't Mick or Keith, they didn't want to know," Wyman explains. "Not Decca, not Andrew—he was only interested in Mick and Keith, he had them on Immediate Records producing Chris Farlowe; he had Jimmy Page on there as well; the rest of us weren't part of it all.

"There was no door to go through to meet people because you were working. You were always traveling, you never got the chance to meet up with other record company people or anything, it was always your own record company, and I didn't have any other friends in the music biz on the recording side. Glyn Johns I knew, and we did do a couple of little production things together, which was the End, but that was it. I didn't have the help beside me to do anything, so it kind of went in spits and sputters, it was never a dedicated project." Wyman in fact financed the End's now-highly regarded (but then completely ignored) *Introspection* album himself, then watched while Decca simply took the tapes and sat on them.

"They never said 'We hate it, we're never going to release it'; it was always 'Another few weeks, another few weeks.' Charlie had the same problem when he produced the People Band; Brian didn't even live to see his *Joujouka* album released."

The End eventually split, resurfacing on the hard rock scene as Tucky Buzzard; Wyman remained alongside that band as well, producing four albums for them between 1969-1973, and recently floated the possibility of releasing a Tucky Buzzard boxed set, again on a limited, collectors-only, basis. Unfortunately, it was not to be.

"Tucky Buzzard did have some success in Europe and America; they toured with Grand Funk and all sorts of people, and I did the four albums with them. But I only have ownership of two of them, I can't get the rights to the others, and the moment I said, 'Can I have the rights to these old Tucky Buzzard albums, I don't mind giving you an over-ride or whatever,' the record label kind of went 'Ooh, money.' So that was the end of that."

By now, too, Wyman had finally realized that no matter how gratifying such projects were, they still didn't quite scratch the itch he was feeling. He also realized that for the first time in the Stones' career, they had a record company they could actually talk to—their own.

"I never thought about trying to record a solo album before, because I never had anyone to help me do it. I knew very few people, I was the bass player in a band that was like a closed shop, and I don't mean in songwriting terms now, it was the Stones/Andrew Oldham/Allan Klein, and the record company was Decca/London and I had no contact with them. When it became Atlantic and Ahmet Ertegun, though, things changed. Because I did know those people, they were friends, they were fans, they weren't typical record company people."

In June 1974, Wyman became the first Stone to step outside of the band when he released the *Monkey Grip* solo album; two years later, he followed it with *Stone Alone*.

Neither album had much in common with the Stones. Wyman's laconic vocals, allied to even more laconic lyrics, stretched even the vaguest comparisons to breaking point, and in many ways, public awareness of his "other" career was the worst thing in the world to hang his solo albums on. Fans wandered in looking for a de-facto Rolling Stones, and came out with a clutch of darkly humorous songs about girls, guns, and cars.

But *Monkey Grip*, at least, did reasonably well: Top 40 in the U.K., it also reached #99 in America; *Stone Alone*, on the other hand, faltered at #136 in this country. Wyman, however, takes such figures philosophically.

"The main thing was, it gave me an opportunity to play with people who I admired, like Dr. John, the Pointer Sisters, Joe Walsh; I picked up anybody I thought was good, and might like to have a bit of fun in the studio, and it was that sort of music, wasn't it? Tongue-in-cheek, happy-go-lucky, simple chord structures, semi-amusing words, and I had some quite good success with some of it, and some of it I had quite good failure. Quite good in America, France, Australia, places like that. It was up and down."

It is also worth noting that both albums were released just weeks ahead of new Stones' records, a serious miscalculation on everybody's part, and one which was guaranteed to swamp Wyman's own, self-confessedly humble efforts.

"Yeah, it did work out like that; *Monkey Grip* was released, and two weeks later, *It's Only Rock 'n' Roll*; it was doing really well in the chart, and then bang, the Stones arrived and that was pretty much the end of it. Then we had *Stone Alone*, and one week later, *Black And Blue*. Unfortunately, I had no control over things like that, so again, it was just— live with it."

Following this initial flurry of mid-decade activity, Wyman's solo ambitions again took a backseat to the Stones' own career. Working though they were to a more relaxed schedule than at any time in the past, with breaks of eighteen months or more between albums, still the mid-late '70s were a fraught time for the group, both personally—Keith Richards' Canadian drug bust cast a very long shadow over band activities; and creatively.

Riding out Mick Taylor's departure in 1974, and the necessary chaos surrounding the recruitment of a replacement, the band then found its most private musical moments leaking out of the studio, as their rehearsal sessions became open house to the bootleggers.

"They were standing outside our truck, just recording through the walls," Wyman marvels. The Stones had never personally taken on the bootleg community, happily acknowledging that a well-produced unauthorized release could often be as valid (and certainly as collectible) as an official album. Indeed, Jagger himself is on permanent (bootlegged) record, seated in an hotel room negotiating with a bootlegger for sundry Stones recordings, while Wyman acknowledges that he has his own collection of the things, that fans have given him over the years.

Leaking out over the years under such titles as *Reggae and Roll* and *Munich Hilton*, however, the rehearsal tapes were a distinctly below the belt blow, and one which could not be allowed to recur. In the future, the Stones' recording sessions would take place within considerably more guarded surroundings, one more slice of regimented life for the individual band members to contend with.

Wyman continued writing, of course, stockpiling songs which "I figured I might do something with sometime," and around 1979-1980, he remembers, "I came up with one which I thought was perfect for Ian Dury."

One of the undisputed stars of the Stiff Records canon, Dury had enjoyed considerable success in recent years, scoring massive European hits with "What A Waste," "Reasons To Be Cheerful," and, most impressively of all, the #1 "Hit Me With Your Rhythm Stick."

"So I wrote 'Si Si, Je Suis Un Rock Star' for Ian. I thought, 'I'm not gonna do any more recording, I'll write for other people,' and that was the first one I came up with."

A pulsing synthpop beat underpinned this delightfully droll tale of rampant pop grandiosity: "then I took a chance," sings Wyman of an unexpected disco pick-up: "come home with me today, I live in France, we'll get there BEA..."; or, "we could take a hovercraft across the water, they'll think I'm your dad, and you're my daughter."

Wyman continues, "I thought Ian would do a great job with it. He'd had a lot of hits around that time, and I love him, he's a good bloke. I knew him a bit as well, but no one would get the song to him. Then people started saying 'It's a hit, you've got to do it yourself.' And they were right."

"Si Si, Je Suis Un Rock Star" hit #14 in Britain in April 1981; it climbed even higher elsewhere, and Wyman recalls, "it really blew a few people away; some people really didn't want it to be a hit—I won't mention any names—and I ended up being the only one in the band who's had a big single hit."

Thoughts immediately turned to rushing out a follow-up; only to be dashed by ("of course!") the imminence of the next Stones' album. Working once again to that sense of impeccable timing which had dogged Wyman's past two albums, "Rock Star" was released just two weeks before *Tattoo You*, and while this time, it would not affect his sales, the accompanying world tour would keep him well clear of the recording studio for the next few months.

"The tour was great," Wyman recalls, "but Mick used to set me up rotten. He didn't really like the single, and he didn't like me having a hit with it... Keith was okay about it, he was already working on solo ideas, so he went 'Well done mate, that's all right.' But Mick was saying 'Ah, that's just a stupid song, that,' and he kinda pooh-poohed it.

"But of course, when we played Europe...when we were onstage, obviously we didn't think about ever doing the song, just like we'd never have thought about doing a Mick or Keith or Woody song; you don't do them on a Stones tour. But 'Rock Star' was a huge hit all over Europe, and when it came to Mick introducing the band—'Charlie, Keith, Bill on the bass,' I would get this big roar. So he'd say 'Do you want him to do his song?' and all the crowd would go 'Yeah, yeah,' so Mick would go, 'Come on Bill, sing the song,' and I had to cop out all the time, just as he knew I would. No one had rehearsed it, no one knew the song, so he kinda set me up; I'd say no, and he'd be 'Ah come on Bill, are you shy?' all that kind of thing. He was just getting his own back."

It would be early 1982 before Wyman followed up "Rock Star," when the infuriatingly contagious "A New Fashion" breached the Top 40; the album Bill Wyman followed, together with two other singles, "Visions" and "Come Back Suzanne," and while none could replicate the success of "Rock Star," Wyman recalls the period with intense pride.

Especially memorable are the videos which accompanied the four singles. The video medium itself was still in its infancy then, as a quick glance at the Stones' own contemporary efforts will reveal. But Wyman pulled out all the stops. "Come Back Suzanne" was especially impressive, a mini-movie in which an increasingly disheveled looking Wyman pleads with his lover to return, while the house falls apart around him, and the simplest domestic chores become unmitigated disasters.

"I really liked 'A New Fashion' as well," muses Wyman. "I thought that one was really nice." Tying the visuals to the song lyrics, it became a smorgasbord of bizarre puns and word association gags, "It was really great, and I thought it would be really, really popular. But it just sort of passed by and nobody really said anything. It's very quick, you need a few viewings to catch it all."

Wyman never bothered following up this latest burst of activity. "I just left it for a while. I'd had four Top 40 singles in Europe and the far east, and everyone was suggesting I should work on the solo career, but I wasn't really interested in pursuing it."

Instead, he spent the 1980s working in a variety of supporting roles, most of which he took on simply because they sounded like fun. He recorded an album with Junior Wells and Buddy Guy, 1980's *Drinkin' TNT, Smokin' Dynamite*; he produced a brave, but barely noticed album by the Sons of Heroes; and scored the Ryan O'Neal movie *Green Ice*, taking considerable pride from seeing the soundtrack land far better reviews than the movie.

"So yeah, I did the movie score, I produced people. It was a period when the band didn't work for about seven years, we did albums but we didn't tour through until 1989, so it was a dead period for me; we were just kinda sitting around."

He did, however, piece together one of the decade's most notable, and successful, all-star aggregations. Coming together in March, 1985, Willie And The Poor Boys was designed to raise funds for, and awareness of, the ARMS multiple sclerosis charity, and paired Wyman with the likes of Jimmy Page, Paul Rodgers, Andy Fairweather-Low, Ringo Starr, Chris Rea, and Kenney Jones. Three years later, he organized a similarly star-studded crew to raise money for London's Great Ormond Street children's hospital.

Wyman also launched AIMS (Ambition, Ideas, Motivation, Success), an attempt to encourage grassroots musicians by touring the country with the Stones mobile and recording unknown bands. He joined Ronnie Wood guesting at Rod Stewart's July 1986, show at Wembley Stadium; and he was at the center of a major controversy when the News Of The World tabloid newspaper published photographs of one Mandy Smith, the 16-year-old model with whom Wyman had been having an affair for the past two years—since Smith was a mere thirteen years old.

Against a riotously self-righteous backdrop of press outrage, revolving both around the potential for statutory rape charges and the vast age difference between the pair, a police investigation cleared Wyman of any wrongdoing, and in June 1989, following Smith's nineteenth birthday, the couple was married in Bury St. Edmunds, Suffolk. Laughing, Wyman recalls that amongst the wedding gifts was one from comedian Spike Milligan—for the groom, a walking frame.

Adding an even more bizarre twist to the story, Wyman's twenty-eight-year-old son Stephen would soon be dating Smith's mother! Bill and Mandy, however, broke up after just seventeen months of marriage, and both swiftly moved on: Smith wed Dutch soccer player Pat Van Den Hauwe (they were divorced in November 1997); Wyman married American fashion designer Suzanne Accosta in April, 1993, and is currently awaiting the birth of the couple's third child.

And in the midst of all this, Wyman finally published *Stone Alone*, the first volume of his long-threatened biography of the Stones. Very long-threatened—reports of this book had been circulating for almost ten years!

"You have to understand, I approach them in the same way as I approach the history of the house, as historical documents, if you like. They're for the fans; *Stone Alone* did well, but I don't write them to have a big selling book like some other people do; if I did I'd have had one out this year or next year, to cash in on the new Stones tour, and it'd be nonstop sex and drugs. But that's not the intention of it.

"So I get slagged off by the critics, because it's too detailed, it's too long, it's too concerned with who recorded what where and when. But I don't write the books for the critics; I write for the fans, and the collectors, and the people who want to know those things."

Nowhere, of course, is this zeal for truth better detailed than in his treatment of Brian Jones' death, in *Stone Alone* itself, a stark and very refreshing response to the increasingly convoluted murder plots which other biographers have woven around the late Golden Stone.

"Oh, they're all crap aren't they?" Wyman can barely conceal his disdain for so many amateur sleuths, so he doesn't even bother trying. "I mean, that murder thing: 'Let's make as much money as we can on that idea.' What happened was, there was this guy, Tom Keylock, who was a wally in himself; he drove us to some TV show, and then Brian took him on as his driver and dogsbody. When Anita left Brian to go with Keith, Keith took Keylock to work with him, and then he kind of hung around with Brian as well, to do things. And when Brian died, he was on the scene and all that. End of story.

"But then he says he went to the deathbed of Thoroughgood, the builder who was working on Brian's house at the time, and Thoroughgood said that he'd murdered Brian. So that was the story. But the moment it started coming out in the English press, this story, the police immediately got in touch with Keylock, interviewed him and he denied everything, said he'd just made all that up for the book, and that was it. But of course, the story just kept going, and now there's books coming out about the other books, and all the conspirators are fighting each other about who got told the story first; it's just stupid.

"The thing with Brian was just a horrible accident. He was doing silly things like a lot of sleepers, and then bottles of brandy on top of that, and I know what that can do to people. I've seen it; you just zonk out, so you can imagine what would happen in a bloody swimming pool. And also he had this asthma problem, and also, he used to have these fits which we didn't know about at the time, but I found out from one of his illegitimate daughters, she suffers from it and it's hereditary.

"So that explains a lot of things we didn't understand at the time as well. It was something you didn't really talk about when people had something weird like that; you kind of left them alone for a few minutes, and they were all right again. And Brian really was a bit strange like that; nothing like that happened when I was with him, but other people I've heard stories from, Suki Poitier and people like that, said he used to just fall over backwards and go all strange, he'd be asleep and all that, so they just used to put him on a bed for half hour, he'd wake up and he'd be normal. And the daughter told me that's exactly how it affected her, so something like that could have happened in the pool as well.

"I don't think we'll ever know exactly what happened, but it was just an unfortunate accident, I think, and I don't believe there was anybody else involved—I don't see the reason; why would they? He was a pathetic guy, there was no good motive, he'd left the band, he wasn't interfering with anyone else's life, there was nothing there. He was just a pathetic wasted guy who had a huge problem with drugs, he had psychological problems, he had health problems, he was quite unwell, and that was that."

Such matter-of-fact reporting disappointed many readers. But there is no doubt, in either history's mind or Wyman's own, that amidst the plethora of Stones biographies, past, present, and possibly future, *Stone Alone* is as close to the truth as we are ever likely to get. *Stone Alone* was published in 1990, as the Stones' own Steel Wheels tour finally ground to a halt. Two years later, Wyman announced that he was indeed a lone Stone, handing in his resignation from the longest-running club in rock history, and celebrating his new found freedom by starting work on what would become his

fourth solo album, Stuff. Unreleased in the U.S., but reasonably successful in Japan (where it appeared in February, 1993) and Europe (July), Stuff successfully avoided clashing with any new Stones project, but did run headfirst into the new Mick Jagger, a topic which does raise a wry smile from Wyman.

"He could make a wonderful solo album, he could do a soul album or a blues, instead of trying to be pop. I kinda gave up listening to them, I didn't really enjoy the first one (1985's *She's The Boss*); I heard bits on the radio and it didn't excite me too much. I just thought if he'd done an album of soul hits, with a really great band, all those wonderful people that played with Aretha and people like that, a great horn section, great piano player, he could have done a wonderful bloody album. But he likes to do pop, current pop, and it doesn't quite suit him sometimes."

Five years on from *Stuff* (and indeed, from *Wandering Spirit*), Wyman has now released his fifth solo album, the similarly titled—but otherwise unrelated—*Strutting Our Stuff*. It was released in Europe one week before the Stones' *Bridges To Babylon*, but Wyman simply shrugs. "Yeah, but I've got two more albums coming out in the next year. I bet they don't."

One part, indeed, of a trilogy which will ultimately paint a very personalized portrait of the history of music in the 20th century, *Strutting Our Stuff* is immediately most notable for the Poor Boys-esque gathering of talent which recorded it, an ad-hoc gathering which he dubbed the Rhythm Kings.

Across the sessions, Wyman's regular band of Beverley Skeete (vocals), Terry Taylor (guitar, organ), Dave Hartley (piano), and one-time David Coverdale/Whitesnake drummer Graham Broad, was augmented by Eric Clapton, Georgie Fame, Peter Frampton, Gary Brooker, Jeff Beck, Chris Rea, Kiki Dee, and Albert Lee, although Wyman is adamant that this time, reputation was less important than his relationship with the individuals.

"All the people I chose, they're nice people, they're great musicians, and they're easy to get along with. They're talented people, but they're friends as well, so there's no egos, there's no tantrums. So it was always a nice, fun atmosphere. We went in for three days every month, and in three days we'd record between five and seven tracks; we did that for over a year and we ended up with fifty-six tracks. And it was bloody wonderful, because I went in saying I've got no problem about image, I don't have to worry about style, I don't have to worry about having a chart hit or an album hit, I've got no pressures at all from record companies or anyone else, I can just do anything I like.

"So, I went through my record collection over a period of six months, and thought of all the songs I liked that might be nice to do, like a Fats Waller; a Billie Holliday; a '20s country blues; a Creedence Clearwater song; a piece of jump music from the '50s like a Louis Jordan or Cab Calloway sort of thing; a '50s Chicago blues; a '30s blues; a bit of country music from the '40s... and one Rolling Stones song.

"I thought, it's crazy not to do a Stones song, there must be something in there, and I was thinking about all the early ones like 'Down The Road Apiece,' early rock things, R&B bluesy rock things, and I kinda went for a few of those, and then I thought of 'Melody'; 'Yeah, that'll work,' because we were doing some jazzy bluesy things as well, and 'Melody' kinda slotted into that sort of feel. I changed the words slightly, so it was girl-boy instead of boy-boy, and it worked. It's a bit more punchy than the original, and I think that's because...the original was done on sixteen tracks, and there's more technology around today. But I also think I approached it in a different way, a more kind of jazzy feel way."

He is still awaiting the song's authors' response, but one Stone at least has heard the record.

"I did play it for Charlie, because he comes round and has a cup of tea with me sometimes, and he said 'Ooh, that's nice innit?'"

Knowing the economically spoken Mr. Watts, that was high praise indeed.

"Anyway, I just went in and did a whole assortment of music with a little rhythm section, five or six people, and they came out wonderful, they came out bloody wonderful. And we ended up with all these tracks, nearly sixty songs, and that's when I thought, 'Now what am I gonna do with them?'"

He admits that he was genuinely surprised when the Velvel label moved in to release all three albums; even more shocked when cuts from *Strutting Our Stuff* began turning up on European radio (the album was released overseas at the end of last year; its American release is scheduled for this month). "It was all uncommercial stuff," Wyman puzzles. "I thought no record company was ever going to be interested; it'd never get played on the radio, and no one was ever gonna hear it, let alone buy it."

Instead, at sixty-one years of age, he found himself playing his first ever live shows as a solo artist, and being completely blown away by the response.

"Three shows, London, Amsterdam, and Hamburg, and we only booked small places, a thousand people or so. But they were completely sold out. We finished the set and—well, what do you do? You run out for one encore, then back to the hotel. That's what the Stones always did. But we were called back again and again; in Hamburg, twenty minutes after the lights went up, we'd all got changed, we'd packed our stuff up, and the promoter came tearing backstage, 'You have to go back on, they're refusing to leave!'

"Another funny thing that happened; before the show, the promoter asked if he could sell copies of the CD at the show, set up a little table and sell them. So I was, 'Ooh, I dunno, isn't that what you do when you don't have a record deal?' But I told him to go ahead, and we ended up selling 500 copies, in a club that only held a thousand people. That was just amazing!"

A longer Rhythm Kings tour is scheduled for early spring, although Wyman regrets that America is unlikely to see it.

"I stopped flying in 1990, after my last Stones tour," he shrugs. "So it'll just be northern Europe, Britain, just a couple of weeks."

He's not hurting for ways of filling his time, though. The owner of a growing chain of Sticky Fingers restaurants, a proud and active family man, Wyman also has three books currently on the go: a photographic collection; an archaeological/historical study of his 1,000-year-old house; and of course, the next volume of *Stone Alone*.

"I've been working on the second one since I finished the first, but I can't do it all the time; it's very hard work constantly checking everything, then having to re-check things I find out against what I have in my diaries or whatever. I've got 300 books on the Stones upstairs in my attic, and I can take any one of them and say 'That's wrong, that's wrong, the date's wrong on that, it's the wrong year, it's the wrong name, that guy wasn't even there.' I can read some of these—there's one that came out, it was written by this Italian guy, and on every page there's like twenty things wrong. It's a joke. But it sells, because people want to know things. So if I'm going to tell them what they want to know, I'm going to make sure that I at least get it right."

Willie Dixon

By Cary Baker
January 1982

No chronicler of American music can do justice to the subject of Willie Dixon, not even Dixon himself.

"I started to write a book on two or three occasions," he says, "and then stopped and started again. I'd get so far and get worn out and decide I'm not going to do it like this—I'm going to do it another way."

But a few facts about the master of the blues pen bear sharing. And that—without pretense of his being a "definitive" Willie Dixon story—is the approach for which we've opted.

There are many Willie Dixons, all factions of one ardent, prolific individual who practically defined Chicago blues just by being in the right place with the right talents and resources. His manifold achievements are known worldwide; Dixon lives for the inkling that blues strikes a nerve transcending race, nationality, and age.

In spreading the blues "gospel," Dixon has worn many hats. Among them:

Willie Dixon the songwriter has written more songs than he can count—somewhere in the middle three digit range. Among his classics: "I Just Want To Make Love To You," "Violent Love," "My Babe," "Back Door Man," "You Shook Me," "Hoochie Coochie Man," "Bring It On Home," "Wang Dang Doodle," "I Can't Quit You Baby," ad infinitum. Themes run the gamut from black art to stops-out hoedowns, hard lovin'and tender lovin'.

Willie Dixon the performer played upright bass with Leonard "Baby Doo" Caston and Ollie Crawford as the Big Three Trio all through the '40s. Following years spent "behind the scenes," due to his value to the Chess brothers as a producer and scribe, Dixon launched the Chicago Blues All-Stars in the late '60s as a full-time entity. Personnel changes notwithstanding, they've flanked him since. Present All-Stars include sons Freddie and Butch.

Willie Dixon the producer... of Koko Taylor (long his fondest protégé), a host of other Chess Blues artists plus a stable of artists on his own Yambo and Spoonful labels and one (the Branding Iron) on Stax/Volt. Some are around today (Buster Benton), others (the Honey Duo Twins), long forgotten.

Willie Dixon the entrepreneur launched the Soul Attractions agency in the '60s. Soul Productions, with greater emphasis on independent recording, ensued through the '70s, based in Dixon's Blues Factory at 7711 S. Racine Ave., on Chicago's South Side. The Blues Factory is active today as a "think tank" for the genre with many activities (such as Dixon's Blues Heaven Foundation) in the works at all times.

Willie Dixon the prizefighter hasn't surfaced in thirty years, but it's interesting to realize that as James Dixon, this gentle, philanthropic man once held the Golden Glove.

The distinctions go on and on. But in the end Willie Dixon is a one-in-a-million person with unparalleled recall of his past and vision for the future. Even over a period of several hours, we barely skimmed the surface of his career in the following interview. However, Dixon would have gone on for hours more, answering any question asked him. One day, his life will be documented in a book of his own authorship.

For information on Dixon's Blues Heaven Foundation, write the Cameron Organization, 320 S. Waiola Ave., LaGrange IL 60525.

Goldmine: Suppose we start by talking a little about the Blues Heaven Foundation you've formed.

Willie Dixon: The Blues Heaven Foundation is an organization I've been intending to start for over thirty years. But I was financially short, and had nobody to work with and nobody would work with me. Now, you know as well as I know that over the years that blues musicians have been branded as drunks: inferior people who didn't give a doggone or just some guy who's sittin' around cryin' the blues about everything. But I have known all my life that it wasn't just that. The things the people see in front isn't the story all the time. It all comes from the facts of life, and the facts of life can exist from the beginning until the end. And this is what the blues is all about—to explain the various facts of life so that other people can understand that their life is the same as yours. And so this Blues Heaven organization that I have just about together now—I figured it would be a good place to let the world know what the blues are. And also, to let the world know what can be done about the blues. Also, it would give a lot of the blues artists various things to get involved in other than hangin' around in the streets, getting loaded and acting like a nut.

You see, the blues is actually the root of all American music, and a lot of folks don't know this. The blues is the facts of life. And blues came from the various experiences that people have had in life all their life, and people decide they're going to sing about it. If a guy doesn't have a lot of education to work with, he has to sing it according to the way he feels. And a lot of times, a guy feels different from you but you don't know it no more than just looking at it, and because if he can't explain it, he can't tell you. But I've been lucky enough—I don't know if you'd call it lucky or unlucky—to have had a bit of experience about all of it from my childhood days until the present day. And I know, when a man is singing about something, what he's singing about and the way he feels about it.

If a guy's singing about goin' up the country and I won't be back no more, and you say, "What does he mean he won't be back no more?" Well, he means what he says. He was probably in the South or somewhere where he wasn't getting the proper treatment or the proper understanding, and he feels like he's downtrodden. And he feels like it's the time to get the heck out of there because he's tired of this place.

There was a fellow that asked me not long ago about, "What do you mean by 'Blues jumped a rabbit and jumped him for a salad now'?" Well, you see, if the guy had come along with me when I was in the South, there were many days when the dog didn't jump a rabbit or my old man didn't shoot a squirrel and we didn't eat before we went to school. Then, when a guy say "Goin' Down Slow," I know many people who could express that better if they could explain it. A fellow having enjoyed the best of his life in many places and then he gets one place where he isn't having so much fun and says, "I'm not going to be here much longer."And he started thinkin' about it and says, "Someone write my mama and tell her the shape I'm in and tell her to don't send no doctor," and all these things. All of these are the facts of life. And when the world understands this as the facts of life and quit trying to ridicule people because they think this is just something that they made up, then they'd make a better understanding. And a better understanding makes a better world all the way around.

So I feel that if the blues were properly understood, the world would be a better place to live in because the average person that don't understand the blues can't realize what a position a person would be in when in the first place, they took his country, in the next place, his language, the next place, his religion, and they took all of his traditions. And they forced him into other things that he disapproved of all around. It would be like you being forced to be an Indian or an African or something. You find you're doing the same thing your foreparents did. They brought them to the States to be a slave and work, and you're still being a slave and working. The other man supposed to be the boss; he's still the boss.

So I feel people can be educated with what I call a blues education. This is what the Blues Heaven Foundation is all about. And also—to produce grants and to teach people to have different kinds of occupations to help themselves.

You're applying for grants to achieve this?

I'm definitely trying to get grants to educate the children to various things that can help them in the future. It's also a good thing to educate them to blues and their heritage, learning to play instrument and the facts of life—this is why the blues needs an organization. We need to have a better understanding of blues so the world will know blues is the root of American music.

What is the Blues Factory, and how does it relate to your Blues Heaven Foundation?

Frankly, what we use the Blues Factory for is to teach the kids different trades and keep 'em off the streets. The average kid gets out onto the streets and makes a little fightin' and raising hell. If they're here in the Blues Factory, they can learn how to play piano, learn to bang on the drums, learn how to play on the guitar. They can learn the art of making sings and instruments. These things can help them in lots of ways.

What about your own recording activities? I know you were recently in Paragon Studios in Chicago updating a song called "It's In The News" from your Peace albums for Mexican reissue.

Oh yeah. I had to update it, because on February 4-5, I'm going to be in Washington, D.C., at the Smithsonian Institution. They have a regular concert—I played that before. But in this particular concert, it is my intention to get over some of the facts of life about the blues, and also I'm thinking of having a record out there that the President and Congress can use to enlighten themselves a little with this one tune, "It don't make sense/You can't make peace."

What do you think Reagan's outlook on the blues is?

Well, I don't know what his outlook is, but I know what everybody else's outlook has been of the past. Because if the world were wise enough to make all these other great things, they still haven't been wise enough to make peace. I don't think this one is going to be any better. But I think if we have a way of getting to 'em and putting a few thoughts in their mind, they might get together and do something else besides fight.

The album originally came out on your own Yambo label. And now it's going to come out on what label in Mexico?

I think it'll be out on my label down there. I'm not sure. It's been on my Yambo label all the time, but I never did push it or anything.

Do you still have the Yambo label?

Sure, I still have it, but I haven't really been using it. The last thing was "The Last Home Run," Hank Aaron. You heard that?

Actually no.

"The Last Home Run" and "Hank Done It Again." You know, another thing about Blues Heaven is I think it can wake up a number of people. Through generations, you can reach back to Memphis Minnie, Robert Johnson—you can reach back to thousands of them. The kids don't know nothing about them, but still they were great artists. And many of the songs that came out in the later years—they never got a call or any recognition.

There have been many people who have dipped in the blues bag to get a rock number, dipped in the blues bag to get a boogie-woogie, or a spiritual, or a Dixieland, or a country and western. They all come out of this one big bag, but the blues never gets the recognition. I go out among the public and people hear me sing "Hoochie Coochie Man," "Make Love To You," "My Babe," all these different things. They say, "That's someone's song and that's someone's song." Hell, no! I made these songs, and I made them first! They think I'm the copier when I'm the original.

Has anyone ever taken credit for one of your compositions outright?

Oh, I've had several different people do that kind of thing. I don't make a big thing of it. But after learning about copyrights and those things, it doesn't matter whose name is on it. I'll get the benefits anyway.

Let's go from the present to the past for a minute. When and where were you born?

I was born in Vicksburg, Mississippi, July 1, 1915.

And you've spoken of having quite a big family.

Oh yeah, it was a big family. My mother was the mother of fourteen kids, but some of them died when they were babies. Her name was Daisy Dixon.

She was an influence on the lyrical side of your songwriting, wasn't she?

Oh yes. My mother wrote a lot of poems herself, but she was kind of spiritually inspired, with the biblical thing. And I can remember when I was in Jerusalem and I sent her back a bible with one side of the page in Hebrew, the other English. They used to sing songs about Jerusalem in my happy home when I was a kid. And they just accepted biblical affairs as the word. And whatever anyone told them, that's what they accepted. And accepting somebody's word without proof—today—you know what you get!

When did you write your first poems or songs?

I started to write when I was a kid going to school, maybe eleven years old, because I always thought poetic form things were pretty. I had books of the stuff. I thought I could sell it as poems, but you couldn't sell no poems or nothing in those days.

So when did you add the music?

Well, you know, once you write these things, you keep a lot of it in your mind. They had some people who'd done blues. The world had branded these people lower class people.

Are we talking about the early '20s?

Oh yeah, because in the early '20s, I met little Brother Montgomery. I used to follow Little Brother all up and down. One day they'd be on a wagon bed with horses and mules, playing a piano up there and a clarinet with a guy with a megaphone...they're going to be playing a dance in the South Side Park in Marcus Bottom. Next two or three days, they'd come on with a Model T Ford truck bed and they'd have the same thing. I was just a barefoot kid. Every night I'd get a whippin' for being out all day and all night chasing this truck around. And Little Brother—he was little at that time!

He was from Vicksburg too, or at least sang the "Vicksburg Blues."

Actually, he was from Kentwood, Louisiana. And we thought because he was little, he was like us. I was bigger than Little Brother, but I wasn't older than him. My sister would go with me to clubs on Washington Street (in Vicksburg) where they would be playing. Zack Lewis had a place down there. And my sister and I got a chance to meet Little Brother and we made friends and that stuff. He was a little guy, and in those days you didn't wear no long suits of clothes until you were grown. A boy who was considered a boy, he had the pants that button above the knees. But when he thought he was grown, he could let them button below the knee. And this was the first time we'd seen a long suit. He had his derby on, and he thought he was really sharp!

Did you go directly to Chicago from Mississippi?

No, the first time I ran away from home, I went out to this place in the country. I was about twelve years old and went to a place called Bovina, about fifteen or sixteen miles out of Vicksburg (in Mississippi). My mother was looking for me, but I didn't know country kids had to work hard. I thought they had the same thing going for them that we have in Vicksburg, which was nothing. I'd go to school and maybe I'd go get slop for the pigs, and that was it. Anyway, I went out there and that's where I found out what work meant. Them guys out there were working like mad! I'd never seen the sun rise in my life. But they said they had to make money so they could come to Vicksburg. I was pretty fat and big, but I'd never done no work! I hadn't even cut wood with an ax. Eight or ten barrels of charcoal sold for fifty cents! That's when I started figuring my arithmetic—that's four of us got to split this! And I ain't got my money yet!

How did you eventually migrate to the North?

The first time I came to Chicago, I was thirteen. And then I had a sister living here named Katy Gibbs. She had married a guy named Ted Gibbs, and was living at 4716 S. Forestville. I was working on an ice wagon here. They used to have a company called the L&N Ice Co. And at that time, they didn't have no Frigidaires, man, you had to put the ice on your shoulder and go all the way up to the fourth floor. Most buildings had three floors, but occasionally there'd be a fourth. And it seemed that everybody on a fourth floor wanted 100 lbs!

I grew up doing that. I thought I was making a lot of money, but I was making $20 a week. I'd go to school now and then, but my sister was trying to keep me in school, and I wouldn't go. They finally sent me back home after about a year, and I had to go back to school in Vicksburg. I went back to school there for a while. Thought I was going to be a fighter. And because I'd worked on the boats with those roustabouts—they pick up a barrel and truck it on off the gangplank. 'Cuz I was a big boy, I thought I was a man. I was pretty strong.

When I was young, I didn't want to stay at home too much because my old man wouldn't be there too much. You saw him about as much as I did! I saw him sometimes, and he didn't have but a lot of baloney to talk. But he did like the blues. And my mama, she liked the spirituals. When they'd meet, there'd always be some kind of heavy discussion going on. I'd always be out on my own, and I felt I could help the family more by being away than I could by being there.

After I got to fighting, I fought at the YMCA two or three times, and I fought at four or five places around there. And then I came to Chicago. It was around 1936. I had a friend with whom I hoboed to New Orleans in 1935. And we didn't know where to find nothing to eat but at the banana cart and the watermelon cart. I went with the Stamer excursion boat going in every night to St. Paul. I came back one day through Rock Island, Illinios, and caught a bus from Rock Island to Chicago. In Chicago, I met my sister. I lived with her, and then I decided I was going to finish my fighting career. I won the Golden Glove in 1937. You see, my name is Willie James Dixon. And I was fighting under the name of James Dixon. People down home always used to call me W.J. Dixon. Well, I did pretty good after I won the Golden Glove.

I don't know much about boxing. How prestigious is the Golden Glove?

Yeah, the Heavyweight Champion in 1937! And

213

then, after I won the Golden Glove, I got me a couple of managers. I had about five good fights, and turned pro in 1938. Anyway, after I turned pro I had three or four really good fights. They were taking a third of my money for management, and so much for my trainer, and I wasn't getting no money. And on top of that, people who'd fought less than me were getting $400 or $500 for their fights. I was getting $200 and thought I deserved more money. One day, we were discussing contracts—they had all the contracts written—but the contracts that I hadn't signed! We got into a heated discussion, and wound up in a fight. We tore up the office and all got expelled. And at that time, I was training our at Eddie Nichols' gym. My manager really wanted us to cover up his dope racket—he didn't really care whether we won or not! But all the while, this fellow "Baby Doo" Caston was playing guitar around the gymnasium. We sat around all day when we wasn't practice for a fight, singing.

Were you playing the bass at the time?

No, I wasn't playing no bass at all. I was just singing. I used to sing bass all the time. So (Caston) said, "Hey, you ain't doin' nothin'. Why don't you come out nightclubbing with us?" I hadn't ever been in a nightclub in my whole life. So he and a guy called Evan Spencer, we got together and we went up and down Madison Street, all of 'em, all of 'em down Clark Street, everywhere... we used to sing the Ink Spots, the Mills Brothers, and everybody.

The Big Three Trio, who you began your recording career with, consisted of yourself on bass, Baby Doo on piano, and...

Ollie Crawford, guitar, and also Bernard Dennis— he was the first one and stayed with us a year. Ollie was the second and stayed about six years. Anyway, we went all the different places and I found out, hell, I was making more passing the hat than I was fighting! We'd wind up over in Jewtown (Maxwell Street) playing on Sunday with a water bucket and people would fill that water bucket up with pennies and nickels and a few dimes, you know. And we just put them in three piles, 'cuz we couldn't count all them pennies all day. Then after that, we worked with that a long time.

Before the Big Three, we had another group called the Four Jumps of Jive, with Leonard, myself, Jimmy Gilmore, and Ellis Hunter.

You recorded for Delta Records as the Big Three.

On Delta, it was Baby Doo, Bernard Dennis, and myself. And on Columbia, it was Baby Doo, Ollie Crawford, and myself.

What was Delta Records?

It was a thing out of Nashville, Tennessee, owned by Jim Bullet. He also had Bullet Records. He finally went to New York.

Did he ever do anything with country, being in Nashville?

He did some things, like "Near You" (begins to sing). Oh never mind! That was before your time. All along, I'd be writing songs. I'd try to turn them into popular tunes and nobody really cared. We was recording blues, even though we were playing a lot of popular things at the clubs, because when you go places playing, passing the hat, everybody's got a request for a different thing. And we had to spend a lot of time getting that together. But we recorded the blues: "Wee Wee Baby, You Sure Look Good To Me" and "The Signifying Monkey"... "88 Boogie"and "Lonesome Blues"...

What years did you have the Big Three Trio?

Well, we started around 1945 and it went 'til about 1951.

Is that when you went over to Chess Records?

Yeah, that's when I started working at Chess, while I still had the Big Three Trio. Because I played pretty good bass. We was right out there on Madison Street, just gigging up and down there, me and Baby Doo. He made me a tin-can bass with just one string, and I played that thing all over Chicago. In fact, I've been trying to find somebody that has pictures of me on that tin can! Anyway, we used to jam with Muddy Waters when he first started out.

While Muddy was on the Aristocrat label?

Well Muddy wasn't on no label when we was jammin'. Him or Walter, either. And we went over there on 35th Street, over on the street where they cut the Dan Ryan Expressway, next to Jefferson— what was that? I know it when I hear it called.

Anyway, we jammed with Muddy and one day he got to record, and he told Chess to call me up and see if I could play bass on his session. Well, he had recorded a couple things ahead of that time. They called me in Omaha, where I'd been working...

Omaha?

That's right, Omaha, Nebraska. I was working at the Dundee Dell. So I came back and recorded with Muddy Waters and Robert Nighthawk. Nighthawk recorded that thing about "Sweet Black Angel."And then he had some girls singing behind him. Well, we'd already recorded "Wee Wee Baby, You Sure Look Good To Me" for both Delta and Bullet, which was the same company, and Columbia too. Then Baby Doo started having matrimonial trouble with his family. And then every time we'd get onstage, there'd come the police and drag him off the stage! So we (the Big Three Trio) gave up for a while and I started working with Chess.

Baby Doo's in Minneapolis now...

That's right. Incidentally, just three weeks ago (approx. Oct. 17), he had a heart operation, a bypass. I was talking to him the other night and he said, "Man I have a new carburetor and everything and I'm rarin' to go!" He said the percolator's working good and they got him walkin' around!

You were hired by Chess, at first, specifically as a bass player?

As a bass player. After they found out I was on the loose, I got a contract from them as a producer. And I was told the contract was as producer, songwriter, and all like this. He started me and had me listen to the artists and see what I could make out of some of the songs they had, or if they didn't have songs that were properly sufficiently, to try to write songs for them. I had a load of songs—I've had a load of songs ever since I was ten! And somehow or other, it looked as if some of them reached different (artists). So as everyone came along, I had a song for them. Even Leonard Allen at the United States label wanted a few. And that's the way it went, up until Leonard (Chess) died. Then I worked with the company a while longer.

You did a few songs as a performer on Chess, but not many—like "Walking The Blues."Why was this?

I did some on Chess. But the thing about it was that when Chess found they could use me more in the studio than a would-be artist, so that's why they kept me in the studio and gave me a salary there. I figured it was a good thing because I got a pretty straight salary there. And I worked on salary 'til after Leonard died. At the same time, I was writing my own songs. I was with Arc Music—he and Chess had a deal. Under Arc Music, all my music was my own.

But you have your own publishing company now.

Oh yeah, I have my own publishing. Most of the songs that they had of mine, in fact all of the songs I don't have, I will have in just a matter of time.

You played bass on a good portion of the Chess output. Did you play any electric?

No, mostly upright.

Did you ever play electric?

Well, I had one for a while, but I never did get accustomed to it, because I sold it to Jack Meyers. I had one of the first because the company wanted me to advertise it, but I never really did get to it because it looked like it took all the show out of my field. I like the sound of (the upright bass) better on certain things, because I could get a better slap sound out of it.

In your new group, your son Freddie plays electric bass.

Right, but I still do occasional things on my bass.

Who's in your current group?

Right now, I have my two sons—Freddie (bass) and Butch (piano). I also have Johnny Watkins on the guitar. I use two harmonica players—Snooky Pryor and Billy Branch.

You're the one who brought Snooky Pryor out of retirement.

Right, and Billy Branch too! Billy really wasn't playing very much harp when I got him. But you know, after a lot of rehearsals, anyone can come out of retirement. And I have Jim Tilman on the drums.

Your last album was the one on Ovation, What Happened To My Blues, right?

Oh yes, that last I actually released was on Ovation. Now I have a new one I just finished last year called A Mighty Earthquake, A Hurricane. This is supposed to be released in England. And then it's supposed to be released in the States too with Stan Lewis, Jewel Records. But I'm going to Washington on February 4 and 5, and I'm going to release a special on "It Don't Make Sense, You Can't Make Peace," and the other side, "It's In The News." And I'm going to see that Congress all has one of those. And I think it might make quite an impact. I just want to know why the great countries of the world say they want peace and end up making war. Now why? That's the only question I want to ask them is why!

I wish I had the answer to that one.

But it don't make sense. You take big countries, small countries, medium countries and they say they want peace. And they have scientists and wise men and smart men. Democrats and Republicans...

And then we have presidents!

And still, nobody can get together to make peace. They ain't talking about stoppin' war. When they going to limit arms? Why make something they say they're not going to use? Why they can't make peace? They can make everything else. They can even make babies without men now!

As a bit of a nonsequitur, let's talk about the final days of Chess Records. You were there after Leonard died?

I was there after he died. Leonard ran that company. There were a lot of understudies around there, but they really didn't understand the business like he did. After you've done business with the headman, and then you have to do business with a substitute, you don't come up with the same agreement. It's that simple. Phil (Chess) took it over. Marshall (Leonard's son) didn't do much because he was on the move all the time and youngsters didn't have much time for it in the first place. I think the only reason Marshall was in it was because he was forced in it. It's like my kids—they wouldn't give a doggone about the music or nothin'

else. They were forced in it because if you're going to eat around me, you got to play music. Or work. So they'd rather play music than work.

Was it during or after Chess that you recorded "I Am The Blues" for Columbia?

I'd written the song long before they had it. I did that album on Columbia for—what's that guy's name? He's out in California now?

Normal Dayron?

No, no...this was another guy. He leased it to Columbia. He used to work around there at Chess occasionally. An Italian fellow...who was that blond guy who sang?

Johnny Winter?

No, not that blond! Less blond. Big guy, muscles.

Wayne Cochran?

Yeah! The guy who managed Wayne Cochran. Anyway, he said, "You've written all these songs for other people but you've never done 'em yourself." And I told him I'd done 'em all at different times but no one put them all together.

Were you satisfied with your Columbia relationship?

I didn't actually have none. He was the go-between. I'd recorded for Columbia years ago with the Big Three Trio, but that was a much better relationship because we had direct contact. But it's better to be a big fish in a little pond than little fish in a big pond. In a big pond, like Columbia, little guys like me got eaten up by big fish.

From there, you started putting out records on Yambo.

Right.

How long have you had this storefront, the Blues Factory?

About ten years. It was a practice studio because there were so many musicians who didn't have a place to practice. But we had a free studio down there, and I kept my own band rehearsin' and making new tunes.

What was this building before you converted it to the Blues Factory?

It was a store. They had shelves all around the wall and everything. The lady got held up a couple of times and figured she'd get rid of it. I ripped all the shelves off the wall and kind of padded it and we've had band rehearsals in here for a long time. When the union had free band rehearsal space, everybody would use it. But when you started putting a tax on it, nobody showed up. So I just used it as a Blues Factory, where I just made songs. And whenever I feel up to par, I come in here and get ideas and hide from all my friends and write a song.

I followed you through the Yambo label. What was the Spoonful label? A continuation?

I did a few things on Yambo but I never did actually go out to sell very many of these things. I attempted to, at first. But when you got to the various disc jockeys that you think are going to promote things, you can forget about it if you ain't got no money! And I didn't have no money to pay no money. I still ain't got no money to pay somebody to play a record. The big companies can afford to pay these guys because the disc jockeys know that while he's playing my record, he could be playing somebody else's record and get a dollar off it 'cause he can't get no dollar off of me. And, if he plays my record, he figures I may not have another record but the big companies gonna have one and that's why he plays the big companies' records.

Next question...will we ever see your book on the blues on the stands?

Oh, sure. One day. No prediction on time, though, because I've gone into so many different things

such as this Blues Heaven Foundation which has required quite a bit of time.

You're called the Master Story Teller, and I hear you're doing some work on the college lecture circuit.

Well, this is because of the many stories of the blues. When you really figure them out, all the stories and the songs, each is the story of somebody's life one way or another. If it's not a story of life, it's a part of life. One guy tells you a story about his old lady left him and he got happy. The other one, his lady left him and he didn't get happy. And the other, his old lady came back, and that was the wrong things to do!

Even in the political thing, the condition of the world is another blues fact. And everything life consists of is another phase of the blues. So your blues may be different from mine, but if we reach a mutual understanding, sooner or later we'll be able to understand each other's blues.

You won some awards in WXOL's recent Blues Awards banquet.

Oh, yeah, that was...I don't know how they got that thing together, but that was a damn thing I paid to be on! Hell, I sent them $125 of my money and they sent me a damn award I could get for $15! I think that's just something somebody's trying to sell on some poor folks and thinks this is a fast way to get some.

You have a column in Living Blues magazine, blues questions and answers...

Yeah, I had it for a while. It was never a big thing. It was a free thing. I was answering questions. Once in a while, one of them asks me different questions. But I've got a lot of questions I'm going to be asking real soon, especially why the world can't make peace.

Del Shannon

By Wayne Jones
July 1976

On April 25, 1976, Del Shannon appeared at a Rock 'n' Roll Revival Show in Springfield, Massachusetts, along with Bo Diddley, Chiffons, Danny and the Juniors, and Jay & the Americans. The show was emceed by Henry "Fonzie" Winkler. Wayne Jones was wandering around backstage with his trusty tape recorder and submits the following interview with Shannon.

Goldmine: *Someone once said that if there's ever a Rock 'n' Roll Hall of Fame, that the song "Runaway" would probably be one of the first to be inducted. We're speaking to the man who was responsible for "Runaway" and so many other great hits of the 1960's, Del Shannon. Del, welcome to New England.*

Del Shannon: Hello Wayne, nice to be here.

Del, I have a number of things that I'd like to ask about. First, how did the name change come about from Charles Westover to Del Shannon?

I was working a club in Battle Creek, Michigan. There was a guy who used to come in a lot that drank heavily. He was a big guy who always was saying that one day he was going to become a wrestler and that well, Shannon, that's a great name. Well, anyhow I knew he never would be a wrestler so in essence I stole the name he wanted to use, Shannon. Then too, I always wanted a Cadillac because I was always poor. My friend had a Cadillac DeVille. So, I took Del from Deville. And that's it. I got it from that.

That's interesting.

(laughing) Yea, I finally got a Cadillac, too.

Who were your early influences?

Jerry Lee Lewis, Elvis, and mainly Hank Williams. He was my idol.

"Runaway", of course, was your biggest record. In 1969, Elvis introduced "Runaway" in his Las Vegas act as being one of his favorites and also a song that he wished he had recorded first. I was wondering if you were aware of these comments?

I was there when he did it and he introduced me from the audience. I was quite thrilled. One of his aides had called me and said "We have a seat for you at Elvis's show; he's doing 'Runaway' so would you like to come up?" So, I said that I was recording but that I guessed I could slip away. I did, and they had a table for me there with about eight bottles of champagne on it. I talked to him for a couple of hours after the show. He's a hell of a guy and I don't care what the press says about him. He's great.

Some followers of the oldies state that they could never understand why a record label pushes some releases and not others. Some of your 45s, in my opinion, that were not hits are much better than some that were. Who decides which ones to push?

Are you talking about within the label?

Right.

Well a record company has to hustle. There's a lot of things that happen in record companies. First of all, I may join a record company just because of one man, whether it be the president of the company who knows what he's doing or because of the promotion man who is also important. I'm with Island records now, with Pat Pipolo who produced a song called "Gypsy Woman." He took eight months to break that record. It sold a million and a half records but once again, it took him eight months to get it off the ground. When he left MCA, I followed him over to Island because he's tops to me in the business. But sometimes, it can all be so confusing. For example, a president of a company could say to a promotion man that he doesn't want to hear a certain record pushed but another one because he may have more of an interest in it. It's all very strange. The record business is insane.

During what many consider to be the height of your musical success, why did you switch to an obscure label like Berlee?

That was my own label.

Is that right? I wasn't aware of that.

I had to do that because I was suing my manager who also leased all my masters. So, no label would sign me at the time, because he threatened to sue them. So, I formed my own company and tried to get around it.

Del, you also hold the distinction for having the first Lennon-McCartney composition to hit the pop charts in America well before the Beatles came to America. This, of course, being "From Me To You" in the summer of 1963. How did you come to record this song?

I was headlining a show at the Albert Hall in London. The place was jammed out and the Beatles were really hot over there. They had something like three No. 1's in a row at the time. So, they were doing this one show with me. I was talking with John Lennon and I told him that "From Me To You" has got a little bit of a falsetto in it. So I'm going to record it. Then Lennon said (imitating an English accent) "That I would be great mate, great stuff." Then he walked up the stairs and turned around and said "Don't you do that!" Then, I saw Lennon again about three to four months later and the first thing he said was "Ah, you did it, didn't you!" And that's how it all came about. It was No. 1 over there and wasn't a big hit for me over here. At the time, no one had heard of the Beatles here, but I knew they were great writers, so I just picked up on one of their songs.

Did the British invasion have any affect on your career?

On my career, no. But record-wise it did. It was like, forget it. So, I went into production and helped produce "Gypsy Woman" for Brian Hyland and I also had a group called Smith who had a hit record called "Baby, It's You." Their album also did great. So, I didn't do anything for three years except

produce. It didn't hurt me because I kept busy.

Del, you've had many hit records besides "Runaway" such as "Hats Off to Larry," "Little Town Flirt," "Keep Searchin," and many others. Out of all the songs that you recorded, do you have a particular favorite?

Well, I don't know... my favorite record really isn't "Runaway." It was for a long time, but I've done it so much that I don't know what's my favorite song any more. I wrote one song called "The Ghost" and that's one of my favorites even though it hasn't been released, yet. I like that. "Jody" was also a nice song, which was the B side of "Runaway."

I like some of the B sides too, like "I Don't Care Anymore" and "The Answer to Everything," the Burt Bacharach tune. This kind of reverts back to what I indicated earlier, and that's some of the flip sides were at times better than the hit sides.

Well, they'll go with anything commercial. Like "Kelly" which was the B side of "Two Kinds of Teardrops" went to No. 6 in England and went to No. 40 or something here. And it's funny because whenever I go to England, I have to do that song ("Kelly") wherever I go. To them it's as popular as "Runaway" even though it was a B side. Australia's the same way; I have to do "Kelly" all the time.

Do you have a complete collection of your own recordings?

Just about; there's maybe one or two that I don't have.

Did you ever turn down any material that perhaps went on to become a hit for someone else?

Well, I was offered "His Latest Flame" at the same time I was ready to do "Hats Off to Larry," which I did. But I think "Hats Off to Larry" was a better record for me. And of course, Presley ended up doing "His Latest Flame," which he got after me. Pomus & Shuman wrote it. His version, to me, was a lot better than mine. There was also another song that I turned down. This was a forced deal. The record company said to me "If you do this song then it has to be your next single." Well, that's dictating to me, and I don't like that. I wouldn't do it that way. I suggested that I would do the song and perhaps a couple of others with it and maybe we'll pick the best. But they said no because this song would be on nationwide TV every week. It was called "Where The Action Is."

The Freddy Cannon hit?

Right, but I think that Freddy did it good. He did it cool.

Do any memorable moments come to mind with regards to any of the earlier tours that you were on during the '60s?

There was one. This was a show with just about everybody in the business on it, about thirty acts total. I think it was in Atlanta at the Gator Bowl, if that's where the Gator Bowl is. It was a giant outside show with about 30,000 people there. They had a stage that was about ten or twelve feet high that was constructed in the middle of a field. Believe it or not, the stage fell in and the piano that was on stage came just over my head and stopped on a barrier which probably saved my life, I guess. I know I ripped my shirt. That was unbelievable.

Del, in the past couple of years, many artists are coming out with songs that were hits years ago, probably with the reasoning that the new generation hasn't heard of these songs yet and will hopefully buy them. Do you have any plans to follow this pattern?

Well, I really don't like to follow but I know if there's a good song like Johnny Rivers redoing "Help Me, Rhonda," well he did that, in my opinion, as good as the original. I do have a record that I may release. I have to go back to Los Angeles and finish it next week and then I also have some original songs, too. But you're right; today's kids never heard those songs. In fact, this song I'm talking about releasing, I played for some neighbor kids the other day and they were saying "Oh wow, that's a great new song." I told them that I didn't write it and that this song was No. 1, seventeen years ago.

What song is that?

"Sea of Love" by Phil Phillips.

Looking back over your career, do you have any regrets, or perhaps is there something that you might like to change if you could do it over?

Yes, when I signed my first contract, I would definitely get a lawyer. I did eventually get a lawyer three years after. Young kids in this business really have to be very careful. I mean, if they're good and the record company really wants them, then they should get a contract to a lawyer and have him read it to them because if you're a kid, they'll try to force you into it. And if you're a kid who questions anything, they'll say "C'mon, are you an egotistical maniac—are you crazy? Do you want to sign or don't you?—get out if you don't want to sign now." Well, this is all crazy, because if they want you to sign, then they want you. So, then you should definitely see a good lawyer.

What are your feelings on today's rock 'n' roll Revival?

I don't call it a revival at all. It's always been there. When they say revival, nostalgia etc., they're nuts because it's always been here. It's only because of the people that grew up with it. That's their music! And there's millions of these people. Twenty years of rock 'n' roll? Are you kidding? It's always been there and it'll be here for a long time.

Good Del. I want to thank you for taking time off your hectic schedule to sit and talk with us and we hope that we can do it again sometime.

I've thoroughly enjoyed it. Thank You.

Wayne Jones would like to extend his thanks to Bruce Edelson in Dekalb, Illinois for his help in contributing some of the questions that were asked in this interview.

Counterfeit Beatles

By Tim Neely

In recent months, the most frequent call I've received here at *Goldmine* magazine is some variation of this:

"I read in (multiple choice: *The National Enquirer/Good Housekeeping* magazine/the fifth edition of your albums price guide) that there's this album called *Introducing The Beatles* that could be worth over $20,000. Well, I think I have one. Can you tell me if it is?"

I usually have to tell them, "No, it's not; you have one of the hundreds of thousands of counterfeits." Most people are not surprised; it's like sending in your Publishers Clearinghouse entry, then watching the Super Bowl and seeing the Prize Patrol go to someone else's house. But they dream anyway, and of course, there's always the off chance that indeed, someone could have an authentic stereo copy.

The most common "real" versions of *Introducing The Beatles* are mono (no reference to stereo on the cover or label), have "Please Please Me" and "Ask Me Why" on the back cover, the label and the record, and have the letters "VJ" in brackets with a rainbow of colors on the border of the label. The most common "fake" versions have a "Stereophonic" banner at the top of the front cover

and list "Love Me Do" and "P.S. I Love You" on the back cover. For years, it was claimed that if the front cover said "Stereophonic" and the song lists on the back cover featured "Love Me Do" and "P.S. I Love You," it was fake without exception. But this is no longer true: one that checked out in every way was sold for $20,000, and another one that seems to check out in every way is in the hands of a *Goldmine* reader.

So in the interests of awareness, we'll give you some of the more obvious ways to tell whether that *Introducing The Beatles* you have is an original or a phony.

On The Cover:

First, almost all the counterfeits claim to be stereo on the cover. Authentic copies of *Introducing The Beatles* in stereo have always been scarce; they were even scarce in 1964!

However, if your jacket lists "Love Me Do" and "P.S. I Love You" and the disc plays "Please Please Me" and "Ask Me Why," it's either fake or someone put the right record in the wrong jacket. But if your back cover has "Please Please Me" and "Ask Me Why," it's probably original. Ditto if your back cover

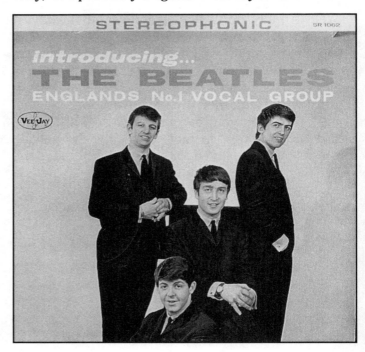

222

has pictures of twenty-five other albums, or if the cover is completely blank.

If your cover has a brown border around the front cover photo, stop right there; it's fake.

If there is no shadow accompanying George Harrison, who is at the far right of the cover photo, you have a fake.

If the cover has a yellow tint and has the word "Stereo" in the upper left, it's counterfeit.

There are some very well-done counterfeit covers; another giveaway is if you have a counterfeit record inside the jacket. Unless someone who owned both put an authentic record into a phony cover (it happens), a phony record implies a phony cover.

On The Record:

The two easiest ways to tell if your alleged stereo *Introducing The Beatles* is the real thing is to look at the record label.

First, does the record say "Stereo" on the label? While some authentic copies say stereo and actually play mono, the reverse is not true. If it doesn't say "Stereo," it's not.

Second, where are the words "Introducing The Beatles" and "The Beatles"? Both real and phony copies have both on them. But on an authentic copy, the words "The Beatles" are directly underneath "Introducing The Beatles," and both lines are above the center hole. If the center hole separates "Introducing The Beatles" and "The Beatles," it's a counterfeit.

There are other considerations as well, but those are the two easiest. For example, almost all real copies of the record have some sort of machine stamping in the dead wax, usually the words "Audio Matrix" or the letters "MR" in a circle. No phonies have machine stamping. Also, phonies often will be on 1970s-style flimsy vinyl as opposed to the sturdier 1960s vinyl.

The Play Test:

If you're still not sure whether your stereo *Introducing The Beatles* is the real thing or not, put Side 1, Song 1 on your turntable. "I Saw Her Standing There," as well as the next four tracks, will be in clean, crisp, true stereo. If the record plays mono or is very poorly rechanneled stereo, and the record doesn't say "Stereo" on it, it's either a real mono copy (check the record label again) or a phony.

Also, if your record doesn't play what's listed on the label, it's a fake. Some phonies list "Love Me Do" and "P.S. I Love You" on the label, but play "Please Please Me" and "Ask Me Why," and vice versa.

And Finally:

If everything checks about your "stereo" copy, before you start counting the dollars, check with a reputable dealer in Beatles records. There are other, even more subtle ways to check for authenticity than I've mentioned here. Good luck!

Ringo Starr

By Robyn Flans
July 29, 1988

There was excitement in the air Feb. 9, 1964. Like millions of others across the United States—perhaps you—I settled in front of the TV to watch the much-anticipated American debut of the Beatles on *The Ed Sullivan Show*. My youthful reaction to these four strange moptops, however, came in a burst of laughter, which got me booted from the room by my sister and her boyfriend. I'll never know what compelled me to beg for forgiveness, re-enter the room, and watch them, but I'm glad I did. My life changed that night; so too did rock 'n' roll and maybe the character of life in this country. How many musicians since that day—twenty-four years ago—have admitted they wouldn't be doing what they do had it not been for the Beatles?

The impact made by Paul McCartney, John Lennon, George Harrison, and Ringo Starr may forever be impossible to explain, but the fact that they altered the course of music and changed sociological norms from fashion to morals to attitudes cannot be denied. First it was little things like hair—the barbering profession must have really hit the skids as of Feb. 10—and later on it was bigger things like war and drugs. People listened to what the Beatles had to say. The Beatles became, for millions all over the world, not merely an object of affection or a group of talented entertainers, but an obsession to be emulated and idolized—a lifestyle.

Their greatest impact was, of course, music. They challenged the field and made experimentation acceptable. Before them, there was no such thing as "growth" when one spoke of a rock 'n' roll artist. The idea was just to keep getting hits, and when you stopped doing that, your time was up. Few artists challenged the hitmaking process by altering a proven formula; that was commercial suicide. The Beatles never sat still, from start to finish, and whatever they did worked. They were gifted with talent, charisma, and everything else it took to become a phenomenon the like of which hadn't been seen before or since.

They even altered the almighty music business itself. Before them, it was the record companies, the producers, the publishers who came first, who determined who and what was a hit. The Beatles largely took hold of their own destiny instead; they decided what they would sing and how they would look, and nobody was going to tell them otherwise. Within a couple of years after their initial burst of success, they were even responsible for the album taking over from the single as the dominant format in which rock was heard.

For this Beatles fan, their effect was such that it determined my profession; without the Beatles, it is unlikely that I would be a music journalist. Needless to say, one of my dreams as such was to interview a member of the Beatles. When I expressed that desire to a drummer named Jim Keltner a few years ago, he made that dream come true by arranging for me to meet with Ringo Starr for an interview with *Modern Drummer* magazine.

Walking into his rented Beverly Hills house, I was nervous. I had been warned by other reporters that Ringo was not receptive to talking about the Beatles, that he was temperamental and difficult. I was worried that if he was indeed like that, it might damage my feelings for the music that had played such a large part in my childhood and has remained with me since. Ringo always seemed so lovable, the Beatle who kept out of the bickering at the end and just wanted to play his drums.

But that was an occupational risk I had to take. I'm sure there are many among us who have met a long-admired celebrity, only to be disappointed by finding out what they were really like away from their image. A tainted personal impression of a musical artist can forever sour the artist's music in one's mind.

But Ringo was nothing like the description I had gotten from others. He was warm and sincere, witty and humorous. Sitting in his garden, he spoke about the Beatles and anything else I wanted to know, to my heart's content. The transcript of that interview, minus some of the more technical questions about drumming which he answered for *Modern Drummer*'s readers, follows.

225

Today, incredibly, Ringo Starr is without a record contract. He has been for several years; his last album, 1983's *Old Wave*, was not even released in America. That's sad commentary, considering just who this man is. But rather than set a down tone for an interview with a man who's brought happiness to so many, and whose own demeanor always seems so cheery, let's just lead off by saying... Heeeeere's Ringo!

Goldmine: Why drums?

Ringo Starr: I tried everything else. Originally, my grandfather and grandmother were very musical and played mandolin and banjo, and we had a piano, which I used to walk on as a child. Being an only child and a spoiled brat, my mother would let me do most things, so I used to walk on the piano, but never actually learned it. Then when I was seven, my grandfather brought me a mouth organ, which I never got into either, and then they died and I sort of ended up with the banjos, but never got into that.

Drums were just the ones I always felt an affinity with. At thirteen, in the hospital, we used to play on the little cupboard next to the bed, and then once a week, they had a band to keep us occupied, since we were in there for a year. So they fetched this band around and this guy would have these big green, yellow, and red notes, and if he pointed to the red note, you would hit the drum, or the yellow was the cymbal or the triangle, and things like that. It was a percussion band, but it was just to keep us entertained while we were in bed.

They used to come once a week to the hospital, and we used to knit and do all stuff like that, anything to keep us occupied. So in the hospital, I wouldn't play in the band unless I had the drum. When I came out, it was always the only instrument I wanted. So at sixteen, I bought a $3 bass drum, made a pair of sticks out of firewood, and used to pound that, much to the joy of all the neighbors. I couldn't really play; I used to just hit it. Then I made a kit out of tin cans, with little bits of metal on the snare. Flat tins were the cymbals, and a big biscuit tin with some depth in it was the tom, and a shallow biscuit tin was the snare drum, and so forth.

Then my stepfather, Harry Graves, who came from the south of England (we're from the north), went down to see his family one Christmas, and one of his uncles was selling a kit of drums for £12 (roughly $30). It was a great old kit—a great trap

and all the wood blocks and everything—so I had that. I got that kit in January 1958. There were two problems, though. One, I didn't have a car to carry it and, two, I wasn't in a band. But in February, one month later, I joined a band, although I couldn't play. Nobody knew, though, because they couldn't play well, either. We were all just starting out playing. It was the skiffle days in 1958 in England.

What was the name of the band?

It was called the Eddie Clayton Skiffle Group. The guy next door used to play guitar, a friend of mine used to play tea-chest bass, and we played "Hey Lidy Lidy Lo"and all skiffle songs. We used to play for the men at lunch hour in the factory. It was mainly, if you had an instrument, you could join a band. It didn't matter if you could play. But my problem was I was always traveling on the bus, so I couldn't carry the kit.

Then we started auditioning, and we did every audition in the world, every free show we could do. We had no sense of time, so we'd start with the count of "one, two, three, four,"and then it would be like an express train because we'd get faster and faster and faster. People were just dropping like flies on the dance floor because it was like, "Can't you slow it down, can't you slow it down?"

So we did a lot of free shows. In that band, I didn't really need the full kit, but I always wanted to play it. Anyway, I got the kit, and I set it up in the back bedroom like a professional, thinking, "I'll practice and everything." I only did that one night and we had all the neighbors yelling "Shurup (shutup), get out of here," because we were in very close proximity to everyone else. So I never practiced since that day, except with a band. I made all the mistakes onstage, as it were.

Did you have any drum idols?

No, the only drum record I ever bought was Cozy Cole's *Top Parts I and II*. I used to like Gene Krupa although I never bought any of his records. It was that type of drumming though, heavy kind of tom-tom stuff, and Cozy Cole was another tom-tom person. But I was never really into drummers and I never did solos. I hated solos. I wanted to be the drummer within the band, not the frontman. The longest solo I ever did was thirteen bars.

I read somewhere that part of the reason you

changed your last name was that in the beginning, they wanted to bill your solo time as "Starr Time."

We used to have "Starr Time" when I had the solo spot about two years later with Rory Storme and the Hurricanes. We all were professional as it were. The difference is that they pay you for playing. That's the only difference in being a professional from being an amateur.

What was your first professional job?

On the first profess they offered me ten shillings, which was about a dollar and a half in those days, and the guy got so drunk at the end of the night that he didn't pay us anyway. We were really down about that, but it was the first paying gig. We (the Eddie Clayton band) had done all the auditions and won a few competitions and stuff like that, but also still worked in the factory.

Then I joined a couple of other bands, a skiffle group, and I ended up with Rory Storme, which was basically a skiffle group, but we were going rock. We were the first band to be thrown out of the Cavern for playing rock 'n' roll because it was a jazz club. The only thing we used to have different was that our lead guitarist used to come out of a radio. That was his amp. He used to plug into this little radio onstage, so suddenly we were too rock 'n' roll for this jazz club, and they threw us off the stage. It was all in good fun at the time.

When did you join up with Rory Storme?

1959. In 1960, we all decided to leave our jobs and go real professional, where that's all we'd do. So I left the factory.

That must have been a major commitment, the money being so poor in that business, particularly at that time.

It was a major commitment, but it was all I wanted to do. The family said, "It's all right as a hobby, but keep the job."

"You'll never make a living by being a musician."

My mother still thinks that to this day, I think: "It's all right as a hobby, son." Anyway, this is a roundabout way of saying how the names came about. We decided to go away to play Butlin's Holiday Camp in England, which is a camp where people go for two weeks' holiday. So when we went professional and bought the red suits and the shoes and everything, we all thought we'd change our names, because show biz means changing your name. That's what's so great about it; you can call

Photo/Chuck Boyd/Flower Children

yourself anything you like, like Zinc Alloy.

So the guitarist called himself Johnny Guitar, and in the end, I think because we're English, we all picked cowboy names like Ty Hardin, Lou O'Brien, Rory Storme, and Ringo Starr, because of the rings which I always wore then. But then, to get back to your point, I used to do a twenty-minute spot with vocals. I used to sing songs, because we used to do hours, so anyone could sing, play a solo or anything. The guitarist would do a couple of guitar numbers, then the singer would come on, and then I'd do a couple of numbers, and that's why it was called "Starr Time." So I'd do "Let's Twist Again," "Holly Gully," "Sticks And Stones," a Ray Charles number, and a couple of other numbers like that. God, it's all so long ago. I was even doing "Boys" in those days.

So you never did any drum solos?

I never did any drum solos, no. Never have; never wanted to—even at the beginning. While we were still at this holiday camp, we used to play in the Rockin' Calypso, but on Sunday, the big night, they had a big theater there, and they'd have name acts, and the local people working there would be on the bill. So we were working with the Happy Wanderers, an English street band with a big walking bass drum, trumpet, clarinet, and they were like a walking jazz band. They used to walk around the streets of London playing songs, and then the guy would walk around with the hat. They became very well known. At the end of the show, it used to get to the solo and I used to let their drummer take the solo on the bass drum: "boom, boom, boom, boom." I would never do the solo, even then. Never liked them. So anyway, that's when we got our names.

Why did you grow up with such a fascination for the American West?

As children in England, your cowboys were great heroes to us. To an English kid, a cowboy was a fascinating thing, you know, in his leather waistcoat and his black gloves and all of that, so that's part of it.

Photo/Chuck Boyd/Flower Children

Had rock come into the picture yet in England?

Rock 'n' roll was very big here, and Elvis was out in 1957. We're talking about '59 and '60, so we were just getting into rock and away from the skiffle stuff. We suddenly got amplifiers and played different songs. Rock was coming in, and that's where I went; that was my direction. I was purely rock 'n' roll. Drummers or musicians were either going for jazz or rock.

There used to be coffee shops and things like that in those days, and we'd sit around, and I used to get so mad at the drummers who wanted to play jazz because I was just strictly rock 'n' roll. I always felt it was like rats running around the kit if you played jazz, and I just liked it solid. So we'd have these great deep discussions about drums. It was all so exciting then. It's still exciting, but...

Were you a drum fanatic in those days?

No, just a rock fanatic, but my instrument was drums. I never wanted to play anything else. But I also wanted every other drummer to play rock. I didn't want them to play anything else (laughs). "You've got to be kidding. Just rock! Listen to it. Get into it." There was more emotion in rock than in jazz. We went through jazz, in my opinion, just listening to it. I went through it in one week and knew I had had enough of that. Rock never ceases to make me happy when it's good.

How far into your Rory Storme gig were you when you came in contact with the Beatles?

I was playing with Rory about eighteen months or two years. We'd all played the same venues and, at the time, Rory and the Hurricanes used to be top of the bill. There'd be all these other bands on and occasionally, the Beatles would play. It ended up that they were the only band I ever watched because they were really good, even in those days. One morning, I was in bed, as usual—I don't like getting up in the day because I live at night. So a knock came at the door, and Brian Epstein said, "Would you play a lunchtime session at the Cavern with the Beatles?" And I said, "Okay, okay, I'll get out of bed," and I went down and played. I thought it was really good. I thought the band was good, and it was great for me to play.

Were they different from other bands playing at the time?

Yeah, they were playing better stuff. They were doing very few of their own songs then, but they were doing really great old tracks: Shirelles tracks and Chuck Berry tracks, but they did it so well. They had a good style. I don't know; there was a whole feel about Paul, George, and John. And Pete, it's no offense, but I never felt he was a great drummer. He had sort of one style, which was very good for them in those years, I suppose, but they felt, I think, that they wanted to move out of it more. So I just played the session and then we went and got drunk and then I went home.

So it was a one-shot deal.

It was a one-shot, but we knew each other. We met in Germany when Rory played there and so did the Beatles, but we didn't play with each other. There was heavy competition because we used to play weekends, twelve hours a night between the two bands, and we'd try to get the audience in the club, so there was a lot of competition. And then, at 4 a.m. or 5 a.m. in the morning set, if the Beatles were left on, I'd usually still hang around because I was drunk, asking them to play some sort of soft sentimental songs, which they did. So basically, they were at one club and we were at another club and we ended up at the same club. That's how we sort of said hello. We never played with each other, but then out of the blue, Brian came and asked me to play.

Was that an audition for you from their standpoint?

No, Pete wasn't well or something, so they needed a drummer for the session and asked me, or asked Brian to ask me. So I went and played and that was all there was to it. This went on for about six months, where every couple of weeks I'd play, for whatever reasons. Then there was talk about me joining, and I was asked if I would like to. I said, "Yeah," and then went away with Rory to play this holiday camp again because it was good money for three months, and we just played what we wanted.

About five weeks into this three month gig, Brian called and asked if I would join the Beatles. I said, "Yeah, I'd love to. When?" He called me on a Wednesday, and he said, "Tonight." I said, "No, I can't leave the band without a drummer. They'd lose a six-week gig, which they have left to go." So I said I'd join Saturday, which gave Rory the rest of the week to find a drummer.

Why did you choose to join the Beatles if both bands, in essence, were starving young bands?

Well, I'd rather starve with a better band, and I felt the Beatles were a better band. By then, we weren't actually starving. We were making, not great money, but enough to live on. And the Beatles were making a bit more; they were coming up real fast. But I loved the band so much. I thought it was a better band, and I thought I had done everything our band could do at the time. We were just repeating ourselves. So it was time to move on again, and that's why. And I liked the boys as well as the music.

So you joined them that Saturday.

I left Saturday, played on Saturday night, and it was in every newspaper. There were riots. It was okay when I just joined in and played a gig and left, but suddenly I was the drummer. Pete had a big following, but I had been known for years in Liverpool, so I had quite a following too. So there was this whole shouting match, "Ringo never, Pete forever,"and "Pete never, Ringo forever." There was this whole battle going on, and I'm just trying to drum away.

But they got over it, and then we went down to make a record. I'm not sure about this, but one of the reasons they also asked Pete to leave was George Martin, the producer, didn't like Pete's drumming. So then, when I went down to play, he didn't like me either, so he called a drummer named Andy White, a professional session man, to play the session. But George has repented since (laughs). He did come out one day saying it, only when he said it, it was ten years later. In the end, I didn't play that session. I played every session since, but the first session, he brought in a studio drummer.

There were two versions of the first tune ("Love Me Do"); one where Andy White plays and one where you play.

You're right. There are two versions. I'm on the album and he's on the single. You can't spot the difference, though, because all I did was what he did. Because that's what they wanted for the song.

I heard that Martin handed you a tambourine.

Yeah, and told me to get lost. I was really brought down. I mean, the idea of making a record was real heavy. You just wanted a piece of plastic. That was the most exciting period of records—the first couple of records. Every time it moved into the fifties on the charts, we'd go out and have dinner and celebrate. Then when it was in the forties, we'd celebrate. And we knew every time it was coming on the radio and we'd all be waiting for it in cars or in someone's house. We wouldn't move for that three minutes.

And then, of course, the first gold disc and the first number one. But like everything else, when you've had five number ones, one after the other, and as many gold discs as you can eat, it's not boring, but it's just that the first couple of records were so exciting. I think they are for everybody. It's like sweets every day, though. You get used to it.

So I was really brought down when he had this other drummer, but the record came out and made it quite well, and from then on, I was on all the other records, with my silly style and silly fills. They used to call it "silly fills."

Who?

Everyone used to sort of say, "Those silly fills he does."

And yet, it turned drumming around for a lot of people.

But we didn't know that then. Everyone put me down—said that I couldn't play. They didn't realize that was my style and I wasn't playing like anyone else—that I couldn't play like anyone else.

How did it come to be that George Martin allowed you to play the second session?

I think I drove him mad, because we rehearsed for the next record and I had a tambourine in one hand and maracas in the other and played the kit with them. George was just flabbergasted. I didn't have a stick in my hand; I just had a tambourine and maracas, and I was hitting the cymbals and smashing the tom with the maracas, so he thought he'd better do something about it. So he said, "Well, if you use sticks, I'll let you play."

He never said that really, but I think he just

thought I'd gone mad, so he'd better please me and let me play on the next record. And from then on, I played, except for *Back In The U.S.S.R.*, which Paul played on because I wasn't there. We just carried on from there, and then it got to where John and Paul were always the writers and the bass player and rhythm guitar, and George was getting some notice as a lead guitarist, but I was still getting, "He's all right,"so it was a bit of a putdown at the time.

Let's talk about sessions. How much creative input were you allowed, and how much did George Martin dictate?

Well, at the beginning, George Martin dictated a certain amount, and then it was John and Paul's writing to consider. See, what helped me a lot was that I had three frustrated drummers around, because everyone wants to be a drummer for some reason. John could play and Paul could play and George could play, but they each had one standard style. We all have one standard style, but they only had one sort of groove, where I have two or three.

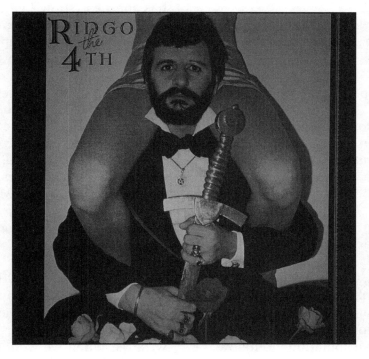

John and I used to have, not arguments, but discussions, because we'd be playing all these records and he'd say, "Like that," and I'm saying "But John, there's two drummers on there," and he could never hear there were two drummers. They'd play stuff with two drummers on it and the three of them each had their own idea of what the drummer should do, and then I had my idea. So all I would do was combine my idea, their three ideas, and the ideas of the two drummers on a record. They got what they were given, and it worked. But that helped me to play. Also, the long hours in Germany, you know, you soon get your act together.

So we were playing and making these records, and then we sort of got freeform rock in our own way, though it was a lot tighter than acid-rock because we had songwriters and we did songs and

didn't just jam. We went through a lot of changes on records. Then in '68, I got the kit with the calf skins and that changed everything. Then it really became tom-tom city because of the calf and wood.

When you're touring, everyone thanks God that the plastic heads were invented because you're playing outside in the heat, or the wet, or whatever, and skins are very hard to handle. But since '66, we were in a controlled environment, in the studio, so the temperature was always the same and you could deal with calf. You can't deal with them outside, although drummers have for thousands of years. So plastic heads were a godsend on the road, but then when we were just in the studio, I ordered this kit and I had calf skins put on.

To backtrack even further: I'd had this kit that my stepfather got for £12. It was a great old kit, but it was old-fashioned. I joined a band when I was eighteen, and in my silliness, thought "I want a new kit." So I bought an Ajax kit, which is an English company. It was a black pearl kit, about £47, roughly $125, complete with a pair of sticks. "You can take it away and play it"; it was one of those. You had everything you needed.

Then one of the band got a car so we could carry the kit, because in the old days, as I was saying, we were on the bus, so you couldn't take a kit. I would only take a snare drum, a hi-hat and cymbal, and beg all the other drummers for their kits. Some of them wouldn't give them to me, so I'd just have to play with a snare. I never like to let the kit out, either, unless I know the person. You never let anyone use the snare. The only two times I ever lent a snare, it was broken. And it takes a long time to get it to how you want it to sound. I would understand others not lending the kit, but I thought they were real mean.

One time, I remember a guy asking me if he could use my kit and I said, "Well, can you play?"And he said, "Yeah, I've been playing for years,"and if you can imagine, a guy gets on your kit and puts his foot on the beater of the bass drum pedal and thinks it's a motorbike starter, kick starting. So I just went over and grabbed him off the kit and threw him offstage. It blew me away! The man never played in his life, and he thought it was a motor bike. That was one time I lent the kit out.

So you had this Ajax set.

Right up to the Beatles, and then we were getting new instruments and things and I wanted a new kit. I wanted a Ludwig kit. It was good, for their own good and my good, because while we were touring, of course, they would give me a couple of free kits because I was a Ludwig drummer. I used to play that mini-kit on stage. Couldn't hear a thing! But it was good for me to get behind because I'm not that tall, so I looked bigger with a small kit, so at least you could see me.

But it didn't matter much what you sounded like in concert, did it?

No. That's why we stopped.

George Harrison said that he felt the response to the Beatles was some sort of hysterical outlet for people. The four of you must have sat around and conjectured as to what the hell was going on. That had to be mind-blowing.

Well, we enjoyed them letting their hysterical needs out because no one came to listen to our gigs. They bought records to listen to. They just came to scream and shout, which was fine, but after four years, I was becoming such a bad player because I couldn't hear anything. Because of the noise going on, all I had to do was just constantly keep the time, so we'd have something to follow. If you look at films, you'll see I'm looking at their mouths—I'm lip-reading where we're up to in the song because I couldn't hear the amps or anything. We were becoming bad musicians, so we had the discussion about it. Besides, we could play in any town or country in the world and get the same response, but only the four of us would know if we played any good, and that was very seldom because we couldn't hear. So you're getting the same response for a bad gig and it wasn't any help. You only wanted applause if you did something that worked, so we decided to go into the studio. It was pointless playing on stage anymore.

I guess I wonder what you thought. I mean, that response had never happened before.

I don't know. The media and the madness of the time, I guess. Things were very dead just up to when we came out and that was just part of what we did.

So onstage, you were absolutely reading lips at that point?

Yeah, just to find out where we were up to in the song, and just carrying a beat. So then we went back into the studio where we could get back to playing with each other again, because we'd do the same twelve numbers every night and we'd do a thirty-minute show. That seems amazing now, because Bruce Springsteen does four hours. He still has the best show I've seen in the last ten years, and I only watched two hours of that, and it was enough. But every group does at least an hour and a half, and Bruce, who is the extreme, does four hours.

We did a thirty-minute show, and if we didn't like the place, we'd play a bit fast and do it in twenty-five minutes. We were getting real despondent playing live, so we went into the studio for months and months. It got us playing again and exploring a lot of avenues of the technology of the studio, which compared to now, was Mickey Mouse.

Eight-track was a big deal then.

And we didn't have one. We begged for one because we did everything on four-track up to *Pepper (Sgt. Pepper's Lonely Hearts Club Band)* and four-to-four, but EMI was technically a very, very good studio with their engineers and electronic wizards. When we went four-to-four, to go tape-to-tape, there's usually a loss, but the loss was so slight, because their engineers were technically so good that no one missed it. You can't miss it anyway because the public didn't know what they were missing so they only got what they got. But we put the drums through phasers and things like that.

How did you feel about all that?

It was great, because it worked with the tracks we were doing and it was magic. Just like magic. And we put it through the Hammond speaker and it goes round and round, whatever that's called, and just tricks like that. We put the guitar through something going backwards and it was all experimental madness to us, but it was in the form of a song. It wasn't us just freaking out, playing, which we did quite a lot, but we never released any tapes like that.

And you knew you wouldn't have to reproduce it onstage anyway.

We knew we weren't going out onstage and it ended up, like on *Pepper*, that if we wanted to go out, we'd have to take an orchestra with us. But no one was interested in going out. We were only interested in making records. So that was exciting, the sound we could get. And then the group broke up. So I started playing with a lot of other people. One year I did Leon Russell, Stephen Stills, B.B. King, and Howlin' Wolf, which was good for my head. After being in one band so long, suddenly playing with such a diverse group of people was good for me.

I wondered if during the Beatles, you ever felt you wanted to get out and do something else.

No, never did. That was always good enough for me. I never played any other sessions. I only did a few, like Jackie Lomax and a couple of other people. But then it was exciting when the group had split and I just started playing with a lot of people. In 1970, England was the place everyone wanted to make albums, so I played a lot of different sessions, like with Jimmy Webb and Harry Nilsson.

After the Beatles, I heard that you really felt that you didn't want to play drums anymore, for a while at least.

It wasn't that I didn't want to play drums; I didn't know what to do with my life. I'd been playing with the band for so long and suddenly it ended. I just

sat there wondering what to do with my life, because I wasn't a producer and I wasn't a writer.

To backtrack for a second: The White Album. *I read that you left for about a week.*

I left for two weeks. I felt I wasn't part of the group. I felt that the other three were really together and close and I wasn't part of the group, so because of that feeling, I felt I wasn't playing well. I went around to John, knocked on the door and said, "I'm leaving the band, man. You three are really close and I'm getting out." And he said, "I thought it was you three." So I went around to Paul and said the same thing: "I'm leaving; I'm not playing well because you three are real close and I'm not in the band anymore." And he said, "I thought it was you three." I said, "Well, I don't know who it is, but I'm going on holiday," and I went to Sardinia for a couple of weeks to clear my head. That's when they made *U.S.S.R.*, which I wasn't on. Then I came back to the *While Album*, which I felt, for me, was a better album than *Pepper* for the group.

Why do you say that?

Well, we were much more like a band. We're like session players on *Pepper*, using all those orchestras and sound effects. I mean it was good fun, but I felt we were getting more like a group on the *White Album* again, though it was a double album, and double albums give too much information for me, anyway. But that and *Abbey Road*, besides *Rubber Soul*, are a few of the finest albums.

The music became a lot more sophisticated, and I'm sure you were called on to do more sophisticated kinds of things.

Never. You got what you got. I don't know if it got more sophisticated. I don't think you'd call the *White Album* sophisticated, but I enjoyed it more than *Pepper*, which you could call sophisticated. But you'd only call that sophisticated because of what you put on top; the brass section and such. The idea behind *Pepper*, which never got fully realized, was that it was going to be a whole show, but we only got into two tracks and then we made it just a regular album.

A show as far as a concept album, or something to take on the road?

Just a concept album of a show, and we segued from *Sgt. Pepper* into the next track with the cheer, and there's Billy Shears, and then we did it for two tracks and we got bored with that and just made another album. The *White Album* was not to do tricks; it was for us to get together, I felt, and play together as a group, which is what we were, and best at.

I read that Paul had been very critical of your playing on the White Album *before you left for two weeks, and that's one of the reasons you left.*

No, I left for the very reason I told you. I thought I just had to go away and straighten my head out because it was getting too silly. And while I was away, I got telegrams from John saying, "The best rock 'n' roll drummer in the world," and when I came back, George had the whole studio decorated with flowers. So Paul may have been pissed off. I don't know; he never did anything. But he never actually said to me, "That's not good," or whatever, so I don't know where that rumor came from. He was never that critical.

Dispelled that rumor.

I've never read that one, even, (laughs); I've read most of them. There was a guy in New York who said he played on everything. All that bull has gone down. You have to let those things pass. Some

RINGO ST★RR STOP AND SMELL THE ROSES

drummer in New York wanted to make a name for himself and said he played on everything, and I never played on anything. So what was I doing? I know on some sessions I wasn't all there, but I wasn't off completely away.

Obviously, John and Paul were the most integral portion of what went on in the studio.

It was their songs.

But what would happen? Take us through a typical session, or even a song.

Well, what would happen is that someone would say, "Well, I've got this" because it was very early on that John and Paul didn't write together. It was their own songs, and then a lot of them would start as jams and someone would put lyrics to them; like "Helter Skelter" was a full-on jam, and "Birthday," just to mention jams where we had nothing when we went in. Other songs would have a verse and a chorus and they'd finish them, or anyone could shout a line and if the line was good, they'd use it. The roadies, the tea lady, if anyone had a line, it would be used.

It was always open like that, and always the best line would be used. It wouldn't matter who said it. No one had the ego big enough to say, "I have to write this." Not all the time; I mean, they wrote ninety percent finished songs, but not musically, because they could only use what we could play. "Birthday" was one case. "They say it's your birthday," do you know that track?

Of course.

We went over to Paul's and came back and wanted to do a sort of rowdy rock 'n' roll track because Little Richard had freaked us out yet again, so we just took a couple of chord sequences and played them sort of raucous and loud and there was a newspaper on the floor and it was about someone's birthday. So Paul started singing and we all just hopped on behind him. That's how that came about, but we never went in with anything. We just went in and I sat behind the kit and they stood behind their instruments and that came about like that.

On the finished tunes, would you get called into the session, come in and listen to the tune, and just supply what you felt was right?

No. On the finished tunes, they'd sit at the piano and play them. Then we'd go through several different changes of how we all felt it should be done. Mainly, the writer had the definite idea, but if anyone did anything to change it and it was good and moved into a place they enjoyed, that's how it would be. There was a lot of open-mindedness. There were very few tracks with the definite idea, this is how it has to be. Mostly, if someone came up with anything that was different and worked, then everyone would go along with it.

In those days, for a drummer to have that kind of creative allowance was somewhat unusual.

Well, I was allowed to create anything I could as long as it worked, and it was the same with the guitar or the bass or the piano. It was all the same, but the difference was that it had to fit around their song.

What about when you began to write?

First of all, I used to rewrite Jerry Lee Lewis B-sides and not really know it. I just put new words to all the songs. It took me years to fetch a song in because I, as much as anyone else, was in awe of our two writers, who I felt were the best writers around. So I'd write my little songs and I'd be embarrassed to fetch them in because of John and Paul.

So then I started fetching them in and they'd all be laughing on the floor, "Oh, you've rewritten 'Crazy Arms,'"or something. So then I started writing a bit more, like, "I listen for your footsteps coming up the drive,"some song I wrote, don't know the title anymore ("Don't Pass Me By"). That was the first one that we did of mine. But they used to write songs for me tailor-made, because they

knew my range and it was like a personality thing I used to put across. Or then I'd pick the country song, because I always liked country 'n' western: "Boys" I had done for years, then they started writing songs just for me. Then I started writing my own, and then I wrote "Octopus's Garden." I always mention "Octopus's Garden."

That was the first one you were proud of, really, wasn't it?

Well, it was so silly.

That was written on your holiday in Sardinia?

Yeah. We were on this boat and they offered us this meal and we'd ordered fish and chips, and the fish came and I said, "What's that?" There were legs and things. And the guy said, "Oh, it's octopus," and being English and food-wise, that blew me away. "Are you kidding? Octopus? You've got be to crazy. Nobody eats that. Tentacles? It's not fish; it's jet-propelled."

Then I got talking to the captain, and he was telling me the story of octopuses building gardens under the sea. They find shiny rocks and tins and whatever and they build these gardens, and I found it fascinating. I was just sitting on the pier one day and I wrote "Octopus's Garden" for me and the children. And some days you really feel like you'd like to be there, under the sea, in an octopus's garden, because it gets a bit tough out here, and it was a tough period then. So I felt it would be very nice to be real quiet under the ocean.

Was the breakup gradual? I presume it didn't happen in just one day.

No, the breakup came because everyone had ideas of what he wanted to do, whereas everyone used to have ideas of what we would do, as a group. Then we weren't really fulfilling John's musical ambitions or Paul's or George's, or my own, in the end, because it was separate. We weren't working for one aim, just the one band. Everyone wanted to do other things as well. So you could see it coming, but like everything else, we all held it off for a while.

Then it just got too silly and we had a meeting about what everyone wanted to do. You can't keep a band together. We never did it for the money; we did it for the playing. I mean, the money is very nice but we were players first. As anyone will tell you, if we had wanted, we could have just carried on and made fortunes, but that was not our game. Our game was actually making music. So it became too strange, because there was a lot of stuff I didn't want to play on that I felt just wasn't exciting anymore.

Can you be specific?

Well, John is the easiest to talk about. He wanted to do stuff which was avant-garde in its way. Besides, I had no place being on it and I wasn't on some of it. He wanted to do that more than play with the group, and Paul wanted to do another thing, and George was wanting something else.

What did you want?

Well, I just wanted to play really good music—not that any of it's bad. I enjoyed the group thing, and then people wanted to do other things, which could have included us if we had wanted to. But half the time, we didn't want to get involved with certain tracks because it just wasn't what we were there to do as a group. We were there to do it individually, but not as a group. So the regression started about '68 and it was over by '70. So that was the end of that, and I did feel lost, as we talked about before.

I would imagine it was an adjustment personally, but did you feel lost musically?

Well, I'd never played with a better band, you see, so I think that's the loss I felt.

Where does one go from the best?

It's not even just the best. A lot of it was telepathy. We all felt so close. We knew each other so well that we'd know when any of us would make a move up or down within the music, and we'd all make it. No one would say anything or look at each other; we'd just know. The easiest word is telepathy. The band worked so well, and we were four good friends a lot of the time. But like any four friends, we had rows and shouted and disliked each other for a moment.

Then it ended, and I started playing sessions and had a really good time, but I was just playing. You can play with any band, but that band was something special to me, and it's never been like that again. I've had great sessions, great tracks, but it's

never been like that, and you can't expect that if you walk into a studio and play someone's session. You're strangers.

We had all lived together so close; we knew each other so well that it crossed over into the music. We knew exactly what the other was doing. That's even the wrong way to explain it. We just knew that the chemistry worked! The excitement! If things were just jogging along and one of us felt, "I'm going to lift it here," it was just a feeling that went through the four of us and everyone lifted it, or everyone lowered it, or whatever. It was just telepathy. When I do sessions now, I'm playing the best I can, and some sessions are really great. But I've never played on anyone's album all the way through, because I always felt it was boring, so I'd do three or four tracks.

Can you define what you think is a good drummer?

Yeah, me. It took me a long time to think of myself like that, but I am probably the best rock drummer.

Why do you say that?

Because I play with emotion and feeling, and that's what rock is. Rock is not reading, and I'm not putting reading down, although it's something that I don't do and something I never wanted to do. I did have one lesson in the old days and the guy wrote all those dots on the paper, but I felt it wasn't the way I wanted to play. I only wanted to play, and some days it's a real bummer for people, because if I'm on a downer, I still have to play, and you only get what's in my soul at the time. But that's life. We all make a choice. A lot of session guys can go in and read and play five different sessions a day, totally different types of music. He just reads it and plays it, but that's a different musician to me.

There was never a time where you felt you should have lessons or you'd like to take lessons?

Only in the very early days when I first got the kit, because you think that's what you should do. So I had one lesson and realized that wasn't what I should be doing.

Did you play along with records?

No, I never practiced in my life. I just practiced one day and then joined a band and made every mistake I could on stage.

That's incredible.

Well, it was easier then. I don't know if it was easier then, but it seems like it was. Now, you've got to be an amazing player to get a job, even in the local band that plays a Bar Mitzvah. You've got to read and play. As I told you before, back then if you had an instrument, you were in a band. That was how easy it was when I started. And a month after I had the kit, I had one lesson, gave that up, practiced once in the back room and joined a group and I've played with groups ever since. I think it's better for you. Well, I don't know if it's better for you, but it was for me.

I have a son who is a drummer, who played for three years, three hours a day, practicing with headphones on to records and to himself, but that's his style. He plays a totally different style from me, and he plays, not better, but technically he can do more than I can do. And he's interested in all those words they keep mentioning like flams and para-diddies and things like that, which I never understood.

So you really feel that what made you special was that you worked from your gut emotion?

Well, I think that the drums are an emotional instrument and there's no melody. It's not like you can sit in a room with a guitar or piano and play. It's only "boom-boom-boom" or "ratta-tat-tat,"and there's no real melody there. That's why I dislike solos. I don't care which drummer does a solo; it's not melodic, and he just has an ego problem.

When did you decide to make your first solo album?

After the breakup, I was sitting around, wondering what to do with myself. I had done a few sessions, but it was the end of that gig and I was wondering what to do next. I realized I had to do something, so I ran and did a standard album. I did all tracks I was brought up with at the parties at the house: "Sentimental Journey"and "Stardust"and all those '40s tunes.

Was "Sentimental Journey" really a gift to your mother?

Yeah. It was a gift for her, and it got me off my ass. So I did that, and then I was working on George's album and he flew Pete Drake in because Pete had done something with Dylan's album and they were friends. I lent Pete my car, and he noticed I had a lot of country cassettes in the car. I told him I liked country music. So he said, "Well, why don't you do a country album?"

And I said, "I'm not going to live in Nashville for six months,"which was how long the Beatles would be there to make an album. He said, "Are you kidding? We did Bob's album in two days." I was blown away, even though the Beatles' first album took twelve hours, but it had been so long ago my memory had failed. So I said, "Okay, I'll come over next week and we'll do an album."And we did the album in three days. It was just all to get me moving.

I did the *Sentimental Journey* album and then the Nashville album (*Beaucoups Of Blues*), and then Harry Nilsson called me. Harry and I had been invited to present some Grammy awards, so I thought, "I'm not going to fly all the way to America just to present a Grammy award and then go home. Why don't I do some sessions in Nashville again?" So I phoned Richard Perry, who I had met in England while playing on some sessions for Harry, and said, "Why don't we do some sessions while we're in Nashville?" Then he called back saying, "Well, why don't you leave Nashville and fly to L.A. and we'll do some sessions there?"

So I figured I'd make two weeks out of it, and that's how the *Ringo* album came about. I came into L.A. just to do the album, and it just happened that John had flown into L.A. and George was in L.A. I was making an album, and we're all friends even if we had split up, so I said, "Have you got any songs, boys?" and John said, "Yeah, I've got a song," so I said, "Well, come and play."So he came down, and I asked George if he had one and he came down, and then I called Paul in England and said, "You can't be left out of this"—like it was the big deal of his life— so we came to England and did the track. That's how that came about. It was all accidental, not planned.

How did you feel, suddenly becoming the focal point of a project in an album that revolved around you?

It was really good. Before that, we had had the two singles, which George had produced, "It Don't

Come Easy"and "Back Off Boogaloo," which were number one. I had written them and George finished them. So that was exciting, and I was getting excited about the business again as a solo career, so I was back in the music trade as a solo. It just took time for me to get used to the idea, because I had never been a solo artist. I had always been in a band, since drummers are usually in the band.

Are there specific recordings you are particularly proud of?

There's different styles, though it's the one attitude. I still think the finest stuff I did was on "Rain." "Rain" is, to me, my all-time favorite drum track.

Why?

Because of what I did; wherever my head was at the time. It is a vague departure for me. And *Abbey Road*, and there's lots of things in between; bits here and bits there. "Get A Woman," by B.B. King; I felt I played some real solid drums on that. "A Day In The Life"; I felt the drums were as colorful as the song and the guitars. There's one, "It's been a long time..." ("Wait"). That has really fine tom-tom work on it.

It's fine on everything, really, but some of them knock me out. And it took me awhile to listen to Beatle records without going through the emotions of the day: how we felt, what was going on, who was saying hello to who.

After we broke up, it took me a couple of years to really listen. You know, you'd make the record and really enjoy making it, and when it was finished, you'd enjoy listening to it in the studio and enjoy having it at home as a piece of plastic in a sleeve, but then I would never play them again. Only in the last several years could I listen to them as tracks. And you can also look back and see the stages you were going through or you went through.

What about highlights, playing or personal?

There's too many. Well, there's high and high. How high do you want to get? You know what I'm saying? As an act, which we were, the Palladium or the *Ed Sullivan Show*, because they were definite moves in a career. I always thought, though we played music, we still wanted to be the biggest band in the world. Not that we knew it would be a monster, but we knew we were aiming somewhere, and the only degree of saying it is popularity. And we did become the most popular group on earth, so there's all those moves.

But like the "Rain" session, where something just comes out of the bag; that just arrives, that's exciting. It's not a conscious thing; it just happens, and some sessions can get exciting. Musically, sometimes you would be blown away with what came out, but not every time. Other times you did the best you could and if it worked, great. But sometimes a lot of magic, a lot of magic, just came out of the blue, and it comes out for everybody. To play with three other people, any other people, when it works is when everyone is hitting it together, no one is racing, no one's dragging, the song is good or the track is good and the music is good, and you're all just hitting it together.

If you're not a musician, I don't know if you'll understand that, when just three, four, ten of you, a hundred-piece orchestra, hit it together for as much time as you can—because there's very few times it goes through the whole track, never mind the whole album—there's magic in that that is unexplainable. I can't explain what I get from that. It's getting high for me. Just a pure musical high.

How does someone maintain his perspective on being a human being when the world has made him larger than life?

I think you're born it. Also, at certain periods, I did go over the edge and believe the myth, but three great friends told me, "You're fooling yourself."

But weren't they going over the edge as well?

Yes, but they had three friends, too, to tell them they're fooling themselves. It's not that we actually all did it at once.

During all the talk about a Beatles reunion and all of that, was there ever a time when you thought if you got together for a night that...

Well, we did. The four of us never got together, but at certain times after the breakup, three of us got together.

Was that magic still there?

Well, we looked at each other and smiled. It was interesting. Now, it's impossible to put it all back together, of course, but I don't think any of us really thought we'd get back together. Everyone got too busy. No matter how much money they offered us, we never did it for the money, then or now. Then, when we were doing it in the '60s, and when they were offering us $50 million in the '70s, it wasn't an incentive to play. Money is no incentive for musicians. It's nice to have, but it's not enough.

I think it was John and Paul who said they felt that spark couldn't be re-created. I wondered whether you agreed, or how you felt.

I don't believe that. I think, had the four of us gotten down and played, that spark would have been there. But the reasons would have been different, and that was the difference.

What kind of effect would you say the Beatles, the fame, all that, has had on you today?

I don't know. It's hard to say where I'd be if it hadn't happened. But it did, so I'm exactly where I feel I should be. Does anybody know what he would have done if he hadn't been doing what he did do at the time he was doing something? It's impossible to tell. The difference would be that you wouldn't be interested in talking to me if I had just been playing some little club somewhere. But whether I would have been a different human being... it's hard to tell. I'm sure I must have changed, but would I have changed had I gone through a whole different type of life? I don't know. The effect it all had from being born today and everything that went on in between is that we're here in the garden, trying to say hello.

The Top 50 Most Valuable Beatles Albums

Compiled by Tim Neely from the *Goldmine British Invasion Record Price Guide*

Key: For many listings, you'll see a letter or two before the title. These designate something special about the listing as follows:

B: for LPs, a record listed as stereo has both mono and stereo tracks on it, and as far as we know none of it is rechanneled stereo.

DJ: some sort of promotional copy, usually for radio stations, and not meant for public sale.

M: for any record pressed in both mono and stereo, a mono record.

P: for LPs, a record listed as stereo has some tracks in true stereo and some tracks in rechanneled stereo. The stereo or the rechanneled tracks are often listed below.

PD: picture disc (artwork is actually part of the record).

PS: for 45s and some EPs, a picture sleeve (this is the value for the sleeve alone, combine the record and sleeve value to get an estimated worth for the two together). UK EPs are assumed to have a picture sleeve unless noted.

R: for LPs, a record listed as stereo is entirely rechanneled stereo.

S: for any record pressed in both mono and stereo, a stereo record. Either the entire record is known to be true stereo or we don't know whether it's all stereo. In general, rechanneled stereo was not used in the UK.

	Label, Catalog #		Title	Value
1.	Vee Jay SR 1062	S	Introducing the Beatles	$20,00
	Song titles cover; with "Love Me Do" and "P.S. I Love You"; oval Vee Jay logo with colorband only! Perhaps half a dozen authentic copies have been discovered, with hundreds of thousands of counterfeits.			
2.	Vee Jay PRO 202	DJ	Hear the Beatles Tell All	15,000
	White label promo with blue print; only three known copies, a NM copy sold for $16,500 on April 24, 1997.			

3.   United Artists UAS 6366   S   A Hard Day's Night   12,000
Pink vinyl; only one copy known, probably privately (and secretly) done by a pressing-plant employee.

4.   Decca 31382   My Bonnie/The Saints   10,000
By "Tony Sheridan and the Beat Brothers;" black label with color bars (all-black label with star under "Decca" is likely a counterfeit).

4.   Vee Jay Spec. DJ No. 8   Ask Me Why/Anna   10,000
Unusual promo used to push the Beatles' Vee Jay EP.

4.   Vee Jay SR 1062   S   Introducing the Beatles   10,000
"Ad back" cover; with "Love Me Do" and "P.S. I Love You" (both mono); oval Vee Jay logo with colorband only!

4.   Vee Jay SR 1085   S   The Beatles and Frank Ifield on Stage   10,000
Portrait of Beatles cover; "Stereo" on both cover and label.

8.   Apple SO-385   DJ   The Beatles Again   8,000
Prototypes with "The Beatles Again" on cover; not released to the general public.

8.   Capitol ST 2553   S   Yesterday and Today   8,000
"First state" butcher cover (never had other cover on top); cover will be the same size as other Capitol Beatles LPs.

8.   Vee Jay 1-903   PS   Misery/Taste of Honey/Ask Me Why/Anna   8,000
"Ask Me Why/The Beatles" plugged on promo-only sleeve.

11.   Capitol 5150   Can't Buy Me Love/You Can't Do That   4,000
Yellow vinyl (unauthorized); value is conjecture.

11.   Capitol ST 2553   S   Yesterday and Today   4,000
"Third state" butcher cover (trunk cover removed, leaving butcher cover intact); cover will be about 3/16-inch narrower than other Capitol Beatles LPs; value is highly negotiable depending upon the success of removing the paste-over.

11.   Capitol T 2553   M   Yesterday and Today   4,000
"First state" butcher cover (never had other cover on top); cover will be the same size as other Capitol Beatles LPs.

11.   Vee Jay LP 1085   M   The Beatles and Frank Ifield on Stage   4,000
Portrait of Beatles cover; counterfeits are poorly reproduced and have no spine print.

11.   Vee Jay SR 1062   S   Introducing the Beatles   4,000
Blank back cover; with "Love Me Do" and "P.S. I Love You"; oval Vee Jay logo with colorband only!

16.	Decca 31382	DJ	My Bonnie/The Saints	3,000

By "Tony Sheridan and the Beat Brothers"; pink label, star on label under "Decca."

16.	United Artists UA-Help-Show	DJ	United Artists Presents Help!	3,000

One-sided interview with script (blue label).

16.	United Artists UAL 3366	M-DJ	A Hard Day's Night	3,000

White label promo.

16.	Vee Jay DXS-30	(2) S	The Beatles vs. The Four Seasons	3,000

Combines "Introducing the Beatles" with "Golden Hits of the Four Seasons" (Vee Jay 1065).

16.	Vee Jay LP 1062	M	Introducing the Beatles	3,000

"Ad back" cover; with "Love Me Do" and "P.S. I Love You"; oval Vee Jay logo with colorband only!

21.	Vee Jay 581	PS	Please Please Me/From Me to You	2,500

Special "The Record That Started Beatlemania" promo-only sleeve.

22.	Apple Films KAL 004	DJ	The Yellow Submarine (A United Artists Release)	2,000

One-sided LP with radio spots for movie.

22.	Apple/Capitol (no #)	(17)	The Beatles 10th Anniversary Box Set	2,000

22.	Capitol 5112	PS	I Want to Hold Your Hand/WMCA Good Guys	2,000

Giveaway from New York radio station with photo of WMCA DJs on rear.

22.	Capitol 5150		Can't Buy Me Love/You Can't Do That	2,000

Yellow and black vinyl (unauthorized); value is conjecture.

22.	Apple/Americom 5715		Yellow Submarine/Eleanor Rigby	2,000

Four-inch flexi-disc sold in vending machines.

22.	Capitol ST 2553	S	Yesterday and Today	2,000

"Second state" butcher cover (trunk cover pasted over original cover).

22.	Capitol T 2553	M	Yesterday and Today	2,000

"Third state" butcher cover (trunk cover removed, leaving butcher cover intact); cover will be about 3/16-inch narrower than other Capitol Beatles LPs; value is highly negotiable depending upon the success of removing the paste-over.

22.	United Artists SP-2359/60	DJ	United Artists Presents A Hard Day's Night	2,000

Open-end interview with script.

22.	United Artists UA-Help-INT	DJ	United Artists Presents Help!	2,000

Open-end interview with script (red label).

22.	Vee Jay 498		Please Please Me/Ask Me Why	2,000

Correct spelling; number is "VJ 498"; brackets label.

22.	Vee Jay LP 1062	M	Introducing the Beatles	2,000

Blank back cover; with "Love Me Do" and "P.S. I Love You;" oval Vee Jay logo with colorband only!

22.	Vee Jay SR 1062	S	Introducing the Beatles	2,000

Song titles cover; with "Please Please Me" and "Ask Me Why;" oval Vee Jay logo with colorband.

22.	Vee Jay SR 1062	S	Introducing the Beatles	2,000

Song titles cover; with "Please Please Me" and "Ask Me Why;" plain Vee Jay logo on solid black label.

22.	Vee Jay VJS 1092	S	Songs, Pictures and Stories of the Fabulous Beatles	2,000

All copies have gatefold cover with 2/3 width on front; also, all copies have "Introducing the Beatles" records. Oval Vee Jay logo with colorband.

22.	Vee Jay VJS 1092	S	Songs, Pictures and Stories of the Fabulous Beatles	2,000

See above; brackets Vee Jay logo with colorband.

22.	Vee Jay VJS 1092	S	Songs, Pictures and Stories of the Fabulous Beatles	2,000

See above; plain Vee Jay logo on solid black label. Note: Any non-gatefold copy or any copy called "Songs and Pictures of the Fabulous Beatles" is a counterfeit.

38.	Vee Jay SR 1062	S	Introducing the Beatles	1,800

Song titles cover; with "Please Please Me" and "Ask Me Why;" brackets Vee Jay logo with colorband.

39.	Vee Jay 498		Please Please Me/Ask Me Why	1,600

Misspelled "The Beattles"; number is "#498."

39.	Vee Jay 498		Please Please Me/Ask Me Why	1,600

Correct spelling; number is "#498."

41.	Capitol 5555		We Can Work It Out/Day Tripper	1,500

Red and white "Starline" label (mispress).

41.	I-N-S Radio News DOC-1	DJ	Beatlemania Tour Coverage	1,500

Promo-only open-end interview with script in plain white jacket.

41.	Savage BM-69	M	The Savage Young Beatles	1,500
	Yellow label, glossy orange cover.			
41.	United Artists SP-2357	DJ	A Hard Day's Night Theatre Lobby Spot (45)	1,500
41.	United Artists SP-2362/3	DJ	United Artists Presents A Hard Day's Night	1,500
	Radio spots for movie.			
41.	United Artists T 90828	M	A Hard Day's Night	1,500
	Capitol Record Club edition.			
41.	United Artists UA-Help-A/B	DJ	United Artists Presents Help!	1,500
	Radio spots for movie.			
41.	United Artists UAEP 10029	DJ	A Hard Day's Night Open End Interview (45)	1,500
41.	Vee Jay 498		Please Please Me/Ask Me Why	1,500
	Misspelled "The Beattles"; number is "VJ 498."			
50.	Apple (no #)	(10)	The Beatles Special Limited Edition	1,200
	Promo-only set issued in 1974.			
50.	Vee Jay LP 1062	M	Introducing the Beatles	1,200
	Song titles cover; with "Please Please Me" and "Ask Me Why"; brackets Vee Jay logo on solid black label (versions with colorband, or versions with all-black labels and other logos, have less value).			
50.	United Artists ULKP-42370	DJ	Let It Be Radio Spots (45)	1,200
	Special disc with commercials promoting the movie Let It Be.			

Photo/Chuck Boyd/Flower Children

Frank Zappa

By William Ruhlmann
January 27, 1989

Frank Zappa is arguably the most prolific and versatile composer/performer of the last twenty-five years. Primarily known as a rock musician, his work has employed the structure and instrumentation of classical music as often as it has the improvisations of jazz. And that work has been heard on nearly fifty albums of original material in the last twenty-two years.

Born in Baltimore on Dec. 21, 1940, Zappa moved with his family to California at the age of ten. He began composing music in his sophomore year in high school, and by the age of twenty, had written the score to a low-budget film, *The World's Greatest Sinner*. At twenty-two, he appeared on the Steve Allen television show, where he played a duet with Allen on a bicycle. He also took over a recording studio in Cucamonga, called Studio Z, where he recorded local bands and his own work. Examples of the results can be heard on the "Mystery Disc" that accompanies the *Old Masters Box One*, issued in 1986, and on *Rare Meat*, an EP of Zappa productions released on Del-Fi/Rhino in 1983.

Zappa joined a group called the Soul Giants in 1964, and by 1965 they had been renamed the Mothers. The group was signed to the Verve division of MGM Records in 1966 by Tom Wilson, an A&R man and producer who had worked on albums by Bob Dylan. Rechristened the Mothers of Invention, they released their first album, *Freak Out!*, a two-record set, in the summer of 1966.

Freak Out! was one of the strangest and most original albums of the '60s. It was followed by a series of equally challenging works, including *We're Only In It For The Money*, a parody of *Sgt. Pepper's Lonely Hearts Club Band*, and *Lumpy Gravy*, a Zappa solo album recorded with a fifty-piece orchestra. In the summer of 1967, the band rented the Garrick Theatre in New York and put on a series of avant-garde theatrical shows.

After numerous personnel changes, Zappa disbanded the Mothers at the end of the '60s and subsequently produced a series of acts for his Bizarre and Straight record labels (licensed to Warner Brothers through Reprise, and soon to be reissued through Enigma) including Captain Beefheart and his Magic Band, Alice Cooper, and the GTO's, a groupie group. Commissioned to write a piece for the Los Angeles Symphony Orchestra, Zappa put together a new Mothers band, eventually including former Turtles Howard Kaylan and Mark Volman, and made the film 200 Motels.

This edition of the band continued until Dec. 10, 1971, when Zappa was thrown from the stage of the Rainbow Theatre in London by , as he said, "an irate individual who later told police that we hadn't given him his money's worth and that I had been making 'eyes' at his girlfriend. I spent a month in the hospital and the best part of the following year in a wheelchair."

Zappa and a new group of Mothers returned to active duty with *Over-nite Sensation* in the fall of 1973, their highest charting album to this point, and went back on tour in 1974. In the fall, "Don't Eat the Yellow Snow" became Zappa's first hit single, and the album *Apostrophe* (') went into the Top 10.

The mid- and late '70s was a period of heavy touring and recording, during which Zappa eventually dropped the Mothers name and performed under his own name. The band became a school for aspiring musicians, featuring future jazz stars like George Duke and future pop-rockers like the various members of Missing Persons.

Zappa and Warner Brothers parted company by 1979, with the company issuing the contractual obligation albums *Studio Tan*, *Sleep Dirt*, and *Orchestral Favorites*. (Zappa now owns the rights to these out-of-print LPs, but has no plans at present to reissue them.) After leaving the major label association, Zappa became more prolific than ever, releasing, for example, two double record sets along with three LPs of instrumental guitar work in 1981 alone.

The early '80s also saw Zappa turning to more orchestral works, recording with Pierre Boulez and with the London Symphony Orchestra. On his own, he turned increasingly to the Synclavier, a form of studio synthesizer, to replace his bands.

Nevertheless, Zappa returned to the concert

stage in 1984 for the "Smell the Glove" tour, again playing rock. 1984 also saw the first release in a series of reissues of Zappa's early material, as the *Old Masters Box One*, a six-record set, appeared.

In 1985, Zappa appeared before Congress to testify against the Parents Music Resource Center (PMRC) and its attempts to censor rock music. Around the same time, he contracted with Rykodisc to begin reissuing his recordings on compact disc. These reissues continue, with more expected in early 1989.

An even more ambitious project is *You Can't Do That Onstage Anymore*, a series of six double-CDs presenting previously unreleased live material from the last twenty years. To date, two volumes have been released. In 1988, Zappa mounted his first tour in three and a half years, the "Broadway the Hard Way" tour, featuring an eleven-piece band, during which he helped to register voters around the country. A single-disc LP from the tour has been released, and will be followed by a longer CD early this year.

In this interview, conducted at Zappa's home in Los Angeles, he talks about his recording career, from Studio Z to an upcoming project call *Phase Three*.

Goldmine*: Lets start by taking it back as far as possible and talk about the recording studio that you had before the Mothers.*

Frank Zappa: In Cucamonga.

There was an album that came out on Rhino a couple of years ago that had some productions that were done at that time.

Really?

It was called Rare Meat.

What, the masters that were released to Del-Fi?

Yes. Is that all the stuff that ever came out or are there other things as well?

There's much more that was recorded there, but it's never been released.

How did you come to have a recording studio?

I was introduced to Paul Buff, the guy who owned the studio, by Ronnie Williams, a guitar player that I was working with in some local bands at that time, and we just would go up there and record. And Paul—I don't know whether you know anything about him. I think he's a genius guy. He invented a number of pieces of equipment that are standards of the recording industry right now. But before you can understand the studio and how I got it, you'd have to know how Paul got it. He was a local boy from Cucamonga who had decided he could go into the Marine Corps in order to learn about electronics, and he did. He got out and decided he was going to be a recording artist and he was going to make his own studio. He built his own five-track recorder at a time when four-track was an absolutely exotic piece of equipment in the industry. Three-track was something that they used for filmwork. Four-track was rare.

And the only person who had a machine that was truly capable of overdubbing was Les Paul. He had that eight-track. Well, Paul Buff built this five-track recorder and then proceeded to teach himself how to play just enough notes on the bass to play a bass part, just enough beats on the drum to keep a background beat, just a little bit of piano, little bit of organ, little bit of guitar, little bit of alto saxophone, and taught himself to sing, and proceeded to make pop records that were clones of hits.

He would take all the hooks, he would listen to whatever was on the tracks and he would grasp what the hook element was and then build his version of something that contained the same hook-type material. And he was there doing this all by himself, just multiple recording.

I don't know how he met Ronnie Williams, but Ronnie had joined him up there and was putting guitar parts on some of his things and then Ronnie brought me over and I worked with him on some stuff, and I brought in Ray Collins, who would up doing a lot of singing on some of these things. So, he (Paul) got into debt. He was many months behind in his rent, on his lease payments for the studio. And I came into some money because I'd done a film score for a Western, and so I made a deal with him where I would agree to take over his payments on the studio, and that's how I got it. He showed me how to work the stuff, and I went from being kind of an incompetent commercial artist to a full-time obsessive overdub maniac, working in this studio.

How much of that stuff has ever been released?

Little or none.

Was any of it released at the time, on local labels?

Photo/Chuck Boyd/Flower Children

No. The only thing that has come out, I believe "Charva" is on the first *Mystery Disc*.

How long were you doing that?

I don't know; I think maybe four or five months.

Does anyone have rights to that stuff now or does it still exist anywhere?

I've got all the tapes. As far as rights to it go, I have absolute right to the stuff wherein I'm the guy that's playing all the parts, and I think that some of the other tapes, I actually have some of the masters that Buff made before I took the place over, and some of them are hilarious. They really should be released, but I have no idea how I would contact the people who are singing on them.

There's one song that was done by a guy named Sonny Wilson called "Lonely Lips," which I think is a great song. He was not exactly an Elvis imperson-

ator, but he had an Elvis-type voice, and it's a slow country-pop song with a good hook. I always thought it was a great tune, but I have no idea where Sonny Wilson is or how one would go about releasing "Lonely Lips."

And there's a few other odd things like that. The master tapes, the five-track masters, are unplayable now because the machine upon which they were recorded doesn't exist anymore. You just can't play them back without that original head stack. So the only thing that remains of the material that would be releasable would be the two-track mixes that were done at the time.

Let's jump ahead and go immediately up to talking about Verve. I suppose the unusual thing to me is that the Mothers of Invention would be signed to a label like Verve, which I associate with Norman Granz and jazz recordings, so I'm curious about how that happened.

It happened because of Tom Wilson, who was the staff producer for—they called it "blue" Verve. The regular Verve label was black and silver, but blue Verve was for the rock 'n' roll and/or underground stuff. And Wilson was an interesting guy. He's dead now, but he would take a chance on just about anything. I remember one day he came in and announced that he had just signed a Japanese psychedelic artist named Harumi, and Harumi was making some kind of a flower-power album. I never heard the album, I don't know if it was in Japanese or what. But it was the idea that, "Okay, today we're gonna record a Japanese psychedelic record."

A lot of the credit for the odd stuff that went on the label has to go to him because he was the one who would stand up to the people that wrote the paychecks and say, "Yeah, I wanna record and/or produce these things." Without Wilson, we never would have got a contract.

So he was the A&R guy as well as the producer.

Yeah.

And, I guess, your connection to the company, too. I mean, they must have had trouble figuring out what kind of band it was or how to deal with it.

They had no idea what kind of band it was. As a matter of fact, when I went to New York for the first time and was taken to the MGM/Verve office, they had a cafeteria in the building for the employees. They wouldn't even let me in, 'cause I had long hair. That's the kind of world it was, it was just bizarre. And I went in there with Wilson; they threw us both out. He was black and I had long hair.

In the first Old Masters *book, you talk a little bit about the difficulty of wresting the Verve tapes from whatever vault they were in. I wondered if you could elaborate on that, and then I wanted to talk about the matter of some of the re-recordings that had to be done. But what was the legal status and when did the recordings go out of print and what were the rights to them? Or is there a simple way of describing that?*

There is no simple way of describing that, but basically, there was a lawsuit that lasted eight years and at the end of the eight years, I got the rights to all my old masters back and when the actual tapes were returned to me, the ones that were in possession of MGM/UA were in pitiful condition. The oxide was actually falling off of the tape.

I mean, you could unreel the tape, and you could see through it. It was like Scotch tape with black flakes on it, was what it looked like. And so, if you played it, what you'd hear would be a piece of music and then silence and then scratchy sound, or the volume dropped real low and then came back, and there was no way you could take the original mixes and treat them, there was no scientific method that would allow you to doctor up the original mixes in order to release them. They had to be reconstructed from the four-track master tapes or the eight-track master tapes.

I'm sorry, I'm confused because I thought you were talking about the master tapes.

No, no, there's two. The word "master" applies to several different classifications of tape. The original master for *Freak Out!* was four-track, and also for *Absolutely Free*, and then, by the time *We're Only In It For The Money* came along, we were up to eight-track, and two of the songs on that album were actually twelve-track. We didn't do a sixteen-track recording until Hot Rats. That's how the world progressed. The other word "master" applies to the two-track mix, or the mono mix that would be made from the original master. Both of them are called "master." The thing with the flakes coming off was the two-track mix.

Okay, but did you have either the four-track master or the eight-track master to go back to?

For some things, yes, some things, no. I do not have the four-track masters for *Lumpy Gravy*. Nobody knows where they are.

That was an album that originally came out on Capitol, is that right?

That's right. I was offered a chance to write for and conduct an orchestra by Nik Venet at Capitol Records, and he presumed that even though I was signed to Verve as an artist, my contract was a rock 'n' roll performer/vocalist, it had nothing to do with my work as a composer or a conductor. It wasn't even mentioned in the contract.

But in spite of that, at the point where Capitol had invested about $40,000 into recording this orchestra, MGM/Verve threatened Capitol with a lawsuit, and so the thing was unresolved for about thirteen months and finally, Verve bought the masters from Capital at cost and at that point it was possible to release it. But nobody at Verve would ever have given me—$40,000 in those days, to record an album with an orchestra in a studio? No way. With all respect to Tom Wilson, nobody at that company had the vision of Nik Venet.

(Author's note: *Nik Venet is probably best known as the A&R man who signed the Beach Boys to Capitol and worked with Brian Wilson on the production of their early albums.*)

There's been some controversy about what you did with We're Only In It For The Money *for the* Old Masters *set and the Rykodisc CD, the bass and drum tracks that were added to it. Was that the only solution to this tape problem?*

No, bass and drums added was not a solution to the tape problem. The tape problem had to be dealt with with a remix, no matter what. The idea of putting digitally recorded bass and drums into those tracks was a creative decision that I made because I've always thought that this material in *We're Only In It For The Money* was good material, but I hated the technical quality of the recording; we were just trapped into that level of technical quality because that's the way the world was then. I mean, we were virtually using a prototype eight-track machine when that album was done.

We were working in a studio in New York that had

one speaker for every track. You sat in front of eight speakers. And you couldn't punch in and out without leaving an enormous click on the tape. It was living hell to mix something from that machine because every time you had punched in to add a part, in advance of pushing that part up in the mix, you had to first duck it out to get rid of the click. You had to either duck it out or cut it out with a razor blade, which would screw up the rhythm of the tape. So it was a nightmare to mix that stuff.

Now, some of those things, we could never get them out. There's just no way, because there are clicks right in the middle of vocals and things like that. But I've always had kind of fondness for the tunes that were in there, and I wanted to enhance that album above and beyond the level of 1967 technical development. So that's why as a creative decision, I decided to put it on.

The problem with people who are collectors and purists and stuff like that is their regard is not for the music, it is for some imaginary intrinsic value of vinyl and cardboard. People who demand to have the original release of this, that, and the other thing in the original wrapper and all that stuff, that's fetishism. And I think that's fine, if you want to be a fetishist and have that kind of a hobby. But it is a type of attitude that I don't share when it comes to re-releasing the material. I think that the material should have a chance to sound as good as you can make it sound, given the technical tools that are at your disposal.

So when digital audio came along and you had the possibility of a 95-db dynamic range, and, in 1967, it might have been, maybe 40-db or something like that, the chance to make those tunes punchier, and the same thing on Ruben & The Jets, the chance to have some aspect of 1980's transience and top end on those tapes was something that I felt was worth the time and the money that I spent redoing it.

If it was just a matter of re-releasing stuff and dumping it out on the market, you wouldn't take any time with it at all. But everything that is released here has been completely gone over in terms of either equalization or, in the case of those two albums, new parts added to it. In the case of *Absolutely Free*, there were a couple of bad edits that were in the original two-track album which I was able to fix using a digital editor, but everything else is pretty much the same. There's a few of the tunes in that that have been remixed from the original four-track, but nothing added to it.

I don't have any more plans for taking older material and adding stuff to it—those are the only two albums that it was done—and I would describe any criticism of the addition of the bass and drums as something less than a tempest in a teapot. If you've got time to worry about that, you really must have time on your hands. There's too many other important musical, social, and intellectual problems floating around the country today to give a rat's ass as to whether or not I swapped the bass and drums on *We're Only In It For The Money*.

Part of the way to look at that, too, though, is to say, who are you reissuing them for? Are you reissuing them for people who heard them then and remember them in a certain way or are you reissuing them for potentially a new audience?

It's for a new audience, because I think that a lot of the things that were said in those lyrics, like "Mom And Dad" and some of the other songs that are in there, they have a relevance today. And the problem with appealing to the younger audience today is they have become accustomed to a level of audio excellence and would psychologically reject certain older recordings just because of the way they sound without ever stopping to listen to what the content was. The tone quality of the recording itself would turn them off or dissuade them from in-depth listening. So, in an attempt to meet those new customers halfway, I would like to spiff the stuff up as much as possible, so that they can tolerate the sound of it while they're listening to the content that's in there.

The last time I saw you play, there was a point where you said something to the audience about voting for Richard Nixon and then you paused and you said, "I mean, your parents voted for Richard Nixon." Do you think you're speaking to a different audience now from the audience that you were speaking to before, at least in concert?

In terms of what?

I mean, are they different people?

You mean, have they mutated?

Well, no, I mean, are they literally different people from the people who were listening to you twenty years ago?

Oh, absolutely. What, you think there's a bunch of people on crutches and wheelchairs that come stumbling into the auditorium every time I'm booked to do a concert?

Well, you're not on crutches and wheelchairs.

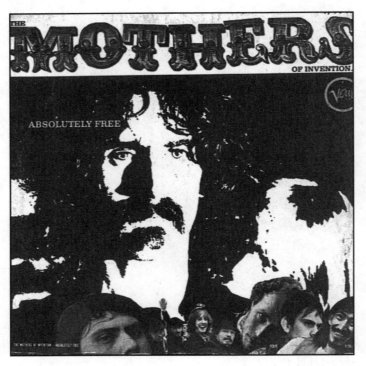

There's a lot of people who write about me that think the people who are coming there are dressed up like Grateful Dead followers and there's just old hippies and stuff. First of all, we never had a hippie audience. The hippies went directly for the Dead. They didn't stop anywhere, they went straight for the Dead. And they've stayed there and God bless them. Our audience has always been really mixed, in terms of age, in terms of geographical back-grounds, whatever. We have strange appeal; it's really hard to describe.

For example, the age range at our concerts could be anywhere from fourteen to sixty, with a prepon-derance of the individuals in the concert right around eighteen to twenty-five. I don't think very many other groups have that kind of range. But the idea that the people who come to the live concerts are all just remnants from the Garrick Theatre is completely without merit. Most of the ones who come are new customers. Get it out of your mind once and for all that what we do is to be consumed by people who were going to concerts in 1967. That's not true. Very few of those people have an interest in what we're doing now or have an incli-nation to leave their homes to go to a concert.

Anybody's concert.

Anybody's concert, 'cause usually the older you get, the lower your tolerance for having people vomit on your shoe. And if you leave your home to go to a concert, a rock 'n' roll concert, and that concert usually has a lot of young people who are chemically altered in some way, there is always the chance that you're going to come up with something on your clothes that wasn't there when you went in the door. So a lot of the older people stay home.

So, in a way, it's a trib-ute to us that anybody in that older age bracket would leave their house and come to the show. They're doing it at some peril, I would imagine. And the younger ones that come to the audience are not just there out of curiosity. They come there and they know the words to the songs. So, some-how or another, they got ahold of the material, and if we're playing something that is repertoire, some-thing that is from the older albums, I'll look out there and there's kids who know the words.

There's a development in terms of the personnel that appear on your records, and even on the billings that appear on your records, it gradually goes from the Mothers of Invention to Frank Zappa/Mothers to

Frank Zappa. *Would it be fair to say that there was ever actually a band, a group in the typical sense called the Mothers, or was it always a band that you employed and they were employees, if you know what I mean.*

Basically it's always been an employee situation, even with the earliest group. They had an employment contract. I was the one who had to guarantee them a weekly salary whether they worked or not. We're not talking about The Beatles here. It was run like a business, as much as you could run something like that like a business during that period in American musical history. I had to, one way or another, come up with the cash to pay people to be Mothers of Invention. This was not a cooperative, voluntary organization.

In the notes that you make in You Can't Do That Onstage Anymore, Vol. 1, *you talk about trying to defeat a nostalgic notion about the original Mothers. Part of that nostalgic notion is that there was this group of six people and they were a real group.*

Well, you tell me, what is a real group?

Well, I suppose it isn't a case where one person is paying the others, but in which there are group decisions made and it's a group situation financially. U2, for instance, one might argue, is a group.

I don't know anything about U2.

For instance, the songwriters credits are all listed as "U2." That kind of thing.

Well, this was a different way to do business, okay? I wrote the music. I paid the bills. I took the risk. This is called capitalism. And for those of you who don't like capitalism, please consider the alternatives.

There was a Warner Brothers album that came out of various productions that you had done that was sort of a promotion record in 1970.

Zapped?

Right, and on the back, it said, "Before Zappa dissolved (the Mothers) in the fall of 1969, sneering bitterly about the inability of youngsters to recognize good rock music even when it comes up and bites them on the ass"—the phrase "dissolved the Mothers": was that actually a period when there was a hiatus in the band or was that just record company nonsense?

That was record company nonsense, 'cause basically, the tour at which the Mothers stopped existing as a band—and we're talking about that original bunch of guys. The end came in 1969 after a concert in the Carolinas. We were on a Geroge Wein Jazz tour and we were booked with Roland Kirk, Gary Burton, and Duke Ellington. And I witnessed a situation backstage with Duke Ellington begging the road manager of the tour for a $10 advance, Duke Ellington *begging* for a $10 advance.

And we were booked into a hall—it was one of those large, circular halls like an arena, big place—and the PA system was jukebox speakers around the room. And there we are, a ten- or eleven-piece band that I had then. And I started the tour off, I had to take $400 out of my bank account to eat on while I was doing the tour and I was still responsible to pay the weekly salaries of the band and crew that was out there. At the end of that tour, I was $10,000 in debt. I felt like, I'm Duke Ellington here, in that sense of the word.

So after that gig, I just said, 'There's no way I can continue this,' because, to be honest about it, with very few exceptions, most of the people in the band didn't want to rehearse. It was just a job to them.

You couldn't get them to put in extra effort to make the group move forward to do anything spectacular. They didn't have any faith in it, it was their gig.

And when I said we're not gonna do this anymore, they were upset. It was like somebody canceling their Social Security. There's no way I could have afforded to give them more money to keep them going. It's not coming in to me, what am I supposed to do? And one of the last things that I did as that group broke up was, Jimmy Carl Black came to see me, he and five kids, and he came to me and said, "Look"—at that point, his playing had certainly gone into a slump since the first time I saw him playing at the Broadside in Pomona—and he said he wanted to take drum lessons. And I said, this is good. I game him $100 to take drum lessons. I don't know whether he ever took the lessons. I'd done everything that I could with those guys to help them out, but there's no logical way you could expect any employer to just keep shoveling out money for no services rendered.

And I don't think there's a logical person reading this that could put themselves in that position and say, yeah, they would voluntarily hock everything that they owned in order to keep a bunch of guys going who didn't even want to do the job. They didn't give a shit. Anybody who takes the risk to put a band together, especially a big band, is taking a big risk, because you can make a far bigger profit with a power trio.

You don't make as interesting music, I don't think. But if you want to have a band with a lot of guys in it and be able to produce music with those kind of tone colors to it, you have to be just a little bit crazy. And I learned the same lesson all over again on this last tour. It was an eleven-piece band. We rehearsed for four months, we toured for four months. I lost $400,000. But the tapes are unbelievable. And the audiences that saw the show really got a big thrill out of it. They liked the band. There's no way I could keep it going.

So that was just a function of the economics of having that many people.

Yeah, it was five trucks, two buses, forty-three guys, all on the road in a band and support crew and the rest of that stuff. And we weren't doing fireworks or anything spectacular out there, it was like a basic touring package: enough lights to see the show, enough PA to hear the music and enough crew to set up the gear. It's not like taking a glamorous entourage out there. Just was not a money-making proposition. In a way, I'm glad I did it, though, just because of some of the musical things that did get recorded.

I know there's a Broadway The Hard Way *CD. Do you think that you have sufficient material that there may be later releases as well from this tour?*

Oh, part of this stuff, because it is repertory material, is ideal for *You Can't Do That Onstage Anymore*, so it'll be incorporated in there. One of the reasons why I did *You Can't Do That Onstage Anymore* is for the people who have seen the band grow over the years. It gives them a chance to compare different versions of the same song played by different bands year after year.

And some of the versions that were played by this band really are the accumulation of all of the skill of musicians through the ages totaling on the repertoire that are just plain hard songs. And every band wrestles with the technical difficulties of playing those songs. "Black Page" is hard, things like that. "Strictly Genteel." All the ones that require a high level of musical competence, this band basically did a good job playing those songs. It will be nice to put those versions into the albums.

When we say that you broke up the band at that point, back in '69, what we mean is you stopped paying them the weekly wage whether they worked or they didn't work, and you stopped going on the road.

I said, no, this is it. I don't want to do Mothers of Invention anymore. That's it, bye.

This was about the same time that you were doing a whole series of outside productions for Bizarre and Straight?

No. Those hadn't really got rolling yet.

Was that the next thing that followed after that, though?

Yeah. I mean, I had to do something.

You were at that point on Warner Brothers.

Not on Warners. We were on Bizarre.

Which was not associated at that time.

Distributed by Reprise which was a subsidiary of Warner Brothers. Got it?

Yes, sir.

Not quite as bad as all those multiple credits that you see at the beginning of a movie, a so-and-so production of a film by blah, blah, blah.

I suppose as a result of that you didn't have trouble getting the rights to the albums that appeared either on DiscReet or Bizarre or whatever at a later time. Did you always own those and they were just being released to or distributed by this giant conglomerate of many names?

Those masters were always supposed to revert.

Having dropped the band for these good reasons, why did you then put together another band only, what, about a year later or so?

Well, after I broke that band up, I made the Hot Rats album, I did some recording with Sugarcane Harris and...

Jean-Luc Ponty?

Yeah, just for a minute with Jean-Luc. I didn't really get involved with Jean-Luc till several years after that. Then we had this offer from the Los Angeles Philharmonic, they wanted to do some kind of a performance with a rock 'n' roll group and a symphony orchestra.

And when we finally did that, Mark and Howard from the Turtles were in the audience and they came backstage after the show and they said they had either quit the Turtles or the Turtles had broke up—something like that—and they wanted to do something. So, I had met them before on the road, and I thought they were funny guys, so we started rehearsing together, put something together. It was just a fluke. If they hadn't been to the show and come backstage and expressed some interest in doing something, I doubt whether I ever would have called them.

But the result of that was a band that stayed together for, what about a year and a half, something like that?

Yeah, something like that.

With a few recordings until that concert in London.

'Till I got knocked off the stage.

That was the death of that band.

Yep.

Let me go ahead and get into the Onstage *thing in a kind of roundabout way in that sense that anyone who's followed your career over a fair amount of time has, at one time or another, heard about a ten-record set or a twelve-record set, with various titles; I thing one of them was* No Commercial Potential. *There's even a little Warners promotional thing that you included in the* Masters.

It got so far as test pressings. But, see, the problem was that Warners wanted a rate on the publishing and refused to pay full publishing on the thing, so I said forget it.

What was on that record at that time? Was it ten records, or how many records was it?

It was ten.

And what was that material that was on there?

It was live recordings, basically, that were done either using Scully two-track or a Uher two-track with a portable mixer, mostly from '68 and '69.

Do you still have that stuff?

Yeah.

And do you have any plans to include any of it with—I guess a couple of things have already turned up on the first Onstage.

Yeah. But I just think that there's so much better material since that time and there's no reason to dwell on the 68-69 period, just in terms of listening quality. Unless you're an archive freak or a music historian or something like that, it is not necessarily a pleasurable experience to listen to the technology of 1968, and some of the tunes that were played by that band have been played by other bands so much better.

The aesthetic goals of that series, *You Can't Do That Onstage Anymore,* have more to do with the growth of the music and a celebration of the good parts of live performance. There are a lot of good things to be said about playing on the stage in terms of unique events that will happen one time only for that particular audience and if you've got a tape running and you've captured it, you've got a little miracle on your hands.

And so, the things that are included in the series, I generally give the nod to that particular version of a tune that may have occurred on one of those nights when the performance was unique. Sometimes the recording quality is not as good as some other version of it, but I want to put as much of the unique stuff in there as possible.

And I don't know whether it's because the frequency of recording has increased over the years or that the bands did more unique things, but is seems in listening to the material available that the more entertaining or unique events are not of the early Mothers of Invention period. In fact, there are very few that exist on tape from the early MOI period. The most unique things that that band ever did were all at the Garrick Theatre in 1967 and there's no tape of that. I have no tape of the Garrick Theatre.

There's no record of that at all?

I think some people may have booted some stuff, but I have nothing in my collection. We actually had the opportunity to tape the whole show and Verve wouldn't do it. We had a deal with Wally Heider who, at that time, had a recording truck in New York City; he had all this gear in a van and he needed a place to park his van. And I wanted to make a deal with him that we'd give him parking space for the van outside of this theatre which we had rented. All he had to do was just turn the tape on every night. And we could have had it. Verve wouldn't do it.

Did going from the band that had been put together at one time in the '60s, to a situation where you were auditioning people and changing musicians cause a jump up in the musical abilities of the band, the musical quality of the band?

Well, let's just say that the first band was put together partly by accident and partly by—there was just no other way to get any players to do it. You couldn't go out and audition. You just couldn't. Especially if you wanted to do technical stuff.

If you look at recent musical history you'll notice that in those early days there were very few people with conservatory chops who would venture into the world of rock 'n' roll. It simply wasn't done. If you had conservatory skill, you might play jazz, but you certainly wouldn't go out and play this stuff. And I was lucky enough to have a few conservatory type of people in that band: Ian Underwood, Art Tripp, Ruth Underwood, these were people with great musical skill.

But the rest of the guys were regular guys. So at the point where it was possible to audition and select from a variety of choices of people to be in the band, I think the musical quality of the bank shot up about a thousand percent.

I think at this point you have the sort of reputation in rock that Miles Davis has in jazz; one sees people going off from your band to—well, actually often to a lot of jazz things. Do you get a lot of people auditioning or calling you to get in your bands?

Yeah, it's been that way since I first started auditioning. I mean, we have file drawers full of resumes and cassettes that people have sent in and that kind of stuff. There's a guy who just called two days ago, wanted to be the new "stunt" guitar player. I don't know how he got my phone number, but he called right here to the house and I have no plans of touring in the near future, so I just filed his stuff away.

I guess a lot of recording you're doing now is stuff that you're doing with machines by yourself. You're not bringing in other musicians too much.

Most of the stuff I'm working on right now is just to mix what happened on this last tour. The only time I'll put a musician in front of a microphone in this studio is to do sampling. We haven't had a real recording session in here since 1981.

Since we had left off somewhere in the '70s, let me ask you about The Helsinki Concert, which is the newest volume of Onstage. *Tell me about those tapes, about what's special about them, especially in the philosophy you were talking about regarding this series.*

Each band had its devotees. There were people who thought that the early Mothers of Invention were a pinnacle of their idea of musical entertainment and won't listen to anything else. There are people who like the band with Mark and Howard and think the Fillmore East album is their favorite, don't want to hear anything else. And there are also people (who) like that group with Napoleon (Murphy Brock) and George Duke and Ruth (Underwood), and here is an opportunity to take one complete concert, which was basically a good show, and release it in a way that the listener would get the sense of what that band was like onstage. And one of the things that was good about that show was that there was a lot of improvised, funny talking and witty stuff in there. So it's got part of the attitude of the band and I think it's a good record. It's got some good spirit in it.

Let me ask a question having to do with the way critics view your work, although I wouldn't think you care too much about the way critics view your work. There was sort of a turning in the way people wrote about you in the '70s. I think especially at the point that we're talking about, the Helsinki period, where at least it gave the appearance the records were selling more records, like Over-Nite Sensation *and* Apostrophe *were.*

Over-Nite didn't sell that well when it came out. Apostrophe was the first one that sold a quarter of a million, or whatever it was, and that was our first gold record. And that was an accident, because a radio station in Pittsburgh took "Don't Eat The Yellow Snow," cut it down from ten minutes to three minutes, and put it on the station, which was part of a chain, part of their format of playing novelty records from the '60s.

The guy who did it heard the song, perceived it as modern-day novelty record and put it on right alongside of "Teeny Weeny Bikini" and it became a hit. And at this time, we were touring in Europe. We hadn't even released it as a single, and I was informed in Europe that I had a hit single on this chain of stations in the East Coast and what do you want to do about it? And I told the engineer, who was still in Los Angeles, who worked on the album,

to edit a version of "Don't Eat The Yellow Snow" to match the way in which this guy had cut it, and put it out. And it was a hit.

But it was nothing that Warner Brothers ever foresaw, it was nothing that I could have foreseen as a guy at DiscReet Records, a subsidiary of a subsidiary of a subsidiary. Who knew? The credit goes to the DJ. And the same thing goes with "Valley Girl." Nobody knew that was going to be a hit.

And as far as critics viewing my work, the fact of the matter is, if a guy sets himself up as a record reviewer, if he has any knowledge of music history or music structure, chances are he's not writing about rock 'n' roll; he's writing about something else. If the guy's in the business of reviewing rock 'n' roll records, the chances are he couldn't get a job doing anything else.

And so, the actual musical opinion is of no interest to me, because most of what they're talking about is either connected to my personality or fantasies about my personality imagined by people who have never met me. And the other aspect of it is, in order for a guy to build a reputation as a rock critic, you don't get that reputation for being a sensational critic by saying nice things about people.

And I'm sure, along with the musicians who have been through my band who have moved on to bigger and better things, there have been a number of rock critics who have made their reputation by bashing me, one way or another. I'm pretty reliable, I'm always there. When there's nothing else, say something about him, everybody will understand it. But the fact of the matter is I am still here, and a few of the ones who bashed me, they're dead!

Talking about the music through time, one of the things that's striking about the first volume of the Onstage *record, given the way you've sequenced it, where it's going back and forth in time, often very suddenly back and forth in the consistency of the music; not only that but a consistency in terms of vision. You come off as someone who knew exactly what he wanted twenty-five years ago and still wants the same things, and there's a great consistency to that. Do you see an evolution in what you've been doing musically or artistically, or is that the case, are you sort of out of the head of Zeus?*

There's certain things I am interested in musically, and certain things I am limited to musically, simply because I have to hire human beings to do it. That's one of the reasons why I'm so enthusiastic about the Synclavier, because you can bypass all the human limitations. I already know how to run a band. I know how to do live music. Okay? I've done it. Now there are other things that are more interesting to me, and by the time the complete *You Can't Do That Onstage Anymore* collection comes out, and anybody who wants to take a scholarly approach to it and follow the stuff through and look at the continuity that you're talking about, the way in which things were done, I think that anything that has been written about me in a negative way in the past will certainly be put to rest by what the actual taped evidence is of what lives on the record.

People who said there was nothing happening musically during the '70s certainly didn't listen to any of our stuff. There has been, consistently, from the minute that the band was formed, creative, exploratory, investigative, humorous, multi-dimensional stuff going on with this band, just because it has been like a little research laboratory going on in one way or another, to try things. Where other people wouldn't dare try it, because they would be afraid of what it might do to their career, we would

try it, because they've already said every bad thing in the world about us. What the hell can they say? We're immune. We're totally Teflon to that stuff. They can say whatever they want. It turns out to be untrue. They can't do anything about it.

And so, with that virtual license to explore, I've been happy to take advantage of that and to all kinds of stuff that other people wouldn't try, for one reason or another. I want to try it, I want to find out what happens if you do this. Sometimes it works, sometimes it doesn't, but at least, if you want to find out what happens if you put this kind of a chord with that kind of note or this kind of a rhythm with that kind of a rhythm, or these kind of words in a certain kind of a setting, the evidence is there. It's almost like a textbook of odd techniques and things that would be useful for a musician or a composer to learn. The experiment is there for you to see. It's just like watching Mr. Wizard on television: when he pours the vinegar into the baking soda, it makes bubbles. Thanks a lot, Mr. Wizard, now we know. But there's a certain element of that in this collection.

If you have certain basic musical knowledge and want to find out what might happen on the fringes of musical experience, it's in there. There are some very strange things lurking in that album, and also some basic good musical performances. You have to consider what the average level of musical skill was during each of the years when those tapes were made, and if you have some knowledge of that, which unfortunately most people don't, then the level of expertise that is exhibited by these

258

bands is amazing. People just didn't do stuff like that back then.

Let me ask you two questions about the Onstage collection. One is about the sequencing. What really is the sequencing logic?

The sequencing rules are determined by things like—I like to do shows seamless, nonstop. Used to be, we would stop after every song and then you would tune up. Then came the strobe tuner and roadies who could do it for you and so you wouldn't have to do that. And also, the idea of doing the shows seamless, the albums often edited with songs slammed up against each other, and when I first got the idea of making people play edits live onstage, it turned out to be pretty funny, and so that's another one of the impossible things that you wouldn't expect: the whole band being able to make that unbelievable tempo change at a certain point and just evolve from one musical texture into another and then come back and—that kind of continuity. So the source material for *You Can't Do That Onstage* would probably have one song blending into another song, and so my first choice would be, do I continue with the next tune from this year, or do I keep the same song title, which was the natural sequence, and jump to another year, or do I let the intro start from this year and then change to another thing, or whatever?

That's number one. The other thing that you would decide is, how many slow songs have been in a row, how many fast songs in a row, what is the dynamic of the side? Then you also have to realize that each side is constructed hopefully with some sort of talking in the front, and then the side either goes to an apparent intermission or an apparent concert conclusion. I'm trying to avoid fading out the last tune on the side.

So you're talking about vinyl.

No, CD, too. So that you have the feeling that you're at a concert, but it's an impossible concert. There's no way you could ever see all those people onstage at the same time, but if you've got a fairly decent imagination, you could especially put the earphones on and be at a show that spans, what, twenty-five years, with some of the most amazing musicians that were ever put onto a record and

there they are, just performing their little hearts out for you. And the digital medium is the perfect medium for that. First of all, it allows you enough time on one side that you can give the illusion of sitting in a concert and that happening to you.

Could you just sketch out what the rest of the volumes of the Onstage *will be?*

Oh, what's in 'em? That's hard, because there's so many titles. It's all about random sequencing. There may be one other volume (in addition to *Vol. 2, The Helsinki Concert*) that has a complete concert from a complete band, and that would be something from the '88 band, but everything else is all mix and match and some of the edits are—as edits, they're works of art, I must say.

The last thing I wanted to talk about, since all of what we've been talking about is stuff that has been created in the past that you are in various ways arranging, just to ask about what you're writing or composing now. I had a sense a few years ago that you might be moving more toward symphonic stuff in general.

Everything that I'm writing now, with the exception of the tunes that I wrote while I was on this tour, is all stuff that is on the Synclavier and that can be any kind of a texture, symphonic, chamber music, whatever. Even though I've got a busy schedule editing albums and doing all the mechanical stuff to stay in that part of the record business, I still manage thirty hours a week on the Synclavier.

So we'll be seeing some of that at some point, as well.

Yes, you will. You'll be seeing, the beginning of this year, something called *Phase Three*, which takes all the missing dialogue parts of *Lumpy Gravy* and integrates them with all-new music, which will either be completely from the Synclavier or live from this tour, which is a mixture of an eleven-piece band with Synclavier with audience, all of them fitting together to be in the same style of the original *Lumpy Gravy* album, but taking it to a level of technical perfection that was impossible at the time the first *Lumpy* came out.

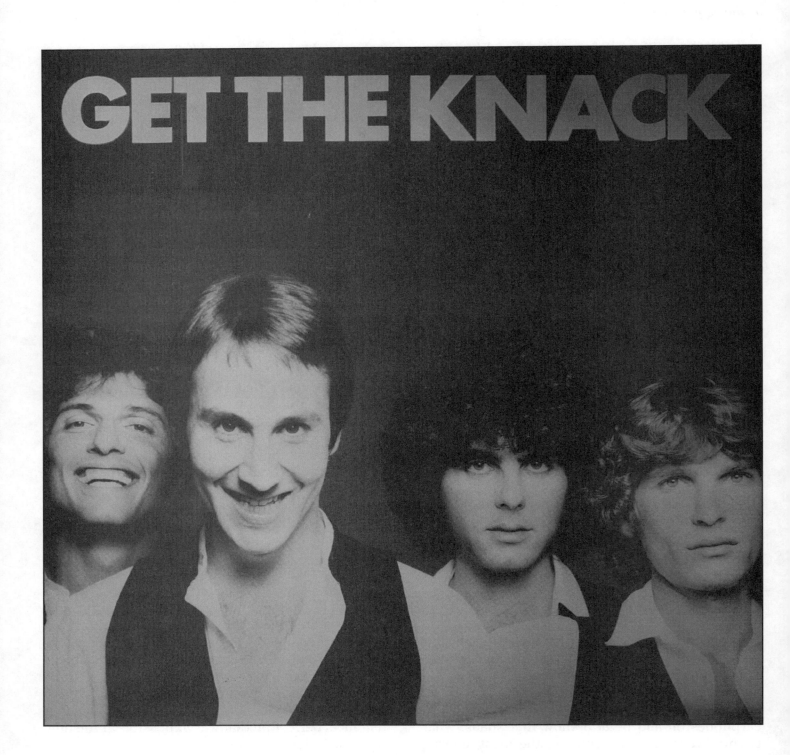

The Knack

By Jeff Tamarkin
December 1981

You remember the Knack, right? "My Sharona," "Good Girls Don't," "the next Beatles" and all that? Why are you laughing? The poor Knack. In 1979, the L.A. based rock 'n' roll quartet was riding high. "My Sharona," that teen type tale of love and romance, set to an irresistible funky riff and imbued with the frothy pop sensibilities that marked all those great '60s hits by the Beatles, and countless other British and American bands, was the year's biggest hit. Everyone loved it—if for no other reason, it was the first outright simple rock song to push dreaded disco away from its top-of-the-charts perch. The group came out of nowhere, released a single and an album (Get The Knack) that blasted from every radio in sight, and spearheaded a return to roots rock that so many had been clamoring for since the arrival of punk and new wave.

The Knack were the first band with any tenuous connection to new wave to dent the upper reaches of the charts. In the wake of "Sharona" came more "the" bands than anyone could (or wanted to) keep track of: the Pop, the Now, the Shoes, the this, the that. Then the Knack put out another album on the heels of the debut. *But The Little Girls Understand*, also on Capitol, came and went… it went Ka-blooey! Suddenly, the Knack, who had just been proclaimed the newest sensation, was the newest joke. "Knuke The Knack" buttons were even big for awhile. The album sold respectably, but nowhere near as well as the first. What went wrong?

Doug Fieger, the Knack's lead singer, rhythm guitarist, and principal songwriter, recently discussed that question and others, detailing the band's phenomenal rise and subsequent fall from grace. "We made some mistakes," he admitted from L.A. before the recent release of the third Knack album on Capitol, Round Trip.

Basically, what it amounts to is that the Knack had a tough act to follow: a smash debut album released at the right time and place and marketed as if it truly was the second coming of the Liverpudlian Fab Four. Adding on the fact that the Knack and their management decided to keep a mysterious air about the band by not giving interviews to the press—which might have helped them explain just what they were doing, looking and sounding like updated early Beatles—it's easy to understand why the resentment and ridicule mounted to the point that it hurt

the band. Fieger hopes that the new album, which finds the Knack departing somewhat from its earlier trademark sound, will put the band back on the public's good side.

Why, Fieger was asked, did people turn so vehemently against the Knack after raving about them and scooping up millions of their records? "We were successful," he replied, "and because they didn't know us, because they weren't allowed in, there was an element of 'Fuck you.' And to an extent, I understand that. That's not to make apologies, though, because we can't do that—we didn't allow the press to do their job. So nobody knew that we had worked so hard to get where we were, and that was our own fault because we didn't let them know that. If you don't let people know the truth, they'll draw their own conclusions, right or wrong. Some were saying that we were the second coming to God and some were calling us the Monkees. But that was interesting to us, because it was the first time in a long time that we saw any rock 'n' roll band have an effect like that. So we must have meant something to someone."

Another reason for the Knack backlash was because when some people found out that the group was not composed of teens but of men in their late twenties, there was a certain amount of criticism over the lyrics of their songs. They were blasted for writing songs about being young and in love, about having teenage desires and thoughts, when they were not teens themselves—as if writers had never written in the third person before. Fieger said he finds those charges absurd.

"I don't think there's anything wrong when you consider that Bill Haley was thirty or thirty-two when had did 'Rock Around The Clock' and 'See You Later Alligator.' I think that's an agist point of view and I don't go for it. I was twenty-six when our first album came out. That's not that far from being fifteen and I can remember those feelings. I reject that argument."

Fieger agreed that perhaps he could have helped thwart the backlash by giving interviews, and although he said that it was basically a management decision, he takes some of the blame for not speaking up. "At the very beginning, we wanted to present a project along the lines of the bands in the '60s—not necessarily the Beatles but all those bands. Back then, *16 Magazine* was the only magazine and they asked questions like: 'What's your favorite color?' 'What's your fave type of girl?' 'What do you eat for breakfast?' (Curiously, the press kit accompanying the debut album had the Knack answering just those type of questions.) Our management felt that there was mileage to be gained by being mysterious and they carried it too far. It got out of control and that's our fault. We paid for it."

Fieger continued: "If I was a kid and a fan now, which I actually am, and I listened to Steely Dan, I'd want to know a little more about Becker and Fagen. There's a strangeness that comes through in their music that's intriguing and sometimes it would be interesting to read what they say. Sometimes it might also be bullshit. We have things to say in our music, but we are reasonably articulate so we should have spoken more. We made a mistake."

Still, it would seem that the group was going to run up against trouble eventually. The debut album had Beatles written all over it. From the title (*Get The Knack* isn't that far from *Meet The Beatles*) to the fact that the label (Capitol) was the same as the Beatles', to the photo on the back cover picturing the group in a scene almost precisely like the classic shots of the Beatles on the "Ed Sullivan Show" or in A Hard Day's Night, the Knack were, in a sense, asking for trouble. While those factors might have helped them sell truckloads of records, they also made them easy targets for the band's detractors.

"Those pictures were the first the band had ever taken," reported Fieger. "We weren't trying to consciously say we were the Beatles. It was, if anything, to say that that was ridiculous. But there was another element to the back cover: the use of TV cameras. When we were little kids, we didn't go to rock 'n' roll shows; we saw the groups on TV. And since our eleven, twelve, thirteen-year-old souls were coming through in these songs, we wanted that to come through on the back cover. It was a joke, but I think we should have at least considered telling people that it was a joke."

Fieger believes that the anti-Knack criticism got out of hand, and in retrospect, he's probably right— of the crop of "power pop" bands that emerged (and mostly disappeared) in 1979 (most after the Knack hit it big), their music still holds up as some of the best of the period. And if it was derivative, so what? Didn't the Beatles themselves start out by covering songs by Little Richard, Chuck Berry, et al? If the second album wasn't as good as the first, those things happen—most bands have trouble following up a strong debut with an equally strong followup. The Knack's only crime was releasing the followup too soon. But some of the criticism, like the 'Knuke The Knack' campaign organized by a disgruntled Californian, was a bit much after the initial goof.

"At first," said Fieger, "we were amused because it was a commercial effort; he sold 'Knuke The Knack' kits at $10 a shot. He was calling himself an artist but frankly he was another businessman trying to cash in. But when he started personally attacking friends of ours (Fieger doesn't get specific, but this writer does recall seeing bumper stickers saying 'Honk If You've Slept With Sharona'), then it got uncomfortable. I thought that was mean and low. At first, we thought it was funny and we even went out and bought them. We were amused that anyone would take the time to hate a band, like we were Democrats or Republicans."

Sharona, it should be noted, was not only the subject of the song that launched the Knack into platinum-land, but also a real person, and the subject of Fieger's affections. To date, they are still close to inseparable. Fieger described how that song came about over two years ago.

"Berton (Averre, lead guitarist—the other Knacks are Prescott Niles, bass, and Bruce Gary, drums) had this lick for a long time and we never worked on it. I had met this girl Sharona and fell very deeply in love with her—she was inspirational and moved me on a very basic level. I was just trying to put my feelings about her into the beat that Berton had come up with. Then it made sense—the whole feeling of sexual frustration in the lyrics come out of the implicit frustration in the beat. It was very organic and we wrote it in one afternoon.

"None of us," continued Fieger, "ever expected the song to do as well as it did. We were totally unprepared that it would be the number one song of 1979, and one of the only rock 'n' roll songs to become number one in the 1970s."

Although the Knack's rise from obscurity to the top was rather speedy, success for the four individuals involved was by no means an overnight affair. Fieger traced the band's roots.

"I moved to L.A. in 1970 and I was playing in a band called Sky," he recalled. "I was young, just out of high school, and had visions of being a big rock star. But it got crazy, and the band broke up. I then met Bruce Gary through a mutual friend and we started playing together, in the garage at his mom's house. I played bass at the time and he played drums, so I was looking for a guitar-playing, songwriting partner. It took four years of playing in bar bands and then I met Berton. I thought he was a great player and we talked, and it turned out he had a beat on what I was trying to do. That was in '73."

From the start, Fieger and friends knew they wanted to have a basic rock 'n' roll band, although that wasn't fashionable at the time. "We had songs like 'Good Girls Don't' and 'That's What The Little Girls Do' on tape, but no one was buying them. So around '77, I gave up the idea and started playing with other bands—a German synthesizer band and then the Sunset Bombers, an L.A. punk band. One day I called Berton and said 'Fuck this, let's stop trying to get a deal with our tapes and just get a group together.' We got Bruce, and then six days later we found Prescott. This was 1978. We played the Whisky, and the rest, as they say, is history."

In spite of the band's leaning toward '60s style pop rock, Fieger claims that his influences are more varied than one might imagine. Going way, way back, he explained, "My parents couldn't afford a babysitter so they would put me in a high chair and put on a stack of pop records—Julius LaRosa, Frankie Laine, Peggy Lee, Johnnie Ray, Perry Como, Dean Martin, Sinatra.

"Then I learned about rock music early from watching TV—Elvis, Bill Haley, Little Richard. Also, my parents were sort of liberal, radical laborites— my mom was a teacher's union organizer and my dad a labor lawyer—so they listened to Pete Seeger, the Weavers. I knew about Dylan in '61, and Woody Guthrie. My mom was also into opera. So by the time the Beatles came out, I was primed and ready.

"The Beatles blew my mind. They changed my life. I'll never forget it: me and my sister were watching Ed Sullivan and we begged my father to let us watch it on the big TV. He used to watch The Defenders, which was on the same time. So we had to watch it on the shitty TV in my sister's room. But I'll never forget it—especially Lennon. He was one of the most powerful and confident young people I'd ever seen and he was somebody to trust. As a kid you looked at him and even though he was a little older, he was still a kid."

Years after watching the Beatles on TV, how did Fieger feel when his group was compared to them? "I was dumbfounded. We were making a joke, saying tongue-in-cheek that, 'Hey, people, if you're looking for the next big thing, it ain't coming. The Beatles were the best you're ever going to get and if you want the next best thing, it's just a rehash.' But by not giving interviews, a lot of people didn't get the joke. A lot of people take rock 'n' roll seriously."

In 1979, punk and new wave—the return to simple rock—had been around for a while already without any great commercial success. Why did the spotlight fall on the Knack? Why was it that particular group that broke through? "I think it was our tunes," offered Fieger. "Rock 'n' roll is based on the song, and the kids knew we had the songs. Plus, there was an intangible chemistry that the four of us had."

"My Sharona" skyrocketed to the top, but the album actually went to number one first; before long, word was out that celebs such as Tom Petty, Bruce Springsteen, and Stephen Stills were digging— and sitting in with—this new L.A. pop group. The Knack sold out all of its L.A. dates at clubs such as the Troubador and Madame Wong's. By the time the group got to New York after having the hits (a pre-album four generated little response), the Knack was booked into no less a prestigious venue than Carnegie Hall—where the Beatles had played some fifteen years before. Everything was happening for the Knack, and the band went back to L.A. to record its second album, with Mike "The Commander" Chapman producing for the second time. The project was completed in seven days—four days less than the debut—and "Baby Talks Dirty" was released as a single. Both album and single fared modestly, but were no match for the success of the first time around. "Everyone says we're calculated," mentioned Fieger. "But if we are, then we're also stupid." Next came the grand re-thinking of strategy which led to album number three, *Round Trip*.

The new album does find the group expanding its base, and Fieger said that they took time to find new directions that would widen the Knack's musical scope while maintaining the basic Knack sound. "We let our fans down with the second album," admitted Fieger. "We were trying to recapture the feeling of the first one so we said, 'Well, let's do this one in even less time,' and we did it in seven days. But we weren't true to the material. Nobody wanted to be the one to say, 'Wait, slow down.' The success of the first album gave us a false euphoria.

"One of the reasons for the changes now is that we were moving too fast. We had to say stop and wait. We want to be able to have fun with this again and take time to be human beings again. We've got to have real experiences instead of the fake life you live on the road, which is a false reality. So we took time and realized that we didn't like the way we were being handled, and that we had different directions we wanted to take musically."

The songs of *Round Trip* (produced by Jack Douglas), according to Fieger, "runs the gamut from straight rock 'n' roll to dance music to ersata R&B to fusion to a country waltz to cynical joking. The lyrical approach is more adult (one song described a friend being shot during a robbery) and the playing more sophisticated. But there's enough of a tie to the old sound so that we won't leave people behind. We wanted more control over the recording and agreed it wasn't going to work with Mike Chapman, so we got Jack Douglas, who was the perfect guy for the kind of record we wanted to make. We wanted to stretch out musically and we called up Jack. It was one-two-three, very simple.

"I think our fans were ready for change. When I was a kid I used to like it when the new Who album came out and it was so different than the last one. We want to change and we want our audience to come with us."

Now, that's not so funny, is it?

Collectible Hendrix

By Tim Neely

What makes one artist more collectible than another?

For the most part, three things come into play. Jimi Hendrix, profiled extensively in this issue, fits very nicely in all three:

The artist must have importance in the history of whatever music they do. Big sales aren't necessary.

The artist must have continuing influence.

There must be some records the artist put out that are very hard to find, or what's the challenge in collecting them?

We are going to look at some of the most collectible Jimi Hendrix releases, focusing on the United States. Plenty of overseas rarities exist as well.

Singles

Hendrix was probably the first true "album rock" artist, based on the following definition: An album rock artist is one whose albums were bigger and more important than their singles.

The biggest Hendrix 45 in the U.S. was "All Along The Watchtower," which peaked at a measly No. 20 in *Billboard*. Seven of his albums, both during and after his life, made the Top 10 in the same magazine, with *Electric Ladyland* spending two weeks at No. 1 in 1968. Needless to say, original Hendrix 45s, even "Watchtower," are scarce, and some are downright impossible to find.

Here's a sampling of current values in Near Mint (basically brand-new-looking) condition for U.S. singles:

Reprise PRO 595, "...And a Happy New Year," $200 with picture sleeve (this was a promo-only item with Hendrix performing "Little Drummer Boy," "Silent Night," and "Auld Lang Syne").

Reprise 0572, "Hey Joe"/ "51st Anniversary," $100 (this was the first U.S. Hendrix single).

Reprise 1000, "Stepping Stone"/ "Izabella," $100 (this was withdrawn shortly after its release).

Reprise 0665, "Up From The Skies"/"One Rainy Wish," $20.

Most others not in the Back to Back Hits series, $15.

The only regular Hendrix 45 to be issued with a picture sleeve in the States was the first one, Reprise 0572. The sleeve is one of the rarest of all, and is listed at $600 Near Mint, but could go for much more depending on the buyer and seller.

Another selling point of Hendrix U.S. 45s: All of the 1960s and early 1970s singles have mono mixes of the songs. When you see how much the original mono albums are worth, the 45s may actually be undervalued compared to their rarity.

Albums

You might think that with the vast quantities of albums Hendrix sold, only a handful would have any value. You think incorrectly.

The most collectible Hendrix albums are his U.S. monaural pressings, without a doubt.

When *Are You Experienced* was released in 1967, mono was on its last legs, and it was basically extinct a year later. Two Hendrix LPs were released in the U.S. in mono, and one was released that way as a promotional copy for radio stations. In Near Mint condition, *Are You Experienced* (Reprise R 6261) is about a $150 item, *Axis: Bold As Love* (Reprise R 6281) a $600 item, and the two-record promo-only *Electric Ladyland* (Reprise 2R 6307, white labels) can go for $3,000 or more.

Promotional copies of Hendrix albums—provided they are identified on the label as such and not merely stamped that way on the cover—are almost always worth more than their stock counterparts. Promo copies of the aforementioned mono LPs go for $500 Near Mint for *Experienced*, and as much as $2,000 for *Axis*. A stereo white-label promo for *Electric Ladyland* is a $200 item; the same for *Smash Hits*, a $100-plus piece. Most of the others with promo editions are $25-$50.

A promo-only 12-inch single, "The Jimi Hendrix Medley," compiled during the infamous medley craze of the early 1980s (Reprise PRO-A-840), is a $75 item.

The original stereo pressing of *Are You Experienced*, with a pink, gold, and green Reprise label (not any other label—the LP was in print on vinyl into the late 1980s and exists on at least four later label designs) is up to $50 Near Mint. *Axis: Bold As Love* on the same label is a $40 piece. The original two-record stereo *Electric Ladyland* on the two-tone orange Reprise label with a "W7" logo (from the brief time when Warner Bros, was owned by 7 Arts in the late 1960s) is a $40 item; *Smash Hits* is a $25 item (make that $60 if it has a poster inside); and *The Cry Of Love* on the two-tone orange label is a nifty $500, because it wasn't supposed to be pressed that way. By that time, the Warner Bros.-7 Arts merger had failed, and the Reprise label was redesigned as an all-orange (or tan) label.

One rarity is of recent vintage. In 1986, Capitol released *Band Of Gypsys* 2, more live tracks from the Hendrix/Billy Cox/Buddy Miles collaboration. Some copies have four unreleased tracks on Side 2 that are not supposed to be there! You have to count the tracks to identify this, because the label lists the three tracks that are supposed to be there. This goodie, though barely a decade old, can go for $150.

The one import most Americans have heard about isn't as rare as you think worldwide. For the British release of *Electric Ladyland*, which came out after the American issue, Jimi is surrounded by naked ladies. In England, because it's the common version, it's worth about the same as the American version. But in America, copies can exchange for astronomical prices.

For more information on U.S. Hendrix albums, see the *Goldmine Price Guide To Collectible Record Albums, Fifth Edition* by Neal Umphred.

Compact Discs

If CDs were collected the same way LPs were, using the same criteria, some Hendrix CDs would be quite collectible right now. But many CD collectors want the best sounding version, not necessarily the first version. I list few values for these, but I throw them out as things that could be collectible.

All of Hendrix's CDs on Reprise are now out of print and have been since 1992. Most of the early ones were remastered at least once while they were in print; the longboxes will mention this on a sticker (assuming you still have the longbox). The most significant change was in *Electric Ladyland*; originally this came out as a 2-CD set ($50) before it was discovered that the whole LP would fit on one disc.

Also, the Alan Douglas-supervised reissues on MCA, released from 1993-95, are now out of print. Some of them may never appear again; only time will tell which ones those will be. I'd bet you'll never see *Voodoo Soup* again, for one. And you certainly won't see the garish covers that came with the reissues.

Some promo CDs were released in conjunction with albums; one exists for the Rykodisc issue of *Radio One* and another for the Reprise box set *Lifelines*, among others.

One interesting oddity: The nude-cover version of *Electric Ladyland* was distributed briefly in the United States on a 2-CD set (Polydor 823 359-2). It's also a $50 item.

Addendum

Since this column was first published in Goldmine, *some of the newer releases have become quite collectible.*

The 180-gram vinyl versions of the MCA reissues of Are You Experienced?, *Axis:* Bold As Love, Electric Ladyland, *and* First Rays Of The New Rising Sun *disappeared from the primary market shortly after their release. The U.S. versions, which originally sold in the $20-$25 range, have topped $50-$60 already. American versions are individually numbered; the European versions are not. (The exports also were pressed in the United States.)*

Happy collecting!

Neil Young

By Bill DeYoung
December 5, 1997

One of rock 'n' roll's most mercurial figures, Neil Young has been known to say something one minute, and then turn around and do the complete opposite the next. Since his earliest public incarnation, as the "Hollywood Indian" tearing up the lead guitar in Buffalo Springfield, he's been a mystery man, coming and going in various combinations of shadow and light, never explaining himself, never staying in one place long enough to be pigeonholed. He's switched from acoustic to electric, from techno to rockabilly, to country, pop and blues, back to acoustic and back to electric. He's a confounding fellow. Millions of people love him for these very reasons.

Yet over the course of his thirty-plus years in the music business, Young has been assailed as often as he's been praised: He's too whiny, his songs are weird, his songs are boring, his guitar playing is rudimentary. All true, in a way, but one man's ceiling is another man's floor—or so said another gifted songwriter long ago—and the very qualities that so irritate Neil Young's detractors are what make him special to the people who believe his best intentions run comfortably in their blood.

There is no one in rock 'n' roll who sings and plays electric guitar with the symphonic crudeness of Neil Young, not another musician within 100 light years who can hammer an acoustic the way he can, and make it sound like something freshly hewn from the forest. He writes strange, beautiful songs.

His songs—the long, repetitive ones with Crazy Horse, his longtime backing band—are hypnotic in their simplicity. Anyone who's ever tranced through the studio version of "Cortez the Killer" can vouch for that. Or "Danger Bird." Or any of the epic pieces on the *Ragged Glory* album.

For that matter, anyone who saw Young and Crazy Horse, rockin' the hell out of the free world on this summer's H.O.R.D.E. tour, knows first-hand just how intimate Neil Young is with his guitar.

This interview was conducted over the phone just before Young and his mates took the stage to mesmerize another H.O.R.D.E. crowd of never-say-die hippies and slackjawed Squirrel Nut Zippers fans.

Every stop on the tour, this fifty-two-year-old guy blew everybody away like a hurricane.

Lately he's been riding the rails, figuratively, as part owner of the legendary Lionel Train company. There was another Farm Aid in October, at which he made a long (for him) and impassioned speech about the huge factory farms that are taking over America's heartland, and another benefit concert for the Bridge School, a facility for physically challenged youngsters operated by his wife, Pegi, in Northern California.

He's got a movie out, too: Directed by Jim "Dead Man" Jarmusch, *Year of the Horse* is a documentary about Young's sometimes stormy relationship with the guys in Crazy Horse.

Notoriously opinionated about what he sees as the "inferior" digital sound of the compact disc, Young is adamant about keeping his six remaining catalog albums, and his planned retrospective of unreleased work, *Archives*, out of the public's hands until things start to sound better.

Of course, he's said this before, and then announced the release dates, and pulled them back, then announced them again. Ever the will o' the wisp, he may just change his mind for more than a few minutes and the "lost" albums will see the light of CD day.

Then again, maybe they won't.

For the record, the missing titles are *Journey Through the Past, Time Fades Away, On the Beach, American Stars 'n' Bars, Hawks & Doves,* and *Re*Ac*Tor.*

Goldmine: *Six of your catalog albums remain unavailable on compact disc. Recently, you told an interviewer you would burn the tapes before you let them come out on CD. Why?*

Neil Young: Until we get the technology. I'm pushing for better technology. And CDs don't cut it, to me. HDCD is a real great improvement on digital sound, no matter what the format of the sound is. That's a process you can make CDs through, and it makes them sound more detailed. If you have an HDCD playback system, it sounds incredibly more detailed.

267

Is that one of those technologies that we'll 'see by the year 2000'?

It's out there now. There's about forty different companies, small audiophile companies that make stereo equipment that carries the HDCD chip.

There are something like fifteen of your albums out on CD on Reprise. How come they're out, and these six aren't?

Those were made during the beginning of CDs. When it hadn't really dawned on everybody how inferior the CD was. But during the mastering of all of those, and listening to what we ended up with compared to what we started with, everyone became aware of the problems. And that was maybe more than fifteen years ago. And there's been no improvement, in fifteen years, from a bad standard.

Meanwhile, we got 64-bit video games, and 32-bit this, and 16-bit sound. Running at a slow speed. So we really need to get a standard together for recorded sound that doesn't destroy it.

But Reprise is still making those discs.

Oh yeah, that's right, you can't stop that. But I'm not gonna do any new ones until there's a standard.

Let me play devil's advocate. Since you're committed to this, can't you just put a stop to those that are still in print? Can't you tell the label 'They sound like shit; let's take 'em out'?

You can do that with the new ones. When you put out a master, you put it out—OK, it's out. Until then, you have it.

You know, those six albums aren't available on vinyl or cassettes, either. They've all been deleted.

I'm trying to use that leverage to get some tonal quality on the recordings.

Well, what can I do? I'll make a call. As a fan, it bugs me that I can't put, say, American Stars 'n' Bars *on the CD player.*

It's tough for me, too, but I'm not gonna put out *Hurricane* sounding like a piece of shit. That's the way it is. There's the ability to have it better, and I can make a statement. I'm not gonna let it keep happening.

Hawks and Doves, *a great record. Can't hear it. That makes me a little sad.*

Right, me too! I feel the same way. When it comes out, it'll sound great.

What about your long-rumored multi-disc Archives *project?*

It's the same thing there. We're close enough to the new standard. There's all kinds of people throwing ideas for the new standard around. The latest new standard that came out for sound is worse than the CD. That's the DVD. That is totally a piece of crap. A thousand times more distortion, and I'm not exaggerating. That is a clinical number.

It's a terrible thing, and they say that you can play CDs on it. You can play 'em, but they have to be interpolated and translated and everything before your ear hears 'em; by then, they're so distorted, they're just not there any more.

So what they've done is, they're killing an art form through greed, and not being able to focus on using a decent standard. They're more interested, it seems, in putting out more product, and more real time information on a disc, than they are in putting out more quality on a disc. And one plays against the other.

So a lot of things have to be worked out before the new standard is set, but the wheels are turning right now, it's happening.

Do you have a time frame, i.e. 'They'll be out in four years or something?"

They may never be out on the market if the standard's not right.

What exactly is the Archives? *And how close to getting it done did you get?*

Pretty close, now. It's a set of volumes. Each volume carries a number of CDs, but none of those numbers are locked in.

Will it be a mail-order thing, or will it come out through the label?

No, it's a label. It's on Warner Brothers.

Didn't you record Time Fades Away *digitally in '73?*

No, it was recorded through a Quad-8 CompuMix board, one of the first computer boards. It was mixed directly to masters; instead of copying masters, it made masters over and over again. But actually it was kind of a misfire.

You turned down the Lollapalooza tour. What appealed to you about H.O.R.D.E.?

Really, the diversity of the music. There's just so many different bands out that are all so different, and all of the different kinds of music, from the Mighty Mighty Bosstones to the Squirrel Nut Zippers, and on the tour we've had other groups that have visited and stayed for two or three weeks, like Beck, Primus, Blues Traveler.

There's always new bands that nobody knows too much about, which is always cool because their energy is so good and they're so positive. It's just good to be around all of that, for me.

Does that make the audience primed and already vibrating when you get out there?

Well, actually, they get a day of music that's all different, so they're wide open by the time I see them. So it works real well. I just like the energy out here.

Is it a younger crowd, or is it really mixed aged groups?

Oh, it's definitely a younger crowd. I have to say that at least fifty percent of the people I play for have never seen me. So that's great; that's a big plus. Because it's just more of a challenge...it's just different. And at this stage, something different is something great.

Does it have to be Crazy Horse for this audience; could you, for example, have used the acoustic band or the Bluenotes for H.O.R.D.E.? Is that what makes the most sense for you?

Yeah, I would say that's true, that Crazy Horse is the band for this. And that's had a lot to do with us choosing this, and doing it this way. Whereas the Bluenotes would have been great, but not as the position I'm in, as the headliner. They would have been a great band to play during the day or in the afternoon, if it wasn't 'Neil Young.' The band itself, without having to drag my name along with it, would've been fantastic at this show. Because the same kind of diversity represented in that band is represented all over this show.

You're doing a lot of re-arranging lately. It was nice to hear "Barstool Blues" again, on the live album Year of the Horse. *Can you take any song out of your bag and say 'Crazy Horse could do this'? An acoustic song, or something from* Trans, *for example.*

Well, "Barstool Blues" was a Crazy Horse song in the first place. And Crazy Horse was on a lot of *Trans*, on the songs I sang with the vocoder, so it would be possible.

See, they're there all the time. People seem to think that through all these changes and everything that they're gone, but the core of Crazy Horse is always around, on most of the albums. And of course the other albums that I've done that don't have this core music thing happening, that I have with Crazy Horse, a lot of those songs don't fit with Crazy Horse.

The opposite to that is true of the album I did with Pearl Jam, where most of the songs on that album fit great with Crazy Horse.

I just go through my songs to figure out what would be the right ones to do that night.

Down the road, does that mean Crazy Horse might play songs from Harvest Moon? *Is that conceivable?*

Hey, anything's possible.

Tell me about the Year of the Horse *movie. Was*

Dead Man *your first collaboration with Jim Jarmusch, and did it lead to this?*

Dead Man was definitely first. That was just getting to know Jim. And we did a video together, for Dead Man, and then we did a video for "Broken Arrow," and then we decided to do this—actually, we didn't really decide to make a film, we just decided 'Let's film some stuff and see what we get. If it looks like it's gonna be good, and fun, we'll keep going.'

The Dead Man *soundtrack was issued on your label, Vapor Records. Does Vapor Records still exist?*

Yeah! We're not a big record company, we're a real record company. Real small, too.

You cut your hand a while ago. What was the deal with that?

It was just a regular accident. If I hadn't been so famous, it wouldn't have made any difference. I was slicing a sandwich.

And you had to cancel some dates in Europe?

Yeah. If it had been Joe Schmoe, it wouldn't have made any darn difference, but now I gotta live with people going 'Hey, you cut your hand a few months ago...' Pretty soon it's gonna be like 'Hey, back in '97, you cut your finger..." When I'm eighty-eight.

Back in January, you declined to go to the Rock and Roll Hall of Fame for Buffalo Springfield's induction. Was that something you had to think about, or was there never any question that you would go to the ceremony?

No, I went back and forth several times, trying to make up my mind. But there was always something stopping me from getting excited about going; there was always something there. Finally, what it really came down to was the television of it. I just didn't want to go.

I'd already been to four or five of those things where it wasn't televised, and I knew how cool it was. Then I was at one where they televised it, and I could see the difference.

Then, when it went to VH1... you know, the world does not need another awards show. So who cares? I'm saying it's great to be in the Hall of Fame. I'm already in it. It's great to be in the Buffalo Springfield, but I've already been in the Buffalo Springfield.

And here I'm talking to guys in the Springfield who would like to bring some of their families with them, but can't afford it because the seats are so expensive. And then the place is filled up with all these high rollers, and it's all on VH1's bill, or the TV station, or whoever the heck it is. They all make the money; everybody gets the big sponsorship money, and people in the bands can't afford to bring their families to the ceremony. There were a lot of things about it that kind of bothered me.

Now, it was expensive to go to the Waldorf in New York, but there wasn't a big television thing involved in it. No 'We're going to cash in,' or 'We're going to make a donation to the Hall of Fame to shore up the building' or something. I don't know. So I left that off my itinerary of things that I thought were cool to do.

Did Dewey, Bruce, and Richie understand when you made your statement, or were they just pissed off?

Well, I know Dewey and Bruce understood. I guess everybody else understood it—I never really spoke to Richie about it. But I did speak to the other guys about it. I just told them where I was at with it. And they're used to me.

What was it Stills said onstage: 'Well, Rich, he quit again.'

Yeah, right. That was great.

Your induction as a solo artist, and performance with Pearl Jam, had been televised just two years earlier. I remember thinking that was great TV. You said you could tell it was different then. How was it different?

What's different is that your speech, whatever you want to say... this is the moment of a lifetime for a musician. Did you see the Grammys when they gave Frank Sinatra his Lifetime Achievement Award? How did you feel about that?

Pretty upset.

Well, television. That's the way television has to be. They have a corporate thing going there, they got their commercials, they got their slot, and with

VH1 it was even worse because they didn't even do it live. I mean they didn't even have that excuse.

Later on, they went in and Editor D, from Room C, was designated by Executive A to leave half of some guy's heartfelt speech on the cutting room floor. And cut out almost everything that he said, and put in just what VH1 thought was cool. As far as I'm concerned, that's not hip. Doesn't get it for me.

It reminded me, and a lot of people, of this "This Note's For You" thing with MTV. That was the last TV controversy I could think of involving you.

Well, you know, there's a place for 'em. They do a good service to the community. (laughs) Wasn't that diplomatic? You won't be seeing any of my videos on VH1, I'll tell you that.

As I remember, MTV didn't play "This Note's For You" until it won their big award.

Yeah, they didn't play it until it won Video of the Year, so they aired it.
How did you feel about that?

For me, it was a lucky break. I didn't have to have anybody see it, so they didn't recognize me when I was walking down the street.

How much of Lionel Trains do you own?

Well, the partners and I have control of the company.

How did you get involved with Lionel? I know it had something to do with your son.

Well, I bought part of Lionel along with my partners, Wellspring, an investment group. I had a history with Lionel before that, where I developed a control system that the company uses for controlling the trains. It was developed with an eye for doing a lot of things with my son, using a controller that was accessible to a physically challenged individual who had different ways of accessing switches.
So I came up with this idea, and came up with

concepts for supplying auditory feedback, and visual feedback, for every command issued. So that every time you made a command, you heard or saw something happen. You got action back.

And then you can select the commands by remote control, with a wireless controller, that can be accessed by your physically challenged friend. And so whatever you do with the controller, then when they hit their switch, it happens. So there's no plugging things in or changing things. It's fast and easy.

Were you a model train aficionado before this?

Yeah! I sort of developed this because of that. I kept thinking how all my kids loved trains so much, and I did too, so we just enjoyed playing with them.
And I just happen to have this son, Ben, who's physically challenged, and wants to have a lot of fun. So we share this together.
And it just turns out that through the development of it, it's made it possible for a lot of other things to happen for everybody who plays with trains that really couldn't happen before.

There's a tent at H.O.R.D.E. with a train setup.

Yeah, Lionel has a display of electric trains, and a thing called LionelVision, which is cameras mounted in the trains. The trains fly around with little color cameras and stereo microphones mounted in them, listening and looking everywhere they go.

So will we eventually see your face on the packaging? 'Neil Young says…'

No. (Laughing). No, I don't think so.

You're fifty-one now. What does life look like to you?

Well, I love playing. I love playing music, and I love being around lots of other people who play music. That's why the H.O.R.D.E. tour is so much fun.
It absolutely feels just as good.

Photo/Chuck Boyd/Flower Children

Ginger Baker

By Gene Kalbacher
October 11, 1985

Peter (Ginger) Baker, one of the most flamboyant drummers in the history of rock, has died so many times over the past seventeen years that rock coroners, er, critics have lost count.

The reports of his demise have been insubstantial and, of course, untrue. But this founding member of Cream, the short-lived (1966-68) band that played the loudest, fastest, most technically proficient and ferocious blues-rock (spawning, in its wake, the boogie and heavy-metal bands that reign today), has been a favorite target of rock's doomsayers.

At once the most mysterious and most maligned drummer of the era, the most imitated and the most castigated, Baker, forty-three, has seldom stood still long enough to quiet his detractors. Born in Lewisham, London in 1939, Baker took to the drums as a youngster after a reportedly brief flirtation with the trumpet. Goaded by friends to try his hand at the traps, and having intently watched drummers in concert, young Baker discovered that he possessed natural ability; drumming came quickly and easily to him, although in later years he would faithfully practice the drum basics, or rudiments, for hour after hour.

Jazz drummers, in particular Baby Dodds, Big Sid Catlett, Max Roach, and Elvin Jones, made lasting impressions on Baker. And under the tutelage of Phil Seamen, probably England's most celebrated drummer at the time, Baker started to make his own way. His earliest professional associations were jazz bands—the Storyville Jazzmen, the Terry Lightfoot big band, Acker Bilk and Alexis Korner's Blues Incorporated (in the latter, he replaced future Rolling Stone Charlie Watts)—and Baker found his first niche in early 1963 when he joined the Graham Bond Trio, which later became the Graham Bond Organization and also included future Cream partner Jack Bruce on bass.

Three years of rhythm and blues activity with the saxist Bond laid the ground-work for Cream, which Baker himself initiated. Concurrent with his budding genius at the drums, Baker acquired a reputation for wild, erratic behavior. Though many considered him a wildman on the skins, due in part to his intense flamming, crossrhythms, and booming shots on double bass drums, all was not climax and crescendo. He was equally capable of shimmering delicacy on the cymbals (hear "Tales of Brave Ulysses") and locomotive precision with wire brushes on snare ("Train Time").

On stage in Cream with Bruce and guitarist Eric Clapton, Baker cast a foreboding, if not downright frightening, spell over his audience. The tall, rakish Baker, seated behind a sea of cymbals and a kit dominated by two bass drums, pounded the skins with such pagan fury, his outrageously long, flaming-orange hair and psychedelic robes billowing before him, that some thought him Mephistopheles incarnate. And when he spoke, introducing a song, one heard a croaking, seemingly disembodied voice that all the more accentuated his craggy facial features and sallow, milk-blue complexion.

When Cream disbanded in 1969, Baker joined or formed a succession of equally short-lived bands—Blind Faith, Ginger Baker's Air Force, and the Baker Gurvitz Army. In between, he spent several years in Nigeria, opening a recording studio and producing several African percussion ensembles. At last report, he had moved to Italy from his native England, where government agents were reportedly on his trail for failure to pay back taxes.

This was three years ago, so Baker's recent visit to the Bottom Line nightclub in New York City—where he performed with a power blues trio featuring Italians Enzo Pietropaule on bass and Roberto Ciocci on guitar—not only confirmed his status among the living but aroused interest in his on-again/off-again career.

Slouched on the bed in his room at the Doral Inn in mid-Manhattan, Baker wore a black T-shirt and dungarees (not designer jeans) rolled up at the bottoms. Though fatigued from a sleepless flight from Italy and a snowbound tour stopover in Buffalo, Baker was as attentive and jovial as one can be after thirty sleepless hours. Smoking a pipe, Baker was alternately magisterial and avuncular as he answered questions.

"Strange things have been happening on this tour," he admitted. For one thing, a man claiming to be Mario Lanza telephoned during the interview; for another, the master drummer, the master time-keeper, never knew what time it was. Nobody wore a watch.

Goldmine: *What's the actual name of this band? Is it the Ginger Baker Band?*

Ginger Baker: ...For this tour it is, I suppose. When we play in Italy, it's Roberto's band.

Tell me about the band's book.

Books?

The repertoire.

The writing's being done by various people, quite a number of whom are dead (laughs). We're doing a lot of old blues things. Things we were doing in 1963.

Twenty years later, the tunes of Robert Johnson, Skip James, and Willie Dixon, to name but three bluesmen, still sound potent.

Yeah. Even 1963—they go back to 1933.

The blues revival in England in the mid-'60s, in which you played a part, paved the way for Cream and many other bands, including those imitators of imitators now known under the rubric of heavy metal. The British musicians seemed to have a far greater reverence for blues, an American music form, than most Americans did. Why was that?

Alexis Korner and Cyril Davies were the two people that really got that thing together there.

Maybe racism kept blues from reaching the American masses. But blues and jazz and rock 'n' roll essentially come from black music, I would think.

Oh, would you?

Yes, wouldn't you?

No, not exactly quite like that (chuckles). I think the blues, whichever way you look at it, wouldn't have happened if the white man hadn't been involved as well (casts knowing, sidelong glance at the interviewer).

Yes. Touché. Great retort. Without the oppressor there wouldn't be the expression of the oppressed.

Yes. Also, what about the whites' use of chords coming to the blues from Western music?

And, at the same time, retaining much of the African call-and-response dynamic.

It was the influence of one culture on another... You're getting racialistic. You seem to be supercon-scious about that in America; you seem to be super-sensitive about it... I don't know, man. It (racism) is there everywhere, but it's also not there every-where. It's the not there that I'm really interested in. Human beings, man, are really strange creatures. Really strange.

In the early '70s, you moved to Africa and set up a recording studio. Did you produce many indigenous percussionists and groups?

I produced some things, yeah. Quite a few. A lot of the music was sold in Nigeria only. It wasn't music that anybody else would be interested in because it was all in local dialects. I didn't have the recording studio to record what I was doing. What it was about was a contribution to an economy (laughs softly, as if savoring an inside joke).

Did you have any contact in Nigeria with Fela (Ransome-Kuti)?

Yeah, an awful lot. I met Fela first in London in about 1960. Fela used to come sit in with us on a jazz gig, all night Friday and Saturday. The other act was Georgie Fame's band, playing all the hit records. And we did a jazz hour in the middle.

What jazz band was this, the Storyville Jazzmen?

No, man, this was modern jazz. That (Storyville Jazzmen) was old-fashioned jazz. That was the first jazz. When I started off playing, I started playing the first (traditional) jazz, and gradually came up to playing mainstream and big bands.

I needed to read (music) to get into a big band, right (laughs)? I got a two-week try (out). I've got very good ears, so I was just listening to everybody and watching the parts.

So you had to fake it?

Yeah. I didn't know what repeat signs were for the first week (laughs). I couldn't figure out why the part was finished long before the band...I couldn't figure out what was going on after the first chorus.

After Blind Faith broke up, you formed Ginger Baker's Air Force, a wild-and-woolly aggregation that recorded two albums, the first one a double album. What prompted you to form this band?

Just to get some old friends together. I decided I'd made enough money by this point (1970), so I dedicated all the funds to the band (laughs). It went down rather well. We had a really good time in that band; there were some hilarious incidents. I mean, you can imagine fourteen or fifteen lunatic musicians on the run. Incredible happenings.

Was the band rehearsed or was it just a very loose grouping?

No, we rehearsed. You can hear from that double album that we got quite a few numbers together.

I'm not suggesting that the music sounded haphazard.

...Well, (that gig at London's Royal Albert Hall) was our second gig. You don't really start getting a band together in that time. The band was only formed for two gigs, one at Town Hall and one at the Albert Hall.

Air Force was only together for two gigs?

Yeah. The office decided it would be a good idea to keep it going. All they were interested in was their twenty-five percent (laughs). So I said, "Yeah, I'll keep it going, only on that basis." But Stevie (Winwood) couldn't do it; he'd got his own thing together.

That must have been the reformed Traffic.

Well, it was already virtually reformed after the

Blind Faith tour of the States.

Blind Faith recorded one hit album and followed with a sellout tour of America, as critics were proclaiming the quartet the first "supergroup." Yet the band was finished, it seemed, before it really got started. Did Blind Faith record any material that has yet to be released?

I don't think so, no.

Why did the band break up?

I don't know, really.

The music was happening.

It was certainly happening. I think that's the best band (voice trails off)...

Was it lack of material?

No, Christ, it wasn't that at all. It just broke to bits. I don't know because I wasn't there at the time. I was in Hawaii, followed by six weeks in Jamaica, followed by three on a boat going home. I didn't get back from the end of the Blind Faith tour till three months (laughs) after the tour ended. I was trying to get straight, actually.

One of the tunes on the only Blind Faith album was yours, "Do What You Like." Even the Cream albums always featured one or two of your tunes.

Most of them were terrible.

But very distinctive. Everyone knew it was your voice, just as everyone recognized Ringo Starr whenever he sang on a Beatles record. You're a world-renowned drummer, but scant attention has been paid to you as a composer. How did your songwriting get started?

That came about in the very first big band I played with, the one I learned to read (music) in. It involved reading lots of new parts. We played every night. I started reading off the saxophone parts (laughs). The horn player, who used to sit in front of me, caught me at this. I wasn't reading the drum parts anymore; I started reading over his shoulder, because I've got really long (eye) sight. I was reading his part (laughs).

He got me these books on basic harmony and 5/2/1s and all this rubbish. It's not rubbish, actually, it's quite interesting. So I studied this, and he told me what books to get. It was just one book, and it was very precise. I understand immediately, so I understood the basic harmony... That was it, and that got me into writing. But I don't know, I don't think I'm a very good writer, really. What I enjoy doing best is arranging for horns. You can play games with the patterns of the notes.

"Sweet Wine," from Fresh Cream and "Those Were The Days," from Wheels Of Fire, are among your better tunes. Were you the lyricist for these numbers?

"Sweet Wine" I wasn't, no. That was Janet (Godfrey), Jack's wife.

And Mike Taylor is credited as your co-composer on "Those Were The Days."

Mike didn't write any words. Mike's dead. He died a long, long time ago. He was a good musician, a piano player, a jazz player. I used to play with him. He was very, very straight when I first met him, and in a very short time he sort of went the other way. Graham Bond was another one. Bondy was the same. When I first met him, his hair was all short and he had suit and a shirt and a tie always.

I remember seeing pictures of him at the time.

No, that was the band uniform; we all wore uniforms then (laughs).

A few years ago, you dispensed with your patented double-bass-drum configuration. Now you're using it again. What brought that about?

I am using two bass drums. A lot of people asked me to. Quite recently I got another bass drum back again. I don't use it very much.

When and why did you choose this setup?

When Cream started.

Did the demands of Cream's music necessitate two bass drums?

No, it was just me going mad, I think. It was an Ellington concert that got me into it. All the drum-

mers with Ellington played with two-bass-drum kits. It was a specification of the gig. Dave Black, Louis Bellson, and Sam Woodyard all used two bass drums. They played some incredible fill-ins, simple ones but really nice, using the two bass drums. What a sound!

Your whole presence on stage, indeed your flamboyance, has led some listeners, the untrained ones, to label you a wildman. Yet you have a strong grasp of the drum rudiments, and you've elaborated upon them.

Well, I've got some rudiments that are more than the others. Things that make your hands work.

Rudiments of your own creation?

Yeah. And Phil's (Seamen). Phil had some rudiments as well that were really nice.

Jack Bruce told me that there were times on stage with Cream, during long stretches of soloing, when he'd get so absorbed in his improvising that he'd forget what song you were playing. He said he had to think real hard when it came time to bring the tune around to the theme. That's a strange state of affairs for a bassist. Did you ever have similar experiences?

(Laughs) I hope not, but it did happen a few times with Cream. Eric used to turn around sometimes and say to me, "Where is it, man?" I'd say, "One, two, one-two-three-four," and it was away again. It did go like that sometimes. I would always like to know where it is (laughs). It's important if you play the drums.

To many fans, Cream was, in a sense, two bands—a live band, with extensive jamming, and a studio unit playing shorter, more structured tunes. Was Cream two bands or was it manifestations of the same band?

Yeah, two bands. Live, we were playing jazz (laughs); in the studio, we were playing music, much more arranged, obviously.

Was it difficult for Cream to reconcile after two sensibilities?

No. Yes and no. No and yes. I don't know. It's a problem because you get a sort of studio technique and a live thing, and it's wrong, really, because you should play the same in the studio as you do live. Then it's up to the sound engineers to make it sound right.

With Cream you had Tom Dowd, of course, as the engineer. And the producer was Felix Pappalardi, who was also a versatile musician.

Felix, bless his soul. (Pappalardi was shot to death in 1983 by his wife, Gail Collins, who co-wrote such Cream tunes as "Strange Brew" and "World Of Pain"; she was indicted for his murder and convicted on a lesser charge.)

On stage, Cream was a together, tight, integrated band. In a sense, the interaction among the trio was telepathic...

Not in a sense. It was telepathic.

Okay, telepathic. But for all its cohesion on stage, the band in its final stages, according to Jack Bruce, reached the point where the only time the three of you met was on stage for the gig. You traveled in separate limousines and airplanes.

Gradually these big stacks arrived. It started with one little box. Then two boxes, one as big as the other and standing on top of it. Then it was four. It got incredibly loud. Friends of mine would come to the gigs and say, "Yeah, man, it was great, but the only time I heard you was during the drum solo." ("Toad" was his featured tune) The rest of the night I was completely inaudible.

There was this incredible cacophony. It used to make me very bad-tempered, I know that. You'd come off stage and your ears are ringing. There's this buzzing in your ears. You're in bed, trying to go to sleep, and you've still got this RRRRRrrrrr going on. It's terrible, man.

The first gigs were different... Cream was a very short-lived band, and Cream didn't make it just like that. The first gigs we did, we got #45. I got Cream together because I couldn't take it with Graham (Bond) anymore (laughs). I'd been with Graham three-and-a-half years.

Sadly, Cream broke up at the height of its popularity. Did Cream record any material other than what's been released?

There was "The Coffee Song" or something (laughs). I don't remember what that was about. It was in the very early days. Obviously one of Robert Stigwood's brainstorms.

In Cream, who decided what songs would be recorded and performed live?

Everybody.

Was the songwriting done in anticipation of the

No, we didn't take our own airplanes. Sometimes it happened that somebody goofed and missed a plane. Jack missed a plane (laughs). But that was a different story altogether. We did see our problems. Musicians are silly people, I suppose.

The bone of contention with me (in Cream) was the incredible volume. Having two guitars flat out right beside you, man—we didn't use to mike drums. In the beginning, we didn't. First of all, there were just small, little amps. Then they started building these big stacks. The Who and everything.

album to come, or were songs germinating for a period of time?

For an album. Once we'd done all the numbers we did on stage, we had to think of some more to put on records. A lot of stuff on the records we didn't play live. We'd put 'em on record and not play 'em again (laughs).

Your song "Passing The Time," from Wheels Of Fire, *wasn't performed live. The studio version boasted some nice colors and textures. Jack Bruce played cello and you added glockenspiel.*

Felix had a lot to do with that sort of thing. He was really good to work with. The horn thing on "Pressed Rat And Warthog," that was Felix. Mike (Taylor, the composer) was at the piano, and I was trying to get Eric to play this part. Felix said, "That would sound great on the cornet." He came in the next day and he played it on this trumpet. He was really blowing it.

"Pressed Rat And Warthog" features some of your most abstract, surreal lyrics. Strange creature-creations.

That was one of the good ones. It's poetry, jazz and poetry.

"What A Bringdown," from Goodbye Cream, *lies in a similar vein. Something like "Moby Dick and Albert making out with Captain Bligh." What the hell does that mean?*

"Moby Dick" is when you're sick. "Moby Dick"—sick. It's rhyme and slang. That whole song is rhyme and slang. "Captain Bligh," you know who he is. "…in a jam jar" (becomes) it's cold in the car; the heater doesn't work…"Parson's collar" (becomes) half a dollar. You're sitting in the car, it's cold, and all you've got in your pocket is half a dollar.

And "Pressed Rat And Warthog"?

"Pressed Rat," I don't know how he arrived (laughs). He arrived one day. "Pressed Rat" arrived on the three of us in the early days. We used to just sit around and incredible things would happen. One of them was "Pressed Rat".

There was such a person?

No! "Pressed Rat" was "pressed rat." It was a joke among us.
A condition?

No, it had nothing to do with that. It was "Pressed Rat." If you don't understand "pressed rat," then I'm sorry. We did, okay (snickers).

Two live Cream albums, volumes one and two, were released by RSO Records in 1970 and '72, several years after the group had split up. Where were they recorded? The albums don't specify.

(Examining the covers) Some of them were at the Fillmore East. Some of them were somewhere else. And some of them were somewhere else. (The live portion of 1968's double-pocket *Wheels Of Fire* was recorded at the Fillmore West.)

You're not doing any writing for this new band, you mentioned a while ago. Beside the old blues numbers, is the band doing any of Roberto's or Enzo's songs?

We do one of Roberto's tunes, and on one of Enzo's we do sort of a chase.

Do you have any plans to record this band?

Doing this stuff? No. But Roberto's doing an album in Italian, and I'm playing on that. That's for the Italian market.

I saw the guest list for the gig tonight. I see that (drummers) Max Roach and Elvin Jones are on the list.

I've heard about it. I know Elvin, but I've not met Max Roach.

Tell me this, Ginger. I know you dug Jones' playing with John Coltrane, and I'm sure he respected your work. Why all the acrimonious remarks surrounding the famous drum battle you two had in 1970? (At the time, Jones was quoted in the rock press as saying something to the effect, "They should put that cat into a capsule and shoot his ass into space.")

It was game, man. He said I was suffering from delusions of grandeur. Which I was.

Have you gotten over those delusions of grandeur?

No, I don't have delusions of grandeur (anymore). I know I can play the drums, though (laughs). That's all I want to do.

Many would say it's neither a delusion nor an illusion, but simply drumming grandeur.

Oh, well (shrugs), that's up to you.

Why is it, Ginger, that the British press has attacked you so viciously. "Ginger Baker is burned out, Ginger Baker is dead," they would write.

That happened in America, man. It was announced on the radio in America that I was dead. That I was even in a dead band with Jimi (Hendrix) and Janis (Joplin) and people like that. Why, I really don't know. Yes, I did have a problem, but a problem I was in control of, so much so that I don't have it anymore. I think life is what you make it.

When did you get your first kit and what attracted you to the drums?

I discovered I could do it. It was as simple as that. I didn't sort of have to sit down and say, "I'm going to be a drummer," and start (practicing) and doing all these things. I could do it straight away, I just did it. I sat on a kit and played.

I knew what to do, because I'd been watching drummers since I was a little kid. Every time I went to see a band of any description, I only used to watch the drummer, man, I didn't watch anybody else.

So you were a drummer the first time you sat behind a kit.

Yeah, I played it, yeah. All the kids got me to sit in with a band at a party. We all left school and we got together at a party. There was a band playing, and somebody said [to me], "Play the drums!" the

drummer, of course, didn't want me to, and I wanted to but I wasn't going to ask or anything. Finally, I sat on the drums. The trombone player turned to me after the first chorus and said, "Great, a drummer!"

That was it, right. I got a kit the very next week, for three pounds.

You've always been fascinated by movement, Ginger. You're an avid cyclist and, I'm told, an accomplished polo player.

It's all down to time, yeah, with a horse as well as with a drum kit. I don't play polo anymore at the moment. I wasn't accomplished, but my side used to win.

That's what counts.

Yeah, polo is a bit of aggression and suss, and being able to handle a horse is a very large part of the game.

You just said, "It's all down to time." What do you think about drum machines? Do you find them interesting or are you threatened by them?

I've got a friend of mine in Italy who's got a recording studio. He does all these disco records. He's got one of these machines in there, so one day I went in there and set up the drums. He put this (drum) machine on and I sat there and drummed to it. It was good. Quite enjoyable. He set a pattern (on the machine) and I just played on top of it. It was quite fun.

Do you keep copies of all the albums you played on over the years?

I don't have any of them. I don't like the way I sound (on any of the Cream albums).

Photo/Chuck Boyd/Flower Children

Chuck Berry

By Dan Fries
November 1, 1979

In the minds of many people, Chuck Berry was and is the poet of the rock 'n' roll generation. Since his first hit "Maybellene" in 1955, he has been a giant on the music scene, and he still packs auditoriums around the country and abroad. He started out by forming the Chuck Berry Trio in the early '50s, but he had little success until 1955 when he met Muddy Waters, who introduced him to the people at Chess Records... and the rest, as they say, is history.

Berry has always been an enigmatic figure and he runs true to form in the following interview. His life as a rock 'n' roll superstar is fairly well-known up to about 1959, when he was reportedly tried and convicted for violation of the Mann Act. There are many versions of what happened and unfortunately, Mr. Berry has not seen fit to 'clear the air' as yet. As this interview was being readied for publication, Chuck was sentenced to spend 120 days in prison and to perform 1,000 hours of public service work after pleading guilty to Income Tax evasion for the year 1973. The amount due is still in dispute, but reportedly lies somewhere between $100,000 and $200,000. He was due to report to Lompoc prison on August 10 after completion of his twelve-day European tour. Newspapers reported that he was visibly shaken at the sentencing and said that he planned a series of benefit concerts to deter young people from using drugs.

This interview took place last year in Houston, Texas where he was the headliner of a '50s revival show.

Goldmine: *Chuck, suppose we start out with your early career. Could you fill us in on your childhood and how you got started in music?*

Chuck Berry: Well as to my childhood, there's really not much to tell, I mean, everyone was a child at some time...

I read that you sang in the church choir; is that true?

Truth is whatever you believe, but yes, I did sing in the choir.

What got you started in music as a career?

I have always been into music as far back as I can remember, but since you are referring to my 'career' as a musician, I guess you could say it all really started when I met the great Muddy Waters and Mr. Leonard Chess of Chess Records.

The story of how you wrote your first hit— "Maybellene"—has been told before, but is there anything you could add to that story now?

Well, I don't know what 'story' you refer to. I wrote "Maybellene" with a different title—"Ida Red"—and the people at Chess Records told me that there was already another song with this name and I could not use it, so... we did it over as "Maybellene."

Is it true that "Maybellene" was the name of a cow that belonged to your aunt?

If you say so!

No, I'm asking you where the title "Maybellene" came from, in the light of the fact that you were once an aspiring hairdresser at about that time, right?

"Maybellene" had nothing to do with the cosmetic thing. I was through with hairdressing by that time, and the cow's name was Maybelle. I just got to playing with the song, trying different names and Maybellene popped up. Anyway, Maybelle wouldn't fit.

What was life like for you after "Maybellene" become a hit? Did success change your lifestyle very much?

It was good, very good, to be in demand and to

see something of your own creation appeal to a wide audience. I enjoyed it. I still do.

Many rock stars of the '50s said that they were 'ripped off,' and some of them received little or nothing from their hit records. Did you have any problems like this yourself?

When you say 'ripped-off"... you must define your statement.

Do you feel that you got all that was due you from your records?

I don't know, did I? Does anybody really know? How can you tell what is 'due' someone who creates? Oh, you can sit down with pencil and paper and do marvelous things with figures—and I have no doubt some of these things were done. Did I get money from my records? Yes I did and I do, but I don't say I was ripped-off. I was basically unknowledgeable about this business and when the time came to sign certain papers, well, I signed! And these are things you learn with time like in any other business, and this is a business! You write songs and you sing and you are in business for yourself. You struggle and you learn and you pay to learn just as if you went to a school. I'm still learning and I'm still paying.

Can we explore this a little further? I have heard that Alan Freed appeared as a co-writer on your hit record of "Maybellene."

I have no collaborators.

(continuing) ...but here on this LP Chuck Berry's Golden Decade, *the label states: "all selections by C. Berry." Can you explain about this a little?*

What?

Did Alan Freed write any songs with you?

There's nothing I can tell you about Alan Freed writing songs. I don't know how his name came to be on my record, but if it was, it was there for a reason.

Do you have any idea who might have made a deal with Alan Freed to do that?

I don't know that there was a deal. I know that I wrote certain songs and I recorded them with Chess Records and any deals, if there were any, were done by them, I guess.

How did you feel when you found out?

How did I feel about Freed's name on my record? How could I feel? He was an important man in the business and if this was the way it was done, it was done, and as I said, no one can say what is due someone who creates. All things have their price. I paid and I was paid and I'm still paying and being paid.

It's rumored that Chuck Berry doesn't go onstage until he is paid "up front"... is that true? Because on the movie American Hot Wax, *you ended up playing for "Rock 'n' Roll," free, in other words.*

In the movies, the truth isn't always on the screen; in real life it is what you know, what you believe you know.

Have you ever performed and then not been paid your fee?

(Grins, but doesn't answer.)

You don't want to answer that?

(Starts playing with a guitar string, doesn't speak.)

Okay, let's move on. You've been rocking and rolling for almost twenty-five years now. Do you have any plans to retire, or will you stay out on the road indefinitely?

It's hard to say how long I'll be out. It's a question of need or obligation. I don't know how long I'll need to be out on the road, but as long as a need or obligation exists, I guess I'll be out. No, I have no plans to retire.

Let's talk about your famous "duck-walk." How did you invent that?

It wasn't invented! It's something I do.

I once read that you first did it during one of your early appearances and you were crouching down to hide the wrinkles in your suit. Is there anything to that?

Is there? I don't know that story! (Laughing) I've always done that. Did it as a kid even.

As a kid? When? Performing or what?

No, I just did it around the house, like a kid goes under tables and things, well—this was just my way of doing that. The family thought it was funny and I used to do it every time company came. It got laughs, and later, well I just sort of went into it on stage one time, and it went over big. So I've been doing it on certain numbers ever since.

When was the first time you did it on stage?

Who knows? I think it was at one of Alan Freed's shows, most likely.

How well did you know Alan Freed?

Well enough. I did his shows, he played my records. We weren't what you might call close friends. If that's what you mean, but I knew him.

I don't want to re-open that can of worms, but let me ask you this: What was your opinion of Freed's alleged involvement in payola?

Payola?

Yes. "Play for pay," that sort of thing.

I wouldn't know about that. I know a man does what he has to do, what he wants to do, needs to do or likes to do—

What does that mean?

It means whatever you take it to mean. What does it all mean anyway? I don't know what all—what the whole fuss was about, and I still don't; it's done all the time.

You mean now?

Now, then, what's the problem? You can't fault a man who accepts a gift, or a token of gratitude or...

Is that how you see it? A token of gratitude?

A man does certain things to get paid for it. Who pays for it and how it's paid for is of consequence only to those party to it. "Payola" is only a made-up word, to be used. It's all the same thing—I will do this or that if you will pay me to do it and we are all guilty if guilt must be assigned. I feel no guilt. I don't know if Freed did either.

Can we talk about your trouble with the law?

What trouble was that?

I was referring to your trials for violation of the Mann Act. Didn't you serve some time in jail?

(Grins, but just shakes his head and does not answer.)

Well, to wrap this up; how does it feel to be called the "Granddaddy of Rock & Roll" and "A Living Legend"?

Well, I don't know—it feels good. Nothing is changed, yet nothing's the same. I'm older, and that "Granddaddy" part, well... legends are fantasies and dreams and I'm a man... who creates, who puts words and a melody together. I play my guitar and I sing my songs, but am I a legend? I guess I am if it's said that I am, but if you speak of legends, you must speak of Elvis Presley, because he's gone, you see, and I'm still here. It's good to me and it's a shame that his time had come.

Well, Chuck, I want to say thanks for the time you've given me today. I really enjoyed it...

I seldom allow people into my dressing room.

I thought that you'd be the hardest to get to, with all the guards, and you were!

(Laughs) It's the price you pay when you're a legend!

Todd Rundgren

By Deron Bissett
March 29, 1996

During his career, Todd Rundgren has demonstrated his talents as a singer, songwriter, guitarist, keyboardist, recording engineer, producer, concert performer, radio show host, and technological innovator. He has produced thirty albums of his own music, as well as provided musical scores for three movie soundtracks, four television series, and the New York performance of the Beatles' screenplay, *Up Against It*. His involvement in an additional eighty productions for other groups has contributed to the success of a wide range of artists, from Badfinger, Grand Funk, XTC, and the Band to first-time efforts by Jesse Winchester, Michael Stanley, the New York Dolls, and Jill Sobule.

That he has also contributed so much to the future of visual and technological creativity is an added measure of Rundgren's energy and talents. It was back in 1974, long before the idea would occur to most other musicians, that Rundgren first merged computer-generated electronic music, video images, and rock 'n' roll on national television, and on tour with his band Utopia.

Among Rundgren's landmark achievements:

* In 1978, he organized and performed the first interactive television concert on the QUBE network.

* In 1981, Rundgren's video of "Time Heals" was the first to use compositing of live action with computer-generated graphics. The video was the second video ever broadcast on MTV.

* In 1989, Rundgren generated enough cover graphics associated with the *No World Order* album project to provide for a gallery presentation in Tokyo that year.

* Rundgren has created album covers for the majority of his thirty albums spanning twenty-six years.

* Rundgren continues to support the institutionalization of technology for creative purposes. He has recently put songs from his most recent album, *The Individualist*, on the Internet's World Wide Web so fans can have immediate access to them.

* Rundgren continues to refine the CD+ interactive technologies which combine recorded music with computer graphics, short musical clips, interactive games, and images for consumer interplay.

Rundgren has been labeled an enigma, a genius, a provocateur, and a paradox. His fans regard him as a wizard, a true star. But he shuns the labels and the limelight of guaranteed success for the challenge of the future; and has achieved success in an ongoing focus on continuous innovation and evolution. Paul Fishkin of Bearsville Records, reflecting on Rundgren's penchant for defying classification, said Rundgren is seeking success on his own terms.

Rundgren's take on his own muse is that his musical works are a reflection of his own personal odyssey.

Todd Rundgren was born in Philadelphia on June 22, 1948, and raised in Upper Darby, Pennsylvania, a middle class suburb near Philly. Rundgren's experience with the guitar began at an early age. He dabbled with his father's guitar; occasionally, he played the guitar like a violin. Eventually Rundgren broke the guitar trying to tune it with a pair of pliers. So his parents purchased an inexpensive Japanese-made guitar for him at age eight. The deal included guitar lessons. When lessons ran out, Rundgren continued to experiment with the guitar.

With little happening in school to warrant his attention, he instead focused his energy on music, and became immersed in the Motown and Memphis soul sounds and the British Invasion, along with a rich mix of Philadelphia soul. Rundgren formed his first group, Money, at age sixteen. The band played the usual assortment of frat parties, high school competitions, and local canteen, on occasion dressed in nehru jackets.

After graduating from high school in 1966 at eighteen, with no marketable skill except to play the guitar, Rundgren headed for the New Jersey shore, where he settled in Wildwood, a resort town strewn with clubs and venues for new bands to market their talents. Rundgren met up with a local band, Woody's Truck Stop, which let him set in and play backup guitar. The band found gigs around Philadelphia at the Second of Autumn, the Second Fret and, eventually, by 1967, the Electric Factory, a converted tire warehouse with a psychedelic light show installed.

In his nine months with the band, Rundgren developed his blues guitar-playing style as the backup player. The band members included Alan Miller (lead guitar), who distinguished himself in high school by refusing to cut his hair, thereby being confined to school-by-telephone; Bobby Radeloff (lead vocals), Kenny Radeloff (vocalists and organ), Carson Van Osted (bass), and Rundgren (second guitar).

One story surrounding Rundgren's involvement with Woody's Truck Stop relates how a local Philly high school wanted the band to play its senior prom. When the senior in charge of booking the band tracked Rundgren down at a makeshift rehearsal studio in a converted motorcycle shop, he made it clear to Rundgren that the band would have to wear ties, but minus shirts and jackets!

The band changed personnel regularly, going through some twenty-three members in a three-year period. When the band turned its focus to psychedelics, and thought about moving to the country to "get back to nature," Rundgren left to form his next band, the Nazz.

Rundgren selected the other members of his band from an assortment of local groups. Rundgren and Carson Van Osten knew each other from Woody's Truckstop. (Van Osten had recently completed his degree at the Philadelphia College of Art.) Recruited to fill in the lineup were Robert "Stewkey" Antoni (lead singer and organ player from Elizabeth) and Thom Mooney, (drummer from the Munchkins). The quartet chose the Nazz for its name, from a Yardbirds 45 flip side, "The Nazz Are Blue." In Mod slang of the day, Nazz was loosely translated as the ultimate.

The Nazz debuted in July 1967 at Town Hall in Philadelphia, opening for the Doors. The band also made an early appearance at the Philadelphia Folk Festival in August 1967. The tour program for the festival shows Rundgren nonchalantly poised on a motorcycle; another page shows the Nazz in four live cameo shots, one of each band member. They continued to play in Wildwood, sometimes with only peanut butter to eat and no place to sleep other than the floor of a club.

By the end of summer 1967, the Nazz got some financial backing from the owners of a Philly record store, Bartoff and Warfield. The band practiced extensively in a small apartment above the store. Eventually, Bartoff and Warfield contacted John Kurland, a record promoter who formerly worked with Barbara Streisand. Kurland was in Philly attending a Who concert, and Bartoff and Warfield convinced him to meet the band. On Labor Day 1967, the Nazz met Kurland at his home on Long Island. The band had the look, if not the sound Kurland sought, so he signed the Nazz to a management contract. They set up a studio in the basement of a rented house in Great Neck, New York, where they practiced extensively. The Nazz gigged less frequently at local Philly clubs like the Second of Autumn, and the Cheetah Club in New York City, but only when their managers let them appear.

Michael Friedman and John Kurland managed the group with the intent of building its image as fashionable pop-rockers. Dressed and coifed to the max, the band's appearances in local clubs was somewhat limited by the logic of its managers, who believed that less exposure increased their demand. As it turned out, the band practiced a lot, but actually appeared only at a few local clubs.

The Nazz produced four separate demos at an assortment of studios from late 1967 to early 1968, as they honed their sound for record deals. Four demos have surfaced in the past twenty years on four different labels. Most of these songs were included in refined form on Nazz and Nazz Nazz. On the four demos are a series of rough mixes and versions of Nazz tunes played live in the studio, and two unreleased songs: "It Must Be Everywhere" and "Sidney's Lunch Box," credited to Stewkey.

The Nazz was signed by John Kurland and Michael Friedman in June 1968 to Screen Gems/Columbia (SGC) Records, a subsidiary of Atlantic. The band received an advance of about $100,000. The promotion for the band's debut was formidable. A press kit, containing a promo poster, an eight-page bio, cartoon drawings of each band member, and six photos of the band members, represented hopes for a smash act to challenge the Boston and New York bands, including Ultimate Spinach, Beacon Street Union, and the Velvet Underground. The album, titled simply *Nazz*, appeared in late August 1968. Its ten songs reflected proficient and fresh playing, catchy tunes, and a tip of the hat to a number of British influences, including the Yardbirds, Stones, Beatles, and the Who. An unusual version, the debut album was released with Rundgren counting into the opening cut, "Open My Eyes." This rare album variation is currently valued at $100.

In the U.S., promotion for Nazz succeeded in getting needed visibility for the band. *16 Magazine*, *Cash Box*, and *Hullabaloo* stressed aspects for the band's dress, hair, and attitudes. Some articles spoke of the electricity the band emanated in its live performances. Others focused more on its attire, looks, and vital statistics. The album sold moderately well, based upon the worldwide marketing of the band in Canada, Europe, and Japan. In the U.K., *New Musical Express*, *Variety* and *Record Mirror* hyped the first single, "Hello It's Me"/"Open My Eyes," as well as details on the band's talent in concert. Nazz peaked at #118 in *Billboard* in late 1968.

Nazz singles would eventually appear in eight foreign nations, including Britain, France, Belgium, Spain, Italy, Germany, Japan, and Australia; several include picture sleeves which have become quite collectible. The rarest Nazz single, "Under The Ice" (Japan), came with a photo insert that illustrated the band hanging on a jungle gym in a park. (Valued at $250, its rarity is legendary, even in Japan.)

In November 1968, the Nazz embarked on a trip to London to record their second LP. They met with difficulties in short order. Since John Lennon had been having trouble getting a visa to work in the U.S. over his anti-war activities, the British Musician's Union denied Nazz's request to record in the U.K. The union claimed that the band had misrepresented itself as an instrumental group when, in fact, the group actually both played and sang. So, after purchasing some British fashions, the Nazz returned to the U.S. with only one song, "Christopher Columbus," recorded.

Settling in a Regent Sound Studio in New York, the Nazz resumed recording of some twenty-four tracks, sufficient music for a two-record album. Its working title was *Fungo Bat*. Other cuts were mastered in Hollywood. It was to be a diverse collection consisting of romantic ballads ("Only One Winner"), tight rock songs ("Forget All About It"), and expansive classical-oriented tunes ("A Beautiful Song"). The acetates of *Fungo Bat* reveal additional long blues pieces and one unique unreleased song, "Sing You A Song."

Rundgren also performed lead vocals on five songs; his vocal tracks were replaced by Stewkey's voice when Rundgren left the Nazz in 1969. Released in April 1969, the fragments of *Fungo Bat* became *Nazz Nazz*, a single LP. The songs "Not Wrong Long"/"Under the Ice" were released on a single.

The first issue of *Nazz Nazz* was pressed on red vinyl, followed by a more limited pressing on black vinyl and as a record club issue. The album peaked at #80 in May 1969.

The Nazz toured the East coast and the South, reaching Dallas in summer of 1969 to play at the Dallas International Pop Festival. (Led Zeppelin also appeared on the bill during their first American tour.) The Nazz's set was interrupted by rain and a less than adequate sound system. A few fans recall the band playing in New Orleans and Corpus Christi that year, with Rundgren still present on guitar.

Eventually, personality differences led to discord and low morale in the band. This led to the departure of the bass player, Carsen Van Osten, followed by Rundgren. A tour band made up of Philly musicians Greg Simpler (bass) and Craig Bolan (guitar) joined with Stewkey and Mooney to finish out the tour of the Southwest states until mid-1970. Stewkey would persist for a number of months by linking with an Illinois-based band called Fuse.

(Stewkey and some members of Fuse later moved to Philadelphia and reconvened as Sick Man of Europe, which included future members of Cheap Trick. The group's demos would be bootlegged as *Retrospective Foresight*, a collection of tunes misrepresented as "Nazz outtakes.")

Van Osten eventually went to work for Walt Disney studios as an artist and comic book designer. Mooney also moved to California, where he played with Wally Bryson in Bamboo and, some time later, linked up with Rita Coolidge's band. A third album, *Nazz III*, was released in May 1971 as a collections of outtakes and remaining cuts from the *Nazz Nazz* sessions two years before. The single released, "Some People"/"Magic Me," appeared primarily as a white label promotion of *Nazz III*. Few stock copies of the latter were pressed, making it the rarer U.S. Nazz single, currently valued at $80. The Nazz was history.

Meanwhile, Rundgren began to learn the trade of production and engineering. Albert Grossman, manager of Janis Joplin and Bob Dylan, hired Rundgren as the resident engineer/producer for his management company, and provided a studio,

Bearsville, in upstate New York for Rundgren to work. Rundgren engineered or produced a diverse group of local and West coast bands: the American Dream, Jericho, Halfnelson, Janis Joplin, Libby Titus, and a Tennessee artist named Jesse Winchester. As Rundgren's proficiency at mixing and recording improved, he was provided an opportunity to record his own LP.

Called *Runt*, the collection provided a single, "We Gotta Get You A Woman," that received wide airplay across the U.S., reaching #20 in Billboard in November 1970. The album contained hard rock ("Devil's Bite"), spacy experimental tunes ("There Are No Words"), and love songs ("Believe In Me"). Runt sold only 50,000 units, but got favorable reviews. *Rolling Stone* complimented Rundgren for his engineering skill in its review of *Runt* in October 1970. A *Crawdaddy* reviewer saw *Runt* as "difficult to categorize, less for its limited complexities than its subtle eccentricities and stylized point of view."

The music reflected a white pop consciousness and a bluesy, wistful air. Three versions of the Ampex *Runt* were eventually pressed and issued. The most common version, pressed in May 1970, Ampex pressed a version with two additional songs, "Say No More" and "Hope I'm Around," and an extended version of "Baby Let's Swing" with a verse devoted to singer Laura Nyro. To complicate the matter even more, a few copies of a third version were pressed with just one extra song, "Say No More," on side two in late 1970. The version with two extra cuts is currently valued at $60; and the one extra cut version at $75, respectively, based upon rarity. Bearsville reissued *Runt* in 1971 with the original ten-song pressing on the Bearsville label.

Rundgren signed a recording contract with Bearsville Records in 1971, to be distributed by Warner Brothers. That year, he began recording his next album for Ampex/Bearsville at Bearsville studio in Woodstock, New York. Titled *The Ballad Of Todd Rundgren*, the cover portrayed Rundgren in a solitary mood, sitting forlornly at the piano with a hangman's noose around his neck. The music reflected a romantic artist infused with a tone of irony and mischief. Released as singles were "Be Nice To Me" (Ampex 10002), followed by "A Long Time, A Long Way To Go" (Ampex 10004).

A curious variation of the second single was created with an alternate flip, "Long Flowing Robe," on a few hundred promotional copies. Intended as a promotional coup to encourage airplay, the idea bombed, as neither song reached the ears of the AM radio community. In an ironic twist, Bearsville Records' promotion coordinator Marc Nathan and the Bearsville staff flew most of the alternate singles out the second story window of a rented house, thus creating more scarce collectors items in those few discs that remained in radio station archives. Only three copies are known to have survived destruction. *Ballad* sold only 15,000 units, amid ecstatic reviews in *Rolling Stone* and *Rock*, the lowest-selling album of Rundgren's career.

Runt was primarily a studio group. For a brief tour with the band called Runt, Rundgren recruited Tony Sales and N.D. Smart to support him at several gigs. Tommy Cosgrove and Stu Woods, two blues players, and Marc Klingman joined Rundgren on the tour. One of the concerts was broadcast live by WMMR from Sigma Sound Studio on June 30, 1971. It was to be his first of twenty-eight live concerts simulcast over radio waves in the next twenty years.

The band was not flashy, but lyrically strong and melodic, according to *Fusion* magazine that year. Patti Smith assessed Rundgren's music as a personal statement, a solo vision, in a review in

Rock Magazine in July 1971. Rundgren continued to engineer and produce artists for Bearsville and Capitol Records, including the James Cotton Blues Band, Moogy Klingman, Badfinger (Straight Up), and the Band (Stage Fright).

Meanwhile, Rundgren continued to lay and produce his own music. He has been in the studio for most of 1971. According to Rundgren, the forthcoming album was about "what that experience (of recording music) does to your head." The twenty-three songs, recorded at the Record Plant in New York, became a two-record set for Bearsville, which was to become his musical tour-de-force for its variety, creativity, and musicianship. Titled *Something/Anything?*, it would become Rundgren's largest-selling album. The leadoff single, "I Saw The Light," was promoted with a light blue vinyl version. In all, *Something/Anything?* generated four singles: "Hello It's Me," "I Saw The Light," "Wolfman Jack," and "Couldn't I Just Tell You." The fiery guitar tune, "Black Maria," was included on a 1972 three-song EP in the U.K.

The album was marketed in the music press with a picture of Rundgren holding a stick of dynamite, with a challenge: "Go Ahead, Ignore Me." Radio stations and record stores received special versions of the album pressed in a translucent red and blue vinyl, encouraging airplay. (These very limited pressings are now valued at $250.) Rundgren also produced a promotional album, *The Todd Rundgren Radio Show* to provide an audio history of his musical career. (It's valued at $200.) *Something/Anything?* peaked at #29 in *Billboard* in summer, 1972.

Rundgren began touring to support *Something/Anything?* in April 1972. For five shows, Rundgren opened for Alice Cooper; for two shows, Van Morrison; and for other stops on the tour, the Jeff Beck Group. His backup band was a six-member mime group, the Hello People. The reviews of the show were mixed, with Rundgren being characterized as loose, entertaining and likable. High regard for Rundgren's guitar playing was evident. But in Boston, he was booed off the stage by overzealous Jeff Beck fans. The album went gold in February 1975, having sold 500,000 units on the strength and variety of the songs.

In late 1972, Rundgren returned to the newly-built Secret Sound Studio in New York City to begin production of his next album. Titled *A Wizard , A True Star*, it was a substantial departure from the expectations of the rock world for another *Some-thing/Anything?*. Rundgren designed the surrealistic album cover from a cryptic painting he saw in a gallery window on New York street. Rundgren explained the departure as "the first time that I reflected truly personal attitudes in terms of things that I like to hear."

The album was labeled as radical, bizarre, and electric by a number of reviewers. Fans heard the music differently. "Todd Rundgren is a wizard, (the reviewer) is a doorknob," commented a fan in Rolling Stone. Patti Smith called Rundgren's new music, "Rock and Roll for the skull" in *Circus* magazine. *Wizard* was released in March 1973, and sold 150,000 units, peaking at #86 in *Billboard*. A curious variation of the album cover was released in Holland, printed with a lime green cover, with graphics that were color complements of the U.S. album cover. This Dutch variation of *Wizard* is now valued at $75.

In 1973, Rundgren found time to tour with a new band, including Moogy Klingman (organ), David Mason (bass), M. Frog, aka Jean Yves Labat (Moog synthesizer), and the Sales brothers. Initially marketed as Todd Rundgren's Utopia, they soon shortened their name to Utopia.

On tour, Rundgren's hair was now tinted in a variety of colors, which did not go unnoticed by fans and reviewers along the tour. It elicited strong reactions both ways. Observed in Chicago that year, sporting flashy clothes, the band members were visibly awesome. "Jean Yves Labat is sporting a bright lime green do, Hunt Sales has had his sharply skunked, his brother Tony's (Sales) is day-glo pink, while Todd's is every color they have a name for and then some." (*Creem*, Nov. 1974)

In concert, Utopia concentrated on the theatrical element in the performances. Initially, the tour was to run for three weeks. Tour dates included Philadelphia, C.W. Post College on Long Island; Buffalo, New York; Cleveland, Ohio (where they played live in the studio over WMMS-FM); Cincinnati (another live simulcast on WKRQ); Massey Hall in Toronto, Canada; and Chicago at Crown Erie. The tour was cut short due to technical factors, because of the weakening of Rundgren's voice. "I was going to pull it off the road anyway to get some technical things together. But once I pulled it off I got to thinking. I decided that I didn't want to be just another glitter rocker. I didn't want to be considered another standard rock 'n' roll act. We got mixed response to the show, but a lot of the old fans were shocked and frightened, so I decided

I'd have to smarten 'em up a little—bring them around to a different attitude—to re-educate my audience." (*Rolling Stone*, August 16, 1973)

Rundgren also found time in 1973 to produce a number of other bands, including the Hello People, Moggy Klingman, Fanny, the New York Dolls, and Grand Funk. Of those experiences, Rundgren's reflections on the New York Dolls and Grand Funk were ambivalent: "The Dolls were the first of a whole set of New York groups who were springing up at the time, and I felt that as their album was the first, and therefore, most important product to come from that whole scene, it better be at least half-decent—and I succeeded. The Dolls themselves were only barely capable of a half-decent effort anyway. I always had to keep the first take that wasn't literally offensive to the ears, and that first album was in fact more than half-decent."(*NME*, September 14, 1974)

The combination of drug abuse in the band, a management that did not support the band's image in New York, and insistence by the band that it participated in Rundgren's final mixing of the album, all led to a less-than-ideal working situation for Rundgren.

The Grand Funk production experience was more satisfying to Rundgren. He was interested in the "We're an American Band" project because the band had received less that adequate production in the past, and had been the focus of poor reviews among music critics for their muddled mix on previous albums. So Rundgren agreed to produce the band. His recollection of Grand Funk was that of a professional band that had written the songs for the album and practiced them extensively before entering the studio to record the album. The result was a successful production of a highly listenable album with solid musicianship that sold well, earning a gold record in 1973.

Bearsville had agreed to re-release Rundgren's two Ampex albums as a two-fer budget album called *Todd Rundgren's Rack Job*. All that emerged from the *Rack Job* idea was a cover slick, a photograph of Rundgren roaming the sultry streets of New York in summer. But the project was not to be completed. It was not until 1987 that *Runt* and *Ballad* would be reissued on vinyl and compact disc in the United States.

Rundgren's next album, titled *Todd*, required some negotiating with Warners, his record company. Warners had wanted a single album—the energy shortage had made vinyl an expensive commodity. Rundgren had produced enough new music for a two-record set. Warners proposed to cull some hits from the *Todd* masters, and release them as a single LP. In exchange, Rundgren offered an album of new material from a new band.

But it became more and more difficult negotiating with the record company. *Todd* was released on February 14, 1974. The album included a computer graphic of Rundgren, composed of the names of all the fans who sent in a postcard included in the *A Wizard, A True Star* album the year before. *Todd* contained elements of his early hits like "A Dream Goes On Forever" (romantic ballad), "Izzat Love" (a sugary love song which Rundgren refused to release as a single), along with complex electronic experiments like "Everybody's Going To Heaven," and the down dirty blues tune, "Number 1 Lowest Common Denominator." Sales were good, but not brisk. Todd would peak at #54, and would eventually sell 200,000 units.

Rundgren offered a new LP of material in October 1974 by his reconfigured version of Todd Rundgren's Utopia. He reasoned that his voice would be better supported by a group that could assist on vocals, allowing him the flexibility to devote his energy to theatrics and guitar playing. The new configuration of Utopia included Moogy Klingman (organ and vocals) and members of his band, the Rhythm Kings: Ralph Schuckett (keyboards and vocals), John Siegler (bass and vocals), and Kevin Ellman (drums and vocals), and Jean Yves Labat (Moog), who had released a synthesizer album on Bearsville in 1973.

The first tour date of the second Utopia tour was Vermillion, South Dakota. On this tour, Rundgren opened with a solo set, playing selections from the *Todd* album. After intermission, the Utopia band played new material from the Utopia album, including the "Utopia Theme," "Freedom Fighters," "Freak Parade," and "The Ikon." Playing music that combined expansive classical movements, complex harmonies and utopian themes, Utopia was compared by some to Yes; by others to Mahavishnu Orchestra. The *Utopia* album reached #34 in *Billboard* in November 1974.

By late that year, the rainbow of hair-colors was gone, according to Rundgren, "for practical reasons, for now." Roger Powell would replace the jazz-focused and increasingly erratic M. Frog Labat on synthesizers in October 1974. Powell had released *Cosmic Furnace* on Atlantic Records in 1973, an innovative solo album on which he demonstrated his mastery of electronic composition with his "Fourneau cosmique—the alchemical furnace of Cleopatra." Powell was respected for his creativity in the development of synthesized music on ARP and Moog, and recognized for his proficiency in playing a variety of synthesizers in harmony.

The Utopia band began a tour of the United Kingdom in October 1975; the band played five concerts at concert halls across Britain, including one at Hammersmith Odeon on October 9, 1975 that was recorded live for the BBC Rock Hour. British reviews were very positive, as Rundgren's musicianship, humor, and theatrics entertained the U.K. fans. During the U.K. tour, Rundgren's candid and outspoken remarks on the state of contemporary music, and the decline of rock music in particular, were printed in a number of U.K. music publications, raising the ire of a handful of British music critics; and the avid interest of a growing number of U.K. fans.

Songs recorded live in 1974-75 at several U.S. and Canadian concerts were released as the band's next album, *Another Live*, in 1975. A highlight of the album, "The Seven Rays," reflected in its lyrics the Utopian optimism:

"Red—the ruler seeking freedom; Gold—the father seeking unity; Orange—the thinker seeking understanding; Yellow—the poet seeking harmony; Green—the scientist seeking truth; Blue—the disciple seeking goodness; Indigo—the artist seeking beauty."— "The Seven Rays."(1974)

The British version of *Another Live* was designed with a cover photograph of Rundgren playing live onstage from the first U.K. tour. This album variation is currently valued at $45.

Initiation, Rundgren's solo production for 1975, was marketed by Bearsville with a flyer inserted in promo copies which conveyed the message to "stand up for what you believe in." The first single, "Real Man," became a success after Utopia's appearance on The Midnight Special in 1975. Rundgren also sang a mantra-like solo meditation, "Born To Synthesize," in another segment of the show. "Real Man" became a Top AM hit in Cleveland, and was played on FM radio in other U.S. markets, including Boston, Philadelphia, and New York.

Upon the departure of Kevin Ellman, Rundgren recruited John "Willie" Wilcox, a jazz-focused drummer who he knew from Hall and Oates's War Babies recording session. Ellman had left to pursue his Buddhist faith. Moogy Klingman left the band in

fall 1975 to produce Bette Midler. Then Ralph Schuckett resigned. Rundgren selected three backup singers, led by a then unknown Luther Vandross, to beef up the vocal support.

Rundgren's solo release for 1976, Faithful, was a mix of melodic and diverse songs, with one side devoted to cover versions of Hendrix, Beach Boys, Yardbirds, and Dylan tunes, and a side of diverse original tunes which were straightforward and honest. It became traditional for Rundgren to play "Love of The Common Man" and "Cliché" from Faithful at live shows well into the 1980s. The plain white cover represented a spartan strategy that was utilized on the tour that year, as Utopia played in white, loose outfits, thereby focusing more attention to the music. "Black And White" and "When I Pray" were highlights of the Utopia tour that year. John Siegler left the band in 1976 to get married.

Later in 1976, Utopia produced a series of instrumental tunes for a project titled, *Disco Jets*. The collection of songs included an expansive musical piece, "Mad Men and Metal Machines," driven by Roger Powell's synthesizers and harmonic vocals. The project was not finalized for release, and has become somewhat of a mystery among Utopia fans.

By its second visit to the U.K. in August 1976 to play at the Knebworth Festival, the Utopia band had attracted a number of fans to the Utopian ideal, and raised the eyebrows of some acerbic U.K. reviewers. The critics did not know what to make of Rundgren, whose theatrical antics onstage and strong philosophical views in the British music press were viewed by some critics as both confrontational and quirky. Rundgren's criticism of the solo Beatles' recent music and John Lennon in particular had fed the controversy surrounding Rundgren's views during and after the 1975 tour. Lennon's tongue-in-cheek response to Rundgren's comments in *Melody Maker* (see sidebar) had fed the fire.

So a wide range of curious, devoted and amused fans flocked to Knebworth on August 21, 1976. Other bands playing that day included 10cc, Lynyrd Skynyrd, and the Rolling Stones. Utopia performed a rousing set of tunes from Faithful, and their upcoming album, *Ra*. The Utopia set at Knebworth was enthusiastically reviewed by Pete Makowski in Sounds.

A most ambitious set and sound, the album *Ra* took the Utopian band to a more technological level. Rundgren described *Ra* as a "soundtrack to a pyramid stage show." A large eighteen-foot golden sphinx, affectionately named Maurice by the band, was the backdrop for Utopia on the road. Incorporating an Egyptian motif, the band played unique instruments ranging from an Ankh-shaped guitar to a Probe (hand-held) synthesizer keyboard, designed by Roger Powell, which controlled five synthesizers located offstage. The $2 million stage show was well-received by a growing number of fans, enamored by the Egyptian stage set, and kinetic atmosphere generated by the band. The newly configured Utopia included bassist Kasim Sulton (a studio engineer who sang with the New York City band Cherry Vanilla), Willie Wilcox, and Roger Powell.

Utopia highlighted the *Ra* Tour with a series of four Japanese shows in December 1976. Rundgren was profiled and interviewed by that country's *Music Life* for its December 1976 issue. Utopia would return to Japan in January 1979 during the Adventures World Tour, and several times during the 1980s and '90s. The Japanese continue to be strong supporters of Utopia, as reflected in a fan-sponsored publication, *One World*, currently at issue #30.

Rundgren and Utopia began a European tour on January 11, 1977, playing shows in Sweden, France, Germany, and Holland. While in Germany, Utopia played a concert live at the Rockpalast, which was transmitted across western Europe on public television. Utopia played dates in the U.K. on four college campuses in late January, beginning at Oxford Polytech on January 25. That lively concert showcasing the *Ra* album was recorded and aired in December 1977 on the BBC Rock Hour.

The band also played at the Glasgow Apollo, and in London at the New Victoria Theater. A reviewer of the New Victoria shows in *New Musical Express* highlighted Rundgren's humor and animated performances on melodic tunes from *Wizard* and *Faithful*, but was chagrined with the bombatic emissions of the band as Utopia played songs from the "blitzkrieg bog" of *Ra*. Witnessed in the lobby during the two shows were members of the Sex Pistols and the Damned, "looking bored." (*NME*, February 12, 1977)

Rundgren produced a debut album, *Bat Out Of Hell*, by a large Texan named Meat Loaf in 1977. Rundgren was amazed when the album went gold, then platinum, then platinum again and again and again. To date, *Bat Out Of Hell* has reportedly sold

twenty-three million albums worldwide, certainly Rundgren's most successful production and one of the best-selling albums of all time, despite its peak position of #14 upon its initial release.

Oops! Wrong Planet followed in the fall of 1977. A balanced mix of songs from all of the band members, *Oops!* was described by Roger Powell as "an Armageddonish earth-on-the-skids opera." Kasim Sulton's vocals added dimension to the band's sound on "The Martyr." Powell stepped out on "Abandon City." Rundgren reprised a bluesy growl in "Love In Action" and "Trapped." Recently reissued on a Mobile Fidelity Ultradisc, it retains its power pop/Blade Runner ambiance.

In March 1978, Rundgren produced a strong album of melodic songs and angst-heavy tunes, *Hermit Of Mink Hollow*. He reflected at the time that after touring with Utopia for two years, he was inclined to take a break from the band to record a solo record on which he played all of the instruments. Rather than reflect a theme, the album included high harmonic tunes ("All The Children Sing"), intensely emotional songs ("Too Far Gone"), and defiant anthems ("Determination"). *Hermit* was promoted with the single "Can We Still Be Friends." The song would be covered by Colin Blunstone (1979) and Rod Stewart (1984). The Canadian versions of *Hermit* were pressed in both red and green vinyl, making these pressings collectible at $25 today.

Later in 1978, Rundgren was asked by Paul Fishkin, Bearsville Records president, if he would be interested in re-recording a collection of his previous songs live on the road in venues like the Bottom Line in New York and Roxy in L.A. for a retrospective album. The product of those shows was released as the two-album *Back To The Bars*. A reprise of the Nazz song "Hello It's Me" became a hit for the third time.

Rundgren was joined by Stevie Nicks and Hall and Oates at the Roxy in L.A. that spring for a simulcast on the King Biscuit Flower Hour. Several of the tour shows were broadcast over local radio links and via national radio. Rundgren and Utopia traveled to the U.K. in December 1978 to play a week-long engagement at the London Venue. One of the concerts was to be broadcast throughout the U.K. over BBC Radio, another was to be broadcast in Europe via Radio Luxembourg, and a third was to be televised internationally. (*Rolling Stone*, April 5, 1979). Due to a dispute with the British Musician's Union, however, these "Back to the

Bars" shows were not broadcast by the BBC. Rundgren filed suit in 1979, disputing the union action and the suit was settled in 1982.

Rundgren and Utopia returned again to the U.K. in August 1979 to play two shows at the Knebworth Festival. Other artists appearing were the Commander Cody Band, Southside Johnny and the Asbury Jukes, and Led Zeppelin. Utopia received an enthusiastic reception from the concert-goers, playing music from *Oops! Wrong Planet* and *Faithful*.

In 1979, Rundgren and Utopia played a benefit for the Vietnamese boat people at the International Relief Committee (IRC) Concert in New York. He would take part in a dozen benefits for environmental, voter registration, and humanitarian causes over the next twelve years.

The next Utopia album, *Adventures In Utopia* (1980), took the best elements of the Ra Tour and turned them into an extended road trip with Utopia. The tour and heavy promotion produced three singles, and three videos on the newly-burgeoning MTV: "Set Me Free," "You Make Me Crazy," and "Love Alone." Utopia made several appearances on television, including the Mike Douglas and John Davidson variety shows. *Adventures* reached #32 on the *Billboard* chart by mid-1980, making *Adventures* Utopia's most successful album. A limited Australian album variation pressed on red vinyl has become a scarcity, valued at $100.

Rundgren produced a variety of artists in the late 1970s, including Hall and Oates, Patti Smith, Tom Robinson Band, Rick Derringer and the Tubes. Rundgren reflected on some of his varied production duties: "To be at the helm of some of those crazed Nazi ghost ships sometimes is a heavy responsibility."(*Collage*, Sept.1980)

Riding the success of the *Ra* and *Adventures* tours, Utopia played a concert in November 1979 that was recorded and later distributed by the NBC Source Radio Network to radio stations for broadcast on January 1, 1980 as the "First Concert of the Decade."

Ever prolific, Rundgren designed a parody on the Beatles, with a set of heavily British songs, in October 1980, titled *Deface The Music*. The inspiration for the album originated when Utopia was asked to provide a song for a movie, *Roadie*. When the song "I Just Want To Touch You" was considered "too Beatlesque," and not used, the band was inspired to create an entire album of "'60s British-style tunes." For the tour, members of Utopia dressed in Beatlesque attire, and played like the Fab Four. The tongue-in-cheek effort was humorously received by fans on the tour. The single, "I Just Want To Touch You" appeared around the world. The Australian release of the single was pressed on light blue vinyl, with a blue wrap-around sleeve; a rare version, today valued at $40. Utopia played a Halloween 1980 concert promoting the *Deface The Music* album, which was broadcast across the entire United States live.

The Japanese release of "I Just Want To Touch You" from *Deface* has an unusual picture insert that superimposes the heads of band members on Beatle-era suits. Powell's head appears twice: once with short hair, and once with a Prince Valiant cut. In addition, Willie Wilcox is conspicuously absent on the sleeve, a comical oversight.

For his next solo effort, in early 1981, Rundgren produced a set of songs which focused on a theme of personal choice and philosophical insight, called *Healer*, which met with some controversy by elements of the Christian right that year. From *Healer* came the single "Tiny Demons." "Time Heals," an innovative video which combined computer images imposed with live human actions, received heavy airplay on MTV. In Europe, the single "Compassion" was popular in Spain and Holland.

Rundgren produced an autobiographical video, *The Ever Popular Tortured Artist Effect*. The video was eventually released on Passport Video in 1983, along with a retrospective video collection, and a live Utopia concert from 1981 at the Royal Oak Theater in Detroit.

Swing To The Right (1982) was a pop collection of tunes that addressed the '80s' indulgences head on. It was initially rejected by Bearsville, which wanted a more Rundgren-sounding album. Rundgren insisted on defending the album as a band effort. An agreement was reached whereby the *Swing To The Right* album would be released as a Utopia album, releasing Utopia from the Bearsville label. Rundgren agreed to produce two additional solo albums. The single releases from *Swing*, "One World" and "Hideaway," got extensive FM play that summer.

A cover song from *Swing*, "For the Love of Money" (the O'Jays hit), carries an interesting anecdote. Joe Tarsia, producer at Sigma Sound Studio in Philadelphia, commented in a 1992 interview that "For the Love of Money" utilized bass licks and drum and vocal effects that were inspired by Rundgren during the 1968 recording Nazz. "He was the instigator for me to record 'For the Love of Money' the way I did—Some day I'd like to tell him, 'You didn't copy the O'Jays. You copied yourself,'" Tarsia commented. (*Philadelphia Daily News*, 8/14/92)

Rundgren visited the U.K. in March 1982 to play a set at Whistle Test Studio, following settlement of the Musician Union dispute. In April 1982, Rundgren returned to the U.K. for a tour of small clubs, marketed as the "Man and His Piano" tour. The concert, which reprised songs from *Something/Anything?* to *Swing To The Right*, received very good press reviews; and Rundgren was interviewed in the British press, and by the BBC.

In *New Musical Express*, Rundgren reflected on his own lifestyle: "I think that the things I'm involved in, the kind of things that I do, and the ideas that I have, are as accessible and as fascinating as anyone's in music. It's not my loss if no one discovers it. I'm living it all the time. I have more important priorities. By the time people discover where I am, if they ever do, I'll be someplace else anyway. So it's more important to me that I evolve rather than crystallize to the point where everyone goes, 'Oh, yes, I understand now.' If I crystallize so that they understand, I will have lost something that is of prime importance to me."(NME, April 24, 1982)

Utopia negotiated a new contract with the Network Label in 1982. The band soon delivered a new album of songs simply titled *Utopia*; fans know the album as the "Network Album." Promoted well, the album reached #84 on the Billboard albums chart, and produced two singles, "Feet Don't Fail Me Now" and "Hammer In My Heart." The marketing effort by Network led to a substantial road show, but Network could not continue as a record company after this album release, and Utopia found itself without a record company again.

Utopia signed with the Passport label for its next three albums: *Oblivion* (1983), *POV* (1984), and *Trivia* (1985). From *Oblivion* came "Crybaby," a futuristic doomsday video which received airplay on MTV. From *POV* came "Mated," a love song. An unreleased song, "Man Of Action," appeared as the B-side in the U.K. The *POV* acronym's meaning elicited a variety of possible options, from "Point of View" to "Persistence of Vision." Utopia continued to tour the U.S. to promote the Passport albums. *Trivia*, a compilation album, included two unreleased songs, "Fix Your Gaze (a powerful guitar-driven rocker) and "Monument," a love anthem.

Rundgren's next solo album reflected in its title his growing disenchantment with record companies; he called it *The Ever Popular Tortured Artist Effect*. Rundgren released "Bang The Drum All Day" as the single, a song he dreamed in his sleep. It turned out to be another of Rundgren's most popular songs. Utopia toured extensively throughout the U.S. from 1982-84.

Rundgren utilized computer-generated rhythms and human voices on his next solo effort, *A Cappella*, in 1985. Initially held up by Bearsville, the album was bootlegged before Warner Brothers agreed to release it as the final product due under Rundgren's extended contract with Bearsville. "Something To Fall Back On" was released as the single in both 7-inch and 12-inch versions in the U.S. and the U.K. "Johnny Jingo" was released with a unique picture sleeve in Germany. On tour, an "11-Voice Orchestra," a group of talented professional singers, provided the rhythms and vocals, with minimum musical accompaniment. One A Cappella show was recorded and broadcast on the King Biscuit Flower Hour in late 1985.

In 1987, Rhino Records began reissuing all of Rundgren's catalog on vinyl and compact disc. In all, twenty-three albums, many long out-of-print, were made available to fans again. Included were the rare Nazz LPs, the Ampex solo albums, all of Rundgren's Bearsville releases, and Utopia's albums. The Japanese *Music Magazine* profiled Rundgren's musical archives in October 1987. A special issue of the Japanese Record Collector Magazine profiled Rundgren collectible memorabilia in February-March, 1988.

In the late 1980s, Rundgren produced or played on musical products by artists including Jim Steinman, the Psychedelic Furs, XTC, Jules Shear, and Laura Nyro. He contributed songs to tribute albums for Thelonious Monk and Kurt Weill.

Rundgren became focused once again on recording live music. For his next album, *Nearly Human* (1989), Rundgren convened a group of singers for a series of recording sessions to be produced and recorded live in the studio. The album generated three singles, including "The Want Of A Nail" (with Bobby Womack)," "Can't Stop Running" (a song Rundgren composed as an Olympic Games tune), and "Parallel Lines," a song from the musical *Up*

Against It, based upon the screenplay for the unreleased Beatles' third film by Joe Orton. The Nearly Human Tour was well-attended by Rundgren's network of fans, who supported the upbeat atmosphere, harmonic vocals, and spirited playing of the tour band.

In 1991, Rundgren returned to the live recording approach with his album *Second Wind*. Rundgren's tour that year showcased his affinity for theater and live harmonies. An imaginative video, "Change Myself," superimposed computer-generated graphics with human actions and was aired on VH-l.

Utopia reunited in May 1992 for a brief tour which took them to Japan in June for a Utopia Redux Tour. The Tokyo concert was released by Rhino on CD, as well as on video and laser disc. The kinetic performance who cased the band's precise timing and strong vocal harmonies as they opened with "Fix Your Gaze," and moved quickly through "Windows," Trapped," and a reprise of songs from the seven Utopia albums which showcased the band's talents in live performance.

Later in summer 1992, Rundgren joined Ringo Starr and his All Starr Band on the road for a number of shows. Members of the band at various shows included Joe Walsh, Burton Cummings, Dave Edmunds, Nils Lofgren, and some special guests, including Kasim Sulton at the Waterloo Village, New Jersey show. Rundgren showcased his guitar prowess on his screaming rendition of "Black Maria," and a lively version of "Bang The Drum."

Rundgren signed with Rhino Records' Forward label in 1992; and produced a set of powerful songs which combined rap, hard rock, and rhythmic electronic motifs. Titled No World Order, this interactive compact disc was a dramatic departure from the mainstream of 1990s rock. Rundgren produced an interactive CD-i version of NWO (the first of its kind), which allowed the listener to select from a variety of song options and sequences while listening to the CD-i. Rundgren toured the U.S., Europe, and Japan for much of 1993-94. Rhino released three singles, "Property," "Fascist Christ," and "Day Job" was also released in an unusual variation as a 12-inch dance single. In a 1993 interview in Seconds, Rundgren reflected that he was in the process of "aggression personal evolution."

In August 1994, Rundgren set up an interactive technological tent, christened the "Todd Pod," on site at the Woodstock '94 festival in New York. He played a series of ten shows, until the rainy weather forced his act to cancel the last four presentations. But those who caught the shows enjoyed the performances, which included dancer Michelle Gay and guitarist Jesse Gress at some of the shows, as well as the interactive video messages.

In 1995, Rundgren released *The Individualist*, his most recent solo album, on the Pony Canyon label in Japan. *The Individualist* was released in the U.S. on cassette last September. An enhanced CD version of the album was released in December 1995, which allowed listeners to experience video versions of the songs, and to select alternate versions and sequences of the songs.

In the 1990s, Rundgren has produced or arranged music by artists including Hiroshi Takano, the Pursuit of Happiness, Paul Shaffer, Jill Sobule, and Meat Loaf.

A two-CD collection of Rundgren's songs performed by other musicians, *Still There's More*, was released by Third Lock Records in 1995. This collection was a follow-up to the fan-generated tribute CD, *For The Love Of Todd*, released by Third Lock in 1991.

After extensive Japanese and U.S. tours last summer, Rundgren began making arrangements to build a recording studio in Hawaii. He is taking a hiatus from touring to devote energy to his computer and technological interests. His radio show, The Difference, is currently broadcast weekly over thirty-five radio stations nationwide. Rhino Records is currently compiling a collection of Rundgren's rare recordings for a retrospective boxed set scheduled for release this summer.

Goldmine: *In your first formal rock group, the Nazz, you apparently did a lot of practicing. Was that the result of your limited visibility, or of seeking a record deal?*

Todd Rundgren: In those days, there weren't home studios, and if you wanted to get signed, you had to do it on the basis of your performance skills. The only break is that you didn't have to sing the vocals at the same time. Most people who went into the studio to make a demo had to be able to perform the song. The Nazz, when we first got together, had to rehearse over a record store on Chestnut Street in Philadelphia. We were managed, in a manner of speaking, by the men who owned the record store. They were real nice to us, and gave us the space above the record store to practice in.

I would say that we did a reasonable amount of practicing. The material we first started out with was often used as a springboard for some kind of jamming thing. Songs became free works for extended jams. But as time went on, we started evolving a little bit more of an actual song style. We actually were not on an aggressive "let's go get a record contract" campaign. We thought it would be nice; but we really thought we had to win that opportunity through our performances. We got discovered before I think we were ready to make that move. And it was more or less on the basis of our looks.

In other words, the guy had not actually heard us play. Me and Thom Mooney were hanging around in a bar after a Who concert in Philadelphia, and this guy was looking for a band. He was actually the publicist for the Mamas and the Papas, who oddly enough were sharing the bill with the Who. And he just thought we had the look. So he started with the look and then the next day came to hear us play in our little rehearsal space, and he thought we had a serviceable sound.

Was that Michael Friedman or (Nazz manager) John Kurland?

John Kurland, with Michael Friedman with him, came to hear us play. Anyway, from that point, we got this Zvengali treatment; they took a lot of control on where we played and how many times we played. So if we played at all, it was doing a lot of rehearsing. And we started doing the rounds of studio demos. We did some demos independently, to get some people initially interested. And they were engineered by Chris Andersen in some little studio he was using somewhere. And we essentially went through a lot of the stuff we did live. I don't even recall if the vocals were overdubbed, or whether they were done live. One time, I think they literally were performed in the studio.

And I recall we went to a couple of places and worked with several engineers on a few occasions.

Nazz demo discs are from Atlantic Recording Studio, Columbia Records, and National Recording Studios in New York.

The discs could have been recorded on tape at one studio and cut elsewhere, mastered, and relabeled at another studio. We didn't have to do a terrible amount of demoing. We did maybe a total of four demos for various labels.

There were actually songs on the demos that didn't appear on the albums.

Some were songs that weren't originals. When we came to doing the records, we never did songs that weren't originals.

There was a song on the Atlantic Nazz demo that Stewkey apparently wrote, "Sidney's Lunch Box," that didn't appear on the first Nazz LP (1968).

That may not have evolved into anything, or that may have been the working title for something. Some of it was extemporaneous goofing around. By the second album, we were comfortable enough in the studio to just sort of goof around in the basement.

Rhino Records is working on a Todd Rundgren Rarities Box and they are interested in the rare demos that are available. Gary Peterson at Rhino is doing a formidable job of assembling it.

I've located something for him. I was looking for the missing reel for *A Wizard, A True Star* and found a song that was relatively fully-produced that never made it to the record because it was too sappy. I still think it's sappy but it has all of these background vocals that make it interesting.

Your early experiences with Woody's Truck Stop, American Dream, and those early bands extend back to 1965. In a concert program for the Philadelphia Folk Festival there is a photograph of you sitting on a motorcycle, and on another page, the phrase, "NAZZ—What are they doing here?" with pictures of the Nazz band members in the program. Were you aware of that?

No, but I think we may have played the Philadelphia Folk Festival in 1967.

At one time (1984), you guest-DJed on the Rolling Stone *magazine radio show. More recently, you're a DJ in your own right on your syndicated radio show,* The Difference. *Do you have a fondness for working in that context, or do you find that to be some form of distraction?*

Promoting to radio is not a fondness so much as a reality. Everyone does it at some stage of their life, usually early on in their career, and sporadically later on in their career trying to promote something. A couple of shows were fun, like Rockline, a national call-in show where people called in from all over the nation. The shows that are professionally-handled are fun. But often locally you get a DJ who doesn't give a damn. He's been there forever, and has seen everybody who has come through town, so that often can be humiliating.

But in terms of being a DJ, the appeal of that is to expose listeners to music that you think they should hear, and protect them from music that you don't think is worthwhile. In The Difference, I need to be comfortable with what goes on the show. That's the more appealing part.

Could you elaborate on some of those artists that you would like to hear on the radio?

Artists that I've heard once on the radio, or not at all but that I discovered through another channel, all varieties of music. It's kind of fun to discover hip-hop artists, and other artists that are out of character that don't get played; and a Cinco de Mayo show that allows us to play Tito Puente; or St. Patrick's Day—Irish music. Some of the music we play is far off the beaten path, as long as we conform to a level of thematic integrity

In an interview about ten years ago, you referred to the "institutionalization of technology" for creative purposes. Obviously you were far ahead on linkages between technology and music. Do you still feel that technology is a key tool to improve the quality of music or do you believe that "organic" music is preferable.

To me, organic means saxophone, stand-up bass and drums, and no amp at all. There's a lot of subjective latitude in what some folks consider to be organic.

But you tend to balance the high-tech and the quality recording strategy with a real clean natural mix. What allows you to get that fine tone and quality to your recordings rather than muddling them up? How do you do that with bands that normally are not able to get the quality?

I tend not to get involved in projects where the music can't be performed in a way that is interesting without being tarted up all the time. There are certain justifications for production tricks and even certain kinds of ambiances and sonorities to give a record a certain kind of style. But I don't like to go into the studio thinking that I have to make up the difference between the way a band wants to sound. They really have to have a grasp of how to get the sound they want, and then I can put that in a setting that ideally allows you to hear what's going on.

Beyond that, it's bold techniques and methodologies that I've acquired over time that at this point just second nature to me so I don't think about it too much. The objective is to have a song that is worth listening to, to secondly have it performed in a way that is engaging at least, and finally, the thing I worry about least is the sound. Everything else imposes a certain sound on it in the end. That sound is ideally one that is not light years away from what the musicians are actually doing in the first place.

Recordings you worked on that might be considered unique to the public and unique to the artists themselves were XTC's Skylarking *and Hiroshi*

Takano's two LPs from Japan.

There are kinds of similarities. Takano has been very influenced by XTC as one of his favorite artists. That whole XTC thing had some bearing on me getting involved with certain artists. That XTC album was seminal in some ways. It was one of those things where the material suggests everything that happens beyond that. More than any other record that I've worked on, it was a record of details. It really kind of highlighted something that I've always believed, and that is, it's not the grandiose kinds of things as the little details that go on in it that really define the lasting experience.

And so that's found its way over into Takano's records. The albums were done in my studio, and we did the singles in Japan, because the singles would precede the album recordings. And essentially once I get into that environment, I don't even have to think about it much in terms of getting the sound; even if the artist wants to do something radical, it's easy to arrive at. It becomes a question of how much you've experienced in creating a particular sound, in order to create something that's similar in sound to something I created in my own studio (in Woodstock, New York).

Oddly enough, when some artists go back and try and do the same thing, they find it difficult. Part of my problem is that I make it look too easy, partly because I've been doing it so long. And I know what I'm going for and know how to get there. Some artists, particularly the Japanese who have fascination with technology for some reason, think that it can be reduced to some checklist of things that you do. They've often told me that when they go back afterwards, that it doesn't seem like I do anything on the records, and they go back and try to do it, and it becomes an incredible nightmare to do something similar in terms of sound. I don't understand why either. While it seems relatively easy for me, given that in some of these projects, it seems like I'm baby sitting. What the essential difference is, it's something catalytic, not so much obvious as kind of subtle and natural, and very easily overlooked in some way.

You're saying that you facilitate the success of groups without dabbling in what makes them a unique group.

Ideally not. There was a time when my fingers would be all over my productions. It becomes hard afterwards to delegate responsibility—good and bad. After the project's done, you would like to know at least in sonic general terms what the contributing factors were, in case you have to do it again, you know what's involved. In many cases, my influence might be too obvious on a particular part of the record, and the artist will react in varying degrees to that. Some artists will say it's obvious, while others will say, "Hey, that's over the line."

I really want what I do to be recognizable. So my style has evolved to something where I minimize the degree to which I get involved rather than go in desiring to have things changed to something that I've visualized.

We won't get into Andy Partridge's comments over the years, but let's talk about some others you've produced: Jesse Winchester, Tom Robinson Band's Two and Patti Smith's Wave. You're really not clearly fingerprinted on those records, and yet they sound good, whereas others are more easily compared to you, like the later Tubes albums.

A measure of how well-directed the artist is when we go in to do the record. The Tubes records have historically been situations when I come into the life of the band when they are in a state of turmoil, they are kind of up against the wall with a record company that is demanding a record with sonic semblance of commercial possibilities to it, and also the band, when they get into that mode, they kind of get into a dithering state, afraid to make decisions. When that happens, my presence gets much larger and I become more of a member of the band at that point. Nothing would be accomplished otherwise. They get to a point where they just can't finish the song—they have verses but they're just pointless babbling.

It's that way for a lot of people when it comes down to it: You've just got to finish this song. And particularly with a band of players, and a band that has been around for some time and has already expressed their seminal ideas, things just sort of grind to a halt. So someone has to get in there and start making up the difference. My job description is sort of generalized in that way. It really depends on what is necessary for me to do.

That makes it possible for me to become quasi-invisible in some productions, in that all that they ask is quality in the engineering and the final mix, and maybe very little else other than maybe just an outside opinion about what's going on. In other cases, there may be huge amounts of organizational and musical input necessary—string arrangements.

The XTC thing—I had the entire album concept mapped out before we ever recorded a note of it. So it's variable from project to project the degree to which I'm compelled to become involved in the composition and arrangement of the music, rarely any more in the performance of it, but it's certainly possible. In some cases, I would be playing guitar on the record. So it varies from production to production.

At the South-by-Southwest Multimedia Conference in Austin (March 1995), you drew an analogy comparing "Smells Like Teen Spirit" to "More Than A Feeling" to "Louie Louie." Do your own songs connect in a similar way in regard to the comparison of your songs from your early career to more recent creations? In the past, you've said that you sometimes dream your songs.

I have done that, but not all the time. If I get into a state of mind that I'm making a record, that will often happen. Some people would like to imply that there's something extremely mystical about that. In some instances the realization is so complete that it mystifies me as well. But just as revelatory is that the same things have happened when I'm fully awake. Some confluence of events, such as the full realization of how a piece of music is supposed to be, will come to me, and all I have to do is keep that thought alive long enough to get it down.

So dreaming it or having it pop into your head when you're awake are two ways of receiving the same information. It mostly has to do with the state of equipoise that I get in when I'm making a record, which usually involves a degree of isolation for a while, and kind of paring down other things that I have to think about, and concentrating solely on what to me is a process of accumulated ideas. That requires me to not talk, but to listen, essentially to myself. To get someplace where I get some degree of solitude where I start to hear what I really think. And then to find a way to essentially transcribe that.

The thing about music is that it is a very small palate. Musicians are always a product of their influences. A number of factors: one is the limit of the palate. That's because we work with the 12-tone scale. And also because there are cultural limitations on what kind of music you hear, and what kinds of music a population is willing to accept. So you can make some very weird and peculiar music, people indeed do make that, but that's music you make for yourself, because no one wants to hear it. It's no less solid from a musical perspective; it's just that in the realm of commercial art, what actually gets distributed and listened to, you've got a limited area to work in, so every single song you hear on the radio has some two-four drum pattern on it. The rule of thumb is that you will have some two-four or four-four drum pattern in your song.

But you have a sort of complex series of motifs in your library. "Black Maria" is not a simple song. The actual flow of the song goes through a lot of changes.

Syncopations—yeah, every time that song has to be relearned, it's a challenge learning it.

"International Feel" is another one in regards to its innovative sound.

Some of it is just turning beats upside down to make it more interesting. Generally, musical exploration—if I have a drum pattern, what do I have to do with the drum pattern so I don't get too bored with it? In the realm of pop music there are certain rules that you labor under. So you could say that most of my creations could be traced back to a series of songs or pieces of music, songs that along the way have had some big impact on me, and therefore stuck in my mind and had some influence on how I might have written other things.

Like Marvin Gaye, "What's Going On." And that particular era and other associated, slightly earlier Motown acts, like Stevie Wonder. And also there's the Philadelphia thing. All of that influences the kind of music that I do that sometimes dominates my composition and performance, and sometimes falls into the background. You could say that in an album like *Nearly Human*, that's where that influence came full force to the front, and ever since it's been falling into the background again. Sort of that Philadelphia, Motown, R&B influence. When I was a teenager, that's what we heard on the radio. The kind of music I ignored was Brian Hyland and that really "arch-white" music; that silly white music I just had no interest in. So the kind of music I really paid attention to was Philadelphia, or Memphis.

You got to hear a lot of that R&B music on Philadelphia radio.

I was fortunately in a place for music, because it's close enough to the South that a lot of that Memphis-style music could appear on the radio, and some of that Detroit-style music, and some of that hard R&B, but not so far into the South to be a redneck and therefore trying to keep it off the radio, So Philadelphia was a really good area to grow up in, particularly in exposure to black music; Philadelphia has always been a great jazz capital. A lot of great jazz musicians came out of the Philadelphia area. So you could always hear good jazz on the radio.

In the past twenty years, you have occasionally played tribute songs like the Who's "Anyhow, Anyway, Anywhere" and the Mysterians' "96 Tears." Is there any other music that you continue to fall back to as being your derivative music, beside Motown, from the eclectic standpoint?

I always had that influence of classical and show tunes. The reason that I can't get into *Cats, Phantom Of The Opera,* (is that) it's something that parents used to listen to a lot. My dad was not much into pop music a lot—he would not allow it to appear on his turntable. But in return, we had highbrow tastes, actually middlebrow tastes, which was better than highbrow. Otherwise we would have been inundated with Baroque music, which was the most archly-repetitive music there is. I got to hear things like Debussy and Ravel and Bernstein, and Richard Rodgers, and Kismet, and more high/middlebrow music that was available.

What about guitar players of the era? Who did you enjoy listening to?

What I could hear on the radio. Of course, there was Duane Eddy, but he was not a spectacular guitar player; all he did was wiggle that bar around a lot. I really had no real true jazz experience until I was sixteen or seventeen. I started listening to Horace Silver and Bill Evans, and something beyond Jimmy Smith. Jimmy Smith is easy to like. Some jazz is just more bluesy and funky; and, to the uninitiated, a little harder to understand.

I didn't get hip to that until I was sixteen or seventeen. But then I started to get hip to a lot of interesting music that I never heard before because I had a enough money to buy a few records. I wouldn't go down and buy the new Gerry and the Pacemakers; I would go down to the Nonesuch (Records) bin, and find a seventy-nine cent record of Eastern European electronic music. I've always been more fascinated with the exploration of music rather than with settling into a style and minding that for however long the vein holds out.

Are there any recent guitar players that are easy to listen to because of their clarity?

Guitar playing has changed so much. It is a highly technical exercise. But I've heard some music recently that I really enjoyed listening to that was guitar-based. Lyle Workman has played with me, and he did a whole solo album. Now he plays with Frank Black. So he plays a style of guitar that is appropriate to that music. Perhaps as the whole Internet thing expands, his music will find an audience.

You use a lot of percussion. Any particular percussion motifs that you relate to, like Latin America or Far Eastern?

A lot of it is just simple coloration for me. I have no preference for a style of percussion. There are instances where percussion has been used to a great advantage. For example, how percussion is used to color something like "Mysterious Ways," the U2 song, in the context of an electrified pop song. And in "Can't Stop Running" (from *Nearly Human,* 1990), which was supposed to be done with a quasi-international feel to it because it was originally done at the behest of the Olympics. Even though they never used the song, when I did a version in a live band, it kind of evolved. Quasi-collection of instruments and sound, but not one particular ethnicity, just the idea of something of a general tribalism.

"When I Pray" from *Faithful* (1975) was an attempt to elicit a kind of African-Christian thing. I guess it was a precursor to that kind of South African craze, which became big later.

In an interview you did for the San Francisco Chronicle *(5/7/92), you once said that your motivation is based on being deathly afraid of being conditioned. In your career, you tend to make dramatic reversals in direction. The melodicism of* Nearly Human *(1990) to the cacophony of* No World Order *(1992) is an example. Can you reflect on how that occurs.*

I remember a particularly epiphanal moment that I had just after *Something/Anything* (1972) or in that period. I was listening to "I Saw The Light," and I realized that it had taken fifteen minutes to twenty minutes to write the song from beginning to end. And everybody liked it. Everyone was immediately taken by the song. And I suddenly had this horrific feeling of myself being trapped in this existence of some kind of Tin Pan Alley guy who sat down at the piano like Steve Allen. I could see everyone being fascinated by the facility of the thing, but me getting no personal reward out of it, like being a musical trained monkey. Even since, my greatest nightmare is that I wake up and for the past five years, I've been doing this on autopilot. And therefore, it makes it extremely difficult for me to defend what I've done.

This is something that extends to all realms of human endeavor, which is, if you do things without thinking about them, and someone asks, "Why did you do that?" you don't have very good legs to stand on. So I'm always asking myself the musical question, "What is the real reason that you're doing this? Is it because you're learning something? Is it because you're expressing something that you're fixated on that you have to get out? Is it because you're just doing it out of formula? Are you doing it because it's easy for you."

It's not to say that I won't do something out of formula, but I have to know at the time. I have to recognize soon after I've done it, that "Hey, now I know where I got the idea for that. It was this other song that I did three or four or five years ago, and this is its direct antecedent. That was easy, but take it easy, you can't get away with that too often."

I wonder if that is another way of saying, "I keep myself honest, because no one else will."

More or less, yeah. It would be very easy to simply respond to what people respond to. I have some idea of the amount of challenge in any of the musical things I do and the way that people respond to them because there is a degree of challenge in them for me in conceptualizing and performing them. But at the same time, I'm also cognizant of the fact that a lot of the records I have done have not been recognized for what they truly are until some years later, when they're put in the context of a period of musical mutation. Therefore, I don't form strong opinions about the value of the things I do musically They'll fall into their proper perspective as time goes on.

You mentioned recently that not only have you worked on music, but also graphically on your album covers; and you use interactivity in your technical work. Which album covers did you take the most time in designing?

I've always considered the album artwork as being part of the overall expression of the concept; it's the setup, the opening act, the experience of listening to the record. In some cases, it's merely advertising for what's inside; in other cases, it expands on what's inside. In general, it sets a certain tone that often primes the listener for the listening experience. So I've always invested a lot in the covers in one way or another. Not to say that every one represents a crowning achievement in any way, or that there is not some other agenda. I've allowed others to do things on one or two occasions to design the way the cover will come out, and let it be their expression rather than mine, because they have more honesty than the idea that I would have in mind.

But for the most part, I do get highly involved in the generation of the album graphics, to the point that it may be 100% my doing, and in other cases, it may represent the organized contribution of many people. I'd say that *No World Order* (1992) represented a high degree of investment in that we spent weeks on that doing computer graphics, designing and rendering computer graphic pictures that ultimately aren't on the final product. Others are more simple and straight-ahead. The *A Cappella* album (1986) was essentially two photographs and some type.

What about the Wizard, A True Star *LP cover? Did you design that?*

I contracted somebody to do that. I was walking down the street and looked in a gallery that was up near Carnegie Hall, and I saw these paintings that were a combination of very classical painting techniques and these peculiar mystical and geometric elements all jumbled together in weird psychedelic perspectives on things. So I contracted the artist to do the cover, and I actually sat for a while where he did some sketches of me, a little bit of portraiture. Then he did the rest of it more or less without my supervision. He showed me sketches as it evolved as it was going, and I kind of approved the whole thing. The photo session that was inside were a couple of friends of mine who did that themselves. The most I had to do was print out the lyrics.

At the South by Southwest Multimedia Conference presentation in Austin, you mentioned that the CD-ROM would be a short-lived phenomenon. In 1989, you commented that CD-ROM could be useful for music education and for the archives of musical creations over time. Do you see a changing perception of the value and fundamental utility of technology, or are you separating the CD-ROM from what you're currently doing with the interactive element of technology?

Since what I do is principally musical-computers, I have a tough time presenting in traditional music with quality that we expect from a CD player or a video tape deck, or cable television, or other methods of delivery of sound and pictures.

The reason that CD-ROM, as something specific to computers, will be a short-lived phenomenon is because, in the long run, people don't want to be entertained sitting in an office chair. They would rather go to the couch, or sit in their rumpus room. In that sense, as the bandwidth of wire that is connected to your television and your stereo begins to increase, less and less will be necessary to go out and purchase that actual artifact that contains the sounds and pictures on it. You will simply order it up and experience it, and then pay what will probably be a fraction of the normal cost of buying a CD-ROM in a store. What you won't get with it is all the dead trees, the printed material. And a lot of people miss that. But people will have to get used to missing it, because there are going to be fewer and fewer paper products in the world, and that's as it should be, since we've destroyed all of our forests.

There was a song you did in the early '80s that never made it on an album, called "God And Me." Another aspect of that theme on Healing *was a song ("Healer") that positively and deliberately focused on a feeling about God. What would you like to say about the themes of these songs that reflect the spiritual feeling that you have, or is that something that we don't want to talk about?*

None of those reflect a specifically spiritual feeling. I've kind of given up on describing the indescribable, The common thread in all those is what I consider to be the mistake in the course of people trying to get close to God through other people. Like, if you couldn't discover it in yourself, how would you discover it in someone else? That to me is all basically illusory, the idea that you get any greater knowledge of, or more intimate experience of, the truly mystical and spiritual aspect of life by listening to somebody else talk about it or tell you what you're supposed to think about it. To me, that is basically flawed.

Every once in a while the topic comes up in one way or another. In the case of "God And Me," it's specific about the idea that something that's particular to Christianity or religions that grew out of the Mediterranean area is this idea of the personification of evil in the Christian religion called the Devil.

To me, the Devil's work would be, and ostensibly, is described in Christian publications to be, that the Devil is trying to get between you and the Christian God, and to influence you to do things his way, and to fool you into thinking that he is the Christian God. Therefore, explicit in that, is that whenever you listen to another human being try to tell you what the spiritual side of life is about, then essentially you're being misled. So that's what that song is about, the idea that if you really want the truth, you have to be willing to examine yourself for it.

"Healer" was metaphorical. "Healer" was this whole idea of what happens to someone when they are able to control some extraordinary power, or are at least thought to do so. It's that phenomenon from the other way around—people insisting on placing sonic divine significance on what you do and say. And the hubris and the ultimate downfall that comes with that as evidenced by the constant string of martyrs to their religion—some phenomenological thing that is more animal than god-like—it's more of a product of the herd mentality than the product of some divine inspiration.

You've been called, in various articles, a provocateur, a wizard, a genius, a weirdo and, more recently, puzzling.

We do jigsaw puzzles, so puzzling is legitimate. (laughs) We have Flow-Fazer and Grokgazer jigsaw puzzles. Puzzling works because it represents some closure—some continual threat. When I was just a child, one thing we knew about my relationship with my parents and the rest of the world was that it was puzzling, and that it didn't seem to make a whole lot of sense. And it wasn't until I became a "free agent" at the age of eighteen that any of it started to make any sense. But that's all nominal anyway. Because most of the things that people seem to take for granted in their own lives are always open to question in mine. That's why I do what I do. And that's just the way it's always going to be.

Is there anything about the latest album, The Individualist, that you're excited to talk about?

Having blitzkrieged everybody with *No World Order*, the fact that it was musically and technically new in so many different ways, and really I'm just letting this record lay there. But I'm wary at this time to editorialize on the music because I don't want people to have to go through what they went through last time. Eventually there will be the interactive version of it, and all the other ramifications involved, this ongoing merging of music and technology. But for the time being, I'd just as soon have people listen to the music and evaluate it without any consideration of the other issues.

John Fogerty

By Craig Werner
July 18, 1997

The history of rock 'n' roll bears witness to the power of the unmistakably individual voice bubbling up from subterranean reservoirs of the blues, gospel, and country music: Chuck Berry's ringing guitar; little Richard's gospel whoops; the young Elvis' rockabilly drawl; the James Jamerson bass lines propelling the great Motown records of the mid-sixties. If you can name the artist in three notes, chances are pretty good they're going to wind up in the Rock and Roll Hall of Fame.

Creedence Clearwater Revival (CCR) was inducted into the Hall by Bruce Springsteen in 1993 mostly because of John Fogerty's absolutely distinctive guitar and voice. Patron saint of garage bands throughout America, Fogerty wrote, produced, sang lead, and played lead guitar on the records that made CCR's politically-charged "swamp rock" one of the defining sounds of sixties rock 'n' roll. Between 1968—when CCR emerged from nearly a decade of playing bars, high school dances, and military bases up and down the west coast—and the band's 1982 break-up, Fogerty and CCR released at least a dozen songs that seem to flow up out of the deepest wellsprings of American music: "Bad Moon Rising," "Green River," "Run Through the Jungle," "Who'll Stop the Rain," "Lodi," "Fortunate Son," "Proud Mary," etc. If you make it to the end of the list without at least a few Fogerty riffs echoing in your head, it's probably time to put down this article and locate a copy of *Yuppie Nostalgia*'s special issue on James Taylor.

Like Elvis, Little Richard, and James Brown, Fogerty produced music that resonates with the sounds of the American South. Reflecting on his recent "pilgrimage" through the Mississippi Delta, Fogerty pinpoints the curious fact that the poorest, most oppressed and oppressive parts of the nation gave rise to something like a shared interracial heritage.

"I think about what Muddy Waters really did and he's every bit as seminal, as ground-breaking, as epochal, as Elvis Presley. It's funny that they're both from Mississippi. It's kind of the same journey, just some years apart. Initially, they went to different parts of our culture, but they ended up in the same place."

When Fogerty's voice drawls out the opening lines of CCR's "Green River"—"Take me back down where cool water flows, y'all/ Help me remember things I don't know"—he's staking a claim to his corner of the mythic American soil where, if race doesn't go away, it at least doesn't keep us from hearing each other's voices. More like Springsteen than Elvis and Muddy Waters, Fogerty came to his soulful rock 'n' roll through radio rather than regional upbringing. Fogerty's story belongs to a profoundly American mythic tradition that allows you to reinvent yourself as a way of discovering something better and deeper than what you "really" are. It's a way of imagining community into the broken world. Fogerty's music belongs as much to the Louisiana swamps as to the San Francisco Bay area where he was born and raised. Which doesn't change the fact that CCR's claim to being the quintessential San Francisco band is as strong as the Grateful Dead's and a whole lot stronger than those of the Jefferson Airplane or Big Brother and the Holding Company.

After nearly a decade away from performance—broken only by appearances at benefits for Vietnam Veterans, earthquake victims, and AIDS research—Fogerty is bringing his classic sound back to the stage. During a June performance at Chicago's House of Blues, Fogerty created a perfectly seasoned gumbo of songs from his new CD Blue Moon Swamp, blended with the CCR classics he hadn't performed regularly for over two decades as a result of sometimes bitter disputes with Creedence's record label, Fantasy.

During an interview with Goldmine at his Chicago hotel, Fogerty talked about how a kid from a working class California suburb near Berkeley came by his "Southern" voice: "It was totally unconscious," Fogerty said in a speaking voice that bears no trace of Memphis or New Orleans. "I didn't even know it was Southern. I knew from the inside that I liked talking about swamps and spooky stuff, but I didn't set out to do anything in particular. It just felt real good when I finished a song like 'Born on the Bayou.' I'd go, 'Yeah, I like that, I'd buy a record like that.'"

Fogerty remembers being somewhat surprised when "people kept pointing out it seemed so Southern, so swampy. I've thought about this for years. Where did that come from? Because I grew up in El Cerrito, California, and there wasn't much Southern about it."

The answer to Fogerty's meditations arrived, appropriately enough, at the 1986 Rock and Roll Hall of Fame dinner where he delivered an induction speech for Buddy Holly. Holly was part of the initial group of inductees alongside Elvis, Ray Charles, Little Richard, Jerry Lee Lewis, James Brown, and Chuck Berry. "That was when I finally got my answer," Fogerty recalls with a smile, "I'd been thinking about this for twenty-five years. That night I stood there and either the people who were being honored were there at the same time or their posters. There were pictures of everybody all around. I looked and looked at each one of them and realized they were all from the South. The only one I wasn't sure was from the South was Sam Cooke.

"So it was at least nine out of ten," Fogerty continues. "And I found out later Sam Cooke was from Clarksdale, Mississippi, so it was really ten out of ten. Rock 'n' roll is Southern and that's why I'm Southern. Because what I learned from was Southern. I rest my case." Fogerty frames the question as one of regional roots that impart a distinct Southern family, resemblance to rock 'n' roll everywhere.

"If you imitate your father and other people say, 'Hey, you imitated your father,' you don't even have a choice. You just do what you see."

As it has for white rock 'n' rollers from Keith Richards to Lowell George, black music provided Fogerty with an alternative to the sanitized music that dominated the pop charts.

"The blues came to me on the R&B radio out of San Francisco and I really did appreciate the fire on those records," he recalls. "But when you're a kid, you're not researching in the library or going through the bins at the record store."

There's a smile on Fogerty's face as he describes his distinctly limited access to musical variety when he was growing up: "If there was a record store anywhere near where I lived, which did not have any Muddy Waters, that's for sure. The only records for miles around were in the furniture store, which was a very common connection because the record player was piece of furniture so they sold the records to go with the furniture. In the fifties, the furniture store in El Cerrito was selling Patti Page and Tony Bennett, that sort of thing. I doubt there were more than fifty different titles. I never bought any R&B records in that store. I bought Elvis Presley and I remember seeing a Hank Williams with strings album. I saw that and said 'What?' I really stayed away from that one," Fogerty concludes with a laugh.

Not that Fogerty was totally isolated from the deeper roots of American music. "I grew up with the blues," he says, reemphasizing the role radio played in his musical education. "It's not like I was for Tibet or Mars. But I was doing it from afar. I was listening to Muddy Waters but I barely knew anything 'bout his real life. I knew he had a great band."

Fogerty remembers feeling a deep sense of dissatisfaction with the way the blues were presented by critics such as Ralph J. Gleason, who was later to write the liner notes for the first Creedence album. Parodying the dry voice of an academic lecturer, Fogerty intones, "The blues came up the Mississippi and landed in Chicago. My may my." He switches back to his regular speaking voice: "There'd be all these paragraphs showing off his college education. But it's so much more awesome to realize this guy who's barely literate comes up to Chicago and plugs in. I mean any rock and roller can appreciate that, wow, when everybody else was sitting on their porches playing on their acoustic guitars, he organized it and plugged into it. We call it a blues band, but that was a rock 'n' roll band. It was loud."

Fogerty's quest for deeper understanding of his musical influences and ancestors led him to the Mississippi Delta in 1990. "As far as I know, it was the first time I'd ever been in the state of Mississippi, certainly in the Delta," Fogerty reflects. "The state line is only a few miles south of Memphis, so I might have been there by accident when I went to see (Memphis bass player) Duck Dunn and he took me somewhere, but it was the first time I knew I was in Mississippi. That's kind of strange. I'd been in Tennessee a lot; I'd been in Louisiana a lot. So it was just sort of a gap in my knowledge."

Almost reverent in his attitude toward both country and blues musicians, Fogerty is careful to emphasize that he doesn't consider his music part of any musical tradition other than straight rockin' roll. The distinctions he makes between rock, country, and the blues involve both technique and attitude.

Fogerty marvels at the virtuosity of the country pickers who inspired his 1973 album, *The Blue Ridge Rangers*: "I have so much reverence for the people who play really good, like a Jerry Douglas or a James Burton or there's a guy in Nashville now, Brett Mason, who's just a hot picker. That's something else you tend to see more in country music than in rock'n' roll or even the blues. In

country, people are just flat out pickers on their instrument. They're just amazing players," Fogerty continues. "When rock 'n' roll guys become amazing players, it's almost like they're not rock 'n' roll anymore. They become too high falutin'. 'Cause rock 'n' roll folks kind of have an attitude and a sound with some dirt in it."

While Fogerty recognizes "dirt" as a shared element of rock and the blues, he points to some crucial differences in the blues tradition: "The blues has a definite attitude about how you play, at least to my mind. Once you get too citified and become scientific, like a college professor, then it's not rooted anymore, that's for sure.

"That's why I always say I'm not a blues man and I'm not pretending to be a blues man," Fogerty continues. "I have such reverence for the music. Blues are disciplined, they're regimented, so you have to stay in that format. If you go outside, you can't come back in again. You're just not accepted. I don't really want to buy a blues record by some middle class white guy from Iowa. I have strong feelings about this. It's just not the blues anymore. It's fine if he calls it something else, but he shouldn't say, anymore than I would, it's the blues. Because it's not."

Describing his attempt to find the right version of a song for inclusion on *Blue Moon Swamp*, Fogerty makes a similar point about the country tradition: "There's a song on the album called 'Rambunctious Boy' and I had arrangement prior to this one that's not on the record. I came to the realization one day that it was really just too flat-out country. And I remember it was bothering me and I was saying, why is this bugging me? It was because it wasn't honest. And I finally said, well, I love Buck Owens and I think everybody knows that. I name Buck Owens in one of my songs ('Lookin' Out My Back

Door'), but I'm not Buck Owens. He does what he does; that's his job. I shouldn't imitate him. That's me not doing my job. So I changed the arrangement and made in more like a rock 'n' roll approach. I love Buck Owens' music, but I shouldn't try to clone myself into somebody else. I don't want that."

Fogerty's insistence on something like authenticity—the idea that you sing what you're born to—seems strange coming from the man who opened the distinctly bluesy "Wrote a Song for Everyone" with: "Met myself comin' country welfare line/I was feelin' strung out, hung out on the line." It's a safe bet that the black listener whose response took Ike and Tina Turner's remake of "Proud Mary" to #5 of the R&B charts in 1971—it rose to #4 pop—heard more than a touch of the blues in Tina's incendiary performance. From the opening guitar riffs through CCR's unforgettable harmonies on "rollin' on the river," Fogerty's original flows down from Memphis through the heart of a mythic South that would have been equally familiar to Howlin' Wolf and Hank Williams.

The key to understanding Fogerty's relationship to the blues lies in distinguishing between the blues as a musical form—usually twelve bars with an AAB lyrical pattern—and the blues as what black intellectuals have called a "cultural impulse." Fogerty's right when he insists on the dangers of uprooting the blues from the soil of the rural black south. Even when they traveled up the Mississippi to Chicago, where Muddy Waters and Elmore James plugged in their guitars and laid down the fundamentals of rock 'n' roll, the Delta blues spoke directly out of the historical experiences of slavery and segregation. A white middle class kid from Iowa, or El Cerrito, California, is venturing onto risky ground if he presents himself as the voice of Stovall's Plantation.

But there's another way of thinking about the blues that helps explain why, for example, CCR's "Who'll Stop the Rain" and "Run Through The Jungle" can legitimately be called the best blues songs written about Vietnam. Black novelist Ralph Ellison, best known for the classic Invisible Man, defines the blues as "an impulse to keep the painful details and episodes of a brutal experience alive in one's aching consciousness, to finger its jagged grain, and to transcend it, not by the consolation of philosophy but by squeezing from it near-tragic, near-comic lyricism."

Later in the same essay, Ellison redefines the blues as "an autobiographical chronicle of personal catastrophe expressed lyrically," without confusing the issue of who has the right to sing about the inside meaning of blackness in the Jim Crow South. Ellison's definition testifies to the fact that we all have our brutal experiences to deal with and that the blues peak to our dilemmas, not just a specific music but as a way of confronting the human condition. The idea of the blues impulse helps us hear the shared conversation between Bob Dylan's "Desolation Row" and Bessie Smith's "Downhearted Blues"; Springsteen's "Backstreets" and Howlin Wolf's "Killin' Floor"; Fogerty's "Run Through The Jungle" and Robert Johnson's "Hellbound on My Trail."

None of that was in Fogerty's mind when he embarked on his recent trips to the Mississippi Delta. "I actually didn't know what I was doing," he says. "It wasn't scientific, like if a guy got a grant from a university or something like that. I'd had this feeling for more than a year before I finally went and I just kept telling myself, 'you don't know what you're doing,' so I didn't go. I just kept pushing the feeling aside, but I finally decided that what was behind it was that I wanted to understand more about the lineage."

At least initially, Fogerty pursued the blues as a kind of amateur historian: "I was trying to straighten out who all the people were—John Lee Hooker and Jimmy Reed and Muddy Waters—and what order they came in, who was influenced by who and who knew each other, who played with each other, that sort of thing," he says. "When I started out, that's all I had to go on. It's like anything you're fond of but don't know a lot about. You start out making a lot of mistakes."

Especially after the first of several trips, Fogerty began to focus his search on more specific parts of the blues heritage. "The first trip was just sort of testing the water and I really didn't get much done," he recalls. "But when I went back down, what I did was to make an itinerary each day, where I wanted to go and what I wanted to see. So I knew Charlie Patton had stayed a lot at Dockery's Plantation outside of Clarksdale and I also knew there were churches in the area with their graveyards. Of course, I always ran out of time and I never did get everything accomplished."

Fogerty takes special pleasure in minor discoveries, such as the moment when he located the grave of Charlie Patton's sister, Viola Cannon. "I was all excited when I found where she was buried.

There's not a big sign on the road—Charlie Patton's sister buried here, Look!", Fogerty laughs. "I was walking through this sacred place, this graveyard and there was her name. I went, 'Oh my God.' It's not the same name so you gotta know a little bit.

"It's part of my reverence for the lineage of things; it's a joy of discovery," Fogerty concludes. "It's like a new thing and all the details became an end to themselves finally. I have to keep telling people I'm not an expert, I couldn't write a book. I just feel a lot fuller because of those journeys."

Although Fogerty wasn't seeking out inspiration for his own music on the trips south, at least one song on *Blue Moon Swamp* grew directly out of the experience. "A Hundred and Ten in the Shade," which sounds like it originated with the Swan Silverstones or Dixie Hummingbirds, came to Fogerty as what he calls a "visitation."

"It was a direct blessing from my trips to Mississippi," he says. "It came to me as a complete song, not like this agonizing back-breaking stuff you go through with a lot of songs. This just sorta landed with a feeling and a sound. It was a direct memory of Mississippi, the heat and the humidity and the feelings."

Fogerty gives full credit to the gospel group the Fairfield Four, whose backup harmonies make "A Hundred and Ten in the Shade" one of the highlights of the new album. "I knew exactly what it should sound like, but it took from 1992 'til 1996 to finally find the Fairfield Four, who had exactly the right sound. There are things you can't really verbalize, the words get in the way. Your ears either tell you it's true or it's not true; it's right or it's not right. They got it right."

Early in his career, it must have seemed to Fogerty that he'd never get anywhere near the point where he could take four or five years working on a single song. Fogerty grew up in a household where fights frequently broke out. "I was always ashamed," he told Time magazine in 1969. "I never brought my friends home. My room was in the basement—cement floor, cement walls. I just grabbed music and withdrew."

"Porterville," the first single released under the Creedence Clearwater Revival name in 1967, reflects Fogerty's attempt to come to terms with the difficulties at home. Not quite biographical—Fogerty's father chose to leave home when John was nine—the song fingers the jagged grain in a way that speaks to anyone else who's shared the singer's brutal experience: "They came and took my dad away, to serve some time/ But it was me that paid the debt he left behind/ Folks said I was full of sin because I was the next of kin."

Between 1959 and 1968, when CCR seemed to come from nowhere to become one of the most popular and successful American bands—they received $10,000 for their appearance at the Woodstock Festival—the band went through several name changes, appearing as the Blue Velvets, the Visions and the Golliwogs, the latter monstrosity foisted on them by the executives at the Fantasy record label, who thought it sounded more in tune with the British invasion.

During Creedence's long apprenticeship, Fogerty saw an awful lot of the places described in "Lodi," which became the anthem of garage bands throughout the United States: "If I only had a dollar for every song I've sung/ Every time I've had to play while people sat there drunk/ You know I'd catch the next train back to where I live/ Oh lord, stuck in Lodi again." As rock critic Dave Marsh observes, the song's complaint about having been on the road for a whole year without making it sounds curious once you realize that Fogerty, his brother and rhythm guitarist Tom, bass player Stu Cook, and drummer Doug Clifford struggled almost a decade before finally breaking through with "Suzie Q" (#11) in 1968.

Cook, Clifford, and Fogerty formed the earliest version of Creedence while they were attending El Cerrito's Portola Junior High in 1959. John had learned guitar chords from a Burl Ives songbook. He invited Clifford to sign on as drummer despite the fact that Clifford had never played the instrument. Converting an old pool cue into a set of drumsticks and buying a used snare drum, Clifford became the drummer of a band that soon included Cook on piano and Tom Fogerty on bass. Before long the group was performing as Tommy Fogerty and the Blue Velvets with the older Fogerty singing lead. When the younger members graduated from high school in 1963, the group expanded its geographical range, playing in numerous clubs and bars around the Bay area.

Fogerty remembers the early incarnations of the group as "a very typical American band; your basic high school rock 'n' roll band," whose playlist included Duane Eddy, Johnny and the Hurricanes, "a little bit of Ventures, 'Wipe Out,' 'Louie, Louie,' right down the rock and roll line." In the early days, the group performed little of the R&B or soul music that emerged as a major part of the swamp rock sound.

"We weren't heavily off into James Brown, any more than most white high school kids would have been. We weren't Delta relics at all. That wasn't in our consciousness at the time. We did 'Midnight Hour,' but then everybody did," Fogerty says. "We never did 'Mustang Sally.' For some reason, we skipped that one. Going back to ninth grade, we did 'Hully Gully' and 'Annie Had a Baby.'" Fogerty smiles as he remembers the Blue Velvet version of Hank Ballard's sexually explicit classic. "We were really gettin' down."

When asked whether his bands ever had a sizable black audience, Fogerty shakes his head and offers a description of the groups performance at the tenth reunion of the El Cerrito High School class of 1953. "We'd played 'Green Onions,' and this black guy came up, his name was R.B. King. He would have been about twenty-eight years old. And he says, 'You boys do that rock 'n' roll pretty good. But when you do 'Green Onions' there's this in-between you're missin'.' Later, he would have said 'soul.' He was trying to compliment us, but it was absolutely the truth. We were high school kids and we couldn't play a shuffle to save our lives. It's something most white people can't do. 'There's that little in-between you're missing, when you get that, then you'll have 'Green Onions' down.' I thought about that a lot over the years."

Although they would not make the national charts until 1968, the Fogertys, Clifford and Cook, began their recording career in 1964. Tom Fogerty had gotten a job as a packing and shipping clerk at Berkeley-based Fantasy Records, best known for its jazz releases. In 1963, a nationally televised documentary had focused on the label's success in making the Vince Guaraldi Trio's light jazz classic "Cast Your Fate to the Wind" a popular hit. Tom succeeded in getting the group an audition with Fantasy which released "Don't Tell Me No Lies," sung by Tom, under the Golliwogs name in November. Neither their debut nor the 1965 follow-ups "Where You Been" and "You Can't Be True," attracted much attention outside the Bay area. The first indication that the Golliwogs might finally break out of the cycle of local bars and clubs came when "Brown-Eyed Girl," released on Fantasy's new teen-oriented Scorpio imprint, sold 10,000 copies in the regional market.

But before they had a chance to capitalize on the success, Fogerty and Clifford were drafted. In 1966, the American public had not yet begun to worry much about Vietnam. The domestic economy was booming; the anti-war movement was limited to a relatively small group of activists portrayed in the media as an un-American lunatic fringe. In public President Lyndon Johnson downplayed the extent of American involvement while in private he told advisors: "I don't think it's worth fighting for; I don't think that we can get out. It's just the biggest damn mess I ever saw. This is a terrible thing that we're getting ready to do."

Even though Fogerty was "able to finagle my way into a reserve unit," he shared the GI's knowledge of how sharply the reality differed from its image. "It was actually at the height of the war, so all the rules were changing," he recalls. "There were National Guard guys whose units got shipped over to Vietnam. It was amazing. Things got real altered, but luckily for me, I didn't have to go overseas or serve three years in the hard-core Army."

The fact that Johnson attempted to hide the escalation by refusing to call up reserve units—which in effect shifted the burden of the fighting to draftees who were more likely to be from black, rural, and working-class backgrounds—simply reflects how confused the experience of Vietnam was for everyone who came anywhere close to it.

In 1967, when Fogerty finished serving his six months of active duty at Ft. Bragg, Ft. Knox, and Ft. Lee, the "Summer of Love" was establishing San Francisco as the center of a counterculture based in large part on its opposition to what was beginning to be seen more widely as a corrupt and futile war. Like Jimi Hendrix, who served in the Army's elite "Screaming Eagles" parachute unit in the early '60s, Fogerty never confused hatred for the war with hostility to the draftees who found themselves fighting it. He appreciates the intense response his music received from the "grunts"—"you weren't really a vet until after you got back," Fogerty notes—who served in Vietnam.

Although numerous CCR songs have been used in soundtracks for movies on Vietnam and at least a half dozen were adopted by the anti-war movement, Fogerty wrote only two of them with Vietnam specifically in mind: the blistering "Fortunate Son" and the meditative "Who'll Stop the Rain." But there's no question that CCR's music played a much broader role in the musical culture of Vietnam. Marsh places "Fortunate Son" alongside "Don't Look Now" and "Bad Moon Rising" on his list of the top fifteen protest songs of the 1960s;

"Who'll Stop the Rain" was used as the title of the movie version of Robert Stone's classic Vietnam novel *Dog Soldiers*; "Run Through the Jungle" appears on the soundtrack of the film adaptation of Ron Kovac's memoir *Born on the Fourth of July*.

Fogerty finds it interesting that "Run Through the Jungle" is almost always heard as a song about Vietnam. "It definitely got adopted by the guys in that country," he says. "But it was really my remark about American society, the metaphor being society as a jungle. When I sang 'two hundred million guns are loaded,' I was talking about the ease with which guns are purchased in America. And it is a jungle.

"It's even worse now. To me it's a sad thing. 'Satan cries take aim.' We're all killing each other. That part of it was an anti-gun statement." Fogerty pauses to consider his words carefully, "You may think that's a paradox because I love to go hunting. I enjoy the ownership of guns. Guns have a history and a lore like guitars and cars and even women," he says with a laugh.

But he quickly turns serious when he asserts that: "I'm not confused. I don't need an AK-47 to go deer hunting. It's pretty clear that if you have something like that, you want to kill people. I think it's respectable to waste a lot of

Photo/Henry Diltz

time with an old hunting rifle or an old Colt six-shooter. That's cool because it's a kind of American history and lore. But I don't think any true gun freak would mind being regulated." Fogerty speaks with passion when he says, "I think it's the nut cases that are bothered by that. Charlton Heston scares the shit out of me. A lot of the NRA guys are hunters, but the NRA itself hasn't done the country any good with its endorsements of Teflon bullets, which were only meant to go through armored plate and kill policemen. The NRA's just had it all wrong."

During the Vietnam era, garage bands playing for racially-mixed audiences on military bases back home found they could get by mixing in Creedence jams with some Chicago blues and the sorts of R&B standards that began to appear more frequently in the performances of the newly renamed Creedence Clearwater Revival.

There are competing versions of how the band's name was put together. Everyone agrees that "Revival" was chosen to symbolize the band's new direction. But at different times Creedence has been attributed to either the band's belief in itself or the name of Tom Fogerty's friend Creedence Nuball. Similarly, some have said "Clearwater" came from a commercial praising a beer's "sparkling clear waters" despite John's 1969 statement that it indicated "something deep, true and pure through which the light always shines."

Fogerty remembers the period leading up to the release of the group's first album as a period of self-definition. After "Porterville," which, despite a strong lyric, has a somewhat generic blues rock feel, failed to attract much attention, he set about creating a more distinctive sound.

"I wanted the band to sound mysterious, to have its own definition," he remembers. "So I decided to mess around with 'Suzie Q', which was a cool rock 'n' roll song by Dale Hawkins. I kind of did the same thing with 'I Put a Spell on You.' Those songs took us to another place than where we'd been for ten years." When a demo version of "Suzie Q" began to receive extensive airplay in the Bay area, Fantasy decided to re-record an extended version of the song, which was released as both sides of CCR's first hit single (#11).

The group's debut album *Creedence Clearwater Revival* (#52, 1968) reflected Fogerty's interest in moving beyond a straight rock'n' roll sound. Alongside "I Put a Spell On You," which reached #58 as the follow-up to "Suzie Q," the album places several Fogerty originals ("The Working Man," "Get

Down Woman," "Walk on the Water") that would have sounded at home on an album by blues rockers Canned Heat or the Paul Butterfield Band. A cover of Wilson Pickett's "Ninety-Nine and a Half" provides evidence of the band's continuing attempts to find that "little shuffle." Later CCR and Fogerty albums included versions of Jackie Wilson's "Lonely Teardrops" and the Motown classic "I Heard It Through the Grapevine." Despite some nice moments in the extended guitar breaks on "Grapevine," the relatively static rhythms made it clear Marvin Gaye and Gladys Knight had nothing to worry about.

The liner notes to *Creedence Clearwater Revival* provided a peculiar, and somewhat lukewarm, introduction. Written by *Rolling Stone* consulting editor Ralph J. Gleason, a leading jazz critic who had enthusiastically embraced rock 'n' roll, the notes present a panoramic overview of San Francisco's emerging scene. Praising area groups as "the dominant force in a popular music which is the most universal expression of attitudes and ideas we've ever seen," Gleason divided San Francisco groups into three echelons, the top one headed by the Jefferson Airplane, the Grateful Dead, Big Brother and the Holding Company, and Moby Grape. According to Gleason, the bands performed in venues divided into "three concentric circles," descending from the gaudy heights of the major ballrooms to small clubs like the Lion's Share, Deno-Carlo, and the New Monk.

Creedence, who Gleason gets around to naming only in the final paragraph of the lengthy essay, had spent most of its existence playing in spots Gleason would have placed somewhere between circles eight and fourteen. Belatedly getting around to the business at hand, Gleason closes with a tepid endorsement of CCR as a band "which gives every indication... of keeping the strength of the San Francisco sound undiminished."

"It was nice of him to mention our name in the very last sentence, on our own record," Fogerty says, with a lingering touch of exasperation. "The whole rest of the thing went to declaring San Francisco the center of the universe. Airplane, Dead, Moby Grape, Quicksilver Messenger Service. 'In future years, everyone will know the San Francisco sound permeated the world, one of the greatest influences. Creedence Clearwater is a fine example of the third generation,'" Fogerty breaks from his professor's voice. "What? We'd been there when those guys were off in Texas or someplace. So it

kind of pissed us off.

"San Francisco sound, great. You mean like Peter Wheat and the Breadmen? San Francisco sound? You mean like We Five," Fogerty names two of the numerous groups active in the Bay area long before the Summer of Love. "It was all sort of a concoction. I have to say I looked at it with a bit of a jaundiced eye. We knew that many of those people came to San Francisco later. I thought the whole myth, the mythology of the San Francisco sound, was a concoction, almost like a Chamber of Commerce thing."

Creedence had relatively little contact with Gleason's "first echelon" bands: "The Grateful Dead were always a little off from our circle. They did things differently. And the Airplane, at least in those days, gave off this vibe, this attitude like Creedence somehow didn't fit into those circles. It was very real. I could never put my finger on what it was, but we were considered outsiders in our own town."

Once CCR's records began to appear, their peculiar outsider status didn't keep them from advancing into the top circle of Bay area venues. In May 1968, as "Suzie Q" began to appear on the radio, the group made its Avalon Ballroom debut on a bill with bluesman Taj Mahal; in July then played the Fillmore West, along with the Paul Butterfield Blues Band. In September, with "Suzie Q" rising on the national charts, they played the Fillmore West three more times. In early 1969, they were back at the Fillmore West on bills with Fleetwood Mac, then in its Peter Green-era blues incarnation, and Jethro Tull.

Fogerty emphasizes that Creedence admired and developed friendships with some San Francisco-based bands. He expresses a special admiration and fondness for Santana. "Carlos and the guys in the band were up and coming at the same time. Carlos was a smoking guitar player and the band was hot. They were doing something quite different from everyone else. They were relaxed and genuine, really nice people. That was fun. I was meeting guys with a dream in their eyes, guys who were going someplace."

By the start of the summer of 1969, no one could question Creedence's right to share any stage at any rock 'n' roll show in the U.S. The turning point was "Proud Mary," (#2) the first of nine consecutive top-ten singles over the next three years, one of the most consistent creative outputs in American music history. "Bad Moon Rising," "Green

River," "Travlin' Band," "Up Around The Bend," and "Lookin' Out My Back Door" also rose to #2. "Down on the Corner" peaked at #3, "Up Around the Bend" at #4, "Sweet Hitch-Hiker" at #6, and "Have You Ever Seen the Rain" at #8. When you look over the list of Creedence hits, what's striking is the absence of all of the explicitly anti-war songs. "Fortunate Son" did rise to #14 but DJs flipped the record and made "Down on the Corner" the top side. Neither "Run Through The Jungle" nor "Who'll Stop the Rain" charted on its own. It's a mark of Fantasy's limited experience with marketing pop material that no CCR song ever reached #1.

Riding the wave of their success, CCR began to appear regularly at the festivals that had featured rockers from Britain and the United States, often alongside some of the blues artists who influenced their sound. At the Denver Pop Festival, for example, Creedence appeared alongside Frank Zappa's Mothers of Invention, the Jimi Hendrix Experience, and Big Mama Thornton. At the Newport '69 Pop Festival in Northridge, California, they played with Hendrix, Jethro Tull, and the Byrds. At the Atlanta Pop Festival the line-up included Joe Cocker,

Canned Heat, Johnny Winter, and Led Zeppelin. Capping the hectic summer, Creedence was one of the star attractions at Woodstock, although they refused to allow their performance to be incorporated into either the follow-up movie or its soundtrack album.

The surge in CCR's popularity resulted from Fogerty's success in pinning down the swamp rock sound on their second album, Bayou Country (#7). The first album crediting Fogerty as producer, Bayou Country opens with the feedback from Fogerty's guitar which gradually yields to the signature "Born on the Bayou" riff that made the song a perfect opener for most of the band's live sets; even a quarter century after Creedence broke up, "Born on the Bayou" maintains all of its power, as Fogerty demonstrated at the House of Blues.

Bayou Country includes garage rock standards "Good Golly Miss Molly," which Fogerty would rework into "Travlin' Band" a year later, and his own composition "Keep On Chooglin'," a boogie classic that Creedence frequently used to close its live shows. But the core of the album consists of the southern-sounding cuts that provide an ideal setting for "Proud Mary." You can still hear echoes of the first album's blues rock in "Graveyard Train" and "Penthouse Pauper," but it's blues rock Fogerty dreamed up out of the mythic Louisiana he'd found in his southern musical ancestors.

Like "Born on the Bayou," "Bootleg" could have been recorded by no one else. As he does on "Proud Mary," Fogerty locates the accent that allowed him to cross over the Mason-Dixon line without providing proof of identity. There are some specific elements of the accent that place Fogerty in Louisiana, close to New Orleans rather than, say, Memphis or Charleston. It's in the way he puts the Brooklyn twist on the vowels in the line "woiking for the man every night and day," the way he reduces the word "bootleg" to the near-Cajun "boo-lay." No one ever really talked that way, but no one who came under Fogerty's spell was likely to notice, or mind.

After *Bayou Country* and "Proud Mary," swamp rock remained a constant part of the musical soundtrack that carried the sixties into the seventies. The pace was grueling. While the band continued to tour, Fantasy released four CCR singles in 1969 and three more in 1970. By the time "Someday Never Comes" (#25) brought the band's run of Top Ten singles to an end in 1972, Fogerty was showing signs of creative burnout. There would be only one more Creedence single, a re-release of "I Heard It Through The Grapevine," which reached #43 when Fantasy released it in 1976 amidst legal battles which helped drive Fogerty out of the music business intermittently throughout the seventies and eighties.

But between *Bayou Country* and the last CCR studio album, *Mardi Gras*, Fogerty was responsible for a string of albums that stand beside the classics of American rock 'n' roll. Two of them—*Green River* (1969) and *Cosmo's Factory* (1970)—reached #1, while *Willy And The Poor Boys* (1970) peaked at #3 and *Pendulum* reached #5. Even *Mardi Gras*, clearly the group's weakest work, in large part because Fogerty divided song-writing and production duties with Cook and Clifford, made #12.

In a recent issue honoring the most important albums of the rock 'n' roll era, *Rolling Stone* chose *Willy And The Poor Boys* to represent Creedence.

"I'm flattered that *Rolling Stone* would do that," said Fogerty, "but my personal favorite is *Green River*. I like where that music is, the sound of it, the cover, everything. It's the style, the sound of the song 'Green River.'

"It's a little more a Sun record," Fogerty continues, referring to the Memphis studio where Sam Phillips brought together blues (Howlin' Wolf, Little Milton), country (Johnny Cash) and rockabilly (Carl Perkins, Jerry Lee Lewis) musicians in the early fifties, providing a perfect setting for the emergence of Elvis Presley's rock 'n' roll. "It's a little more rockabilly. 'Cross-Tie Walker,' 'Bad Moon Rising;' that's kind of more my center. *Green River* was close to the sound you may notice on *Blue Moon Swamp*."

As long as you're not making a top 200 list, there's no particular reason to choose between Green River and Willy And The Poor Boys, which were released just three months apart in the fall and winter of 1969. On Green River, Fogerty perfects the "spooky" sound that summons up the bayou shadows as a metaphor for what's going down in Richard Nixon's America, where it was getting harder to tell the difference between paranoia and common sense. Sounding like something out of the *Old Testament* prophets, Fogerty's poetic images tap a power similar to that of Robert Johnson's classic Delta blues. When Creedence sang about that bad moon rising, it meant one thing to the grunts in the Mekong Delta, something else to the crowd at the Denver Pop Festival, which had been tear-gassed three times prior to CCR's closing set. No one listening to "Sinister Purpose" or "Commotion" in 1970 had any trouble at all coming up with a point of reference.

At once angrier and more exuberant than *Green River*, *Willy And The Poor Boys* includes two of Fogerty's most explicit political statements. "Fortunate Son" calls down a righteous wrath on the heads of the folks who "wave the flag to prove they're red, white, and blue," "while sending the poor off to die in a war no one even pretends to believe in," "and when the band plays 'Hail to the Chief'/ they point the cannon at you," "some folks inherit star-spangled eyes, then they send you off to war." The chorus makes it clear where Fogerty stands: "It ain't me/ it ain't me/ I ain't no senator's son, no/ It ain't me/ it ain't me/ I ain't no fortunate one." As he said in 1969, "I see things through lower class eyes. If you sit around and think about all that money, you can never write a song about where you came from."

Equally clear about the political dynamics of a time when too many people were making promises "you don't have to keep," "Don't Look Now" lays down a country-tinged variation on the straight ahead rock'n' roll of "Fortunate Son." Where Fogerty rips into "Fortunate Son" with Little Richard style screams, he delivers the crucial lines of "Don't Look Back" in something closer to a whisper: "Don't look now, someone's done your starvin'/ don't look now, someone's done your prayin' too."

Fogerty ends the crucial three-song sequence that defines *Willy and the Poor Boys'* social vision with "The Midnight Special," bringing back the exuberant sound of "Down on the Corner," which opens the album. Creedence's adaptation of Leadbelly's song which, along with "Cotton Fields" gives the album a strong African-American presence, contrasts an almost cheerful syncopated rhythm— CCR shows definite signs of having figured out "that little shuffle"—with a lyric line that raises images of incarceration, police violence, and death; in the black southern tradition, the "midnight special" could refer either to a train heading north to freedom or to the suicide that some preferred to life in the fields. Mix in swamp rock classic "Feelin' Blue," the haunting "Effigy" and "It Came Out of the Sky," one of the classic pieces of rock 'n' roll science fiction, and it's clear that *Willy and the Poor Boys* deserves whatever honors anyone cares to pass its way.

The last of Creedence's classic albums, *Cosmo's Factory*, represents what Fogerty calls a "culmination" of the group's career.

"It may actually be our best record," he says. "I always thought it was the culmination. By that time, Creedence had all these records and we looked back and put everything on it. It was almost redemptive, you might say. We'd done all these things and it was like 'Boom! there, I said it again.'"

It's a good description. *Cosmo's Factory* features three Top Ten singles ("Travlin' Band," "Up Around the Bend," and "Long As I Can See the Light"); two of Fogerty's strongest political lyrics ("Who'll Stop the Rain," "Run Through the Jungle"); a shot of rockabilly rhythm ("Ooby Dooby") and a couple shots of blues ("Before You Accuse Me," "My Baby Left Me"); and the extended jams on "Ramble Tamble" and "I Heard It Through the Grapevine," that let Fogerty stretch out like he had on "Suzie Q."

But there's little question that the hectic pace of the previous three years was beginning to take its toll on the band, both creatively and personally. Fogerty admits to suffering from burnout. In addition to almost constant recording, Creedence had

begun to tour internationally, beginning with a 1970 tour that took them to London's Royal Albert Hall, where they performed alongside Booker T. and the MGs, the originators of "Green Onions." Members of the MGs backed up Fogerty during his 1985 appearance on an A&M Records Soundstage show and again in 1995 when Fogerty appeared at the Concert for the Rock and Roll Hall of Fame in Cleveland. Presumably, the shuffle thing worked out fine.

By 1971, however, it seemed clear that serious tensions were developing within CCR. Clifford, Cook, and Tom Fogerty all expressed desires for greater input into the band's creative decisions. Those concerts played a part in Tom's decision to withdraw from CCR in early 1971, ostensibly to spend more time with his family. That September, while the group was in the midst of its second European tour, Clifford collapsed following a concert in Amsterdam, suffering from scarlet fever. But in early 1972, CCR was back on the road, touring Australia and Japan.

In October, the company holding the copyright to Little Richard's "Good Golly, Miss Molly" filed a suit, later settled out of court, accusing Fogerty of plagiarism on "Travin' Band." It's an issue rock 'n' roll has never really come to terms with. In a field defined by three chords and a half dozen rhythm patterns, there's bound to be a lot of family resemblance between songs. Certainly, if Fogerty had a dollar for every time a rock band's written a song as similar to one of his as "Travlin' Band" is to "Good Golly Miss Molly," he'd be set for the next couple of centuries. But for Fogerty, what would become an absurdist drama on the theme of plagiarism was just beginning.

In the midst of these changes, CCR released its last two albums: *Pendulum*, the last album on which Tom appears, and *Mardi Gras*, the first album on which John shared producing credits with Cook and Clifford. Highlighted by the up tempo rocker "Hey Tonight" and Fogerty's moving ballad "Have You Ever Seen the Rain?," *Pendulum* reveals an increasing interest in instrumental textures that move beyond the four-piece rock format CCR had held to from the beginning. "Sailor's Lament," for example, incorporates saxophone, and what sounds like some unobtrusive synthesizer effects; "Chameleon" opens with an R&B riff from a horn section modeled on the Memphis Horns' "Wish I Could Hideaway" with an organ solo. *Pendulum* isn't really a bad album, but it was a long way down the bayou from *Green River*.

And it stood head and shoulders above *Mardi Gras*, the next record. Commenting on *Rolling Stone*'s selection of *Willy and the Poor Boys* for the top 200, Fogerty laughs and says: "You remember of course that *Rolling Stone* also had a comment about Mardi Gras back in '72. They called it the worst album ever made by a major rock band, and John agreed when he read it." Fogerty smiles again. "You can't escape what you do. You're better off just being honest about it. Anyway, it's nice that they didn't choose to put that one on the list."

There's no escaping the fact that the problems on *Mardi Gras* grow directly out of Fogerty's surrender of the creative control that had made CCR something special. The only songs that bear comparison with the earlier work are the ones with the distinctive Fogerty stamp: "Someday Never Comes," "Sweet Hitch-Hiker," and "Lookin' for a Reason." The Tom Fogerty, Clifford, and Cook material reveals nothing to suggest bright post-Creedence careers. Before his death from tuberculosis in 1990, Tom recorded seven solo albums and played occasionally with Merl Saunders and Jerry Garcia. Clifford, who also released a solo album, and Cook, who would join Southern Pacific in the mid-eighties, would later provide the rhythm section on albums by Doug Sahm and the Don Harrison Band. Enough said.

Although he shows few signs of the bitterness that developed between him and his former bandmates in the late '70 s and '80s, Fogerty makes no attempt to downplay his central role in the creation of the CCR sound. In a recent interview with Michael Goldberg, Fogerty meditated on "this mythical character that I invented called Creedence. And we all tend to say 'Oh yeah, Creedence songs.' It's a cartoon I invented. And basically, it became a recording entity well before it became an in-person entity... Because I created this alter ego thing, this Creedence thing, it was allowed to kind of bubble under in a unspoken way, kind of like a deformed half brother in the closet or something."

The monster in the closet began to emerge after Creedence formally broke up in October 1972. Fogerty continued to work in the studio, pursuing the country sound he had begun to explore on songs like "Lookin' Out My Back Door." His first solo album, a compilation of country classics released as The Blue Ridge Rangers (#47), featured a cover of Hank Williams' "Jambalaya (On the Bayou)," which reached #16; a second single, "Hearts of Stone," made it to #37. But Fogerty looks back on The Blue Ridge Rangers as a good idea gone wrong.

"I wouldn't do it the way I did it then," he admits. "Meaning, I wouldn't play all the instruments. I love that music; The Blue Ridge Rangers was a really cool idea. It was just limited by John Fogerty playing all the instruments. That's a dumb idea," he laughs. "But those songs are great songs, and then just arrange it through a rock 'n' roll guy's eyes."

"Will The Blue Ridge Rangers ever surface again?" Fogerty asks himself. He stops to think. He's still working on his country licks, having learned to play dobro for one of the songs on *Blue Moon Swamp*. On the current tour, he's performing an updated version of "Working on a Building" from the *Blue Ridge Rangers* album. "Yeah, I think it will. But with real people. I have every intention of making a record eventually with people like Jerry Douglass who just scares me, he's so great. I would like some of that on a record I do some day."

Fogerty sounds less enthusiastic about the first post-Creedence album released under his own name, *John Fogerty* (#78). The strongest cuts on the album, where Fogerty again plays all the instruments, are the two singles, "Rockin' All Over The World" (#27) and "Almost Saturday Night" (#78). Although neither meets the standards established by "Fortunate Son" or "Green River," the compositions had enough going for them to become substantial hits in England in cover version. Dave Edmunds had a hit with "Almost Saturday Night," while the Status Quo took "Rockin' All Over the World" to #3 on the British charts in 1977. Like other rock immortals, Fogerty has made a strong impact on a range of other musicians. John Lennon praised Creedence for resisting the pretense that infiltrated late '60s rock; Bruce Springsteen has incorporated "Run Through The Jungle," "Who'll Stop the Rain," and "Rockin' All Over the World" into his live performances. Even before Ike and Tina, Solomon Burke and the Checkmates had placed "Proud Mary" on the R&B charts. Country-rock bands associated with the "No Depression" movement—Wilco, Son Volt, the Jayhawks—cite Fogerty as a primary influence. Sonic Youth named an album after "Bad Moon Rising;" an early incarnation of Pearl Jam was named Green River.

During the mid-seventies, major problems began to develop between Fogerty, his former bandmates, and, most crucially, Fantasy Records president Saul Zaentz. Convinced that Fantasy had mismanaged CCR's financial affairs, Fogerty abandoned his plans for an album tentatively titled *Hoodoo* and retired to a farm in Oregon. Meanwhile, Fantasy continued to release packages of greatest hits and live albums, including Live in Europe (#143), which had been recorded during the group's 1971 tour, and The Concert (#62). Originally released as The Royal Albert Hall Concert, the latter was retitled when Fantasy discovered it had inadvertently mastered the record using tapes from a 1970 Oakland Coliseum performance.

For most of the next decade, Fogerty remained withdrawn from public life, reuniting briefly with Creedence to play at his brother's wedding reception in 1980 and a school reunion in El Cerrito in 1983. Two years later, he released a comeback album on Warner which reached #1. A blend of Creedence style rock 'n' roll and Memphis rockabilly, *Centerfield* demonstrated Fogerty's undiminished ability as a singer, songwriter, and instrumentalist. The first single from the album, "The Old Man Down The Road" reached the Top Ten, and Fogerty followed up with a two-sided hit pairing "Rock And Roll Girls" (#20) and "Centerfield" (#44). Yet another cut from Centerfield, "Big Train From Memphis" hit #36 on the country and western charts. The album also included a song titled "Zaentz Can't Dance," a direct tirade against the Fantasy executive that climaxed with the chorus: "Zaentz can't dance, but he'll steal your money." When Zaentz threatened to sue, Fogerty sarcastically reworked the song into "Vanz Kant Danz."

What should have been a moment of triumph rapidly came to resemble a Kafka parable when Fantasy, supported by Clifford and Cook, brought suit against Fogerty for plagiarism. Citing the similarity in sound and structure between "The Old Man Down The Road" and "Run Through the Jungle," the suit forced Fogerty into the bizarre position of having to defend himself in court against charges of sounding like himself. At one point in the trial, after demonstrating the relatively limited harmonic structure of swamp rock on his guitar, Fogerty said in exasperation, "Yeah, it's the same interval. What am I supposed to do, get an inoculation?

"I proved that, no, I didn't copy myself, I invented something new that really sounds a lot like me," Fogerty told Goldberg. "Do you find fault with Elvis for sounding like Elvis? When McCartney sounds like McCartney or Dylan sounds like Dylan? No one else ever had to go through that." Ultimately the main legal issues were resolved in Fogerty's favor, but persistent appeals kept the final financial settlement in litigation until 1993. As a result, an angry Fogerty refused to play any Creedence material on his 1986 tour.

Looking back on the battle with Fantasy today, Fogerty sounds at peace: "The real reason that I'm not going to hide under a rock again is that I feel a lot better about myself. I'm not going to worry about the things Saul Zaentz has done, or the other guys from Creedence. Mostly what they've done is lack support." Fogerty pauses. "Abandonment is a pretty strong word in that situation. But a lot of the things that hurt me personally, or even in a professional way, caused a lot of diversions. I have to go this way, I have to go that way."

Fogerty credits his recovery primarily to the influence of his wife, Julie. "With the help of my wife," he says, "I've gotten past worrying about that too much anymore. They are the way they are and things I'm sure will continue because it's their nature. But me being me is more important. I should be writing songs, making music, singing in front of people rather than defending myself. That's my real job in life."

When someone in the audience called out a request of "Vanz Kant Danz" during the House of Blues performance, Fogerty laughed and responded, "I ain't that pissed off anymore. We'll save that one for some other tour."

Between *Centerfield* and *Blue Moon Swamp*, which Fogerty once vowed "won't sound sort of like a Creedence album, it'll sound exactly like a Creedence album," he recorded only one record, *Eye of the Zombie* (#26). Released as the conflict with Zaentz was heating up, *Eye of the Zombie* sounds not at all like a Creedence album. An interesting, if unsuccessful, experiment with Stax-style Memphis soul, the album expresses Fogerty's disgust with the political situation in Ronald Reagan's America. "Headlines," "Violence Is Golden," and the title cut, which died at #81 as the album's only single, provide a strong sense of America as a nightmare landscape ruled by the living dead.

But the songs really don't work musically or lyrically, which is one of the reasons *Blue Moon Swamp* isn't filled with explicitly topical songs. "I made a conscious effort not to be so heavy-handed as *Zombie* was," he says. "I'm a rock 'n' roll guy and a music maker first. I consider *Zombie* kind of an over-indulgent mistake. Just too much preaching, too much soap boxing. Where do I get off coming off with all that stuff?

"It was just too much and the album became something almost unlistenable," Fogerty says, overstating his case considerably. "It wasn't something you'd gravitate back to. If I was lucky, somebody'd buy it and maybe listen to it once. I mean, I could barely listen to it. I don't listen to it now. It has some moments, but it's not well constructed and I don't encourage anybody to buy that record. Life is a learning process and the foremost lesson being that what I do should be entertaining. You don't scare people to death or over-preach them. You tell a kid 'God's gonna punish you,' they'd rather go fishing."

A decade later, Fogerty isn't worried about repeating that mistake. On *Blue Moon Swamp*, he set out "to get it just right," to make "a record that really rocks." A great rock 'n' roll record, Fogerty observes, "is about more than just the songs. It's about the playing. If you're calling it a rock 'n' roll record and it's not rocking, it hasn't got most of what it really needs. When I was making this album, I said, 'this can't just be some guys impression of a rock 'n' roll album, it's got to be a rock and roll album.'"

Fogerty's return to the concert stage was spurred both by his desire to play the new songs for a live audience and his wife's suggestions that he return to music. "She ribbed me, saying 'When are you going to stop playing benefits? When are you going to play something where you actually earn some money?'" Fogerty laughs. "It's true. I've done a lot of benefits because I believe in them. But they're sort of quirky. It's a little strange when you prepare for a month for just one night. And then you come out and it's all over."

Looking ahead to his summer tour, Fogerty underlined the connection between his old and his new material. "I didn't just walk out one day and say, 'Hey, I'm gonna go play the old songs, that'll put me back with the in crowd, that'll save my career.' It wouldn't have been honest for me to play the old songs until I could make it all one life again, which is what I think I've done now. The old John and the new John are really the same guy."

Blue Moon Swamp takes the new John Fogerty back to the mythic American South the old John Fogerty helped define, the South where the music resonates with truths that the history books hide. Like *Cosmo's Factory*, *Blue Moon Swamp* maps the corners of the landscape Fogerty's explored and gives you an idea of where he may want to go. The two songs that open the CD—"Southern Streamline" and "Hot Rod Heart"—establish movement as the image that holds the album together. There's no question that the sounds on the album evoke a rural past: the country pedal steel guitar on "Southern Streamline"; the gospel harmonies on "A Hundred and Ten in the Shade"; the honky-tonk twang of "Bring It Down to Jellyroll"; and the hayride rockabilly of "Blue Moon Nights," which sounds like a song recovered from Elvis's Sun Sessions.

Some of Fogerty's new lyrics contain images that resonate in ways that recall "Bad Moon Rising" or "Who'll Stop the Rain"; "Walking In A Hurricane," for example, could be about Bill Clinton's America as well as a volatile love affair; "A Hundred and Ten in the Shade" isn't just about the thermometer. But the spiritual center of *Blue Moon Swamp* lies in a sense of the past that walks the borderline between myth and nostalgia. Nowhere is it clearer than on "Swamp River Days," where Fogerty revisits both his childhood and the early days of CCR's career. He traces the song to his family's summer vacations in Northern California, remembering "a blazing-hot summer romance with Susie when we were both four years old." But when Fogerty sings "Sweet Susie, do you think about me/ that was good as it's ever gonna be/ give me those swamp river days again," he's obviously thinking about Creedence's breakthrough single, which came out back when people still thought music was going to change the world. Fogerty admits, "It's a mythic state of mind."

Fogerty's southern pilgrimages flooded him with new thoughts on the tangled web of history, myth, and his own complicated life. He describes leaving Memphis in explicitly mythic terms: "Lula and Robinsonville are just a little south of Memphis. They're the first true Delta towns and it's strong with Robert Johnson and Charlie Patton, their presence and history and lore. It's like learning about Canaan or learning about Galilee. Just the names, you go, 'yeah and then he went down to Lula.'"

An important moment in Fogerty's quest took place at Robert Johnson's grave. Meditating on Johnson's troubled life and history, Fogerty experienced an epiphany that helped him come to terms with some of his anger toward those he'd felt betrayed him. As he told Dave DiMartino, Fogerty realized that "There's this guy buried there and maybe some guy named Morris Stealum of Cheatem, Beatem & Whatever owns his songs in some big building in Manhattan. (But) it's Robert Johnson who owns those songs; he's the spiritual owner of those songs. Muddy Waters owns his songs; Howlin' Wolf owns his songs. And someday somebody is gonna be standing where I'm buried, and they won't know about Saul Zaentz—screw him. What they'll know is if they thought the life's work was valuable or not. Standing among all those giants, I went, 'That's the deal here. It's time to jump back into your own stream.'"

No question about it: *Blue Moon Swamp* flows out of the same headwaters as Fogerty's earlier work. But it also raises a new set of questions, intertwined with his thoughts about American music and the American South. As Marsh points out, despite Fogerty's determination to avoid preaching, *Blue Moon Swamp* presents a "sermon on pastoralism and authenticity." Fogerty realizes that whatever authenticity means, it's under constant pressure from a changing present.

"I haven't been back in a few years," he says. "But a friend was telling me about what Lula's like today. Mississippi legalized gambling and they set it up right there on the river, just south of Memphis. So you fly in and boom! It's like Atlantic City. I got there just in time because if that's what I'd seen, it would have all been different. So for some reason I was called and allowed to be there before all that hit."

The changes in the South go deeper, Fogerty observes, touching the musical traditions that fathered his creative spirit. "Young black kids today, even down south, like the music of their day, of their time. They like rap because that's what's going on in black music. R&B is sort of an old-fashioned music; blues is a relic. So what could be weirder to a young kid than to see some white guy playing blues? That's gotta be like the weirdest thing. 'Oh, so you stealin' my Granddaddy's music here at the mall.' It's a real strange concept." Fogerty pauses and says slowly, "It's almost beyond being black or white anymore. It's really more a vintage thing."

That's just one of the questions that makes Blue Moon Swamp's engagement with the Southern myth more suggestive than definitive. The other one concerns power. Fogerty is fully aware that the burden of southern history remains very real in the lives of black Mississippians.

"It's a different place," he observes. "You see many more black people in Mississippi than most places I've been. They're the majority, but they're not in control of the power."

Reflecting on an often-noted and little understood aspect of American racial experience, Fogerty identifies the seeming contradiction between political context and personal experience in the South. "But in Mississippi, I always felt I could walk safely anywhere I wanted to. Now maybe if I went down around over the levee where no one could see, maybe that would be a bad place to go in the middle of the night. But as far as walking into an all-black club, people always treated me with great respect as a stranger, trying to make me welcome."

Almost immediately, Fogerty balances that perception with the observation that there were some places he chose not to go. "There are joke joints out away with names like Mad Dog Disco. Their aspirations are to something grand, but it's painted in hand-writing. It's all dripping and funky. One of them had a picture of Michael Jackson hand-painted. So the picture in the patron's mind would be something grand, but you're looking at this thing in stark fluorescent light going 'Oh, that's God-awful looking.'" Fogerty pauses. "I thought I'd better not go in there and disrupt what was going on."

Fogerty's meditations on his Mississippi experiences belong to an unending song—part celebration, part lament—about what authenticity means in an America where a California boy can make a South of his own. Like the songs sung by Elvis and Muddy Waters when they set out on their different roads toward the same place—and you can add Mahalia Jackson and Buddy Holly, Bruce Springsteen and Sam Cooke to the list of travelers—the song Fogerty is singing reverberates with unanswered questions: About who we are, where we can walk, and the sounds of our voices, together and alone.

The Top 15 Most Collectible Miles Davis Albums

by Tim Neely

There are some musicians whose work transcends time or genre and Miles Davis is one of them. His influence was not only felt on jazz, but he also influenced a bevy of classic rock stars and crossed paths with many more. Understandably, his rarest records command a pretty penny on the collector's market. Here are the most valuable.

	Label, Catalog #	Title	Value
1.	Blue Note BLP-5013	(10") Young Man With A Horn	$300
1.	Blue Note BLP-5022	(10") Miles Davis, Volume 2	300
1.	Blue Note BLP-5040	(10") Miles Davis, Volume 3	300
4.	Capitol H-459	(10") Jeru	250
		Contains the 1949 "Birth Of The Cool" sessions.	
4.	Prestige PRLP-124	(10") The New Sounds Of Miles Davis	250
4.	Prestige PRLP-140	(10") Blue Period	250
4.	Prestige PRLP-154	(10") Miles Davis Plays Al Cohn Compositions	250
4.	Prestige PRLP-161	(10") Miles Davis Featuring Sonny Rollins	250
4.	Prestige PRLP-182	(10") Miles Davis Sextet	250
4.	Prestige PRLP-185	(10") Miles Davis Quintet	250
4.	Prestige PRLP-187	(10") Miles Davis Quintet Featuring Sonny Rollins	250
4.	Prestige PRLP-196	(10") Miles Davis All Stars, Vol. 1	250
4.	Prestige PRLP-200	(10") Miles Davis All Stars, Vol. 2	250
14.	Blue Note BLP-1501	(M) Miles Davis, Volume 1 (deep groove)	200
14.	Blue Note BLP-1502	Miles Davis, Volume 2 (deep groove)	200